S0-BAR-325

THE RISE OF MODERN RELIGIOUS IDEAS IN AMERICA

– Editorial Director –

SYDNEY E. AHLSTROM, American Studies Program, Yale University

JAMES FREEMAN CLARKE

Ten Great Religions

An Essay in Comparative Theology

Reprint Edition
with a New Introduction

THE REGINA PRESS

CARL A. RUDISILL LIBRARY
LENOIR RHYNE COLLEGE

Reprint Edition 1975

THE REGINA PRESS
7 Midland Avenue
Hicksville, New York 11801

New Introduction © 1975 by The Regina Press

Library of Congress Catalog Number: 74-78284
International Standard Book Number: 0-88271-020-6

291
C54π
95051
Oct1925

This volume is reprinted according to the standards
established in 1972 by the Rare Book Libraries' Con-
ference on Facsimiles.

Manufactured in the United States of America.

NEW INTRODUCTION TO THE REPRINT EDITION
by George H. Williams,
Harvard Divinity School

WHEN *Ten Great Religions: An Essay on Comparative Theology* was published by James Freeman Clarke in 1871, after having been copiously serialized in the *Atlantic Monthly* during the year 1869, it documented a major achievement of Transcendental Unitarianism in New England. Interest in the other religions of the world, to be sure, was not new. Two New England writers had preceded Clarke in the field, Hannah Adams in 1784 and Lydia Maria Child in 1855. But Clarke's work showed a far greater command of the growing body of European scholarship in this exceedingly complex field of study. The book placed its author in the forefront among American scholars in this new field of intellectual and theological endeavor.

Clarke grew up in Boston, received his B. A. from Harvard College in 1829 and graduated from the Harvard Divinity School in 1833. For the next seven years he was minister to a Unitarian congregation in Louisville, Kentucky. Returning to Boston in 1841, he founded the Church of the Disciples on new and liberal principles and remained its minister to the end of his life. During these same years he played an active role in the affairs of the Unitarian denomination, though he always insisted that he belonged to "the Church of Christ" and not to any particular sect of Christians. From 1867 to 1877 he was a part-time teacher at the Harvard Divinity School. In the course of a busy life he produced an enormous body of writings, including over a dozen books on very diverse subjects, but his work in comparative religion is probably his most significant writing.

Two developments in New England help account for the enlarged interest in non-Christian religions. Most important, perhaps, was the Transcendentalist view of universal Reason and the accompanying dissatisfactions with the narrowness of the traditional churches. More immediate in Clarke's case were the ideas of Friedrich Schleiermacher, especially his definition of religion as the "feeling of dependence."

Because Clarke deemed all non-Christian religions to be fundamentally ethnic, and saw the Christian religion as "steadily progressive" and ever tending to universality, he did not place the Christianity among the Ten Religions but treated it comparatively at the end of each chapter. In a final chapter he then brought these observations together synoptically so as to stress the fullness of Christianity. All that was living in other religions could, to his mind, be eventually included by sublimation.

In the opening chapter he promises "to show that all the religions of the earth are providential, and that all tend to benefit mankind." He also saw religion as a universal response to the divine power illuminating the world. Alluding to Paul's address on Mars Hill, he linked the faith of all men to a primordial religion instituted by the Creator.

The shortcomings of religion, on the other hand, were usually attributed to the effects of priestcraft; and in illustrating this point Clarke was not reluctant about discussing the First Vatican Council then recently concluded, or the churches of the Irish and other Roman Catholic immigrants. Due to his disdain and antipathy for latter-day Celts, who were then changing the religious atmosphere and political institutions of Boston, he dealt with the ancient Celts solely by way of hostile characterizations from Tacitus.

Clarke broke from the traditional practice of presenting the religions of China before those of India. About these Indian religions, moreover, he had clearly formed ideas, regarding Buddhism, for example, as "the Protestantism of the East."

Far more bold and innovative in Clarke's account is his use of the theory of biological evolution as a rationale for the universal phenomenon of religion. Perhaps for the first time in America, he makes an unambiguous and utterly comprehensive affirmation of the theory of progressive relevation: "Instead of degenerating toward something worse, they [religions] come to prepare the way for something better." "If heathen religions are a step, a preparation for Christianity, then this law of degrees [obtaining in the evolution from lower to highter forms] appears also in religion . . . . Then we can understand why Christ's coming was delayed till the fulness of time had come."

In finding his basic distinction between ethnic and fully universal religion in the words of Paul and then in Jesus himself Clarke expresses amazement that Christian divines should have so long speculated about the fate of the heathen when Jesus so clearly said that he had other sheep not of the Jewish [Christian] fold (John 10:16). He also cites ancient Christian Apologists in support of his conviction "that God had one great plan for educating the world, of which Christianity was the final step." Clarke could even interpret the one principal post-Christian religion, Islam, as universalizing with respect to classes and nationalities and therefore as taking the place of Judaism in the preparation for Christianity in the modern world. A view like this was all the easier for Clarke because the kind of Christianity overwhelmed by Islam during its era of expansion was to him so encrusted with theological and liturgical complications as to be ethically immobilized. Thus Clarke was opposed to the radical Transcendentalist view that all the great religions could be put on the same level with Christianity or admired uncritically.

Ten Religions went through innumerable editions without significant alteration. The last before the present reprint was by the Beacon Press in Boston in 1920. Clarke chose to put most of his revisionary energy not into improving his bestseller but into preparing a second volume, entitled *Ten Great Religions, Part II: A Comparison of All Religions* (Boston, 1883). After this, every reprinting of the book before us was marked on the binding to indicate that it was in effect Part I of a two-volume work.

Bibliographical Suggestions:
John Wesley Thomas, *James Freeman Clarke: Apostle of German Culture of America* (Boston: J. N. Luce, 1949); Arthur S. Bolster, Jr., *James Freeman Clarke: Disciple to Advancing Truth* (Boston: Beacon Press, 1954); Edward Everett Hale, ed., *Autobiography, Diary and Correspondence of James Freeman Clarke* (Boston, 1891); J. W. Thomas, ed., *The Letters of James Freeman Clarke to Margaret Fuller* (Hamburg, Germany, 1957); George H. Williams, "The Attitude of Liberals in New England Toward Non-Christian Religions," *The Crane Review*, IV:2 (1967), pp. 59-89; Sydney E. Ahlstrom, *The American Protestant Encounter with World Religions* (1962).

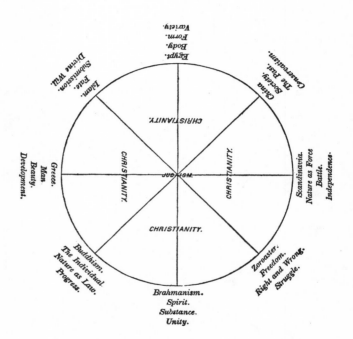

Egypt.
Body.
Form.
Variety.

China
Society.
The Past.
Conservatism.

Scandinavia.
Nature as Force.
Battle.
Independence.

Zoroaster.
Freedom.
Right and Wrong.
Struggle.

Brahmanism.
Spirit.
Substance.
Unity.

Buddhism.
The Individual.
Nature as Law.
Progress.

Greece.
Man.
Beauty.
Development.

Islam.
Fate.
Submission.
Divine Will.

CHRISTIANITY.
CHRISTIANITY.
CHRISTIANITY.
CHRISTIANITY.

JUDAISM.

TEN GREAT RELIGIONS

An Essay in Comparative Theology

BY

JAMES FREEMAN CLARKE

Prophets who have been since the world began. — LUKE i. 70.

Gentiles . . . who show the work (or influence) of the (that) law which is written in their hearts. — ROMANS ii. 15.

God . . . hath made of one blood all nations of men for to dwell on all the face of the earth . . . that they should seek the Lord, if haply they may feel after him and find him. — ACTS xviii. 24–27.

TWENTY-FOURTH EDITION

BOSTON AND NEW YORK
HOUGHTON, MIFFLIN AND COMPANY
The Riverside Press, Cambridge
1887

Entered according to Act of Congress, in the year 1871,

BY JAMES FREEMAN CLARKE,

in the Office of the Librarian of Congress, at Washington.

TO

WÍLLIAM HENRY CHANNING,

MY FRIEND AND FELLOW-STUDENT

DURING MANY YEARS,

𝕿𝖍𝖎𝖘 𝖂𝖔𝖗𝖐

IS AFFECTIONATELY INSCRIBED.

PREFACE.

—◆—

THE first six chapters of the present volume are composed from six articles prepared for the Atlantic Monthly, and published in that magazine in 1868. They attracted quite as much attention as the writer anticipated, and this has induced him to enlarge them, and add other chapters. His aim is to enable the reader to become acquainted with the doctrines and customs of the principal religions of the world, without having to consult numerous volumes. He has not come to the task without some preparation, for it is more than twenty-five years since he first made of this study a speciality. In this volume it is attempted to give the latest results of modern investigations, so far as any definite and trustworthy facts have been attained. But the writer is well aware of the difficulty of being always accurate in a task which involves such interminable study and such an amount of details. He can only say, in the words of a Hebrew writer: "If I have done well, and as is fitting the story, it is that which I desired; but if slenderly and meanly, it is that which I could attain unto."

CONTENTS.

—◆—

CHAPTER I.

INTRODUCTION. — ETHNIC AND CATHOLIC RELIGIONS.

CHAPTER II.

CONFUCIUS AND THE CHINESE, OR THE PROSE OF ASIA.

CHAPTER III.

BRAHMANISM.

CHAPTER IV.

BUDDHISM, OR THE PROTESTANTISM OF THE EAST.

CHAPTER V.

ZOROASTER AND THE ZEND AVESTA.

CHAPTER VI.

THE GODS OF EGYPT.

CHAPTER VII.

THE GODS OF GREECE.

CHAPTER VIII.

THE RELIGION OF ROME.

CHAPTER IX.

THE TEUTONIC AND SCANDINAVIAN RELIGION.

CHAPTER X.

THE JEWISH RELIGION.

CHAPTER XI.

MOHAMMED AND ISLAM.

CHAPTER XII.

THE TEN RELIGIONS AND CHRISTIANITY.

TEN GREAT RELIGIONS.

CHAPTER I.

INTRODUCTION. — ETHNIC AND CATHOLIC RELIGIONS.

§ 1. Object of the present Work. § 2. Comparative Theology; its Nature, Value, and present Position. § 3. Ethnic Religions. Injustice often done to them by Christian Apologists. § 4. How Ethnic Religions were regarded by Christ and his Apostles. § 5. Comparative Theology will furnish a new Class of Evidences in Support of Christianity. § 6. It will show that, while most of the Religions of the World are Ethnic, or the Religions of Races, Christianity is Catholic, or adapted to become the Religion of all Races. § 7. It will show that Ethnic Religions are Partial, Christianity Universal. § 8. It will show that Ethnic Religions are arrested, but that Christianity is steadily progressive.

§ 1. *Object of the present Work.*

THE present work is what the Germans call a *Versuch*, and the English an Essay, or attempt. It is an attempt to compare the great religions of the world with each other. When completed, this comparison ought to show what each is, what it contains, wherein it resembles the others, wherein it differs from the others; its origin and development, its place in universal history; its positive and negative qualities, its truths and errors, and its influence, past, present, or future, on the welfare of mankind. For everything becomes more clear by comparison. We can never understand the nature of a phenomenon when we contemplate it by itself, as well as when we look at it in its relations to other phenomena of the same kind The qualities of each become more clear in contrast with those of the others. By comparing together, therefore,

1

the religions of mankind, to see wherein they agree and wherein they differ, we are able to perceive with greater accuracy what each is. The first problem in Comparative Theology is therefore analytical, being to distinguish each religion from the rest. We compare them to see wherein they agree and wherein they differ. But the next problem in Comparative Theology is synthetical, and considers the adaptation of each system to every other, to determine its place, use, and value, in reference to universal or absolute religion. It must, therefore, examine the different religions to find wherein each is complete or defective, true or false; how each may supply the defects of the other or prepare the way for a better; how each religion acts on the race which receives it, is adapted to that race, and to the region of the earth which it inhabits. In this department, therefore, it connects itself with Comparative Geography, with universal history, and with ethics. Finally, this department of Comparative Theology shows the relation of each partial religion to human civilization, and observes how each religion of the world is a step in the progress of humanity. It shows that both the positive and negative side of a religion make it a preparation for a higher religion, and that the universal religion must root itself in the decaying soil of partial religions. And in this sense Comparative Theology becomes the science of missions.

Such a work as this is evidently too great for a single mind. Many students must co-operate, and that through many years, before it can be completed. This volume is intended as a contribution toward that end. It will contain an account of each of the principal religions, and its development. It will be, therefore, devoted to the natural history of ethnic and catholic religions, and its method will be that of analysis. The second part, which may be published hereafter, will compare these different systems to show what each teaches concerning the great subjects of religious thought, — God, Duty, and Immortality. Finally, it will compare them with Christianity, and will inquire whether or not that is capable of becoming the religion of the human race.

§ 2. *Comparative Theology ; its Nature, Value, and present Position.*

The work of Comparative Theology is to do equal justice to all the religious tendencies of mankind. Its position is that of a judge, not that of an advocate. Assuming, with the Apostle Paul, that each religion has come providentially, as a method by which different races " should seek the Lord, if haply they might feel after him and find him," it attempts to show how each may be a step in the religious progress of the races, and " a schoolmaster to bring men to Christ." It is bound, however, to abstain from such inferences until it has accurately ascertained all the facts. Its first problem is to learn what each system contains; it may then go on, and endeavor to generalize from its facts.

Comparative Theology is, therefore, as yet in its infancy. The same tendency in this century, which has produced the sciences of Comparative Anatomy, Comparative Geography, and Comparative Philology, is now creating this new science of Comparative Theology.* It will be to any special theology as Comparative Anatomy is to any special anatomy, Comparative Geography to any special geography, or Comparative Philology to the study of any particular language. It may be called a science, since it consists in the study of the facts of human history, and their relation to each other. It does not dogmatize : it observes. It deals only with phenomena, — single phenomena, or facts ; grouped phenomena, or laws.

Several valuable works, bearing more or less directly on Comparative Theology, have recently appeared in Germany, France, and England. Among these may be mentioned those of Max Müller, Bunsen, Burnouf, Döllinger, Hardwicke, St. Hilaire, Düncker, F. C. Baur, Rénan, Creuzer, Maurice, G. W. Cox, and others.

In America, except Mr. Alger's admirable monograph on the " Doctrine of the Future Life," we have scarcely anything worthy of notice. Mrs. Lydia Maria Child's

---

* It is one of the sagacious remarks of Goethe, that "the eighteenth century tended to analysis, but the nineteenth will deal with synthesis."

work on the " Progress of Religious Ideas" deserves the
greatest credit, when we consider the time when it was
written and the few sources of information then accessible.* Twenty-five years ago it was hardly possible to procure any adequate information concerning Brahmanism,
Buddhism, or the religions of Confucius, Zoroaster, and
Mohammed. Hardly any part of the Vedas had been
translated into a European language. The works of
Anquetil du Perron and Kleuker were still the highest
authority upon the Zendavesta. About the Buddhists
scarcely anything was known. But now, though many
important *lacunæ* remain to be filled, we have ample
means of ascertaining the essential facts concerning most
of these movements of the human soul. The time seems
to have come to accomplish something which may have
a lasting value.

§ 3. *Ethnic Religions. Injustice often done to them by
Christian Apologists.*

Comparative Theology, pursuing its impartial course as
a positive science, will avoid the error into which most
of the Christian apologists of the last century fell, in
speaking of ethnic or heathen religions. In order to
show the need of Christianity, they thought it necessary
to disparage all other religions. Accordingly they have
insisted that, while the Jewish and Christian religions
were revealed, all other religion were invented; that,
while these were from God, those were the work of man ;
that, while in the true religions there was nothing false,
in the false religions there was nothing true. If any trace
of truth was to be found in Polytheism, it was so mixed
with error as to be practically only evil. As the doctrines of heathen religions were corrupt, so their worship
was only a debasing superstition. Their influence was to
make men worse, not better ; their tendency was to produce sensuality, cruelty, and universal degradation. They
did not proceed, in any sense, from God; they were not

* Professor Cocker's work on "Christianity and Greek Philosophy,"
should also be mentioned.

even the work of good men, but rather of deliberate imposition and priestcraft. A supernatural religion had become necessary in order to counteract the fatal consequences of these debased and debasing superstitions. This is the view of the great natural religions of the world which was taken by such writers as Leland, Whitby, and Warburton in the last century. Even liberal thinkers, like James Foster * and John Locke,† declare that, at the coming of Christ, mankind had fallen into utter darkness, and that vice and superstition filled the world. Infidel no less than Christian writers took the same disparaging view of natural religions. They considered them, in their source, the work of fraud; in their essence, corrupt superstitions; in their doctrines, wholly false; in their moral tendency, absolutely injurious; and in their result, degenerating more and more into greater evil.

A few writers, like Cudworth and the Platonists, endeavored to put in a good word for the Greek philosophers, but the religions of the world were abandoned to unmitigated reprobation. The account which so candid a writer as Mosheim gives of them is worth noticing, on account of its sweeping character. "All the nations of the world," he says, "except the Jews, were plunged in the grossest superstition. Some nations, indeed, went beyond others in impiety and absurdity, but all stood charged with irrationality and gross stupidity in matters of religion." "The greater part of the gods of all nations were ancient heroes, famous for their achievements and their worthy deeds, such as kings, generals, and founders of

* James Foster has a sermon on "The Advantages of a Revelation," in which he declares that, at the time of Christ's coming, "just notions of God were, in general, erased from the minds of men. His worship was debased and polluted, and scarce any traces could be discerned of the genuine and immutable religion of nature."

† John Locke, in his "Reasonableness of Christianity," says that when Christ came "men had given themselves up into the hands of their priests, to fill their heads with false notions of the Deity, and their worship with foolish rites, as they pleased; and what dread or craft once began, devotion soon made sacred, and religion immutable." "In this state of darkness and ignorance of the true God, vice and superstition held the world." Quotations of this sort might be indefinitely multiplied. See an article by the present writer, in the "Christian Examiner," March, 1857.

cities." "To these some added the more splendid and useful objects in the natural world, as the sun, moon, and stars ; and some were not ashamed to pay divine honors to mountains, rivers, trees, etc." " The worship of these deities consisted in ceremonies, sacrifices, and prayers. The ceremonies were, for the most part, absurd and ridiculous, and throughout debasing, obscene, and cruel. The prayers were truly insipid and void of piety, both in their form and matter." " The priests who presided over this worship basely abused their authority to impose on the people." " The whole pagan system had not the least efficacy to produce and cherish virtuous emotions in the soul; because the gods and goddesses were patterns of vice, the priests bad men, and the doctrines false." *

This view of heathen religions is probably much exaggerated. They must contain more truth than error, and must have been, on the whole, useful to mankind. We do not believe that they originated in human fraud, that their essence is superstition, that there is more falsehood than truth in their doctrines, that their moral tendency is mainly injurious, or that they continually degenerate into greater evil. No doubt it may be justly predicated of all these systems that they contain much which is false and injurious to human virtue. But the following considerations may tend to show that all the religions of the earth are providential, and that all tend to benefit mankind.

To ascribe the vast phenomena of religion, in their variety and complexity, to man as their author, and to suppose the whole a mere work of human fraud, is not a satisfactory solution of the facts before us. That priests, working on human ignorance or fear, should be able to build up such a great mass of belief, sentiment, and action, is like the Hindoo cosmogony, which supposes the globe to rest on an elephant, the elephant on a turtle, and the turtle on nothing at all.

If the people were so ignorant, how happened the priests to be so wise ? If the people were so credulous, why were not the priests credulous too ? " Like people,

---

* Mosheim's Church History, Vol. I. Chap. I.

like priests," is a proverb approved by experience. Among so many nations and through so many centuries, why has not some one priest betrayed the secret of the famous imposition? Apply a similar theory to any other human institution, and how patent is its absurdity! Let a republican contend that all other forms of government— the patriarchal system, government by castes, the feudal system, absolute and limited monarchies, oligarchies, and aristocracies — are wholly useless and evil, and were the result of statecraft alone, with no root in human nature or the needs of man. Let one maintain that every system of *law* (except our own) was an invention of lawyers for private ends. Let one argue in the same way about medicine, and say that this is a pure system of quackery, devised by physicians, in order to get a support out of the people for doing nothing. We should at once reply that, though error and ignorance may play a part in all these institutions, they cannot be based on error and ignorance only. Nothing which has not in it some elements of use can hold its position in the world during so long a time and over so wide a range. It is only reasonable to say the same of heathen or ethnic religions. They contain, no doubt, error and evil. No doubt priestcraft has been carried very far in them, though not further perhaps than it has sometimes been carried in Christianity. But unless they contained more of good than evil, they could not have kept their place. They partially satisfied a great hunger of the human heart. They exercised some restraint on human wilfulness and passion. They have directed, however imperfectly, the human conscience toward the right. To assume that they are wholly evil is disrespectful to human nature. It supposes man to be the easy and universal dupe of fraud. But these religions do not rest on such a sandy foundation, but on the feeling of dependence, the sense of accountability, the recognition of spiritual realities very near to this world of matter, and the need of looking up and worshipping some unseen power higher and better than ourselves. A decent respect for the opinions of mankind forbids us to ascribe pagan religions to priestcraft as their chief source.

And a reverence for Divine Providence brings us to the same conclusion. Can it be that God has left himself without a witness in the world, except among the Hebrews in ancient times and the Christians in modern times ? This narrow creed excludes God from any communion with the great majority of human beings. The Father of the human race is represented as selecting a few of his children to keep near himself, and as leaving all the rest to perish in their ignorance and error. And this is not because they are prodigal children who have gone astray into a far country of their own accord; for they are just where they were placed by their Creator. HE "has determined the times before appointed and the bounds of their habitation." HE has caused some to be born in India, where they can only hear of him through Brahmanism ; and some in China, where they can know him only through Buddha and Confucius. The doctrine which we are opposing is ; that, being put there by God, they are born into hopeless error, and are then punished for their error by everlasting destruction. The doctrine for which we contend is that of the Apostle Paul, that God has " determined beforehand the bounds of their habitation, that they should seek the Lord, IF HAPLY THEY MAY FEEL AFTER HIM AND FIND HIM." Paul teaches that " all nations dwelling on all the face of the earth " may not only seek and feel after God, but also FIND him. But as all living in heathen lands are heathen, if they find God at all, they must find him through heathenism. The pagan religions are the effort of man to feel after God. Otherwise we must conclude that the Being without whom not a sparrow falls to the . ground, the Being who never puts an insect into the air or a polyp into the water without providing it with some appropriate food, so that it may live and grow, has left the vast majority of his human children, made with religious appetences of conscience, reverence, hope, without a corresponding nutriment of truth. This view tends to atheism ; for if the presence of adaptation everywhere is the legitimate proof of creative design, the absence of adaptation in so important a sphere tends, so far, to set aside that proof.

The view which we are opposing contradicts that law of progress which alone gives meaning and unity to history. Instead of progress, it teaches degeneracy and failure. But elsewhere we see progress, not recession. Geology shows us higher forms of life succeeding to the lower. Botany exhibits the lichens and mosses preparing a soil for more complex forms of vegetation. Civil history shows the savage state giving way to the semi-civilized, and that to the civilized. If heathen religions are a step, a preparation for Christianity, then this law of degrees appears also in religion; then we see an order in the progress of the human soul, — " first the blade, then the ear, afterward the full corn in the ear." Then we can understand why Christ's coming was delayed till the fulness of the time had come. But otherwise all, in this most important sphere of human life, is in disorder, without unity, progress, meaning, or providence.

These views, we trust, will be amply confirmed when we come to examine each great religion separately and carefully. We shall find them always feeling after God, often finding him. We shall see that in their origin they are not the work of priestcraft, but of human nature; in their essence not superstitions, but religions; in their doctrines true more frequently than false; in their moral tendency good rather than evil. And instead of degenerating toward something worse, they come to prepare the way for something better.

§ 4. *How Ethnic Religions were regarded by Christ and his Apostles.*

According to Christ and the Apostles, Christianity was to grow out of Judaism, and be developed into a universal religion. Accordingly, the method of Jesus was to go first to the Jews; and when he left the limits of Palestine on a single occasion, he declared himself as only going into Phœnicia to seek after the lost sheep of the house of Israel. But he stated that he had other sheep, not of this fold, whom he must bring, recognizing that there were, among the heathen, good and honest hearts

1 *

prepared for Christianity, and already belonging to him; sheep who knew his voice and were ready to follow him. He also declared that the Roman centurion and the Phœnician woman already possessed great faith, the centurion more than he had yet found in Israel. But the most striking declaration of Jesus, and one singularly overlooked, concerning the character of the heathen, is to be found in his description of the day of judgment, in Matthew (chap. xxv.). It is very curious that men should speculate as to the fate of the heathen, when Jesus has here distinctly taught that all good men among them are his sheep, though they never heard of him. The account begins, "Before him shall be gathered all the Gentiles" (or heathen). It is not a description of the judgment of the Christian world, but of the heathen world. The word here used (τὰ ἔθνη) occurs about one hundred and sixty-four times in the New Testament. It is translated "gentiles" oftener than by any other word, that is, about ninety-three times; by "heathen" four or five times; and in the remaining passages it is mostly translated "nations." That it means the Gentiles or heathen here appears from the fact that they are represented as ignorant of Christ, and are judged, not by the standard of Christian faith, but by their humanity and charity toward those in suffering. Jesus recognizes, therefore, among these ethnic or heathen people, some as belonging to himself, — the "other sheep," not of the Jewish fold.

The Apostle Paul, who was especially commissioned to the Gentiles, must be considered as the best authority upon this question. Did he regard their religions as wholly false? On the contrary, he tells the Athenians that they are already worshipping the true God, though ignorantly. "Whom ye ignorantly worship, Him declare I unto you." When he said this he was standing face to face with all that was most imposing in the religion of Greece. He saw the city filled with idols, majestic forms, the perfection of artistic grace and beauty. Was his spirit then moved *only* with indignation against this worship, and had he no sympathy with the spiritual needs which it expressed? It does not seem so. He recognized

piety in their souls.   " I see that ye are, in all ways, exceedingly pious." He recognized their worship as passing
beyond the idols, to the true God.   He did not profess
that he came to revolutionize their religion, but to reform
it.   He does not proceed like the backwoodsman, who
fells the forest and takes out the stumps in order to plant
a wholly different crop ; but like the nurseryman, who
grafts a native stock with a better fruit.   They were already ignorantly worshipping the true God.   What the
apostle proposed to do was to enlighten that ignorance by
showing them who that true God was, and what was his
character.   In his subsequent remarks, therefore, he does
not teach them that there is one Supreme Being, but he
assumes it, as something already believed.   He assumes
him to be the creator of all things ; to be *omnipotent,* —
" the Lord of heaven and earth " ; *spiritual,* — " dwelleth
not in temples made with hands " ; *absolute,* — " not needing anything," but the source of all things.   He says this,
as not expecting any opposition or contradiction ; he re-
serves his criticisms on their idolatry for the end of his
discourse.   He then states, quite clearly, that the different
nations of the world have a common origin, belong to one
family, and have been providentially placed in space and
time, that each might seek the Lord in its own way.   He
recognized in them a power of seeking and finding God,
the God close at hand, and in whom we live ; and he
quotes one of their own poets, accepting his statement of
God's fatherly character.   Now, it is quite common for
those who deny that there is any truth in heathenism, to
admire this speech of Paul as a masterpiece of ingenuity
and eloquence.   But he would hardly have made it, unless he thought it to be true.   Those who praise his
eloquence at the expense of his veracity pay him a poor
compliment.   Did Paul tell the Athenians that they were
worshipping the true God *when they were not,* and that
for the sake of rhetorical effect ?   If we believe this concerning him, and yet admire him, let us cease henceforth
to find fault with the Jesuits.

No ! Paul believed what he said, that the Athenians
were worshipping the true God, though ignorantly.   The

sentiment of reverence, of worship, was lifting them to its true object. All they needed was to have their understanding enlightened. Truth he placed in the heart rather than the understanding, but he also connected Christianity with Polytheism where the two religions touched, that is, on their pantheistic side. While placing God *above* the world as its ruler, " seeing he is Lord of heaven and earth," he placed him *in* the world as an immanent presence, — " in him we live, and move, and have our being." And afterward, in writing to the Romans, he takes the same ground. He teaches that the Gentiles had a knowledge of the eternal attributes of God (Rom. i. 19) and saw him in his works (v. 20), and that they also had in their nature a law of duty, enabling them to do the things contained in the law. This he calls " the law written in the heart " (Rom. ii. 14, 15). He blames them, not for ignorance, but for disobedience. The Apostle Paul, therefore, agrees with us in finding in heathen religions essential truth in connection with their errors.

The early Christian apologists often took the same view. Thus Clement of Alexandria believed that God had one great plan for educating the world, of which Christianity was the final step. He refused to consider the Jewish religion as the only divine preparation for Christianity, but regarded the Greek philosophy as also a preparation for Christ. Neander gives his views at length, and says that Clement was the founder of the true view of history.* Tertullian declared the soul to be naturally Christian. The Sibylline books were quoted as good prophetic works along with the Jewish prophets. Socrates was called by the Fathers a Christian before Christ.

Within the last few years the extravagant condemnation of the heathen religions has produced a reaction in their favor. It has been felt to be disparaging to human nature to suppose that almost the whole human race should consent to be fed on error. Such a belief has been seen to be a denial of God's providence, as regards nine tenths of mankind. Accordingly it has become more

---

* Neander, Church History, Vol. I. p. 540 (Am. ed.).

usual of late to rehabilitate heathenism, and to place it on the same level with Christianity, if not above it. The *Vedas* are talked about as though they were somewhat superior to the Old Testament, and Confucius is quoted as an authority quite equal to Paul or John. An ignorant admiration of the sacred books of the Buddhists and Brahmins has succeeded to the former ignorant and sweeping condemnation of them. What is now needed is a fair and candid examination and comparison of these systems from reliable sources.

§ 5. *Comparative Theology will furnish a new Class of Evidences in Support of Christianity.*

Such an examination, doing full justice to all other religions, acknowledging their partial truth and use, will not depreciate, but exalt the value of Christianity. It will furnish a new kind of evidence in its favor. But the usual form of argument may perhaps be changed.

Is Christianity a supernatural or a natural religion? Is it a religion attested to be from God by miracles? This has been the great question in evidences for the last century. The truth and divine origin of Christianity have been made to depend on its supernatural character, and to stand or fall with a certain view of miracles. And then, in order to maintain the reality of miracles, it became necessary to prove the infallibility of the record ; and so we were taught that, to believe in Jesus Christ, we must first believe in the genuineness and authenticity of the whole New Testament. "All the theology of England," says Mr. Pattison,* "was devoted to proving the Christian religion credible, in this manner." "The apostles," said Dr. Johnson, "were being tried one a week for the capital crime of forgery." This was the work of the school of Lardner, Paley, and Whately.

But the real question between Christians and unbelievers in Christianity is, not whether our religion is or is not supernatural; not whether Christ's miracles were or not violations of law; nor whether the New

Essays and Reviews, Article VI.

Testament, as it stands, is the work of inspired men. The main question, back of all these, is different, and not dependent on the views we may happen to take of the universality of law. It is this: Is Christianity, as taught by Jesus, intended by God to be the religion of the human race? Is it only one among natural religions? is it to be superseded in its turn by others, or is it the one religion which is to unite all mankind? "Art thou he that should come, or look we for another?" This is the question which we ask of Jesus of Nazareth, and the answer to which makes the real problem of apologetic theology.

Now the defenders of Christianity have been so occupied with their special disputes about miracles, about naturalism and supernaturalism, and about the inspiration and infallibility of the apostles, that they have left uncultivated the wide field of inquiry belonging to Comparative Theology. But it belongs to this science to establish the truth of Christianity by showing that it possesses all the aptitudes which fit it to be the religion of the human race.

This method of establishing Christianity differs from the traditional argument in this: that, while the last undertakes to *prove* Christianity to be true, this *shows* it to be true. For if we can make it appear, by a fair survey of the principal religions of the world, that, while they are ethnic or local, Christianity is catholic or universal; that, while they are defective, possessing some truths and wanting others, Christianity possesses all; and that, while they are stationary, Christianity is progressive; it will not then be necessary to discuss in what sense it is a supernatural religion. Such a survey will show that it is adapted to the nature of man. When we see adaptation we naturally infer design. If Christianity appears, after a full comparison with other religions, to be the one and only religion which is perfectly adapted to man, it will be impossible to doubt that it was designed by God to be the religion of our race; that it is the providential religion sent by God to man, its truth God's truth, its way the way to God and to heaven.

§ 6. *It will show that, while most of the Religions of the World are Ethnic, or the Religions of Races, Christianity is Catholic, or adapted to become the Religion of all Races.*

By ethnic religions we mean those religions, each of which has always been confined within the boundaries of a particular race or family of mankind, and has never made proselytes or converts, except accidentally, outside of it. By catholic religions we mean those which have shown the desire and power of passing over these limits, and becoming the religion of a considerable number of persons belonging to different races.

Now we are met at once with the striking and obvious fact, that most of the religions of the world are evidently religions limited in some way to particular races or nations. They are, as we have said, *ethnic*. We use this Greek word rather than its Latin equivalent, *gentile*, because *gentile*, though meaning literally " of, or belonging to, a race," has acquired a special sense from its New Testament use as meaning all who are not Jews. The word " ethnic" remains pure from any such secondary or acquired meaning, and signifies simply *that which belongs to a race.*

The science of ethnology is a modern one, and is still in the process of formation. Some of its conclusions, however, may be considered as established. It has forever set aside Blumenbach's old classification of mankind into the Caucasian and four other varieties, and has given us, instead, a division of the largest part of mankind into Indo-European, Semitic, and Turanian families, leaving a considerable penumbra outside as yet unclassified.

That mankind is so divided into races of men it would seem hardly possible to deny. It is proved by physiology, by psychology, by glossology, and by civil history. Physiology shows us anatomical differences between races. There are as marked and real differences between the skull of a Hindoo and that of a Chinaman as between the skulls of an Englishman and a negro. There is not as great a difference, perhaps, but it is as real and as constant. Then the characters of races remain distinct, the same traits reappearing after many centuries exactly as at first. We find the same difference of character between the Jews and Arabs, who are merely different families of the same Semitic race, as existed between their ancestors, Jacob and Esau, as described in the Book of Genesis. Jacob and the Jews are prudent, loving trade, money-making, tenacious of their ideas, living in cities; Esau and the Arabs, careless, wild, hating cities, loving the desert.

A similar example of the maintaining of a moral type is found in the characteristic differences between the German and Kelts, two families of the same Indo-European race. Take an Irishman and a German, working side by side on the Mississippi, and they present the same characteristic differences as the Germans and Kelts described by Tacitus and Cæsar. The German loves liberty, the Kelt equality; the one hates the tyrant, the other the aristocrat; the one is a serious thinker, the other a quick and vivid thinker; the one is a Protestant in religion, the other a Catholic. Ammianus Marcellinus, living in Gaul in the fourth century, describes the Kelts thus (see whether it does not apply to the race now).

"The Gauls," says he, "are mostly tall of stature,* fair and red-haired, and horrible from the fierceness of their eyes, fond of strife, and haughtily insolent. A whole band of strangers would not endure one of them, aided in his brawl by his powerful and blue-eyed wife, especially when with swollen neck and gnashing teeth, poising her huge white arms, she begins, joining kicks to blows, to put forth her fists like stones from a catapult. Most of their voices are terrific and threatening, as well when they are quiet as when they are angry. All ages are thought fit for war. They are a nation very fond of wine, and invent many drinks resembling it, and some of the poorer sort wander about with their senses quite blunted by continual intoxication."

Now we find that each race, beside its special moral qualities, seems also to have special religious qualities, which cause it to tend toward some one kind of religion

---

* In this respect the type has changed.

more than to another kind. These religions are the flower of the race; they come forth from it as its best aroma. Thus we see that Brahmanism is confined to that section or race of the great Aryan family which has occupied India for more than thirty centuries. It belongs to the Hindoos, to the people taking its name from the Indus, by the tributaries of which stream it entered India from the northwest. It has never attempted to extend itself beyond that particular variety of mankind. Perhaps one hundred and fifty millions of men accept it as their faith. It has been held by this race as their religion during a period immense in the history of mankind. Its sacred books are certainly more than three thousand years old. But during all this time it has never communicated itself to any race of men outside of the peninsula of India. It is thus seen to be a strictly ethnic religion, showing neither the tendency nor the desire to become the religion of mankind.

The same thing may be said of the religion of Confucius. It belongs to China and the Chinese. It suits their taste and genius. They have had it as their state religion for some twenty-three hundred years, and it rules the opinions of the rulers of opinion among three hundred millions of men. But out of China Confucius is only a name.

So, too, of the system of Zoroaster. It was for a long period the religion of an Aryan tribe who became the ruling people among mankind. The Persians extended themselves through Western Asia, and conquered many nations, but they never communicated their religion. It was strictly a national or ethnic religion, belonging only to the Iranians and their descendants, the Parsees.

In like manner it may be said that the religion of Egypt, of Greece, of Scandinavia, of the Jews, of Islam, and of Buddhism are ethnic religions. Those of Egypt and Scandinavia are strictly so. It is said, to be sure, that the Greeks borrowed the names of their gods from Egypt, but the gods themselves were entirely different ones. It is also true that some of the gods of the Romans were borrowed from the Greeks, but their life was left behind. They

B

merely repeated by rote the Greek mythology, having no power to invent one for themselves. But the Greek religion they never received. For instead of its fair humanities, the Roman gods were only servants of the state, — a higher kind of consuls, tribunes, and lictors. The real Olympus of Rome was the Senate Chamber on the Capitoline Hill. Judaism also was in reality an ethnic religion, though it aimed at catholicity and expected it, and made proselytes. But it could not tolerate unessentials, and so failed of becoming catholic. The Jewish religion, until it had Christianity to help it, was never able to do more than make proselytes here and there. Christianity, while preaching the doctrines of Jesus and the New Testament, has been able to carry also the weight of the Old Testament, and to give a certain catholicity to Judaism. The religion of Mohammed has been catholic, in that it has become the religion of very different races, — the Arabs, Turks, and Persians, belonging to the three great varieties of the human family. But then Mohammedanism has never sought to make *converts*, but only *subjects ;* it has not asked for belief, but merely for submission. Consequently Mr. Palgrave, Mr. Lane, and Mr. Vambery tell us, that, in Arabia, Egypt, and Turkistan, there are multitudes who are outwardly Mohammedan, but who in their private belief reject Mohammed, and are really Pagans. But, no doubt, there is a catholic tendency both in Judaism and Mohammedanism ; and this comes from the great doctrine which they hold in common with Christianity, — the *unity of God.* Faith in that is the basis of all expectation of a universal religion, and the wish and the power to convert others come from that doctrine of the Divine unity.

But Christianity teaches the unity of God not merely as a supremacy of power and will, but as a supremacy of love and wisdom ; it teaches God as Father, and not merely as King ; so it seeks not merely to make proselytes and subjects, but to make converts. Hence Christianity, beginning as a Semitic religion, among the Jews, went across the Greek Archipelago and converted the

Hellenic and the Latin races ; afterward the Goths, Lombards, Franks, Vandals ; later still, the Saxons, Danes, and Normans. Meantime, its Nestorian missionaries, pushing east, made converts in Armenia, Persia, India, and China. In later days it has converted negroes, Indians, and the people of the Pacific Islands. Something, indeed, stopped its progress after its first triumphant successes during seven or eight centuries. At the tenth century it reached its term. Modern missions, whether those of Jesuits or Protestants, have not converted whole nations and races, but only individuals here and there. The reason of this check, probably, is, that Christians have repeated the mistakes of the Jews and Mohammedans. They have sought to make proselytes to an outward system of worship and ritual, or to make subjects to a *dogma ;* but not to make converts to an idea and a life. When the Christian missionaries shall go and say to the Hindoos or the Buddhists : " You are already on your way toward God, — your religion came from him, and was inspired by his Spirit ; now he sends you something more and higher by his Son, who does not come to destroy but to fulfil, not to take away any good thing you have, but to add to it something better," then we shall see the process of conversion, checked in the ninth and tenth centuries, reinaugurated.

Judaism, Islam, and Christianity, all teaching the strict unity of God, have all aimed at becoming universal. Judaism failed because it sought proselytes instead of making converts. Islam, the religion of Mohammed (in reality a Judaizing Christian sect) failed because it sought to make subjects rather than converts. Its conquests over a variety of races were extensive, but not deep. To-day it holds in its embrace at least four very distinct races, — the Arabs, a Semitic race, the Persians, an Indo-European race, the Negroes, and the Turks or Turanians. But, correctly viewed, Islam is only a heretical Christian sect, and so all this must be credited to the interest of Christianity. Islam is a John the Baptist crying in the wilderness, " Prepare the way of the Lord " ; Mohammed is a schoolmaster to bring men to Christ. It does for the nations just what Judaism did, that is, it teaches the Divine unity. Esau has taken the place of Jacob in the economy of Providence. When the Jews rejected Christ they ceased from their providential work, and their cousins, the Arabs, took their place. The conquests of Islam, therefore, ought to be regarded as the preliminary conquests of Christianity.

There is still another system which has shown some tendencies toward catholicity. This is Buddhism, which has extended itself over the whole of the eastern half of Asia. But though it includes a variety of nationalities, it is doubtful if it includes any variety of races. All the Buddhists appear to belong to the great Mongol family. And although this system originated among the Aryan race -in India, it has let go its hold of that family and transferred itself wholly to the Mongols.

But Christianity, from the first, showed itself capable of taking possession of the convictions of the most different races of mankind. Now, as on the day of Pentecost, many races hear the apostles speak in their own tongues, in which they were born, — Parthians, Medes, Elamites, dwellers in Mesopotamia, Judæa, and Cappadocia, Pontus and Asia, Phrygia and Pamphylia, Egypt and the parts of Lybia about Cyrene, strangers of Rome, Cretes and Arabians. The miracle of tongues was a type of the effect of the truth in penetrating the mind and heart of different nationalities. The Jewish Christians, indeed, tried to repeat in Christianity their old mistake which had prevented Judaism from becoming universal. They wished to insist that no one should become a Christian unless he became a Jew at the same time. If they had succeeded in this, they would have effectually kept the Gospel of Christ from becoming a catholic religion. But the Apostle Paul was raised up for the emergency, and he prevented this suicidal course. Consequently Christianity passed at once into Europe, and became the religion of Greeks and Romans as well as Jews. Paul struck off from it its Jewish shell, told them that as Christians they had nothing to do with the Jewish law, or with Jewish Passovers, Sabbaths, or ceremonies. As Christians they were only to know Christ, and they were not to know him according to the flesh, that is, not as a Jew. So Christianity became at once a catholic religion, consisting in the diffusion of great truths and a divine life. It overflowed the nationalities of Greece and Rome, of North Africa, of Persia and Western Asia, at the very beginning. It conquered the Gothic and German conquerors of the Roman Empire. Under Arian missionaries, it converted Goths, Vandals, Lombards. Under Nestorian missionaries, it penetrated as far east as China, and made converts there. In like manner the Gospel spread over the whole of North Africa, whence it was afterwards expelled by the power of Islam. It has shown itself, therefore, capable of adapting itself to every variety of the human race.

§ 7. *Comparative Theology will probably show that the Ethnic Religions are one-sided, each containing a Truth of its own, but being defective, wanting some corresponding Truth. Christianity, or the Catholic Religion, is complete on every Side.*

Brahmanism, for example, is complete on the side of spirit, defective on the side of matter; full as regards the infinite, empty of the finite; recognizing eternity but not time, God but not nature. It is a vast system of spiritual pantheism, in which there is no reality but God, all else being Maya, or illusion. The Hindoo mind is singularly pious, but also singularly immoral. It has no history, for history belongs to time. No one knows when its sacred books were written, when its civilization began, what caused its progress, what its decline. Gentle, devout, abstract, it is capable at once of the loftiest thoughts and the basest actions. It combines the most ascetic self-denials and abstraction from life with the most voluptuous self-indulgence. The key to the whole system of Hindoo thought and life is in this original tendency to see God, not man; eternity, not time; the infinite, not the finite.

Buddhism, which was a revolt from Brahmanism, has exactly the opposite truths and the opposite defects. Where Brahmanism is strong, it is weak; where Brahmanism is weak, it is strong. It recognizes man, not God; the soul,

not the all; the finite, not the infinite; morality, not piety
Its only God, Buddha, is a man who has passed on through
innumerable transmigrations, till, by means of exemplary
virtues, he has reached the lordship of the universe.   Its
heaven, Nirvana, is indeed the world of infinite bliss; but,
incapable of cognizing the infinite, it calls it nothing.
Heaven, being the inconceivable infinite, is equivalent to
pure negation.   Nature, to the Buddhist, instead of being
the delusive shadow of God, as the Brahman views it, is
envisaged as a nexus of laws, which reward and punish
impartially both obedience and disobedience.

The system of Confucius has many merits, especially
in its influence on society.   The most conservative of all
systems, and also the most prosaic, its essential virtue is
reverence for all that is.   It is not perplexed by any fear or
hope of change; the thing which has been is that which
shall be; and the very idea of progress is eliminated from
the thought of China.   Safety, repose, peace, these are
its blessings.   Probably merely physical comfort, earthly
bien-être, was never carried further than in the Celestial
Empire.   That virtue so much exploded in Western civilization, of respect for parents, remains in full force in
China.   The emperor is honored as the father of his people; ancestors are worshipped in every family; and the
best reward offered for a good action is a patent of nobil-
ity, which does not reach forward to one's children, but
backward to one's parents.   This is the bright side of
Chinese life; the dark side is the fearful ennui, the moral
death, which falls on a people among whom there are no
such things as hope, expectation, or the sense of progress.
Hence the habit of suicide among this people, indicating
their small hold on life.   In every Chinese drama there
are two or three suicides.   A soldier will commit suicide
rather than go into battle.   If you displease a Chinaman,
he will resent the offence by killing himself on your door-
step, hoping thus to give you some inconvenience.   Such
are the merits and such the defects of the system of Confucius.

The doctrine of Zoroaster and of the Zend Avesta is far
nobler.   Its central thought is that each man is a soldier,

bound to battle for good against evil. The world, at the present time, is the scene of a great warfare between the hosts of light and those of darkness. Every man who thinks purely, speaks purely, and acts purely is a servant of Ormazd, the king of light, and thereby helps on his cause. The result of this doctrine was that wonderful Persian empire, which astonished the world for centuries by its brilliant successes; and the virtue and intelligence of the Parsees of the present time, the only representatives in the world of that venerable religion. The one thing lacking to the system is unity. It lives in perpetual conflict. Its virtues are all the virtues of a soldier. Its defects and merits are, both, the polar opposites of those of China. If the everlasting peace of China tends to moral stagnation and death, the perpetual struggle and conflict of Persia tends to exhaustion. The Persian empire rushed through a short career of flame to its tomb; the Chinese empire vegetates, unchanged, through a myriad of years.

If Brahmanism and Buddhism occupy the opposite poles of the same axis of thought, — if the system of Confucius stands opposed, on another axis, to that of Zoroaster, — we find a third development of like polar antagonisms in the systems of ancient Egypt and Greece. Egypt stands for Nature; Greece for Man. Inscrutable as is the mystery of that Sphinx of the Nile, the old religion of Egypt, we can yet trace some phases of its secret. Its reverence for organization appears in the practice of embalming. The bodies of men and of animals seemed to it to be divine. Even vegetable organization had something sacred in it: "O holy nation," said the Roman satirist, "whose gods grow in gardens!" That plastic force of nature which appears in organic life and growth made up, in various forms, as we shall see in the proper place, the Egyptian Pantheon. The life-force of nature became divided into the three groups of gods, the highest of which represented its largest generalizations. Kneph, Neith, Sevech, Pascht, are symbols, according to Lepsius, of the World-Spirit, the World-Matter, Space and Time. Each circle of the gods shows us some working of the mysterious powers of nature, and of its occult laws. But when we come to Greece, these personified laws turn into men. Everything in the Greek Pantheon is human. All human tendencies appear transfigured into glowing forms of light on Mount Olympus. The gods of Egypt are powers and laws; those of Greece are persons.

The opposite tendencies of these antagonist forms of piety appear in the development of Egyptian and Hellenic life. The gods of Egypt were mysteries too far removed from the popular apprehension to be objects of worship; and so religion in Egypt became priestcraft. In Greece, on the other hand, the gods were too familiar, too near to the people, to be worshipped with any real reverence. Partaking in all human faults and vices, it must sooner or later come to pass that familiarity would breed contempt. And as the religion of Egypt perished from being kept away from the people, as an esoteric system in the hands of priests, that of Greece, in which there was no priesthood as an order, came to an end because the gods ceased to be objects of respect at all.

We see, from these examples, how each of the great ethnic religions tends to a disproportionate and excessive, because one-sided, statement of some divine truth or law. The question then emerges at this point: "Is Christianity also one-sided, or does it contain in itself *all* these truths?" Is it *teres atque rotundus,* so as to be able to meet every natural religion with a kindred truth, and thus to supply the defects of each from its own fulness? If it can be shown to possess this amplitude, it at once is placed by itself in an order of its own. It is not to be classified with the other religions, since it does not share their one family fault. In every other instance we can touch with our finger the weak place, the empty side. Is there any such weak side in Christianity? It is the office of Comparative Theology to answer.

The positive side of Brahmanism we saw to be its sense of spiritual realities. That is also fully present in Christianity. Not merely does this appear in such New Testament texts as these: "God is spirit," "The letter killeth, the spirit giveth life": not only does the New Testament just graze and escape Pantheism in such passages as "From whom, and through whom, and to whom are all things," "Who is above all, and through all, and in us all," "In him we live and move and have our being," but the whole history of Christianity is the record of a spiritualism almost too excessive. It has appeared in the worship of the Church, the hymns of the Church, the tendencies to asceticism, the depreciation of earth and man. Christianity, therefore, fully meets Brahmanism on its positive side, while it fulfils its negations, as we shall see hereafter, by adding as full a recognition of man and nature.

The positive side of Buddhism is its cognition of the human soul and the natural laws of the universe. Now, if we look into the New Testament and into the history of the Church, we find this element also fully expressed. It appears in all the parables and teachings of Jesus, in which man is represented as a responsible agent, rewarded or punished according to the exact measure of his works; receiving the government of ten or five cities according to his stewardship. And when we look into the practical working of Christianity we find almost an exaggerated stress laid on the duty of saving one's soul. This excessive estimate is chiefly seen in the monastic system of the Roman Church, and in the Calvinistic sects of Protestantism. It also comes to light again, curiously enough, in such books as Combe's "Constitution of Man," the theory of which is exactly the same as that of the Buddhists; namely, that the aim of life is a prudential virtue, consisting in wise obedience to the natural laws of the universe. Both systems substitute prudence for Providence as the arbiter of human destiny. But, apart from these special tendencies in Christianity, it cannot be doubted that all Christian experience recognizes the positive truth of Buddhism in regarding the human soul as a substantial, finite, but progressive monad, not to be absorbed, as in Brahmanism, in the abyss of absolute being.

2

The positive side of the system of Confucius is the organization of the state on the basis of the family. The government of the emperor is paternal government, the obedience of the subject is filial obedience. Now, though Jesus did not for the first time call God " the Father," he first brought men into a truly filial relation to God. The Roman Church is organized on the family idea. The word " Pope " means the " Father"; he is the father of the whole Church. Every bishop and every priest is also the father of a smaller family, and all those born into the Church are its children, as all born into a family are born sons and daughters of the family. In Protestantism, also, society is composed of families as the body is made up of cells. Only in China, and in Christendom, is family life thus sacred and worshipful. In some patriarchal systems, polygamy annuls the wife and the mother; in others the father is a despot, and the children slaves; in other systems, the crushing authority of the state destroys the independence of the household. Christianity alone accepts with China the religion of family life with all its conservative elements, while it fulfils it with the larger hope of the kingdom of heaven and brotherhood of mankind.

This idea of the kingdom of heaven, so central in Christianity, is also the essential motive in the religion of Zoroaster. As, in the Zend Avesta, every man is a soldier, fighting for light or for darkness, and neutrality is impossible ; so, in the Gospel, light and good stand opposed to darkness and evil as perpetual foes. A certain current of dualism runs through the Christian Scriptures and the teaching of the Church. God and Satan, heaven and hell, are the only alternatives. Every one must choose between them. In the current theology, this dualism has been so emphasized as even to exceed that of the Zend Avesta. The doctrine of everlasting punishment and an everlasting hell has always been the orthodox doctrine in Christianity, while the Zend Avesta probably, and the religion in its subsequent development certainly, teaches universal restoration, and the ultimate triumph of good over evil. Nevertheless, practically, in consequence of the greater richness and fulness of Christianity, this tendency to dualism has been neutralized by its mono-theism, and evil kept subordinate; while, in the Zend religion, the evil principle assumed such proportions as to make it the formidable rival of good in the mind of the worshipper. Here, as before, we may say that Christianity is able to do justice to all the truth involved in the doc-trine of evil, avoiding any superficial optimism, and rec-ognizing the fact that all true life must partake of the nature of a battle.

The positive side of Egyptian religion we saw to be a recognition of the divine element in nature, of that plas-tic, mysterious life which embodies itself in all organisms. Of this view we find little stated explicitly in the New Testament. But that the principles of Christianity con-tain it, implicitly, in an undeveloped form, appears, (1.) Because Christian monotheism differs from Jewish and Mohammedan monotheism, in recognizing God "*in all things*" as well as God "*above all things.*" (2.) Because Christian art and literature differ from classic art and literature in the *romantic* element, which is exactly the sense of this mysterious life in nature. The classic artist is a ποιητής, a maker; the romantic artist is a troubadour, a finder. The one does his work in giving form to a dead material; the other, by seeking for its hidden life. (3.) Because modern science is *invention*, i. e. finding. It recog-nizes mysteries in nature which are to be searched into, and this search becomes a serious religious interest with all truly scientific men. It appears to such men a pro-fanity to doubt or question the revelations of nature, and they believe in its infallible inspiration quite as much as the dogmatist believes in the infallible inspira-tion of Scripture, or the churchman in the infallible in-spiration of the Church. We may, therefore, say, that the essential truth in the Egyptian system has been taken up into our modern Christian life.

And how is it, lastly, with that opposite pole of re-ligious thought which blossomed out in "the fair human-ities of old religion" in the wonderful Hellenic mind? The gods of Greece were men. They were not abstract

ideas, concealing natural powers and laws. They were
open as sunshine, bright as noon, a fair company of men
and women idealized and gracious, just a little way off, a
little way up. It was humanity projected upon the skies,
divine creatures of more than mortal beauty, but thrill-
ing with human life and human sympathies. Has Christianity anything to offer in the place of this charming
system of human gods and goddesses ?

We answer that the fundamental doctrine of Christianity is the incarnation, the word made flesh. It is
God revealed in man. Under some doctrinal type this
has always been believed. The common Trinitarian doctrine states it in a somewhat crude and illogical form.
Yet somehow the man Christ Jesus has always been seen
to be the best revelation of God. But unless there were
some human element in the Deity, he could not reveal
himself so in a human life. The doctrine of the incarnation, therefore, repeats the Mosaic statement that " man
was made in the image of God." Jewish and Mohammedan monotheism separate God entirely from the world.
Philosophic monotheism, in our day, separates God from
man, by teaching that there is nothing in common between the two by which God can be mediated, and so
makes him wholly incomprehensible. Christianity gives
us Emmanuel, God with us, equally removed from the
stern despotic omnipotence of the Semitic monotheism
and the finite and imperfect humanities of Olympus.
We see God in Christ, as full of sympathy with man, God
" in us all "; and yet we see him in nature, providence,
history, as " above all " and " through all." The Roman
Catholic Church has, perhaps, humanized religion too far.
For every god and goddess of Greece she has given us, on
some immortal canvas, an archangel or a saint to be
adored and loved. Instead of Apollo and the Python
we have Guido's St. Michael and the Dragon; in place
of the light, airy Mercury she provides a St. Sebastian;
instead of the " untouched " Diana, some heavenly Agnes
or Cecilia. The Catholic heaven is peopled, all the way
up, with beautiful human forms ; and on the upper throne
we have holiness and tenderness incarnate in the queen

of heaven and her divine Son. All the Greek humanities are thus fulfilled in the ample faith of Christendom.

By such a critical survey as we have thus sketched in mere outline it will be seen that each of the great ethnic religions is full on one side, but empty on the other, while Christianity is full all round. Christianity is adapted to take their place, not because they are false, but because they are true as far as they go. They "know in part and prophesy in part ; but when that which is perfect is come, then that which is in part shall be done away."

§ 8. *Comparative Theology will probably show that Ethnic Religions are arrested, or degenerate, and will come to an End, while the Catholic Religion is capable of a progressive Development.*

The religions of Persia, Egypt, Greece, Rome, have come to an end ; having shared the fate of the national civilization of which each was a part. The religions of China, Islam, Buddha, and Judæa have all been arrested, and remain unchanged and seemingly unchangeable. Like great vessels anchored in a stream, the current of time flows past them, and each year they are further behind the spirit of the age, and less in harmony with its demands. Christianity alone, of all human religions, seems to possess the power of keeping abreast with the advancing civilization of the world. As the child's soul grows with his body, so that when he becomes a man it is a man's soul and not a child's, so the Gospel of Jesus continues the soul of all human culture. It continually drops its old forms and takes new ones. It passed out of its Jewish body under the guidance of Paul. In a speculative age it unfolded into creeds and systems. In a worshipping age it developed ceremonies and a ritual. When the fall of Rome left Europe without unity or centre, it gave it an organization and order through the Papacy. When the Papacy became a tyranny, and the Renaissance called for free thought, it suddenly put forth

Protestantism, as the tree by the water-side sends forth its shoots in due season. Protestantism, free as air, opens out into the various sects, each taking hold of some human need ; Lutheranism, Calvinism, Methodism, Swedenborgianism, or Rationalism. Christianity blossoms out into modern science, literature, art, — children who indeed often forget their mother, and are ignorant of their source, but which are still fed from her breasts and partake of her life. Christianity, the spirit of faith, hope, and love, is the deep fountain of modern civilization. Its inventions are for the many, not for the few. Its science is not hoarded, but diffused. It elevates the masses, who everywhere else have been trampled down. The friend of the people, it tends to free schools, a free press, a free government, the abolition of slavery, war, vice, and the melioration of society. We cannot, indeed, here *prove* that Christianity is the cause of these features peculiar to modern life ; but we find it everywhere associated with them, and so we can say that it only, of all the religions of mankind, has been capable of accompanying man in his progress from evil to good, from good to better.

We have merely suggested some of the results to which the study of Comparative Theology may lead us. They will appear more fully as we proceed in our examination of the religions, and subsequently in their comparison. This introductory chapter has been designed as a sketch of the course which the work will take. When we have completed our survey, the results to which we hope to arrive will be these, if we succeed in what we have undertaken : —

1. All the great religions of the world, except Christianity and Mohammedanism, are ethnic religions, or religions limited to a single nation or race. Christianity alone (including Mohammedanism and Judaism, which are its temporary and local forms) is the religion of all races.

2. Every ethnic religion has its positive and negative side. Its positive side is that which holds some vital truth ; its negative side is the absence of some other essential truth. Every such religion is true and providential, but each limited and imperfect.

3. Christianity alone is a πλήρωμα, or a fulness of truth, not coming to destroy but to fulfil the previous religions; but being capable of replacing them by teaching all the truth they have taught, and supplying that which they have omitted.

4. Christianity, being not a system but a life, not a creed or a form, but a spirit; is able to meet all the changing wants of an advancing civilization by new developments and adaptations, constantly feeding the life of man at its roots by fresh supplies of faith in God and faith in man.

CHAPTER II.

CONFUCIUS AND THE CHINESE, OR THE PROSE OF ASIA.

§ 1. *Peculiarities of Chinese Civilization.*

IN qualifying the Chinese mind as prosaic, and in calling the writings of Confucius and his successors *prose*, we intend no disrespect to either.   Prose is as good as poetry.   But we mean to indicate the point of view from which the study of the Chinese teachers should be approached.   Accustomed to regard the East as the land of imagination; reading in our childhood the wild romances of Arabia; passing, in the poetry of Persia, into an atmosphere of tender and entrancing song; then, as we go farther East into India, encountering the vast epics of the Mahá-Bhárata and the Rámáyana; — we might naturally expect to find in far Cathay a still wilder flight of the Asiatic Muse.   Not at all.   We drop at once from unbridled romance into the most colorless prose.   Another race comes to us, which seems to have no affinity with Asia, as we have been accustomed to think of Asia.   No more aspiration, no flights of fancy, but the worship of order, decency, propriety, and peaceful commonplaces.   As the people, so the priests.   The works of Confucius and his commentators are as level as the valley of their great river, the Yang-tse-kiang, which the tide ascends for four hundred miles.   All in these writings is calm, serious, and moral.   They assume that all men desire to be made better, and will take the trouble to find out how they can be made so. It is not thought necessary to entice them into goodness by the attractions of eloquence, the charm of imagery, or the fascinations of a brilliant wit. These philosophers have a Quaker style, a dress of plain drab, used only for clothing the thought, not at all for its ornament.

And surely we ought not to ask for any other attraction than the subject itself, in order to find interest in China and its teachers. The Chinese Empire, which contains more than five millions of square miles, or twice the area of the United States, has a population of five hundred millions, or half the number of the human beings inhabiting the globe. China proper, inhabited by the Chinese, is half as large as Europe, and contains about three hundred and sixty millions of inhabitants. There are eighteen provinces in China, many of which contain, singly, more inhabitants than some of the great states of Europe. But on many other accounts this nation is deeply interesting.

China is the type of permanence in the world. To say that it is older than any other *existing* nation is saying very little. Herodotus, who has been call'd the Father of History, travelled in Egypt about 450 B. C. He studied its monuments, bearing the names of kings who were as distant from his time as he is from ours, — monuments which even then belonged to a gray antiquity. But the kings who erected those monuments were possibly posterior to the founders of the Chinese Empire. Porcelain vessels, with Chinese mottoes on them, have been found in those ancient tombs, in shape, material, and appearance precisely like those which are made in China to-day ; and Rosellini believes them to have been imported from China by kings contemporary with Moses, or before him. This nation and its institutions have outlasted everything. The ancient Bactrian and Assyrian kingdoms, the Persian monarchy, Greece and Rome, have all risen, flourished, and fallen, — and China continues still the same. The dynasty has been occasionally changed ; but the laws, customs, institutions, all that makes national life, have

2 *   c

continued. The authentic history of China commences some two thousand years before Christ, and a thousand years in this history is like a century in that of any other people. The oral language of China has continued the same that it is now for thirty centuries. The great wall bounding the empire on the north, which is twelve hundred and forty miles long and twenty feet high, with towers every few hundred yards, — which crosses mountain ridges, descends into valleys, and is carried over rivers on arches, — was built two hundred years before Christ, probably to repel those fierce tribes who, after ineffectual attempts to conquer China, travelled westward till they appeared on the borders of Europe five hundred years later, and, under the name of Huns, assisted in the downfall of the Roman Empire. All China was intersected with canals at a period when none existed in Europe. The great canal, like the great wall, is unrivalled by any similar existing work. It is twice the length of the Erie Canal, is from two hundred to a thousand feet wide, and has enormous banks built of solid granite along a great part of its course. One of the important mechanical inventions of modern Europe is the Artesian well. That sunk at Grenelle, in France, was long supposed to be the deepest in the world, going down eighteen hundred feet. One at St. Louis, in the United States, has since been drilled to a depth, as has recently been stated, of about four thousand.* But in China these wells are found by tens of thousands, sunk at very remote periods to obtain salt water. The method used by the Chinese from immemorial time has recently been adopted instead of our own as being the most simple and economical. The

---

* The actual depth reached in the St. Louis well, before the enterprise was abandoned, was 3,843½ feet on August 9, 1869. This well was bored for the use of the St. Louis County Insane Asylum, at the public expense. It was commenced March 31, 1866, under the direction of Mr. Charles H. Atkeson. At the depth of 1,222 feet the water became saltish, then sulphury. The temperature of the water, at the bottom of the well, was 105° F. Toward the end of the work it seemed as if the limit of the strength of wood and iron had been reached. The poles often broke at points two or three thousand feet down. "Annual Report (1870) of the Superintendent of the St. Louis County Insane Asylum."

Chinese have been long acquainted with the circulation of the blood ; they inoculated for the small-pox in the ninth century ; and about the same time they invented printing. Their bronze money was made as early as 1100 B. C., and its form has not been changed since the beginning of the Christian era. The mariner's compass, gunpowder, and the art of printing were made known to Europe through stories told by missionaries returning from Asia. These missionaries, coasting the shores of the Celestial Empire in Chinese junks, saw a little box containing a magnetized needle, called Ting-nan-Tchen, or "needle which points to the south." They also noticed terrible machines used by the armies in China called Ho-pao or fire-guns, into which was put an inflammable powder, which produced a noise like thunder and projected stones and pieces of iron with irresistible force.

Father Huc, in his " Christianity in China," says that "the Europeans who penetrated into China were no less struck with the libraries of the Chinese than with their artillery. They were astonished at the sight of the elegant books printed rapidly upon a pliant, silky paper by means of wooden blocks. The first edition of the classical works printed in China appeared in 958, five hundred years before the invention of Gutenberg. The missionaries had, doubtless, often been busied in their convents with the laborious work of copying manuscript books, and the simple Chinese method of printing must have particularly attracted their attention. Many other marvellous productions were noticed, such as silk, porcelain, playing-cards, spectacles, and other products of art and industry unknown in Europe. They brought back these new ideas to Europe ; 'and from that time,' says Abel Remusat, 'the West began to hold in due esteem the most beautiful, the most populous, and the most anciently civilized of all the four quarters of the world. The arts, the religious faith, and the languages of its people were studied, and it was even proposed to establish a professorship for the Tartar language in the University of Paris. The world seemed to open towards the East ; geography made immense strides, and ardor for discovery opened a new vent for the adventurous spirit of the Europeans. As our own hemisphere became better known, the idea of another ceased to appear a wholly improbable paradox ; and in seeking the Zipangon of Marco Polo, Christopher Columbus discovered the New World.' "

The first aspect of China produces that impression on the mind which we call the grotesque. This is merely because the customs of this singular nation are so opposite to our own. They seem morally, no less than physically, our antipodes. Their habits are as opposite to ours as the direction of their bodies. We stand feet to feet in everything. In boxing the compass they say " westnorth " instead of northwest, " eastsouth " instead of southeast, and their compass-needle points south instead of north. Their soldiers wear quilted petticoats, satin boots, and bead necklaces, carry umbrellas and fans, and go to a night attack with lanterns in their hands, being more afraid of the dark than of exposing themselves to the enemy. The people are very fond of fireworks, but prefer to have them in the daytime. Ladies ride in wheelbarrows, and cows are driven in carriages. While in Europe the feet are put in the stocks, in China the stocks are hung round the neck. In China the family name comes first, and the personal name afterward. Instead of saying Benjamin Franklin or Walter Scott they would say Franklin Benjamin, Scott Walter. Thus the Chinese name of Confucius, Kung-fu-tsee, means the Holy Master Kung ;— Kung is the family name. In the recent wars with the English the mandarins or soldiers would sometimes run away, and then commit suicide to avoid punishment. In getting on a horse, the Chinese mount on the right side. Their old men fly kites, while the little boys look on. The left hand is the seat of honor, and to keep on your hat is a sign of respect. Visiting cards are painted red, and are four feet long. In the opinion of the Chinese, the seat of the understanding is the stomach. They have villages which contain a million of inhabitants. Their boats are drawn by men, but their carriages are moved by sails. A married woman while young and pretty is a slave, but when she becomes old and withered is the most powerful, respected, and beloved person in the family. The emperor is regarded with the most profound reverence, but the empress mother is a greater person than he. When a man furnishes his house, instead of laying stress, as we do, on rosewood pianos and carved mahogany, his first ambition is for a handsome camphor-wood coffin, which he keeps in the best place in his room. The interest of money is thirty-six per cent, which, to be sure, we also give in hard times to stave off a stoppage, while with them it is the legal rate. We once heard a bad dinner described thus : " The meat was cold, the wine was hot, and everything was sour but the vinegar." This would not so much displease the Chinese, who carefully warm their wine, while we ice ours. They understand good living, however, very well, are great epicures, and somewhat gourmands, for, after dining on thirty dishes, they will sometimes eat a duck by way of a finish. They toss their meat into their mouths to a tune, every man keeping time with his chop-sticks, while we, on the contrary, make anything but harmony with the clatter of our knives and forks. A Chinaman will not drink a drop of milk, but he will devour birds'-nests, snails, and the fins of sharks with a great relish. Our mourning color is black and theirs is white ; they mourn for their parents three years, we a much shorter time. The principal room in their houses is called " the hall of ancestors," the pictures or tablets of whom, set up against the wall, are worshipped by them ; we, on the other hand, are only too apt to send our grandfather's portrait to the garret.*

---

* Andrew Wilson (" The Ever-Victorious Army, Blackwood, 1868 ") says that "the Chinese people stand unsurpassed, and probably unequalled, in regard to the possession of freedom and self-government." He denies that infanticide is common in China. " Indeed," says he, "there is nothing a Chinaman dreads so much as to die childless. Every Chinaman desires to have as large a family as possible ; and the labors of female children are very profitable."

§ 2. *Chinese Government based on Education.   Civil-Service Examinations.*

Such are a few of the external differences between the Chinese customs and ours.   But the most essential peculiarity of this nation is the high value which they attribute to knowledge, and the distinctions and rewards which they bestow on scholarship.   All the civil offices in the Empire are given as rewards of literary merit.   The government, indeed, is called a complete despotism, and the emperor is said to have absolute authority.   He is not bound by any written constitution, indeed; but the public opinion of the land holds him, nevertheless, to a strict responsibility. He, no less than his people, is bound by a law higher than that of any private will, — the authority of custom. For, in China, more than anywhere else, "what is gray with age becomes religion."   The authority of the emperor is simply authority to govern according to the ancient usages of the country, and whenever these are persistently violated, a revolution takes place and the dynasty is changed.   But a revolution in China changes nothing but the person of the monarch ; the unwritten constitution of old usages remains in full force.   "A principle as old as the monarchy," says Du Halde, "is this, that the state is a large family, and the emperor is in the place of both father and mother.   He must govern his people with affection and goodness ; he must attend to the smallest matters which concern their happiness.   When he is not supposed to have this sentiment, he soon loses his hold on the reverence of the people, and his throne becomes insecure."   The emperor, therefore, is always studying how to preserve this reputation.   When a province is afflicted by famine, inundation, or any other calamity, he shuts himself in his palace, fasts, and publishes decrees to relieve it of taxes and afford it aid.

The true power of the government is in the literary class.   The government, though nominally a monarchy, is really an aristocracy.   But it is not an aristocracy of birth, like that of England, for the humblest man's son can obtain a place in it ; neither is it an aristocracy of wealth, like ours in the United States, nor a military aristocracy, like that of Russia, nor an aristocracy of priests, like that of ancient Egypt, and of some modern countries, — as, for instance, that of Paraguay under the Jesuits, or that of the Sandwich Islands under the Protestant missionaries; but it is a literary aristocracy.

The civil officers in China are called mandarins. They are chosen from the three degrees of learned men, who may be called the bachelors, licentiates, and doctors. All persons may be candidates for the first degree, except three excluded classes, — boatmen, barbers, and actors. The candidates are examined by the governors of their own towns. Of those approved, a few are selected after another examination. These again are examined by an officer who makes a circuit once in three years for that purpose. They are placed alone in little rooms or closets, with pencils, ink, and paper, and a subject is given them to write upon. Out of some four hundred candidates fifteen may be selected, who receive the lowest degree. There is another triennial examination for the second degree, at which a small number of the bachelors are promoted. The examination for the highest degree, that of doctor, is held at Pekin only, when some three hundred are taken out of five thousand. These are capable of receiving the highest offices. Whenever a vacancy occurs, one of those who have received a degree is taken by lot from the few senior names. But a few years since, there were five thousand of the highest rank, and twenty-seven thousand of the second rank, who had not received employment.

The subjects upon which the candidates are examined, and the methods of these examinations, are thus described in the Shanghae Almanac (1852).*

The examinations for the degree of Keujin (or licentiate) takes place at the principal city of each province once in three years. The average number of bachelors in the large province of Keang-Nan (which contains seventy millions of inhabitants) is twenty thousand, out of whom

---

* Quoted by Mr. Meadows, who warrants the correctness of the account. "The Chinese and their Rebellions," p. 404.

only about two hundred succeed. Sixty-five mandarins are deputed for this examination, besides subordinate officials. The two chief examiners are sent from Pekin. When the candidates enter the examination hall they are searched for books or manuscripts, which might assist them in writing their essays. This precaution is not superfluous, for many plans have been invented to enable mediocre people to pass. Sometimes a thin book, printed on very small type from copperplates, is slipped into a hole in the sole of the shoe. But persons detected in such practices are ruined for life. In a list of one hundred and forty-four successful candidates, in 1851, thirteen were over forty years of age, and one under fourteen years; seven were under twenty; and all, to succeed, must have known by heart the whole of the Sacred Books, besides being well read in history.

Three sets of themes are given, each occupying two days and a night, and until that time is expired no one is allowed to leave his apartment, which is scarcely large enough to sleep in. The essays must not contain more than seven hundred characters, and no erasure or correction is allowed. On the first days the themes are taken from the Four Books; on the next, from the older classics; on the last, miscellaneous questions are given. The themes are such as these: " Choo-tsze, in commenting on the Shoo-King, made use of four authors, who sometimes say too much, at other times too little; sometimes their explanations are forced, at other times too ornamental. What have you to observe on them ? " " Chinshow had great abilities for historic writing. In his Three Kingdoms he has depreciated Choo-ko-leang, and made very light of E and E, two other celebrated characters. What is it that he says of them ? "

These public-service examinations are conducted with the greatest impartiality. They were established about a thousand years ago, and have been gradually improved during the intervening time. They form the basis of the whole system of Chinese government. They make a good education universally desirable, as the poorest man may see his son thus advanced to the highest position.

All of the hundreds of thousands who prepare to compete are obliged to know the whole system of Confucius, to commit to memory all his moral doctrines, and to become familiar with all the traditional wisdom of the land. Thus a public opinion in favor of existing institutions and the fundamental ideas of Chinese government is continually created anew.

What an immense advantage it would be to our own country if we should adopt this institution of China! Instead of making offices the prize of impudence, political management, and party services, let them be competed for by all who consider themselves qualified. Let all offices now given by appointment be hereafter bestowed on those who show themselves best qualified to perform the duties. Each class of offices would of course require a different kind of examination. For some, physical culture as well as mental might be required. Persons who wished diplomatic situations should be prepared in a knowledge of foreign languages as well as of international law. All should be examined on the Constitution and history of the United States. Candidates for the Post-Office Department should be good copyists, quick at arithmetic, and acquainted with book-keeping. It is true that we cannot by an examination obtain a certain knowledge of moral qualities; but industry, accuracy, fidelity in work would certainly show themselves. A change from the present corrupt and corrupting system of appointments to that of competitive examinations would do more just now for our country than any other measure of reconstruction which can be proposed. The permanence of Chinese institutions is believed, by those who know best, to result from the influence of the literary class. Literature is naturally conservative; the tone of the literature studied is eminently conservative; and the most intelligent men in the empire are personally interested in the continuance of the institutions under which they hope to attain position and fortune.

The highest civil offices are seats at the great tribunals or boards, and the positions of viceroys, or governors, of the eighteen provinces.

The boards áre : —

Ly Pou, Board of Appointment of Mandarins.

Hou Pou, Board of Finance.

Lee Pou, Board of Ceremonies.

Ping Pou, Board of War.

Hing Pou, Board of Criminal Justice.

Kong Pou, Board of Works, — canals, bridges, &c.

The members of these boards, with their councillors and subordinates, amount to twelve hundred officers. Then there is the Board of Doctors of the Han Lin College, who have charge of the archives, history of the empire, &c. ; and the Board of Censors, who are the highest mandarins, and have a peculiar office. Their duty is to stand between the people and the mandarins, and between the people and the emperor, and even rebuke the latter if they find him doing wrong. This is rather a perilous duty, but it is often faithfully performed. A censor, who went to tell the emperor of some faults, took his coffin with him, and left it at the door of the palace. Two censors remonstrated with a late emperor on the expenses of his palace, specifying the sums uselessly lavished for perfumes and flowers for his concubines, and stating that a million of taels of silver might be saved for the poor by reducing these expenses. Sung, the commissioner who attended Lord Macartney, remonstrated with the Emperor Kiaking on his attachment to play-actors and strong drink, which degraded him in the eyes of the people. The emperor, highly irritated, asked him what punishment he deserved for his insolence. "Quartering," said Sung. "Choose another," said the emperor. "Let me be beheaded." "Choose again," said the emperor ; and Sung asked to be strangled. The next day the emperor appointed him governor of a distant province, — afraid to punish him for the faithful discharge of his duty, but glad to have him at a distance. Many such anecdotes are related, showing that there is some moral courage in China.

The governor of a province, or viceroy, has great power. He also is chosen from among the mandarins in the way described. The only limitations of his power are these : he is bound to make a full report every three years of the affairs of the province, *and give in it an account of his own faults,* and if he omits any, and they are discovered in other ways, he is punished by degradation, bambooing, or death. It is the right of any subject, however humble, to complain to the emperor himself against any officer, however high ; and for this purpose a large drum is placed at one of the palace gates. Whoever strikes it has his case examined under the emperor's eye, and if he has been wronged, his wrongs are redressed, but if he has complained unnecessarily, he is severely punished. Imperial visitors, sent by the Board of Censors, may suddenly arrive at any time to examine the concerns of a province ; and a governor or other public officer who is caught tripping is immediately reported and punished.

Thus the political institutions of China are built on literature. Knowledge is the road to power and wealth. All the talent and knowledge of the nation are interested in the support of institutions which give to them either power or the hope of it. And these institutions work well. The machinery is simple, but it produces a vast amount of happiness and domestic virtue. While in most parts of Asia the people are oppressed by petty tyrants, and ground down by taxes, — while they have no motive to improve their condition, since every advance will only expose them to greater extortion, — the people of China are industrious and happy. In no part of the world has agriculture been carried to such perfection. Every piece of ground in the cultivated parts of the empire, except those portions devoted to ancestral monuments, is made to yield two or three crops annually, by the careful tillage bestowed on it. The ceremony of opening the soil at the beginning of the year, at which the emperor officiates, originated two thousand years ago. Farms are small, — of one or two acres, — and each family raises on its farm all that it consumes. Silk and cotton are cultivated and manufactured in families, each man spinning, weaving, and dyeing his own web. In the manufacture of porcelain, on the contrary, the division of labor is carried very far. The best is made at the village of Kiangsee, which contains a million of inhabitants. Seventy hands are sometimes employed on a single cup. The Chinese are very skilful in working horn and ivory. Large lanterns are made of horn, transparent and without a flaw. At Birmingham men have tried with machines to cut ivory in the same manner as the Chinese, and have failed.

§ 3. *Life and Character of Confucius.*

Of this nation the great teacher for twenty-three centuries has been Confucius. He was born 551 B. C., and was contemporary with the Tarquins, Pythagoras, and Cyrus. About his time occurred the return of the Jews from Babylon and the invasion of Greece by Xerxes. His descendants have always enjoyed high privileges, and there are now some forty thousand of them in China, seventy generations and more removed from their great ancestor. His is the oldest family in the world, unless we consider the Jews as a single family descended from Abraham. His influence, through his writings, on the minds of so many millions of human beings is greater than that of any man who ever lived, excepting the writers of the Bible ; and in saying this we do not forget the names of Mohammed, Aristotle, St. Augustine, and Luther. So far as we can see, it is the influence of Confucius which has maintained, though probably not originated, in China, that profound reverence for parents, that strong family affection, that love of order, that regard for knowledge and deference for literary men, which are fundamental principles underlying all the Chinese institutions. His minute and practical system of morals, studied as it is by all the learned, and constituting the sum of knowledge and the principle of government in China, has exerted and exerts an influence on that innumerable people which it is impossible to estimate, but which makes us admire the power which can emanate from a single soul.

To exert such an influence requires greatness. If the tree is to be known by its fruits, Confucius must have been one of the master minds of our race. The supposition that a man of low morals or small intellect, an impostor or an enthusiast, could influence the world, is a theory which is an insult to human nature. The time for such theories has happily gone by. We now know that nothing can come of nothing, — that a fire of straw may make a bright blaze, but must necessarily soon go out. A light which illuminates centuries must be more than an ignis fatuus. Accordingly we should approach Confucius with respect, and expect to find something good and wise in his writings. It is only a loving spirit which will enable us to penetrate the difficulties which surround the study, and to apprehend something of the true genius of the man and his teachings. As there is no immediate danger of becoming his followers, we can see no objections to such a course, which also appears to be a species of mental hospitality, eminently in accordance with the spirit of our own Master.

Confucius belongs to that small company of select ones whose lives have been devoted to the moral elevation of their fellow-men. Among them he stands high, for he sought to implant the purest principles of religion and morals in the character of the whole people, and succeeded in doing it. To show that this was his purpose it will be necessary to give a brief sketch of his life.

His ancestors were eminent statesmen and soldiers in the small country of Loo, then an independent kingdom, now a Chinese province. The year of his birth was that in which Cyrus became king of Persia. His father, one of the highest officers of the kingdom, and a brave soldier, died when Confucius was three years old. He was a studious boy, and when fifteen years old had studied the five sacred books called Kings. He was married at the age of nineteen, and had only one son by his only wife. This son died before Confucius, leaving as his posterity a single grandchild, from whom the great multitudes of his descendants now in China were derived. This grandson was second only to Confucius in wisdom, and was the teacher of the illustrious Mencius.

The first part of the life of Confucius was spent in attempting to reform the abuses of society by means of the official stations which he held, by his influence with princes, and by travelling and intercourse with men. The second period was that in which he was recalled from his travels to become a minister in his native country, the kingdom of Loo. Here he applied his theories of government, and tested their practicability. He was then fifty years old. His success was soon apparent in the growing prosperity of the whole people. Instead of the tyranny which before prevailed, they were now ruled according to his idea of good government, — that of the father of a family. Confidence was restored to the public mind, and all good influences followed. But the tree was not yet deeply enough rooted to resist accidents, and all his wise arrangements were suddenly overthrown by the caprice of the monarch, who, tired of the austere virtue of Confucius, suddenly plunged into a career of dissipation. Confucius resigned his office, and again became a wanderer, but now with a new motive. He had before travelled to learn, now he travelled to teach. He collected disciples around him, and, no longer seeking to gain the ear of princes, he diffused his ideas among the common people by means of his disciples, whom he sent out everywhere to communicate his doctrines. So, amid many vicissitudes of outward fortune, he lived till he was seventy-three years old. In the last years of his life he occupied himself in publishing his works, and in editing the Sacred Books. His disciples had become very numerous, historians estimating them at three thousand, of whom five hundred had attained to official station, seventy-two had penetrated deeply into his system, and ten, of the highest class of mind and character, were continually near his person. Of these Hwuy was especially valued by him, as having early attained superior virtue. He frequently referred to him in his conversations. " I saw him continually advance," said he, " but I never saw him stop in the path of knowledge." Again he says : " The wisest of my disciples, having one idea, understands two. Hwuy, having one understands ten." One of the select ten disciples, Tszee-loo, was rash and impetuous like the Apostle Peter. Another, Tszee-Kung, was loving and tender like the Apostle John ; he built a house near the grave of Confucius, wherein to mourn for him after his death.

The last years of the life of Confucius were devoted to editing the Sacred Books, or Kings. As we now have them they come from him. Authentic records of Chinese history extend back to 2357 B. C., while the Chinese philosophy originated with Fuh-he, who lived about 3327 B. C. He it was who substituted writing for the knotted strings which before formed the only means of record. He was also the author of the Eight Diagrams, — each consisting of three lines, half of which are whole and half broken in two, — which by their various combinations are supposed to represent the active and passive principles of the universe in all their essential forms. Confucius edited the Yih-King, the Shoo-King, the She-King, and the Le-Ke, which constitute the whole of the ancient literature of China which has come down to posterity.* The Four Books, which contain the doctrines of Confucius, and of his school, were not written by himself, but composed by others after his death.

One of these is called the "Immutable Mean," and its object is to show that virtue consists in avoiding extremes. Another — the Lun-Yu, or Analects — contains the conversation or table-talk of Confucius, and somewhat resembles the Memorabilia of Xenophon and Boswell's Life of Johnson.*

* Dr. Legge thus arranges the Sacred Books of China, or the Chinese Classics : —

  A. The Five *King*. [*King* means a web of cloth, or the warp which keeps the threads in their place.]
    (a) *Yih-King*. (Changes.)
    (b) *Shoo-King*. (History.)
    (c) *She-King*. (Odes.)
    (d) *Le-Ke-King*. (Rites.)
    (e) *Ch'un-Ts'eu*. (Spring and Autumn. Annals from B. C. 721 to 480.)

  B. The Four Books.
    (a) *Lun-Yu*. (Analects, or Table-Talk of Confucius.)
    (b) *Ta-Hio*. (Great Learning. Written by *Tsang-Sin*, a disciple of Confucius.)
    (c) *Chung-Yung* (or Doctrine of the Mean), ascribed to *Kung-Keih*, the grandson of Confucius.
    (d) Works of *Mencius*.

After the death of Confucius there was a period in which the Sacred Books were much corrupted, down to the *Han* dynasty (B. C. 201 to

The life of Confucius was thus devoted to communicating to the Chinese nation a few great moral and religious principles, which he believed would insure the happiness of the people. His devotion to this aim appears in his writings. Thus he says : —

" At fifteen years I longed for wisdom. At thirty my mind was fixed in the pursuit of it. At forty I saw clearly certain principles. At fifty I understood the rule given by heaven. At sixty everything I heard I easily understood. At seventy the desires of my heart no longer transgressed the law."

" If in the morning I hear about the right way, and in the evening I die, I can be happy."

He says of himself : " He is a man who through his earnestness in seeking knowledge forgets his food, and in his joy for having found it loses all sense of his toil, and thus occupied is unconscious that he has almost reached old age."

Again : " Coarse rice for food, water to drink, the bended arm for a pillow, — happiness may be enjoyed even with these ; but without virtue both riches and honor seem to me like the passing cloud."

" Grieve not that men know not you ; grieve that you know not men."

A. D. 24), which collected, edited, and revised them : since which time they have been watched with the greatest care.

" The evidence is complete that the Classical Books of China have come down from at least a century before our era, substantially the same as we have them at present." — *Legge*, Vol. I. Chap. I. § 2.

The Four Books have been translated into French, German, and English. Dr. Marshman translated the Lun-Yu. Mr. Collie afterward published at Calcutta the Four Books. But within a few years the labors of previous sinologues have been almost superseded by Dr. Legge's splendid work, still in process of publication. We have, as yet, only the volumes containing the Four Books of Confucius and his successors, and a portion of the Kings. Dr. Legge's work is in Chinese and English, with copious notes and extracts from many Chinese commentators. In his notes, and his preliminary dissertations, he endeavors to do justice to Confucius and his doctrines. Perhaps he does not fully succeed in this, but it is evident that he respects the Chinese sage, and is never willingly unfair to him. If to the books above mentioned be added the works of Pauthier, Stanislas Julien, Mohl, and other French sinologues, and the German works on the same subject, we have a sufficient apparatus for the study of Chinese thought.

"To rule with equity is like the North Star, which is fixed, and all the rest go round it."

"The essence of knowledge is, having it, to apply it; not having it, to confess your ignorance."

"Worship as though the Deity were present."

"If my mind is not engaged in my worship, it is as though I worshipped not."

"Formerly, in hearing men, I heard their words, and gave them credit for their conduct; now I hear their words, and observe their conduct."

"A man's life depends on virtue; if a bad man lives, it is only by good fortune."

"Some proceed blindly to action, without knowledge; I hear much, and select the best course."

He was once found fault with, when in office, for not opposing the marriage of a ruler with a distant relation, which was an offence against Chinese propriety. He said: "I am a happy man; if I have a fault, men observe it."

Confucius was humble. He said: "I cannot bear to hear myself called equal to the sages and the good. All that can be said of me is, that I study with delight the conduct of the sages, and instruct men without weariness therein."

"The good man is serene," said he, "the bad always in fear."

"A good man regards the ROOT; he fixes the root, and all else flows out of it. The root is filial piety; the fruit brotherly love."

"There may be fair words and an humble countenance when there is little real virtue."

"I daily examine myself in a threefold manner: in my transactions with men, if I am upright; in my intercourse with friends, if I am faithful; and whether I illustrate the teachings of my master in my conduct."

"Faithfulness and sincerity are the highest things."

"When you transgress, do not fear to return."

"Learn the past and you will know the future."

The great principles which he taught were chiefly based on family affection and duty. He taught kings that they

3   D

were to treat their subjects as children, subjects to respect the kings as parents ; and these ideas so penetrated the national mind, that emperors are obliged to seem to govern thus, even if they do not desire it. Confucius was a teacher of reverence, — reverence for God, respect for parents, respect and reverence for the past and its legacies, for the great men and great ideas of former times. He taught men also to regard each other as brethren, and even the golden rule, in its negative if not its positive form, is to be found in his writings.

Curiously enough, this teacher of reverence was distinguished by a remarkable lump on the top of his head, where the phrenologists have placed the organ of veneration.* Rooted in his organization, and strengthened by all his convictions, this element of adoration seemed to him the crown of the whole moral nature of man. But, while full of veneration, he seems to have been deficient in the sense of spiritual things. A personal God was unknown to him ; so that his worship was directed, not to God, but to antiquity, to ancestors, to propriety and usage, to the state as father and mother of its subjects, to the ruler as in the place of authority. Perfectly sincere, deeply and absolutely assured of all that he knew, he said nothing he did not believe. His power came not only from the depth and clearness of his convictions, but from the absolute honesty of his soul.

Lao-tse, for twenty-eight years his contemporary, founder of one of the three existing religions of China, — Tao-ism, — was a man of perhaps equal intelligence. But he was chiefly a thinker ; he made no attempt to elevate the people ; his purpose was to repress the passions, and to preserve the soul in a perfect equanimity. He was the Zeno of the East, founder of a Chinese stoicism. With him virtue is sure of its reward ; everything is arranged by a fixed law. His disciples afterwards added to his system a thaumaturgic element and an invocation of departed spirits, so that now it resembles our modern Spiritism ; but the original doctrine of Lao-tse was rationalism

---

* " On the top of his head was a remarkable formation, in consequence of which he was named Kew." — Legge, Vol. 1. Chap. VI. (note).

in philosophy and stoicism in morals. Confucius is said, in a Chinese work, to have visited him, and to have frankly confessed his inability to understand him. " I know how birds fly, how fishes swim, how animals run. The bird may be shot, the fish hooked, and the beast snared. But there is the dragon. I cannot tell how he mounts in the air, and soars to heaven. To-day I have seen the dragon."

But the modest man, who lived for others, has far surpassed in his influence this dragon of intelligence. It certainly increases our hope for man, when we see how these qualities of perfect honesty, good sense, generous devotion to the public good, and fidelity to the last in adherence to his work, have made Confucius during twenty-three centuries the daily teacher and guide of a third of the human race.

Confucius was eminently distinguished by energy and persistency. He did not stop working till he died. His life was of one piece, beautiful, noble. " The general of a large army," said he, " may be defeated, but you cannot defeat the determined mind of a peasant." He acted conformably to this thought, and to another of his sayings. " If I am building a mountain, and stop before the last basketful of earth is placed on the summit, I have failed of my work. But if I have placed but one basketful on the plain, and go on, I am really building a mountain."

Many beautiful and noble things are related concerning the character of Confucius, — of his courage in the midst of danger, of his humility in the highest position of honor. His writings and life have given the law to Chinese thought. He is the patron saint of that great empire. His doctrine is the state religion of the nation, sustained by the whole power of the emperor and the literary body. His books are published every year by societies formed for that purpose, who distribute them gratuitously. His descendants enjoy the highest consideration. The number of temples erected to his memory is sixteen hundred and sixty. One of them occupies ten acres of land. On the two festivals in the year sacred to his memory there are sacrificed some seventy thousand animals of different

kinds, and twenty-seven thousand pieces of silk are
burned on his altars. Yet his is a religion without priests,
liturgy, or public worship, except on these two occasions.

§ 4. *Philosophy and subsequent Development of Confucianism.*

According to Mr. Meadows, the philosophy of China, in
its origin and present aspect, may be thus briefly described.* Setting aside the Buddhist system and that
of Tao-ism, which supply to the Chinese the element of
religious worship and the doctrine of a supernatural world,
wanting in the system of Confucius, we find the latter as
the established religion of the state, merely tolerating the
others as suited to persons of weak minds. The Confucian system, constantly taught by the competitive examinations, rules the thought of China. Its first development
was from the birth of Confucius to the death of Mencius
(or from 551 B. C. to 313 B. C.). Its second period was
from the time of Chow-tsze (A. D. 1034) to that of Choo-
tsze (A. D. 1200). The last of these is the real fashioner
of Chinese philosophy, and one of the truly great men of
the human race. His works are chiefly Commentaries on
the Kings and the Four Books. They are committed to
memory by millions of Chinese who aspire to pass the
public-service examinations. The Chinese philosophy,
thus established by Choo-tsze, is as follows.†

There is one highest, ultimate principle of all existence,
— the Tae-keih, or Grand Extreme. This is absolutely
immaterial, and the basis of the order of the universe.
From this ultimate principle, operating from all eternity,
come all animate and inanimate nature. It operates in
a twofold way, by expansion and contraction, or by cease-
less active and passive pulsations. The active expansive
pulsation is called Yang, the passive intensive pulsation
is Yin, and the two may be called the Positive and Negative Essences of all things. When the active expansive
phase of the process has reached its extreme limit, the op-

---

* Meadows, " The Chinese and their Rebellions," p. 332.
† Meadows, p. 342.

eration becomes passive and intensive ; and from these vi-
brations originate all material and mortal existences. Creation is therefore a perpetual process, — matter and spirit
are opposite results of the same force. The one tends to
variety, the other to unity ; and variety in unity is a permanent and universal law of being. Man results from
the utmost development of this pulsatory action and passion ; and man's nature, as the highest result, is perfectly
good, consisting of five elements, namely, charity, righteousness, propriety, wisdom, and sincerity. These constitute the inmost, essential nature of man ; but as man
comes in contact with the outward world evil arises by
the conflict. When man follows the dictates of his nature
his actions are good, and harmony results. When he is
unduly influenced by the outward world his actions are
evil, and discord intervenes. The holy man is one who
has an instinctive, inward sight of the ultimate principle
in its twofold operation (or what we should call the sight
of God, the beatific vision), and who therefore spontane-
ously and easily obeys his nature. Hence all his thoughts
are perfectly wise, his actions perfectly good, and his
words perfectly true. Confucius was the last of these
holy men. The infallible authority of the Sacred Books
results from the fact that their writers, being holy men,
had an instinctive perception of the working of the ultimate principle.

All Confucian philosophy is pervaded by these principles : first, that example is omnipotent; secondly, that to
secure the safety of the empire, you must secure the happiness of the people ; thirdly, that by solitary persistent
thought one may penetrate at last to a knowledge of the
essence of things ; fourthly, that the object of all government is to make the people virtuous and contented.

§ 5. *Lao-tse and Tao-ism.*

One of the three religious systems of China is that of
the Tao, the other two being that of Confucius, and that of
Buddhism in its Chinese form. The difficulty in understanding Tao-ism comes from its appearing under three

entirely distinct forms: (1) as a philosophy of the absolute or unconditioned, in the great work of the Tse-Lao, or old teacher; * (2) as a system of morality of the utilitarian school, † which resolves duty into prudence; and (3) as a system of magic, connected with the belief in spirits. In the Tao-te-king we have the ideas of Lao himself, which we will endeavor to state; premising that they are considered very obscure and difficult even by the Chinese commentators.

The Tao (§ 1) is the unnamable, and is the origin of heaven and earth. As that which can be named, it is the mother of all things. These two are essentially one. Being and not-being are born from each other (§ 2). The Tao is empty but inexhaustible (§ 4), is pure, is profound, and was before the Gods. It is invisible, not the object of perception, it returns into not-being (§§ 14, 40). It is vague, confused, and obscure (§ 25, 21). It is little and strong, universally present, and all beings return into it (§ 32). It is without desires, great (§ 34). All things are born of being, being is born of not-being (§ 40).

From these and similar statements it would appear that the philosophy of the Tao-te-king is that of absolute being, or the identity of being and not-being. In this point it anticipated Hegel by twenty-three centuries.‡ It teaches that the absolute is the source of being and of not-being. Being is essence, not-being is existence. The first is the noumenal, the last the phenomenal.

As being is the source of not-being (§ 40), by identifying one's self with being one attains to all that is not-being, i. e. to all that exists. Instead, therefore, of aiming at acquiring knowledge, the wise man avoids it; instead of acting, he refuses to act. He "feeds his mind with a wise passiveness." (§ 16.) "Not to act is the source of all power," is a thesis continually present to the mind of Lao (§§ 3, 23, 38, 43, 48, 63). The wise man

---

* "Le Tao-te-king, le livre de la voie et de la vertu, composé dans le vie siècle avant l'ère Chrétienne, par le philosophe Lao-tseu, traduit par Stanislas Julien. Paris, 1842."

† "Le livre des Récompenses et des Peines. Julien, 1835."

‡ "Seyn and Nichts ist Dasselbe." Hegel.

is like water (§§ 8, 78), which seems weak and is strong; which yields, seeks the lowest place, which seems the softest thing and breaks the hardest thing. To be wise one must renounce wisdom, to be good one must renounce justice and humanity, to be learned one must renounce knowledge (§§ 19, 20, 45), and must have no desires (§§ 8, 22), must detach one's self from all things (§ 20) and be like a new-born babe. From everything proceeds its opposite, the easy from the difficult, the difficult from the easy, the long from the short, the high from the low, ignorance from knowledge, knowledge from ignorance, the first from the last, the last from the first. These antagonisms are mutually related by the hidden principle of the Tao (§§ 2, 27). Nothing is independent or capable of existing save through its opposite. The good man and bad man are equally necessary to each other (§ 27). To desire aright is not to desire (§ 64). The saint can do great things because he does not attempt to do them (§ 63). The unwarlike man conquers.* He who submits to others controls them. By this negation of all things we come into possession of all things (§ 68). *Not to act* is, therefore, the secret of all power (§§ 3, 23, 38, 43, 48, 63).

We find here the same doctrine of opposites which appears in the Phædo, and which has come up again and again in philosophy. We shall find something like it in the Sánkhya-karika of the Hindoos. The Duad, with the Monad brooding behind it, is the fundamental principle of the Avesta.

The result, thus far, is to an active passivity. Lao teaches that not to act involves the highest energy of being, and leads to the greatest results. By not acting one identifies himself with the Tao, and receives all its power. And here we cannot doubt that the Chinese philosopher was pursuing the same course with Sakya-Muni. The Tao of the one is the Nirvana of the other. The different motive in each mind constitutes the difference of their career. Sakya-Muni sought Nirvana, or

* "The meek shall inherit the earth."

the absolute, the pure knowledge, in order to escape from evil and to conquer it. Lao sought it, as his book shows, to attain power. At this point the two systems diverge. Buddhism is generous, benevolent, humane ; it seeks to help others. Tao-ism seeks its own. Hence the selfish morality which pervades the Book of Rewards and Punishments. Every good action has its reward attached to it. Hence also the degradation of the system into pure magic and spiritism. Buddhism, though its course runs so nearly parallel, always retains in its scheme of merits a touch of generosity.

We find thus, in the Tao-te-king, the element afterwards expanded into the system of utilitarian and eudæmonic ethics in the Book of Rewards and Punishments. We also can trace in it the source of the magical tendency in Tao-ism. The principle, that by putting one's self into an entirely passive condition one can enter into communion with the unnamed Tao, and so acquire power over nature, naturally tends to magic. Precisely the same course of thought led to similar results in the case of Neo-Platonism. The ecstatic union with the divine element in all nature, which Plotinus attained four times in his life, resulted from an immediate sight of God. In this sight is all truth given to the soul. The unity, says Plotinus, which produces all things, is an essence behind both substance and form. Through this essential being all souls commune and interact, and magic is this interaction of soul upon soul through the soul of souls, with which one becomes identified in the ecstatic union. A man therefore can act on demons and control spirits by theurgic rites. Julian, that ardent Neo-Platonician, was surrounded by diviners, hierophants, and aruspices.*

In the Tao-te-king (§§ 50, 55, 56, etc.) it is said that he who knows the Tao need not fear the bite of serpents nor the jaws of wild beasts, nor the claws of birds of prey. He is inaccessible to good and to evil. He need fear neither rhinoceros nor tiger. In battle he needs neither cuirass nor sword. The tiger cannot tear him, the

---

* See " La Magie et l'Astrologie, par Alfred Maury."

soldier cannot wound him. He is invulnerable and safe from death.*

If Neo-Platonism had not had for its antagonist the vital force of Christianity, it might have established itself as a permanent form of religion in the Roman Empire, as Tao-ism has in China. I have tried to show how the later form of this Chinese system has come naturally from its principles, and how a philosophy of the absolute may have degenerated into a system of necromancy.

§ 6. *Religious Character of the "Kings."*

We have seen that, in the philosophy of the Confucians, the ultimate principle is not necessarily identical with a living, intelligent, and personal God. Nor did Confucius, when he speaks of Teen, or Heaven, express any faith in such a being. He neither asserted nor denied a Supreme God. His worship and prayer did not necessarily imply such a faith. It was the prayer of reverence addressed to some sacred, mysterious, unknown power, above and behind all visible things. What that power was, he, with his supreme candor, did not venture to intimate. But in the She-King a personal God is addressed. The oldest books recognize a Divine person. They teach that there is one Supreme Being, who is omnipresent, who sees all things, and has an intelligence which nothing can escape, — that he wishes men to live together in peace and brotherhood. He commands not only right actions, but pure desires and thoughts; that we should watch all our behavior, and maintain a grave and majestic demeanor, " which is like a palace in which virtue resides "; but especially that we should guard the tongue. " For a blemish may be taken out of a diamond by carefully polishing it; but, if your words have the least blemish, there is no way to efface that." " Humility is the solid foundation of all the virtues." " To acknowledge one's incapacity is the way to be soon prepared to teach others; for from the

---

* Was it some pale reflection of this Oriental philosophy which took form in the ode of Horace, " Integer vitæ " (i. 22), in which he describes the portentous wolf which fled from him ?

moment that a man is no longer full of himself, nor puffed
up with empty pride, whatever good he learns in the
morning he practises before night." " Heaven penetrates
to the bottom of our hearts, like light into a dark chamber.   We must conform ourselves to it, till we are like
two instruments of music tuned to the same pitch.   We
must join ourselves with it, like two tablets which appear
but one.   We must receive its gifts the very moment its
hand is open to bestow.   Our irregular passions shut up
the door of our souls against God."

Such are the teachings of these Kings, which are unquestionably among the oldest existing productions of
the human mind.   In the days of Confucius they seem
to have been nearly forgotten, and their precepts wholly
neglected.   Confucius revised them, added his own explanations and comments, and, as one of the last acts of
his life, called his disciples around him and made a
solemn dedication of these books to Heaven.   He erected
an altar on which he placed them, adored God, and returned thanks upon his knees in a humble manner for
having had life and health granted him to finish this
undertaking.

§ 7. *Confucius and Christianity.   Character of the Chinese.*

It were easy to find defects in the doctrine of Confucius.   It has little to teach of God or immortality.   But
if the law of Moses, which taught nothing of a future life,
was a preparation for Christianity ; if, as the early Christian Fathers asserted, Greek philosophy was also a schoolmaster to bring men to Christ; who can doubt that the
truth and purity in the teachings of Confucius were providentially intended to lead this great nation in the right
direction ?   Confucius is a Star in the East, to lead his
people to Christ.   One of the most authentic of his sayings is this, that " in the West the true Saint must be
looked for and found."   He had a perception, such as
truly great men have often had, of some one higher than
himself, who was to come after him.   We cannot doubt,
therefore, that God, who forgets none of his children, has

given this teacher to the swarming millions of China to lead them on till they are ready for a higher light. And certainly the temporal prosperity and external virtues of this nation, and their long-continued stability amid the universal changes of the world, are owing in no small degree to the lessons of reverence for the past, of respect for knowledge, of peace and order, and especially of filial piety, which he inculcated. In their case, if in no other, has been fulfilled the promise of the divine commandment, " Honor thy father and thy mother, that thy days may be long in the land which the Lord·thy God giveth thee."

In comparing the system of Confucius with Christianity, it appears at. once that Christianity differs from this system, as from most others, in its greater completeness. Jesus says to the Chinese philosopher, as he said to the Jewish law, " I have not come to destroy, but to fulfil." He fulfils the Confucian reverence for the past by adding hope for the future ; he fulfils its stability by progress, its faith in man with faith in God, its interest in this world with the expectation of another, its sense of time with that of eternity. Confucius aims at peace, order, outward prosperity, virtue, and good morals. All this belongs also to Christianity, but Christianity adds a moral enthusiasm, a faith in the spiritual world, a hope of immortal life, a sense of the Fatherly presence of God. So that here, as before, we find that Christianity does not exclude other religions, but includes them, and is distinguished by being deeper, higher, broader, and more far-reaching than they.

A people with such institutions and such a social life as we have described cannot be despised, and to call them uncivilized is as absurd in us as it is in them to call Europeans barbarians. They are a good, intelligent, and happy people. Lieutenant Forbes, who spent five years in China, — from 1842 to 1847, — says : " I found myself in the midst of as amiable, kind, and hospitable a population as any on the face of the earth, as far ahead of us in some things as behind us in others." As to the charge of dishonesty brought against them by those who judge the whole nation by the degraded population of the suburbs of Canton, Forbes says, "My own property suffered more in landing in England and passing the British frontier than in my whole sojourn in China."

"There is no nation," says the Jesuit Du Halde, "more laborious and temperate than this. They are inured to hardships from their infancy, which greatly contributes to preserve the innocence of their manners. . . . . They are of a mild, tractable, and humane disposition." He thinks them exceedingly modest, and regards the love of gain as their chief vice. "Interest," says he, "is the spring of all their actions; for, when the least profit offers, they despise all difficulties and undertake the most painful journeys to procure it." This may be true; but if a Chinese traveller in America should give the same account of us, would it not be quite as true? One of the latest writers — the author of "The Middle Kingdom" — accuses the Chinese of gross sensuality, mendacity, and dishonesty. No doubt these are besetting sins with them, as with all nations who are educated under a system which makes submission to authority the chief virtue. But then this writer lived only at Canton and Macao, and saw personally only the refuse of the people. He admits that "they have attained, by the observance of peace and good order, to a high security of life and property; that the various classes are linked together in a remarkably homogeneous manner by the diffusion of education; and that property and industry receive their just reward of food, raiment, and shelter." He also reminds us that the religion of China differs from all Pagan religions in this, that it encourages neither cruelty nor sensuality. No human victims have ever been offered on its altars, and those licentious rites which have appeared in so many religions have never disgraced its pure worship.

The Chinese citizen enjoys a degree of order, peace, and comfort unknown elsewhere in Asia. "He can hold and sell landed property with a facility, certainty, and security which is absolute perfection compared with the nature of English dealings of the same kind." * He can traverse the country for two thousand miles unquestioned by any

* Meadows, p. 28.

official. He can follow what occupation he pleases. He can quit his country and re-enter it without a passport. The law of primogeniture does not exist. The emperor appoints his heir, but a younger son quite as often as an elder one. The principle that no man is entitled by birth to rule over them is better known to the three hundred and sixty millions of China than to the twenty-seven millions of Great Britain that they have a right to a trial by their peers.* The principle of Chinese government is to persuade rather than to compel, to use moral means rather than physical. This rests on the fundamental belief in human goodness. For, as Mr. Meadows justly observes: "The theory that man's nature is radically vicious is the true psychical basis of despotic or physical-force government; while the theory that man's nature is radically good is the basis of free or moral-force government." The Chinese government endeavors to be paternal. It has refused to lay a tax on opium, because that would countenance the sale of it, though it might derive a large income from such a tax. The sacred literature of the Chinese is perfectly free from everything impure or offensive. There is not a line but might be read aloud in any family circle in England. All immoral ceremonies in idol worship are forbidden. M. Huc says that the birth of a daughter is counted a disaster in China ; but well-informed travellers tell us that fathers go about with little daughters on their arms, as proud and pleased as a European father could be.

Slavery and concubinage exist in China, and the husband has absolute power over his wife, even of life and death. These customs tend to demoralize the Chinese, and are a source of great evil. Woman is the slave of man. The exception to this is in the case of a mother. She is absolute in her household, and mothers, in China, command universal reverence. If an officer asks leave of absence to visit his mother it must be granted him. A mother may order an official to take her son to prison, and she must be obeyed. As a wife without children woman is a slave, but as a mother with grown-up sons she is a monarch.

* Meadows, p. 18.

§ 8. *The Tae-ping Insurrection.*

Two extraordinary events have occurred in our day in China, the results of which may be of the utmost importance to the nation and to mankind. The one is the Tae-ping insurrection, the other the diplomatic mission of Mr. Burlingame to the Western world. Whatever may be the immediate issue of the great insurrection of our day against the Tartar dynasty, it will remain a phenomenon of the utmost significance. There is no doubt, notwithstanding the general opinion to the contrary, that it has been a religious movement, proceeding from a single mind deeply moved by the reading of the Bible. The hostility of the Chinese to the present Mantchoo Tartar monarchs no doubt aided it ; but there has been in it an element of power from the beginning, derived, like that of the Puritans, from its religious enthusiasm. Its leader, the Heavenly Prince, Hung-sew-tseuen, son of a poor peasant living thirty miles northeast of Canton, received a tract, containing extracts from the Chinese Bible of Dr. Morison, from a Chinese tract distributor in the streets of Canton. This was in 1833, when he was about twenty years of age. He took the book home, looked over it carelessly, and threw it aside. Disappointed of his degree at two competitive examinations, he fell sick, and saw a vision of an old man, saying : " I am the Creator of all things. Go and do my work." After this vision six years passed by, when the English war broke out, and the English fleet took the Chinese forts in the river of Canton. Such a great national calamity indicated, according to Chinese ideas, something rotten in the government ; and such success on the part of the English showed that, in some way, they were fulfilling the will of Heaven. This led Hung-sew-tseuen to peruse again his Christian books ; and alone, with no guide, he became a sincere believer in Christ, after a fashion of his own. God was the Creator of all things, and the Supreme Father. Jesus was the Elder Brother and heavenly Teacher of mankind. Idolatry was to be overthrown, virtue to be practised. Hung-sew-tseuen believed that the Bible confirmed his former visions. He accepted his mission and began to make converts. All his converts renounced idolatry, and gave up the worship of Confucius. They travelled to and fro teaching, and formed a society of "God-worshippers." The first convert, Fung-yun-san, became its most ardent missionary and its disinterested preacher. Hung-sew-tseuen returned home, went to Canton, and there met Mr. Roberts, an American missionary, who was induced by false charges to refuse him Christian baptism. But he, without being offended with Mr. Roberts, went home and taught his converts how to baptize themselves. The society of " God-worshippers " increased in number. Some of them were arrested for destroying idols, and among them Fung-yun-san, who, however, on his way to prison, converted the policemen by his side. These new converts set him at liberty and went away with him as his disciples. Various striking phenomena occurred in this society. Men fell into a state of ecstasy and delivered exhortations. Sick persons were cured by the power of prayer. The teachings of these ecstatics were tested by Scripture ; if found to agree therewith, they were accepted ; if not, rejected.

It was in October, 1850, that this religious movement assumed a political form. A large body of persons, in a state of chronic rebellion against the Chinese authorities, had fled into the district, and joined the " God-worshippers." Pursued by the imperial soldiers, they were protected against them. Hence war began. The leaders of the religious movement found themselves compelled to choose between submission and resistance. They resisted, and the great insurrection began. But in China an insurrection against the dynasty is in the natural order of things. Indeed, it may be said to be a part of the constitution. By the Sacred Books, taught in all the schools and made a part of the examination papers, it is the duty of the people to overthrow any bad government. The Chinese have no power to legislate, do not tax themselves, and the government is a pure autocracy. But it is not a despotism ; for old usages make a constitution, which the government must respect or be overthrown. "The right to rebel," says Mr. Meadows, " is in China a chief element

of national stability." The Tae-ping (or Universal-Peace)
Insurrection has shown its religious character throughout.
It has not been cruel, except in retaliation. At the taking of Nan-king orders were given to put all the women
together and protect them, and any one doing them an
injury was punished with death. Before the attack on
Nan-king a large body of the insurgents knelt down and
prayed, and then rose and fought, like the soldiers of
Cromwell. The aid of a large body of rebels was refused,
because they did not renounce idolatry, and continued to
allow the use of opium. Hymns of praise to the Heavenly
Father and Elder Brother were chanted in the camp.
And the head of the insurrection distinctly announced
that, in case it succeeded, the Bible would be substituted
in all public examinations for office in the place of Confucius. This would cause the Bible to be at once studied
by all candidates for office among three hundred and sixty
millions of people. It would constitute the greatest event
in the history of Christianity since the days of Constan-
tine, or at least since the conversion of the Teutonic races.
The rebellion has probably failed; but great results must
follow this immense interest in Christianity in the heart
of China, — an interest awakened by no Christian mission,
whether Catholic or Protestant, but coming down into
this great nation like the rain from heaven.

In the "History of the Ti-Ping Revolution" (published
in London in 1866), written by an Englishman who held
a command among the Ti-Pings, there is given a full, interesting, and apparently candid account of the religious
and moral character of this great movement, from which
I take the following particulars : —

"I have probably," says this writer,* "had a much greater

* Ti-Ping Tien-Kwoh ; The History of the Ti-Ping Revolution, by
Lin-Le, special agent of the Ti-Ping General-in-Chief, &c. Davy and
Son, London, 1866. Vol. I. p. 306.
    Mr. Andrew Wilson, author of "The Ever-Victorious Army" (Black-
wood, 1868), speaks with much contempt of Lin-Le's book. In a note
(page 389) he brings certain charges against the author. Mr. Wilson's
book is written to glorify Gordon, Wood, and others, who accepted rov-
ing commissions against the Ti-Pings ; and of course he takes their view
of the insurrection. The accusations he brings against Lin-Le, even if
correct, do not detract from the apparent accuracy of that writer's story,
nor from the weight of his arguments.

experience of the Ti-Ping religious practices than any other European, and as a Protestant Christian I have never yet found occasion to condemn their form of worship. The most important part of their faith is the Holy Bible, — Old and New Testaments entire. These have been printed and circulated gratuitously by the government through the whole population of the Ti-Ping jurisdiction." Abstracts of the Bible, put into verse, were circulated and committed to memory. Their form of worship was assimilated to Protestantism. The Sabbath was kept religiously on the seventh day. Three cups of tea were put on the altar on that day as an offering to the Trinity. They celebrated the communion once a month by partaking of a cup of grape wine. Every one admitted to their fellowship was baptized, after an examination and confession of sins. The following was the form prescribed in the " Book of Religious Precepts of the Ti-Ping Dynasty " : — *

Forms to be observed when Men wish to forsake their Sins. — They must kneel down in God's presence, and ask him to forgive their sins. They may then take either a basin of water and wash themselves, or go to the river and bathe themselves ; after which they must continue daily to supplicate Divine favor, and the Holy Spirit's assistance to renew their hearts, saying grace at every meal, keeping holy the Sabbath day, and obeying all God's commandments, especially avoiding idolatry. They may then be accounted the children of God, and their souls will go to Heaven when they die."

The prayer offered by the recipient of Baptism was as follows : —

" I (A. B.), kneeling down with a true heart, repent of my sins, and pray the Heavenly Father, the great God, of his abundant mercy, to forgive my former sins of ignorance in repeatedly breaking the Divine commands, earnestly beseeching him also to grant me repentance and newness of life, that my soul may go to Heaven, while I henceforth truly forsake my former ways, abandoning idolatry and

* Ibid., Vol. I. p. 315. These forms are given, says the writer, partly from memory.

E

all corrupt practices, in obedience to God's commands.   I
also pray that God would give me his Holy Spirit to
change my wicked heart, deliver me from all temptation,
and grant me his favor and protection, bestowing on me
food and raiment, and exemption from calamity, peace in
this world and glory in the next, through the mercies of
our Saviour and Elder Brother, Jesus, who redeemed us
from sin."

In every household throughout the Ti-Ping territory
the following translation of the Lord's Prayer was hung
up for the use of the children, printed in large black characters on a white board : —

"Supreme Lord, our Heavenly Father, forgive all our
sins that we have committed in ignorance, rebelling against
thee.   Bless us, brethren and sisters, thy little children.
Give us our daily food and raiment ; keep from us all
calamities and afflictions ; that in this world we may have
peace and finally ascend to heaven to enjoy everlasting
happiness.   We pray thee to bless our brethren and sisters
of all nations.   We ask these things for the redeeming
merits of our Lord and Saviour, our heavenly brother,
Jesus.   We also pray, Heavenly Father, that thy will
may be done on earth as in heaven : for thine are all the
kingdoms, glory, and power.   Amen."

The writer says he has frequently watched the Ti-Ping
women teaching the children this prayer ; " and often, on
entering a house, the children ran up to me, and pulling
me toward the board, began to read the prayer."

The seventh day was kept very strictly.   As soon as
midnight sounded on Friday, all the people throughout
Ti-Pingdom were summoned to worship.   Two other services were held during the day.   Each opened with a
doxology to God, Jesus, and the Holy Spirit.   Then was
sung this hymn : —

> " The true doctrine is different from the doctrine of this world ;
> It saves men's souls and gives eternal bliss.
> The wise receive it instantly with joy ;
> The foolish, wakened by it, find the way to Heaven.
> Our Heavenly Father, of his great mercy,
> Did not spare his own Son, but sent him down
> To give his life to redeem sinners.
> When men know this, and repent, they may go to Heaven."

The rest of the services consisted in a chapter of the Bible read by the minister ; a creed, repeated by the congregation standing ; a prayer, read by the minister and repeated by the whole congregation kneeling. Then the prayer was burned, the minister read a sermon, an anthem was chanted to the long life of the king ; then followed the Ten Commandments, music, and the burning of incense and fire-crackers. No business was allowed on the Sabbath, and the shops were closed. There was a clergy, chosen by competitive examination, subject to the approval of the Tien-Wong, or supreme religious head of the movement. There was a minister placed over every twenty-five families, and a church, or Heavenly Hall, assigned to him in some public building. Over every twenty-five parishes there was a superior, who visited them in turn every Sabbath. Once every month the whole people were addressed by the chief Wong.

The writer of this work describes his attendance on morning prayers at Nan-king, in the Heavenly Hall of the Chung-Wang's household. This took place at sunrise every morning, the men and women sitting on opposite sides of the hall. " Oftentimes," says he, " while kneeling in the midst of an apparently devout congregation, and gazing on the upturned countenances lightened by the early morning sun, have I wondered why no British missionary occupied my place, and why Europeans generally preferred slaughtering the Ti-Pings to accepting them as brothers in Christ. When I look back," he adds, " on the unchangeable and universal kindness I always met with among the Ti-Pings, even when their dearest relatives were being slaughtered by my countrymen, or delivered over to the Manchoos to be tortured to death, their magnanimous forbearance seems like a dream. Their kind and friendly feelings were often annoying. To those who have experienced the ordinary dislike of foreigners by the Chinese, the surprising friendliness of the Ti-Pings was most remarkable. They welcomed Europeans as " brethren from across the sea," and claimed them as fellow-worshippers of " Yesu."

Though the Ti-Pings did not at once lay aside all hea

then customs, and could not be expected to do so, they took some remarkable steps in the right direction. Their women were in a much higher position than among the other Chinese; they abolished the custom of cramping their feet; a married woman had rights, and could not be divorced at will, or sold, as under the Manchoos. Large institutions were established for unmarried women. Slavery was totally abolished, and to sell a human being was made a capital offence. They utterly prohibited the use of opium; and this was probably their chief offence in the eyes of the English. Prostitution was punished by death, and was unknown in their cities. Idolatry was also utterly abolished. Their treatment of the people under them was merciful; they protected their prisoners, whom the Imperialists always massacred. The British troops, instead of preserving neutrality, aided the Imperialists in putting down the insurrection in such ways as this. The British cruisers *assumed* that the Ti-Ping junks were pirates, because they captured Chinese vessels. The British ship Bittern and another steamer sank every vessel but two in a rebel fleet, and gave up the crew of one which they captured to be put to death. This is the description of another transaction of the same kind, in the harbor of Shi-poo : " The junks were destroyed, and their crews shot, drowned, and hunted down, until about a thousand were killed; the Bittern's men aiding the Chinese on shore to complete the wholesale massacre." *

It is the deliberate opinion of this well-informed English writer that the Ti-Ping insurrection would have succeeded but for British intervention; that the Tartar dynasty would have been expelled, the Chinese regained their autonomy, and Christianity have been established throughout the Empire. At the end of his book he gives a table of *forty-three* battles and massacres in which the British soldiers and navy took part, in which about four hundred thousand of the Ti-Pings were killed, and he estimates that more than two millions more died of starvation in 1863 and 1864, in the famine occasioned by the operations of the allied English, French, and Chinese troops,

* Hong-Kong Gazette, October 12, 1855.

when the Ti-Pings were driven from their territories. In view of such facts, well may an English writer say: " It is not once or twice that the policy of the British government has been ruinous to the best interests of the world. Disregard of international law and of treaty law in Europe, deeds of piracy and spoliation in Asia, one vast system of wrong and violence, have everywhere for years marked the dealings of the British government with the weaker races of the globe." *

Other Englishmen, beside " Lin-Le " and Mr. Meadows, give the same testimony to the Christian character of this great movement in China. Captain Fishbourne, describing his visit in H. M. S. Hermes to Nan-king, says : " It was obvious to the commonest observer that they were practically a different race." They had the Scriptures, many seemed to him to be practical Christians, serious and religious, believing in a special Providence, thinking that their trials were sent to purify them. " They accuse us of magic," said one. " The only magic we employ is prayer to God." The man who said this, says Captain Fishbourne, " was a little shrivelled-up person, but he uttered words of courageous confidence in God, and could utter the words of a hero. He and others like him have impressed the minds of their followers with their own courage and morality."

The English Bishop of Victoria has constantly given the same testimony. Of one of the Ti-Ping books Dr. Medhurst says : " There is not a word in it which a Christian missionary might not adopt and circulate as a tract for the benefit of the Chinese."

Dr. Medhurst also describes a scene which took place in Shanghae, where he was preaching in the chapel of the London Missionary Society, on the folly of idolatry and the duty of worshipping the one true God. A man arose in the middle of the congregation and said : " That is true ! that is true ! the idols must perish. I am a Ti-Ping; we all worship one God and believe in Jesus, and we everywhere destroy the idols. Two years ago when we began we were only three thousand ; now we have

* Intervention and Non-Intervention, by A. G. Stapleton.

marched across the Empire, because God was on our side."
He then exhorted the people to abandon idolatry and to
believe in Jesus, and said : " We are happy in our religion,
and look on the day of our death as the happiest moment
of life.   When any of our number dies, we do not weep,
but congratulate each other because he has gone to the
joy of the heavenly world."

The mission of Mr. Burlingame indicated a sincere desire on the part of the sagacious men who then governed
China, especially of Prince Kung, to enter into relations
with modern civilization and modern thought.   From the
official papers of this mission,* it appears that Mr. Burlingame was authorized " to transact all business with the
Treaty Powers in which those countries and China had a
common interest," (communication of Prince Kung, December 31, 1867).   The Chinese government expressly states
that this step is intended as adopting the customs of diplomatic intercourse peculiar to the West, and that in so
doing the Chinese Empire means to conform to the law of
nations, as understood among the European states.   It
therefore adopted " Wheaton's International Law " as the
text-book and authority to be used in its Foreign Office,
and had it carefully translated into Chinese for the use of
its mandarins.   This movement was the result, says Mr.
Burlingame, of the " co-operative policy " adopted by
the representatives in China of the Treaty Powers, in
which they agreed to act together on all important questions, to take no cession of territory, and never to menace
the autonomy of the Empire.   They agreed " to leave her
perfectly free to develop herself according to her own form
of civilization, not to interfere with her interior affairs, to
make her waters neutral, and her land safe " (Burlingame's
speech at San Francisco).   There is no doubt that if
the states known as the " Treaty Powers," namely, the
United States, Belgium, Denmark, France, Great Britain,
Holland, Italy, North Germany, Russia, Spain, and Sweden, will loyally abstain from aggression and interference
in China and respect her independence, that this great

* Official Papers of the Chinese Legation.   Berlin : T. Calvary & Co.,
Oberwasser Square. 1870.

Empire will step forth from her seclusion of fifty centuries, and enter the commonwealth of nations.

The treaty between the United States and China of July 28, 1868, includes provisions for the neutrality of the Chinese waters ; for freedom of worship for United States citizens in China, and for the Chinese in the United States ; for allowing voluntary emigration, and prohibiting the compulsory coolie trade ; for freedom to travel in China and the United States by the citizens of either country ; and for freedom to establish and attend schools in both countries.

We add to this chapter a Note, containing an interesting account, from Huc's " Christianity in China," of an inscribed stone, proving that Christian churches existed in China in the seventh century. These churches were the result of the efforts of Nestorian missionaries, who were the Protestant Christians of their age. Their success in China is another proof that the Christianity which is to be welcomed there must be presented in an intelligible and rational form.

NOTE.

THE NESTORIAN INSCRIPTION IN CHINA.*

In 1625 some Chinese workmen, engaged in digging a foundation for a house, outside the walls of the city of Si-ngau-Fou, the capital of the province of Chen-si, found buried in the earth a large monumental stone resembling those which the Chinese are in the habit of raising to preserve to posterity the remembrance of remarkable events and illustrious men. It was a dark-colored marble tablet, ten feet high and five broad, and bearing on one side an inscription in ancient Chinese, and also some other characters quite unknown in China.

. . . . .

Several exact tracings from the stone were sent to Europe by the Jesuits who saw it. The library of their house at Rome had one of t'ie first, and it attracted numerous visitors ; subsequently, another authentic copy of the dimensions of the tablet was sent to Paris, and deposited at the library in the Rue Richelieu, where it may still be seen in the gallery of manuscripts.

* From Huc's " Christianity in China."

This monument, discovered by chance amidst rubbish in the environs of an ancient capital of the Chinese Empire, excited a great sensation; for on examining the stone, and endeavoring to interpret the inscription, it was with surprise discovered that the Christian religion had had numerous apostles in China at the beginning of the seventh century, and that it had for a long time flourished there. The strange characters proved to be those called *estrangélhos*, which were in use among the ancient inhabitants of Syria, and will be found in some Syriac manuscripts of earlier date than the eighth century.

Monument of the great Propagation of the Luminous Doctrine in the Central Empire, composed by Khing-Tsing, a devout Man of the Temple of Ta-Thsin.

1. There has always been only one true Cause, essentially the first, and without beginning, supremely intelligent and immaterial; essentially the last, and uniting all perfections. He placed the poles of the heavens and created all beings; marvellously holy, he is the source of all perfection. This admirable being, is he not the *Triune*, the true Lord without beginning, *Oloho?*

He divided the world by a cross into four parts. After having decomposed the primordial air, he gave birth to the two elements. Chaos was transformed, and then the sun and the moon appeared. He made the sun and the moon move to produce day and night. He elaborated and perfected the ten thousand things; but in creating the first man, he endowed him with perfect interior harmony. He enjoined him to watch over the sea of his desires. His nature was without vice and without error; his heart, pure and simple, was originally without disorderly appetites.

2. But Sa-Thang propagated lies, and stained by his malice that which had been pure and holy. He proclaimed, as a truth, the equality of greatness, and upset all ideas. This is why three hundred and sixty-five sects, lending each other a mutual support, formed a long chain, and wove, so to speak, a net of law. Some put the creature in the place of the Eternal, others denied the existence of beings, and destroyed the two principles. Others instituted prayers and sacrifices to obtain good fortune; others proclaimed their own sanctity to deceive mankind. The minds of men labored, and were filled with anxiety; aspirations after the supreme good were trampled down; thus perpetually floating about they attained to nothing, and all went from bad to worse. The darkness thickened, men lost their sight, and for a long time they wandered without being able to find it again.

3. Then our Triune God communicated his substance to the very venerable Mi-chi-ho (Messiah), who, veiling his true majesty, appeared in the world in the likeness of a man. The celestial spirits manifested their joy, and a virgin brought forth the saint in Ta-Thsin. The most splendid constellations announced this happy

event; the Persians saw the splendor, and ran to pay tribute. He fulfilled what was said of old by the twenty-four saints; he organized, by his precepts, both families and kingdoms; he instituted the new religion according to the true notion of the Trinity in Unity; he regulated conscience by the true faith; he signified to the world the eight commandments, and purged humanity from its pollutions by opening the door to the three virtues. He diffused life and extinguished death; he suspended the luminous sun to destroy the dwelling of darkness, and then the lies of demons passed away. He directed the bark of mercy towards the palace of light, and all creatures endowed with intelligence have been succored. After having consummated this act of power, he rose at midday towards the Truth. Twenty-seven books have been left. He has enlarged the springs of mercy, that men might be converted. The baptism by water and by the Spirit is a law that purifies the soul and beautifies the exterior. The sign of the cross unites the four quarters of the world, and restores the harmony that had been destroyed. By striking upon a piece of wood, we make the voice of charity and mercy resound; by sacrificing towards the east we indicate the way of life and glory.

Our ministers allow their beards to grow, to show that they are devoted to their neighbors. The tonsure that they wear at the top of their heads indicates that they have renounced worldly desires. In giving liberty to slaves we become a link between the powerful and weak. We do not accumulate riches, and we share with the poor that which we possess. Fasting strengthens the intellectual powers, abstinence and moderation preserve health. We worship seven times a day, and by our prayers we aid the living and the dead. On the seventh day we offer sacrifice, after having purified our hearts and received absolution for our sins. This religion, so perfect and so excellent, is difficult to name, but it enlightens darkness by its brilliant precepts. It is called the Luminous Religion.

5. Learning alone without sanctity has no grandeur, sanctity without learning makes no progress. When learning and sanctity proceed harmoniously, the universe is adorned and resplendent.

The Emperor Tai-Tsoung illustrated the Empire. He opened the revolution, and governed men in holiness. In his time there was a man of high virtue named Olopen, who came from the kingdom of Ta-Thsin. Directed by the blue clouds, he bore the Scriptures of the true doctrine; he observed the rules of the winds, and traversed difficult and perilous countries

In the ninth year of Tching-Kouan (636) he arrived at Tchang-ngan. The Emperor ordered Fang-hi-wen-Ling, first minister of the Empire, to go with a great train of attendants to the western suburb, to meet the stranger and bring him to the palace. He had the Holy Scriptures translated in the Imperial library. The court listened to the doctrine, meditated on it profoundly, and understood the great unity of truth. A special edict was promulgated for its publication and diffusion.

3

In the twelfth year of Tching-Kouan, in the seventh moon, during the autumn, the new edict was promulgated in these terms : —

The doctrine has no fixed name, the holy has no determinate substance ; it institutes religions suitable to various countries, and carries men in crowds in its tracks. Olopen, a man of Ta-Thsin, and of a lofty virtue, bearing Scriptures and images, has come to offer them in the Supreme Court. After a minute examination of the spirit of this religion, it has been found to be excellent, mysterious, and pacific. The contemplation of its radical principle gives birth to perfection and fixes the will. It is exempt from verbosity ; it considers only good results. It is useful to men, and consequently ought to be published under the whole extent of the heavens. I, therefore, command the magistrates to have a Ta-Thsin temple constructed in the quarter named T-ning of the Imperial city, and twenty-one religious men shall be installed therein.

10. Sou-Tsoung, the illustrious and brilliant emperor, erected at Ling-ou and other towns, five in all, *luminous* temples. The primitive good was thus strengthened, and felicity flourished. Joyous solemnities were inaugurated, and the Empire entered on a wide course of prosperity.

11. Tai-Tsoung (764), a lettered and a warlike emperor, propagated the holy revolution. He sought for peace and tranquillity. Every year, at the hour of the Nativity (Christmas), he burnt celestial perfumes in remembrance of the divine benefit; he prepared imperial feasts, to honor the *luminous* (Christian) multitude.

21. This stone was raised in the second year of Kien-Tchoung of the great dynasty of Thang (A. D. 781), on the seventh day of the moon of the great increase. At this time the devout Ning-Chou, lord of the doctrine, governed the luminous multitude in the Eastern country.

Such is the translation of the famous inscription found at Si-ngau-Fou, in 1625. On the left of the monument are to be read the following words in the Syriac language : " In the days of the Father of Fathers, Anan-Yeschouah, Patriarch *Catholicos*." To the right can be traced, " Adam, Priest, and Chor-Episcopus " ; and at the base of the inscription: " In the year of the Greeks one thousand nine hundred and two (A. D. 781), Mar Yezd-bouzid, Priest and Chor-Episcopus of the Imperial city of Komdam, son of Millesins, priest of happy memory, of Balkh, a town of Tokharistan (Turkistan), raised this tablet of stone, on which are described the benefits of our Saviour, and the preaching of our fathers in the kingdom of the Chinese. Adam, Deacon, son of Yezd-bouzid, Chor-Episcopus ; Sabar-Jesu, Priest ; Gabriel, Priest, Archdeacon, and Ecclesiarch of Komdam and Sarage."

The abridgment of Christian doctrine given in the Syro-Chinese inscription of Si-ngau-Fou shows us, also, that the propagators of the faith in Upper Asia in the seventh century professed the Nestorian errors.

Through the vague and obscure verbiage which characterizes the Chinese style, we recognize the mode in which that heresiarch admitted the union of the Word with man, by indwelling plenitude of grace superior to that of all the saints. One of the persons of the Trinity communicated himself to the very illustrious and venerable Messiah, "veiling his majesty." That is certainly the doctrine of Nestorius; upon that point the authority of the critics is unanimous.

History, as we have elsewhere remarked, records the rapid progress of the Nestorian sects in the interior of Asia, and their being able to hold their ground, even under the sway of the Mussulmans, by means of compromises and concessions of every kind.

Setting out from the banks of the Tigris or the Euphrates, these ardent and courageous propagators of the Gospel probably proceeded to Khorassan, and then crossing the Oxus, directed their course toward the Lake of Lop, and entered the Chinese Empire by the province of Chen-si. Olopen, and his successors in the Christian mission, whether Syrians or Persians by birth, certainly belonged to the Nestorian church.

Voltaire, who did not like to trouble himself with scientific arguments, and who was much stronger in sarcasm than in erudition, roundly accuses the missionaries of having fabricated the inscription on the monument of Si-ngau-Fou, from motives of " pious fraud." " As if," says Remusat, " such a fabrication could have been practicable in the midst of a distrustful and suspicious nation, in a country in which magistrates and private people are equally ill-disposed towards foreigners, and especially missionaries, where all eyes are open to their most trivial proceedings, and where the authorities watch with the most jealous care over everything relating to the historical traditions and monuments of antiquity. It would be very difficult to explain how the missionaries could have been bold enough to have printed and published in China, and in Chinese, an inscription that had never existed, and how they could have imitated the Chinese style, counterfeited the manner of the writers of the dynasty of Thang, alluded to customs little known, to local circumstances, to dates calculated from the mysterious figures of Chinese astrology, and the whole without betraying themselves for a moment; and with such perfection as to impose on the most skilful men of letters, induced, of course, by the singularity of the discovery to dispute its authenticity. It could only have been done by one of the most erudite of Chinese scholars, joining with the missionaries to impose on his own countrymen."

" Even that would not be all, for the borders of the inscription are covered with Syrian names in fine *estranghélo* characters. The forgers must, then, have been not only acquainted with these characters, but have been able to get engraved with perfect exactness

ninety lines of them, and in the ancient writing, known at present
to very few."

"This argument of Remusat's," says another learned Orientalist,
M. Felix Neve, "is of irresistible force, and we have formerly
heard a similar one maintained with the greatest confidence by M.
Quatremère, of the Academy of Inscriptions and Belles-Lettres, and
we allow ourselves to quote the opinion of so highly qualified a
judge upon this point. Before the last century it would have been
absolutely impossible to forge in Europe a series of names and titles
belonging to a Christian nation of Western Asia; it is only since
the fruits of Assemani's labors have been made public by his
family at Rome, that there existed a sufficient knowledge of the
Syriac for such a purpose; and it is only by the publication of the
manuscripts of the Vatican, that the extent to which Nestorianism
spread in the centre of Asia, and the influence of its hierarchy in the
Persian provinces could have been estimated. There is no reason
to suppose that missionaries who left Europe in the very beginning
of the seventeenth century could have acquired a knowledge which
could only be obtained from reading the originals and not vague
accounts of them."

The sagacity of M. Saint Martin, who was for a long time the
colleague of M. Quatremère, has pointed out in a note worthy of
his erudition, another special proof, which is by no means to be
neglected.

"Amongst the various arguments," he says, "that might be urged
in favor of the legitimacy of the monument, but of which, as yet, no
use has been made, must not be forgotten the name of the priest
by whom it is said to have been erected. The name *Yezdbouzid*
is Persian, and at the epoch when the monument was discovered
it would have been impossible to invent it, as there existed no
work where it could have been found. Indeed, I do not think that,
even since then, there has ever been any one published in which it
could have been met with.

"It is a very celebrated name among the Armenians, and comes
to them from a martyr, a Persian by birth, and of the royal race,
who perished towards the middle of the seventh century, and
rendered his name illustrious amongst the Christian nations of the
East." Saint Martin adds in the same place, that the famous monument of Si-ngau-Fou, whose authenticity has for a long time been
called in question from the hatred entertained against the Jesuit
missionaries who discovered it, rather than from a candid examination of its contents, is now regarded as above all suspicion.

CHAPTER III.

BRAHMANISM.

§ 1. Our Knowledge of Brahmanism. Sir William Jones. § 2. Difficulty of this Study. The Complexity of the System. The Hindoos have no History. Their Ultra-Spiritualism. § 3. Helps from Comparative Philology. The Aryans in Central Asia. § 4. The Aryans in India. The Native Races. The Vedic Age. Theology of the Vedas. § 5. Second Period. Laws of Manu. The Brahmanic Age. § 6. The Three Hindoo Systems of Philosophy, — the Sánkhya, Vedanta, and Nyasa. § 7. Origin of the Hindoo Triad. § 8. The Epics, the Puranas, and Modern Hindoo Worship. § 9. Relation of Brahmanism to Christianity.

§ 1. *Our Knowledge of Brahmanism. Sir William Jones.*

IT is more than forty years since the writer, then a boy, was one day searching among the heavy works of a learned library in the country to find some entertaining reading for a summer afternoon. It was a library rich in theology, in Greek and Latin classics, in French and Spanish literature, but contained little to amuse a child. Led by some happy fortune, in turning over a pile of the " Monthly Anthology " his eye was attracted by the title of a play, " Sácontala,* or the Fatal Ring ; an Indian Drama, translated from the original Sanskrit and Pracrit. Calcutta, 1789," and reprinted in the Anthology in successive numbers. Gathering them together, the boy took them into a great chestnut-tree, amid the limbs of which he had constructed a study, and there, in the warm, fragrant shade, read hour after hour this bewitching story. The tale was suited to the day and the scene, — filled with images of tender girls and religious sages, who lived amid a tropical abundance of flowers and fruits ; so blending the beauty of nature with the charm of love. Nature becomes in it alive, and is interpenetrated with human sentiments.

* Now usually written Sákoontalá or Sákuntalá.

Sákuntalá loves the flowers as sisters; the Késara-tree beckons to her with its waving blossoms, and clings to her in affection as she bends over it. The jasmine, the wife of the mango-tree, embraces her lord, who leans down to protect his blooming bride, "the moonlight of the grove." The holy hermits defend the timid fawn from the hunters, and the birds, grown tame in their peaceful solitudes, look tranquilly on the intruder. The demons occasionally disturb the sacrificial rites, but, like well-educated demons, retire at once, as soon as the protecting Raja enters the sacred grove. All breathes of love, gentle and generous sentiment, and quiet joys in the bosom of a luxuriant and beautiful summer land. Thus, in this poem, written a hundred years before Christ, we find that romantic view of nature, unknown to the Greeks and Romans, and first appearing in our own time in such writers as Rousseau, Goethe, and Byron.

He who translated this poem into a European language, and communicated it to modern readers, was Sir William Jones, one of the few first-class scholars whom the world has produced. In him was joined a marvellous gift of language with a love for truth and beauty, which detected by an infallible instinct what was worth knowing, in the mighty maze of Oriental literature. He had also the rare good fortune of being the first to discover this domain of literature in Asia, unknown to the West till he came to reveal it. The vast realm of Hindoo, Chinese, and Persian genius was as much a new continent to Europe, when discovered by Sir William Jones, as America was when made known by Columbus. Its riches had been accumulating during thousands of years, waiting till the fortunate man should arrive, destined to reveal to our age the barbaric pearl and gold of the gorgeous East, — the true wealth of Ormus and of Ind.

Sir William Jones came well equipped for his task. Some men are born philologians, loving *words* for their own sake, — men to whom the devious paths of language are open highways; who, as Lord Bacon says, "have come forth from the second general curse, which was the confusion of tongues, by the art of grammar." Sir William

Jones was one of these, perhaps the greatest of them. A paper in his own handwriting tells us that he knew critically eight languages, — English, Latin, French, Italian, Greek, Arabic, Persian, and Sanskrit; less perfectly eight others, — Spanish, Portuguese, German, Runic, Hebrew, Bengali, Hindi, Turkish ; and was moderately familiar with twelve more, — Tibetian, Pâli, Phalavi, Deri, Russian, Syriac, Ethiopic, Coptic, Welsh, Swedish, Dutch, and Chinese. There have been, perhaps, other scholars who have known as many tongues as this. But usually they are crushed by their own accumulations, and we never hear of their accomplishing anything. Sir William Jones was not one of these, "deep versed in books, and shallow in himself." Language was his instrument, but knowledge his aim. So, when he had mastered Sanskrit and other Oriental languages, he rendered into English not only Sákuntalá, but a far more important work, "The Laws of Manu" ; "almost the only work in Sanskrit," says Max Müller, "the early date of which, assigned to it by Sir William Jones from the first, has not been assailed." He also translated from the Sanskrit the fables of Hitopadesa, extracts from the Vedas, and shorter pieces. He formed a society in Calcutta for the study of Oriental literature, was its first president, and contributed numerous essays, all valuable, to its periodical, the "Asiatic Researches." He wrote a grammar of the Persian language, and translated from Persian into French the history of Nadir Shah. From the Arabic he also translated many pieces, and among them the Seven Poems suspended in the temple at Mecca, which, in their subjects and style, seem an Arabic anticipation of Walt Whitman. He wrote in Latin a Book of Commentaries on Asiatic Poetry, in English several works on the Mohammedan and Civil Law, with a translation of the Greek Orations of Isæus. As a lawyer, a judge, a student of natural history, his ardor of study was equally apparent. He presented to the Royal Society in London a large collection of valuable Oriental manuscripts, and left a long list of studies in Sanskrit to be pursued by those who should come after him. His generous nature showed itself in his opposition to slavery and the slave-trade, and his open sympathy with the American Revolution. His correspondence was large, including such names as those of Benjamin Franklin, Sir Joseph Banks, Lord Monboddo, Gibbon, Warren Hastings, Dr. Price, Edmund Burke, and Dr. Parr. Such a man ought to be remembered, especially by all who take an interest in the studies to which he has opened the way, for he was one who had a right to speak of himself, as he has spoken in these lines : —

> " Before thy mystic altar, heavenly truth,
> I kneel in manhood, as I knelt in youth.
> Thus let me kneel, till this dull form decay,
> And life's last shade be brightened by thy ray,
> Then shall my soul, now lost in clouds below,
> Soar without bound, without consuming glow."

Since the days of Sir William Jones immense progress has been made in the study of Sanskrit literature, especially within the last thirty or forty years, from the time when the Schlegels led the way in this department. Now, professors of Sanskrit are to be found in all the great European universities, and in this country we have at least one Sanskrit scholar of the very highest order, Professor William D. Whitney, of Yale. The system of Brahmanism, which a short time since could only be known to Western readers by means of the writings of Colebrooke, Wilkins, Wilson, and a few others, has now been made accessible by the works of Lassen, Max Müller, Burnouf, Muir, Pictet, Bopp, Weber, Windischmann, Vivien de Saint-Martin, and a multitude of eminent writers in France, England, and Germany.*

* To avoid multiplying footnotes, we refer here to the chief sources on which we rely in this chapter. *C. Lassen*, Indische Altherthumskunde ; *Max Müller*, History of Ancient Sanskrit Literature (and other works) ; *J. Muir*, Sanskrit Texts ; *Pictet*, Les Origines Indo-Européennes ; *Sir William Jones*, Works, 13 vols. ; *Vivien de Saint-Martin*, Étude, &c., and articles in the Revue Germanique ; *Monier Williams*, Sákoontalá (a new translation), the Rámayána, and the Mahá Bhárata ; *Horace Hayman Wilson*, Works (containing the Vischnu Purana, &c.) ; *Burnouf*, Essai sur la Véda, Le Bhagavata Purana ; *Stephenson*, the Sanhita of the Sama Veda ; *Ampère*, La Science en Orient ; *Bunsen*, Gott in der Geschichte ; *Shea* and *Troyer*, The Dabistan ; *Hardwick*, Christ and other Masters ; *J. Talboys Wheeler*, History of India from the Earliest Times ; Works published by the Oriental Translation Fund ; *Max Duncker*, Die Geschichte der Arier ; *Rammohun Roy*, The Veds ; *Mullens*, Hindoo Philosophy.

§ 2. *Difficulty of this Study. The Complexity of the System. The Hindoos have no History. Their Ultra-Spiritualism.*

But, notwithstanding these many helps, Brahmanism remains a difficult study. Its source is not in a man, but in a caste. It is not the religion of a Confucius, a Zoroaster, a Mohammed, but the religion of the Brahmans. We call it Brahmanism, and it can be traced to no individual as its founder or restorer. There is no personality about it.* It is a vast world of ideas, but wanting the unity which is given by the life of a man, its embodiment and representative.

But what a system? How large, how difficult to understand! So vast, so complicated, so full of contradictions, so various and changeable, that its very immensity is our refuge! We say, It is impossible to do justice to such a system; therefore do not demand it of us.

India has been a land of mystery from the earliest times. From the most ancient days we hear of India as the most populous nation of the world, full of barbaric wealth and a strange wisdom. It has attracted conquerors, and has been overrun by the armies of Semiramis, Darius, Alexander; by Mahmud, and Tamerlane, and Nadir Shah; by Lord Clive and the Duke of Wellington. These conquerors, from the Assyrian Queen to the British Mercantile Company, have overrun and plundered India, but have left it the same unintelligible, unchangeable, and marvellous country as before. It is the same land now which the soldiers of Alexander described, — the land of grotto temples dug out of solid porphyry; of one of the most ancient Pagan religions of the world; of social distinctions fixed and permanent as the earth itself; of the sacred Ganges; of the idols of Juggernaut, with its bloody worship; the land of elephants and tigers; of fields of rice and groves of palm; of treasuries filled with chests of gold, heaps of pearls, diamonds, and incense. But, above all, it is the land of unintelligible

* " The soul knows no persons." — EMERSON.

4 *

systems of belief, of puzzling incongruities, and irreconcilable contradictions.

The Hindoos have sacred books of great antiquity, and a rich literature extending back twenty or thirty centuries ; yet no history, no chronology, no annals. They have a philosophy as acute, profound and, spiritual as any in the world, which is yet harmoniously associated with the coarsest superstitions. With a belief so abstract that it almost escapes the grasp of the most speculative intellect, is joined the notion that sin can be atoned for by bathing in the Ganges or repeating a text of the Veda. With an ideal pantheism resembling that of Hegel, is united the opinion that Brahma and Siva can be driven from the throne of the universe by any one who will sacrifice a sufficient number of wild horses. To abstract one's self from matter, to renounce all the gratification of the senses, to macerate the body, is thought the true road to felicity ; and nowhere in the world are luxury, licentiousness and the gratification of the appetites carried so far. Every civil right and privilege of ruler and subject is fixed in a code of laws, and a body of jurisprudence older far than the Christian era, and the object of universal reverence ; but the application of these laws rests (says Rhode) on the arbitrary decisions of the priests, and their execution on the will of the sovereign. The constitution of India is therefore like a house without a foundation and without a roof. It is a principle of Hindoo religion not to kill a worm, not even to tread on a blade of grass, for fear of injuring life ; but the torments, cruelties, and bloodshed inflicted by Indian tyrants would shock a Nero or a Borgia. Half the best informed writers on India will tell you that the Brahmanical religion is pure monotheism ; the other half as confidently assert that they worship a million gods. Some teach us that the Hindoos are spiritualists and pantheists ; others that their idolatry is more gross than that of any living people.

Is there any way of reconciling these inconsistencies ? If we cannot find such an explanation, there is at least one central point where we may place ourselves ; one elevated position, from which this mighty maze will not seem wholly without a plan. In India the whole tendency of thought is ideal, the whole religion a pure spiritualism. An ultra, one-sided idealism is the central tendency of the Hindoo mind. The God of Brahmanism is an intelligence, absorbed in the rest of profound contemplation. The good man of this religion is he who withdraws from an evil world into abstract thought.

Nothing else explains the Hindoo character as this does. An eminently religious people, it is their one-sided spiritualism, their extreme idealism, which gives rise to all their incongruities. They have no history and no authentic chronology, for history belongs to this world, and chronology belongs to time. But this world and time are to them wholly uninteresting ; God and eternity are all in all. They torture themselves with self-inflicted torments ; for the body is the great enemy of the soul's salvation, and they must beat it down by ascetic mortifications. But asceticism, here as everywhere else, tends to self-indulgence, since one extreme produces another. In one part of India, therefore, devotees are swinging on hooks in honor of Siva, hanging themselves by the feet, head downwards, over a fire, rolling on a bed of prickly thorns, jumping on a couch filled with sharp knives, boring holes in their tongues, and sticking their bodies full of pins and needles, or perhaps holding the arms over the head till they stiffen in that position. Meantime in other places whole regions are given over to sensual indulgences, and companies of abandoned women are connected with different temples and consecrate their gains to the support of their worship.

As one-sided spiritualism will manifest itself in morals in the two forms of austerity and sensuality, so in religion it shows itself in the opposite direction of an ideal pantheism and a gross idolatry. Spiritualism first fills the world full of God, and this is a true and Christian view of things. But it takes another step, which is to deny all real existence to the world, and so runs into a false pantheism. It first says, truly, " There is nothing *without* God." It next says, falsely, " There is nothing *but* God." This second step was taken in India by means of the doctrine of *Maya*, or *Illusion*. *Maya* means the delusive shows which spirit assumes. For there is nothing but spirit; which neither creates nor is created, neither acts nor suffers, which cannot change, and into which all souls are absorbed when they free themselves by meditation from the belief that they suffer or are happy, that they can experience either pleasure or pain. The next step is to polytheism. For if God neither creates nor destroys, but only seems to create and destroy, these *appearances* are not united together as being the acts of one Being, but are separate, independent phenomena. When you remove personality from the conception of God, as you do in removing will, you remove unity. Now if creation be an illusion, and there be no creation, still the *appearance* of creation is a fact. But as there is no substance but spirit, this *appearance* must have its cause in spirit, that is, is a *divine* appearance, is God. So destruction, in the same way, is an appearance of God, and reproduction is an appearance of God, and every other appearance in nature is a manifestation of God. But the unity of will and person being taken away, we have not one God, but a multitude of gods, — or polytheism.

Having begun this career of thought, no course was possible for the human mind to pursue but this. An ultra spiritualism must become pantheism, and pantheism must go on to polytheism. In India this is not a theory, but a history. We find, side by side, a spiritualism which denies the existence of anything but motionless spirit or Brahm, and a polytheism which believes and worships Brahma the Creator, Siva the Destroyer, Vischnu the Preserver, Indra the God of the Heavens, the Sactis or energies of the gods, Krishna the Hindoo Apollo, Doorga, and a host of others, innumerable as the changes and appearances of things.

But such a system as this must necessarily lead also to idolatry. There is in the human mind a tendency to worship, and men must worship something. But they believe in one Being, the absolute Spirit, the supreme and only God, — Para Brahm; *him* they cannot worship, for he is literally an unknown God. He has no qualities,

no attributes, no activity. He is, neither the object of
hope, fear, love, nor aversion. Since there is nothing in
the universe but spirit and illusive appearances, and they
cannot worship spirit because it is absolutely unknown,
they must worship these appearances, which are at any
rate *divine* appearances, and which do possess some traits,
qualities, character ; *are* objects of hope and fear. But
they cannot worship them as appearances, they must
worship them as persons. But if they have an inward
personality or soul, they become real beings, and also beings independent of Brahm, whose appearances they are.
They must therefore have an outward personality ; in
other words, a body, a shape, emblematical and characteristic ; that is to say, they become idols.

Accordingly idol-worship is universal in India. The
most horrible and grotesque images are carved in the
stone of the grottos, stand in rude, block-like statues in
the temple, or are coarsely painted on the walls. Figures
of men with heads of elephants or of other animals, or
with six or seven human heads, — sometimes growing in a
pyramid, one out of the other, sometimes with six hands
coming from one shoulder, — grisly and uncouth monsters, like nothing in nature, yet too grotesque for symbols, — such are the objects of the Hindoo worship.

§ 3. *Helps from Comparative Philology. The Aryans in
Central Asia.*

We have seen how hopeless the task has appeared of
getting any definite light on Hindoo chronology or history. To the ancient Egyptians events were so important that the most trivial incidents of daily life were
written on stone and the imperishable records of the
land, covering the tombs and obelisks, have patiently
waited during long centuries, till their decipherer should
come to read them. To the Hindoos, on the other hand,
all events were equally unimportant. The most unhis-
toric people on earth, they cared more for the minutiæ of
grammar, or the subtilties of metaphysics, than for the
whole of their past. The only date which has emerged

from this vague antiquity is that of Chandragupta, a contemporary of Alexander, and called by the Greek historians Sandracottus. He became king B. C. 315, and as, at his accession, Buddha had been dead (by Hindoo statement) one hundred and sixty-two years, Buddha may have died B. C. 477. We can thus import a single date from Greek history into that of India. This is the whole.

But all at once light dawns on us from an unexpected quarter. While we can learn nothing concerning the history of India from its literature, and nothing from its inscriptions or carved temples, *language* comes to our aid. The fugitive and airy sounds, which seem so fleeting and so changeable, prove to be more durable monuments than brass or granite. The study of the Sanskrit language has told us a long story concerning the origin of the Hindoos. It has rectified the ethnology of Blumenbach, has taught us who were the ancestors of the nations of Europe, and has given us the information that one great family, the Indo-European, has done most of the work of the world. It shows us that this family consists of seven races, — the Hindoos, the Persians, the Greeks, the Romans, who all emigrated to the south from the original ancestral home ; and the Kelts, the Teutons, and Slavi, who entered Europe on the northern side of the Caucasus and the Caspian Sea. This has been accomplished by the new science of Comparative Philology. A comparison of languages has made it too plain to be questioned, that these seven races were originally one ; that they must have emigrated from a region of Central Asia, at the east of the Caspian, and northwest of India ; that they were originally a pastoral race, and gradually changed their habits as they descended from those great plains into the valleys of the Indus and the Euphrates. In these seven linguistic families the roots of the most common names are the same ; the grammatical constructions are also the same ; so that no scholar, who has attended to the subject, can doubt that the seven languages are all daughters of one common mother-tongue.

Pursuing the subject still further, it has been found

possible to conjecture with no little confidence what was the condition of family life in this great race of Central Asia, before its dispersion. The original stock has received the name Aryan. This designation occurs in Manu (II. 22), who says : " As far as the eastern and western oceans, between the two mountains, lies the land which the wise have named Ar-ya-vesta, or *inhabited by honorable men.*" The people of Iran receive this same appellation in the Zend Avesta, with the same meaning of *honorable.* Herodotus testifies that the Medes were formerly called Ἄριοι (Herod. VII. 61). Strabo mentions that, in the time of Alexander, the whole region about the Indus was called *Ariana.* In modern times, the word *Iran* for Persia and *Erin* for Ireland are possible reminiscences of the original family appellation.

The Ayrans, long before the age of the Vedas or the Zend Avesta, were living as a pastoral people on the great plains east of the Caspian Sea. What their condition was at that epoch is deduced by the following method: If it is found that the name of any fact is the same in two or more of the seven tribal languages of this stock, it is evident that the name was given to it before they separated. For there is no reason to suppose that two nations living wide apart would have independently selected the same word for the same object. For example, since we find that *house* is in Sanskrit *Dama* and *Dam ;* in Zend, *Demana ;* in Greek, Δόμος ; in Latin, *Domus ;* in Irish, *Dahm ;* in Slavonic, *Domu,* — from which root comes also our English word *Domestic,* — we may be pretty sure that the original Aryans lived in houses. When we learn that *boat* was in Sanskrit *Nau* or *nauka ;* in Persian, *Naw, nawah ;* in Greek, Ναῦς ; in Latin, *Navis ;* in old Irish, *Noi* or *nai ;* in old German, *Nawa* or *nawi ;* and in Polish *Nawa,* we cannot doubt that they knew something of what we call in English *Nau*tical affairs, or Navigation. But as the words designating masts, sails, yards, &c. differ wholly from each other in all these linguistic families, it is reasonable to infer that the Aryans, before their dispersion, went only in boats, with oars, on the rivers of

their land, the Oxus and Jaxartes, and did not sail anywhere on the sea.

Pursuing this method, we see that we can ask almost
any question concerning the condition of the Aryans, and
obtain an answer by means of Comparative Philology.

Were they a pastoral people ? The very word *pastoral*
gives us the answer. For *Pa* in Sanskrit means to watch,
to guard, as men guard cattle, — from which a whole
company of words has come in all the Aryan languages.

The results of this method of inquiry, so far as given
by Pictet, are these. Some 3000 years B. C.,* the Aryans,
as yet undivided into Hindoos, Persians, Kelts, Latins,
Greeks, Teutons, and Slavi, were living in Central Asia,
in a region of which Bactriana was the centre. Here
they must have remained long enough to have developed
their admirable language, the mother-tongue of those
which we know. They were essentially a pastoral, but
not a nomad people, having fixed homes. They had oxen,
horses, sheep, goats, hogs, and domestic fowls. Herds of
cows fed in pastures, each the property of a community,
and each with a cluster of stables in the centre. The
daughters † of the house were the dairy-maids ; the food
was chiefly the products of the dairy and the flesh of the
cattle. The cow was, however, the most important animal, and gave its name to many plants, and even to the
clouds and stars, in which men saw heavenly herds passing over the firmament above them.

But the Aryans were not an exclusively pastoral people ;
they certainly had barley, and perhaps other cereals, before their dispersion. They possessed the plough, the
mill for grinding grain ; they had hatchet,‡ hammer, auger.
The Aryans were acquainted with several metals, among

---

* All Indian dates older than 300 B. C. are uncertain. The reasons
for this one are given carefully and in full by Pictet.

† Our English word *daughter*, together with the Greek θυγάτηρ, the
Zend *daghdar*, the Persian *dochtar*, &c., corresponds with the Sanskrit
duhitar, which means both daughter and milkmaid.

‡ *Hatchet*, in Sanskrit *takshani*, in Zend *tasha*, Greek
τόχος, Irish *tuagh*, Old German *deksa*, Polish *tasak*, Russian *tesaku*.
And what is remarkable, the root *tak* appears in the name of the hatchet
in the languages. of the South Sea Islanders and the North American
Indians.

which were gold, silver, copper, tin. They knew how to
spin and weave to some extent; they were acquainted
with pottery. How their houses were built we do not
know, but they contained doors, windows, and fireplaces.
They had cloaks or mantles, they boiled and roasted meat,
and certainly used soup. They had lances, swords, the
bow and arrow, shields, but not armor. They had family
life, some simple laws, games, the dance, and wind instruments. They had the decimal numeration, and their
year was of three hundred and sixty days. They worshipped the heaven, earth, sun, fire, water, wind; but
there are also plain traces of an earlier monotheism, from
which this nature-worship proceeded.

§ 4. *The Aryans in India. The Native Races. The
Vedic Age. Theology of the Vedas.*

So far Comparative Philology takes us, and the next
step forward brings us to the Vedas, the oldest works in
the Hindoo literature, but at least one thousand or fifteen
hundred years more recent than the times we have been
describing. The Aryans have separated, and the Hindoos
are now in India. It is eleven centuries before the time
of Alexander. They occupy the region between the Punjaub and the Ganges, and here was accomplished the
transition of the Aryans from warlike shepherds into
agriculturists and builders of cities.*
  The last hymns of the Vedas were written (says St.
Martin) when they arrived from the Indus at the Ganges,
and were building their oldest city, at the confluence of
that river with the Jumna. Their complexion was then
white, and they call the race whom they conquered, and
who afterward were made *Soudras*, or lowest caste, blacks.†

---

* M. Vivien de Saint-Martin has determined more precisely than has
been done before the primitive country of the Aryans, and the route followed by them in penetrating into India. They descended through Cabul
to the Punjaub, having previously reached Cabul from the region between the Jaxartes and the Oxus.
  † The Rig-Veda distinguishes the Aryans from the Dasjus. Mr. Muir
quotes a multitude of texts in which Indra is called upon to protect the
former and slay the latter.

The chief gods of the Vedic age were Indra, Varuna, Agni, Savitri, Soma. The first was the god of the atmosphere; the second, of the Ocean of light, or Heaven; the third, of Fire;* the fourth, of the Sun; and the fifth, of the Moon. Yama was the god of death. All the powers of nature were personified in turn, — as earth, food, wine, months, seasons, day, night, and dawn. Among all these divinities, Indra and Agni were the chief.† But behind this incipient polytheism lurks the original monotheism, — for each of these gods, in turn, becomes the Supreme Being. The universal Deity seems to become apparent, first in one form of nature and then in another. Such is the opinion of Colebrooke, who says that "the ancient Hindoo religion recognizes but one God, not yet sufficiently discriminating the creature from the Creator." And Max Müller says: "The hymns celebrate Varuna, Indra, Agni, &c., and each in turn is called supreme. The whole mythology is fluent. The powers of nature become moral beings."

Max Müller adds: "It would be easy to find, in the numerous hymns of the Veda, passages in which almost every single god is represented as supreme and absolute. Agni is called 'Ruler of the Universe'; Indra is celebrated as the Strongest god, and in one hymn it is said, 'Indra is stronger than all.' It is said of Soma that 'he conquers every one.'"

But clearer traces of monotheism are to be found in the Vedas. In one hymn of the Rig-Veda it is said: "They call him Indra, Mitra, Varuna, Agni; then he is the well-winged heavenly Garutmat; that which is One, the wise call it many ways; they call it Agni, Yama, Matarisvan."

Nothing, however, will give us so good an idea of the character of these Vedic hymns as the hymns themselves. I therefore select a few of the most striking of those which have been translated by Colebrooke, Wilson, M. Müller, E. Bumont, and others.

In the following, from one of the oldest Vedas, the unity of God seems very clearly expressed.

---

* Agni, whence Ignis, in Latin.
† See Talboys Wheeler, "History of India."

Rig-Veda, X. 121.

" In the beginning there arose the Source of golden light. He was the only born Lord of all that is. He established the earth, and this sky. Who is the God to whom we shall offer our sacrifice ?

" He who gives life. He who gives strength ; whose blessing all the bright gods desire; whose shadow is immortality, whose shadow is death. Who is the God to whom we shall offer our sacrifice ?

" He who through his power is the only king of the breathing and awakening world. He who governs all, man and beast. Who is the god to whom we shall offer our sacrifice ?

" He whose power these snowy mountains, whose power the sea proclaims, with the distant river. He whose these regions are, as it were his two arms. Who is the god to whom we shall offer our sacrifice ?

" He through whom the sky is bright and the earth firm. He through whom heaven was stablished ; nay, the highest heaven. He who measured out the light in the air. Who is the god to whom we shall offer our sacrifice ?

" He to whom heaven and earth, standing firm by his will, look up, trembling inwardly. He over whom the rising sun shines forth. Who is the god to whom we shall offer our sacrifice ?

" Wherever the mighty water-clouds went, where they placed the seed and lit the fire, thence arose he who is the only life of the bright gods. Who is the god to whom we shall offer our sacrifice ?

" He who by his might looked even over the water-clouds, the clouds which gave strength and lit the sacrifice ; *he who is God above all gods.* Who is the god to whom we shall offer our sacrifice ?

"May he not destroy us, — he the creator of the earth, — or he, the righteous, who created heaven ; he who also created the bright and mighty waters. Who is the god to whom we shall offer our sacrifices ? " *

* Müller's Ancient Sanskrit Literature, page 569. He adds the following remarks: "There is nothing to prove that this hymn is of a particularly ancient date. On the contrary, there are expressions in it which seem to belong to a later age. But even if we assign the lowest possible date to this and similar hymns, certain it is that they existed during the Mantra period, and before the composition of the Brâhmanas. For, in spite of all the indications of a modern date, I see no possibility how

The oldest and most striking account of creation is in the eleventh chapter of the tenth Book of the Rig-Veda. Colebrooke, Max Müller, Muir, and Goldstücker, all give a translation of this remarkable hymn and speak of it with admiration. We take that of Colebrooke, modified by that of Muir : —

"Then there was no entity nor non-entity; no world, no sky, nor aught above it; nothing anywhere, involving or involved; nor water deep and dangerous. Death was not, and therefore no immortality, nor distinction of day or night. But THAT ONE breathed calmly * alone with Nature, her who is sustained within him. Other than Him, nothing existed [which] since [has been]. Darkness there was; [for] this universe was enveloped with darkness, and was indistinguishable waters; but that mass, which was covered by the husk, was [at length] produced by the power of contemplation. First desire † was formed in his mind; and that became the original productive seed; which the wise, recognizing it by the intellect in their hearts, distinguish as the bond of nonentity with entity.

"Did the luminous ray of these [creative acts] expand in the middle, or above, or below? That productive energy became providence [or sentient souls], and matter [or the elements]; Nature, who is sustained within, was inferior; and he who sustains was above.

" Who knows exactly, and who shall in this world declare, whence and why this creation took place? The gods are subsequent to the production of this world: then who can know whence it proceeded, or whence this varied world arose, or whether it upholds [itself] or not? He who in the highest heaven is the ruler of this universe, — he knows, or does not know."

If the following hymn, says Müller, were addressed only to the Almighty, omitting the word "Varuna," it would not disturb us in a Christian Liturgy : —

we could account for the allusions to it which occur in the Brâhmanas, or for its presence in the Sanhitâs, unless we admit that this poem formed part of the final collection of the Rig-veda-Sanhitâ, the work of the Mantra period.

   * Max Müller translates "breathed, breathless by itself; other than it nothing since has been."

   † Max Müller says, "Love fell upon it."

1. " Let me not yet, O Varuna, enter into the house of clay ; have mercy, almighty, have mercy.

2. " If I go along trembling, like a cloud driven by the wind, have mercy, almighty, have mercy !

3. " Through want of strength, thou strong and bright god, have I gone to the wrong shore ; have mercy, almighty, have mercy !

4. " Thirst came upon the worshipper, though he stood in the midst of the waters ; have mercy, almighty, have mercy !

5. " Whenever we men, O Varuna, commit an offence before the heavenly host ; whenever we break thy law through thoughtlessness ; have mercy, almighty, have mercy ! "

Out of a large number of hymns addressed to Indra, Müller selects one that is ascribed to Vasishtha.

1. " Let no one, not even those who worship thee, delay thee far from us ! Even from afar come to our feast ! Or, if thou art here, listen to us !

2. " For these who here make prayers for thee, sit together near the libation, like flies round the honey. The worshippers, anxious for wealth, have placed their desire upon Indra, as we put our foot upon a chariot.

3. " Desirous of riches, I call him who holds the thunderbolt with his arm, and who is a good giver, like as a son calls his father.

4. " These libations of Soma, mixed with milk, have been prepared for Indra : thou, armed with the thunderbolt, come with the steeds to drink of them for thy delight ; come to the house !

5. " May he hear us, for he has ears to hear. He is asked for riches ; will he despise our prayers ? He could soon give hundreds and thousands ; — no one could check him if he wishes to give."

13. " Make for the sacred gods a hymn that is not small, that is well set and beautiful ! Many snares pass by him who abides with Indra through his sacrifice.

14. " What mortal dares to attack him who is rich in thee ? Through faith in thee, O mighty, the strong acquires spoil in the day of battle."

17. " Thou art well known as the benefactor of every one, whatever battles there be. Every one of these kings of the earth implores thy name, when wishing for help.

18. " If I were lord of as much as thou, I should support the

sacred bard, thou scatterer of wealth, I should not abandon him to misery.

19. " I should award wealth day by day to him who magnifies ; I should award it to whosoever it be. We have no other friend but thee, no other happiness, no other father, O mighty ! "

22. " We call for thee, O hero, like cows that have not been milked ; we praise thee as ruler of all that moves, O Indra, as ruler of all that is immovable.

23. " There is no one like thee in heaven and earth ; he is not born, and will not be born. O mighty Indra, we call upon thee as we go fighting for cows and horses."

" In this hymn," says Müller, " Indra is clearly conceived as the Supreme God, and we can hardly understand how a people who had formed so exalted a notion of the Deity and embodied it in the person of Indra, could, at the same sacrifice, invoke other gods with equal praise. When Agni, the lord of fire, is addressed by the poet, he is spoken of as the first god, not inferior even to Indra. While Agni is invoked Indra is forgotten ; there is no competition between the two, nor any rivalry between them and other gods. This is a most important feature in the religion of the Veda, and has never been taken into consideration by those who have written on the history of ancient polytheism." *

" It is curious," says Müller, " to watch the almost imperceptible transition by which the phenomena of nature, if reflected in the mind of the poet, assume the character of divine beings. The dawn is frequently described in the Veda as it might be described by a modern poet. She is the friend of men, she smiles like a young wife, she is the daughter of the sky." " But the transition from *devî*, the bright, to *devî*, the goddess, is so easy ; the daughter of the sky assumes so readily the same personality which is given to the sky, Dyaus, her father, that we can only guess whether in every passage the poet is speaking of a bright apparition, or of a bright goddess ; of a natural vision, or of a visible deity. The following hymn of Vashishtha will serve as an instance : —

* Müller, Sanskrit Lit., p. 546.

"She shines upon us, like a young wife, rousing every living being to go to his work. The fire had to be kindled by men; she brought light by striking down darkness.

"She rose up, spreading far and wide, and moving towards every one. She grew in brightness, wearing her brilliant garment. The mother of the cows (of the morning clouds), the leader of the days, she shone gold-colored, lovely to behold.

"She, the fortunate, who brings the eye of the god, who leads the white and lovely steed (of the sun), the Dawn was seen, revealed by her rays; with brilliant treasures she follows every one.

"Thou, who art a blessing where thou art near, drive far away the unfriendly; make the pastures wide, give us safety! Remove the haters, bring treasures! Raise wealth to the worshipper, thou mighty Dawn.

"Shine for us with thy best rays, thou bright Dawn, thou who lengthenest our life, thou the love of all, who givest us food, who givest us wealth in cows, horses, and chariots.

"Thou, daughter of the sky, thou high-born Dawn, whom the Vasishthas magnify with songs, give us riches high and wide : all ye gods, protect us always with your blessings!"

"This hymn, addressed to the Dawn, is a fair specimen of the original simple poetry of the Veda. It has no reference to any special sacrifice, it contains no technical expressions, it can hardly be called a hymn, in our sense of the word. It is simply a poem expressing, without any effort, without any display of far-fetched thought or brilliant imagery, the feelings of a man who has watched the approach of the Dawn with mingled delight and awe, and who was moved to give utterance to what he felt in measured language." *

"But there is a charm in these primitive strains discoverable in no other class of poetry. Every word retains something of its radical meaning, every epithet tells, every thought, in spite of the most intricate and abrupt expressions, is, if we once disentangle it, true, correct, and complete." †

The Vedic literature is divided by Müller into four periods, namely, those of the Chhandas, Mantra, Brâhmana, and Sûtras. The Chhandas period contains the oldest

---

* Müller, Sanskrit Lit., p. 552.   † Ibid., p. 553.

hymns of the oldest, or Rig-Veda. To that of the Mantras belong the later hymns of the same Veda. But the most modern of these are older than the Brâhmanas. The Brâhmanas contain theology; the older Mantras are liturgic. Müller says that the Brâhmanas, though so very ancient, are full of pedantry, shallow and insipid grandiloquence and priestly conceit. Next to these, in the order of time, are the Upanishads. These are philosophical, and almost the only part of the Vedas which are read at the present time. They are believed to contain the highest authority for the different philosophical systems, of which we shall speak hereafter. Their authors are unknown. More modern than these are the Sûtras. The word "Sûtra" means *string*, and they consist of a string of short sentences. Conciseness is the aim in this style, and every doctrine is reduced to a skeleton. The numerous Sûtras now extant contain the distilled essence of all the knowledge which the Brahmans have collected during centuries of meditation. They belong to the non-revealed literature, as distinguished from the revealed literature, — a distinction made by the Brahmans before the time of Buddha. At the time of the Buddhist controversy the Sûtras were admitted to be of human origin and were consequently recent works. The distinction between the Sûtras and Brâhmanas is very marked, the second being revealed. The Brâhmanas were composed by and for Brahmans and are in three collections. The Vedângas are intermediate between the Vedic and non-Vedic literature. Pânini, the grammarian of India, was said to be contemporary with King Nanda, who was the successor of Chandragupta, the contemporary of Alexander, and therefore in the second half of the fourth century before Christ. Dates are so precarious in Indian literature, says Max Müller, that a confirmation within a century or two is not to be despised. Now the grammarian Kâtyâyana completed and corrected the grammar of Pânini, and Patanjeli wrote an immense commentary on the two which became so famous as to be imported by royal authority into Cashmere, in the first half of the first century of our era. Müller considers the limits of the

Sûtra period to extend from 600 B. C. to 200 B. C. Buddhism before Asoka was but modified Brahmanism. The basis of Indian chronology is the date of Chandra-gupta. All dates before his time are merely hypothetical. Several classical writers speak of him as founding an empire on the Ganges soon after the invasion of Alexander. He was grandfather of Asoka. Indian traditions refer to this king.

Returning to the Brâhmana period, we notice that between the Sûtras and Brâhmanas come the Aranyakas, which are books written for the recluse. Of these the Upanishads, before mentioned, form part. They presuppose the existence of the Brâhmanas.

Rammohun Roy was surprised that Dr. Rosen should have thought it worth while to publish the hymns of the Veda, and considered the Upanishads the only Vedic books worth reading. They speak of the divine SELF, of the Eternal Word in the heavens from which the hymns came. The divine SELF they say is not to be grasped by tradition, reason, or revelation, but only by him whom he himself grasps. In the beginning was Self alone. Atman is the SELF in all our selves, — the Divine Self concealed by his own qualities. This Self they sometimes call the Undeveloped and sometimes the Not-Being. There are ten of the old Upanishads, all of which have been published. Anquetil Du Perron translated fifty into Latin out of Persian.

The Brâhmanas are very numerous. Müller gives stories from them and legends. They relate to sacrifices, to the story of the deluge, and other legends. They substituted these legends for the simple poetry of the ancient Vedas. They must have extended over at least two hundred years, and contained long lists of teachers.

Müller supposes that writing was unknown when the Rig-Veda was composed. The thousand and ten hymns of the Vedas contain no mention of writing or books, any more than the Homeric poems. There is no allusion to writing during the whole of the Brâhmana period, nor even through the Sûtra period. This seems incredible to us, says Müller, only because our memory has been systematically debilitated by newspapers and the like during many generations. It was the business of every Brahman to learn by heart the Vedas during the twelve years of his student life. The Guru, or teacher, pronounces a group of words, and the pupils repeat after him. After writing was introduced, the Brahmans were strictly forbidden to read the Vedas, or to write them. Cæsar says the same of the Druids. Even Pânini never alludes to written words or letters. None of the ordinary modern words for book, paper, ink, or writing have been found in any ancient Sanskrit work. No such words as *volumen*, volume ; *liber*, or inner bark of a tree ; *byblos*, inner bark of papyrus ; or book, that is beech wood. But Buddha had learnt to write, as we find by a book translated into Chinese A. D. 76. In this book Buddha instructs his teacher ; as in the " Gospel of the Infancy " Jesus explains to his teacher the meaning of the Hebrew alphabet. So Buddha tells his teacher the names of sixty-four alphabets. The first authentic inscription in India is of Buddhist origin, belonging to the third century before Christ.

In the most ancient Vedic period the language had become complete. There is no growing language in the Vedas.

In regard to the age of these Vedic writings, we will quote the words of Max Müller, at the conclusion of his admirable work on the " History of Ancient Sanskrit Literature," from which most of this section has been taken : —

" Oriental scholars are frequently suspected of a desire to make the literature of the Eastern nations appear more ancient than it is. As to myself, I can truly say that nothing would be to me a more welcome discovery, nothing would remove so many doubts and difficulties, as some suggestions as to the manner in which certain of the Vedic hymns could have been added to the original collection during the Brâhmana or Sûtra periods, or, if possible, by the writers of our MSS., of which most are not older than the fifteenth century. But these MSS., though so modern, are checked by the Anukramanîs. Every hymn which stands in our MSS. is counted in the Index of Saunaka, who is anterior to the invasion of Alexander. The Sûtras, belonging to the same period as Saunaka, prove the previous existence of every chapter of the Brâhmanas ; and I

doubt whether there is a single hymn in the Sanhitâ of the
Rig-Veda which could not be checked by some passage of the
Brâhmanas and Sûtras. The chronological limits assigned to
the Sûtra and Brâhmana periods will seem to most Sanskrit
scholars too narrow rather than too wide, and if we assign but
two hundred years to the Mantra period, from 800 to 1000
B. C., and an equal number to the Chhandas period, from 1000
to 1200 B. C., we can do so only under the supposition that
during the early periods of history the growth of the human
mind was more luxuriant than in later times, and that the
layers of thought were formed less slowly in the primary than
in the tertiary ages of the world."

The Vedic age, according to Müller, will then be as
follows : —

Sûtra period,	from B. C.	200 to	B. C.	600.
Brâhmana period,	"	"	600	"	800.
Mantra period,	"	"	800	"	1000.
Chhandas period,	"	"	1000	"	1200.

Dr. Haug, a high authority, considers the Vedic period
to extend from B. C. 1200 to B. C. 2000, and the very oldest
hymns to have been composed B. C. 2400.

The principal deity in the oldest Vedas is Indra, God
of the air. In Greek he becomes Zeus ; in Latin, Jupiter. The hymns to Indra are not unlike some of the
Psalms of the Old Testament. Indra is called upon as
the most ancient god whom the Fathers worshipped.
Next to India comes Agni, fire, derived from the root Ag,
which means "to move." * Fire is worshipped as the principle of motion on earth, as Indra was the moving power
above. Not only fire, but the forms of flame, are worshipped and all that belongs to it. Entire nature is
called Aditi, whose children are named Adityas. M.
Maury quotes these words from Gotama : " Aditi is
heaven ; Aditi is air ; Aditi is mother, father, and son ;
Aditi is all the gods and the five races ; Aditi is whatever is born and will be born ; in short, the heavens and
the earth, the heavens being the father and the earth the
mother of all things. This reminds one of the Greek
Zeus-pateer and Gee-mêteer. Varuna is the vault of

* That heat was "a form of motion " was thus early discovered.

heaven. Mitra is often associated with Varuna in the Vedic hymns. Mitra is the sun, illuminating the day, while Varuna was the sun with an obscure face going back in the darkness from west to east to take his luminous disk again. From Mitra seems to be derived the Persian Mithra. There are no invocations to the stars in the Veda. But the Aurora, or Dawn, is the object of great admiration ; also, the Aswins, or twin gods, who in Greece become the Dioscuri. The god of storms is Rudra, supposed by some writers to be the same as Siva. The two hostile worships of Vishnu and Siva do not appear, however, till long after this time. Vishnu appears frequently in the Veda, and his three steps are often spoken of. These steps measure the heavens. But his real worship came much later.

The religion of the Vedas was of odes and hymns, a religion of worship by simple adoration. Sometimes there were prayers for temporal blessings, sometimes simple sacrifices and libations. Human sacrifices have scarcely left any trace of themselves if they ever existed, unless it be in a typical ceremony reported in one of the Vedas.

§ 5. *Second Period. Laws of Manu. The Brahmanic Age.*

Long after the age of the elder Vedas Brahmanism begins. Its text-book is the Laws of Manu.* As yet Vishnu and Siva are not known. The former is named once, the latter not at all. The writer only knows three Vedas. The Atharva-Veda is later. But as Siva is mentioned in the oldest Buddhist writings, it follows that the laws of Manu are older than these. In the time of Manu the Aryans are still living in the valley of the Ganges. The caste system is now in full operation, and the authority of the Brahman is raised to its highest point. The Indus and Punjaub are not mentioned ; all this is forgotten. This work could not be later than B. C. 700, or earlier than B. C. 1200. It was probably written about

---

* It is the opinion of Maine ("Ancient Law") and other eminent scholars, that this code was never fully accepted or enforced in India, and remained always an ideal of the perfect Brahmanic state.

B. C. 900 or B. C. 1000. In this view agree Wilson, Lassen, Max Müller, and Saint-Martin. The Supreme Deity is now Brahma, and sacrifice is still the act by which one comes into relation with heaven. Widow-burning is not mentioned in Manu; but it appears in the Mahabharata, one of the great epics, which is therefore later.

In the region of the Sarasvati, a holy river, which formerly emptied into the Indus, but is now lost in a desert, the Aryan race of India was transformed from nomads into a stable community.* There they received their laws, and there their first cities were erected. There were founded the Solar and Lunar monarchies.

The Manu of the Vedas and he of the Brahmans are very different persons. The first is called in the Vedas the father of mankind. He also escapes from a deluge by building a ship, which he is advised to do by a fish. He preserves the fish, which grows to a great size, and when the flood comes acts as a tow-boat to drag the ship of Manu to a mountain.† This account is contained in a Brahmana.

The name of Manu seems afterward to have been given by the Brahmans to the author of their code. Some extracts from this very interesting volume we will now give, slightly abridged, from Sir William Jones's translation.‡ From the first book, on Creation : —

"The universe existed in darkness, imperceptible, undefinable, undiscoverable, and undiscovered ; as if immersed in sleep."

"Then the self-existing power, undiscovered himself, but making the world discernible, with the five elements and other principles, appeared in undiminished glory, dispelling the gloom."

"He, whom the mind alone can perceive, whose essence eludes the external organs, who has no visible parts, who exists from eternity, even he, the soul of all beings, shone forth in person.

* See Vivien de Saint-Martin, Revue Germanique, July 16, 1862. The Sarasvati is highly praised in the Rig-Veda. Talboys Wheeler, II. 429.
† Max Müller, Sanskrit Lit., p. 425.
‡ Institutes of Hindu Law, or the Ordinances of Menu, according to the Gloss of Calluca, Calcutta, 1796, §§ 5, 6, 7, 8.

CARL A. RUDISILL LIBRARY
LENOIR RHYNE COLLEGE

" He having willed to produce various beings from his own divine substance, first with a thought created the waters, and placed in them a productive seed."

" The seed became an egg bright as gold, blazing like the luminary with a thousand beams, and in that egg he was born himself, in the form of Brahma, the great forefather of all spirits.

" The waters are called Nárá, because they were the production of Nara, or the spirit of God; and hence they were his first ayana, or place of motion; he hence is named Nara yana, or moving on the waters.

" In that egg the great power sat inactive a whole year of the creator, at the close of which, by his thought alone, he caused the egg to divide itself.

" And from its two divisions he framed the heaven above and the earth beneath; in the midst he placed the subtile ether, the eight regions, and the permanent receptacle of waters.

" From the supreme soul he drew forth mind, existing substantially though unperceived by sense, immaterial; and before mind, or the reasoning power, he produced consciousness, the internal monitor, the ruler.

" And before them both he produced the great principle of the soul, or first expansion of the divine idea; and all vital forms endued with the three qualities of goodness, passion, and darkness, and the five perceptions of sense, and the five organs of sensation.

" Thus, having at once pervaded with emanations from the Supreme Spirit the minutest portions of fixed principles immensely operative, consciousness and the five perceptions, he framed all creatures.

" Thence proceed the great elements, endued with peculiar powers, and mind with operations infinitely subtile, the unperishable cause of all apparent forms.

" This universe, therefore, is compacted from the minute portions of those seven divine and active principles, the great soul, or first emanation, consciousness, and five perceptions; a mutable universe from immutable ideas.

" Of created things, the most excellent are those which are animated; of the animated, those which subsist by intelligence; of the intelligent, mankind; and of men, the sacerdotal class.

" Of priests, those eminent in learning; of the learned,

those who know their duty; of those who know it, such as perform it virtuously; and of the virtuous, those who seek beatitude from a perfect acquaintance with scriptural doctrine.

"The very birth of Brahmans is a constant incarnation of Dharma, God of justice; for the Brahman is born to promote justice, and to procure ultimate happiness.

"When a Brahman springs to light, he is born above the world, the chief of all creatures, assigned to guard the treasury of duties, religious and civil.

"The Brahman who studies this book, having performed sacred rites, is perpetually free from offence in thought, in word and in deed.

"He confers purity on his living family, on his ancestors, and on his descendants as far as the seventh person, and he alone deserves to possess this whole earth."

The following passages are from Book II., " On Education and the Priesthood " : —

"Self-love is no laudable motive, yet an exemption from self-love is not to be found in this world : on self-love is grounded the study of Scripture, and the practice of actions recommended in it.

"Eager desire to act has its root in expectation of some advantage; and with such expectation are sacrifices performed; the rules of religious austerity and abstinence from sins are all known to arise from hope of remuneration.

"Not a single act here below appears ever to be done by a man free from self-love; whatever he perform, it is wrought from his desire of a reward.

"He, indeed, who should persist in discharging these duties without any view to their fruit, would attain hereafter the state of the immortals, and even in this life would enjoy all the virtuous gratifications that his fancy could suggest.

"The most excellent of the three classes, being girt with the sacrificial thread, must ask food with the respectful word Dhavati at the beginning of the phrase; those of the second class with that word in the middle; and those of the third with that word at the end.

"Let him first beg food of his mother, or of his sister, or of his mother's whole sister; then of some other female who will not disgrace him.

"Having collected as much of the desired food as he has occasion for, and having presented it without guile to his preceptor, let him eat some of it, being duly purified, with his face to the east.

"If he seek long life, he should eat with his face to the east; if prosperity, to the west; if truth and its reward, to the north.

"When the student is going to read the Veda he must perform an ablution, as the law ordains, with his face to the north; and having paid scriptural homage, he must receive instruction, wearing a clean vest, his members being duly composed.

"A Brahman beginning and ending a lecture on the Veda must always pronounce to himself the syllable óm; for unless the syllable óm precede, his learning will slip away from him; and unless it follow, nothing will be long retained.

"A priest who shall know the Veda, and shall pronounce to himself, both morning and evening, that syllable, and that holy text preceded by the three words, shall attain the sanctity which the Veda confers.

"And a twice-born man, who shall a thousand times repeat those three (or óm, the vyáhrítis, and the gáyatri) apart from the multitude, shall be released in a month even from a great offence, as a snake from his slough.

"The three great immutable words, preceded by the triliteral syllable, and followed by the gáyatri, which consists of three measures, must be considered as the mouth, or principal part of the Veda.

"The triliteral monosyllable is an emblem of the Supreme; the suppressions of breath, with a mind fixed on God, are the highest devotion; but nothing is more exalted than the gáyatri; a declaration of truth is more excellent than silence.

"All rites ordained in the Veda, oblations to fire, and solemn sacrifices pass away; but that which passes not away is declared to be the syllable óm, thence called acshara; since it is a symbol of God, the Lord of created beings.

"The act of repeating his Holy Name is ten times better than the appointed sacrifice; an hundred times better when it is heard by no man; and a thousand times better when it is purely mental.

"To a man contaminated by sensuality, neither the Vedas, nor liberality, nor sacrifices, nor strict observances, nor pious austerities, ever procure felicity.

"As he who digs deep with a spade comes to a spring of water, so the student, who humbly serves his teacher, attains the knowledge which lies deep in his teacher's mind.

" If the sun should rise and set, while he sleeps through sensual indulgence, and knows it not, he must fast a whole day repeating the gáyatri.

" Let him adore God both at sunrise and at sunset, as the law ordains, having made his ablution, and keeping his organs controlled ; and with fixed attention let him repeat the text, which he ought to repeat in a place free from impurity.

" The twice-born man who shall thus without intermission have passed the time of his studentship shall ascend after death to the most exalted of regions, and no more again spring to birth in this lower world.

The following passages are from Book IV., " On Private Morals " : —

" Let a Brahman, having dwelt with a preceptor during the first quarter of a man's life, pass the second quarter of human life in his own house, when he has contracted a legal marriage.

" He must live with no injury, or with the least possible injury, to animated beings, by pursuing those means of gaining subsistence, which are strictly prescribed by law, except in times of distress.

" Let him say what is true, but let him say what is pleasing ; let him speak no disagreeable truth, nor let him speak agreeable falsehood ; this is a primeval rule.

" Let him say ' well and good,' or let him say ' well' only ; but let him not maintain fruitless enmity and altercation with any man.

" All that depends on another gives pain ; and all that depends on himself gives pleasure ; let him know this to be in few words the definition of pleasure and pain.

" And for whatever purpose a man bestows a gift, for a similar purpose he shall receive, with due honor, a similar reward.

" Both he who respectfully bestows a present, and he who respectfully accepts it, shall go to a seat of bliss ; but, if they act otherwise, to a region of horror.

" Let not a man be proud of his rigorous devotion ; let him not, having sacrificed, utter a falsehood ; let him not, though injured, insult a priest ; having made a donation, let him never proclaim it.

" By falsehood the sacrifice becomes vain ; by pride the merit of devotion is lost ; by insulting priests life is diminished ; and by proclaiming a largess its fruit is destroyed.

" For in his passage to the next world, neither his father,

5 *

nor his mother, nor his wife, nor his son, nor his kinsmen will remain his company ; his virtue alone will adhere to him.

"Single is each man born ; single he dies ; single he receives the reward of his good, and single the punishment of his evil deeds.

From Book V., " On Diet" : —

" The twice-born man who has intentionally eaten a mushroom, the flesh of a tame hog, or a town cock, a leek, or an onion, or garlic, is degraded immediately.

" But having undesignedly tasted either of those six things, he must perform the penance sántapana, or the chándráyana, which anchorites practise ; for other things he must fast a whole day.

" One of those harsh penances called prájápatya the twice-born man must perform annually, to purify him from the unknown taint of illicit food ; but he must do particular penance for such food intentionally eaten.

" He who injures no animated creature shall attain without hardship whatever he thinks of, whatever he strives for, whatever he fixes his mind on.

" Flesh meat cannot be procured without injury to animals, and the slaughter of animals obstructs the path to beatitude ; from flesh meat, therefore, let man abstain.

" Attentively considering the formation of bodies, and the death or confinement of embodied spirits, let him abstain from eating flesh meat of any kind.

" Not a mortal exists more sinful than he who, without an oblation to the manes or the gods, desires to enlarge his own flesh with the flesh of another creature.

" By subsisting on pure fruit and on roots, and by eating such grains as are eaten by hermits, a man reaps not so high a reward as by carefully abstaining from animal food.

" In lawfully tasting meat, in drinking fermented liquor, in caressing women, there is no turpitude ; for to such enjoyments men are naturally prone, but a virtuous abstinence from them produces a signal compensation.

" Sacred learning, austere devotion, fire, holy aliment, earth, the mind, water, smearing with cow-dung, air, prescribed acts of religion, the sun, and time are purifiers of embodied spirits.

" But of all pure things purity in acquiring wealth is pronounced the most excellent : since he who gains wealth with clean hands is truly pure ; not he who is purified merely with earth and water.

"By forgiveness of injuries, the learned are purified; by liberality, those who have neglected their duty; by pious meditation, those who have secret faults; by devout austerity, those who best know the Veda.

"Bodies are cleansed by water; the mind is purified by truth; the vital spirit, by theology and devotion; the understanding, by clear knowledge.

"No sacrifice is allowed to women apart from their husbands, no religious rite, no fasting; as far only as a wife honors her lord, so far she is exalted in heaven.

"A faithful wife, who wishes to attain in heaven the mansion of her husband, must do nothing unkind to him, be he living or dead.

"Let her emaciate her body by living voluntarily on pure flowers, roots, and fruit; but let her not, when her lord is deceased, even pronounce the name of another man.

"Let her continue till death forgiving all injuries, performing harsh duties, avoiding every sensual pleasure, and cheerfully practising the incomparable rules of virtue, which have been followed by such women as were devoted to one only husband."

The Sixth Book of the Laws of Manu relates to devotion. It seems that the Brahmans were in the habit of becoming ascetics, or, as the Roman Catholics would say, entering Religion. A Brahman, or twice-born man, who wishes to become an ascetic, must abandon his home and family, and go to live in the forest. His food must be roots and fruit, his clothing a bark garment or a skin, he must bathe morning and evening, and suffer his hair to grow. He must spend his time in reading the Veda, with a mind intent on the Supreme Being, "a perpetual giver but no receiver of gifts; with tender affection for all animated bodies." He is to perform various sacrifices with offerings of fruits and flowers, practise austerities by exposing himself to heat and cold, and "for the purpose of uniting his soul with the Divine Spirit he must study the Upanishads."

"A Brahman, having shuffled off his body by these modes, which great sages practise, and becoming void of sorrow and fear, is exalted into the divine essence."

"Let him not wish for death. Let him not wish for life. Let him expect his appointed time, as the hired servant expects his wages."

" Meditating on the Supreme Spirit, without any earthly desire, with no companion but his own soul, let him live in this world seeking the bliss of the next."

The anchorite is to beg food, but only once a day ; if it is not given to him, he must not be sorrowful, and if he receives it he must not be glad ; he is to meditate on the " subtle indivisible essence of the Supreme Being," he is to be careful not to destroy the life of the smallest insect, and he must make atonement for the death of those which he has ignorantly destroyed by making six suppressions of his breath, repeating at the same time the triliteral syllable A U M. He will thus at last become united with the Eternal Spirit, and his good deeds will be inherited by those who love him, and his evil deeds by those who hate him.

The Seventh Book relates to the duties of rulers. One of these is to reward the good and punish the wicked. The genius of punishment is a son of Brahma, and has a body of pure light. Punishment is an active ruler, governs all mankind, dispenses laws, preserves the race, and is the perfection of justice. Without it all classes would become corrupt, all barriers would fall, and there would be total confusion. Kings are to respect the Brahmans, must shun vices, must select good counsellors and brave soldiers. A King must be a father to his people. When he goes to war he must observe the rules of honorable warfare, must not use poisoned arrows, strike a fallen enemy, nor one who sues for life, nor one without arms, nor one who surrenders. He is not to take too little revenue, and so " cut up his own root " ; nor too much, and so " cut up the root of others " ; he is to be severe when it is necessary, and mild when ĭt is necessary.

The Eighth Book relates to civil and criminal law. The Raja is to hold his court every day, assisted by his Brahmans, and decide causes concerning debts and loans, sales, wages, contracts, boundaries, slander, assaults, larceny, robbery, and other crimes. The Raja, " understanding what is expedient or inexpedient, but considering only what is law or not law," should examine all disputes. He must protect unprotected women, restore property to its rightful owner, not encourage litigation, and decide according to the rules of law. These rules correspond very nearly to our law of evidence. Witnesses are warned to speak the truth in all cases by the consideration that, though they may think that none see them, the gods distinctly see them and also the spirit in their own breasts.

" The soul itself is its own witness, the soul itself is its own refuge ; offend not thy conscious soul, the supreme internal witness of men."

" The fruit of every virtuous act which thou hast done, O good man, since thy birth, shall depart from thee to the dogs, if thou deviate from the truth."

" O friend to virtue, the Supreme Spirit, which is the same with thyself, resides in thy bosom perpetually, and is an all-knowing inspector of thy goodness or wickedness."

The law then proceeds to describe the punishments which the gods would inflict upon false witnesses ; but, curiously enough, allows false witness to be given, from a benevolent motive, in order to save an innocent man from a tyrant. This is called " the venial sin of benevolent falsehood." The book then proceeds to describe weights and measures, and the rate of usury, which is put down as five per cent. It forbids compound interest. The law of deposits occupies a large space, as in all Eastern countries, where investments are difficult. A good deal is said about the wages of servants, especially of those hired to keep cattle, and their responsibilities. The law of slander is carefully laid down. Crimes of violence are also minutely described, and here the *Lex Talionis* comes in. If a man strikes a human being or an animal so as to inflict much pain, he shall be struck himself in the same way. A man is allowed to correct with a small stick his wife, son, or servant, but not on the head or any noble part of the body. The Brahmans, however, are protected by special laws.

" Never shall the king flay a Brahman, though convicted of all possible crimes ; let him banish the offender from his realm, but with all his property secure and his body unhurt."

" No greater crime is known on earth than flaying a Brahman ; and the king, therefore, must not even form in his mind the idea of killing a priest."

The Ninth Book relates to women, to families, and to the law of castes. It states that women must be kept in a state of dependence.

" Their fathers protect them in childhood ; their husbands protect them in youth ; their sons protect them in age. A woman is never fit for independence."

It is the duty of men to watch and guard women, and very unfavorable opinions are expressed concerning the female character.

" Women have no business with the text of the Veda ; this is fully settled ; therefore having no knowledge of expiatory texts, sinful women must be as foul as falsehood itself. This is a fixed law."

It is, however, stated that good women become like goddesses, and shall be joined with their husbands in heaven ; and that a man is only perfect when he consists of three persons united, — his wife, himself, and his son. Manu also attributes to ancient Brahmans a maxim almost verbally the same as that of the Bible, namely, " The husband is even one person with his wife." Nothing is said by Manu concerning the cremation of widows, but, on the other hand, minute directions are given for the behavior of widows during their life. Directions are also given concerning the marriage of daughters and sons and their inheritance of property. The rest of the book is devoted to a further description of crimes and punishments.

The Tenth Book relates to the mixed classes and times of distress.

The Eleventh Book relates to penance and expiation. In this book is mentioned the remarkable rite which consists in drinking the fermented juice of the moon-plant (or acid asclepias) with religious ceremonies. This Hindu sacrament began in the Vedic age, and the Sanhita of the

Sama-Veda consists of hymns to be sung at the moon-plant sacrifice.* This ceremony is still practised occasionally in India, and Dr. Haug has tasted this sacred beverage, which he describes as astringent, bitter, intoxicating, and very disagreeable.† It is stated by Manu that no one has a right to drink this sacred juice who does not properly provide for his own household. He encourages sacrifices by declaring that they are highly meritorious and will expiate sin. Involuntary sins require a much lighter penance than those committed with knowledge. Crimes committed by Brahmans require a less severe penance than those performed by others; while those committed against Brahmans involve a much deeper guilt and require severer penance. The law declares:—

"From his high birth alone a Brahman is an object of veneration, even to deities, and his declarations are decisive evidence."

"A Brahman, who has performed an expiation with his whole mind fixed on God, purifies his soul."

Drinking intoxicating liquor (except in the Soma sacrifice) is strictly prohibited, and it is even declared that a Brahman who tastes intoxicating liquor sinks to the low caste of a Sudra. If a Brahman who has tasted the Soma juice even smells the breath of a man who has been drinking spirits, he must do penance by repeating the Gayatri, suppressing his breath, and eating clarified butter. Next to Brahmans, cows were the objects of reverence, probably because, in the earliest times, the Aryan race, as nomads, depended on this animal for food. He who kills a cow must perform very severe penances, among which are these:—

"All day he must wait on a herd of cows and stand quaffing the dust raised by their hoofs; at night, having servilely attended them, he must sit near and guard them."

"Free from passion, he must stand while they stand, follow when they move, and lie down near them when they lie down."

* See translation of the Sanhita of the Sama-Veda, by the Rev. J. Stevenson. London, 1842.

† Max Müller, "Chips," Vol. I. p. 107.

"By thus waiting on a herd for three months, he who has killed a cow atones for his guilt."

For such offences as cutting down fruit-trees or grasses, or killing insects, or injuring sentient creatures, the penance is to repeat so many texts of the Veda, to eat clarified butter, or to stop the breath. A low-born man who treats a Brahman disrespectfully, or who even overcomes him in argument, must fast all day and fall prostrate before him. He who strikes a Brahman shall remain in hell a thousand years. Great, however, is the power of sincere devotion. By repentance, open confession, reading the Scripture, almsgiving, and reformation, one is released from guilt. Devotion, it is said, is equal to the performance of all duties; and even the souls of worms and insects and vegetables attain heaven by the power of devotion. But especially great is the sanctifying influence of the Vedas. He who can repeat the whole of the Rig-Veda would be free from guilt, even if he had killed the inhabitants of the three worlds.

The last book of Manu is on transmigration and final beatitude. The principle is here laid down that every human action, word, and thought bears its appropriate fruit, good or evil. Out of the heart proceed three sins of thought, four sins of the tongue, and three of the body, namely, covetous, disobedient, and atheistic thoughts; scurrilous, false, frivolous, and unkind words; and actions of theft, bodily injury, and licentiousness. He who controls his thoughts, words, and actions is called a triple commander. There are three qualities of the soul, giving it a tendency to goodness, to passion, and to darkness. The first leads to knowledge, the second to desire, the third to sensuality. To the first belong study of Scripture, devotion, purity, self-command, and obedience. From the second proceed hypocritical actions, anxiety, disobedience, and self-indulgence. The third produces avarice, atheism, indolence, and every act which a man is ashamed of doing. The object of the first quality is virtue; of the second, worldly success; of the third, pleasure. The souls in which the first quality is supreme rise after death to the condition of deities; those in whom the second rules pass into the bodies of other men; while those under the dominion of the third become beasts and vegetables. Manu proceeds to expound, in great detail, this law of transmigration. For great sins one is condemned to pass a great many times into the bodies of dogs, insects, spiders, snakes, or grasses. The change has relation to the crime : thus, he who steals grain shall be born a rat; he who steals meat, a vulture; those who indulge in forbidden pleasures of the senses shall have their senses made acute to endure intense pain.

The highest of all virtues is disinterested goodness, performed from the love of God, and based on the knowledge of the Veda. A religious action, performed from hope of reward in this world or the next, will give one a place in the lowest heaven. But he who performs good actions without hope of reward, " perceiving the supreme soul in all beings, and all beings in the supreme soul, fixing his mind on God, approaches the divine nature."

" Let every Brahman, with fixed attention, consider all nature as existing in the Divine Spirit ; all worlds as seated in him ; he alone as the whole assemblage of gods; and he the author of all human actions."

" Let him consider the supreme omnipresent intelligence as the sovereign lord of the universe, by whom alone it exists, an incomprehensible spirit ; pervading all beings in five elemental forms, and causing them to pass through birth, growth, and decay, and so to revolve like the wheels of a car."

" Thus the man who perceives in his own soul the supreme soul present in all creatures, acquires equanimity toward them all, and shall be absolved at last in the highest essence, even that of the Almighty himself."

We have given these copious extracts from the Brahmanic law, because this code is so ancient and authentic, and contains the bright consummate flower of the system, before decay began to come.

§ 6. *The Three Hindoo Systems of Philosophy, — Sánkhya, Vedanta, and Nyasa.*

Duncker says * that the Indian systems of philosophy were produced in the sixth or seventh century before Christ. As the system of Buddha implies the existence of the Sánkhya philosophy, the latter must have preceded Buddhism.† Moreover, Kapila and his two principles are distinctly mentioned in the Laws of Manu,‡ and in the later Upanishads.§ This brings it to the Brahmana period of Max Müller, B. C. 600 to B. C. 800, and probably still earlier. Dr. Weber at one time was of the opinion that Kapila and Buddha were the same person, but afterward retracted this opinion.|| Colebrooke says that Kapila is mentioned in the Veda itself, but intimates that this is probably another sage of the same name.¶ The sage was even considered to be an incarnation of Vischnu, or of Agni. The Vedanta philosophy is also said by Lassen to be mentioned in the Laws of Manu.** This system is founded on the Upanishads, and would seem to be later than that of Kapila, since it criticises his system, and devotes much space to its confutation.†† But Duncker regards it as the oldest, and already beginning in the Upanishads of the Vedas.‡‡ As the oldest works now extant in both systems are later than their origin, this question of date can only be determined from their contents. That which logically precedes the other must be chronologically the oldest.

The Sánkhya system of Kapila is contained in many works, but notably in the Káriká, or Sánkhya-Káriká, by Iswara Krishna. This consists in eighty-two memorial

* Geschichte der Arier, Buch V. § 8.
† Lassen, I. 830.
‡ Laws of Manu (XII. 50) speaks of "the two principles of nature in the philosophy of Kapila."
§ Duncker, as above.
|| Müller, Ancient Sanskrit Literature, p. 102.
¶ Colebrooke, Miscellaneous Essays, I. 349.
** Lassen, I. 834.
†† Colebrooke, I. 350, 352.
‡‡ Duncker, I. 204 (third edition, 1867).

verses, with a commentary.* The Vedanta is contained in the Sutras, the Upanishads, and especially the Brahma-Sutra attributed to Vyasa.† The Nyaya is to be found in the Sutras of Gotama and Canade.‡

These three systems of Hindoo philosophy, the Sánkhya, the Nyaya, and the Vedanta, reach far back into a misty twilight, which leaves it doubtful when they began or who were their real authors. In some points they agree, in others they are widely opposed. They all agree in having for their object deliverance from the evils of time, change, sorrow, into an eternal rest and peace. Their aim is, therefore, not merely speculative, but practical. All agree in considering existence to be an evil, understanding by existence a life in time and space. All are idealists, to whom the world of sense and time is a delusion and snare, and who regard the Idea as the only substance. All agree in accepting the fact of transmigration, the cessation of which brings final deliverance. All consider that the means of this deliverance is to be found in knowledge, in a perfect knowledge of reality as opposed to appearance. And all are held by Brahmans, who consider themselves orthodox, who honor the Vedas above all other books, pay complete respect to the Hinduism of the day, perform the daily ceremonies, and observe the usual caste rules.§ The systems of philosophy supplement the religious worship, but are not intended to destroy it. The Vedantists hold that while in truth there is but one God, the various forms of worship in the Vedas, of Indra, Agni, the Maruts, etc., were all intended for those who could not rise to this sublime monotheism. Those who believe in the Sánkhya maintain that though it wholly omits God, and is called " the system without a God," it merely omits, but does not deny, the Divine existence. ||

* The Sánkhya-Káriká, translated by Colebrooke. Oxford, 1837.
† Essay on the Vedanta, by Chunder Dutt. Calcutta, 1854.
‡ Colebrooke, I. 262.
§ The Religious Aspects of Hindu Philosophy : A Prize Essay, by Joseph Mullens, p. 43. London, 1860. See also Dialogues on the Hindu Philosophy, by Rev. K. M. Banerjea. London, 1861.
|| Mullens, p. 44.

Each of these philosophies has a speculative and a practical side. The speculative problem is, How did the universe come ? The practical problem is, How shall man be delivered from evil ?

In answering the first question, the Vedanta, or Mimansa doctrine, proceeds from a single eternal and uncreated Principle ; declaring that there is only ONE being in the universe, God or Brahm, and that all else is Maya, or illusion. The Sánkhya accepts TWO eternal and uncreated substances, Soul and Nature. The Nyaya assumes THREE eternal and uncreated substances, — Atoms, Souls, and God.

The solution of the second problem is the same in all three systems. It is by knowledge that the soul is emancipated from body or matter or nature. Worship is inadequate, though not to be despised. Action is injurious rather than beneficial, for it implies desire. Only knowledge can lead to entire rest and peace.

According to all three systems, the transmigration of the soul through different bodies is an evil resulting from desire. As long as the soul wishes anything, it will continue to migrate and to suffer. When it gathers itself up into calm insight, it ceases to wander and finds repose.

The *Vedanta* or *Mimansa* is supposed to be referred to in Manu.* *Mimansa* means " searching." In its logical forms it adopts the method so common among the scholastics, in first stating the question, then giving the objection, after that the reply to the objection, and lastly the conclusion. The first part of the Mimansa relates to worship and the ceremonies and ritual of the Veda. The second part teaches the doctrine of Brahma. Brahma is the one, eternal, absolute, unchangeable Being. He unfolds into the universe as Creator and Created. He becomes first ether, then air, then fire, then water, then earth. From these five elements all bodily existence proceeds. Souls are sparks from the central fire of Brahma, separated for a time, to be absorbed again at last.

Brahma, in his highest form as Para-Brahm, stands for the Absolute Being. The following extract from

* Duncker, I. 205.   He refers to Manu, II. 160.

the Sáma-Veda (after Haug's translation) expresses this :
" The generation of Brahma was before all ages, unfolding
himself evermore in a beautiful glory ; everything which
is highest and everything which is deepest belongs to him.
Being and Not-Being are unveiled through Brahma."

The following passage is from a Upanishad, translated
by Windischmann : —

" How can any one teach concerning Brahma ? he is
neither the known nor the unknown. That which cannot
be expressed by words, but through which all expression
comes, this I know to be Brahma. That which cannot be
thought by the mind, but by which all thinking comes,
this I know is Brahma. That which cannot be seen by
the eye, but by which the eye sees, is Brahma. If thou
thinkest that thou canst know it, then in truth thou
knowest it very little. To whom it is unknown, he
knows it ; but to whom it is known, he knows it not."

This also is from Windischmann, from the Kathaka
Upanishad : " One cannot attain to it through the word,
through the mind, or through the eye. It is only reached
by him who says, ' It is ! It is !' He perceives it in its
essence. Its essence appears when one perceives it as
it is."

The old German expression *Istigkeit*, according to Bunsen, corresponds to this. This also is the name of Jehovah as given to Moses from the burning bush : " And
God said unto Moses, I AM THE I AM. Thus shalt thou
say unto the children of Israel, I AM hath sent me unto
you." The idea is that God alone really exists, and that
the root of all being is in him. This is expressed in
another Upanishad : " He WHO EXISTS is the root of all
creatures ; he WHO EXISTS is their foundation, and in him
they rest."

In the Vedanta philosophy this speculative pantheism
is carried further. Thus speaks Sankara, the chief teacher
of the Vedanta philosophy (" Colebrooke's Essays ") : " I
am the great Brahma, eternal, pure, free, one, constant,
happy, existing without end. He who ceases to contemplate other things, who retires into solitude, annihilates
his desires, and subjects his passions, he understands that

Spirit is the One and the Eternal. The wise man annihilates all sensible things in spiritual things, and contem-
plates that one Spirit who resembles pure space. Brahma
is without size, quality, character, or division."

According to this philosophy (says Bunsen) the world
is the Not-Being. It is, says Sankara, "appearance without Being; it is like the deception of a dream." "The
soul itself," he adds, "has no actual being."

There is an essay on Vedantism in a book published in
Calcutta, 1854, by a young Hindoo, Shoshee Chunder
Dutt, which describes the creation as proceeding from
Maya, in this way: "Dissatisfied with his own solitude,
Brahma feels a desire to create worlds, and then the
volition ceases so far as he is concerned, and he sinks
again into his apathetic happiness, while the desire, thus
willed into existence, assumes an active character. It
becomes Maya, and by this was the universe created,
without exertion on the part of Brahma. This passing
wish of Brahma carried, however, no reality with it.
And the creation proceeding from it is only an illusion.
There is only one absolute Unity really existing, and
existing without plurality. But he is like one asleep.
Krishna, in the Gita, says: 'These works (the universe)
confine not me, for I am like one who sitteth aloof uninterested in them all.' The universe is therefore all
illusion, holding a position between something and nothing. It is real as an illusion, but unreal as being. It is
not true, because it has no essence; but not false, because its existence, even as illusion, is from God. The
Vedanta declares: 'From the highest state of Brahma to
the lowest condition of a straw, all things are delusion.'"
Chunder Dutt, however, contradicts Bunsen's assertion
that the soul also is an illusion according to the Vedanta.
"The soul," he says, "is not subject to birth or death, but
is in its substance, from Brahma himself." The truth
seems to be that the Vedanta regards the individuation
of the soul as from Maya and illusive, but the substance
of the soul is from Brahma, and destined to be absorbed
into him. As the body of man is to be resolved into its
material elements, so the soul of man is to be resolved

into Brahma. This substance of the soul is neither born nor dies, nor is it a thing of which it can be said, " It was, is, or shall be." In the Gita, Krishna tells Arjun that he and the other princes of the world " never were not." *

The Vedantist philosopher, however, though he considers all souls as emanations from God, does not believe that all of them will return into God at death. Those only who have obtained a knowledge of God are rewarded by absorption, but the rest continue to migrate from body to body so long as they remain unqualified for the same. "The knower of God becomes God." This union with the Deity is the total loss of personal identity, and is the attainment of the highest bliss, in which are no grades and from which is no return. This absorption comes not from good works or penances, for these confine the soul and do not liberate it. " The confinement of fetters is the same whether the chain be of gold or iron." " The knowledge which realizes that everything is Brahm alone liberates the soul. It annuls the effect both of our virtues and vices. We traverse thereby both merit and demerit, the heart's knot is broken, all doubts are split, and all our works perish. Only by perfect abstraction, not merely from the senses, but also from the thinking intellect and by remaining in the knowing intellect, does the devotee become identified with Brahm. He then remains as pure glass when the shadow has left it. He lives destitute of passions and affections. He lives sinless ; for as water wets not the leaf of the lotus, so sin touches not him who knows God." He stands in no further need of virtue, for " of what use can be a winnowing fan when the sweet southern wind is blowing." His meditations are of this sort : " I am Brahm, I am life. I am everlasting, perfect, self-existent, undivided, joyful."

If therefore, according to this system, knowledge alone unites the soul to God, the question comes, Of what use are acts of virtue, penances, sacrifices, worship ? The answer is, that they effect a happy transmigration from

* The Bhagavat-Gita, an episode in the Maha-Bharata, in an authority with the Vedantists.

the lower forms of bodily life to higher ones. They do
not accomplish the great end, which is absorption and
escape from Maya, but they prepare the way for it by
causing one to be born in a higher condition.

The second system of philosophy, the Sánkhya of
Kapila, is founded not on one principle, like the Vedanta,
but on two. According to the seventy aphorisms, Nature
is one of these principles. It is uncreated and eternal.
It is one, active, creating, non-intelligent. The other of
the two principles, also uncreated and eternal, is Soul, or
rather Souls. Souls are many, passive, not creative, intelligent, and in all things the opposite to Nature. But
from the union of the two all the visible universe proceeds, according to the law of cause and effect.

God not being recognized in this system, it is often
called atheism. Its argument, to show that no one
perfect being could create the universe, is this. Desire
implies want, or imperfection. Accordingly, if God desired
to create, he would be unable to do so ; if he was able, he
would not desire to do it. In neither case, therefore, could
God have created the universe. The gods are spoken of
by the usual names, Brahma, Indra, etc., but are all finite
beings, belonging to the order of human souls, though
superior.

Every soul is clothed in two bodies, — the interior original body, the individualizing force, which is eternal as
itself and accompanies it through all its migrations ; and
the material, secondary body, made of the five elements,
ether, air, fire, water, and earth. The original body is
subtile and spiritual. It is the office of Nature to liberate
the Soul. Nature is not what we perceive by the senses,
but an invisible plastic principle behind, which must be
known by the intellect. As the Soul ascends by goodness, it is freed by knowledge. The final result of this
emancipation is the certainty of non-existence, — " neither
I am, nor is aught mine, nor do I exist," — which seems
to be the same result as that of Hegel, Being = Not-
Being. Two or three of the aphorisms of the Karika are
as follows : —

" LIX. As a dancer, having exhibited herself to the spectator, desists from the dance, so does Nature desist, having manifested herself to the Soul."

" LX. Generous Nature, endued with qualities, does by manifold means accomplish, without benefit (to herself), the wish of ungrateful Soul, devoid of qualities."

" LXI. Nothing, in my opinion, is more gentle than Nature ; once aware of having been seen, she does not again expose herself to the gaze of Soul."

" LXVI. Soul desists, because it has seen Nature. Nature desists, because she has been seen. In their (mere) union there is no motive for creation."

Accordingly, the result of knowledge is to put an end to creation, and to leave the Soul emancipated from desire, from change, from the material body, in a state which is Being, but not Existence (*esse,* not *existere;* Seyn, not Da-seyn).

This Sánkhya philosophy becomes of great importance, when we consider that it was the undoubted source of Buddhism. This doctrine which we have been describing was the basis of Buddhism.*

M. Cousin has called it the sensualism of India,+ but certainly without propriety. It is as purely ideal a doctrine as that of the Vedas. Its two eternal principles are both ideal. The plastic force which is one of them, Kapila distinctly declares cannot be perceived by the senses. ‡ Soul, the other eternal and uncreated principle, who " is witness, solitary, bystander, spectator, and passive," § is not only spiritual itself, but is clothed with a spiritual body, within the material body. In fact, the Karika declares the material universe to be the result of the contact of the Soul with Nature, and consists in chains with which Nature binds herself, for the purpose (uncon-

* Burnouf, Introduction à l'Histoire du Buddhisme Indien, I. 511, 520. He says that Sakya-Muni began his career with the ideas of the Sánkhya philosophy, namely, absence of God ; multiplicity and eternity of human souls ; an eternal plastic nature ; transmigration ; and Nirvâna, or deliverance by knowledge.

† Cours de l'Histoire de Philosophie, I. 200 (Paris, 1829) ; quoted by Hardwick, I. 211.

‡ Karika, 8. "It is owing to the subtilty of Nature . . . . that it is not apprehended by the senses."

§ Karika, 19.

6

scious) of delivering the Soul. When by a process of knowledge the Soul looks through these, and perceives the ultimate principle beyond, the material universe ceases, and both Soul and Nature are emancipated.*

One of the definitions of the Karika will call to mind the fourfold division of the universe by the great thinker of the ninth century, Erigena. In his work, περὶ φύσεως μερισμοῦ, he asserts that there is, (1.) A Nature which creates and is not created. (2.) A Nature which is created and creates. (3.) A Nature which is created and does not create. (4.) A Nature which neither creates nor is created. So Kapila (Karika, 3) says, " Nature, the root of all things, is productive but not a production. Seven principles are productions and productive. Sixteen are productions but not productive. Soul is neither a production nor productive."

Mr. Muir (Sanskrit Texts, Part III. p. 96) quotes the following passages in proof of the antiquity of Kapila, and the respect paid to his doctrine in very early times : —

Svet. Upanishad. " The God who superintends every mode of production and all forms, who formerly nourished with various knowledge his son Kapila the rishi, and beheld him at his birth."

" *Bhagavat Purana* (I. 3, 10) makes Kapila an incarnation of Vischnu. In his fifth incarnation, in the form of Kapila, he declared to Asuri the Sankhya which defines the collection of principles.

" *Bhagavat Purana* (IX. 8, 12) relates that Kapila, being attacked by the sons of King Sangara, destroyed them with fire which issued from his body. But the author of the Purana denies that this was done in *anger*. ' How could the sage, by whom the strong ship of the Sankhya was launched, on which the man seeking emancipation crosses the ocean of existence, entertain the distinction of friend and foe' ? "

The Sánkhya system is also frequently mentioned in the Mahabarata.

The Nyaya system differs from that of Kapila, by assuming a third eternal and indestructible principle as the basis of matter, namely, *Atoms*. It also assumes the

---

* Karika, 58, 62, 63, 68.

existence of a Supreme Soul, Brahma, who is almighty and allwise. It agrees with Kapila in making all souls eternal, and distinct from body. Its evil to be overcome is the same, namely, transmigration; and its method of release is the same, namely *Buddhi*, or knowledge. It is a more dialectic system than the others, and is rather of the nature of a logic than a philosophy.

Mr. Banerjea, in his Dialogues on the Hindu philosophy, considers the Buddhists' system as closely resembling the Nyaya system. He regards the Buddhist Nirvana as equivalent to the emancipation of the Nyaya system. Apavarga, or emancipation, is declared in this philosophy to be final deliverance from pain, birth, activity, fault, and false notions. Even so the Pali doctrinal books speak of Nirvana as an exemption from old age, disease, and death. In it desire, anger, and ignorance are consumed by the fire of knowledge. Here all selfish distinctions of mine and thine, all evil thoughts, all slander and jealousy, are cut down by the weapon of knowledge. Here we have an experience of immortality which is cessation of all trouble and perfect felicity.*

§ 7. *Origin of the Hindoo Triad.*

There had gradually grown up among the people a worship founded on that of the ancient Vedas. In the West of India, the god RUDRA, mentioned in the Vedic hymns, had been transformed into Siva. In the Rig-Veda Rudra is sometimes the name for Agni.† He is described as father of the winds. He is the same as Maha-deva. He is fierce and beneficent at once. He presides over medicinal plants. According to Weber (Indische Stud., II. 19) he is the Storm-God. The same view is taken by Professor Whitney.‡ But his worship gradually extended, until, under the name of Siva, the Destroyer, he became one of

---

* Quoted from the Lalita Vistara in Dialogues on the Hindu Philosophy. By Rev. R. M. Banerjea. London: Williams and Nordgate. 1861.

† Muir, Sanskrit Texts, Part IV. p. 253.

‡ Journal Am. Orient. Soc., III. 318.

the principal deities of India. Meantime, in the valley of the Ganges, a similar devotion had grown up for the Vedic god VISCHNU, who in like manner had been promoted to the chief rank in the Hindoo Pantheon. He had been elevated to the character of a Friend and Protector, gifted with mild attributes, and worshipped as the life of Nature. By accepting the popular worship, the Brahmans were able to oppose Buddhism with success.

We have no doubt that the Hindoo Triad came from the effort of the Brahmans to unite all India in one worship, and it may for a time have succeeded. Images of the Trimurtti, or three-faced God, are frequent in India, and this is still the object of Brahmanical worship. But beside this practical motive, the tendency of thought is always toward a triad of law, force, or elemental substance, as the best explanation of the universe. Hence there have been Triads in so many religions : in Egypt, of *Osiris* the Creator, *Typhon* the Destroyer, and *Horus* the Preserver ; in Persia, of *Ormazd* the Creator, *Ahriman* the Destroyer, and *Mithra* the Restorer ; in Buddhism, of *Buddha* the Divine Man, *Dharmma* the Word, and *Sangha* the Communion of Saints. Simple monotheism does not long satisfy the speculative intellect, because, though it accounts for the harmonies of creation, it leaves its discords unexplained. But a dualism of opposing forces is found still more unsatisfactory, for the world does not appear to be such a scene of utter warfare and discord as this. So the mind comes to accept a Triad, in which the unities of life and growth proceed from one element, the antagonisms from a second, and the higher harmonies of reconciled oppositions from a third. The Brahmanical Triad arose in the same way.*

Thus grew up, from amid the spiritual pantheism into which all Hindoo religion seemed to have settled, another system, that of the Trimurtti, or Divine Triad ; the Indian Trinity of *Brahma, Vischnu,* and *Siva.* This Triad ex-

---

* Even in the grammatical forms of the Sanskrit verb, this threefold tendency of thought is indicated. It has an active, passive, and middle voice (like that of the cognate Greek), and the reflex action of its middle voice corresponds to the Restorer or Preserver.

presses the unity of Creation, Destruction, and Restoration. A foundation for this already existed in a Vedic saying, that the highest being exists in three states, that of creation, continuance, and destruction.

Neither of these three supreme deities of Brahmanism held any high rank in the Vedas. Siva (Çiva) does not appear therein at all, nor, according to Lassen, is Brahma mentioned in the Vedic hymns, but first in a Upanishad. Vischnu is spoken of in the Rig-Veda, but always as one of the names for the sun. He is the Sun-God. His three steps are sunrise, noon, and sunset. He is mentioned as one of the sons of Aditi ; he is called the " wide-stepping," " measurer of the world," " the strong," " the deliverer," " renewer of life," " who sets in motion the revolutions of time," " a protector," " preserving the highest heaven." Evidently he begins his career in this mythology as the sun.

BRAHMA, at first a word meaning prayer and devotion, becomes in the laws of Manu the primal God, first-born of the creation, from the self-existent being, in the form of a golden egg. He became the creator of all things by the power of prayer. In the struggle for ascendency which took place between the priests and the warriors, Brahma naturally became the deity of the former. But, meantime, as we have seen, the worship of Vischnu had been extending itself in one region and that of Siva in another. Then took place those mysterious wars between the kings of the Solar and Lunar races, of which the great epics contain all that we know. And at the close of these wars a compromise was apparently accepted, by which Brahma, Vischnu, and Siva were united in one supreme God, as creator, preserver, and destroyer, all in one.

It is almost certain that this Hindoo Triad was the result of an ingenious and successful attempt, on the part of the Brahmans, to unite all classes of worshippers in India against the Buddhists. In this sense the Brahmans edited anew the Mahabharata, inserting in that epic passages extolling Vischnu in the form of Krishna. The Greek accounts of India which followed the invasion of Alexander speak of the worship of Hercules as prevalent

in the East, and by Hercules they apparently mean the
god Krishna.* The struggle between the Brahmans and
Buddhists lasted during nine centuries (from A. D. 500
to A. D. 1400), ending with the total expulsion of Buddhism, and the triumphant establishment of the Triad, as
the worship of India.†

Before this Triad or Trimurtti (of Brahma, Vischnu,
and Siva) there seems to have been another, consisting of Agni, Indra, and Surya.‡ This may have given the
hint of the second Triad, which distributed among the
three gods the attributes of Creation, Destruction, and
Renovation. Of these Brahma, the Creator, ceased soon to
be popular, and the worship of Siva and Vischnu as
Krishna remain as the popular religion of India.

One part, and a very curious one, of the worship of
Vischnu is the doctrine of the Avatars, or incarnations
of that deity. There are ten of these Avatars, — nine
have passed and one is to come. The object of Vischnu
is, each time, to save the gods from destruction impending
over them in consequence of the immense power acquired
by some king, giant, or demon, by superior acts of austerity and piety. For here, as elsewhere, extreme spiritualism
is often divorced from morality ; and so these extremely
pious, spiritual, and self-denying giants are the most cruel
and tyrannical monsters, who must be destroyed at all
hazards. Vischnu, by force or fraud, overcomes them all.

His first Avatar is of the Fish, as related in the Mahabharata. The object was to recover the Vedas, which had
been stolen by a demon from Brahma when asleep. In
consequence of this loss the human race became corrupt,
and were destroyed by a deluge, except a pious prince and
seven holy men who were saved in a ship. Vischnu, as a
large fish, drew the ship safely over the water, killed the
demon, and recovered the Vedas. The second Avatar was
in a Turtle, to make the drink of immortality. The third
was in a Boar, the fourth in a Man-Lion, the fifth in the
Dwarf who deceived Bali, who had become so powerful

* See Colebrooke, Lassen, &c.
† Lassen, I. 838 ; II. 446.
‡ See Muir, Sanskrit Texts, Part IV. p. 136.

by austerities as to conquer the gods and take possession
of Heaven. In the eighth Avatar he appears as Krishna
and in the ninth as Buddha.

This system of Avatars is so peculiar and so deeply
rooted in the system, that it would seem to indicate some
law of Hindoo thought. Perhaps some explanation may be
reached thus : —

We observe that, —

Vischnu does not mediate between Brahma and Siva,
but between the deities and the lower races of men or
demons.

The danger arises from a certain fate or necessity which
is superior both to gods and men. There are laws which
enable a man to get away from the power of Brahma and
Siva.

But what is this necessity but nature, or the nature
of things, the laws of the outward world of active existences ? It is not till essence becomes existence, till spirit
passes into action, that it becomes subject to law.

The danger then is from the world of nature. The
gods are pure spirit, and spirit is everything. But, now
and then, nature *seems to be something*, it will not be ignored or lost in God. Personality, activity, or human
nature rebel against the pantheistic idealism, the abstract
spiritualism of this system.

To conquer body, Vischnu or spirit enters into body,
again and again. Spirit must appear as body to destroy
Nature. For thus is shown that spirit cannot be excluded
from anything, — that it can descend into the lowest
forms of life, and work *in* law as well as above law.

But all the efforts of Brahmanism could not arrest the
natural development of the system. It passed on into
polytheism and idolatry. The worship of India for many
centuries has been divided into a multitude of sects.
While the majority of the Brahmans still profess to recognize the equal divinity of Brahma, Vischnu, and Siva, the
mass of the people worship Krishna, Rama, the Lingam,
and many other gods and idols. There are Hindoo atheists who revile the Vedas ; there are the Kabirs, who are
a sort of Hindoo Quakers, and oppose all worship ; the

Ramanujas, an ancient sect of Vischnu worshippers; the
Ramavats, living in monasteries; the *Panthis,* who oppose
all austerities; the *Maharajas,* whose religion consists
with great licentiousness. Most of these are worshippers
of Vischnu or of Siva, for Brahma-worship has wholly
disappeared.

§ 8. *The Epics, the Puranas, and modern Hindoo Worship.*

The Hindoos have two great epics, the Ramayana and
the Mahabharata, each of immense length, and very
popular with the people. Mr. Talboys Wheeler has recently incorporated both epics (of course much abridged)
into his History of India, and we must refer our readers
to his work for a knowledge of these remarkable poems.
The whole life of ancient India appears in them, and certainly they are not unworthy products of the genius of
that great nation.

According to Lassen,* the period to which the great
Indian epics refer follows directly on the Vedic age.
Yet they contain passages inserted at a much later epoch,
probably, indeed, as long after as the war which ended in
the expulsion of the Buddhists from India.† Mr. Talboys
Wheeler considers the war of Rama and the Monkeys
against Ravana to refer to this conflict, and so makes the
Ramayana later than the Mahabharata. The majority
of writers, however, differ from him on this point. The
writers of the Mahabharata were evidently Brahmans,
educated under the laws of Manu.‡ But it is very difficult to fix the date of either poem with any approach to
accuracy. Lassen has proved that the greater part of the
Mahabharata was written before the political establishment of Buddhism.§ These epics were originally transmitted by oral tradition. They must have been brought
to their present forms by Brahmans, for their doctrine is
that of this priesthood. Now if such poems had been

---

* Lassen, Ind. Alterthum, I. 357.
† Max Müller, Sanskrit Lit., 37.
‡ Ibid., p. 46.
§ Ind. Alterthum, I. 483 – 499.   Müller, Sanskrit Lit., 62, *note.*

composed after the time of Asoka, when Buddhism became a state religion in India, it must have been often
referred to. No such references appear in these epics,
except in some solitary passages, which are evidently
modern additions.* Hence the epics must have been
composed before the time of Buddhism. This argument
of Lassen's is thought by Max Müller to be conclusive,
and if so it disproves Mr. Talboys Wheeler's view of the
purpose of the Ramayana.

Few Hindoos now read the Vedas. The Puranas and
the two great epics constitute their sacred books. The
Ramayana contains about fifty thousand lines, and is held
in great veneration by the Hindoos. It describes the
youth of Rama, who is an incarnation of Vischnu, his
banishment and residence in Central India, and his war
with the giants and demons of the South, to recover his
wife, Sita. It probably is founded on some real war
between the early Aryan invaders of Hindostan and the
indigenous inhabitants.

The Mahabharata, which is probably of later date,
contains about two hundred and twenty thousand lines,
and is divided into eighteen books, each of which would
make a large volume. It is supposed to have been collected by Vyasa, who also collected the Vedas and
Puranas. These legends are very old, and seem to refer
to the early history of India. There appear to have been
two Aryan dynasties in ancient India, — the Solar and
Lunar. Rama belonged to the first and Bharata to the
second. Pandu, a descendant of the last, has five brave
sons, who are the heroes of this book. One of them,
Arjuna, is especially distinguished. One of the episodes
is the famous Bhagavat-gita. Another is called the Brahman's Lament. Another describes the deluge, showing
the tradition of a flood existing in India many centuries
before Christ. Another gives the story of Savitri and
Satyavan. These episodes occupy three fourths of the
poem, and from them are derived most of the legends of

* As of the Atheist in the Ramayana, Javali, who advises Rama to
disobey his dead father's commands, on the ground that the dead are
nothing.

the Puranas. A supplement, which is itself a longer
poem than the Iliad and Odyssey combined (which
together contain about thirty thousand lines), is the
source of the modern worship of Krishna. The whole
poem represents the multilateral character of Hinduism.
It indicates a higher degree of civilization than that of
the Homeric poems, and describes a vast variety of fruits
and flowers existing under culture. The characters are
nobler and purer than those of Homer. The pictures
of domestic and social life are very touching; children
are dutiful to their parents, parents careful of their
children; wives are loyal and obedient, yet independent
in their opinions; and peace reigns in the domestic
circle.

The different works known as the Puranas are derived
from the same religious system as the two epics. They
repeat the cosmogony of the poems, and they relate more
fully their mythological legends. Siva and Vischnu are
almost the sole objects of worship in the Puranas. There
is a sectarian element in their devotion to these deities
which shows their partiality, and prevents them from
being authorities for Hindoo belief as a whole.*

The Puranas, in their original form, belong to a period,
says Mr. Wilson, a century before the Christian era.
They grew out of the conflict between Buddhism and
Brahmanism. The latter system had offered no personal
gods to the people and given them no outward worship,
and the masses had been uninterested in the abstract
view of Deity held by the Brahmans.†

According to Mr. Wilson,‡ there are eighteen Puranas
which are now read by the common people. They are
read a great deal by women. Some are very ancient, or at
least contain fragments of more ancient Puranas. The
very word signifies "antiquity." Most of them are devoted to the worship of Vischnu. According to the
Bhagavat Purana,§ the only reasonable object of life is

---

* Preface to the Vischnu Purana, translated by Horace Hayman Wil-
son. London, 1864.
† Duncker, Geschichte, &c., II. 318.
‡ Preface to his English translation of the Vischnu Purana.
§ Translated by E. Burnouf into French.

to meditate on Vischnu. Brahma, who is called in one place "the cause of causes," proclaims Vischnu to be the only pure absolute essence, of which the universe is the manifestation. In the Vischnu Purana, Brahma, at the head of the gods, adores Vischnu as the Supreme Being whom he himself cannot understand.

The power of ascetic penances is highly extolled in the Puranas, as also in the epics. In the Bhagavat it is said that Brahma, by a penitence of sixteen thousand years, created the universe. It is even told in the Ramayana, that a sage of a lower caste became a Brahman by dint of austerities, in spite of the gods who considered such a confusion of castes a breach of Hindoo etiquette.* To prevent him from continuing his devotions, they sent a beautiful nymph to tempt him, and their daughter was the famous Sakuntala. But in the end, the obstinate old ascetic conquered the gods, and when they still refused to Brahmanize him, he began to create new heavens and new gods, and had already made a few stars, when the deities thought it prudent to yield, and allowed him to become a Brahman. It is also mentioned that the Ganges, the sacred river, in the course of her wanderings, overflowed the sacrificial ground of another powerful ascetic, who incontinently drank up, in his anger, all its waters, but was finally induced by the persuasions of the gods to set the river free again by discharging it from his ears. Such were the freaks of sages in the times of the Puranas.

Never was there a more complete example of piety divorced from morality than in these theories. The most wicked demons acquire power over gods and men, by devout asceticism. This principle is already fully developed in the epic poems. The plot of the Ramayana turns around this idea. A Rajah, Ravana, had become so powerful by sacrifice and devotion, that he oppressed the gods; compelled Yama (or Death) to retire from his dominions; compelled the sun to shine there all the year, and the moon to be always full above his Raj. Agni (Fire) must not burn in his presence; the Maruts (Winds)

* The Ramayana, &c., by Monier Williams Baden Professor of Sanskrit at Oxford.

must blow only as he wishes. He cannot be hurt by
gods or demons. So Vischnu becomes incarnate as Rama
and the gods become incarnate as Monkeys, in order to
destroy him. Such vast power was supposed to be attained by piety without morality.

The Puranas are derived from the same system as the
epic poems, and carry out further the same ideas. Siva
and Vischnu are almost the only gods who are worshipped,
and they are worshipped with a sectarian zeal unknown to
the epics. Most of the Puranas contain these five topics,
— Creation, Destruction and Renovation, the Genealogy of
the gods, Reigns of the Manus, and History of the Solar
and Lunar races. Their philosophy of creation is derived
from the Sánkhya philosophy. Pantheism is one of their
invariable characteristics, as they always identify God
and Nature ; and herein they differ from the system of
Kapila. The form of the Puranas is always that of a
dialogue. The Puranas are eighteen in number, and
the contents of the whole are stated to be one million six hundred thousand lines.*

The religion of the Hindoos at the present time is very
different from that of the Vedas or Manu. Idolatry is
universal, and every month has its special worship, —
April, October, and January being most sacred. April
begins the Hindoo year. During this sacred month bands
of singers go from house to house, early in the morning,
singing hymns to the gods. On the 1st of April Hindoos of all castes dedicate pitchers to the shades of their
ancestors. The girls bring flowers with which to worship
little ponds of water dedicated to Siva. Women adore
the river Ganges, bathing in it and offering it flowers.
They also walk in procession round the banyan or sacred
tree. Then they worship the cow, pouring water on her
feet and putting oil on her forehead. Sometimes they
take a vow to feed some particular Brahman luxuriously
during the whole month. They bathe their idols with
religious care every day and offer them food. This lasts
during April and then stops.

In May the women of India worship a goddess friendly

* Preface to the translation of the Vischnu Purana, by H. H. Wilson.

to little babies, named Shus-ty. They bring the infants to be blessed by some venerable woman before the image of the goddess, whose messenger is a cat. Social parties are also given on these occasions, although the lower castes are kept distinct at four separate tables. The women also, not being allowed to meet with the men at such times, have a separate entertainment by themselves.

The month of June is devoted to the bath of Jugger-naut, who was one of the incarnations of Vischnu. The name, Jugger-naut, means Lord of the Universe. His worship is comparatively recent. His idols are extremely ugly. But the most remarkable thing perhaps about this worship is that it destroys, for the time, the distinction of castes. While within the walls which surround the temple Hindoos of every caste eat together from the same dish. But as soon as they leave the temple this equality disappears. The ceremony of the bath originated in this legend. The idol Jugger-naut, desiring to bathe in the Ganges, came in the form of a boy to the river, and then gave one of his golden ornaments to a confectioner for something to eat. Next day the ornament was missing, and the priests could find it nowhere. But that night in a dream the god revealed to a priest that he had given it to a certain confectioner to pay for his lunch; and it being found so, a festival was established on the spot, at which the idol is annually bathed.

The other festival of this month is the worship of the Ganges, the sacred river of India. Here the people come to bathe and to offer sacrifices, which consist of flowers, incense, and clothes. The most sacred spot is where the river enters the sea. Before plunging into the water each one confesses his sins to the goddess. On the surface of this river castes are also abolished, the holiness of the river making the low-caste man also holy.

In the month of July is celebrated the famous ceremony of the car of Jugger-naut, instituted to commemorate the departure of Krishna from his native land. These cars are in the form of a pyramid, built several stories high, and some are even fifty feet in height. They are found in every part of India, the offerings of wealthy people, and some contain costly statues. They are drawn by hundreds of men, it being their faith that each one who pulls the rope will certainly go to the heaven of Krishna when he dies. Multitudes, therefore, crowd around the rope in order to pull, and in the excitement they sometimes fall under the wheels and are crushed. But this is accidental, for Krishna does not desire the suffering of his worshippers. He is a mild divinity, and not like the fierce Siva, who loves self-torture.

In the month of August is celebrated the nativity of Krishna, the story of whose birth resembles that in the Gospel in this, that the tyrant whom he came to destroy sought to kill him, but a heavenly voice told the father to fly with the child across the Jumna, and the tyrant, like Herod, killed the infants in the village. In this month also is a feast upon which no fire must be kindled or food cooked, and on which the cactus-tree and serpents are worshipped.

In September is the great festival of the worship of Doorga, wife of Siva. It commences on the seventh day of the full moon and lasts three days. It commemorates a visit made by the goddess to her parents. The idol has three eyes and ten hands. The ceremony, which is costly, can only be celebrated by the rich people, who also give presents on this occasion to the poor. The image is placed in the middle of the hall of the rich man's house. One Brahman sits before the image with flowers, holy water, incense. Trays laden with rice, fruit, and other kinds of food are placed near the image, and given to the Brahmans. Goats and sheep are then sacrificed to the idol on an altar in the yard of the house. When the head of the victim falls the people shout, " Victory to thee, O mother !" Then the bells ring, the trumpets sound, and the people shout for joy. The lamps are waved before the idol, and a Brahman reads aloud from the Scripture. Then comes a dinner on each of the three days, to which the poor and the low-caste people are also invited and are served by the Brahmans. The people visit from house to house, and in the evening there is music, dancing, and public shows. So that the worship of the Hindoos is by no means all of it ascetic, but much is social and joyful, especially in Bengal.

In October, November, and December there are fewer ceremonies. January is a month devoted to religious bathing. Also, in January, the religious Hindoos invite Brahmans to read and expound the sacred books in their houses, which are open to all hearers. In February there are festivals to Krishna.

The month of March is devoted to ascetic exercises, especially to the famous one of swinging suspended by hooks. It is a festival in honor of Siva. A procession goes through the streets and enlists followers by putting a thread round their necks. Every man thus enlisted must join the party and go about with it till the end of the ceremony under pain of losing caste. On the day before the swinging, men thrust iron or bamboo sticks through their arms or tongues. On the next day they march in procession to the swinging tree, where the men are suspended by hooks and whirled round the tree four or five times.

It is considered a pious act in India to build temples, dig tanks, or plant trees by the roadside. Rich people have idols in their houses for daily worship, and pay a priest who comes every morning to wake up the idols, wash and dress them, and offer them their food. In the evening he comes again, gives them their supper and puts them to bed.

Mr. Gangooly, in his book, from which most of the above facts are drawn, denies emphatically the statement so commonly made that Hindoo mothers throw their infants into the Ganges. He justly says that the maternal instinct is as strong with them as with others; and in addition to that, their religion teaches them to offer sacrifices for the life and health of their children.

§ 9. *Relation of Brahmanism to Christianity.*

Having thus attempted, in the space we can here use, to give an account of Brahmanism, we close by showing its special relation as a system of thought to Christianity.

Brahmanism teaches the truth of the reality of spirit, and that spirit is infinite, absolute, perfect, one; that it is the substance underlying all existence. Brahmanism glows through and through with this spirituality. Its literature, no less than its theology, teaches it. It is in the dramas of Calidasa, as well as in the sublime strains of the Bhagavat-gita. Something divine is present in all nature and all life, —

> " Whose dwelling is the light of setting suns,
> And the round ocean and the living air."

Now, with this Christianity is in fullest agreement. We have such passages in the Scripture as these : " God is a Spirit "; " God is love ; whoso dwelleth in love dwelleth in God, and God in him " ; " In him we live, and move, and have our being "; " He is above all, and through all, and in us all." But beside these texts, which strike the key-note of the music which was to come after, there are divine strains of spiritualism, of God all in all, which come through a long chain of teachers of the Church, sounding on in the Confessions of Augustine, the prayers of Thomas Aquinas, Anselm, Bonaventura, St. Bernard, through the Latin hymns of the Middle Ages, and develop themselves at last in what is called romantic art and romantic song. A Gothic cathedral like Antwerp or Strasburg, — what is it but a striving upward of the soul to lose itself in God ? A symphony of Beethoven, — what is it but the same unbounded longing and striving toward the Infinite and Eternal ? The poetry of Wordsworth, of Goethe, Schiller, Dante, Byron, Victor Hugo, Manzoni, all partake of the same element. It is opposed to classic art and classic poetry in this, that instead of limits, it seeks the unlimited ; that is, it believes in spirit, which alone is the unlimited ; the *in*finite, that which *is*, not that which appears ; the *essence* of things, not their *ex*istence or outwardness.

Thus Christianity meets and accepts the truth of Brahmanism. But how does it fulfil Brahmanism ? The deficiencies of . Brahmanism are these, — that holding to eternity, it omits time, and so loses history. It therefore is incapable of progress, for progress takes place in time. Believing in spirit, or infinite unlimited substance, it loses person, or definite substance, whether infinite or finite. The Christian God is the infinite, definite substance, self-limited or defined by his essential nature. He is good and not bad, righteous and not the opposite, perfect love, not perfect self-love. Christianity, therefore, gives us God as a person, and man also as a person, and so makes it possible to consider the universe as order, kosmos, method, beauty, and providence. For, unless we can conceive the Infinite Substance as definite, and not undefined; that is, as a person with positive characters; there is no difference between good and bad, right and wrong, to-day and to-morrow, this and that, but all is one immense chaos of indefinite spirit. The moment that creation begins, that the spirit of the Lord moves on the face of the waters, and says, " Let there be light," and so divides light from darkness, God becomes a person, and man can also be a person. Things then become " separate and divisible " which before were " huddled and lumped."

Christianity, therefore, fulfils Brahmanism by adding to eternity time, to the infinite the finite, to God as spirit God as nature and providence. God in himself is the unlimited, unknown, dwelling in the light which no man can approach unto ; hidden, not by darkness, but by light. But God, as turned toward us in nature and providence, is the infinite definite substance, that is, having certain defined characters, though these have no bounds as regards extent. This last view of God Christianity shares with other religions, which differ from Brahmanism in the opposite direction. For example, the religion of Greece and of the Greek philosophers never loses the definite God, however high it may soar. While Brahmanism, seeing eternity and infinity, loses time and the finite, the Greek religion, dwelling in time, often loses the eternal and the spiritual. Christianity is the mediator, able to mediate, not by standing between both, but by standing beside both. It can lead the Hindoos to an Infinite Friend, a perfect Father, a Divine Providence, and so make the possibility for them of a new progress, and give to that ancient and highly endowed race another chance in history. What they want is evidently moral power, for they have all intellectual ability. The effeminate quality which has made them slaves of tyrants during two thousand years will be taken out of them, and a virile strength substituted, when they come to see God as law and love, — perfect law and perfect love, — and to see that communion with him comes, not from absorption, contemplation, and inaction, but from active obedience, moral growth, and personal development. For Christianity certainly teaches that we unite ourselves with God, not by sinking into and losing our personality, in him, but by developing it, so that we may be able to serve and love him.

CHAPTER IV.

BUDDHISM, OR THE PROTESTANTISM OF THE EAST.

§ 1. Buddhism, in its Forms, resembles Romanism ; in its Spirit, Protestantism.   § 2. Extent of Buddhism.   Its Scriptures.   § 3. Sakya-
muni, the Founder of Buddhism.   § 4. Leading Doctrines of Buddhism.
§ 5. The Spirit of Buddhism Rational and Humane.   § 6. Buddhism
as a Religion.   § 7. Karma and Nirvana.   § 8. Good and Evil of
Buddhism.   § 9. Relation of Buddhism to Christianity.

§ 1. *Buddhism, in its Forms, resembles Romanism ; in its Spirit, Protestantism.*

ON first becoming acquainted with the mighty and
ancient religion of Buddha, one may be tempted to
deny the correctness of this title, " The *Protestantism* of
the East." One might say, "Why not rather the *Romanism* of the East ?" For so numerous are the resemblances between the customs of this system and those
of the Romish Church, that the first Catholic missionaries
who encountered the priests of Buddha were confounded,
and thought that Satan had been mocking their sacred
rites. Father Bury, a Portuguese missionary,* when he
beheld the Chinese bonzes tonsured, using rosaries, praying in an unknown tongue, and kneeling before images,
exclaimed in astonishment : "There is not a piece of
dress, not a sacerdotal function, not a ceremony of the
court of Rome, which the Devil has not copied in this
country." Mr. Davis (Transactions of the Royal Asiatic
Society, II. 491) speaks of "the celibacy of the Buddhist
clergy, and the monastic life of the societies of both
sexes ; to which might be added their strings of beads,
their manner of chanting prayers, their incense, and their
candles." Mr. Medhurst (" China," London, 1857) men-

---

* Kesson, "The Cross and the Dragon" (London, 1854), quoted by
Hardwick.

tions the image of a virgin, called the " queen of heaven,"
having an infant in her arms, and holding a cross.   Confession of sins is regularly practised.   Father Huc, in his
" Recollections of a Journey in Tartary, Thibet, and China,"
(Hazlitt's translation), says : " The cross, the mitre, the
dalmatica, the cope, which the grand lamas wear on
their journeys, or when they are performing some ceremony out of the temple, — the service with double choirs,
the psalmody, the exorcisms, the censer suspended from
five chains, and which you can open or close at pleasure,
— the benedictions given by the lamas by extending the
right hand over the heads of the faithful, — the chaplet,
ecclesiastical celibacy, religious retirement, the worship
of the saints, the fasts, the processions, the litanies, the
holy water, — all these are analogies between the Buddhists and ourselves."   And in Thibet there is also a
Dalai Lama, who is a sort of Buddhist pope.   Such numerous and striking analogies are difficult to explain.
After the simple theory " que le diable y était pour beau-
coup " was abandoned, the next opinion held by the Jesuit
missionaries was that the Buddhists had copied these
customs from Nestorian missionaries, who are known to
have penetrated early even as far as China.*   But a serious
objection to this theory is that Buddhism is at least five
hundred years older than Christianity, and that many
of these striking resemblances belong to its earliest period.   Thus Wilson (Hindu Drama) has translated plays
written before the Christian era, in which Buddhist
monks appear as mendicants.   The worship of relics is
quite as ancient.   Fergusson † describes topes, or shrines
for relics, of very great antiquity, existing in India, Ceylon, Birmah, and Java.   Many of them belong to the
age of Asoka, the great Buddhist emperor, who ruled all
India B. C. 250, and in whose reign Buddhism became
the religion of the state, and held its third Œcumenical
Council.

    The ancient Buddhist architecture is very singular, and
often very beautiful.   It consists of topes, rock-cut tem-

    * See Note to Chap. II. on the Nestorian inscription in China.
    † Illustrated Handbook of Architecture, p. 67.

ples, and monasteries. Some of the topes are monolithic columns, more than forty feet high, with ornamented capitals. Some are immense domes of brick and stone, containing sacred relics. The tooth of Buddha was once preserved in a magnificent shrine in India, but was conveyed to Ceylon A. D. 311, where it still remains an object of universal reverence. It is a piece of ivory or bone two inches long, and is kept in six cases, the largest of which, of solid silver, is five feet high. The other cases are inlaid with rubies and precious stones.* Besides this, Ceylon possesses the "left collar-bone relic," contained in a bell-shaped tope, fifty feet high, and the thorax bone, which was placed in a tope built by a Hindoo Raja, B. C. 250, beside which two others were subsequently erected, the last being eighty cubits high. The Sanchi tope, the finest in India,† is a solid dome of stone, one hundred and six feet in diameter and forty-two feet high, with a basement and terrace, having a colonnade, now fallen, of sixty pillars, with richly carved stone railing and gateway.

The rock-cut temples of the Buddhists are very ancient, and are numerous in India. Mr. Fergusson, who has made a special personal study of these monuments, believes that more than nine hundred still remain, most of them within the Bombay presidency. Of these, many date back two centuries before our era. In form they singularly resemble the earliest Roman Catholic churches. Excavated out of the solid rock, they have a nave and side aisles, terminating in an apse or semi-dome, round which the aisle is carried. One at Karli, built in this manner, is one hundred and twenty-six feet long and forty-five wide, with fifteen richly carved columns on each side, separating the nave from the aisles. The façade of this temple is also richly ornamented, and has a great open window for lighting the interior, beneath an elegant gallery or rood-loft.

The Buddhist rock-cut monasteries in India are also numerous, though long since deserted. Between seven

* Hardy, Eastern Monachism, p. 224. Fergusson, p. 9.
† Fergusson, p. 10 Cunningham, Bhilsa Topes of India.

and eight hundred are known to exist, most of them having been excavated between B. C. 200 and A. D. 500. Buddhist monks, then as now, took the same three vows of celibacy, poverty, and obedience, which are taken by the members of all the Catholic orders.   In addition to this, *all* the Buddhist priests are mendicants. They shave their heads, wear a friar's robe tied round the waist with a rope, and beg from house to house, carrying their wooden bowl in which to receive boiled rice. The old monasteries of India contain chapels and cells for the monks.   The largest, however, had accommodation for only thirty or forty ; while at the present time a single monastery in Thibet, visited by MM. Huc and Gabet (the lamasery of Kounboum), is occupied by four thousand lamas.   The structure of these monasteries shows clearly that the monkish system of the Buddhists is far too ancient to have been copied from the Christians.

Is, then, the reverse true ?   Did the Catholic Christians derive their monastic institutions, their bells, their rosary, their tonsure, their incense, their mitre and cope, their worship of relics, their custom of confession, etc., from the Buddhists ?   Such is the opinion of Mr. Prinsep (Thibet, Tartary, and Mongolia, 1852) and of Lassen (Indische Alterthumskunde).   But, in reply to this view, Mr. Hardwicke objects that we do not find in history any trace of such an influence.   Possibly, therefore, the resemblances may be the result of common human tendencies working out, independently, the same results.   If, however, it is necessary to assume that either religion copied from the other, the Buddhists may claim originality, on the ground of antiquity.

But, however this may be, the question returns, Why call Buddhism the Protestantism of the East, when all its external features so much resemble those of the Roman Catholic Church ?

We answer : Because deeper and more essential relations connect Brahmanism with the Romish Church, and the Buddhist system with Protestantism.   The human mind in Asia went through the same course of experience, afterward repeated in Europe.   It protested, in the interest of humanity, against the oppression of a priestly caste. Brahmanism, like the Church of Rome, established a system of sacramental salvation in the hands of a sacred order. Buddhism, like Protestantism, revolted, and established a doctrine of individual salvation based on personal character. Brahmanism, like the Church of Rome, teaches an exclusive spiritualism, glorifying penances and martyrdom, and considers the body the enemy of the soul. But Buddhism and Protestantism accept nature and its laws, and make a religion of humanity as well as of devotion. To such broad statements numerous exceptions may doubtless be always found, but these are the large lines of distinction.

The Roman Catholic Church and Brahmanism place the essence of religion in sacrifices. Each is eminently a sacrificial system. The daily sacrifice of the mass is the central feature of the Romish Church. So Brahmanism is a system of sacrifices. But Protestantism and Buddhism save the soul by teaching. In the Church of Rome the sermon is subordinate to the mass; in Protestantism and in Buddhism sermons are the main instruments by which souls are saved. Brahmanism is a system of inflexible castes; the priestly caste is made distinct and supreme; and in Romanism the priesthood almost constitutes the church. In Buddhism and Protestantism the laity regain their rights. Therefore, notwithstanding the external resemblance of Buddhist rites and ceremonies to those of the Roman Catholic Church, the internal resemblance is to Protestantism. Buddhism in Asia, like Protestantism in Europe, is a revolt of nature against spirit, of humanity against caste, of individual freedom against the despotism of an order, of salvation by faith against salvation by sacraments. And as all revolts are apt to go too far, so it has been with Buddhism. In asserting the rights of nature against the tyranny of spirit, Buddhism has lost God. There is in Buddhism neither creation nor Creator. Its tracts say : " The rising of the world is a natural case." " Its rising and perishing are by nature itself." " It is natural that the world should rise and perish." * While

---

* Upham, Sacred and Historical Books of Ceylon.

in Brahmanism absolute spirit is the only reality, and
this world is an illusion, the Buddhists know only this
world, and the eternal world is so entirely unknown as to
be equivalent to nullity. But yet, as no revolt, however
radical, gives up *all* its antecedents, so Buddhism has the
same *aim* as Brahmanism, namely, to escape from the
vicissitudes of time into the absolute rest of eternity.
They agree as to the object of existence ; they differ as to
the method of reaching it. The Brahman and the Roman
Catholic think that eternal rest is to be obtained by intellectual submission, by passive reception of what is taught
us and done for us by others : the Buddhist and Protestant believe it must be accomplished by an intelligent and
free obedience to Divine laws. Mr. Hodgson, who has
long studied the features of this religion in Nepaul, says :
" The one infallible diagnostic of Buddhism is a belief in
the infinite capacity of the human intellect." The name
of Buddha means the Intelligent One, or the one who is
wide awake. And herein also is another resemblance to
Protestantism, which emphasizes so strongly the value of
free thought and the seeking after truth. In Judaism we
find two spiritual powers, — the prophet and the priest.
The priest is the organ of the pardoning and saving love
of God ; the prophet, of his inspiring truth. In the
European Reformation, the prophet revolting against the
priest founded Protestantism ; in the Asiatic Reformation
he founded Buddhism. Finally, Brahmanism and the
Roman Catholic Church are more religious ; Buddhism
and Protestant Christianity, more moral. Such, sketched
in broad outline, is the justification for the title of this
chapter ; but we shall be more convinced of its accuracy
after looking more closely into the resemblances above
indicated between the religious ceremonies of the East
and West.

These resemblances are chiefly between the Buddhists
and the monastic orders of the Church of Rome. Now it
is a fact, but one which has never been sufficiently noticed,
that the whole monastic system of Rome is based on a
principle foreign to the essential ideas of that church.
The fundamental doctrine of Rome is that of salvation by

sacraments. This alone justifies its maxim, that "out of communion with the Church there is no salvation." The sacrament of Baptism regenerates the soul; the sacrament of Penance purifies it from mortal sin; the sacrament of the Eucharist renews its life; and that of Holy Orders qualifies the priest for administering these and the other sacraments. But if the soul is saved by sacraments, duly administered and received, why go into a religious order to save the soul? Why seek by special acts of piety, self-denial, and separation from the world that which comes sufficiently through the usual sacraments of the church? The more we examine this subject, the more we shall see that the whole monastic system of the Church of Rome is an *included Protestantism*, or a Protestantism within the church.

Many of the reformers before the Reformation were monks. Savonarola, St. Bernard, Luther himself, were monks. From the monasteries came many of the leaders of the Reformation. The Protestant element in the Romish Church was shut up in monasteries during many centuries, and remained there as a foreign substance, an alien element included in the vast body. When a bullet, or other foreign substance, is lodged in the flesh, the vital powers go to work and build up a little wall around it, and shut it in. So when Catholics came who were not satisfied with a merely sacramental salvation, and longed for a higher life, the sagacity of the Church put them together in convents, and kept them by themselves, where they could do no harm. One of the curious homologons of history is this repetition in Europe of the course of events in Asia. Buddhism was, for many centuries, tolerated in India in the same way. It took the form of a monasticism included in Brahmanism, and remained a part of the Hindoo religion. And so, when the crisis came and the conflict began, this Hindoo Protestantism maintained itself for a long time in India, as Lutheranism continued for a century in Italy, Spain, and Austria. But it was at last driven out of its birthplace, as Protestantism was driven from Italy and Spain; and now only the ruins of its topes, its temples, and its monasteries remain to show

7

how extensive was its former influence in the midst of Brahmanism.

§ 2. *Extent of Buddhism. Its Scriptures.*

Yet, though expelled from India, and unable to maintain its control over any Aryan race, it has exhibited a powerful propagandist element, and so has converted to its creed the majority of the Mongol nations. It embraces nearly or quite (for statistics here are only guess-work)* three hundred millions of human beings. It is the popular religion of China ; the state religion of Thibet, and of the Birman Empire ; it is the religion of Japan, Siam, Anam, Assam, Nepaul, Ceylon, in short, of nearly the whole of Eastern Asia.

Concerning this vast religion we have had, until recently, very few means of information. But, during the last quarter of a century, so many sources have been opened, that at present we can easily study it in its

* Here are a few of the guesses : —

Cunningham, *Bhilsa Topes.*

Christians	270 millions.
Buddhist	222 "

Hassel, *Penny Cyclopædia.*

Christians	120 millions.
Jews	4 "
Mohammedans	252 "
Brahmans	111 "
Buddhists	315 "

Johnston, *Physical Atlas.*

Christians	301 millions.
Jews	5 "
Brahmans	133 "
Mohammedans	110 "
Buddhists	245 "

Perkins, *Johnson's American Atlas.*

Christians	369 millions.
Mohammedans	160 "
Jews	6 "
Buddhists	320 "

New American Cyclopædia.

Buddhists	290 millions.

And Professor Newmann estimates the number of Buddhists at 369 . millions.

original features and its subsequent development. The sacred books of this religion have been preserved independently, in Ceylon, Nepaul, China, and Thibet. Mr. G. Turnour, Mr. Georgely, and Mr. R. Spence Hardy are our chief authorities in regard to the Pitikas, or the Scriptures in the Pali language, preserved in Ceylon. Mr. Hodgson has collected and studied the Sanskrit Scriptures, found in Nepaul. In 1825 he transmitted to the Asiatic Society in Bengal sixty works in Sanskrit, and two hundred and fifty in the language of Thibet. M. Csoma, an Hungarian physician, discovered in the Buddhist monasteries of Thibet an immense collection of sacred books, which had been translated from the Sanskrit works previously studied by Mr. Hodgson. In 1829 M. Schmidt found the same works in the Mongolian. M. Stanislas Julien, an eminent student of the Chinese, has also translated works on Buddhism from that language, which ascend to the year 76 of our era.* More recently inscriptions cut upon rocks, columns, and other monuments in Northern India, have been transcribed and translated. Mr. James Prinsep deciphered these inscriptions, and found them to be in the ancient language of the province of Magadha where Buddhism first appeared. They contain the decrees of a king, or raja, named Pyadasi, whom Mr. Turnour has shown to be the same as the famous Asoka, before alluded to. This king appears to have come to the throne somewhere between B. C. 319 and B. C. 260. Similar inscriptions have been discovered throughout India, proving to the satisfaction of such scholars as Burnouf, Prinsep, Turnour, Lassen, Weber, Max Müller, and Saint-Hilaire, that Buddhism had become almost the state religion of India, in the fourth century before Christ.†

---

* Le Bouddha et sa Religion. Par J. Barthélemy Saint-Hilaire. — Eastern Monachism. By Spence Hardy. — Burnouf, Introduction, etc. — Koeppen, Die Religion des Buddha.

† The works from which this chapter has been mostly drawn are these : — Introduction à l'Histoire du Buddhisme indien. Par E. Burnouf. (Paris, 1844.) Le Bouddha et sa Religion. Par J. Barthélemy Saint-Hilaire. (Paris, 1860.) Eastern Monachism. By R. Spence Hardy. (London, 1850.) A Manual of Buddhism in its Modern Development. By R. Spence Hardy. (London, 1853.) Die Religion des Buddha. Von Karl F. Koeppen. (Berlin, 1857.) Indische Alterthumskunde. Von

§ 3. *Sakya-muni, the Founder of Buddhism.*

North of Central India and of the kingdom of Oude,
near the borders of Nepaul, there reigned, at the end
of the seventh century before Christ, a wise and good
king, in his capital city, Kapilavastu.* He was one of
the last of the great Solar race, celebrated in the ancient
epics of India. His wife, named *Maya* because of her
great beauty, became the mother of a prince, who was
named Siddârtha, and afterward known as the Buddha.†
She died seven days after his birth, and the child was
brought up by his maternal aunt. The young prince distinguished himself by his personal and intellectual qualities, but still more by his early piety. It appears from
the laws of Manu that it was not unusual, in the earliest
periods of Brahmanism, for those seeking a superior piety
to turn hermits, and to live alone in the forest, engaged
in acts of prayer, meditation, abstinence, and the study
of the Vedas. This practice, however, seems to have been
confined to the Brahmans. It was, therefore, a grief to
the king, when his son, in the flower of his youth and

Christian Lassen. (Bonn, 1852.) Der Buddhismus, Seine Dogmen, Ges-
chichte, und Literatur. Von W. Wassiljew. (St. Petersburg, 1860.)
Ueber Buddha's Todesjahr. Von N. L. Westergaard. (Breslau, 1862.)
Gott in der Geschichte. Von C. C. J. Bunsen. (Leipzig, 1858.) The
Bhilsa Topes, or Buddhist Monuments of Central India. By A. Cunning-
ham. (London, 1854.) Buddhism in Thibet. By Emil Schlagintweit.
(Leipzig and London, 1863.) Travels in Eastern countries by Huc and
Gabet, and others. References to Buddhism in the writings of Max
Müller, Maurice, Baur, Hardwick, Fergusson, Pritchard, Wilson, Cole-
brooke, etc.

* At the end of the fourth century of our era a Chinese Buddhist
made a pilgrimage to the birthplace of Buddha, and found the city in
ruins. Another Chinese pilgrim visited it A. D. 632, and was able to
trace the remains of the ruined palace, and saw a room which had been
occupied by Buddha. These travels have been translated from the Chinese by M. Stanislas Julien.

† *Buddha* is not a proper name, but an official title. Just as we ought
not to say Jesus Christ, but always Jesus *the* Christ, so we should say
Siddârtha the Buddha, or *Sakya-muni* the Buddha, or *Gautama* the
Buddha. The first of these names, Siddârtha (contracted from *Sarvârtha-
siddha*) was the baptismal name given by his father, and means " The
fulfilment of every wish." Sakya-muni means " The hermit of the race
of Sakya," — Sakya being the ancestral name of his father's race. The
name *Gautama* is stated by Koeppen to be " der priesterliche Beiname
des Geschlechts der Sakya," — whatever that may mean.

highly accomplished in every kingly faculty of body and mind, began to turn his thoughts toward the life of an anchorite. In fact, the young Siddârtha seems to have gone through that deep experience out of which the great prophets of mankind have always been born. The evils of the world pressed on his heart and brain; the very air seemed full of mortality; all things were passing away. Was anything permanent? anything stable? Nothing but truth; only the absolute, eternal law of things. "Let me see that," said he, "and I can give lasting peace to mankind. Then shall I become their deliverer." So, in opposition to the strong entreaties of his father, wife, and friends, he left the palace one night, and exchanged the position of a prince for that of a mendicant. "I will never return to the palace," said he, "till I have attained to the sight of the divine law, and so become Buddha." *

He first visited the Brahmans, and listened to their doctrines, but found no satisfaction therein. The wisest among them could not teach him true peace, — that profound inward rest, which was already called Nirvana. He was twenty-nine years old. Although disapproving of the Brahmanic austerities as an end, he practised them during six years, in order to subdue the senses. He then became satisfied that the path to perfection did not lie that way. He therefore resumed his former diet and a more comfortable mode of life, and so lost many disciples who had been attracted by his amazing austerity. Alone in his hermitage, he came at last to that solid conviction, that KNOWLEDGE never to be shaken, of the laws of things, which had seemed to him the only foundation of a truly free life. The spot where, after a week of constant meditation, he at last arrived at this beatific vision, became one of the most sacred places in India. He was seated under a tree, his face to the east, not having moved for a day and night, when he attained the triple science, which was to rescue mankind from its woes. Twelve hundred years after the death of the Buddha, a Chinese pilgrim was shown what then passed for the sacred tree. It was

* The Sanskrit root, whence the English " bode " and " forebode," means " to know."

surrounded by high brick walls, with an opening to the east, and near it stood many topes and monasteries. In the opinion of M. Saint-Hilaire, these ruins, and the locality of the tree, may yet be rediscovered. The spot deserves to be sought for, since there began a movement which has, on the whole, been a source of happiness and improvement to immense multitudes of human beings, during twenty-four centuries.

Having attained this inward certainty of vision, he decided to teach the world his truth. He knew well what it would bring him, — what opposition, insult, neglect, scorn. But he thought of three classes of men: those who were already on the way to the truth, and did not need him; those who were fixed in error, and whom he could not help; and the poor doubters, uncertain of their way. It was to help these last, the doubters, that the Buddha went forth to preach. On his way to the holy city of India, Benares, a serious difficulty arrested him at the Ganges, namely, his having no money to pay the boatman for his passage. At Benares he made his first converts, "turning the wheel of the law" for the first time. His discourses are contained in the sacred books of the Buddhists. He converted great numbers, his father among the rest, but met with fierce opposition from the Hindoo Scribes and Pharisees, the leading Brahmans. So he lived and taught, and died at the age of eighty years.

Naturally, as soon as the prophet was dead he became very precious in all eyes. His body was burned with much pomp, and great contention arose for the unconsumed fragments of bone. At last they were divided into eight parts, and a tope was erected, by each of the eight fortunate possessors, over such relics as had fallen to him. The ancient books of the North and South agree as to the places where the topes were built, and no Roman Catholic relics are so well authenticated. The Buddha, who believed with Jesus that "the flesh profiteth nothing," and that "the word is spirit and life," would probably have been the first to condemn this idolatry. But fetich-worship lingers in the purest religions.

The time of the death of Sakya-muni, like most Oriental dates, is uncertain. The Northern Buddhists, in Thibet, Nepaul, etc., vary greatly among themselves. The Chinese Buddhists are not more certain. Lassen, therefore, with most of the scholars, accepts as authentic the period upon which all the authorities of the South, especially of Ceylon, agree, which is B. C. 543. Lately Westergaard has written a monograph on the subject, in which, by a labored argument, he places the date about two hundred years later. Whether he will convince his brother *savans* remains to be seen.

Immediately after the death of Sakya-muni a general council of his most eminent disciples was called, to fix the doctrine and discipline of the church. The legend runs that three of the disciples were selected to recite from memory what the sage had taught. The first was appointed to repeat his teaching upon discipline; "for discipline," said they, "is the soul of the law." Whereupon Upali, mounting the pulpit, repeated all of the precepts concerning morals and the ritual. Then Ananda was chosen to give his master's discourses concerning faith or doctrine. Finally, Kasyapa announced the philosophy and metaphysics of the system. The council sat during seven months, and the threefold division of the sacred Scriptures of Buddhism was the result of their work; for Sakya-muni wrote nothing himself. He taught by conversation only.

The second general council was called to correct certain abuses which had begun to creep in. It was held about a hundred years after the teacher's death. A great fraternity of monks proposed to relax the conventual discipline, by allowing greater liberty in taking food, in drinking intoxicating liquor, and taking gold and silver if offered in alms. The schismatic monks were degraded, to the number of ten thousand, but formed a new sect. The third council, held during the reign of the great Buddhist Emperor Asoka, was called on account of heretics, who, to the number of sixty thousand, were degraded and expelled. After this, missionaries were despatched to preach the word in different lands. The names and success of these missionaries are recorded in the *Mahawanso*, or

Sacred History, translated by Mr. George Turnour from the Singhalese. But what is remarkable is, that the relics of some of them have been recently found in the Sanchi topes, and in other sacred buildings, contained in caskets, with their names inscribed on them. These inscribed names correspond with those given to the same missionaries in the historical books of Ceylon. For example, according to the *Mahawanso*, two missionaries, one named Kassapo (or Kasyapa), and the other called Majjhima (or Madhyama), went to preach in the region of the Himalayan Mountains. They journeyed, preached, suffered, and toiled, side by side, so the ancient history informs us, — a history composed in Ceylon in the fifth century of our era, with the aid of works still more ancient;* and now, when the second Sanchi tope was opened in 1851, by Major Cunningham, the relics of these very missionaries were discovered.† The tope was perfect in 1819, when visited by Captain Fell, — "not a stone fallen." And though afterward injured, in 1822, by some amateur relic-hunters, its contents remained intact. It is a solid hemisphere, built of rough stones without mortar, thirty-nine feet in diameter; it has a basement six feet high, projecting all around five feet, and so making a terrace. It is surrounded by a stone railing, with carved figures. In the centre of this tope was found a small chamber, made of six stones, containing the relic-box of white sandstone, about ten inches square. Inside this were four caskets of steatite (a sacred stone among the Buddhists), each containing small portions of burnt human bone. On the outside lid of one of these boxes was this inscription : " Relics of the emancipated Kasyapa Gotra, missionary to the whole Hemawanta." And on the inside of the lid was carved: " Relics of the emancipated Madhyama." These relics, with those of eight other leading men of the Buddhist Church, had rested in this monument since the age of Asoka, and cannot have been placed there later than B. C. 220.

The missionary spirit displayed by Buddhism distinguishes it from all other religions which preceded Christian-

---

* Saint-Hilaire.   † Bhilsa Topes.

ity. The religion of Confucius never attempted to make converts outside of China. Brahmanism never went beyond India. The system of Zoroaster was a Persian religion; that of Egypt was confined to the Valley of the Nile; that of Greece to the Hellenic race. But Buddhism was inflamed with the desire of bringing all mankind to a knowledge of its truths. Its ardent and successful missionaries converted multitudes in Nepaul, Thibet, Birmah, Ceylon, China, Siam, Japan; and in all these states its monasteries are to-day the chief sources of knowledge and centres of instruction to the people. It is idle to class such a religion as this with the superstitions which debase mankind. Its power lay in the strength of conviction which inspired its teachers; and that, again, must have come from the sight of truth, not the belief in error.

§ 4. *Leading Doctrines of Buddhism.*

What, then, are the doctrines of Buddhism? What are the essential teachings of the Buddha and his disciples? Is it a system, as we are so often told, which denies God and immortality? Has *atheism* such a power over human hearts in the East? Is the Asiatic mind thus in love with eternal death? Let us try to discover.

The hermit of Sakya, as we have seen, took his departure from two profound convictions, — the evil of perpetual change, and the possibility of something permanent. He might have used the language of the Book of Ecclesiastes, and cried, "Vanity of vanities! all is vanity!" The profound gloom of that wonderful book is based on the same course of thought as that of the Buddha, namely, that everything goes round and round in a circle; that nothing moves forward; that there is no new thing under the sun; that the sun rises and sets, and rises again; that the wind blows north and south, and east and west, and then returns according to its circuits. Where can rest be found? where peace? where any certainty? Siddârtha was young; but he saw age approaching. He was in health; but he knew that sick-

7 *

ness and death were lying in wait for him. He could not escape from the sight of this perpetual round of growth and decay, life and death, joy and woe. He cried out, from the depths of his soul, for something stable, permanent, real.

Again, he was assured that this emancipation from change and decay was to be found in knowledge. But by knowledge he did not intend the perception and recollection of outward facts, — not learning. Nor did he mean speculative knowledge, or the power of reasoning. He meant intuitive knowledge, the sight of eternal truth, the perception of the unchanging laws of the universe. This was a knowledge which was not to be attained by any merely intellectual process, but by moral training, by purity of heart and life. Therefore he renounced the world, and went into the forest, and became an anchorite.

But just at this point he separated himself from the Brahmans. They also were, and are, believers in the value of mortification, abnegation, penance. They had their hermits in his day. But they believed in the value of penance as accumulating merit. They practised self-denial for its own sake. The Buddha practised it as a means to a higher end, — emancipation, purification, intuition. And this end he believed that he had at last attained. At last he *saw* the truth. He became "wide awake." Illusions disappeared ; the reality was before him. He was the Buddha, — the MAN WHO KNEW.

Still he was a man, not a God. And here again is another point of departure from Brahmanism. In that system, the final result of devotion was to become absorbed in God. The doctrine of the Brahmans is divine absorption; that of the Buddhists, human development. In the Brahmanical system, God is everything and man nothing. In the Buddhist, man is everything and God nothing. Here is its atheism, that it makes so much of man as to forget God. It is perhaps "without God in the world," but it does not deny him. It accepts the doctrine of the three worlds, — the eternal world of absolute being ; the celestial world of the gods, Brahma, Indra, Vischnu, Siva ; and the finite world, consisting of individual souls and the laws of nature. Only it says, of the world of absolute being, Nirvana, we know nothing. That is our aim and end ; but it is the direct opposite to all we know. It is, therefore, to us as nothing. The celestial world, that of the gods, is even of less moment to us. What we know are the everlasting laws of nature, by obedience to which we rise, disobeying which we fall, by perfect obedience to which we shall at last obtain Nirvana, and rest forever.

To the mind of the Buddha, therefore, the world consisted of two orders of existence, — souls and laws. He saw an infinite multitude of souls, — in insects, animals, men, — and saw that they were surrounded by inflexible laws, — the laws of nature. To know these and to obey them, — this was emancipation.

The fundamental doctrine of Buddhism, taught by its founder and received by all Buddhists without exception, in the North and in the South, in Birmah and Thibet, in Ceylon and China, is the doctrine of the four sublime truths, namely : —

1. All existence is evil, because all existence is subject to change and decay.

2. The source of this evil is the desire for things which are to change and pass away.

3. This desire, and the evil which follows it, are not inevitable ; for if we choose we can arrive at Nirvana, when both shall wholly cease.

4. There is a fixed and certain method to adopt, by pursuing which we attain this end, without possibility of failure.

These four truths are the basis of the system. They are : 1st, the evil ; 2d, its cause ; 3d, its end ; 4th, the way of reaching the end.

Then follow the eight steps of this way, namely : —

1. Right belief, or the correct faith.

2. Right judgment, or wise application of that faith to life.

3. Right utterance, or perfect truth in all that we say and do.

4. Right motives, or proposing always a proper end and aim.

5. Right occupation, or an outward life not involving sin.

6. Right obedience, or faithful observance of duty.

7. Right memory, or a proper recollection of past conduct.

8. Right meditation, or keeping the mind fixed on permanent truth.

After this system of doctrine follow certain moral commands and prohibitions, namely, five, which apply to all men, and five others which apply only to the novices or the monks. The five first commandments are : 1st, do not kill ; 2d, do not steal ; 3d, do not commit adultery ; 4th, do not lie ; 5th, do not become intoxicated. The other five are : 1st, take no solid food after noon ; 2d, do not visit dances, singing, or theatrical representations ; 3d, use no ornaments or perfumery in dress ; 4th, use no luxurious beds ; 5th, accept neither gold nor silver.

All these doctrines and precepts have been the subject of innumerable commentaries and expositions. Every-. thing has been commented, explained, and elucidated. Systems of casuistry as voluminous as those of the Fathers of the Company of Jesus, systems of theology as full of minute analysis as the great *Summa Totius Theologiæ* of St. Thomas, are to be found in the libraries of the monasteries of Thibet and Ceylon. The monks have their Golden Legends, their Lives of Saints, full of miracles and marvels. On this simple basis of a few rules and convictions has arisen a vast fabric of metaphysics. Much of this literature is instructive and entertaining. Some of it is profound. Baur, who had made a special study of the intricate speculations of the Gnostics, compares them with "the vast abstractions of Buddhism."

§ 5. *The Spirit of Buddhism Rational and Humane.*

Ultimately, two facts appear, as we contemplate this system, — first, its rationalism ; second, its humanity.

It is a system of rationalism. It appeals throughout to human reason. It proposes to save man, not from a future but a present hell, and to save him by teach ing. Its great means of influence is the sermon. The Buddha preached innumerable sermons; his missionaries went abroad preaching. Buddhism has made all its conquests honorably, by a process of rational appeal to the human mind. It was never propagated by force, even when it had the power of imperial rajas to support it. Certainly, it is a very encouraging fact in the history of man, that the two religions which have made more converts than any other, Buddhism and Christianity, have not depended for their success on the sword of the conqueror or the frauds of priestcraft, but have gained their victories in the fair conflict of reason with reason. We grant that Buddhism has not been without its superstitions and its errors; but it has not deceived, and it has not persecuted. In this respect it can teach Christians a lesson. Buddhism has no prejudices against those who confess another faith. The Buddhists have founded no Inquisition; they have combined the zeal which converted kingdoms with a toleration almost inexplicable to our Western experience. Only one religious war has darkened their peaceful history during twenty-three centuries, — that which took place in Thibet, but of which we know little. A Siamese told Crawford that he believed all the religions of the world to be branches of the true religion. A Buddhist in Ceylon sent his son to a Christian school, and told the astonished missionary, " I respect Christianity as much as Buddhism, for I regard it as a help to Buddhism." MM. Huc and Gabet converted no Buddhist in Tartary and Thibet, but they partially converted one, bringing him so far as to say that he considered himself at the same time a good Christian and a good Buddhist.

Buddhism is also a religion of humanity. Because it lays such stress on reason, it respects all men, since all possess this same gift. In its origin it broke down all castes. All men, of whatever rank, can enter its priesthood. It has an unbounded charity for all souls, and holds it a duty to make sacrifices for all. One legend tells us that the Buddha gave his body for food to a starved tigress, who could not nurse her young through weakness. An incident singularly like that in the fourth chapter of John is recorded of the hermit, who asked a woman of low caste for water, and when she expressed surprise said, " Give me drink, and I will give you truth." The unconditional command, " Thou shalt not kill," which applies to all living creatures, has had great influence in softening the manners of the Mongols. This command is connected with the doctrine of transmigration of souls, which is one of the essential doctrines of this system as well as of Brahmanism. But Buddhism has abolished human sacrifices, and indeed all bloody offerings, and its innocent altars are only crowned with flowers and leaves. It also inculcates a positive humanity, consisting of good actions. All its priests are supported by daily alms. It is a duty of the Buddhist to be hospitable to strangers, to establish hospitals for the sick and poor, and even for sick animals, to plant shade-trees, and erect houses for travellers. Mr. Malcom, the Baptist missionary, says that he was resting one day in a *zayat* in a small village in Birmah, and was scarcely seated when a woman brought a nice mat for him to lie on. Another brought cool water, and a man went and picked for him half a dozen good oranges. None sought or expected, he says, the least reward, but disappeared, and left him to his repose. He adds : " None can ascend the river without being struck with the hardihood, skill, energy, and good-humor of the Birmese boatmen. In point of temper and morality they are infinitely superior to the boatmen on our Western waters. In my various trips, I have seen no quarrel nor heard a hard word."

Mr. Malcom goes on thus : " Many of these people have never seen a white man before, but I am constantly struck with their politeness. They desist from anything on the slightest intimation ; never crowd around to be troublesome ; and if on my showing them my watch or pencil-case, or anything which particularly attracts them, there are more than can get a sight, the outer ones stand aloof and wait till their turn comes. . . . .

" I saw no intemperance in Birmah. though an intoxicating liquor is made easily of the juice of a palm. . . . .

"A man may travel from one end of the kingdom to the other without money, feeding and lodging as well as the people."

"I have seen thousands together, for hours, on public occasions, rejoicing in all ardor, and no act of violence or case of intoxication. . . . .

"During my whole residence in the country I never saw an indecent act or immodest gesture in man or woman. . . . . I have seen hundreds of men and women bathing, and no immodest or careless act. . . . .

"Children are treated with great kindness, not only by the mother but the father, who, when unemployed, takes the young child in his arms, and seems pleased to attend to it, while the mother cleans the rice or sits unemployed at his side. I have as often seen fathers caressing female infants as male. A widow with male and female children is more likely to be sought in marriage than if she has none. . . . .

"Children are almost as reverent to parents as among the Chinese. The aged are treated with great care and tenderness, and occupy the best places in all assemblies."

According to Saint-Hilaire's opinion, the Buddhist morality is one of endurance, patience, submission, and abstinence, rather than of action, energy, enterprise. Love for all beings is its nucleus, every animal being our possible relative. To love our enemies, to offer our lives for animals, to abstain from even defensive warfare, to govern ourselves, to avoid vices, to pay obedience to superiors, to reverence age, to provide food and shelter for men and animals, to dig wells and plant trees, to despise no religion, show no intolerance, not to persecute, are the virtues of these people. Polygamy is tolerated, but not approved. Monogamy is general in Ceylon, Siam, Birmah; somewhat less so in Thibet and Mongolia. Woman is better treated by Buddhism than by any other Oriental religion.

§ 6. *Buddhism as a Religion.*

But what is the religious life of Buddhism? Can there be a religion without a God? And if Buddhism has no

God, how can it have worship, prayer, devotion ? There
is no doubt that it has all these. We have seen that its
cultus is much like that of the Roman Catholic Church.
It differs from this church in having no secular priests, but
only regulars; all its clergy are monks, taking the three
vows of poverty, chastity, and obedience. Their vows,
however, are not irrevocable ; they can relinquish the yellow robe, and return into the world, if they find they have
mistaken their vocation.

The God of Buddhism is the Buddha himself, the
deified man, who has become an infinite being by entering
Nirvana. To him prayer is addressed, and it is so natural
for man to pray, that no theory can prevent him from
doing it. In Thibet, prayer-meetings are held even in the
streets. Huc says : " There is a very touching custom at
Lhassa. In the evening, just before sundown, all the
people leave their work, and meet in groups in the public
streets and squares. All kneel and begin to chant their
prayers in a low and musical tone. The concert of song
which rises from all these numerous reunions produces an
immense and solemn harmony, which deeply impresses
the mind. We could not help sadly comparing this Pagan
city, where all the people prayed together, with our European cities, where men would blush to be seen making
the sign of the cross."

In Thibet *confession* was early enjoined. Public worship is there a solemn confession before the assembled
priests. It confers entire absolution from sins. It consists in an open confession of sin, and a promise to sin no
more. Consecrated water is also used in the service of
the Pagodas.

There are thirty-five Buddhas who have preceded Sakya-
muni, and are considered the chief powers for taking
away sin. These are called the " Thirty-five Buddhas of
Confession." Sakya-muni, however, has been included in
the number. Some lamas are also joined with them in
the sacred pictures, as Tsonkhapa, a lama born in A. D.
1555, and others. The mendicant priests of Buddha are
bound to confess twice a month, at the new and full
moon.

The Buddhists have also nunneries for women. It is related that Sakya-muni consented to establish them at the earnest request of his aunt and nurse, and of his favorite disciple, Ananda. These nuns take the same vows as the monks. Their rules require them to show reverence even to the youngest monk, and to use no angry or harsh words to a priest. The nun must be willing to be taught ; she must go once a fortnight for this purpose to some virtuous teacher ; she must not devote more than two weeks at a time to spiritual retirement ; she must not go out merely for amusement ; after two years' preparation she can be initiated, and she is bound to attend the closing ceremonies of the rainy season.

§ 7. *Karma and Nirvana.*

One of the principal metaphysical doctrines of this system is that which it called Karma. This means the law of consequences, by which every act committed in one life entails results in another. This law operates until one reaches Nirvana. Mr. Hardy goes so far as to suppose that Karma causes the merits or demerits of each soul to result at death in the production of another consciousness, and in fact to result in a new person. But this must be an error. Karma is the law of consequences, by which every act receives its exact recompense in the next world, where the soul is born again. But unless the same soul passes on, such a recompense is impossible.

" *Karma*," said Buddha, " is the most essential property of all beings ; it is inherited from previous births, it is the cause of all good and evil, and the reason why some are mean and some exalted when they come into the world. It is like the shadow which always accompanies the body." Buddha himself obtained all his elevation by means of the Karma obtained in previous states. No one can obtain Karma or merit, but those who hear the discourses of Buddha.

There has been much discussion among scholars concerning the true meaning of Nirvana, the end of all Buddhist expectation. Is it annihilation ? Or is it absorption in God ? The weight of authority, no doubt, is in favor of the first view. Burnouf's conclusion is : "For Buddhist theists, it is the absorption of the individual life in God ; for atheists, absorption of this individual life in the nothing. But for both, it is deliverance from all evil, it is supreme affranchisement." In the opinion that it is annihilation agree Max Müller, Turnour, Schmidt, and Hardy. And M. Saint-Hilaire, while calling it "a hideous faith," nevertheless assigns it to a third part of the human race.

But, on the other hand, scholars of the highest rank deny this view. In particular, Bunsen (*Gott in der Geschichte*) calls attention to the fact that, in the oldest monuments of this religion, the earliest Sutras, Nirvana is spoken of as a condition attained in the present life. How then can it mean annihilation ? It is a state in which all desires cease, all passions die. Bunsen believes that the Buddha never denied or questioned God or immortality.

The following account of NIRVANA is taken from the Pali Sacred Books : —

"Again the king of Ságal said to Nágaséna : 'Is the joy of Nirvana unmixed, or is it associated with sorrow ? ' The priest replied that it is unmixed satisfaction, entirely free from sorrow.

"Again the king of Ságal said to Nágaséna : 'Is Nirvana in the east, west, south, or north ; above or below ? Is there such a place as Nirvana ? If so, where is it ? ' Nágaséna : ' Neither in the east, south, west, nor north, neither in the sky above, nor in the earth below, nor in any of the infinite sakwalas, is there such a place as Nirvana.' Milinda : ' Then if Nirvana have no locality, there can be no such thing ; and when it is said that any one attains Nirvana, the declaration is false.' Nágaséna : ' There is no such place as Nirvana, and yet it exists ; the priest who seeks it in the right manner will attain it.' ' When Nirvana is attained, is there such a place ? ' Nágaséna : ' When a priest attains Nirvana there is such a place.' Milinda : ' Where is that place ? ' Nágaséna : ' Wherever the precepts can be observed ; it may be anywhere ; just as he who has two eyes can see the sky from any or all places ; or as all places may have an eastern side.' "

The Buddhist asserts Nirvana as the object of all his hope, yet, if you ask him what it is, may reply, " Nothing." But this cannot mean that the highest good of man is annihilation. No pessimism could be more extreme than such a doctrine. Such a belief is not in accordance with human nature. Tennyson is wiser when he writes : —

> " Whatever crazy sorrow saith,
> No life that breathes with human breath
> Has ever truly longed for death.

> " 'T is LIFE, whereof our nerves are scant,
> O life, not death, for which we pant ;
> More life, and fuller, that I want. "

The Buddhist, when he says that Nirvana is *nothing,* means simply that it is *no thing ;* that it is nothing to our present conceptions ; that it is the opposite of all we know, the contradiction of what we call life now, a state so sublime, so wholly different from anything we know or can know now, that it is the same thing as nothing to us. All present life is change ; *that* is permanence : all present life is going up and down ; *that* is stability : all present life is the life of sense ; *that* is spirit.

The Buddhist denies God in the same way. He is the unknowable. He is the impossible to be conceived of.

> " Who shall name Him
> And dare to say,
> ' *I believe in Him* ' ?
> Who shall deny Him,
> And venture to affirm,
> ' *I believe in Him not ?* ' "*

To the Buddhist, in short, the element of time and the finite is all, as to the Brahman the element of eternity is all. It is the most absolute contradiction of Brahmanism which we can conceive.

It seems impossible for the Eastern mind to hold at the same time the two conceptions of God and nature, the infinite and the finite, eternity and time. The Brahmans

---

* Goethe, Faust.

accept the reality of God, the infinite and the eternal, and
omit the reality of the finite, of nature, history, time, and
the world.   The Buddhist accepts the last, and ignores
the first.

This question has been fully discussed by Mr. Alger in
his very able work, " Critical History of the Doctrine of
a Future Life," and his conclusion is wholly opposed to
the view which makes Nirvana equivalent to annihilation.

§ 8. *Good and Evil of Buddhism.*

The good and the evil of Buddhism are thus summed
up by M. Saint-Hilaire.

He remarks that the first peculiarity of Buddhism is
the wholly practical direction taken by its founder.   He
proposes to himself the salvation of mankind.   He ab-
stains from the subtle philosophy of the Brahmans, and
takes the most direct and simple way to his end.   But he
does not offer low and sensual rewards; he does not, like
so many lawgivers, promise to his followers riches, pleasures, conquests, power.   He invites them to salvation by
means of virtue, knowledge, and self-denial.   Not in the
Vedas, nor the books which proceed from it, do we find
such noble appeals, though they too look at the infinite
as their end.   But the indisputable glory of Buddha is the
boundless charity to man with which his soul was filled.
He lived to instruct and guide man aright.   He says in
so many words, " My law is a law of grace for all " (Burnouf, Introduction, etc., p. 198).   We may add to M.
Saint-Hilaire's statement, that in these words the Buddha
plainly aims at what we have called a catholic religion.   In
his view of man's sorrowful life, all distinctions of rank
and class fall away ; all are poor and needy together ; and
here, too, he comes in contact with that Christianity which
says, " Come unto me, all ye that labor and are heavy-
laden."   Buddha also wished to cure the sicknesses, not
only of the Hindoo life, but of the life of mankind.

M. Saint-Hilaire adds, that, in seeking thus to help
man, the means of the Buddha are pure, like his ends.

He tries to convince and to persuade : he does not wish
to compel. He allows confession, and helps the weak
and simple by explanations and parables. He also tries
to guard man against evil, by establishing habits of chastity, temperance, and self-control. He goes forward into
the Christian graces of patience, humility, and forgiveness of injuries. He has a horror of falsehood, a reverence for truth ; he forbids slander and gossip ; he teaches
respect for parents, family, life, home.

Yet Saint-Hilaire declares that, with all these merits,
Buddhism has not been able to found a tolerable social
state or a single good government. It failed in India,
the land of its birth. Nothing like the progress and the
development of Christian civilization appears in Buddhism. Something in the heart of the system makes it
sterile, notwithstanding its excellent intentions. What
is it ?

The fact is, that, notwithstanding its benevolent purposes, its radical thought is a selfish one. It rests on
pure individualism, — each man's object is to save his
own soul. All the faults of Buddhism, according to M.
Saint-Hilaire, spring from this root of egotism in the
heart of the system.

No doubt the same idea is found in Christianity. Personal salvation is herein included. But Christianity *starts*
from a very different point : it is the " kingdom of Heav-
en." " Thy kingdom come : thy will be done on earth."
It is not going on away from time to find an unknown
eternity. It is God with us, eternity here, eternal life
abiding in us now. If some narrow Protestant sects
make Christianity to consist essentially in the salvation
of our own soul hereafter, they fall into the condemnation of Buddhism. But that is not the Christianity of
Christ. Christ accepts the great prophetic idea of a Messiah who brings down God's reign into this life. It is
the New Jerusalem coming down from God out of heav-
en. It is the earth full of the knowledge of God, as the
waters cover the sea. It is all mankind laboring together
for this general good,

This solitary preoccupation with one's own salvation

causes the religious teachers of Buddhism to live apart, outside of society, and take no interest in it. There is in the Catholic and Protestant world, beside the monk, a secular priesthood, which labors to save other men's bodies and souls. No such priesthood exists in Buddhism.

Moreover, not the idea of salvation from evil, — which keeps before us evil as the object of contemplation, — but the idea of good, is the true motive for the human conscience. This leads us up at once to God ; this alone can create love. We can only love by seeing something lovely. God must seem, not terrible, but lovely, in order to be loved. Man must seem, not mean and poor, but noble and beautiful, before we can love him. This idea of the good does not appear in Buddhism, says M. Saint-Hilaire. Not a spark of this divine flame — that which to see and show has given immortal glory to Plato and to Socrates — has descended on Sakya-muni. The notion of rewards, substituted for that of the infinite beauty, has perverted everything in his system.

Duty itself becomes corrupted, as soon as the idea of the good disappears. It becomes then a blind submission to mere law. It is an outward constraint, not an inward inspiration. Scepticism follows. " The world is empty, the heart is dead surely," is its language. Nihilism arrives sooner or later. God is nothing ; man is nothing ; life is nothing ; death is nothing ; eternity is nothing. Hence the profound sadness of Buddhism. To its eye all existence is evil, and the only hope is to escape from time into eternity, — or into nothing, — as you may choose to interpret Nirvana. While Buddhism makes God, or the good, and heaven, to be equivalent to nothing, it intensifies and exaggerates evil. Though heaven is a blank, hell is a very solid reality. It is present and future too. Everything in the thousand hells of Buddhism is painted as vividly as in the hell of Dante. God has disappeared from the universe, and in his place is only the inexorable law, which grinds on forever. It punishes and rewards, but has no love in it. It is only dead, cold, hard, cruel, unrelenting law. Yet Buddhists are not atheists, any more than a child who has never heard of God is an

atheist. A child is neither deist nor atheist: he has *no*
theology.

The only emancipation from self-love is in the perception of an infinite love. Buddhism, ignoring this infinite
love, incapable of communion with God, aiming at morality without religion, at humanity without piety, becomes at last a prey to the sadness of a selfish isolation.
We do not say that this is always the case, for in all systems the heart often redeems the errors of the head. But
this is the logical drift of the system and its usual out-
come.

§ 9. *Relation of Buddhism to Christianity.*

In closing this chapter, let us ask what relation this
great system sustains to Christianity.

The fundamental doctrine and central idea of Buddhism
is personal salvation, or *the salvation of the soul by personal acts of faith and obedience.* This we maintain, notwithstanding the opinion that some schools of Buddhists
teach that the soul itself is not a constant element or a
special substance, but the mere result of past merit or
demerit. For if there be no soul, there can be no transmigration. Now it is certain that the doctrine of transmigration is the very basis of Buddhism, the corner-stone
of the system. Thus M. Saint-Hilaire says: " The chief
and most immovable fact of Buddhist metaphysics is the
doctrine of transmigration." Without a soul to migrate,
there can be no migration. Moreover, the whole ethics
of the system would fall with its metaphysics, on this
theory ; for why urge men to right conduct, in order to
attain happiness, or Nirvana, hereafter, if they are not
to exist hereafter. No, the soul's immortality is a radical
doctrine in Buddhism, and this doctrine is one of its
points of contact with Christianity.

Another point of contact is its doctrine of reward and
punishment, — a doctrine incompatible with the supposition that the soul does not pass on from world to world.
But this is the essence of all its ethics, the immutable,
inevitable, unalterable consequences of good and evil. In

this also it agrees with Christianity, which teaches that
" whatsoever a man soweth that shall he also reap " ; that
he who turns his pound into five will be set over five
cities, he who turns it into ten, over ten cities.

A third point of contact with Christianity, however
singular it may at first appear to say so, is the doctrine
of Nirvana. Nirvana, to the Buddhist, means the absolute, eternal world, beyond time and space ; that which
is nothing to us now, but will be everything hereafter.
Incapable of cognizing both time and eternity, it makes
them absolute negations of each other.

The peculiarity of Plato, according to Mr. Emerson and
other Platonists was, that he was able to grasp and hold
intellectually both conceptions, — of God and man, the
infinite and finite, the eternal and the temporal. The
merit of Christianity is, in like manner, that it is able to
take up and keep, not primarily as dogma, but as life,
both these antagonistic ideas. Christianity recognizes
God as the infinite and eternal, but recognizes also the
world of time and space as real. Man exists as well as
God : we love God, we must love man too. Brahmanism
loves God, but not man ; it has piety, but not humanity.
Buddhism loves man, but not God ; it has humanity, but
not piety ; or if it has piety, it is by a beautiful want of
logic, its heart being wiser than its head. That which
seems an impossibility in these Eastern systems is a fact
of daily life to the Christian child, to the ignorant and
simple Christian man or woman, who, amid daily duty
and trial, find joy in both heavenly and earthly love.

There is a reason for this in the inmost nature of Christianity as compared with Buddhism. Why is it that
Buddhism is a religion without God ? Sakya-muni did not
ignore God. The object of his life was to attain Nirvana,
that is, to attain a union with God, the Infinite Being.
He became Buddha by this divine experience. Why,
then, is not this religious experience a constituent element
in Buddhism, as it is in Christianity ? Because in Buddhism man struggles upward to find God, while in Christianity God comes down to find man. To speak in the
language of technical theology, Buddhism is a doctrine

of works, and Christianity of grace. That which God gives all men may receive, and be united by this community of grace in one fellowship. But the results attained by effort alone, divide men; because some do more and receive more than others. The saint attained Buddha, but that was because of his superhuman efforts and sacrifices; it does not encourage others to hope for the same result.

We see, then, that here, as elsewhere, the superiority of Christianity is to be found in its quantity, in its fulness of life. It touches Buddhism at all its good points, in all its truths. It accepts the Buddhistic doctrine of rewards and punishments, of law, progress, self-denial, self-control, humanity, charity, equality of man with man, and pity for human sorrow; but to all this it adds — how much more! It fills up the dreary void of Buddhism with a living God; with a life of God in man's soul, a heaven here as well as hereafter. It gives us, in addition to the struggle of the soul to find God, a God coming down to find the soul. It gives a divine as real as the human, an infinite as solid as the finite. And this it does, not by a system of thought, but by a fountain and stream of life. If all Christian works, the New Testament included, were destroyed, we should lose a vast deal no doubt; but we should not lose Christianity; for that is not a book, but a life. Out of that stream of life would be again developed the conception of Christianity, as a thought and a belief. We should be like the people living on the banks of the Nile, ignorant for five thousand years of its sources; not knowing whence its beneficent inundations were derived; not knowing by what miracle its great stream could flow on and on amid the intense heats, where no rain falls, and fed during a course of twelve hundred miles by no single affluent, yet not absorbed in the sand, nor evaporated by the ever-burning sun. But though ignorant of its source, they know it has a source, and can enjoy all its benefits and blessings. So Christianity is a full river of life, containing truths apparently the most antagonistic, filling the soul and heart of man and the social state of nations with its impulses

8

and its ideas. We should lose much in losing our positive knowledge of its history ; but if all the books were gone, the tablets of the human heart would remain, and on these would be written the everlasting Gospel of Jesus, in living letters which no years could efface and no changes conceal.

CHAPTER V.

ZOROASTER AND THE ZEND AVESTA.

§ 1. Ruins of the Palace of Xerxes at Persepolis. § 2. Greek Accounts of Zoroaster. Plutarch's Description of his Religion. § 3. Anquetil du Perron and his Discovery of the Zend Avesta. § 4. Epoch of Zoroaster. What do we know of him ? § 5. Spirit of Zoroaster and of his Religion. § 6. Character of the Zend Avesta. § 7. Later Development of the System in the Bundehesch. § 8. Relation of the Religion of the Zend Avesta to that of the Vedas. § 9. Is Monotheism or pure Dualism the Doctrine taught in the Zend Avesta ? § 10. Relation of this System to Christianity. The Kingdom of Heaven.

§ 1. *Ruins of the Palace of Xerxes at Persepolis.*

IN the southwestern part of Persia is the lovely valley of Schiraz, in the province of Farsistan, which is the ancient Persis. Through the long spring and summer the plains are covered with flowers, the air is laden with perfume, and the melody of birds, winds, and waters fills the ear. The fields are covered with grain, which ripens in May ; the grapes, apricots, and peaches are finer than those of Europe. The nightingale (or bulbul) sings more sweetly than elsewhere, and the rose-bush, the national emblem of Persia, grows to the size of a tree, and is weighed down by its luxuriant blossoms. The beauty of this region, and the loveliness of the women of Schiraz awakened the genius of Hafiz and of Saadi, the two great lyric poets of the East, both of whom resided here.

At one extremity of this valley, in the hollow of a crescent formed by rocky hills, thirty miles northwest of Schiraz, stands an immense platform, fifty feet high above the plain, hewn partly out of the mountain itself, and partly built up with gray marble blocks from twenty to sixty feet long, so nicely fitted together that the joints can scarcely be detected. This platform is about fourteen hundred feet long by nine hundred broad, and its faces front the four quarters of the heavens. You rise from the plain by flights of marble steps, so broad and easy that a procession on horseback could ascend them. By these you reach a landing, where stand as sentinels two colossal figures sculptured from great blocks of marble. The one horn in the forehead seems to Heeren to indicate the Unicorn; the mighty limbs, whose muscles are carved with the precision of the Grecian chisel, induced Sir Robert Porter to believe that they represented the sacred bulls of the Magian religion; while the solemn, half-human repose of the features suggests some symbolic and supernatural meaning. Passing these sentinels, who have kept their solitary watch for centuries, you ascend by other flights of steps to the top of the terrace. There stand, lonely and beautiful, a few gigantic columns, whose lofty fluted shafts and elegantly carved capitals belong to an unknown order of architecture. Fifty or sixty feet high, twelve or fifteen feet in circumference, they, with a multitude of others, once supported the roof of cedar, now fallen, whose beams stretched from capital to capital, and which protected the assembled multitudes from the hot sun of Southern Asia. Along the noble upper stairway are carved rows of figures, which seem to be ascending by your side. They represent warriors, courtiers, captives, men of every nation, among whom may be easily distinguished the negro from the centre of Africa. Inscriptions abound, in that strange arrow-headed or wedge-shaped character, — one of the most ancient and difficult of all, — which, after long baffling the learning of Europe, has at last begun yielded to the science and acuteness of the present century. One of the inscriptions copied from these walls was read by Grotefend as follows : —

"Darius the King, King of Kings, son of Hystaspes, successor of the Ruler of the World, Djemchid."

Another : —

"Xerxes the King, King of Kings, son of Darius the King, successor of the Ruler of the World."

More recently, other inscriptions have been deciphered,

one of which is thus given by another German Orientalist, Benfey : — *

"Ahura-Mazda (Ormazd) is a mighty God ; who has created the earth, the heaven, and men ; who has given glory to men ; who has made Xerxes king, the ruler of many. I, Xerxes, King of Kings, king of the earth near and far, son of Darius, an Achæmenid. What I have done here, and what I have done elsewhere, I have done by the grace of Ahura-Mazda."

In another place : —

"Artaxerxes the King has declared that this great work is done by me. May Ahura-Mazda and Mithra protect me, my building, and my people." †

Here, then, was the palace of Darius and his successors, Xerxes and Artaxerxes, famous for their conquests, — some of which are recorded on these walls, — who carried their victorious arms into India on the east, Syria and Asia Minor on the west, but even more famous for being defeated at Marathon and Thermopylæ. By the side of these columns sat the great kings of Persia, giving audience to ambassadors from distant lands. Here, perhaps, sat Cyrus himself, the founder of the Persian monarchy, and issued orders to rebuild Jerusalem. Here the son of Xerxes, the Ahasuerus of Scripture, may have brought from Susa the fair Esther. For this is the famous Persepolis, and on those loftier platforms, where only ruinous heaps of stones now remain, stood that other palace, which Alexander burned in his intoxication three hundred and thirty years before Christ. "Solitary in their situation, peculiar in their character," says Heeren, "these ruins rise above the deluge of years which has overwhelmed all the records of human grandeur around

---

* Die Persischen Keilinscriften. (Leipzig, 1847.) See also the account of the inscription at Behistun, in Lenormant's "Manual of Ancient History."

† Rawlinson, Five Great Monarchies. — Duncker, Geschichte des Alterthums, B. II. — Heeren, The Persians. — Fergusson, Illustrated Handbook of Architecture. — Creuzer, Schriften. See also the works of Oppert, Hinks, Menant, and Lassen.

them, and buried all traces of Susa and Babylon. Their venerable antiquity and majestic proportions do not more command our reverence, than the mystery which involves their construction awakens the curiosity of the most unobservant spectator. Pillars which belong to no known order of architecture, inscriptions in an alphabet which continues an enigma, fabulous animals which stand as guards at the entrance, the multiplicity of allegorical figures which decorate the walls, — all conspire to carry us back to ages of the most remote antiquity, over which the traditions of the East shed a doubtful and wavering light."

Diodorus Siculus says that at Persepolis, on the face of the mountain, were the tombs of the kings of Persia, and that the coffins had to be lifted up to them along the wall of rock by cords. And Ctesias tells us that " Darius, the son of Hystaspes, had a tomb prepared for himself in the double mountain during his lifetime, and that his parents were drawn up with cords to see it, but fell and were killed." These very tombs are still to be seen on the face of the mountain behind the ruins. The figures of the kings are carved over them. One stands before an altar on which a fire is burning. A ball representing the sun is above the altar. Over the effigy of the king hangs in the air a winged half-length figure in fainter lines, and resembling him. In other places he is seen contending with a winged animal like a griffin.

All this points at the great Iranic religion, the religion of Persia and its monarchs for many centuries, the religion of which Zoroaster was the great prophet, and the Avesta the sacred book. The king, as servant of Ormazd, is worshipping the fire and the sun, — symbols of the god ; he resists the impure griffin, the creature of Ahriman ; and the half-length figure over his head is the surest evidence of the religion of Zoroaster. For, according to the Avesta, every created being has its archetype or Fereuer (Ferver, Fravashis), which is its ideal essence, first created by the thought of Ormazd. Even Ormazd himself has his Fravashis,* and these angelic

* Vendidad, Fargard, XIX. – XLVI. Spiegel, translated into English by Bleek.

essences are everywhere objects of worship to the disciple of Zoroaster. We have thus found in Persepolis, not only the palace of the great kings of Persia, but the home of that most ancient system of Dualism, the system of Zoroaster.

§ 2. Greek Accounts of Zoroaster. Plutarch's Description of his Religion.

But who was Zoroaster, and what do we know of him ? He is mentioned by Plato, about four hundred years before Christ. In speaking of the education of a Persian prince he says that "one teacher instructs him in the magic of Zoroaster, the son (or priest) of Ormazd (or Oromazes), in which is comprehended all the worship of the gods." He is also spoken of by Diodorus, Plutarch, the elder Pliny, and many writers of the first centuries after Christ. The worship of the Magians is described by Herodotus before Plato. Herodotus gives very minute accounts of the ritual, priests, sacrifices, purifications, and mode of burial used by the Persian Magi in his time, four hundred and fifty years before Christ; and his account closely corresponds with the practices of the Pârsîs, or fire-worshippers, still remaining in one or two places in Persia and India at the present day. "The Persians," he says, "have no altars, no temples nor images; they worship on the tops of the mountains. They adore the heavens, and sacrifice to the sun, moon, earth, fire, water, and winds." * "They do not erect altars, nor use libations, fillets, or cakes. One of the Magi sings an ode concerning the origin of the gods, over the sacrifice, which is laid on a bed of tender grass." "They pay great reverence to all rivers, and must do nothing to defile them; in burying they never put the body in the ground till it has been torn by some bird or dog; they cover the body with wax, and then put it in the ground." "The Magi think they do a meritorious act when they kill ants, snakes, reptiles." †

* Herodotus, I. 131.
† Herodotus, in various parts of his history.

Plutarch's account of Zoroaster * and his precepts. is very remarkable.   It is as follows : —

" Some believe that there are two Gods, — as it were, two rival workmen ; the one whereof they make to be the maker of good things, and the other bad.   And some call the better of these God, and the other Dæmon ; as doth Zoroastres, the Magee, whom they report to be five thousand years elder than the Trojan times.   This Zoroastres therefore called the one of these Oromazes, and the other Arimanius ; and affirmed, moreover, that the one of them did, of anything sensible, the most resemble light, and the other darkness and ignorance ; but that Mithras was in the middle betwixt them.   For which cause, the Persians called Mithras the mediator.   And they tell us that he first taught mankind to make vows and offerings of thanksgiving to the one, and to offer averting and feral sacrifice to the other.   For they beat a certain plant called homomy † in a mortar, and call upon Pluto and the dark ; and then mix it with the blood of a sacrificed wolf, and convey it to a certain place where the sun never shines, and there cast it away.   For of plants they believe, that some pertain to the good God, and others again to the evil Dæmon ; and likewise they think that such animals as dogs, fowls, and urchins belong to the good ; but water animals to the bad, for which reason they account him happy that kills most of them.   These men, moreover, tell us a great many romantic things about these gods, whereof these are some : They say that Oromazes, springing from purest light, and Arimanius, on the other hand, from pitchy darkness, these two are therefore at war with one another.   And that Oromazes made six gods,‡ whereof the first was the author of benevolence, the second of truth, the third of justice, and the rest, one of wisdom,

---

* " Plutarch's Morals.   Translated from the Greek by several hands. London.   Printed for W. Taylor, at the Ship in Pater-noster Row. 1718."   This passage concerning Zoroaster is from the " Isis and Osiris" in Vol. IV. of this old translation.   We have retained the antique terminology and spelling.   (See also the new American edition of this translation.   Boston, Little and Brown, 1871.)

† This is the Haöma spoken of on page 202.

‡ These, with Ormazd, are the seven Amshaspands enumerated on page 197.

one of wealth, and a third of that pleasure which accrues from good actions; and that Arimanius likewise made the like number of contrary operations to confront them. After this, Oromazes, having first trebled his own magnitude, mounted up aloft, so far above the sun as the sun itself above the earth, and so bespangled the heavens with stars. But one star (called Sirius or the Dog) he set as a kind of sentinel or scout before all the rest. And after he had made four-and-twenty gods more, he placed them all in an egg-shell. But those that were made by Arimanius (being themselves also of the like number) breaking a hole in this beauteous and glazed egg-shell, bad things came by this means to be intermixed with good. But the fatal time is now approaching, in which Arimanius, who by means of this brings plagues and famines upon the earth, must of necessity be himself utterly extinguished and destroyed; at which time, the earth, being made plain and level, there will be one life, and one society of mankind, made all happy, and one speech. But Theopompus saith, that, according to the opinion of the Magees, each of these gods subdues, and is subdued by turns, for the space of three thousand years apiece, and that for three thousand years more they quarrel and fight and destroy each other's works; but that at last Pluto shall fail, and mankind shall be happy, and neither need food, nor yield a shadow.* And that the god who projects these things doth, for some time, take his repose and rest; but yet this time is not so much to him although it seems so to man, whose sleep is but short. Such, then, is the mythology of the Magees."

We shall see presently how nearly this account corresponds with the religion of the Pârsîs, as it was developed out of the primitive doctrine of Zoroaster.†

Besides what was known through the Greeks, and some

---

* See the account, on page 195, of these four periods of three thousand years each.

† Kleuker (Anhang zum Zend-Avesta) has given a full *résumé* of the references to Zoroaster and his religion in the Greek and Roman writers. More recently, Professor Rapp of Tübingen has gone over the same ground in a very instructive essay in the Zeitschrift der Deutschen Morgenländischen Gesellschaft. (Leipzig, 1865.)

accounts contained in Arabian and Persian writers, there was, until the middle of the last century, no certain information concerning Zoroaster and his teachings. But the enterprise, energy, and scientific devotion of a young Frenchman changed the whole aspect of the subject, and we are now enabled to speak with some degree of certainty concerning this great teacher and his doctrines.

§ 3. *Anquetil du Perron and his Discovery of the Zend Avesta.*

Anquetil du Perron, born at Paris in 1731, devoted himself early to the study of Oriental literature. He mastered the Hebrew, Arabic, and Persian languages, and by his ardor in these studies attracted the attention of Oriental scholars. Meeting one day in the Royal Library with a fragment of the Zend Avesta, he was seized with the desire of visiting India, to recover the lost books of Zoroaster, " and to learn the Zend language in which they were written, and also the Sanskrit, so as to be able to read the manuscripts in the *Bibliothèque du Roi*, which no one in Paris understood." * His friends endeavored to procure him a situation in an expedition just about to sail ; but their efforts not succeeding, Du Perron enlisted as a private soldier, telling no one of his intention till the day before setting out, lest he should be prevented from going. He then sent for his brother and took leave of him with many tears, resisting all the efforts made to dissuade him from his purpose. His baggage consisted of a little linen, a Hebrew Bible, a case of mathematical instruments, and the works of Montaigne and Charron. A ten days' march, with other recruits, through wet and cold, brought him to the port from whence the expedition was to sail. Here he found that the government, struck with his extraordinary zeal for science, had directed that he should have his discharge and a small salary of five hundred livres. The East India Company (French) gave him a passage gratis, and he set sail for India, February 7, 1755, being then twenty-four years old. The first two years in

* Anq. du Perron, Zend Avesta ; Disc. Prélim., p. vi.

India were almost lost to him for purposes of science, on account of his sicknesses, travels, and the state of the country disturbed by war between England and France.* He travelled afoot and on horseback over a great part of Hindostan, saw the worship of Juggernaut and the monumental caves of Ellora, and, in 1759, arrived at Surat, where was the Pârsî community from which he hoped for help in obtaining the object of his pursuit. By perseverance and patience he succeeded in persuading the Destours, or priests, of these fire-worshippers, to teach him the Zend language and to furnish him with manuscripts of the Avesta. With one hundred and eighty valuable manuscripts he returned to Europe, and published, in 1771, his great work, — the Avesta translated into French, with notes and dissertations. He lived through the French Revolution, shut up with his books, and immersed in his Oriental studies, and died, after a life of continued labor, in 1805. Immense erudition and indomitable industry were joined in Anquetil du Perron to a pure love of truth and an excellent heart.

For many years after the publication of the Avesta its genuineness and authenticity were a matter of dispute among the learned men of Europe ; Sir William Jones especially denying it to be an ancient work, or the production of Zoroaster. But almost all modern writers of eminence now admit both. Already in 1826 Heeren said that these books had " stood the fiery ordeal of criticism." " Few remains of antiquity," he remarks, " have undergone such attentive examination as the books of the Zend Avesta. This criticism has turned out to their advantage ; the genuineness of the principal compositions, especially of the Vendidad and Izeschne (Yaçna), has been demonstrated ; and we may consider as completely ascertained all that regards the rank of each book of the Zend Avesta."

* At the time Anquetil du Perron was thus laboring in the cause of science in India, two other men were in the same region devoting themselves with equal ardor to very different objects. Clive was laying the foundations of the British dominion in India ; Schwartz was giving himself up to a life of toil in preaching the Gospel to the Hindoos. How little would these three men have sympathized with each other, or appreciated each other's work ! And yet how important to the progress of humanity was that of each !

Rhode (one of the first of scholars of his day in this department) says: "There is not the least doubt that these are the books ascribed in the most ancient times to Zoroaster." Of the Vendidad he says: "It has both the inward and outward marks of the highest antiquity, so that we fear not to say that only prejudice or ignorance could doubt it." *

§ 4. *Epoch of Zoroaster. What do we know of him?*

As to the age of these books, however, and the period at which Zoroaster lived, there is the greatest difference of opinion. He is mentioned by Plato (Alcibiades, I. 37), who speaks of " the magic (or religious doctrines) of Zoroaster the Ormazdian" (μαγείαν — Ζωροάστρου τοῦ 'Ωρομάζου).†
As Plato speaks of his religion as something established in the form of Magism, or the system of the Medes, in West Iran, while the Avesta appears to have originated in Bactria, or East Iran,‡ this already carries the age of Zoroaster back to at least the sixth or seventh century before Christ. When the Avesta was written, Bactria was an independent monarchy. Zoroaster is represented as teaching under King Vistaçpa. But the Assyrians conquered Bactria B. C. 1200, which was the last of the Iranic kingdoms, they having previously vanquished the Medes, Hyrcanians, Parthians, Persians, etc. As Zoroaster must have lived before this conquest, his period is taken back to a still more remote time, about B. C. 1300 or B. C. 1250. §

---

* And with this conclusion the later scholars agree. Burnouf, Lassen, Spiegel, Westergaard, Haug, Bunsen, Max Müller, Roth, all accept the Zend Avesta as containing in the main, if not the actual words of Zoroaster, yet authentic reminiscences of his teaching. The Gâthâs of the Yaçna are now considered to be the oldest part of the Avesta, as appears from the investigations of Haug and others. (See Dr. Martin Haug's translation and commentary of the Five Gâthâs of Zarathustra. Leipzig, 1860.)

† Even good scholars often follow each other in a false direction for want of a little independent thinking. The Greek of Plato was translated by a long succession of writers, "Zoroaster the *son* of Oromazes," until some one happened to think that this genitive might imply a different relation.

‡ Duncker (Gesch. des Alterthums, B. II.) gives at length the reasons which prove Zoroaster and the Avesta to have originated in Bactria.

§ Duncker (B. II. s. 483). So Döllinger.

It is difficult to be more precise than this. Bunsen indeed * suggests that "the date of Zoroaster, as fixed by
Aristotle, cannot be said to be so very irrational. He and
Eudoxus, according to Pliny, place him six thousand
years before the death of Plato ; Hermippus, five thousand
years before the Trojan war," or about B. C. 6300 or B. C.
6350. But Bunsen adds : "At the present stage of the
inquiry the question whether this date is set too high
cannot be answered either in the negative or affirmative."
Spiegel, in one of his latest works,† considers Zoroaster
as a neighbor and contemporary of Abraham, therefore
as living B. C. 2000 instead of B. C. 6350. Professor Whitney of New Haven places the epoch of Zoroaster at "least
B. C. 1000," and adds that all attempts to reconstruct
Persian chronology or history prior to the reign of the
first Sassanid have been relinquished as futile.‡ Döllinger § thinks he may have been "somewhat later than
Moses, perhaps about B. C. 1300," but says, "it is impossible to fix precisely " when he lived. Rawlinson‖ merely
remarks that Berosus places him anterior to B. C. 2234.
Haug is inclined to date the Gâthâs, the oldest songs
of the Avesta, as early as the time of Moses.¶ Rapp,**
after a thorough comparison of ancient writers, concludes
that Zoroaster lived B. C. 1200 or 1300. In this he agrees
with Duncker, who, as we have seen, decided upon the
same date. It is not far from the period given by the
oldest Greek writer who speaks of Zoroaster, — Xanthus
of Sardis, a contemporary of Darius. It is the period
given by Cephalion, a writer of the second century, who
takes it from three independent sources. We have no
sources now open to us which enable us to come nearer
than this to the time in which he lived.

Nor is anything known with certainty of the place
where he lived or the events of his life. Most modern

---

* Egypt's Place in Universal History, Vol. III. p. 471.
† Eran, das Land zwischen dem Indus und Tigris.
‡ Journal of the Am. Or. Soc., Vol. V. No. 2, p. 353.
§ The Gentile and Jew, Vol. I. p. 380.
‖ Five Great Monarchies, Vol. III. p. 94.
¶ Essays, &c., by Martin Haug, p. 255.
** Die Religion und Sitte der Perser. Von Dr. Adolf Rapp. (1865.)

writers suppose that he resided in Bactria. Haug maintains that the language of the Zend books is Bactrian.*
A highly mythological and fabulous life of Zoroaster, translated by Anquetil du Perron, called the Zartusht-Namah,† describes him as going to Iran in his thirtieth year, spending twenty years in the desert, working miracles during ten years, and giving lessons of philosophy in Babylon, with Pythagoras as his pupil. All this is based on the theory (now proved to be false) of his living in the time of Darius. " The language of the Avesta," says Max Müller, " is so much more primitive than the inscriptions of Darius, that many centuries must have passed between the two periods represented by these two strata of language."‡ These inscriptions are in the Achæmenian dialect, which is the Zend in a later stage of linguistic growth.

§ 5. *Spirit of Zoroaster and of his Religion*

It is not likely that Zoroaster ever saw Pythagoras or even Abraham. But though absolutely nothing is known of the events of his life, there is not the least doubt of his existence nor of his character. He has left the impress of his commanding genius on great regions, various races, and long periods of time. His religion, like that of the Buddha, is essentially a moral religion. Each of them was a revolt from the Pantheism of India, in the interest of morality, human freedom, and the progress of the race. They differ in this, that each takes hold of one side of morality, and lets go the opposite. Zoroaster bases his law on the eternal distinction between right and wrong ; Sakya-muni, on the natural laws and their consequences, either good or evil. Zoroaster's law is, therefore, the law of justice ; Sakya-muni's, the law of mercy. The one makes the supreme good to consist in truth, duty, right ; the other, in love, benevolence, and kindness. Zoroaster teaches providence : the monk of India teaches prudence.

---

* Bunsen, Egypt, Vol. III. p. 455.
† Written in the thirteenth century after Christ. An English translation may be found in Dr. J. Wilson's "Pârsî Religion."
‡ Chips, Vol. I. p. 88.

Zoroaster aims at holiness, the Buddha at merit. Zoroaster teaches and emphasizes creation : the Buddha knows nothing of creation, but only nature or law. All these oppositions run back to a single root. Both are moral reformers ; but the one moralizes according to the method of Bishop Butler, the other after that of Archdeacon Paley. Zoroaster cognizes all morality as having its root within, in the eternal distinction between right and wrong motive, therefore in God ; but Sakya-muni finds it outside of the soul, in the results of good and evil action, therefore in the nature of things. The method of salvation, therefore, according to Zoroaster, is that of an eternal battle for good against evil ; but according to the Buddha, it is that of self-culture and virtuous activity.

Both of these systems, as being essentially moral systems in the interest of humanity, proceed from persons. For it is a curious fact, that, while the essentially spiritualistic religions are ignorant of their founders, all the moral creeds of the world proceed from a moral source, i. e. a human will. Brahmanism, Gnosticism, the Sufism of Persia, the Mysteries of Egypt and Greece, Neo-Platonism, the Christian Mysticism of the Middle Ages, — these have, strictly speaking, no founder. Every tendency to the abstract, to the infinite, ignores personality.* Individual mystics we know, but never the founder of any such system. The religions in which the moral element is depressed, as those of Babylon, Assyria, Egypt, Greece, Rome, are also without personal founders. But moral religions are the religions of persons, and so we have the systems of Confucius, Buddha, Zoroaster, Moses, Mohammed.† The Protestant Reformation was a protest of the moral nature against a religion which had become divorced from morality. Accordingly we have Luther as the founder of Protestantism ; but mediæval Christianity grew up with no personal leader.

---

* So Mr. Emerson, in one of those observations which give us a system of philosophy in a sentence, says, "The soul knows no persons." Perhaps he should have said, "The Spirit."

† Islam is, in this sense, a moral religion, its root consisting in obedience to Allah and his prophet. Sufism, a Mohammedan mysticism, is a heresy.

The whole religion of the Avesta revolves around the person of Zoroaster, or Zarathustra. In the oldest part of the sacred books, the Gâthâs of the Yaçna, he is called the *pure* Zarathustra, good in thought, speech, and work. It is said that Zarathustra alone knows the precepts of Ahura-Mazda (Ormazd), and that he shall be made skilful in speech. In one of the Gâthâs he expresses the desire of bringing knowledge to the pure, in the power of Ormazd, so as to be to them strong joy (Spiegel, Gâthâ Ustvaiti, XLII. 8), or, as Haug translates the same passage (Die Gâthâs des Zarathustra, II. 8): "I will swear hostility to the liars, but be a strong help to the truthful." He prays for truth, declares himself the most faithful servant in the world of Ormazd the Wise One, and therefore begs to know the best thing to do. As the Jewish prophets tried to escape their mission, and called it a burden, and went to it " in the heat and bitterness of their spirit," so Zoroaster says (according to Spiegel): "When it came to me through your prayer, I thought that the spreading abroad of your law through men was something difficult."

Zoroaster was one of those who was oppressed with the sight of evil. But it was not outward evil which most tormented him, but spiritual evil, — evil having its origin in a depraved heart and a will turned away from goodness. His meditations led him to the conviction that all the woe of the world had its root in sin, and that the origin of sin was to be found in the demonic world. He might have used the language of the Apostle Paul and said, "We wrestle not with flesh and blood," — that is, our struggle is not with man, but with principles of evil, rulers of darkness, spirits of wickedness in the supernatural world. Deeply convinced that a great struggle was going on between the powers of light and darkness, he called on all good men to take part in the war, and battle for the good God against the dark and foul tempter.

Great physical calamities added to the intensity of this conviction. It appears that about the period of Zoroaster, some geological convulsions had changed the climate of Northern Asia, and very suddenly produced severe cold where before there had been an almost tropical temperature. The first Fargard of the Vendidad has been lately translated by both Spiegel and Haug, and begins by speaking of a good country, Aryana-Vaêjo, which was created a region of delight by Ahura-Mazda (Ormazd). Then it adds that the "evil being, Angra-Mainyus (Ahriman), full of death, created a mighty serpent, and winter, the work of the Devas. Ten months of winter are there, two months of summer." Then follows, in the original document, this statement : " Seven months of summer are (were ?) there ; five months of winter were there. The latter are cold as to water, cold as to earth, cold as to trees. There is the heart of winter; there all around falls deep snow. There is the worst of evils." This passage has been set aside as an interpolation by both Spiegel and Haug. But they give no reason for supposing it such, except the difficulty of reconciling it with the preceding passage. This difficulty, however, disappears, if we suppose it intended to describe a great climatic change, by which the original home of the Aryans, Aryana-Vaêjo, became suddenly very much colder than before. Such a change, if it took place, was probably the cause of the emigration which transferred this people from Aryana-Vaêjo (Old Iran) to New Iran, or Persia. Such a history of emigration Bunsen and Haug suppose to be contained in this first Fargard (or chapter) of the Vendidad. If so, it takes us back further than the oldest part of the Veda, and gives the progress of the Aryan stream to the south from its original source on the great plains of Central Asia, till it divided into two branches, one flowing into Persia, the other into India. The first verse of this venerable document introduces Ormazd as saying that he had created new regions, desirable as homes ; for had he not done so, all human beings would have crowded into this Aryana-Vaêjo. Thus in the very first verse of the Vendidad appears the affectionate recollection of these emigrant races for their fatherland in Central Asia, and the Zoroasterian faith in a creative and protective Providence. The awful convulsion which turned their summer climate into the present Siberian winter of ten months' duration was part of a divine plan. Old Iran would have been too attractive, and all mankind would have crowded into that Eden. So the evil Ahriman was permitted to glide into it, a new serpent of destruction, and its seven months of summer and five of winter were changed to ten of winter and two of summer.[*]

This Aryana-Vaêjo, Old Iran, the primeval seat of the great Indo-European race, is supposed by Haug and Bunsen to be situated on the high plains northeast of Samarcand, between the thirty-seventh and fortieth degrees of north latitude, and the eighty-sixth and ninetieth of east longitude. This region has exactly the climate described, — ten months of winter and two of summer. The same is true of Western Thibet and most of Central Siberia. Malte-Brun says: "The winter is nine or ten months long through almost the whole of Siberia." June and July are the only months wholly free from snow. On the parallel of 60°, the earth on the 28th of June was found frozen, at a depth of three feet.

But is there reason to think that the climate was ever different? Geologists assure us that "great oscillations of climate have occurred in times immediately antecedent to the peopling of the earth by man."[†] But in Central and Northern Asia there is evidence of such fluctuations of temperature in a much more recent period. In 1803, on the banks of the Lena, in latitude 70°, the entire body of a mammoth fell from a mass of ice in which it had been entombed perhaps for thousands of years, but with the flesh so perfectly preserved that it was immediately devoured by wolves. Since then these frozen elephants have been found in great numbers, in so perfect a condition that the bulb of an eye of one of them is in the Museum at Moscow.[‡] They have been found as far north as 75°. Hence Lyell thinks it "reasonable to believe that a large region in Central Asia, including perhaps the southern half of Siberia, enjoyed at no very remote period in the earth's history a temperate climate, sufficiently mild to afford food for numerous herds of elephants and rhinoceroses."

---

[*] Vendidad, Farg. I. 3. "Therefore Angra-Mainyus, the death-dealing, created a mighty serpent and snow." The *serpent* entering into the Iranic Eden is one of the curious coincidences of the Iranic and Hebrew traditions.

[†] Lyell, Principles of Geology (eighth edition), p. 77.

[‡] Idem., p. 83. A similar change from a temperate climate to extreme cold has taken place in Greenland within five or six centuries.

Amid these terrible convulsions of the air and ground, these antagonisms of outward good and evil, Zoroaster developed his belief in the dualism of all things. To his mind, as to that of the Hebrew poet, God had placed all things against each other, two and two. No Pantheistic optimism, like that of India, could satisfy his thought. He could not say, "Whatever is, is right"; some things seemed fatally wrong. The world was a scene of war, not of peace and rest. Life to the good man was not sleep, but battle. If there was a good God over all, as he devoutly believed, there was also a spirit of evil, of awful power, to whom we were not to yield, but with whom we should do battle. In the far distance he saw the triumph of good; but that triumph could only come by fighting the good fight now. But his weapons were not carnal. "Pure thoughts" going out into "true words" and resulting in "right actions"; this was the whole duty of man.

§ 6. *Character of the Zend Avesta.*

A few passages, taken from different parts of the Zend Avesta, will best illustrate these tendencies, and show how unlike it is, in its whole spirit, to its sister, the Vedic liturgy. Twin children of the old Aryan stock, they must have struggled together like Esau and Jacob, before they were born. In such cases we see how superficial is the philosophy which, beginning with synthesis instead of analysis, declares the unity of all religions before it has seen their differences. There *is* indeed, what Cudworth has called "the symphony of all religions," but it cannot be demonstrated by the easy process of gathering a few similar texts from Confucius, the Vedas, and the Gospels, and then announcing that they all teach the same thing. We must first find the specific idea of each, and we may then be able to show how each of these may take its place in the harmonious working of universal religion.

If, in taking up the Zend Avesta, we expect to find a system of theology or philosophy, we shall be disappointed. It is a liturgy,—a collection of hymns, prayers, invocations, thanksgivings. It contains prayers to a multitude of deities, among whom Ormazd is always counted supreme, and the rest only his servants.

" I worship and adore," says Zarathustra (Zoroaster), "the Creator of all things, Ahura-Mazda (Ormazd), full of light! I worship the Amĕsha-çpentas (Amshaspands, the seven archangels, or protecting spirits)! I worship the body of the primal Bull, the soul of the Bull! I invoke thee, O Fire, thou son of Ormazd, most rapid of the Immortals! I invoke Mithra, the lofty, the immortal, the pure, the sun, the ruler, the quick Horse, the eye of Ormazd! I invoke the holy Sraosha, gifted with holiness, and Raçnu (spirit of justice), and Arstat (spirit of truth)! I invoke the Fravashi of good men, the Fravashi of Ormazd, the Fravashi of my own soul! I praise the good men and women of the whole world of purity! I praise the Haŏma, health-bringing, golden, with moist stalks. I praise Sraosha, whom four horses carry, spotless, bright-shining, swifter than the storms, who, without sleeping, protects the world in the darkness."

The following passages are from the oldest part of the Avesta, the Gâthâs : —

" Good is the thought, good the speech, good the work of the pure Zarathustra."

" I desire by my prayer with uplifted hands this joy, — the pure works of the Holy Spirit, Mazda, ... a disposition to perform good actions, ... and pure gifts for both worlds, the bodily and spiritual."

" I have intrusted my soul to Heaven, ... and I will teach what is pure so long as I can."

" I keep forever purity and good-mindedness. Teach thou me, Ahura-Mazda, out of thyself; from heaven, by thy mouth, whereby the world first arose."

" Thee have I thought, O Mazda, as the first, to praise with the soul, ... active Creator, ... Lord of the worlds, ... Lord of good things, ... the first fashioner, ... who made the pure creation, ... who upholds the best soul with his understanding."

" I praise Ahura-Mazda, who has created the cattle, created the water and good trees, the splendor of light, the earth and all good. We praise the Fravashis of the pure men and women, — whatever is fairest, purest, immortal."

" We honor the good spirit, the good kingdom, the good law, — all that is good."

" Here we praise the soul and body of the Bull, then our

own souls, the souls of the cattle which desire to maintain us in life, ... the good men and women, ... the abode of the water, ... the meeting and parting of the ways, ... the mountains which make the waters flow, ... the strong wind created by Ahura-Mazda, ... the Haŏma, giver of increase, far from death."

"Now give ear to me, and hear! the Wise Ones have created all. Evil doctrine shall not again destroy the world."

"In the beginning, the two heavenly Ones spoke — the Good to the Evil — thus; 'Our souls, doctrines, words, works, do not unite together.'"

"How shall I satisfy thee, O Mazda, I, who have little wealth, few men? How may I exalt thee according to my wish! . . . . I will be contented with your desires; this is the decision of my understanding and of my soul."

The following is from the Khordah Avesta: —

"In the name of God, the giver, forgiver, rich in love, praise be to the name of Ormazd, the God with the name, 'Who always was, always is, and always will be'; the heavenly amongst the heavenly, with the name 'From whom alone is derived rule.' Ormazd is the greatest ruler, mighty, wise, creator, supporter, refuge, defender, completer of good works, overseer, pure, good, and just.

"With all strength (bring I) thanks; to the great among beings, who created and destroyed, and through his own determination of time, strength, wisdom, is higher than the six Amshaspands, the circumference of heaven, the shining sun, the brilliant moon, the wind, the water, the fire, the earth, the trees, the cattle, the metals, mankind.

"Offering and praise to that Lord, the completer of good works, who made men greater than all earthly beings, and through the gift of speech created them to rule the creatures, as warriors against the Daêvas.*

"Praise the omniscience of God, who hath sent through the holy Zarathustra peace for the creatures, the wisdom of the law, — the enlightening derived from the heavenly understanding, and heard with the ears, — wisdom and guidance for all beings who are, were, and will be, (and) the wisdom of wisdoms; which effects freedom from hell for the soul at the bridge, and leads it over to that Paradise, the brilliant, sweet-smelling of the pure.

* The Daêvas, or evil spirits of the Zend books, are the same as the Dêvas, or Gods of the Sanskrit religion.

" All good do I accept at thy command, O God, and think, speak, and do it. I believe in the pure law; by every good work seek I forgiveness for all sins. I keep pure for myself the serviceable work and abstinence from the unprofitable. I keep pure the six powers, — thought, speech, work, memory, mind, and understanding. According to thy will am I able to accomplish, O accomplisher of good, thy honor, with good thoughts, good words, good works.

" I enter on the shining way to Paradise; may the fearful terror of hell not overcome me! May I step over the bridge Chinevat, may I attain Paradise, with much perfume, and all enjoyments, and all brightness.

" Praise to the Overseer, the Lord, who rewards those who accomplish good deeds according to his own wish, purifies at last the obedient, and at last purifies even the wicked one of hell. All praise be to the creator, Ormazd, the all-wise, mighty, rich in might; to the seven Amshaspands; to Ized Bahrâm, the victorious annihilator of foes."

"HYMN TO A STAR.

" The star Tistrya praise we, the shining, majestic, with pleasant good dwelling, light, shining, conspicuous, going around, healthful, bestowing joy, great, going round about from afar, with shining beams, the pure, and the water which makes broad seas, good, far-famed, the name of the bull created by Mazda, the strong kingly majesty, and the Fravashi of the holy pure, Zarathustra.

" For his brightness, for his majesty, will I praise him, the star Tistrya, with audible praise. We praise the star Tistrya, the brilliant, majestic, with offerings, with Haŏma bound with flesh, with Maúthra which gives wisdom to the tongue, with word and deed, with offerings with right-spoken speech."

" The star Tistrya, the brilliant, majestic, we praise, who glides so softly to the sea like an arrow, who follows the heavenly will, who is a terrible pliant arrow, a very pliant arrow, worthy of honor among those worthy of honor, who comes from the damp mountain to the shining mountain."

"HYMN TO MITHRA.

" Mithra, whose long arms grasp forwards here with Mithrastrength; that which is in Eastern India he seizes, and that which [is] in the Western he smites, and what is on the steppes of Raúha, and what is at the ends of this earth.

"Thou, O Mithra, dost seize these, reaching out thy arms. The unrighteous destroyed through the just is gloomy in soul. Thus thinks the unrighteous : Mithra, the artless, does not see all these evil deeds, all these lies.

"But I think in my soul : No earthly man with a hundred-fold strength thinks so much evil as Mithra with heavenly strength thinks good. No earthly man with a hundred-fold strength speaks so much evil as Mithra with heavenly strength speaks good. No earthly man with a hundred-fold strength does so much evil as Mithra with heavenly strength does good.

"With no earthly man is the hundred-fold greater heavenly understanding allied as the heavenly understanding allies itself to the heavenly Mithra, the heavenly. No earthly man with a hundred-fold strength hears with the ears as the heavenly Mithra, who possesses a hundred strengths, sees every liar. Mightily goes forward Mithra, powerful in rule marches he onwards ; fair visual power, shining from afar, gives he to the eyes."

"A CONFESSION, OR PATET.*

"I repent of all sins. All wicked thoughts, words, and works which I have meditated in the world, corporeal, spiritual, earthly, and heavenly, I repent of, in your presence, ye believers. O Lord, pardon through the three words.

"I confess myself a Mazdayaçnian, a Zarathustrian, an opponent of the Daêvas, devoted to belief in Ahura, for praise, adoration, satisfaction, and laud. As it is the will of God, let the Zaŏta say to me, Thus announces the Lord, the Pure out of Holiness, let the wise speak.

"I praise all good thoughts, words, and works, through thought, word, and deed. I curse all evil thoughts, words, and works away from thought, word, and deed. I lay hold on all good thoughts, words, and works, with thoughts, words, and works, i. e. I perform good actions, I dismiss all evil thoughts, words, and works, from thoughts, words, and works, i. e. I commit no sins.

"I give to you, ye who are Amshaspands, offering and praise, with the heart, with the body, with my own vital powers, body and soul. The whole powers which I possess I possess in dependence on the Yazatas. To possess in dependence upon the

---

* The Patets are formularies of confession. They are written in Pârsî, with occasional passages inserted in Zend.

Yazatas means (as much as) this : if anything happens so that
it behoves to give the body for the sake of the soul, I give it
to them.

" I praise the best purity, I hunt away the Dévs, I am thankful for the good of the Creator Ormazd, with the opposition
and unrighteousness which come from Ganâ-mainyo, am I
contented and agreed in the hope of the resurrection. The
Zarathustrian law created by Ormazd I take as a plummet.
For the sake of this way I repent of all sins.

" I repent of the sins which can lay hold of the character of
men, or which have laid hold of my character, small and great
which are committed amongst men, the meanest sins as much
as is (and) can be, yet more than this, namely, all evil
thoughts, words, and works which (I have committed) for the
sake of others, or others for my sake, or if the hard sin has
seized the character of an evil-doer on my account, — such
sins, thoughts, words, and works, corporeal, mental, earthly,
heavenly, 1 repent of with the three words : pardon, O Lord,
I repent of the sins with Patet.

" The sins against father, mother, sister, brother, wife, child,
against spouses, against the superiors, against my own relations, against those living with me, against those who possess
equal property, against the neighbors, against the inhabitants
of the same town, against servants, every unrighteousness
through which I have been amongst sinners, — of these sins
repent I with thoughts, words, and works, corporeal as spiritual, earthly as heavenly, with the three words : pardon, O
Lord, I repent of sins.

" The defilement with dirt and corpses, the bringing of dirt
and corpses to the water and fire, or the bringing of fire and
water to dirt and corpses ; the omission of reciting the Avesta
in mind, of strewing about hair, nails, and toothpicks, of not
washing the hands, all the rest which belongs to the category
of dirt and corpses, if I have thereby come among the sinners,
so repent I of all these sins with thoughts, words, and works,
corporeal as spiritual, earthly as heavenly, with the three
words : pardon, O Lord, I repent of sin.

" That which was the wish of Ormazd the Creator, and I
ought to have thought, and have not thought, what I ought
to have spoken and have not spoken, what I ought to have
done and have not done ; of these sins repent I with thoughts,
words, and works," etc.

" That which was the wish of Ahriman, and I ought not to

have thought and yet have thought, what I ought not to have spoken and yet have spoken, what I ought not to have done and yet have done ; of these sins I repent," etc.

" Of all and every kind of sin which I have committed against the creatures of Ormazd, as stars, moon, sun, and the red burning fire, the dog, the birds, the five kinds of animals, the other good creatures which are the property of Ormazd, between earth and heaven, if I have become a sinner against any of these, I repent," etc.

" Of pride, haughtiness, covetousness, slandering the dead, anger, envy, the evil eye, shamelessness, looking at with evil intent, looking at with evil concupiscence, stiff-neckedness, discontent with the godly arrangements, self-willedness, sloth, despising others, mixing in strange matters, unbelief, opposing the Divine powers, false witness, false judgment, idol-worship, running naked, running with one shoe, the breaking of the low (midday) prayer, the omission of the (midday) prayer, theft, robbery, whoredom, witchcraft, worshipping with sorcerers, unchastity, tearing the hair, as well as all other kinds of sin which are enumerated in this Patet, or not enumerated, which I am aware of, or not aware of, which are appointed or not appointed, which I should have bewailed with obedience before the Lord, and have not bewailed, — of these sins repent I with thoughts, words, and works, corporeal as spiritual, earthly as heavenly. O Lord, pardon, I repent with the three words, with Patet.

" If I have taken on myself the Patet for any one and have not performed it, and misfortune has thereby come upon his soul or his descendants, I repent of the sin for every one with thoughts," etc.

" With all good deeds am I in agreement, with all sins am I not in agreement, for the good am I thankful, with iniquity am I contented. With the punishment at the bridge, with the bonds and tormentings and chastisements of the mighty of the law, with the punishment of the three nights (after) the fifty-seven years am I contented and satisfied."

The Avesta, then, is not a system of dogmatics, but a book of worship. It is to be read in private by the laity, or to be recited by the priests in public. Nevertheless, just such a book may be the best help to the knowledge of the religious opinions of an age. The deepest convictions come to light in such a collection, not indeed in a systematic statement, but in sincerest utterance. It will contain the faith of the heart rather than the speculations of the intellect. Such a work can hardly be other than authentic; for men do not forge liturgies, and, if they did, could hardly introduce them into the worship of a religious community.

The Avesta consists of the Vendidad, of which twenty-two Fargards, or chapters, have been preserved; the Vispered, in twenty-seven; the Yaçna, in seventy; and the Khordah Avesta, or Little-Avesta, which contains the Yashts, Patets, and other prayers for the use of the laity. Of these, Spiegel considers the Gâthâs of the Yaçna to be the oldest, next the Vendidad, lastly, the first part of the Yaçna, and the Khordah Avesta.

§ 7. *Later Development of the System in the Bundehesch.*

The Bundehesch is a book later than these, and yet, in its contents, running back to a very early period. Windischmann,* who has recently given us a new translation of this book, says: "In regard to the Bundehesch, I am confident that closer study of this remarkable book, and a more exact comparison of it with the original texts, will change the unfavorable opinion hitherto held concerning it into one of great confidence. I am justified in believing that its author has given us mainly only the ancient doctrine, taken by him from original texts, most of which are now lost. The more thoroughly it is examined the more trustworthy it will be found to be."

The following summary of the Pârsî system is mostly derived from the Bundehesch, and the later writings of the Pârsîs. We have abridged it from Rhode. In the time of Zoroaster himself, it was probably far from being so fully elaborated. Only the germs of it are to be found in the elder books of the Avesta. It has been doubted if the doctrine of Zerâna-Akerana, or the Monad behind the Duad, is to be found in the Avesta; though important texts in the Vendidad † seem indeed to imply a Supreme

---

* Zoroast. Stud. 1863.
† Vendidad, Fargard XIX. 33, 44, 55.

and Infinite Being, the creator both of Ormazd and Ahriman.

In the beginning, the Eternal or Absolute Being (Ze-râna-Akerana) produced two other great divine beings. The first, who remained true to him, was Ahura-Mazda, King of Light. The other was Ahriman (Angra-Mainyus), King of Darkness. Ormazd found himself in a world of light and Ahriman in boundless darkness, and the two became antagonists.

The Infinite Being (Zerâna-Akerana) now determined, in order to destroy the evil which Ahriman had caused, to create the visible world by Ormazd; and he fixed its duration at twelve thousand years. This was divided into four periods of three thousand years each. In the first period Ormazd should rule alone; in the second Ahriman should begin to operate, but still be subordinate; in the third they should both rule together; and in the fourth Ahriman should have the ascendency.

Ormazd began the creation by bringing forth the Fereuers (Fravashi). Everything which has been created, or which is to be created, has its Fravashi, which contains the reason and basis of its existence. Even Ormazd has his Fravashi in relation to Zerâna-Akerana (the Infinite). A spiritual and invisible world preceded, therefore, this visible material world as its prototype.

In creating the material world, which was in reality only an incorporation of the spiritual world of Fravashis, Ormazd first created the firm vault of heaven, and the earth on which it rests. On the earth he created the high mountain Albordj * which soared upward through all the spheres of the heaven, till it reached the primal light, and Ormazd made this summit his abode. From this summit the bridge Chinevat stretches to the vault of heaven, and to Gorodman, which is the opening in the vault above Albordj. Gorodman is the dwelling of the Fravashis and

---

* The Albordj of the Zend books is doubtless the modern range of the Elbrooz. This mighty chain comes from the Caucasus into the northern frontier of Persia. See a description of this region in "Histoire des Perses, par le Comte de Gobineau. Paris, 1869."

of the blessed, and the bridge leading to it is precisely above the abyss Duzahk, — the monstrous gulf, the home of Ahriman beneath the earth.

Ormazd, who knew that after the first period his battle with Ahriman would begin, armed himself, and created for his aid the whole shining host of heaven, — sun, moon, and stars, — mighty beings of light, wholly submissive to him. First he created "the heroic runner, who never dies, the sun," and made him king and ruler of the material world. From Albordj he sets out on his course, he circles the earth in the highest spheres of heaven, and at evening returns. Then he created the moon, which " has its own light," which, departing from Albordj, circles the earth in a lower sphere, and returns ; then the five smaller planets, and the whole host of fixed stars, in the lowest circle of the heavens. The space between the earth and the firm vault of heaven is therefore divided into three spheres, that of the sun, of the moon, and of the stars.

The host of stars — common soldiers in the war with Ahriman — was divided into four troops, with each its appointed leader. Twelve companies were arranged in the twelve signs of the zodiac. All these were grouped into four great divisions, in the east, west, north, and south. The planet Tistrya (Jupiter) presides over and watches that in the east, and is named Prince of the Stars ; Sitavisa (Saturn) presides over the western division ; Vanant (or Mercury) over that of the south ; and Hapto-iringa (Mars) over the stars of the north. In the middle of the heavens is the great star Mesch, Meschgah (Venus). He leads them against Ahriman.

The dog Sirius (Sura) is another watchman of the heavens ; but he is fixed to one place, at the bridge Chinevat, keeping guard over the abyss out of which Ahriman comes.

When Ormazd had completed these preparations in the heavens, the first of the four ages drew to an end, and Ahriman saw, from the gloomy depths of his kingdom, what Ormazd had done. In opposition to this light creation, he created a world of darkness, a terrible community, equal in number and power to the beings of light. Ormazd, knowing all the misery that Ahriman would cause, yet knowing that the victory would remain with himself, offered to Ahriman peace ; but Ahriman chose war. But, blinded by Ormazd's majesty, and terrified by the sight of the pure Fravashis of holy men, he was conquered by Ormazd's strong word, and sank back into the abyss of darkness, where he lay fettered during the three thousand years of the second period.

Ormazd now completed his creation upon the earth. Sapandomad was guardian spirit of the earth, and the earth, as Hethra, was mother of all living. Khordad was chief of the seasons, years, months, and days, and also protector of the water which flowed from the fountain Anduisur, from Albordj. The planet Tistrya was commissioned to raise the water in vapor, collect it in clouds, and let it fall in rain, with the aid of the planet Sitavisa. These cloud-compellers were highly reverenced. Amerdad was general deity of vegetation ; but the great Mithra was the god of fructification and reproduction in the whole organic world ; his work was to lead the Fravashis to the bodies they were to occupy.

Everything earthly in the light-world of Ormazd had its protecting deity. These guardian spirits were divided into series and groups, had their captains and their associated assistants. The seven Amshaspands (in Zend, Amĕsha-çpentas) were the chief among these, of whom Ormazd was first. The other six were Bahman, King of Heaven ; Ardibehescht, King of Fire ; Schariver, King of the Metals ; Sapandomad, Queen of the Earth ; Amerdad, King of Vegetables ; and Khordad, King of Water.

So ended the second age. In it Ormazd had also produced the great primitive Bull, in which, as the representative of the animal world, the seeds of all living creatures were deposited.

While Ormazd was thus completing his light-creation, Ahriman, in his dark abyss, was effecting a corresponding creation of darkness, — making a corresponding evil being for every good being created by Ormazd. These spirits of night stood in their ranks and orders, with their seven presiding evil spirits, or Daêvas, corresponding to the Amshaspands.

The vast preparations for this great war being completed, and the end of the second age now coming, Ahriman was urged by one of his Daêvas to begin the conflict. He counted his host ; but as he found nothing therein to oppose to the Fravashis of good men, he sank back in dejection. Finally the second age expired, and Ahriman now sprang aloft without fear, for he knew that his time was come. His host followed him, but he alone succeeded in reaching the heavens ; his troops remained behind. A shudder ran over him, and he sprang from heaven upon the earth in the form of a serpent, penetrated to its centre, and entered into everything which he found upon it. He passed into the primal Bull, and even into fire, the visible symbol of Ormazd, defiling it with smoke and vapor. Then he assailed the heavens, and a part of the stars were already in his power, and veiled in smoke and mist, when he was attacked by Ormazd, aided by the Fravashis of holy men ; and after ninety days and ninety nights he was completely defeated, and driven back with his troops into the abyss of Duzahk.

But he did not remain there, for through the middle of the earth he built a way for himself and his companions, and is now living on the earth together with Ormazd, — according to the decree of the Infinite.

The destruction which he produced in the world was terrible. Nevertheless, the more evil he tried to do, the more he ignorantly fulfilled the counsels of the Infinite, and hastened the development of good. Thus he entered the Bull, the original animal, and injured him so that he died. But when he died, Kaiomarts, the first man, came out of his right shoulder, and from his left Goshurun, the soul of the Bull, who now became the guardian spirit of the animal race. Also the whole realm of clean animals and plants came from the Bull's body. Full of rage, Ahriman now created the unclean animals, — for every clean beast an unclean. Thus Ormazd created the dog, Ahriman the wolf ; Ormazd all useful animals, Ahriman all noxious ones ; and so of plants.

But to Kaiomarts, the original man, Ahriman had nothing to oppose, and so he determined to kill him.

Kaiomarts was both man and woman, but through his death there came from him the first human pair ; a tree grew from his body, and bore ten pair of men and women. Meschia and Meschiane were the. first. They were originally innocent and made for heaven, and worshipped Ormazd as their creator. But Ahriman tempted them. They drank milk from a goat and so injured themselves. Then Ahriman brought them fruit, they ate it, and lost a hundred parts of their happiness, so that only one remained. The woman was the first to sacrifice to the Daêvas. After fifty years they had two children, Siamak and Veschak, and died a hundred years old. For their sins they remain in hell until the resurrection.

The human race, which had thus become mortal and miserable by the sin of its first parents, assumed nevertheless a highly interesting position. The man stands in the middle between the two worlds of light and darkness, left to his own free will. As a creature of Ormazd he can and ought to honor him, and assist him in the war with evil ; but Ahriman and his Daêvas surround him night and day, and seek to mislead him, in order to increase thereby the power of darkness. He would not be able at all to resist these temptations, to which his first parents had already yielded, had not Ormazd taken pity on him, and sent him a revelation of his will in the law of Zoroaster. If he obeys these precepts he is safe from the Daêvas, under the immediate protection of Ormazd. The substance of the law is the command, " THINK PURELY, SPEAK PURELY, ACT PURELY." All that comes from Ormazd is pure, from Ahriman impure ; and bodily purity has a like worth with moral purity. Hence the multitude and minuteness of precepts concerning bodily cleanliness. In fact the whole liturgic worship turns greatly on this point.

The Fravashis of men originally created by Ormazd are preserved in heaven, in Ormazd's realm of light. But they must come from heaven, to be united with a human body, and to go on a path of probation in this world, called the " Way of the Two Destinies." Those who have chosen the good in this world are received after death by good spirits, and guided, under the protection of the dog Sura, to the bridge Chinevat ; the wicked are dragged thither by the Daêvas.   Here Ormazd holds a tribunal and decides the fate of the souls.   The good pass the bridge into the mansions of the blessed, where they are welcomed with rejoicing by the Amshaspands ; the bad fall over into the Gulf of Duzahk, where they are tormented by the Daêvas.   The duration of the punishment is fixed by Ormazd, and some are redeemed earlier by means of the prayers and intercessions of their friends, but many must remain till the resurrection of the dead.

Ahriman himself effects this consummation, after having exercised great power over men during the last three thousand years.   He created seven comets (in opposition to the seven planets), and they went on their destructive paths through the heavens, filling all things with danger, and all men with terror.   But Ormazd placed them under the control of his planets to restrain them.   They will do so, till by the decree of the Infinite, at the close of the last period, one of the comets will break from his watchman, the moon, and plunge upon the earth, producing a general conflagration.   But before this Ormazd will send his Prophet Sosioçh and bring about the conversion of mankind, to be followed by the general resurrection.

Ormazd will clothe anew with flesh the bones of men, and relatives and friends will recognize each other again. Then comes the great division of the just from the sinners.

When Ahriman shall cause the comet to fall on the earth to gratify his destructive propensities, he will be really serving the Infinite Being against his own will. For the conflagration caused by this comet will change the whole earth into a stream like melted iron, which will pour impetuously down into the realm of Ahriman.   All beings must now pass through this stream : to the righteous it will feel like warm milk, and they will pass through to the dwellings of the just ; but all the sinners shall be borne along by the stream into the abyss of Duzahk.   Here they will burn three days and nights , then, being purified, they will invoke Ormazd, and be received into heaven.

Afterward Ahriman himself and all in the Duzahk shall be purified by this fire, all evil be consumed, and all darkness banished.

From the extinct fire there will come a more beautiful earth, pure and perfect, and destined to be eternal.

Having given this account of the Pârsî system, in its later development, let us say that it was not an *invention* of Zoroaster, nor of any one else. Religions are not invented: they grow. Even the religion of Mohammed grew out of pre-existent beliefs. The founder of a religion does not invent it, but gives it form. It crystallizes around his own deeper thought. So, in the time of Zoroaster, the popular imagination had filled nature with powers and presences, and given them names, and placed them in the heavens. For, as Schiller says : —

> " 'T is not merely
> The human being's pride which peoples space
> With life and mystical predominance ;
> For also for the stricken heart of Love,
> This visible nature and this lower world
> Are all too common."

Zoroaster organized into clearer thought the pre-existing myths, and inspired them with moral ideas and vital power.

§ 8. *Relation of the Religion of the Zend Avesta to that of the Vedas.*

That the Vedic religion and that of the Avesta arose out of an earlier Aryan religion, monotheistic in its central element, but with a tendency to immerse the Deity in nature, seems evident from the investigations of Pictet and other scholars. This primitive religion of the Aryan race diverged early in two directions, represented by the Veda and the Avesta. Yet each retains much in common with the other. The names of the powers, Indra, Sura, Nâoghaithya, are in both systems. In the Veda they are gods, in the Avesta evil spirits. Indra, worshipped

9 *

throughout the Rig-Veda as one of the highest deities, appears in the Avesta as an evil being.* Sura (Çura), one of the most ancient names of Shiva, is also denounced and opposed in the Avesta † as a Daêva, or Dew. And the third (Nâoghaithya, Nâouhaiti), also an evil spirit in the Avesta, is the Nâsatya of the Veda, ‡ one of the Aç-vinas or twins who precede the Dawn. The Dews or Daêvas of the Avesta are demons, in the Vedas they are gods. On the other hand, the Ahuras, or gods, of the Avesta are Asuras, or demons, in the Vedic belief. The original land of the race is called Aryavesta in the Laws of Manu (II. 22), and Aryana-Vaêjo in the Avesta. The God of the Sun is named Mithra, or Mitra, in both religions. The Yima of the Pârsî system is a happy king; the Yama of the Hindoos is a stern judge in the realms of death. The dog is hateful in the Indian system, an object of reverence in that of Zoroaster. Both the religions dread defilement through the touch of dead bodies. In both systems fire is regarded as divine. But the most striking analogy perhaps is to be found in the worship paid by both to the intoxicating fermented juice of the plant *Asclepias acida*, called Soma in the Sanskrit and Haŏma in the Zend. The identity of the Haŏma with the Indian Soma has long been proved.§ The whole of the Sáma-Veda is devoted to this moon-plant worship; an important part of the Avesta is occupied with hymns to Haŏma. This great reverence paid to the same plant, on account of its intoxicating qualities, carries us back to a region where the vine was unknown, and to a race to whom intoxication was so new an experience as to seem a gift of the gods. Wisdom appeared to come from it, health, increased power of body and soul, long life, victory in battle, brilliant children. What Bacchus was to the Greeks, this divine Haŏma, or Soma, was to the primitive Aryans. ‖

* See Burnouf, Comment. sur le Yaçna, p. 528. Flotard, La Religion primitive des Indo-Européens. 1864.
† Vendidad, Fargard X. 17.
‡ See Spiegel's note to the tenth Fargard of the Vendidad.
§ See Windischmann, "Ueber den Soma-Cultus der Arien."
‖ Perhaps one of the most widely diffused appellations is that of the

It would seem, therefore, that the two religions setting out from the same point, and having a common stock of primitive traditions, at last said each to the other, " Your gods are my demons." .The opposition was mutual. The dualism of the Persian was odious to the Hindoo, while the absence of a deep moral element in the Vedic system shocked the solemn puritanism of Zoroaster. The religion of the Hindoo was to dream, that of the Persian to fight. There could be no more fellowship between them than there is between a Quaker and a Calvinist.

§ 9. *Is Monotheism or pure Dualism the Doctrine of the Zend Avesta ?*

We find in the Avesta, and in the oldest portion of it, the tendencies which resulted afterward in the elaborate theories of the Bundehesch. We find the Zeârna-Akerana, in the Vendidad (XIX. 33, 44, 55), — " The Infinite Time," or " All-embracing Time," — as the creator of Ahriman, according to some translations. Spiegel, indeed, considers this supreme being, above both Ormazd and Ahriman, as not belonging to the original Persian religion, but as borrowed from Semitic sources. But if so, then Ormazd is the supreme and uncreated being, and creator of all things. Why, then, has Ormazd a Fravashi, or archetype ? And in that case, he must either himself have created Ahriman, or else Ahriman is as eternal as he ; which latter supposition presents us with an absolute, irreconcilable dualism. The better opinion seems, therefore, to be, that behind the two opposing powers of good and evil, the thesis and antithesis of moral life, remains the obscure background of original being, the identity of both, from which both have proceeded, and into whose abyss both shall return.

This great consummation is also intimated by the fact that in the same Fargard of the Vendidad (XIX. 18) the future restorer or saviour is mentioned, Sosioçh (Caoshy-

divine being. We can trace this very word *divine* back to the ancient root *Div*, meaning to shine. From this is derived the Sanskrit Devas, the Zend Daêva, the Latin Deus, the German Zio, the Greek Zeus, and also Jupiter (from Djaus-piter). See Spiegel, Zend Avesta, Einleitung, Cap. I.

anç), who is expected by the Pârsîs to come at the end of all things, and accomplish the resurrection, and introduce a kingdom of untroubled happiness.* Whether the resurrection belongs to the primitive form of the religion remains as doubtful, but also as probable, as when Mr. Alger discussed the whole question in his admirable monograph on the Doctrine of the Future Life. Our remaining fragments of the Zend Avesta say nothing of the periods of three thousand years' duration. Two or three passages in the Avesta refer to the resurrection.† But the conflict between Ormazd and Ahriman, the present struggle between good and evil, the ideal world of the Fravashis and good spirits, — these unquestionably belong to the original belief.

§ 10. Relation of this System to Christianity. The Kingdom of Heaven.

Of this system we will say, in conclusion, that in some respects it comes nearer to Christianity than any other. Moreover, though so long dead, like the great nation of which it was the inspiration and life, — though swept away by Mohammedanism, — its influence remains, and has permeated both Judaism and Christianity. Christianity has probably received from it, through Judaism, its doctrine of angels and devils, and its tendency to establish evil in the world as the permanent and equal adversary of good. Such a picture as that by Retzsch of the Devil playing chess with the young man for his soul, such a picture as that by Guido of the conflict between Michael and Satan, such poems as Milton's Paradise Lost and Goethe's Faust, could perhaps never have appeared in Christendom, had it not been for the influence of the system of Zoroaster on Jewish, and, through Jewish, on Christian thought. It was after the return from Babylon that the Devil and demons, in conflict with men, became a part of the company of spiritual beings in the Jewish mythology. Angels there were before, as messengers of God, but devils there

---

* Spiegel, Vend. Farg. XIX. note.
† Vendidad, Farg. XVIII. 110.　Farvardin-Yasht, XVI.

were not ; for till then an absolute Providence ruled the world, excluding all interference of antagonistic powers. Satan, in Job, is an angel of God, not a devil; doing a low kind of work, indeed, a sort of critical business, fault-finding, and looking for flaws in the saints, but still an angel, and no devil. But after the captivity the horizon of the Jewish mind enlarged, and it took in the conception of God as allowing freedom to man and angels, and so permitting bad as well as good to have its way. And then came in also the conception of a future life, and a resurrection for ultimate judgment. These doctrines have been supposed, with good reason, to have come to the Jews from the influence of the great system of Zoroaster.

There is no doubt, however, that the Jewish prophets had already prepared a point of contact and attachment for this system, and developed affinities therewith, by their great battle-cry to the nation for right against wrong, and their undying conviction of an ultimate restoration of all good things. But the Jews found also in the Persian faith the one among all religions most like their own, in this, that it had no idols, and no worship but that addressed to the Unseen. Sun and fire were his symbols, but he himself was hidden behind the glorious veil of being. And it seems as if the Jews needed this support of finding another nation also hating idolatry, before they could really rise above their tendency to backslide into it. " In the mouth of two witnesses," the spiritual worship of God was established ; and not till Zoroaster took the hand of Moses did the Jews cease to be idolaters. After the return from the captivity that tendency wholly disappears.

But a deeper and more essential point of agreement is to be found in the special practical character of the two systems, regarding life as a battle between right and wrong, waged by a communion of good men fighting against bad men and bad principles.

Perhaps, in reading the New Testament, we do not always see how much Christianity turns around the

phrase, and the idea behind it, of a " kingdom of Heaven."
The Beatitudes begin " Blessed are the poor in spirit, for
theirs is the kingdom of Heaven."   Both John the Baptist and Christ announce that the *kingdom of Heaven* is at
hand.   The parables revolve round the same idea of " the
kingdom." which is likened first to this, and then to that ;
and so, passing on into the Epistles, we have the " kingdom of Heaven " still as the leading conception of Christianity.   " The kingdom of God is not meat nor drink " ;
— such are common expressions.

The peculiar conception of the Messiah also is of the
King, the Anointed one, the Head of this divine Monarchy.   When we call Jesus the Christ, we repeat this
ancient notion of the kingdom of God among men.   He
himself accepted it ; he called himself the Christ. " Thou
sayest," said he, to Pilate, " that I am a king.   To this
end was I born, and for this cause came I into the world,
that I should bear witness unto the truth."

All through antiquity there ran the longing for a communion or association of the wise and good, in order
to establish truth and justice in the world.   The tendency
of error is to divide ; the tendency of selfishness is to separation.   Only goodness and truth are capable of real communion, interpenetration, and so of organic life and growth.
This is their strength, power, and hope.   Hence all the
efforts at associated action in antiquity, such as the College of Pythagoras, the ideal Republic of Plato, the Spartan
Commonwealth, the communities of the Essenes, the monastic institutions of Asia and Europe ; and hence, too, the
modern attempts, in Protestantism, by Fourier, the Mora-
vians, the Shakers, Saint-Simon, Robert Owen, and others.

But among the Jews this desire appeared, first in their
national organization, as a theosophic and theocratic community, and afterward, when this broke down and the
nation was divided, in a larger prophetic hope of the Mes-
sianic times.   There is a tendency in the human mind,
when it sees a great work to be done, to look for a leader.
So the Jewish hope looked for a leader.   Their true King
was to come, and under him peace and righteousness were
to reign, and the kingdom of heaven begin on earth.   It

was to be on earth. It was to be here and now. And so they waited and longed.

Meantime, in the Persian religion, the seed of the same hope was sown. There also the work of life was, to unite together a community of good men and good angels, against bad men and devils, and so make a kingdom of heaven. Long and sore should the conflict be; but the victory at last would be sure. And they also looked for a Sosioch, or Mediator, who was to be what the Messiah was to be to the Jews. And here was the deep and real point of union between the two religions; and this makes the profound meaning of the story of the Star which was seen in the East and which guided the Magi of Zoroaster to the cradle of Christ.

Jesus came to be the Messiah. He fulfilled that great hope as he did others. It was not fulfilled, in the sense of the letter of a prophecy being acted out, but in the sense of the prophecy being carried up and on to its highest point, and so being filled full of truth and value. The first and chief purpose of Christianity was, not to save the souls of men hereafter, as the Church has often taught, but to found a kingdom of heaven here, on earth and in time. It was not to say, "Lo here!" or "Lo there!" but to say, "*Now* is the accepted time"; "the kingdom of God is among you." In thus continuing and developing to its highest point the central idea of his national religion, Jesus made himself the true Christ and fulfilled all the prophecies. Perhaps what we need now is to come back to that notion of the kingdom of heaven here below, and of Jesus the present king, — present, because still bearing witness to the truth. Christians must give up thinking about Christianity as only a means of escaping a future hell and arriving at a future heaven. They must show now, more than ever, that, by a union of loving and truthful hearts, God comes here, immortality begins here, and heaven lies about us. To fight the good fight of justice and truth, as the disciples of Zoroaster tried to fight it, — this is still the true work of man ; and to make a union of those who wish thus to fight for good against evil, — this is still the true church of Christ.

The old religion of Zoroaster died, but as the corn of wheat, which, if it die, brings forth much fruit.

A small body of Pârsîs remain to-day in Persia, and another in India, — disciples of this venerable faith. They are a good, moral, industrious people. Some of them are very wealthy and very generous. Until Mr. George Peabody's large donations, no one had bestowed so much on public objects as Sir Jamsetjee Jeejeeboy, who had given to hospitals, schools, and charities, some years since, a million and a half of dollars. During our Rebellion, some of the Pârsîs sent gifts to the Sanitary Commission, out of sympathy with the cause of freedom and Union.

Who can estimate the power of a single life? Of Zoroaster we do not know the true name, nor when he lived, nor where he lived, nor exactly what he taught. But the current from that fountain has flowed on for thousands of years, fertilizing the souls of men out of its hidden sources, and helping on, by the decree of Divine Providence, the ultimate triumph of good over evil, right over wrong.

CHAPTER VI.

THE GODS OF EGYPT.

§ 1. *Antiquity and Extent of Egyptian Civilization.*

THE ancient Egyptians have been the object of interest to the civilized world in all ages ; for Egypt was the favorite home of civilization, science, and religion. It was a little country, the gift of the river Nile ; a little strip of land not more than seven miles wide, but containing innumerable cities and towns, and in ancient times supporting seven millions of inhabitants. Renowned for its discoveries in art and science, it was the world's university ; where Moses and Pythagoras, Herodotus and Plato, all philosophers and lawgivers, went to school. The Egyptians knew the length of the year and the form of the earth ; they could calculate eclipses of the sun and moon ; were partially acquainted with geometry, music, chemistry, the arts of design, medicine, anatomy, architecture, agriculture, and mining. In architecture, in the qualities of grandeur and massive proportions, they are yet to be surpassed. The largest buildings elsewhere erected by man are smaller than their pyramids ; which are also the oldest human works still remaining, the beauty of whose masonry, says Wilkinson, has not been surpassed in any subsequent age. An obelisk of a single stone now standing in Egypt weighs three hundred tons, and a colossus of Ramses II. nearly nine hundred. But Herodotus describes a monolithic temple, which must have weighed five thousand tons, and which was carried the whole length of the Nile, to the Delta. And there is a roof of a doorway at Karnak, covered with sandstone blocks forty feet long. Sculpture and bas-reliefs three thousand five hundred years old, where the granite is cut with exquisite delicacy, are still to be seen throughout Egypt. Many inventions, hitherto supposed to be modern, such as glass, mosaics, false gems, glazed tiles, enamelling, were well known to the Egyptians. But, for us, the most fortunate circumstance in their taste was their fondness for writing. No nation has ever equalled them in their love for recording all human events and transactions. They wrote down all the details of private life with wonderful zeal, method, and regularity. Every year, month, and day had its record, and thus Egypt is the monumental land of the earth. Bunsen says that "the genuine Egyptian writing is at least as old as Menes, the founder of the Empire; perhaps three thousand years before Christ." No other human records, whether of India or China, go back so far. Lepsius saw the hieroglyph of the reed and inkstand on the monuments of the fourth dynasty, and the sign of the papyrus roll on that of the twelfth dynasty, which was the last but one of the old Empire. "No Egyptian," says Herodotus, "omits taking accurate note of extraordinary and striking events." Everything was written down. Scribes are seen everywhere on the monuments, taking accounts of the products of the farms, even to every single egg and chicken. "In spite of the ravages of time, and though systematic excavation has scarcely yet commenced," says Bunsen, "we possess chronological records of a date anterior to any period of which manuscripts are preserved, or the art of writing existed in any other quarter." Because they were thus fond of recording everything, both in pictures and in three different kinds of writing; because they were also fond of building and excavating temples and tombs in the imperishable granite; because, lastly, the dryness of the air has preserved for us these paintings, and the sand which has buried the monuments has prevented their destruction, — we have wonderfully preserved, over an interval of forty-five centuries, the daily habits, the opinions, and the religious faith of that ancient time.

The oldest mural paintings disclose a state of the arts of civilization so advanced as to surprise even those who have made archæology a study, and who consequently know how few new things there are under the sun. It is *not* astonishing to find houses with doors and windows, with verandas, with barns for grain, vineyards, gardens, fruit-trees, etc. We might also expect, since man is a fighting animal, to see, as we do, pictures of marching troops, armed with spears and shields, bows, slings, daggers, axes, maces, and the boomerang; or to notice coats of mail, standards, war-chariots; or to find the assault of forts by means of scaling-ladders. But these ancient tombs also exhibit to us scenes of domestic life and manners which would seem to belong to the nineteenth century after our era, rather than to the fifteenth century before it. Thus we see monkeys trained to gather fruit from the trees in an orchard; houses furnished with a great variety of chairs, tables, ottomans, carpets, couches, as elegant and elaborate as any used now. There are comic and *genre* pictures of parties, where the gentlemen and ladies are sometimes represented as being the worse for wine; of dances where ballet-girls in short dresses perform very modern-looking pirouettes; of exercises in wrestling, games of ball, games of chance like chess or checkers, of throwing knives at a mark, of the modern thimblerig, wooden dolls for children, curiously carved wooden boxes, dice, and toy-balls. There are men and women playing on harps, flutes, pipes, cymbals, trumpets, drums, guitars, and tambourines. Glass was, till recently, believed to be a modern invention, unknown to the ancients. But we find it commonly used as early as the age of Osertasen I., more than three thousand eight hundred years ago; and we have pictures of glass-blowing and of glass bottles as far back as the fourth dynasty. The best Venetian glass-workers are unable to rival some of the old Egyptian work; for the Egyptians could combine all colors in one cup, introduce gold between two surfaces of glass, and finish in glass details of feathers, etc., which it now requires a microscope to make out. It is evident, therefore, that they understood the use of the magnifying-glass. The Egyptians also imitated successfully the colors of precious stones, and could even make statues thirteen feet high, closely resembling an emerald. They also made mosaics in glass, of wonderfully brilliant colors. They could cut glass, at the most remote periods. Chinese bottles have also been found in previously unopened tombs of the eighteenth dynasty, indicating commercial intercourse reaching as far back as that epoch. They were able to spin and weave, and color cloth; and were acquainted with the use of mordants, the wonder in modern calico-printing. Pliny describes this process as used in Egypt, but evidently without understanding its nature. Writing-paper made of the papyrus is as old as the Pyramids. The Egyptians tanned leather and made shoes; and the shoemakers on their benches are represented working exactly like ours. Their carpenters used axes, saws, chisels, drills, planes, rulers, plummets, squares, hammers, nails, and hones for sharpening. They also understood the use of glue in cabinet-making, and there are paintings of veneering, in which a piece of thin dark wood is fastened by glue to a coarser piece of light wood. Their boats were propelled by sails on yards and masts, as well as by oars. They used the blow-pipe in the manufacture of gold chains and other ornaments. They had rings of gold and silver for money, and weighed it in scales of a careful construction. Their hieroglyphics are carved on the hardest granite with a delicacy and accuracy which indicates the use of some metallic cutting instrument, probably harder than our best steel. The siphon was known in the fifteenth century before Christ. The most singular part of their costume was the wig, worn by all the higher classes, who constantly shaved their heads, as well as their chins, — which shaving of the head is supposed by Herodotus to be the reason of the thickness of the Egyptian skull. They frequently wore false beards. Sandals, shoes, and low boots, some very elegant, are found in the tombs. Women wore loose robes, ear-rings, finger-rings, bracelets, armlets, anklets, gold necklaces. In the tombs are found vases for ointment, mirrors, combs, needles. Doctors and drugs were not unknown to them; and the passport system is no modern invention, for their deeds contain careful descriptions of the person, exactly in the style with which European travellers are familiar. We have only mentioned a small part of the customs and arts with which the tombs of the Egyptians show them to have been familiar. These instances are mostly taken from Wilkinson, whose works contain numerous engravings from the monuments which more than verify all we have said.

The celebrated French Egyptologist, M. Mariette, has very much enlarged our knowledge of the more ancient dynasties, by his explorations, first under a mission from the French government, and afterward from that of Egypt. The immense temples and palaces of Thebes are all of a date at least B. C. 1000. We know the history of Egypt very well as far back as the time of the Hyksôs, or to the eighteenth dynasty. M. Mariette has discovered statues and Sphinxes which he believes to have been the work of the Hyksôs, the features being wholly different from that of the typical Egyptian. Four of these Sphinxes, found by Mariette on the site of the old Tanis, have the regular body of a lion, according to the canon of Egyptian art, but the human heads are wholly un-Egyptian. Mariette, in describing them, says that in the true Egyptian Sphinx there is always a quiet majesty, the eye calm and wide open, a smile on the lips, a round face, and a peculiar coiffure with wide open wings. Nothing of this is to be found in these Sphinxes. Their eyes are small, the nose aquiline, the cheeks hard, the mouth drawn down with a grave expression.

These Shepherd Kings, the Hyksôs, ruled Lower Egypt, according to Manetho, five hundred and eleven years, which, according to Renan,* brings the preceding dynasty (the fourteenth of Manetho) as early as B. C. 2000. Monuments of the twelfth and thirteenth dynasties are common. The oldest obelisk dates B. C. 2800. Thanks to the excavations of M. Mariette, we now have a large quantity

* Article in Revue des Deux Mondes, April, 1865

of sculptures and statues of a still earlier epoch. **M.**
Renan describes * tombs visited by himself, which he considers to be the oldest known, and which he regards as
being B. C. 4000, † where were represented all the details
of domestic life. The tone of these pictures was glad and
gay ; and, what is remarkable, they had no trace of the
funeral ritual or the god Osiris. These were not like
tombs, but rather like homes. To secure the body from all
profanation, it was concealed in a pit, carefully hidden
in the solid masonry. These tombs belong to the six
first dynasties.

The great antiquity of Egyptian civilization is universally admitted ; but to fix its chronology and precise age
becomes very difficult, from the fact that the Egyptians
had no era from which to date forward or backward.
This question we shall return to in a subsequent section
of this chapter.

§ 2. *Religious Character of the Egyptians. Their Ritual.*

But, wonderful as was the civilization of Egypt, it is
not this which now chiefly interests us. They were
prominent among all ancient nations for their interest in
religion, especially of the ceremonial part of religion, or
worship. Herodotus says : " They are of all men the
most excessively attentive to the worship of the gods."
And beside his statement to that effect, there is evidence
that the origin of much of the theology, mythology, and
ceremonies of the Hebrews and Greeks was in Egypt.
" The names of almost all the gods," says Herodotus, " came
from Egypt into Greece " (Euterpe, 50). The Greek oracles, especially that of Dodona, he also states to have
been brought from Egypt (II. 54 – 57), and adds, moreover, that the Egyptians were the first who introduced
public festivals, processions, and solemn supplications,
which the Greeks learned from them. " The Egyptians,
then," says he, " are beyond measure scrupulous in matters

* Article in Revue des Deux Mondes, April, 1865.
† Other Egyptologists would not agree to this antiquity.

of religion (§ 64). They invented the calendar, and connected astrology therewith. " Each month and day," says Herodotus (II. 82), " is assigned to some particular god, and each person's birthday determines his fate." He testifies (II. 123) that " the Egyptians were also the first to say that the soul of man is immortal, and that when the body perishes it transmigrates through every variety of animal." It seems apparent, also, that the Greek mysteries of Eleusis were taken from those of Isis ; the story of the wanderings of Ceres in pursuit of Proserpine being manifestly borrowed from those of Isis in search of the body of Osiris. With this testimony of Herodotus modern writers agree. " The Egyptians," says Wilkinson, " were unquestionably the most pious nation of all antiquity. The oldest monuments show their belief in a future life. And Osiris, the Judge, is mentioned in tombs erected two thousand years before Christ." Bunsen tells us that " it has at last been ascertained that all the great gods of Egypt are on the oldest monuments," and says : " It is a great and astounding fact, established beyond the possibility of doubt, that the empire of Menes on its first appearance in history possessed an established mythology, that is, a series of gods. Before the empire of Menes, the separate Egyptian states had their temple worship regularly organized."

Everything among the Egyptians, says M. Maury,* took the stamp of religion. Their writing was so full of sacred symbols that it could scarcely be used for any purely secular purpose. Literature and science were only branches of theology. Art labored only in the service of worship and to glorify the gods. Religious observances were so numerous and so imperative, that the most common labors of daily life could not be performed without a perpetual reference to some priestly regulation. The Egyptian only lived to worship. His fate in the future life was constantly present to him. The sun, when it set, seemed to him to die ; and when it rose the next morning, and tricking its beams flamed once more in the forehead of the sky, it was a perpetual symbol of a future

* Revue des Deux Mondes, September 1, 1867.

resurrection. Religion penetrated so deeply into the habits of the land, that it almost made a part of the intellectual and physical organization of its inhabitants. Habits continued during many generations at last become instincts, and are transmitted with the blood.* So religion in Egypt became an instinct. Unaltered by the dominion of the Persians, the Ptolemies, and Romans, it was, of all polytheisms, the most obstinate in its resistance to Christianity, and retained its devotees down to the sixth century of our era.†

There were more festivals in Egypt than among any other ancient people, the Greeks not excepted. Every month and day was governed by a god. There were two feasts of the New-Year, twelve of the first days of the months, one of the rising of the dog-star (Sirius, called Sothis), and others to the great gods, to seed-time and harvest, to the rise and fall of the Nile. The feast of lamps at Sais was in honor of Neith, and was kept throughout Egypt. ‡ The feast of the death of Osiris; the feast of his resurrection (when people called out, "We have found him! Good luck!"); feasts of Isis (one of which lasted four days); the great feast at Bubastis, greatest of all, — these were festivals belonging to all Egypt. On one of them as many as seven hundred thousand persons sailed on the Nile with music. At another, the image of the god was carried to the temple by armed men, who were resisted by armed priests in a battle in which many were often killed.

The history of the gods was embodied in the daily life of the people. In an old papyrus described by De Rougé,§ it is said : " On the twelfth of Chorák no one is to go out

* Revue des Deux Mondes, p. 195.

† Yet this very organic religion, "incorporate in blood and frame," was a preparation for Christianity ; and Dr. Brugsch (Aus dem Orient, p. 73) remarks, that "exactly in Egypt did Christianity find most martyrs ; and it is no accident, but a part of the Divine plan, that in the very region where the rock-cut temples and tombs are covered with memorials of the ancient gods and kings, there, by their side, other numerous rock-cut inscriptions tell of a yet more profound faith and devotion born of Christianity."

‡ It is yet marked in the almanacs as Candlemas Day, or the Purification of the Virgin Mary.

§ De Rougé, Revue Archéologique, 1853.

of doors, for on that day the transformation of Osiris into the bird Wennu took place ; on the fourteenth of Toby no voluptuous songs must be listened to, for Isis and Nepthys bewail Osiris on that day. On the third of Mechir no one can go on a journey, because Set then began a war." On another day no one must go out. Another was lucky, because on it the gods conquered Set ; and a child born on that day was supposed to live to a great age.

Every temple had its own body of priests. They did not constitute an exclusive caste, though they were continued in families. Priests might be military commanders, governors of provinces, judges, and architects. Soldiers had priests for sons, and the daughters of priests married soldiers. Of three brothers, one was a priest, another a soldier, and a third held a civil employment.* Joseph, a stranger, though naturalized in the country, received as a wife the daughter of the High-Priest of On, or Heliopolis.

The priests in Egypt were of various grades, as the chief priests or pontiffs, prophets, judges, scribes, those who examined the victims, keepers of the robes, of the sacred animals, etc.

Women also held offices in the temple and performed duties there, though not as priestesses.

The priests were exempt from taxes, and were provided for out of the public stores. They superintended sacrifices, processions, funerals, and were initiated into the greater and lesser mysteries ; they were also instructed in surveying. They were particular in diet, both as to quantity and quality. Flesh of swine was particularly forbidden, and also that of fish. Beans were held in utter abhorrence, also peas, onions, and garlic, which, however, were offered on the altar. They bathed twice a day and twice in the night, and shaved the head and body every three days. A great purification took place before their fasts, which lasted from seven to forty-two days.

They offered prayers for the dead.

The dress of the priests was simple, chiefly of linen, consisting of an under-garment and a loose upper robe,

---

* Ampère, Revue Arch. 1849, quoted by Döllinger.

with full sleeves, and the leopard-skin above ; sometimes one or two feathers in the head.

Chaplets and flowers were laid upon the altars, such as the lotus and papyrus, also grapes and figs in baskets, and ointment in alabaster vases. Also necklaces, bracelets, and jewelry, were offered as thanksgivings and invocations.

Oxen and other animals were sacrificed, and the blood allowed to flow over the altar. Libations of wine were poured on the altar. Incense was offered to all the gods in censers.

Processions were usual with the Egyptians ; in one, shrines were carried on the shoulders by long staves passed through rings. In others the statues of the gods were carried, and arks like those of the Jews, overshadowed by the wings of the goddess of truth spread above the sacred beetle.

The prophets were the most highly honored of the priestly order. They studied the ten hieratical books. The business of the stolists * was to dress and undress the images, to attend to the vestments of the priests, and to mark the beasts selected for sacrifice. The scribes were to search for the Apis, or sacred bull, and were required to possess great learning.

The priests had no sinecure ; their life was full of minute duties and restrictions. They seldom appeared in public, were married to one wife, were circumcised like other Egyptians, and their whole time was occupied either in study or the service of their gods. There was a gloomy tone to the religion of Egypt, which struck the Greeks, whose worship was usually cheerful. Apuleius says " the gods of Egypt rejoice in lamentations, those of Greece in dances." Another Greek writer says, " The Egyptians offer their gods tears."

Until Swedenborg † arrived, and gave his disciples the

---

* These designations are the Greek form of the official titles.

† I do not know if it has been noticed that the principle of Sweden-borg's heaven was anticipated by Milton (Paradise Lost, V. 573), —

> " What surmounts the reach
> Of human sense I shall delineate so
> By likening spiritual to corporeal forms,
> As may express them best ; *though what if Earth
> Be but the shadow of Heaven, and things therein,
> Each to the other like, more than on earth is thought.*"

precise measure and form of the life to come, no religion has ever taught an immortality as distinct in its outline and as solid in its substance as that of the Egyptians. The Greek and Roman hereafter was shadowy and vague ; that of Buddhism remote ; and the Hebrew Beyond was wholly eclipsed and overborne by the sense of a Divine presence and power immanent in space and time. To the Egyptian, this life was but the first step, and a very short one, of an immense career. The sun (Ra) alternately setting and rising, was the perpetually present type of the progress of the soul, and the Sothiac period (symbolized by the Phœnix) of 1421 years from one heliacal rising of Sirius at the beginning of the fixed Egyptian year to the next, was also made to define the cycle of human transmigrations. Two Sothiac periods correspond nearly to the three thousand years spoken of by Herodotus, during which the soul transmigrates through animal forms before returning to its human body. Then, to use the Egyptian language, the soul arrived at the ship of the sun and was received by Ra into his solar splendor. On some sarcophagi the soul is symbolized by a hawk with a human head, carrying in his claws two rings, which probably signify the two Sothiac cycles of its transmigrations.

The doctrine of the immortality of the soul, says Mr. Birch,* is as old as the inscriptions of the twelfth dynasty, many of which contain extracts from the Ritual of the Dead. One hundred and forty-six chapters of this Ritual have been translated by Mr. Birch from the text of the Turin papyrus, the most complete in Europe. Chapters of it are found on mummy-cases, on the wraps of mummies, on the walls of tombs, and within the coffins on papyri. This Ritual is all that remains of the Hermetic Books which constituted the library of the priesthood. Two antagonist classes of deities appear in this liturgy as contending for the soul of the deceased, — Osiris and his triad, Set and his devils. The Sun-God, source of life, is also present.

An interesting chapter of the Ritual is the one hundred

* Bunsen, Egypt's Place, Vol. V. p. 129, *note.*

and twenty-fifth, called the Hall of the Two Truths. It is the process of " separating a person from his sins," not by confession and repentance, as is usual in other religions, but by denying them. Forty-two deities are said to be present to feed on the blood of the wicked. The soul addresses the Lords of Truth, and declares that it has not done evil privily, and proceeds to specifications. He says : " I have not afflicted any. I have not told falsehoods. I have not made the laboring man do more than his task. I have not been idle. I have not murdered. I have not committed fraud. I have not injured the images of the gods. I have not taken scraps of the bandages of the dead. I have not committed adultery. I have not cheated by false weights. I have not kept milk from sucklings. I have not caught the sacred birds." Then, addressing each god by name, he declares : " I have not been idle. I have not boasted. I have not stolen. I have not counterfeited, nor killed sacred beasts, nor blasphemed, nor refused to hear the truth, nor despised God in my heart." According to some texts, he declares, positively, that he has loved God, that he has given bread to the hungry, water to the thirsty, garments to the naked, and an asylum to the abandoned.

Funeral ceremonies among the Egyptians were often very imposing. The cost of embalming, and the size and strength of the tomb, varied with the position of the deceased. When the seventy days of mourning had elapsed, the body in its case was ferried across the lake in front of the temple, which represented the passage of the soul over the infernal stream. Then came a dramatic representation of the trial of the soul before Osiris. The priests, in masks, represented the gods of the under world. Typhon accuses the dead man, and demands his punishment. The intercessors plead for him. A large pair of scales is set up, and in one scale his conduct is placed in a bottle, and in the other an image of truth. These proceedings are represented on the funeral papyri. One of these, twenty-two feet in length, is in Dr. Abbott's collection of Egyptian antiquities, in New York. It is beautifully written, and illustrated with careful drawings. One represents the Hall of the Two Truths, and Osiris sitting in judgment, with the scales of judgment before him.*

Many of the virtues which we are apt to suppose a monopoly of Christian culture appear as the ideal of these old Egyptians. Brugsch says a thousand voices from the tombs of Egypt declare this. One inscription in Upper Egypt says: "He loved his father, he honored his mother, he loved his brethren, and never went from his home in bad-temper. He never preferred the great man to the low one." Another says: "I was a wise man, my soul loved God. I was a brother to the great men and a father to the humble ones, and never was a mischief-maker." An inscription at Sais, on a priest who lived in the sad days of Cambyses, says: "I honored my father, I esteemed my mother, I loved my brothers. I found graves for the unburied dead. I instructed little children. I took care of orphans as though they were my own children. For great misfortunes were on Egypt in my time, and on this city of Sais."

Some of these declarations, in their "self-pleasing pride" of virtue, remind one of the noble justification of himself by the Patriarch Job.† Here is one of them, from the tombs of Ben-Hassan, over a Nomad Prince: —

"What I have done I will say. My goodness and my kindness were ample. I never oppressed the fatherless nor the widow. I did not treat cruelly the fishermen, the shepherds, or the poor laborers. There was nowhere in my time hunger or want. For I cultivated all my fields, far and near, in order that their inhabitants might have food. I never preferred the great and powerful to the humble and poor, but did equal justice to all."

A king's tomb at Thebes gives us in few words the religious creed of a Pharaoh: —

"I lived in truth, and fed my soul with justice. What I did to men was done in peace, and how I loved God, God and my heart well know. I have given bread to the hungry, water

---

* This Museum also contains three large mummies of the sacred bull of Apis, a gold ring of Suphis, a gold necklace with the name of Menes, and many other remarkable antiquities.

† Book of Job, Chap. xxix.

to the thirsty, clothes to the naked, and a shelter to the stranger. I honored the gods with sacrifices, and the dead with offerings."

A rock at Lycopolis pleads for an ancient ruler thus : " I never took the child from its mother's bosom, nor the poor man from the side of his wife." Hundreds of stones in Egypt announce as the best gifts which the gods can bestow on their favorites, " the respect of men, and the love of women." * Religion, therefore, in Egypt, connected itself with morality and the duties of daily life. But kings and conquerors were not above the laws of their religion. They were obliged to recognize their power and triumphs as not their own work, but that of the great gods of their country. Thus, on a monumental stele discovered at Karnak by M. Mariette, and translated by De Rougé,† is an inscription recording the triumphs of Thothmes III., of the eighteenth dynasty (about B. C. 1600), which sounds like the song of Miriam or the Hymn of Deborah. We give some stanzas in which the god Amun addresses Thothmes : —

"I am come : to thee have I given to strike down Syrian princes ;
Under thy feet they lie throughout the breadth of their country .
Like to the Lord of Light, I made them see thy glory,
Blinding their eyes with light, O earthly image of Amun !

"I am come : to thee have I given to strike down Asian peoples ;
Captive now thou hast led the proud Assyrian chieftains ;
Decked in royal robes, I made them see thy glory ;
In glittering arms and fighting, high in thy lofty chariot.

"I am come : to thee have I given to strike down western nations ;
Cyprus and the Ases have both heard thy name with terror ;
Like a strong-horned bull I made them see thy glory ;
Strong with piercing horns, so that none can stand before him.

"I am come : to thee have I given to strike down Lybian archers ;
All the isles of the Greeks submit to the force of thy spirit ;
Like a regal lion, I made them see thy glory ;
Couched by the corpse he has made, down in the rocky valley.

"I am come : to thee have I given to strike down the ends of the ocean.
In the grasp of thy hand is the circling zone of the waters ;
Like the soaring eagle, I have made them see thy glory,
Whose far-seeing eye there is none can hope to escape from."

* Brugsch, as above.
† Lenormant, Ancient History of the East, I. 234, in the English translation.

A similar strain of religious poetry is in the Papyrus of Sallier, in the British Museum.* This is an epic by an Egyptian poet named Pentaour, celebrating the campaigns of Ramses II., the Sesostris of the Greeks, of the nineteenth dynasty. This great king had been called into Syria to put down a formidable revolt of the Kheta (the Hittites of the Old Testament). The poem seems to have been a famous one, for it had the honor of being carved in full on the walls at Karnak, a kind of immortality which no other epic poet has ever attained. It particularly describes an incident in the war, when, by a stratagem of the enemy, King Ramses found himself separated from the main body of his army and attacked by the enemy in full force. Pentaour describes him in this situation as calling on Amun, God of Thebes, for help, recounting the sacrifices he had offered to him, and asking whether he would let him die in this extremity by the ignoble hands of these Syrian tribes. "Have I not erected to thee great temples? Have I not sacrificed to thee thirty thousand oxen? I have brought from Elephantina obelisks to set up to thy name. I invoke thee, O my father, Amun. I am in the midst of a throng of unknown tribes, and alone. But Amun is better to me than thousands of archers and millions of horsemen. Amun will prevail over the enemy." And, after defeating his foes, in his song of triumph, the king says, "Amun-Ra has been at my right and my left in the battles; his mind has inspired my own, and has prepared the downfall of my enemies. Amun-Ra, my father, has brought the whole world to my feet." †

Thus universal and thus profound was the religious sentiment among the Egyptians.

§ 3. *Theology of Egypt. Sources of our Knowledge concerning it.*

As regards the theology of the Egyptians and their system of ideas, we meet with difficulty from the law of secrecy which was their habit of mind. The Egyptian

---

* Translated by De Rougé. See Revue Contemporaine, August, 1856.
† Egypt 3300 Years ago. By Lanoye.

priesthood enveloped with mystery every opinion, just as they swathed the mummies, fold above fold, in preparing them for the tomb.   The names and number of their gods we learn from the monuments.   Their legends concerning them come to us through Plutarch, Herodotus, Diodorus, and other Greek writers.   Their doctrine of a future life and future judgment is apparent in their ceremonies, the pictures on the tombs, and the papyrus Book of the Dead. But what these gods *mean*, what are their offices, how they stand related to each other and to mankind, what is the ethical bearing of the religion, it is not so easy to learn.

Nevertheless, we may find a clew to a knowledge of this system, if in no other way, at least by ascertaining its central, ruling idea, and pursuing this into its details. The moment that we take this course, light will begin to dawn upon us.   But before going further, let us briefly inquire into the sources of our knowledge of Egyptian mythology.

The first and most important place is occupied by the monuments, which contain the names and tablets of the gods of the three orders.   Then come the sacred books of the Egyptians, known to us by Clemens Alexandrinus.   From him we learn that the Egyptians in his time had forty-two sacred books in five classes.   The first class, containing songs or hymns in praise of the gods, were very old, dating perhaps from the time of Menes.   The other books treated of morals, astronomy, hieroglyphics, geography, ceremonies, the deities, the education of priests, and medicine.   Of these sacred Hermaic books, one is still extant, and perhaps it is as interesting as any of them.   We have two copies of it, both on papyrus, one found by the French at Thebes, the other by Champollion in Turin.   And Lepsius considers this last papyrus to be wholly of the date of the eighteenth or nineteenth dynasty, consequently fifteen hundred or sixteen hundred years before Christ, and the only example of an Egyptian book transmitted from the times of the Pharaohs.   Bunsen believes it to belong to the fourth class of Hermaic books, containing Ordinances as to the First Fruits, Sacrifices, Hymns, and Prayers.   In this book the deceased is the person who officiates. His soul journeying on gives utterance to prayers, confessions, invocations. The first fifteen chapters, which make a connected whole, are headed, " Here begins the Sections of the Glorification in the Light of Osiris." It is illustrated by a picture of a procession, in which the deceased soul follows his own corpse as chief mourner, offering prayers to the Sun-God. Another part of the book is headed, "The Book of Deliverance, in the Hall of twofold Justice," and contains the divine judgments on the deceased. Forty-two gods occupy the judgment-seat. Osiris, their president, bears on his breast the small tablet of chief judge, containing a figure of Justice. Before him are seen the scales of divine judgment. In one is placed the statue of Justice, and in the other the heart of the deceased, who stands in person by the balance containing his heart, while Anubis watches the other scale. Horus examines the plummet indicating which way the beam inclines. Thoth, the Justifier the Lord of the Divine Word, records the sentence.*

§ 4. *Central Idea of Egyptian Theology and Religion. Animal Worship.*

We now proceed to ask what is the IDEA of Egyptian mythology and theology?

We have seen that the idea of the religion of India was

---

* Beside the monuments and the papyri, we have as sources of information the remains of the Egyptian historians Manetho and Eratosthenes ; the Greek accounts of Egypt by Herodotus, Plato, Diodorus Siculus, Plutarch, Jamblichus ; and the modern researches of Heeren, Champollion, Rossalini, Young, Wilkinson. The more recent writers to be consulted are as follows : —

Bunsen's "Ægypten's Stelle in der Weltgeschichte. Hamburg." (First volume printed in 1845.) This great work was translated by C. C. Cottrel in five 8vo volumes, the last published in 1867, after the death of both author and translator. The fifth volume of the translation contains a full translation of the " Book of the Dead," by the learned Samuel Birch of the British Museum.

Essays in the Revue Archéologique and other learned periodicals, by the Vicomte de Rougé, Professor of Egyptian Philology at Paris. Works by M. Chabas, M. Mariette, De Brugsch, "Aus dem Orient," etc., Samuel Sharpe, A. Maury, Lepsius, and others.

Spirit; the One, the Infinite, the Eternal; a pure spiritual Pantheism, from which the elements of time and space are quite excluded. The religion of Egypt stands at the opposite pole of thought as its antagonist. Instead of Spirit, it accepts Body; instead of Unity, Variety; instead of Substance, Form. It is the physical reaction from Brahmanism. Instead of the worship of abstract Deity, it gives us the most concrete divinity, wholly incarnated in space and time. Instead of abstract contemplation, it gives us ceremonial worship. Instead of the absorption of man into God, it gives us transmigration through all bodily forms.* It so completely incarnates God, as to make every type of animal existence divine; hence the worship of animals. It makes body so sacred, that the human body must not be allowed to perish. As the Brahman, contemplating eternity, forgot time, and had

---

* The Egyptian doctrine of transmigration differed from that of the Hindoos in this respect, that no idea of retribution seems to be connected with it. According to Herodotus (II. 123), the soul must pass through all animals, fishes, insects, and birds ; in short, must complete the whole circuit of animated existence, before it again enters the body of a man ; "and this circuit of the soul," he adds, "is performed in three thousand years." According to him, it does not begin "until the body decays." This may give us one explanation of the system of embalming ; for if the circuit of transmigration is limited to three thousand years, and the soul cannot leave the body till it decays (the words of Herodotus are, "the body decaying," τοῦ σώματος δὲ καταφθίνοντος), then if embalming delays decay for one thousand years, so much is taken off from the journey through animals. That the soul was believed to be kept with the body as long as it was undecayed is also expressly stated by Servius (Comm. on the Æneid of Virgil): "The learned Egyptians preserve the corpse from decay in tombs in order that its soul shall remain with it, and not quickly pass into other bodies."

Hence, too, the extraordinary pains taken in ornamenting the tombs, as the permanent homes of the dead during a long period. Diodorus says that they ornamented the tombs as the enduring residences of mankind.

Transmigration in India was retribution, but in Egypt it seems to have been a condition of progress. It was going back into the lower organizations, to gather up all their varied life, to add to our own. So Tennyson suggests, —

"If, through lower lives I came,
Though all experience past became
Consolidate in mind and frame," etc.

Beside the reason for embalming given above, there may have been the motive arising from the respect for bodily organization, so deeply rooted in the Egyptian mind.

no history, so on the other hand the Egyptian priest, to whom every moment of time is sacred, records everything and turns every event into history; and as it enshrines the past time historically on monuments, so it takes hold of future time prophetically through oracles.

The chief peculiarity about the religion of Egypt, and that which has always caused the greatest astonishment to foreigners, was the worship of animals. Herodotus says (Book II. § 65), "That all animals in Egypt, wild and tame, are accounted sacred, and that if any one kills these animals wilfully he is put to death." He is, however, mistaken in asserting that *all* animals are sacred; for many were not so, though the majority were. Wilkinson gives a list of the animals of Egypt to the number of over one hundred, more than half of which were sacred, and the others not. As hunting and fishing were favorite sports of the Egyptians, it is apparent that there must have been animals whom it was lawful to kill. Nevertheless, it is certain that animal worship is a striking peculiarity of the Egyptian system. Cows were sacred to Isis, and Isis was represented in the form of a cow. The gods often wore the heads of animals; and Kneph, or Amun, with the ram's head, is one of the highest of the gods, known among the Greeks as Jupiter Ammon. The worship of Apis, the sacred bull of Memphis, the representative of Osiris, was very important among the Egyptian ceremonies. Plutarch says that he was a fair and beautiful image of the soul of Osiris. He was a bull with black hair, a white spot on his forehead, and some other special marks. He was kept at Memphis in a splendid temple. His festival lasted seven days, when a great concourse of people assembled. When he died his body was embalmed and buried with great pomp, and the priests went in search of another Apis, who, when discovered by the marks, was carried to Memphis, carefully fed and exercised, and consulted as an oracle. The burial-place of the Apis bulls was, a few years ago, discovered near Memphis. It consists of an arched gallery hewn in the rock, two thousand feet long and twenty feet in height and breadth. On each side is a series of re-

cesses, each containing a large sarcophagus of granite,
fifteen by eight feet, in which the body of a sacred bull
was deposited. In 1852 thirty of these had been already
found. Before this tomb is a paved road with lions
ranged on each side, and before this a temple with a ves-
tibule. In different parts of Egypt different animals were held
sacred. The animal sacred in one place was not so regarded in another district. These sacred animals were
embalmed by the priests and buried, and the mummies of
dogs, wolves, birds, and crocodiles are found by thousands
in the tombs. The origin and motive of this worship is
differently explained. It is certain that animals were not
worshipped in the same way as the great gods, but were
held sacred and treated with reverence as containing a
divine element. So, in the East, an insane person is accounted sacred, but is not worshipped. So the Roman
Catholics distinguish between Dulia and Latria, between
the worship of gods and reverence of saints. So, too,
Protestants consider the Bible a holy book and the Sabbath a holy day, but without worshipping them. It is
only just to make a similar distinction on behalf of
the Egyptians. The motives usually assigned for this
worship — motives of utility — seem no adequate explanation. "The Egyptians," says Wilkinson, "may have
deified some animals to insure their preservation, some
to prevent their unwholesome meat being used as food."
But no religion was ever established in this way. Man
does not worship from utilitarian considerations, but from
an instinct of reverence. It is possible, indeed, that such
a reverential instinct may have been awakened towards
certain animals, by seeing their vast importance arising
from their special instincts and faculties. The cow and the
ox, the dog, the ibis, and the cat, may thus have appeared
to the Egyptians, from their indispensable utility, to be
endowed with supernatural gifts. But this feeling itself
must have had its root in a yet deeper tendency of the
Egyptian mind. They reverenced the mysterious manifestation of God in all outward nature. No one can look at
an animal, before custom blinds our sense of strangeness,

without a feeling of wonder at the law of instinct, and the special, distinct peculiarity which belongs to it. Every variety of animals is a manifestation of a divine thought, and yet a thought hinted rather than expressed. Each must mean something, must symbolize something. But what does it mean ? what does it symbolize ? Continually we seem just on the point of penetrating the secret; we almost touch the explanation, but are baffled. A dog, a cat, a snake, a crocodile, a spider, — what does each mean ? why were they made ? why this infinite variety of form, color, faculty, character ? Animals thus in their unconscious being, as expressions of God's thoughts, are mysteries, and divine mysteries.*

Now every part of the religion of Egypt shows how much they were attracted toward *variety*, toward nature, toward the outward manifestations of the Divine Spirit. These tendencies reached their utmost point in their reverence for animal life. The shallow Romans, who reverenced only themselves, and the Greeks, who worshipped nothing but human nature more or less idealized, laughed at this Egyptian worship of animals and plants. "O sacred nation! whose gods grow in gardens!" says Juvenal. But it certainly shows a deeper wisdom to see something divine in nature, and to find God in nature, than to call it common and unclean. And there is more of truth in the Egyptian reverence for animal individuality, than in the unfeeling indifference to the welfare of these poor relations which Christians often display. When Jesus said that "not a sparrow falls to the ground without your Father," he showed all these creatures to be under the protection of their Maker. It may be foolish to worship animals, but it is still more foolish to despise them.

That the belief in transmigration is the explanation of animal worship is the opinion of Bunsen. The human soul and animal soul, according to this view, are essen-

* Animals and plants, more than anything else, and animals more than plants, are the types of variety ; they embody that great law of differentiation, one of the main laws of the universe, the law which is opposed to that of unity, the law of centrifugal force, expressed in our humble proverb, "It takes all sorts of people to make a world."

tially the same, — therefore the animal was considered as sacred as man. Still, we do not *worship* man. Animal worship, then, must have had a still deeper root in the sense of awe before the mystery of organized life.

§ 5. *Sources of Egyptian Theology. Age of the Empire and Affinities of the Race.*

But whence came this tendency in the human mind? Did it inhere in the race, or was it the growth of external circumstances? Something, perhaps, may be granted to each of these causes. The narrow belt of fertile land in Egypt, fed by the overflowing Nile, quickened by the tropical sun, teeming with inexhaustible powers of life, continually called the mind anew to the active, creative powers of nature. And yet it may be suspected that the law of movement by means of antagonism and reaction may have had its influence also here. The opinion is now almost universal, that the impulse of Egyptian civilization proceeded from Asia. This is the conclusion of Bunsen at the end of his first volume. "The cradle of the mythology and language of Egypt," says he, "is Asia. This result is arrived at by the various ethnological proofs of language which finds Sanskrit words and forms in Egypt, and of comparative anatomy, which shows the oldest Egyptian skulls to have belonged to Caucasian races." If, then, Egyptian civilization proceeded from Central Asia, Egyptian mythology and religion probably came as a quite natural reaction from the extreme spiritualism of the Hindoos. The question which remains is, whether they arrived at their nature-worship directly or indirectly; whether, beginning with Fetichism, they ascended to their higher conceptions of the immortal gods; or, beginning with spiritual existence, they traced it downward into its material manifestations; whether, in short, their system was one of evolution or emanation. For every ancient theogony, cosmogony, or ontogony is of one kind or the other. According to the systems of India and of Platonism; the generation of beings is by the method of emanation. Creation is a falling away, or an emanation from the absolute. But the systems of Greek and Scandinavian mythology are of the opposite sort. In these, spirit is evolved from matter; matter up to spirit works. They begin with the lowest form of being, — night, chaos, a mundane egg, — and evolve the higher gods therefrom.

It is probable that we find in Egypt a double tendency. One is the Asiatic spiritualism, the other the African naturalism. The union of the ideal and the real, of thought and passion, of the aspirations of the soul and the fire of a passionate nature, of abstract meditation and concrete life, had for its result the mysterious theology and philosophy which, twenty centuries after its burial under the desert sands, still rouses our curiosity to penetrate the secret of this Sphinx of the Nile.

We have seen in a former section that the institutions of Egypt, based on a theocratic monarchy, reach back into a dim and doubtful antiquity. Monuments, extending through thirty-five centuries, attest an age preceding all written history. These monuments, so far as deciphered by modern Egyptologists, have confirmed the accuracy of the lists of kings which have come to us from Manetho. We have no monument anterior to the fourth dynasty, but at that epoch we find the theocracy fully organized.[*] The general accuracy of Manetho's list has been demonstrated by the latest discoveries of M. Mariette, and has rendered doubtful the idea of any of the dynasties being contemporaneous.

The main chronological points, however, are by no means as yet fixed. Thus, the beginning of the first dynasty is placed by Böckh at B. C. 5702, by Lepsius B. C. 3892, by Bunsen B. C. 3623, by Brugsch B. C. 4455, by Lauth B. C. 4157, by Duncker 3233.[†] The period of the builders of the great Pyramids is fixed by Bunsen at B. C. 3229, by Lepsius at B. C. 3124, by Brugsch at B. C. 3686, by Lauth at B. C. 3450, and by Böckh at B. C. 4933.[‡]

---

[*] Maury, "Revue des Deux Mondes, 1867." "Man's Origin and Destiny, J. P. Lesley, 1868." "Recherches sur les Monumens, etc., par M. de Rougé, 1866."

[†] Article "Ægypten," in Schenkel's Bibel-Lexicon, 1869. Duncker, "Geschichte des Alterthums, Dritte Auflage, 1863."

[‡] See Duncker, as above.

The Egyptian priests told Herodotus that there were three hundred and thirty-one kings, from Menes to Moeris, whose names they read out of a book. After him came eleven others, of whom Sethos was the last. From Osiris to Amasis they counted fifteen thousand years, though Herodotus did not believe this statement. If the three hundred and forty-two kings really existed, it would make Menes come B. C. 9150, — at an average of twenty-five years' reign to each king. Diodorus saw in Egypt a list of four hundred and seventy-nine kings. But he says in another place that Menes lived about four thousand seven hundred years before his time. Manetho tells us that from Menes there were thirty dynasties, who reigned five thousand three hundred and sixty-six years. But he gives a list of four hundred and seventy-two kings in these dynasties, to the time of Cambyses. The contradictions are so great, and the modes of reconciling Manetho, Herodotus, Diodorus, Eratosthenes, and the monuments are so inadequate, that we must regard the whole question of the duration of the monarchy as unsettled. But from the time when the calendar must have been fixed, from the skill displayed in the Pyramids, and other reasons independent of any chronology, Duncker considers the reign of Menes as old as B. C. 3500.

The history of Egypt is divided into three periods, that of the old, the middle, and the new monarchy. The first extends from the foundation of the united kingdom by Menes to the conquest of the country by the Hyksôs. The second is from this conquest by the Hyksôs till their expulsion. The third, from the re-establishment of the monarchy by Amosis to its final conquest by Persia. The old monarchy contained twelve dynasties ; the Hyksôs or middle monarchy, five ; the new monarchy, thirteen : in all, thirty.

The Hyksôs, or Shepherd Kings, were at first supposed to be the Hebrews : but this hypothesis adapted itself to none of the facts. A recent treatise by M. Chabas *
shows that the Hyksôs were an Asiatic people, occupying the country to the northeast of Egypt. After conquer-

* Les Pasteurs en Egypt, par F. Chabas.   Amsterdam, 1868.

ing Lower Egypt, Apapi was king of the Hyksôs and Tekenen-Ra ruled over the native Egyptians of the South. A papyrus, as interpreted by M. Chabas, narrates that King Apapi worshipped only the god Sutech (Set), and refused to allow the Egyptian gods to be adored. This added to the war of races a war of religion, which resulted in the final expulsion of the Shepherds, about B. C. 1700. The Hyksôs are designated on the monuments and in the papyri as the " Scourge " or " Plague," equivalent in Hebrew to the *Tzir'ah*, commonly translated " hornet," but evidently the same as the Hebrew *tzavaath*, " plague,". and the Arabic *tzeria*, " scourge," or " plague." *

According to the learned Egyptologist, Dr. Brugsch, the Hebrew slaves in Egypt are referred to in a papyrus in the British Museum of the date of Ramses II. (B. C. 1400), in a description by a scribe named Pinebsa of the new city of Ramses. He tells how the slaves throng around him to present petitions against their overseers. Another papyrus reads (Lesley, " Man's Origin and Destiny ") : " The people have erected twelve buildings. They made their tale of bricks daily, till they were finished." The first corroboration of the biblical narrative which the Egyptian monuments afford, and the first synchronism between Jewish and Egyptian history, appear in the reign of Ramses II., about B. C. 1400, in the nineteenth dynasty.

It appears from the monuments and from the historians that somewhere about B. C. 2000, or earlier, this great movement of warlike nomadic tribes occurred, which resulted in the conquest of Lower Egypt by the pastoral people known as Hyksôs. It was perhaps a movement of Semitic races, the Bedouins of the desert, like that which nearly three thousand years after united them as warriors of Islam to overflow North Africa, Syria, Persia, and Spain. They oppressed Egypt for five hundred years (Brugsch), and appear on the monuments under the name of Amu (the herdsmen) or of Aadu (the hated ones).

---

* The " hornets," Ex. xxiii. 28, and Josh. xxiv. 11, 12, are not insects, but the Hyksôs, who, driven from Egypt were overrunning Syria. See New York Nation, article on the Hyksôs, May 13, 1869.

Their kings resided at Tanis (in Egyptian Avaris), in the Delta. That their conquests had a religious motive, and were made, like that of Mohammed, in the interest of monotheism, seems possible. At all events, we find one of them, Apapi, erecting a temple to Sutech (the Semitic Baal), and refusing to allow the worship of other deities.*

The majority of Egyptologists believe that the Hebrews entered Egypt while these Hyksôs kings, men of the same Semitic family and monotheistic tendencies, were ruling in Lower Egypt. The bare subterranean temple discovered by M. Mariette, with the well near it filled with broken statues of the Egyptian gods, is an indication of those tendencies. The "other king, who knew not Joseph," was a king of the eighteenth dynasty, who conquered the Hyksôs and drove them out of Egypt. Apparently the course of events was like that which many centuries later occurred in Spain. In both cases, the original rulers of the land, driven to the mountains, gradually reconquered their country step by step. The result of this reconquest of the country would also be in Egypt, as it was in Spain, that the Semitic remnants left in the land would be subject to a severe and oppressive rule. The Jews in Egypt, like the Moors in Spain, were victims of a cruel bondage. Then began the most splendid period of Egyptian history, during the seventeenth, sixteenth, fifteenth, and fourteenth centuries before Christ. The Egyptian armies overran Syria, Asia Minor, and Armenia as far as the Tigris.

Ramses II., the most powerful monarch of this epoch, is probably the king whose history is given by Herodotus and other Greek writers under the name of Sesostris.†
M. de Rougé believes himself able to establish this identity. He found in the Museum at Vienna a stone covered with inscriptions, and dedicated by a person whose name is given as Ramses Mei-Amoun, exactly in the hieroglyphics of the great king. But this person's name is also

* Pap. Tallier (Bunsen IV. 671) as translated by De Rougé, Goodwin, &c. : "In the days when the land of Egypt was held by the invaders, King Apapi (at Avaris) set up Sutekh for his lord ; he worshipped no other god in the whole land."

† I follow here De Rougé, Brugsch, and Duncker, rather than Bunsen.

written elsewhere on the stone *Ses*, and a third time as *Ses Mei-amoun*, showing that *Ses* was a common abbreviation of Ramses. It is also written *Sesu*, or *Sesesu*, which is very like the form in which Diodorus writes Sesostris, namely, *Sesoosis.*[*] Now Ramses II., whose reign falls about B. C. 1400, erected a chain of fortresses to defend the northeastern border of Egypt against the Syrian nomads. One of these fortresses was named from the King Ramses, and another Pachtum. The papyri contain accounts of these cities. One papyrus, in the British Museum,[†] is a description by a scribe named Pinebsa, of the aspect of the city Ramses, and of the petitions of the laborers for relief against their overseers. These laborers are called *Apuru*, Hebrews. In a papyrus of the Leyden Museum, an officer reports to his superior thus: " May my lord be pleased. I have distributed food to the soldiers and to the Hebrews, dragging stones for the great city Ramses Meia-moum. I gave them food monthly." This corresponds with the passage (Exodus i. 11): " They built for Pharaoh treasure-cities, Pithom and Raamses." [‡]

The birth of Moses fell under the reign of Ramses II. The Exodus was under that of his successor, Menepthes. This king had fallen on evil times ; his power was much inferior to that of his great predecessor ; and he even condescended to propitiate the anti-Egyptian element, by worshipping its gods. He has left his inscription on the monuments with the title, " Worshipper of Sutech-Baal in Tanis." The name of Moses is Egyptian, and signifies " the child."

" Joseph," says Brugsch, " was never at the court of an Egyptian Pharaoh, but found his place with the Semitic monarchs, who reigned at Avaris-Tanis in the Delta, and whose power extended from this point as far as Memphis

---

[*] Athenæum Français, 1856.

[†] Lesley, Man's Origin and Destiny, p. 149. Brugsch, Aus dem Orient, p. 37.

[‡] A common title on the monuments for the king is Per-aa, in the dialect of Upper Egypt, Pher-ao in that of Lower Egypt, meaning " The lofty house," equivalent to the modern Turkish title, " The Sublime Porte."

and Heliopolis." The "king who knew not Joseph" was evidently the restored Egyptian dynasty of Thebes. These monarchs would be naturally averse to all the Palestinian inhabitants of the land. And the monuments of their reigns represent the labors of subject people, under task-masters, cutting, carrying, and laying stones for the walls of cities.

To what race do the Egyptians belong ? , The only historic document which takes us back so far as this is the list of nations in the tenth chapter of Genesis. We cannot, indeed, determine the time when it was written. But Bunsen, Ebers,* and other ethnologists are satisfied that the author of this chapter had a knowledge of the subject derived either from the Phœnicians or the Egyptians. Ewald places his epoch with that of the early Jewish kings. According to this table the Egyptians were descended from Ham, the son of Noah, and were consequently of the same original stock with the Japhetic and Semitic nations. They were not negroes, though their skin was black, or at least dark.† According to Herodotus they came from the heart of Africa ; according to Genesis (chap. x.) from Asia. Which is the correct view ?

The Egyptians themselves recognized no relationship with the negroes, who only appear on the monuments as captives or slaves.

History, therefore, helps us little in this question of race. How is it with Comparative Philology and Comparative Anatomy ?

The Coptic language is an idiom of the old Egyptian tongue, which seems to belong to no known linguistic group. It is related to other African languages only through the lexicon, and similarly with the Indo-European. Some traces of grammatic likeness to the Semitic may be found in it ; yet the view of Bunsen and Schwartz, that in very ancient times it arose from the

---

* " Ægypten und die Bücher Mosis, von Dr. Georg Ebers. Leipzig, 1868."   " Bunsen, Bibel-Werk," Erster Theil, p. 63.

† Æschylus calls the Egyptian sailors μελάγχιμος, Lucian calls a young Egyptian " black-skinned," but Ammianus Marcellinus says, " Ægyptii plerique subfusculi sunt et atrati."

union of Semitic and Indo-European languages, remains only a hypothesis.* Merx (in Schenkel's Bibel-Lexicon) says this view " rests upon a wish formed in the interest of the Philosophy of History ; and the belief of a connection between these tongues is not justified by any scientific study of philology. No such ethnological affinity can be granted, — a proof of which is that all facts in its favor are derived from common roots, none from common grammar." Benfey, however, assumed two great branches of Semitic nationalities, one flowing into Africa, the other into Western Asia.† Ebers ‡ gives some striking resemblances between Egyptian and Chaldaic words, and says he possesses more than three hundred examples of this kind ; and in Bunsen's fifth volume are comparative tables which give as their result that a third part of the old Egyptian words in Coptic literature are Semitic, and a tenth part Indo-European. If these statements are confirmed, they may indicate some close early relations between these races.

The anatomy of the mummies seems to show a wide departure from negro characteristics. The skull, chin, forehead, bony system, facial angle, hair, limbs, are all different. The chief resemblances are in the flat nose, and form of the backbone.§ Scientific ethnologists have therefore usually decided that the old Egyptians were an

* " Ægypten und die Bücher Mosis, von Ebers, Vol. I. p. 43."
† " Th. Benfey, Ueber das verhältniss der ägyptischen Sprache zum semitischen Sprachstamme, 1844."
‡ Ægypten, &c.
§ " The skulls of the mummies agree with history in proving that Egypt was peopled with a variety of tribes ; and physiologists, when speaking more exactly, have divided them into three classes. The first is the Egyptian proper, whose skull is shaped like the heads of the ancient Theban statues and the modern Nubians. The second is a race of men more like the Europeans, and these mummies become more common as we approach the Delta. These are perhaps the same as the modern Copts. The third is of an Arab race, and are like the heads of the laborers in the pictures." — Sharpe, Hist. of Egypt, I. 3. He refers to Morton's Crania Ægyptiaca for his authority.

Prichard (Nat. Hist. of Man and Researches, &c.), after a full examination of the question concerning the ethnical relations of the Egyptians, and of Morton's craniological researches, concludes in favor of an Asiatic origin of the Egyptians. connected with an amalgamation with the Afric-an autocthones.

Asiatic people who had become partially amalgamated with the surrounding African tribes. Max Duncker comes to this conclusion,* and says that the Berber languages are the existing representatives of the old Egyptian. This is certainly true as concerns the Copts, whose very name is almost identical with the word " Gupti," the old name from which the Greeks formed the term Ægypti.† Alfred Maury (Revue d. D. Mondes, September, 1867) says that, " according to all appearances, Egypt was peopled from Asia by that Hamitic race which comprised the tribes of Palestine, Arabia, and Ethiopia. Its ancient civilization was, consequently, the sister of that which built Babylon and Nineveh. In the valley of the Nile, as in those of the Euphrates and the Tigris, religion gave the motive to civilization, and in all the three nations there was a priesthood in close alliance with an absolute monarchy." M. de Rougé is of the same opinion. In his examination of the monuments of the oldest dynasties, he finds the name given to the Egyptians by themselves to be merely " the Men " (Rut), — a word which by the usual interchange of R with L, and of T with D, is identical with the Hebrew Lud (plural Ludim), whom the Book of Genesis declares to have been a son of Misraim. This term was applied by the Israelites to all the races on the southeast shore of the Mediterranean. It is, therefore, believed by M. de Rougé that the Egyptians were of the same family with these Asiatic tribes on the shores of Syria. Here, then, as in so many other cases, a new civilization may have come from the union of two different races, — one Asiatic, the other African. Asia furnished the brain, Africa the fire, and from the immense vital force of the latter and the intellectual vigor of the former sprang that wonderful civilization which illuminated the world during at least five thousand years.

* Dieser Völkerschaften gehörten der kaukasischen Race an ; ihre Sprachen waren dem Semitischen am nächsten Verwandt." G. des A. I. 11.
† Brugsch derives it from Ki-Ptah = worshippers of Ptah.

§ 6. *The Three Orders of Gods.*

The Egyptian theology, or doctrine of the gods, was of two kinds, — esoteric and exoteric, that is, an interior theology for the initiated, and an exterior theology for the uninitiated. The exterior theology, which was for the whole people, consisted of the mythological accounts of Isis and Osiris, the judgments of the dead, the transmigration of the soul, and all matters connected with the ceremonial worship of the gods. But the interior, hidden theology is supposed to have related to the unity and spirituality of the Deity.

Herodotus informs us that the gods of the Egyptians were in three orders; and Bunsen believes that he has succeeded in restoring them from the monuments. There are eight gods of the first order, twelve gods of the second order, and seven gods of the third order. The gods of the third order are those of the popular worship, but those of the first seem to be of a higher and more spiritual class. The third class of gods were representative of the elements of nature, the sun, fire, water, earth, air. But the gods of the first order were the gods of the priesthood, understood by them alone, and expressing ideas which they shrank from communicating to the people. The spiritual and ideal part of their religion the priests kept to themselves as something which the people were incapable of understanding. The first eight gods seem to have been a representation of a process of divine development or emanation, and constituted a transition from the absolute spiritualism of the Hindoos to the religion of nature and humanity in the West. The Hindoo gods were emanations of spirit: the gods of Greece are idealizations of Nature. But the Egyptian gods represent spirit passing into matter and form.

Accordingly, if we examine in detail the gods of the first order, who are eight, we find them to possess the general principle of self-revelation, and to constitute, taken together, a process of divine development. These eight, according to Bunsen, are Amn, or Ammon; Khem, or Chemmis; Mut, the Mother Goddess; Num, or Kneph; Seti,

or Sate ; Phtah, the Artist God ; Net, or Neith, the Goddess
of Sais ; and Ra, the Sun, the God of Heliopolis. But
according to Wilkinson they stand in a little different
order : 1. Neph, or Kneph ; 2. Amun, or Ammon ; 3. Pthah ;
4. Khem ; 5. Sate ; 6. Maut, or Mut ; 7. Pasht, or Diana ;
and 8. Neith, or Minerva, in which list Pasht, the Goddess
of Bubastis, is promoted out of the second order and takes
the place of Ra, the Sun, who is degraded.

Supposing these lists to be substantially correct, we
have, as the root of the series, Ammon, the Concealed God,
or Absolute Spirit. His titles indicate this dignity. The
Greeks recognized him as corresponding to their Zeus. He
is styled King of the Gods, the Ruler, the Lord of Heaven,
the Lord of the Thrones, the Horus or God of the Two
Egypts. Thebes was his city. According to Manetho, his
name means concealment ; and the root " Amn " also means
to veil or conceal. His original name was Amn ; thus it
stands in the rings of the twelfth dynasty. But after the
eighteenth dynasty it is Amn-Ra, meaning the Sun.
" Incontestably," says Bunsen, " he stands in Egypt as
the head of the great cosmogonic development."

Next comes Kneph, or God as Spirit, — the Spirit of
God, often confounded with Amn, also called Cnubis and
Num Both Plutarch and Diodorus tell us that his name
signifies Spirit, the Num having an evident relation with
the Greek πνεῦμα, and the Coptic word " Nef," meaning also
to blow. So too the Arabic " Nef " means breath, the Hebrew " Nuf," to flow, and the Greek πνέω, to breathe. At
Esneh he is called the Breath of those in the Firmament ;
at Elephantina, Lord of the Inundations. He wears the
ram's head with double horns (by mistake of the Greeks
attributed to Ammon), and his worship was universal in
Ethiopia. The sheep are sacred to him, of which there
were large flocks in the Thebaid, kept for their wool.
And the serpent or asp, a sign of kingly dominion, — hence
called basilisk, — is sacred to Kneph. As Creator, he appears under the figure of a potter with a wheel. In Philæ
he is so represented, forming on his wheel a figure of Osiris,
with the inscription, " Num, who forms on his wheel the
Divine Limbs of Osiris." He is also called the Sculptor

of all men, also the god who made the sun and moon to revolve. Porphyry says that Pthah sprang from an egg which came from the mouth of Kneph, in which he is supported by high monumental authority.

The result of this seems to be that Kneph represents the absolute Being as Spirit, the Spirit of God moving on the face of the waters, — a moving spirit pervading the formless chaos of matter.

Perhaps the next god in the series is Pthah, by the Greeks called Hephæstus, or Vulcan, representing formation, creation by the truth, stability; called in the inscriptions, Lord of Truth, Lord of the Beautiful Face, Father of the Beginnings, moving the Egg of the Sun and Moon. With Horapollo and Plutarch, we may consider the Scarabeus, or Beetle, which is his sign, as an emblem of the world and its creation. An inscription calls him Creator of all things in the world. Iamblicus says, "The God who creates with truth is Pthah." He was also connected with the sun, as having thirty fingers, — the number of days in a month. He is represented sometimes as a deformed dwarf.

The next god in the series is Khem, the Greek Pan, — the principle of generation, sometimes holding the ploughshare.

Then come the feminine principles corresponding with these three latter gods. Amun has naturally no companion. Mut, the mother, is the consort of Khem the father. Seti, — the Ray or Arrow, — a female figure, with the horns of a cow, is the companion of Kneph. And Neith, or Net, the goddess of Sais, belongs to Pthah. The Greek Minerva Athênê is thought to be derived from Neith by an inversion of the letters,* —the Greeks writing from left to right and the Egyptians from right to left. Her name means, "I came from myself." Clemens says that her great shrine at Sais has an open roof with the inscription, "I am all that was and is and is to be, and no mortal has lifted my garment, and the fruit I bore is Helios." This would seem to identify her with Nature.

* Plato, Timæus. Herod. II. 59. Gutschmidt and others deny this etymologic relation of Neith to Athênê.

11   P

For the eighth god of the first order we may take either Helios or Ra or Phra, the Sun-God; from whence came the name of the Pharaohs, or we may take Pasht, Bubastis, the equivalent of the Greek Diana. On some accounts it would seem that Ra was the true termination of this cycle. We should then have, proceeding from the hidden abyss of pure Spirit, first a breathing forth, or spirit in motion; then creation, by the word of truth; then generation, giving life and growth; and then the female qualities of production, wisdom, and light, completed by the Sun-God, last of the series. Amn, or Ammon, the Concealed God, is the root, then the creative power in Kneph, then the generative power in Khem, the Demiurgic power in Ptah, the feminine creative principle of Nature in Neith, the productive principle in Mut, or perhaps the nourishing principle, and then the living stimulus of growth, which carries all forward in Ra.

But we must now remember that two races meet in Egypt, — an Asiatic race, which brings the ideas of the East; and an Ethiopian, inhabitants of the land, who were already there. The first race brought the spiritual ideas which were embodied in the higher order of gods. The Africans were filled with the instinct of nature-worship. These two tendencies were to be reconciled in the religion of Egypt. The first order of gods was for the initiated, and taught them the unity, spirituality, and creative power of God.* The third order — the circle of Isis and Osiris — were for the people, and were

---

* " There is a profound consolation hidden in the old Egyptian inscribed rocks. They show us that the weird figures, half man and half beast, which we find carved and painted there, were not the true gods of Egypt, but politico-religious masks, concealing the true godhead. These rocks teach that the real object of worship was the one undivided Being, existing from the Beginning, Creator of all things, revealing himself to the illuminated soul as the Mosaic "I AM THE I AM." It is true that this pure doctrine was taught only to the initiated, and the stones forbid it to be published. ' This is a hidden mystery; tell it to no one; let it be seen by no eye, heard by no ear : only thou and thy teacher shall possess this knowledge.'" Brugsch, Aus dem Orient, p. 69.

May not one reason for concealing this doctrine of the unity and spirituality of God have been the stress of the African mind to variety and bodily form ? The priests feared to encounter this great current of sentiment in the people, and so outwardly conformed to it.

representative of the forms and forces of outward nature. Between the two come the second series, — a transition from the one to the other, — children of the higher gods, parents of the lower, — neither so abstract as the one nor so concrete as the other, — representing neither purely divine qualities on the one side, nor merely natural forces on the other, but rather the faculties and powers of man. Most of this series were therefore adopted by the Greeks, whose religion was one essentially based on human nature, and whose gods were all, or nearly all, the ideal representations of human qualities. Hence they found in Khunsu, child of Ammon, their Hercules, God of Strength; in Thoth, child of Kneph, they found Hermes, God of Knowledge; in Pecht, child of Pthah, they found their Artemis, or Diana, the Goddess of Birth, protector of women; in Athor, or Hathor, they found their Aphroditê, Goddess of Love. Seb was Chronos, or Time; and Nutpe was Rhea, wife of Chronos.

The third order of gods are the children of the second series, and are manifestations of the Divine in the outward universe. But though standing lowest in the scale, they were the most popular gods of the Pantheon; had more individuality and personal character than the others; were more universally worshipped throughout Egypt, and that from the oldest times. "The Osiris deities," says Herodotus, "are the only gods worshipped throughout Egypt." "They stand on the oldest monuments, are the centre of all Egyptian worship, and are perhaps the oldest original objects of reverence," says Bunsen. How can this be if they belong to a lower order of Deities, and what is the explanation of it? There is another historical fact also to be explained. Down to the time of Ramses, thirteen hundred years before Christ, Typhon, or Seth, the God of Destruction, was the chief of this third order, and the most venerated of all the gods. After that time a revolution occurred in the worship, which overthrew Seth, and his name was chiselled out of the monuments, and the name of Amun inserted in its place. This was the only change which occurred in the Egyptian religion, so far as we know, from its commencement until the time of the Cæsars.* An explanation of both these facts may be given, founded on the supposed amalgamation in Egypt of two races with their religions. Supposing that the gods of the higher orders represented the religious ideas of a Semitic or Aryan race entering Egypt from Asia, and that the Osiris group were the gods of the African nature-worship, which they found prevailing on their arrival, it is quite natural that the priests should in their classification place their own gods highest, while they should have allowed the external worship to go on as formerly, at least for a time. But, after a time, as the tone of thought became more elevated, they may have succeeded in substituting for the God of Terror and Destruction a higher conception in the popular worship.

The myth of Isis and Osiris, preserved for us by Plutarch, gives the most light in relation to this order of deities.

Seb and Nutpe, or Nut, called by the Greeks Chronos and Rhea, were the parents of this group. Seb is therefore Time, and Nut is Motion or perhaps Space. The Sun pronounced a curse on them, namely, that she should not be delivered, on any day of the year. This perhaps implies the difficulty of the thought of Creation. But Hermes, or Wisdom, who loved Rhea, won, at dice, of the Moon, five days, the seventieth part of all her illuminations, which he added to the three hundred and sixty days, or twelve months. Here we have a hint of a correction of the calendar, the necessity of which awakened a feeling of irregularity in the processes of nature, admitting thereby the notion of change and a new creation. These five days were the birthdays of the gods. On the first Osiris is born, and a voice was heard saying, "The Lord of all things is now born." On the second day, Arueris-Apollo, or the elder Horus; on the third, Typhon, who broke through a hole in his mother's side ; on the fourth, Isis ; and on the fifth, Nepthys-Venus, or Victory. Osiris and Arueris are children of the Sun, Isis of Hermes, Typhon and Nepthys of Saturn.

Isis became the wife of Osiris, who went through the

---

* So says Wilkinson.

world taming it by means of oratory, poetry, and music. When he returned, Typhon took seventy-two men and also a queen of Ethiopia, and made an ark the size of Osiris's body, and at a feast proposed to give it to the one whom it should fit. Osiris got into it, and they fastened down the lid and soldered it and threw it into the Nile. Then Isis put on mourning and went to search for it, and directed her inquiries to little children, who were hence held by the Egyptians to have the faculty of divination. Then she found Anubis, child of Osiris, by Nepthys, wife of Typhon, who told her how the ark was entangled in a tree which grew up around it and hid it. The king had made of this tree a pillar to support his house. Isis sat down weeping ; the women of the queen came to her, she stroked their hair, and fragrance passed into it. She was made nurse to the queen's child, fed him with her finger, and in the night-time, by means of a lambent flame, burned away his impurities. She then turned herself into a swallow and flew around the house, bewailing her fate. The queen watched her operations, and being alarmed cried out, and so robbed her child of immortality. Isis then begged the pillar, took it down, took out the chest, and cried so loud that the younger son of the king died of fright. She then took the ark and the elder son and set sail. The cold air of the river chilled her, and she became angry and cursed it, and so dried it up. She opened the chest, put her cheek to that of Osiris and wept bitterly. The little boy came and peeped in ; she gave him a terrible look, and he died of fright. Isis then came to her son Horus, who was at nurse at Buto. Typhon, hunting by moonlight, saw the ark, with the body of Osiris, which he tore into fourteen parts and threw them about. Isis went to look for them in a boat made of papyrus, and buried each part in a separate place.

After this the soul of Osiris returned out of Hades to train up his son. Then came a battle between Horus and Typhon, in which Typhon was vanquished, but Isis allowed him to escape. There are other less important incidents in the story, among them that Isis had another son by the soul of Osiris after his death, who is the god called Harpocrates, represented as lame and with his finger on his mouth.*

Plutarch declares that this story is symbolical, and mentions various explanations of the allegory. He rejects, at once, the rationalistic explanation, which turns these gods into eminent men, — sea-captains, etc. " I fear," says he, "this would be to stir things that are not to be stirred, and to declare war (as Simonides says), not only against length of time, but also against many nations and families of mankind, whom a religious reverence towards these gods holds fast bound like men astonished and amazed, and would be no other than going about to remove so great and venerable names from heaven to earth, and thereby shaking and dissolving that worship and persuasion that hath entered almost all men's constitutions from their very birth, and opening vast doors to the atheists' faction, who convert all divine matters into human." "Others," he says, "consider these beings as demons intermediate between gods and men. And Osiris afterwards became Serapis, the Pluto of the under-world."

Other explanations of the myth are given by Plutarch. First, the geographical explanation. According to this, Osiris is Water, especially the Nile. Isis is Earth, especially the land of Egypt adjoining the Nile, and overflowed by it. Horus, their son, is the Air, especially the moist, mild air of Egypt. Typhon is Fire, especially the summer heat which dries up the Nile and parches the land. His seventy-two associates are the seventy-two days of greatest heat, according to the Egyptian opinion. Nepthys, his wife, sister of Isis, is the Desert outside of Egypt, but which in a higher inundation of the Nile being sometimes overflowed, becomes productive, and has a child by Osiris, named Anubis. When Typhon shuts Osiris into the ark, it is the summer heat drying up the Nile and confining it to its channel. This ark, entangled in a tree, is where the Nile divides into many mouths at the Delta and is overhung by the wood. Isis, nursing the child of the king, the fragrance, etc., represent the earth nourishing plants and animals. The body of Osiris, torn by Typhon

* The finger on the mouth symbolizes, not silence, but childhood.

into fourteen parts, signifies either the division of the Nile at its mouths or the pools of water left after the drying up of the inundation.

There is so much in this account which accords with the facts, that there can be no doubt of its correctness so far as it goes. At the same time it is evidently an incomplete explanation. The story means this, but something more. Beside the geographical view, Plutarch therefore adds a scientific and an astronomical explanation, as well as others more philosophical. According to these, Osiris is in general the productive, the creative power in nature; Isis, the female property of nature, hence called by Plato the nurse; and Typhon the destructive property in nature; while Horus is the mediator between creation and destruction. And thus we have the triad of Osiris, Typhon, and Horus, essentially corresponding to the Hindoo triad, Brahma, Siva, and Vishnu, and also to the Persian triad, Ormazd, Ahriman, and Mithra. And so this myth will express the Egyptian view of the conflict of good and evil in the natural world.

But it seems very likely that it was the object of the priests to elevate this Osiris worship to a still higher meaning, making it an allegory of the struggles, sorrows, and self-recovery of the human soul. Every human soul after death took the name and symbols of Osiris, and then went into the under-world to be judged by him. Connected with this was the doctrine of transmigration, or the passage of the soul through various bodies, — a doctrine brought out of Egypt by Pythagoras. These higher doctrines were taught in the mysteries. "I know them," says Herodotus, "but must not tell them." Iamblicus professes to explain them in his work on the Mysteries. But it is not easy to say how much of his own Platonism he has mingled therewith. According to him, they taught in the mysteries that before all things was one God immovable in the solitude of unity. The One was to be venerated in silence. Then Emeph, or Neph, was god in his self-consciousness. After this in Amun, his intellect became truth, shedding light. Truth working by art is Pthah, and art producing good is Osiris.

Another remarkable fact must be at least alluded to. Bunsen says, that, according to the whole testimony of the monuments, Isis and Osiris not only have their roots in the second order, but are also themselves the first and the second order. Isis, Osiris, and Horus comprise all Egyptian mythology, with the exception of Amun and Neph. Of this fact I have seen no explanation and know of none, unless it be a sign of the purpose of the priests to unite the two systems of spiritualism and nature-worship into one, and to elevate and spiritualize the lower order of gods.

One reason for thinking that the religious system of the priests was a compromise between several different original tendencies is to be found in the local worship of special deities in various places. In Lower Egypt the highest god was Pthah, whom the Greeks identified with Vulcan ; the god of fire or heat, father of the sun. He was in this region the chief god, corresponding to Ammon in Upper Egypt. Manetho says that Pthah reigned nine thousand years before the other gods, — which must mean that this was by far the oldest worship in Egypt. As Ammon is the head of a cosmogony which proceeds according to emanation from spirit down to matter, so Pthah is at the beginning of a cosmogony which ascends by a process of evolution from matter working up to spirit. For from Pthah (heat) comes light, from light proceeds life, from life arise gods, men, plants, animals, and all organic existence. The inscriptions call Pthah, " Father of the Father of the Gods," " King of both Worlds," the " God of all Beginnings," the " Former of Things." The egg is one of his symbols, as containing a germ of life. The scarabæus, or beetle, which rolls its ball of earth, supposed to contain its egg, is dedicated to Pthah. His sacred city was Memphis, in Lower Egypt. His son, Ra, the Sun-God, had his temple at On, near by, which the Greeks called Heliopolis, or City of the Sun. The cat is sacred to Ra. As Pthah is the god of all beginnings in Lower Egypt, so Ra is the vitalizing god, the active ruler of the world, holding a sceptre in one hand and the sign of life in the other. The goddesses of Lower Egypt were Neith at Sais,

Leto, the goddess whose temple was at Buto, and Pacht at Babastis. In Upper Egypt, as we have seen, the chief deity was Amun, or Ammon, the Concealed God, and Kneph, or Knubis. With them belonged the goddess Mut * (the mother) and Khonso. The two oldest gods were Mentu, the rising sun, and Atmu, the setting sun.

We therefore find traces of the same course of religious thought in Egypt as we shall afterward find in Greece. The earlier worship is of local deities, who are afterwards united in a Pantheon. As Zeus was at first worshipped in Dodona and Arcadia, Apollo in Crete and Delos, Aphroditê in Cyprus, Athênê at Athens, and afterward these tribal and provincial deities were united in one company as the twelve gods of Olympus, so in Egypt the various early theologies were united in the three orders, of which Ammon was made the head. But, in both countries, each city and province persevered in the worship of its particular deity. As Athênê continued to be the protector of Athens, and Aphroditê of Cyprus, so, in Egypt, Set continued to be the god of Ombos, Leto of Buto, Horus of Edfu, Khem of Coptos.

Before concluding this section, we must say a word of the practical morality connected with this theology. We have seen, above, the stress laid on works of justice and mercy. There is a papyrus in the Imperial library at Paris, which M. Chabas considers the oldest book in the world. It is an autograph manuscript written B. C. 2200, or four thousand years ago, by one who calls himself the son of a king. It contains practical philosophy like that of Solomon in his proverbs. It glorifies, like the Proverbs, wisdom. It says that " man's heart rules the man," that " the bad man's life is what the wise know to be death," that " what we say in secret is known to him who made our interior nature," that " he who made us is present with us though we are alone."

Is not the human race one, when this Egyptian four thousand years ago, talks of life as Solomon spoke one thousand years after, in Judæa ; and as Benjamin Franklin spoke, three thousand years after Solomon, in America ?

---

* The name " Mut " was also given to Neith, Pacht, and Isis.

§ 7. *Influence of Egypt on Judaism and Christianity.*

How much of the doctrine and ritual of Egypt were imported into Judaism by Moses is a question by no means easy to settle. Of Egyptian theology proper, or the doctrine of the gods, we find no trace in the Pentateuch. Instead of the three orders of deities we have Jehovah; instead of the images and pictures of the gods, we have a rigorous prohibition of idolatry ; instead of Osiris and Isis, we have a Deity above all worlds and behind all time, with no history, no adventures, no earthly life. But it is perhaps more strange not to find any trace of the doctrine of a future life in Mosaism, when this was so prominent among the Egyptians. Moses gives no account of the judgment of souls after death ; he tells nothing of the long journey and multiform experiences of the next life according to the Egyptians, nothing of a future resurrection and return to the body. His severe monotheism was very different from the minute characterization of gods in the Egyptian Pantheon. The personal character of Jehovah, with its awful authority, its stern retribution and impartial justice, was quite another thing from the symbolic ideal type of the gods of Egypt. Nothing of the popular myth of Osiris, Isis, Horus, and Typhon is found in the Pentateuch, nothing of the transmigration of souls, nothing of the worship of animals; nothing of the future life and judgment to come ; nothing of the embalming of bodies and ornamenting of tombs. The cherubim among the Jews may resemble the Egyptian Sphinx ; the priests' dress in both are of white linen ; the Urim and Thummim, symbolic jewels of the priests, are in both ; a quasi hereditary priesthood is in each ; and both have a temple worship. But here the parallels cease. Moses left behind Egyptian theology, and took only some hints for his ritual from the Nile.

There may perhaps be a single exception to this statement. According to Brugsch * and other writers, the Papyrus buried with the mummy contained the doctrine of the Divine unity. The name of God was not

* Brugsch, Aus dem Orient, p. 48.

given, but instead the words NUK PU NUK, "I am the I am," corresponding to the name given in Exodus iii. 14, Jahveh (in a corrupt form Jehovah). This name, Jahveh, has the same meaning with the Egyptian Nuk pu Nuk, "I am the I am." At least so say Egyptologists. If this is so, the coincidence is certainly very striking.

That some of the ritualism to which the Jews were accustomed in Egypt should have been imported into their new ceremonial, is quite in accordance with human nature. Christianity, also, has taken up many of the customs of heathenism.* The rite of circumcision was probably adopted by the Jews from the Egyptians, who received it from the natives of Africa. Livingstone has found it among the tribes south of the Zambesi, and thinks this custom there cannot be traced to any Mohammedan source. Prichard believes it, in Egypt, to have been a relic of ancient African customs. It still exists in Ethiopia and Abyssinia. In Egypt it existed far earlier than the time of Abraham, as appears by ancient mummies. Wilkinson affirms it to have been "as early as the fourth dynasty, and probably earlier, long before the time of Abraham." Herodotus tells us that the custom existed from the earliest times among the Egyptians and Ethiopians, and was adopted from them by the Syrians of Palestine. Those who regard this rite as instituted by a Divine command may still believe that it already existed among the Jews, just as baptism existed among them before Jesus commanded his disciples to baptize. Both in Egypt and among the Jews it was connected with a feeling of superiority. The circumcised were distinguished from others by a higher religious position. It is difficult to trace the origin of sentiments so alien to our own ways of thought; but the hygienic explanation seems hardly adequate. It may have been a sign of the devotion of the generative power to the service of God, and have been the first step out of the untamed license of the passions, among the Africans.

* See Merivale, Conversion of the Northern Nations, p. 187, note, where he gives examples of "the inveterate lingering of Pagan usages among the nominally converted." But many of these were sanctioned by the Catholic Church.

It has been supposed that the figure of the Cherubim among the Jews was derived from that of the Sphinx. There were three kinds of Sphinxes in Egypt, — the *andro-sphinx*, with the head of a man and the body of a lion; the *crio-sphinx*, with the head of a ram and the body of a lion; and the *hieraco-sphinx*, with the head of a hawk and a lion's body. The first was a symbol of the union of wisdom and strength. The Sphinx was the solemn sentinel, placed to watch the temple and the tomb, as the Cherubim watched the gates of Paradise after the expulsion of Adam. In the Cherubim were joined portions of the figure of a man with those of the lion, the ox, and the eagle. In the Temple the Cherubim spread their wings above the ark; and Wilkinson gives a picture from the Egyptian tombs of two kneeling figures with wings spread above the scarabæus. The Persians and the Greeks had similar symbolic figures, meant to represent the various powers of these separate creatures combined in one being; but the Hebrew figure was probably imported from Egypt.

The Egyptians had in their temples a special interior sanctuary, more holy than the rest. So the Jews had their Holy of Holies, into which only the high-priest went, separated by a veil from the other parts of the Temple. The Jews were commanded on the Day of Atonement to provide a scapegoat, to carry away the sins of the people, and the high-priest was to lay his hands on the head of the goat and confess the national sins, " putting them upon the head of the goat " (Lev. xvi. 21, 22), and it was said that " the goat shall bear upon him all their iniquities unto a land not inhabited." So, among the Egyptians, whenever a victim was offered, a prayer was repeated over its head, " that if any calamity were about to befall either the sacrifices or the land of Egypt, it might be averted on this head." *

Such facts as these make it highly probable that Moses allowed in his ritual many ceremonies borrowed from the Egyptian worship.

That Egyptian Christianity had a great influence on the development of the system of Christian doctrine is not

---

* Kenrick, I. 372 (American edition).

improbable.* The religion of ancient Egypt was very
tenacious and not easily effaced. Successive waves of
Syrian, Persian, Greek, and Roman conquest rolled over
the land, scarcely producing any change in her religion
or worship. Christianity conquered Egypt, but was itself
deeply tinged with the faith of the conquered. Many
customs found in Christendom may be traced back to
Egypt. The Egyptian at his marriage put a gold ring on
his wife's finger, as a token that he intrusted her with all
his property, just as in the Church of England service the
bridegroom does the same, saying, "With all my worldly
goods I thee endow." Clemens tells us that this custom
was derived by the Christians from the Egyptians. The
priests at Philæ threw a piece of gold into the Nile once
a year, as the Venetian Doge did into the Adriatic. The
Feast of Candles at Sais is still marked in the Christian
calendar as Candlemas Day. The Catholic priest shaves
his head as the Egyptian priest did before him. The
Episcopal minister's linen surplice for reading the Liturgy
is taken from the dress of obligation, made of linen, worn
by the priest in Egypt. Two thousand years before the
Pope assumed to hold the keys, there was an Egyptian
priest at Thebes with the title of "Keeper of the two
doors of Heaven." †

In the space which we have here at command we are
unable to examine the question of doctrinal influences
from Egypt upon orthodox Christianity. Four doctrines,
however, are stated by the learned Egyptologist, Samuel
Sharpe, to be common to Egyptian mythology and church
orthodoxy. They are these : —

1. That the creation and government of the world is
not the work of one simple and undivided Being, but of
one God made up of several persons. This is the doctrine
of plural unity.

2. That salvation cannot be expected from the justice
or mercy of the Supreme Judge, unless an atoning sacrifice is made to him by a divine being.

---

* See for proofs, Egyptian Mythology and Egyptian Christianity,
by Samuel Sharpe, 1863.
† Sharpe, Egyptian Mythology and Egyptian Christianity.

3. That among the persons who compose the godhead, one, though a god, could yet suffer pain and be put to death.

4. That a god or man, or a being half god and half a man once lived on earth, born of an earthly mother but without an earthly father.

The gods of Egypt generally appear in triads, and sometimes as three gods in one. The triad of Thebes was Amun-Ra, Athor, and Chonso, — or father, mother, and son. In Nubia it was Pthah, Amun-Ra, and Horus-Ra. At Philæ it was Osiris, Isis, and Horus. Other groups were Isis, Nephthys, and Horus; Isis, Nephthys, and Osiris; Osiris, Athor, and Ra. In later times Horus became the supreme being, and appears united with Ra and Osiris in one figure, holding the two sceptres of Osiris, and having the hawk's head of Horus and the sun of Ra. Eusebius says of this god that he declared himself to be Apollo, Lord, and Bacchus. A porcelain idol worn as a charm combines Pthah the Supreme God of Nature, with Horus the Son-God, and Kneph the Spirit-God. The body is that of Pthah, God of Nature, with the hawk's wings of Horus, and the ram's head of Kneph. It is curious that Isis the mother, with Horus the child in her arms, as the merciful gods who would save their worshippers from the vengeance of Osiris the stern judge, became as popular a worship in Egypt in the time of Augustus, as that of the Virgin and Child is in Italy to-day. Juvenal says that the painters of Rome almost lived by painting the goddess Isis, the Madonna of Egypt, which had been imported into Italy, and which was very popular there.

In the trial of the soul before Osiris, as represented on tablets and papyri, are seen the images of gods interceding as mediators and offering sacrifices on its behalf. There are four of these mediatorial gods, and there is a tablet in the British Museum in which the deceased is shown as placing the gods themselves on the altar as his sin-offering, and pleading their merits.*

The death of Osiris, the supreme god of all Egypt, was a central fact in this mythology. He was killed by

* Sharpe, as above.

Typhon, the Egyptian Satan, and after the fragments of his body had been collected by "the sad Isis," he returned to life as king of the dead and their judge.*

In connection with these facts it is deserving of notice that the doctrine of the trinity and that of the atonement began to take shape in the hands of the Christian theologians of Egypt. The Trinity and its symbols were already familiar to the Egyptian mind. Plutarch says that the Egyptians worshipped Osiris, Isis, and Horus under the form of a triangle. He adds that they considered everything perfect to have three parts, and that therefore their good god made himself threefold, while their god of evil remained single. Egypt, which had exercised so powerful an influence on the old religion of Rome, was destined also greatly to influence Christianity. Alexandria was the head-quarters of learning and profound religious speculations in the first centuries. Clemens, Origen, Dionysius, Athanasius, were eminent teachers in that school. Its doctrines were † that God had revealed himself to all nations by his Logos, or Word. Christianity is its highest revelation. The common Christian lives by faith, but the more advanced believer has gnosis, or philosophic insight of Christianity as the eternal law of the soul. This doctrine soon substituted speculation in place of the simplicity of early Christianity. The influence of Alexandrian thought was increased by the high culture which prevailed there, and by the book-trade of this Egyptian city. All the oldest manuscripts of the Bible now extant were transcribed by Alexandrian penmen. The oldest versions were made in Alexandria. Finally the intense fervor of the Egyptian mind exercised its natural influence on Christianity, as it did on Judaism and Heathenism. The Oriental speculative element of Egyptian life was reinforced by the

---

* The earliest form of the Christian doctrine of the atonement was that the Devil killed Jesus in ignorance of his divine nature. The Devil was thus deceived into doing what he had no right to do, consequently he was obliged to pay for this by giving up the souls of sinners to which he had a right. The Osiris myth of the death of a god, which deeply colored the mysteries of Adonis and Eleusis, took its last form in this peculiar doctrine of atonement.

† Hase, Kirchengeschichte, § 87.

African fire ; and in Christianity, as before in the old religion, we find both working together. By the side of the Alexandrian speculations on the nature of God and the Trinity appear the maniacal devotion of the monks of the Thebaid. The ardor of belief which had overcome even the tenacity of Judaism, and modified it into its two Egyptian forms of the speculations of Philo and the monastic devotion of the Therapeutæ, reappeared in a like action upon Christian belief and Christian practice. How large a part of our present Christianity is due to these two influences we may not be able to say. But palpable traces of Egyptian speculation appear in the Church doctrines of the Trinity and atonement, and the material resurrection* of the same particles which constitute the earthly body. And an equally evident influence from Egyptian asceticism is found in the long history of Christian monasticism, no trace of which appears in the New Testament, and no authority for which can be found in any teaching or example of Christ. The mystical theology and mystical devotion of Egypt are yet at work in the Christian Church. But beside the *doctrines* directly derived from Egypt, there has probably come into Christianity another and more important element from this source. The *spirit* of a race, a nation, a civilization, a religion is more indestructible than its forms, more pervasive than its opinions, and will exercise an interior influence long after its outward forms have disappeared. The spirit of the Egyptian religion was reverence for the divine mystery of organic life, the worship of God in creation, of unity in variety, of each in all. Through the Christian Church in Egypt, the schools of Alexandria, the monks of the Thebaid, these elements filtered into the mind of Christendom. They gave a materialistic tone to the conceptions of the early Church, concerning God, Satan, the angels and devils, Heaven, Hell, the judgment, and the resurrection. They prevented thereby the triumph of a misty Oriental spiritualism. Too gross indeed in themselves, they yet were better than the Donatism which

* Which continues in Christianity, in spite of Paul's plain statement, " Thou sowest *not* the body which shall be."

would have turned every spiritual fact into a ghost or a shadow. The African spirit, in the fiery words of a Tertullian and an Augustine, ran into a materialism, which, opposed to the opposite extreme of idealism, saved to the Church its healthy realism.

The elaborate work of Bunsen on "Egypt's Place in Universal History" does not aid us much in finding the place of Egyptian religion in universal religion. It was strictly an ethnic religion, never dreaming of extending itself beyond the borders of the Nile, until long after the conquest of Egypt by the Romans. Then, indeed, Egyptian temples were welcomed by the large hospitality of Rome, and any traveller may see the ruins of the temple of Serapis * at Pozzuoli, and that of Isis at Pompeii. The gods of Greece, as we have seen, took some hints from Egypt, but the Greek Olympus, with its bright forms, was very different from the mysterious sombre worship of Egypt.

The worship of variety, the recognition of the Divine in nature, the sentiment of wonder before the mystery of the world, the feeling that the Deity is in all life, in all form, in all change as well as in what is permanent and stable, — this is the best element and the most original part of the Egyptian religion. So much we can learn from it positively ; and negatively, by its entire dissolution, its passing away forever, leaving no knowledge of itself behind, we can learn how empty is any system of faith which is based on concealment and mystery. All the vast range of Egyptian wisdom has gone, and disappeared from the surface of the earth, for it was only a religion of the priests, who kept the truth to themselves and did not venture to communicate it to the people. It was only priestcraft, and priestcraft, like all other craft, carries in itself the principle of death. Only truth is immortal, — open, frank, manly truth. Confucius was true ; he did not know much, but he told all he knew. Buddha told all he knew. Moses told all he heard. So they and their

---

* Serapis was not a god of the Pharaonic times, but came into Egypt under the Ptolemies. But lately M. Mariette has shown that Serapis was the dead bull Apis = Osiris-Apis. ('Οσοραπις.)

works continue, being built on faith in men. But the vast fabric of Egyptian wisdom, — its deep theologies, its mysterious symbolism, its majestic art, its wonderful science, — remain only as its mummies remain and as its tombs remain, an enigma exciting and baffling our curiosity, but not adding to our real life.

CHAPTER VII.

THE GODS OF GREECE.

§ 1. The Land and the Race. § 2. Idea and General Character of Greek Religion. § 3. The Gods of Greece before Homer. § 4. The Gods of the Poets. § 5. The Gods of the Artists. § 6. The Gods of the Philosophers. § 7. The Worship of Greece. § 8. The Mysteries. Orphism. § 9. Relation of Greek Religion to Christianity.

§ 1. *The Land and the Race.*

THE little promontory and peninsula, famous in the history of mankind as Greece, or Hellas, projects into the Mediterranean Sea from the South of Europe. It is insignificant on the map, its area being only two thirds as large as that of the State of Maine. But never was a country better situated in order to develop a new civilization. A temperate climate, where the vine, olive, and fig ripened with wheat, barley, and flax; a rich alluvial soil, resting on limestone, and contained in a series of valleys, each surrounded by mountains; a position equally remote from excesses of heat and cold, dryness and moisture; and finally, the ever-present neighborhood of the sea, — constituted a home well fitted for the physical culture of a perfect race of men.

Comparative Geography, which has pointed out so many relations between the terrestrial conditions of nations and their moral attainments, has laid great stress on the connection between the extent of sea-coast and a country's civilization. The sea line of Europe, compared with its area, is more extensive than that of any other continent, and Europe has had a more various and complete intellectual development than elsewhere. Africa, which has the shortest sea line compared with its area, has been most tardy in mental activity. The sea is the highway of nations and the promoter of commerce; and commerce, which brings different races together, awakens the intellect by the contact of different languages, religions, arts, and manners. Material civilization, it is true, does not commence on the sea-shore, but in river intervals. The arts of life were invented in the valleys of the Indus and Ganges, of the Yellow and Blue Rivers of China, of the Euphrates and the Nile. But the Phœnician navigators in the Mediterranean brought to the shores of Greece the knowledge of the arts of Egypt, the manufactures of Tyre, and the products of India and Africa. Every part of the coast of Greece is indented with bays and harbors. The Mediterranean, large enough to separate the nations on its shores, and so permit independent and distinct evolution of character, is not so large as to divide them. Coasting vessels, running within sight of land, could easily traverse its shores. All this tempted to navigation, and so the Greeks learned to be a race of sailors. What the shore line of Europe was to that of the other continents, that the shore line of Greece was to the rest of Europe. Only long after, in the Baltic, the Northern Mediterranean, did a similar land-locked sea create a similar love of navigation among the Scandinavians.*

Another feature in the physical geography of Greece must be noticed as having an effect on the psychical condition of its inhabitants. Mountains intersected every part, dividing its tribes from each other. In numerous valleys, separated by these mountain walls, each clan, left to itself, formed a special character of its own. The great chain of Pindus with its many branches, the lofty ridges of the Peloponnesus, allowed the people of Thessaly, Bœotia, Attica, Phocis, Locris, Argolis, Arcadia, Laconia, to attain those individual traits which distinguish them during all the course of Greek history.

* Mr. Grote (Vol. II. p. 222, American edition) refers to Strabo's remark on the great superiority of Europe over Asia and Africa in regard to the intersection and interpenetration of the land by the sea. He also quotes Cicero, who says that all Greece is in close contact to the sea, and only two or three tribes separated from it, while the Greek islands swim among the waves with their customs and institutions. He says that the ancients remarked the greater activity, mutability, and variety in the life of maritime nations.

Such physical conditions as we have described are eminently favorable to a free and full development of national character. But this word "development," so familiar to modern thought, implies not only outward circumstances to educate, but a special germ to be educated. So long as the human being is regarded as a lump of dough, to be moulded into any shape by external influences, no such term as "development" was needed. But philosophical historians now admit national character to be the result of two factors, — the original ethnic germ in the race, and the terrestrial influences which unfold it.* A question, therefore, of grave moment concerns the origin of the Hellenic people. Whence are they derived ? what are their affinities ? and from what region did they come ?

The science of Comparative Philology, one of the great triumphs of modern scholarship, has enabled us now, for the first time, to answer this question. What no Greek knew, what neither Herodotus, Plato, nor Aristotle could tell us, we are now able to state with certainty. The Greek language, both in its grammar and its vocabulary, belongs to the family of Indo-European languages, of which the Sanskrit is the elder sister. Out of eleven thousand six hundred and thirty-three Greek words, some two thousand are found to be Sanskrit, and three thousand more to belong to other branches of the Indo-European tongues. As the words common to the Greek and the Sanskrit must have been in use by both races before their separation, while living together in Central Asia, we have a clew to the degree of civilization attained by the Greeks before they arrived in Europe. Thus it appears that they brought from Asia a familiarity with oxen and cows, horses, dogs, swine, goats, geese ; that they could work in metals ; that they built houses, and were acquainted with the elements of agriculture, especially with farinaceous grains; they used salt ; they had boats propelled by oars, but not

* Mr. Buckle is almost the only marked exception. He nowhere recognizes the doctrine of race.

sails ; they divided the year by moons, and had a decimal notation.*

The Greeks, as a race, came from Asia later than the Latin races. They belonged to that powerful Indo-European race, to which Europe owes its civilization, and whose chief branches are the Hindoos, the Persians, the Greeks, the Latins, the Kelts, the Teutonic tribes, and the Slavi. The original site of the race was, as we have seen in our chapter on Brahmanism, in Bactria ; and the earliest division of this people could not have been later than three thousand or four thousand years before the Christian era. When the Hellenic branch entered Europe we have now no means of saying. It was so long anterior to Greek history that all knowledge of the time was lost, and only the faintest traditions of an Asiatic origin of their nation are to be found in Greek writers.

The Hellenic tribes, at the beginning of the seventh century before Christ, were divided into four groups, — the Achaians, Æolians, Dorians, and Ionians, — with outlying tribes more or less akin. But this Hellenic people had been preceded in Greece by another race known as Pelasgians. It is so difficult to say who these were, that Mr. Grote, in despair, pronounces them unknowable, and relinquishes the problem. Some facts concerning them may, however, be considered as established. Their existence in Greece is pronounced by Thirwall to be "the first unquestionable fact in Greek history." Homer speaks (Iliad, II. 681) of "Pelasgian Argos," and of "spear-skilled Pelasgians," "noble Pelasgians," "Pelasgians inhabiting fertile Larissa" (II. 840 ; X. 429). Herodotus frequently

---

* The ox is, in Sanskrit *go* or *gaûs*, in Latin *bos*, in Greek βοῦς.

The horse is, in Sanskrit *açva*, in Zend *açpa*, in Greek ἵππος, in Latin *equus.*

The sheep is, in Sanskrit *avis*, in Latin *ovis*, in Greek ὄϊς.

The goose is, in Sanskrit *hansa*, in Latin *anser*, in Old German *kans*, in Greek χήν.

House is, in Sanskrit *dama*, in Latin *domus*, in Greek δόμος. Door is, in Sanskrit *dvâr* or *duâra*, in Greek θύρα, in Irish *doras*.

Boat or ship is, in Sanskrit *naûs*, in Latin *navis*, in Greek ναῦς. Oar is, in Sanskrit *aritram*, in Greek ἐρετμός, in Latin *remus*.

The Greeks distinguished themselves from the Barbarians as a grain-eating race. Barbarians ate acorns.

speaks of the Pelasgians. He says that the Dorians were
a Hellenic nation, the Ionians were Pelasgic; he does not
profess to know what language the Pelasgians used, but
says that those who in his time inhabited Crestona,
Placia, and other regions, spoke a barbarous language,
and that the people of Attica were formerly Pelasgic.
He mentions the Pelasgians as remaining to his time
in Arcadia, after the Dorians had expelled them from the
rest of the Peloponnesus; says that the Samothracians
adopted the mysteries of the Kabiri from the Pelasgians;
that the Pelasgians sacrificed victims to unknown gods at
Dodona, and asked that oracle advice about what names
they should give their gods. These names, taken from
Egypt, the Grecians received from them. Hellas was formerly called Pelasgia. The Athenians expelled the Pelasgians from Attica (whether justly or unjustly, Herodotus
does not undertake to say), where they were living under
Mount Hymettus; whereupon the Pelasgians of Lemnos,
in revenge, carried off a number of Athenian women, and
afterward murdered them; as an expiation of which crime
they were finally commanded by the oracle at Delphi to
surrender that island to Miltiades and the Athenians.
Herodotus repeatedly informs us that nearly the whole
Ionian race were formerly called Pelasgians.[*]

From all this it appears that the Pelasgians were the
ancient occupants of nearly all Greece; that they were
probably of the same stock as their Hellenic successors,
but of another branch; that their language was somewhat different, and contained words of barbaric (that is
Phœnician or Egyptian) origin, but not so different as to
remain distinct after the conquest. From the Pelasgian
names which remain, it is highly probable that this people
was of the same family with the old Italians.[†] They must
have constituted the main stem of the Greek people.
The Ionians of Attica, the most brilliant portion of the
Greeks, were of Pelasgic origin. It may be therefore as-

---

[*] Herod., I. 56, 57, 146; II. 51, 171; IV. 145; V. 26; VI. 137;
VII. 94; VIII. 44, 73.

[†] Maury, Histoire des Religions de la Grèce Antique, Chap. I. p. 5.
He mentions several Pelasgic words which seem to be identical with old
Italian or Etruscan names.

sumed, without much improbability, that while the Dorian element gave the nation its strength and vital force, the Pelasgic was the source of its intellectual activity and success in literature and art. Ottfried Müller remarks that " there is no doubt that most of the ancient religions of Greece owed their origin to this race. The Zeus and Diônê of Dodona, Zeus and Hêrê of Argos, Hêphæstos and Athênê of Athens, Dêmetêr and Cora of Eleusis, Hermês and Artemis of Arcadia, together with Cadmus and the Cabiri of Thebes, cannot properly be referred to any other origin." *

Welcker † thinks that the ethnological conceptions of Æschylus, in his " Suppliants," are invaluable helps in the study of the Pelasgic relations to the Greeks. The poet makes Pelasgos the king of Argos, and represents him as ruling over the largest part of Greece. His subjects he calls Greeks, and they vote in public assembly by holding up their hands, so distinguishing them from the Dorians, among whom no such democracy prevailed. ‡ He protects the suppliant women against their Egyptian persecutors, who claimed them as fugitives from slavery. The character assigned by Æschylus to this representative of the Pelasgian race is that of a just, wise, and religious king, who judged that it was best to obey God, even at the risk of displeasing man.

It is evident, therefore, that from the earliest times there were in Greece two distinct elements, either two different races or two very distinct branches of a common race. First known as Pelasgians and Hellênes, they afterwards took form as the Ionian and Dorian peoples. And it is evident also that the Greek character, so strong yet so flexible, so mighty to act and so open to receive, with its stern virtues and its tender sensibilities, was the result of the mingling of these antagonist tendencies. Two continents may have met in Greece, if to the genius of that wonderful people Asia lent her intellect and Africa her fire. It was the marriage of soul and body, of nature and

---

* Müller, Dorians, Introduction, § 10.
† Griechische Götterlehre, Einleitung, § 6.
‡ See Müller, Dorians.

spirit, of abstract speculation and passionate interest in this life. Darkness rests on the period when this national life was being created; the Greeks themselves have preserved no record of it.

That some powerful influence from Egypt was acting on Greece during this forming period, and contributing its share to the great result, there can hardly be a question. All the legends and traditions hint at such a relation, and if this were otherwise, we might be sure that it must have existed. Egypt was in all her power and splendor when Greece was being settled by the Aryans from Asia. They were only a few hundred miles apart, and the ships of Phœnicia were continually sailing to and fro between them.

The testimony of Greek writers to the early influence of Egypt on their country and its religion is very full. Creuzer * says that the Greek writers differed in regard to the connection of Attic and Egyptian culture, only as to How it was, not as to Whether it was. Herodotus says distinctly and positively † that most of the names of the Greek gods came from Egypt, except some whose names came from the Pelasgians. The Pelasgians themselves, he adds, gave these Egyptian names to the unnamed powers of nature whom they before ignorantly worshipped, being directed by the oracle at Dodona so to do. By "name" here, Herodotus plainly intends more than a mere appellation. He includes also something of the personality and character. ‡ Before they were impersonal beings, powers of nature; afterwards, under Egyptian influence, they became persons. He particularly insists on having heard this from the priestesses of Dodona, who also told him a story of the black pigeon from Egypt, who first directed the oracle to be established, which he interpreted, according to what he had heard in Egypt, to be a black Egyptian woman. He adds that the Greeks

---

* Symbolik und Mythologie, Th. III., Heft 1, chap. 5, § 1.
† Herod. II. 50 *et seq.*
‡ Among the ancients Ὄνομα often had this force. It denoted personality. The meaning, therefore, of Herodotus is that the Egyptians taught the Greeks to give their deities proper names, instead of common names. A proper name is the sign of personality.

12

received, not only their oracles, but their public processions, festivals, and solemn prayers from the Egyptians. M. Maury admits the influence of Egypt on the worship and ceremonies of Greece, and thinks it added to their religion a more serious tone and a sentiment of veneration for the gods, which were eminently beneficial. He doubts the story of Herodotus concerning the derivation of gods from Egypt, giving as a sufficient proof the fact that Homer's knowledge of Egyptian geography was very imperfect.* But religious influences and geographical knowledge are very different things. Because the mediæval Christian writers had an imperfect knowledge of Palestine, it does not follow that their Christianity was not influenced in its source by Judaism. The objection to the derivation of the Greek gods from Egypt, on account of the names on the monuments being different from those of the Hellenic deities, is sufficiently answered by Creuzer, who shows that the Greeks translated the Egyptian word into an equivalent in their own language. Orphic ideas came from Egypt into Greece, through the colonies in Thrace and Samothrace.† The story of the Argive colony from Egypt, with their leader Danaus, connects some Egyptian immigration with the old Pelasgic ruler of that city, the walls of which contained Pelasgic masonry. The legends concerning Cecrops, Io, and Lelex, as leading colonies from Egypt to Athens and Megara, are too doubtful to add much to our argument. The influence of Egypt on Greek religion in later times is universally admitted. ‡

§ 2. *Idea and General Character of Greek Religion.*

The idea of Greek religion, which specially distinguishes it from all others, is the human character of its gods. The gods of Greece are men and women, idealized men and women, men and women on a larger scale, but still intensely human. The gods of India, as they

---

* Maury, Religions de la Grèce, III. 263.
† Diod. Sic., I. 92 – 96.
‡ Gerhard, Griechische Mythologie, § 50, Vol. 1.

appear in the Sacred Books, are vast abstractions ; and as they appear in sculpture, hideous and grotesque idols. The gods of Egypt seem to pass away into mere symbols and intellectual generalizations. But the gods of Greece are persons, warm with life, radiant with beauty, having their human adventures, wars, loves. The symbolical meaning of each god disappears in his personal character.

These beings do not keep to their own particular sphere nor confine themselves to their special parts, but, like men and women, have many different interests and occupations. If we suppose a number of human beings, young and healthy and perfectly organized, to be gifted with an immortal life and miraculous endowments of strength, wisdom, and beauty, we shall have the gods of Olympus.

Greek religion differs from Brahmanism in this, that its gods are not abstract spirit, but human beings. It differs also from Buddhism, the god in which is also a man, in this, that the gods of Greece are far less moral than Buddha, but far more interesting. They are not trying to save their souls, they are by no means ascetic, they have no intention of making progress through the universe by obeying the laws of nature, but they are bent on having a good time. Fighting, feasting, and making love are their usual occupations. If they can be considered as governing the world, it is in a very loose way and on a very irregular system. They interfere with human affairs from time to time, but merely from whim or from passion. With the common relations of life they have little to do. They announce no moral law, and neither by precept nor example undertake to guide men's consciences.

The Greek religion differs from many other religions also in having no one great founder or restorer, in having no sacred books and no priestly caste. It was not established by the labors of a Zoroaster, Gautama, Confucius, or Mohammed. It has no Avesta, no Vedas, no Koran. Every religion which we have thus far considered has its sacred books, but that of Greece has none, unless we accept the works of Homer and Hesiod as its Bible. Still more remarkable is the fact of its having no priestly caste. Brahmanism and Egypt have an hereditary priesthood ; and in all other religions, though the priesthood might not be hereditary, it always constituted a distinct caste. But in Greece kings and generals and common people offer sacrifices and prayers, as well as the priests. Priests obtained their office, not by inheritance, but by appointment or election; and they were often chosen for a limited time.

Another peculiarity of the Greek religion was that its gods were not manifestations of a supreme spirit, but were natural growths. They did not come down from above, but came up from below. They did not emanate, they were evolved. The Greek Pantheon is a gradual and steady development of the national mind. And it is still more remarkable that it has three distinct sources, — the poets, the artists, and the philosophers. Jupiter, or Zeus in Homer, is oftenest a man of immense strength, so strong that if he has hold of one end of a chain and all the gods hold the other, with the earth fastened to it beside, he will be able to move them all. Far more grand is the conception of Jupiter as it came from the chisel of Phidias, of which Quintilian says that it added a new religious sentiment to the religion of Greece. Then came the philosophers and gave an entirely different and higher view of the gods. Jupiter becomes with them the Supreme Being, father of gods and of men, omnipotent and omnipresent.

One striking consequence of the absence of sacred books, of a sacred priesthood, and an inspired founder of their religion, was the extreme freedom of the whole system. The religion of Hellas was hardly a restraint either to the mind or to the conscience. It allowed the Greeks to think what they would and to do what they chose. They made their gods to suit themselves, and regarded them rather as companions than as objects of reverence. The gods lived close to them on Olympus, a precipitous and snow-capped range full of vast cliffs, deep glens, and extensive forests, less than ten thousand feet in height, though covered with snow on the top even in the middle of July.

According to the Jewish religion, man was made in the image of God; but according to the Greek religion the gods were made in the image of men. Heraclitus says, "Men are mortal gods, and the gods immortal men." The Greek fancied the gods to be close to him on the summit of the mountain which he saw among the clouds, often mingling in disguise with mankind; a race of stronger and brighter Greeks, but not very much wiser or better. All their own tendencies they beheld reflected in their deities. They projected themselves upon the heavens, and saw with pleasure a race of divine Greeks in the skies above, corresponding with the Greeks below. A delicious religion; without austerity, asceticism, or terror; a religion filled with forms of beauty and nobleness, kindred to their own; with gods who were capricious indeed, but never stern, and seldom jealous or very cruel. It was a heaven so near at hand, that their own heroes had climbed into it, and become demigods. It was a heaven peopled with such a variety of noble forms, that they could choose among them the protector whom they liked best, and possibly themselves be selected as favorites by some guardian deity. The fortunate hunter, of a moonlight night, might even behold the graceful figure of Diana flashing through the woods in pursuit of game, and the happy inhabitant of Cyprus come suddenly on the fair form of Venus resting in a laurel-grove. The Dryads could be seen glancing among the trees, the Oreads heard shouting on the mountains, and the Naiads found asleep by the side of their streams. If the Greek chose, he could take his gods from the poets; if he liked it better, he could find them among the artists; or if neither of these suited him, he might go to the philosophers for his deities.

The Greek religion, therefore, did not guide or restrain, it only stimulated. The Greek, by intercourse with Greek gods, became more a Greek than ever. Every Hellenic feeling and tendency was personified and took a divine form; which divine form reacted on the tendency to develop it still further. All this contributed unquestionably to that wonderful phenomenon, Greek development. Nowhere on the earth, before or since, has the human being been educated into such a wonderful perfection, such an entire and total unfolding of itself, as in Greece. There, every human tendency and faculty of soul and body opened in symmetrical proportion. That small country, so insignificant on the map of Europe, so invisible on the map of the world, carried to perfection in a few short centuries every human art. Everything in Greece is art; because everything is finished, done perfectly well. In that garden of the world ripened the masterpieces of epic, tragic, comic, lyric, didactic poetry; the masterpieces in every school of philosophic investigation; the masterpieces of history, of oratory, of mathematics; the masterpieces of architecture, sculpture, and painting. Greece developed every form of human government, and in Greece were fought and won the great battles of the world. Before Greece, everything in human literature and art was a rude and imperfect attempt; since Greece, everything has been a rude and imperfect imitation.

§ 3. *The Gods of Greece before Homer.*

The Theogony of Hesiod, or Book of Genesis of the Greek gods, gives us the history of three generations of deities. First come the Uranids; secondly, the Titans; and thirdly, the gods of Olympus. Beginning as powers of nature, they end as persons.[*]

The substance of Hesiod's charming account of these three groups of gods is as follows : —

First of all things was Chaos. Next was broad-bosomed Earth, or Gaia. Then was Tartarus, dark and dim, below the earth. Next appears Eros, or Love, most beautiful among the Immortals. From Chaos came Erebus and black Night, and then sprang forth Ether and Day,

---

[*] Mr. Grote (History of Greece, Part I. Chap. I.) maintains that Heaven, Night, Sleep, and Dream "are Persons, just as much as Zeus and Apollo." I confess that I can hardly understand his meaning. The first have neither personal qualities, personal life, personal history, nor personal experience ; they appear only as vast abstractions, and so disappear again.

children of Erebus and Night. Then Earth brought forth the starry Heaven, Uranos, like to herself in size, that he might shelter her around. Gaia, or Earth, also bore the mountains, and Pontus or the barren Sea.

Then Gaia intermarried with Uranos, and produced the Titans and Titanides, namely, Ocean, Kœos, Krios, Hyperion, Iapetus, Theia and Rhea, Themis, Mnêmosynê, Phœbe with golden coronet, and lovely Thethys. Lastly came Kronos, or Time ; with the Cyclôpes and the hundred-headed giants. All these children were hid in the earth by Uranos, who dreaded them, till by a contrivance of Gaia and Kronos, Uranos was dethroned, and the first age of the gods was terminated by the birth from the sea of the last and sweetest of the children of the Heaven, Aphroditê, or Immortal Beauty, — the only one of this second generation who continued to reign on Olympus ; an awful, beauteous goddess, says Hesiod, beneath whose delicate feet the verdure throve around, born in wave-washed Cyprus, but floating past divine Cythera. Her Eros accompanied, and fair Desire followed.

Thus was completed the second generation of gods, the children of Heaven and Earth, called Titans. These had many children. The children of Ocean and Tethys were the nymphs of Ocean. Hyperion and Theia had, as children, Helios, Selênê and Eôs, or Sun, Moon, and Dawn. Kœos and Phœbê had Lêtô and Asteria. One of the children of Krios was Pallas ; those of Iapetus were Prometheus, Epimetheus, and Atlas. Kronos married his sister Rhea, and their children were Hestia, Dêmêtêr and Hêrê ; Hadês, Poseidôn, and Zeus, — all, except Hadês or Pluto, belonging to the subsequent Olympian deities.

The Olympian gods, with their cousins of the same generation, have grown into persons, ceasing to be abstract ideas, or powers of nature. Five were the children of Kronos, namely, Zeus, Poseidôn, Hêrê, Hestia, and Dêmêtêr ; six were children of Zeus, Apollo and Artemis, Hephæstos and Arês, Hermês and Athênê. The twelfth of the Olympian group, Aphroditê, belonged to the second generation, being daughter of Uranos and of the Ocean. Beauty, divine child of Sky and Sea, was conceived of as older than Power.

These are the three successive groups of deities; the second supplanting the first, the third displacing the second. The earlier gods we must needs consider, not as persons, but as powers of nature, not yet humanized.* The last, seated on Olympus, are " fair humanities."

But now, it is remarkable that there must have been, in point of fact, three stages of religious development, and three successive actual theologies in Greece, corresponding very nearly to these three legendary generations of gods.

When the ancestors of the Hellenic race came from Asia, they must have brought with them a nature-worship, akin to that which subsequently appeared in India in the earliest hymns of the Vedas. Comparative Philology, as we have before seen, has established the rule, that whatever words are common to all the seven Indo-European families must have been used in Central Asia before their dispersion. From this rule Pictet † has inferred that the original Aryan tribes all worshipped the Heaven, the Earth, Sun, Fire, Water, and Wind. The ancestors of the Greeks must have brought with them into Hellas the worship of some of these elementary deities. And we find at least two of them, Heaven and Earth, represented in Hesiod's first class of the oldest deities. Water is there in the form of Pontus, the Sea, and the other Uranids have the same elementary character.

The oldest hymns in the Vedas mark the second development of the Aryan deities in India. The chief gods of this period are Indra, Varuna, Agni, Savitri, Soma. Indra is the god of the air, directing the storm, the lightning, the clouds, the rain; Varuna is the all-embracing circle of the heavens, earth, and sea; Savitri or Surja is the Sun, King of Day, also called Mitra; Agni is Fire; and Soma is the sacred fermented juice of the moon-plant, often indeed the moon itself.

As in India, so in Greece, there was a second develop-

---

* Keats, in his Hyperion, is the only modern poet who has caught the spirit of the mighty Titanic deities and is able to speak

"In the large utterance of the early gods."

† Pictet, Les Origines Indo-Européenes.

ment of gods. They correspond in this, that the powers of nature began, in both cases, to assume a more distinct personality. Moreover, Indra, the god of the atmosphere, he who wields the lightning, the thunderer, the god of storms and rain, was the chief god in the Vedic period. So also in Greece, the chief god in this second period was Zeus. He also was the god of the atmosphere, the thunderer, the wielder of lightning. In the name "Zeus" is a reminiscence of Asia. Literally it means "the god," and so was not at first a proper name. Its root is the Sanskrit *Div*, meaning "to shine." Hence the word *Deva*, God, in the Vedic Hymns, from which comes Θεος and Δις, Διος in Greek, Deus in Latin. Ζευς Πατερ in Greek is Jupiter in Latin, coming from the Sanskrit *Djaus-piter*. Our English words "divine," "divinity," go back for their origin to the same Sanskrit root, *Div*. So marvellously do the wrecks of old beliefs come drifting down the stream of time, borne up in those frail canoes which men call words. In how many senses, higher and lower, is it true that "in the beginning was *the Word*."

This most ancient deity, god of storms, ruler of the atmosphere, favorite divinity of the Aryan race in all its branches, became Indra when he reached India, Jupiter when he arrived in Italy, Zeus when in Epirus he became the chief god of the Pelasgi, and was worshipped at that most ancient oracular temple of all Greece, Dodona. To him in the Iliad (XVI. 235) does Achilles pray, saying: "O King Jove, Dodonean, Pelasgian, dwelling afar off, presiding over wintry Dodona." A reminiscence of this old Pelasgian god long remained both in the Latin and Greek conversation, when, speaking of the weather, they called it Zeus, or Jupiter. Horace speaks of "cold Jupiter" and "bad Jupiter," as we should speak of a cold or rainy day. We also find in Horace (Odes III. 2 : 29) the archaic form of the word "Jupiter," *Diespiter*, which, according to Lassen (I. 755), means "Ruler of Heaven"; being derived from Djaus-piter. *Piter*, in Sanskrit, originally meant, says Lassen, Ruler or Lord, as well as Father.

In Arcadia and Bœotia the Pelasgi declared that their old deities were born. By this is no doubt conveyed the

12 *   R

historic consciousness that these deities were not brought to them from abroad, but developed gradually among themselves out of nameless powers of nature into humanized and personal deities. In the old days it was hardly more than a fetich worship. Hêrê was worshipped as a plank at Samos ; Athênê, as a beam at Lindus ; the Pallas of Attica, as a stake ; Jupiter, in one place, as a rock ; Apollo, as a triangle.

Together with Jupiter or Zeus, the Pelasgi worshipped Gaia or Mother Earth, in Athens, Sparta, Olympia, and other places. One of her names was Diônê ; another was Rhea. In Asia she was Cybele ; but everywhere she typified the great productive power of nature.

Another Pelasgic god was Hêlios, the Sun-God, worshipped with his sister Sêlêne, the Moon. The Pelasgi also adored the darker divinities of the lower world. At Pylos and Elis, the king of Hades was worshipped as the awful Aïdoneus ; and Persephonê, his wife, was not the fair Kora of subsequent times, but the fearful Queen of Death, the murderess, homologous to the savage wife of Çiva, in the Hindoo Pantheon. To this age also belongs the worship of the Kabiri, nameless powers, perhaps of Phœnician origin, connected with the worship of fire in Lemnos and Samothrace.

The Doric race, the second great source of the Hellenic family, entered Greece many hundreds of years after [*] the first great Pelasgic migration had spread itself through Asia Minor, Greece, and Italy. It brought with it another class of gods and a different tone of worship. Their principal deities were Apollo and Artemis, though with these they also worshipped, as secondary deities, the Pelasgic gods whose homes they had invaded. The chief difference between the Pelasgic and Dorian conception of religion was, that with the first it was more emotional, with the second more moral ; the first was a mystic natural religion, the second an intellectual human religion. Ottfried Müller [†] says that the Dorian piety was strong, cheerful, and bright. They worshipped Daylight and

[*] B. C. 1104. Döllinger.
[†] Die Dorier, X. 9.

Moonlight, while the Pelasgians also reverenced Night, Darkness, and Storm. Funeral solemnities and enthusiastic orgies did not suit the Dorian character. The Spartans had no splendid processions like the Athenians, but they prayed the gods "to give them what was honorable and good"; and Zeus Ammon declared that the "calm solemnity of the prayers of the Spartans was dearer to him than all the sacrifices of the Greeks." *

Two facts are to be noticed in connection with this primitive religion. One is the local distribution of the different deities and modes of worship through Greece. Every tribe had its own god and its own worship. In one place it was Zeus and Gaia; in another, Zeus and Cybele; in a third, Apollo and Artemis. At Samothrace prevailed the worship of the Heaven and the Earth.† Dione was worshipped with Zeus at Dodona. ‡ The Ionians were devoted to Poseidôn, god of the sea. In Arcadia, Athênê was worshipped as Tritonia. Hermês was adored on Mount Cyllene; Erôs, in Bœotia; Pan, in Arcadia. These local deities long remained as secondary gods, after the Pan-Hellenic worship of Olympus had overthrown their supremacy. But one peculiarity of the Pre-Homeric religion was, that it consisted in the adoration of different gods in different places. The religion of Hellas, after Homer, was the worship of the twelve great deities united on Mount Olympus.

The second fact to be observed in this early mythology is the change of name and of character through which each deity proceeds. Zeus alone retains the same name from the first.§

Among all Indo-European nations, the Heaven and the Earth were the two primordial divinities. The Rig-Veda calls them "the two great parents of the world." At

---

* Ottfried Müller, Die Dorier.

† Varro, quoted by Maury.

‡ Dione was the female Jupiter, her name meaning simply "the goddess," identical with the Italic "Juno," formed from Διός.

§ But not the same character. At Dodona he was invoked as the Eternal. Pausanias (X. c. 12, § 5) says that the priestesses of that shrine used this formula in their prayer: "Zeus was, Zeus is, Zeus shall be! O great Zeus!" On Olympus he was not conceived as eternal, but only as immortal.

Dodona, Samothrace, and Sparta they were worshipped together. But while in India, Varuna, the Heavens, continued to be an object of adoration in the Vedic or second period, in Greece it faded early from the popular thought. This already shows the opposite genius of the two nations. To the Hindoos the infinite was all important, to the Greeks the finite. The former, therefore, retain the adoration of the Heavens, the latter that of the Earth.

The Earth, Gaia, became more and more important to the Hellenic mind. Passing through various stages of development, she became, successively, Gaia in the first generation, Rhea in the second, and Dêmêtêr (Γή μήτηρ), Mother Earth, in the third. In like manner the Sun is successively Hyperiôn, son of Heaven and Earth; Hêlios, son of Hyperiôn and Theia; and Phœbus-Apollo, son of Zeus and Latona. The Moon is first Phœbe, sister of Hyperiôn; then Selênê, sister of Hêlios; and lastly Artemis, sister of Apollo. Pallas, probably meaning at first "the virgin," became afterward identified with Athênê, daughter of Zeus, as Pallas-Athênê. The Urania Pontus, the salt sea, became the Titan Oceanos, or Ocean, and in another generation Poseidôn, or Neptune.

The early gods are symbolical, the later are personal. The turning-point is reached when Kronos, Time, arrives. The children of Time and Earth are no longer vast shadowy abstractions, but become historical characters, with biographies and personal qualities. Neither Time nor History existed before Homer; when Time came, History began.

The three male children of Time were Zeus, Poseidôn, and Hadês; representing the three dimensions of space, Height, Breadth, and Depth; Heaven, Ocean, and Hell. They also represented the threefold progress of the human soul : its aspiration and ascent to what is noble and good, its descent to what is profound, and its sympathy with all that is various: in other words, its religion, its intelligence, and its affection.

The fable of Time devouring his children, and then reproducing them, evidently means the vicissitudes of customs and the departure and return of fashions. What-

ever is born must die; but what has been will be again.
That Erôs, Love, should be at the origin of things from
chaos, indicates the primeval attraction with which the
order of the universe begins. The mutilation of Uranos,
Heaven, so that he ceased to produce children, suggests
the change of the system of emanation, by which the
gods descend from the infinite, into that of evolution, by
which they arise out of the finite. It is, in fact, the end
of Asia, and the beginning of Europe; for emanation
is the law of the theologies of Asia, evolution that of
Europe. Aphroditê, Beauty, was the last child of the
Heavens, and yet born from the Ocean. Beauty is not
the daughter of the Heavens and the Earth, but of the
Heavens and the Ocean. The lights and shadows of
the sky, the tints of dawn, the tenderness of clouds,
unite with the toss and curve of the wave in creating
Beauty. The beauty of outline appears in the sea, that
of light and color in the sky.*

§ 4. *The Gods of the Poets.*

Herodotus says (II. 53), "I am of opinion that Hesiod
and Homer lived four hundred years before my time, and
not more, and these were they who framed a theogony for
the Greeks, and gave names to the gods, and assigned to
them honors and arts, and declared their several forms.
But the poets, said to be before them, in my opinion,
were after them."

That two poets should create a theology and a worship
for a great people, and so unite its separate tribes into a

---

* Rev. G. W. Cox (A Manual of Mythology, London, 1867. The
Mythology of the Aryan Nations, London, 1870) has shown much
ingenuity in his efforts to trace the myths and legends of the Greeks,
Germans, etc., back to some original metaphors in the old Vedic speech,
most of which relate to the movements of the sun, and the phenomena
of the heavens. It seems probable that he carries this too far; for why
cannot later ages originate myths as well as the earlier? The analogies
by which he seeks to approximate Greek, Scandinavian, and Hindoo
stories are often fanciful. And the sun plays so overwhelming a part in
this drama, that it reminds one of the picture in " Hermann and Doro-
thea," of the traveller who looked at the sun till he could see nothing
else.

"Schweben siehet ihr Bild, wohin er die Blicke nur wendet."

commonwealth of united states, seems to modern minds an absurdity. But the poets of Greece were its prophets. They received, intensified, concentrated, the tendencies of thought already in the air. All the drift was toward Pan-Hellenic worship and to a humanized theology, when the Homeric writers sang their song.

The Greeks must be conceived of as a nation of poets; hence all their mythology was poetry. Poetry was their life and joy, written or unwritten, sung or spoken. They were poets in the deeper sense of the word; not by writing verses, but by looking at all nature and all life from its poetic side. Their exquisite mythology arose out of these spontaneous instincts. The tendency of the Greek mind was to vitalize and harmonize nature.*

All the phenomena of nature, all the powers of the human soul, and all the events of life, became a marvellous tissue of divine story. They walked the earth, surrounded and overshadowed by heavenly attendants and supernatural powers. But a striking peculiarity of this immense spiritualism was that it was almost without superstition. Their gods were not their terror, but their delight. Even the great gods of Olympus were around them as invisible companions. Fate itself, the dark Moira, supreme power, mistress of gods and men, was met manfully and not timorously. So strong was the human element, the sense of personal dignity and freedom, that the Greek lived in the midst of a supernatural world on equal terms.

No doubt the elements of mythology are in all nations the same, consisting of the facts of nature and the facts of life. The heavens and the earth, day and night, the sun and moon, storms, fire, ocean, and rivers, love and beauty, life and progress, war, wisdom, doom, and chance, — these, among all nations, supply the material for myths. But while, with some races, these powers remain solemn abstractions, above and behind nature, among the Greeks they descended into nature and turned to poetry, illuminating all of life.

* See Le Sentiment Religieux en Grèce, d'Homère a Eschyle, par Jules Girard, Paris, 1869.

Let us imagine a Greek, possessed by the spirit of his nation and acquainted with its legendary history, visiting the holy places of that ideal land. On the northern boundary he sees the towering summit of Olympus, on whose solemn heights reside the twelve great gods of his country. When the dark clouds roll along its defiles, and the lightning flashes from their black depths, it is Zeus, striking with his thunderbolt some impious offender. There was held the great council of the Immortals. When the ocean was quiet, Poseidôn had left it to visit Olympus. There came Hephæstos, quitting his subterranean fires and gloomy laborers, to jest and be jested with, sitting by his beautiful queen. There, while the sun hung motionless in mid-heaven, Apollo descended from his burning chariot to join the feast. Artemis and Dêmêtêr came from the woods and fields to unite in the high assembly, and war was suspended while Arês made love to the goddess of Beauty. The Greek looked at Parnassus, "soaring snow-clad through its native sky," with its Delphic cave and its Castalian fount, or at the neighboring summits of Helicon, where Pegasus struck his hoof and Hippocrênê gushed forth, and believed that hidden in these sunny woods might perhaps be found the muses who inspired Herodotus, Homer, Æschylus, and Pindar. He could go nowhere without finding some spot over which hung the charm of romantic or tender association. Within every brook was hidden a Naiad; by the side of every tree lurked a Dryad; if you listen, you may hear the Oreads calling among the mountains; if you come cautiously around that bending hill, you may catch a glimpse of the great Pan himself. When the moonlight showers filled the forests with a magical light, one might see the untouched Artemis gliding rapidly among the mossy trunks. Beneath, in the deep abysses of earth, reigned the gloomy Pluto with the sad Persephonê, homesick for the upper air. By the sea-shore Proteus wound his horn, the Sirens sang their fatal song among the rocks, the Nereids and Oceanides gleamed beneath the green waters, the vast Amphitrite stretched her wide-embracing arms, and Thetis with her water-nymphs lived in their submarine grottos. When the morning dawned, Eôs, or Aurora, went before the chariot of the Sun, dropping flowers upon the earth. Every breeze which stirred the tree-tops was a god, going on some errand for Æolus. The joy of inspired thought was breathed into the soul by Phœbus ; the genial glow of life, the festal mirth, and the glad revel were the gift of Dionysos. All nature was alive with some touch of a divine presence. So, too, every spot of Hellas was made interesting by some legend of Hercules, of Theseus, of Promêtheus, of the great Dioscuri, of Minos, or Dædalus, of Jason and the Argonauts. The Greeks extended their own bright life backward through history, and upward through heroes and demigods to Zeus himself.

In Homer, the gods are very human. They have few traits of divinity, scarcely of dignity. Their ridicule of Vulcan is certainly coarse ; the threats of Zeus are brutal.

As a family, they live together on Olympus, feasting, talking, making love, making war, deceiving each other, angry, and reconciled. They feed on nectar and ambrosia, which makes them immortal ; just as the Amrita makes the Hindoo gods so. So in the Iliad we see them at their feast, with Vulcan handing each the cup, pouring out nectar for them all. " And then inextinguishable laughter arose among the immortal gods, when they saw Vulcan bustling through the mansion. So they feasted all day till sundown ; nor did the soul want anything of the equal feast, nor of the beautiful harp which Apollo held, nor of the Muses, who accompanied him, responding in turn with delicious voice."

" But when the splendid light of the sun was sunk, they retired to repose, each one to his house, which renowned Vulcan, lame of both legs, had built. But Olympian Zeus went to his couch, and laid down to rest beside white-armed Hêrê." *

Or sometimes they fight together, or with mortals; instances of both appear in the Iliad. It must be admitted that they do not appear to advantage in these

---

* Iliad, Book I. v. 600.

conflicts. They usually get the worst of it, and go back to Zeus to complain. In the Twenty-first Book they fight together, Arês against Athênê, Athênê also against his helper, Aphroditê; Poseidôn and Hêrê against Apollo and Artemis, Vulcan against the river god, Scamander. Arês called Athênê impudent, and threatened to chastise her. She seized a stone and struck him on the neck, and relaxed his knees. Seven acres he covered falling, and his back was defiled with dust; but Pallas-Athênê jeered at him; and when Aphroditê led him away groaning frequently, Pallas-Athênê sprang after, and smote her with her hand, dissolving her knees and dear heart. Apollo was afraid of Poseidôn, and declined fighting with him when challenged, for which Artemis rebuked him. On this, Hêrê tells her that she can kill stags on the mountains, but is afraid to fight with her betters, and then proceeds to punish her, holding both the hands of Artemis in one of hers, and beating her over the head with her own bow. A disgraceful scene altogether, we must confess, and it is no wonder that Plato was scandalized by such stories.

Thus purely human were these gods; spending the summer's day in feasting beneath the open sky; going home at sundown to sleep, like a parcel of great boys and girls. They are immortal indeed, and can make men so sometimes, but cannot always prevent the death of a favorite. Above them all broods a terrible power, mightier than themselves, the dark Fate and irresistible Necessity. For, after all, as human gods they were like men, subject to the laws of nature. Yet as men, they are free, and in the feeling of their freedom sometimes resist and defy fate.

The Homeric gods move through the air like birds, like wind, like lightning. They are stronger than men, and larger. Arês, overthrown by Pallas, covers seven acres of ground; when wounded by Diomêdês he bellowed as loud as nine or ten thousand men, says the accurate Homer. The bodies of the gods, inexpressibly beautiful, and commonly invisible, are, whenever seen by men, in an aureola of light. In Homer, Apollo is the god of archery, prophecy, and music. He is the far-darter. He shoots his arrows at the Greeks, because his prophet had been ill-treated. " He descended from Olympus," says Homer, " enraged in heart, having his bow and quiver on his shoulders. But as he moved the shafts rattled on the shoulders of him enraged; and he went onward like the night. Then he sat near the ships, and sent an arrow, and dreadful was the clangor of the silver bow."

Later in the Iliad he appears again, defending the Trojans and deceiving Achilles. In the Homeric Hymn his birth on Delos is sweetly told; and how, when he was born, Earth smiled around, and all the goddesses shouted. Themis fed him on nectar and ambrosia; then he sprang up, called for a lyre and bow, and said he would declare henceforth to men the will of Jove; and Delos, exulting, became covered with flowers.*

The Second Book of the Iliad begins thus: " The rest, both gods and horse-arraying men, slept all the night; but Jove sweet sleep possessed not; but he pondered how he might destroy many at the Greek ships, and honor Achilles. But this device appeared best to his mind, to send a fatal dream to Agamemnon. And he said, ' Haste, pernicious dream, to the swift ships, and bid Agamemnon arm the Achæans to take wide-streeted Troy, since Juno has persuaded all the gods to her will.'"

This was simply a lie, sent for the destruction of the Greeks.

In the First Book, Jupiter complains to Thetis that Juno is always scolding him, and good right had she to do so. Presently she comes in and accuses him of plotting something secretly with Thetis, and never letting her know his plans. He answers her by accusations of perversity: " Thou art always suspecting; but thou shalt produce no effect, but be further from my heart." He then is so ungentlemanly as to threaten her with corporal punishment. The gods murmur; but Vulcan interposes as a peacemaker, saying, " There will be no enjoyment in our delightful banquet if you twain thus contend." Then he

---

* Margaret Fuller used to distinguish Apollo and Bacchus as Genius and Geniality.

arose and placed the double cup in her hands and said, "Be patient, my mother, lest I again behold thee beaten, and cannot help thee."

He here refers to a time when Jupiter hung his wife up in mid-heaven with anvils tied to her heels; and when Vulcan untied them he was pitched from Olympus down into the island of Lemnos, whence came his lameness. A rude and brutal head of a household was the poetic Zeus.

No doubt other and much more sublime views of the gods are to be found in Homer. Thus (Il. XV. 80) he compares the motion of Juno to the rapid thought of a traveller, who, having visited many countries, says, " I was here," " I was there." Such also is the description (Il. XIII. 17) of Neptune descending from the top of Samothrace, with the hills and forests trembling beneath his immortal feet. Infinite power, infinite faculty, the gods of Homer possessed; but these were only human faculty and power pushed to the utmost. Nothing is more beautiful than the description of the sleep of Jupiter and Juno, "imparadised in each other's arms" (Il. XIV. 350), while the divine earth produced beneath them a bed of flowers, softly lifting them from the ground. But the picture is eminently human; quite as much so as that which Milton has imitated from it.

After Homer and Hesiod, among the Greek poets, come the lyrists. Callinus, the Ephesian, made a religion of patriotism. Tyrtæus (B. C. 660), somewhat later, of Sparta, was devoted to the same theme. Pindar, the Theban, began his career (B. C. 494) in the time of the conquests of Darius, and composed one of his Pythian odes in the year of the battle of Marathon. He taught a divine retribution on good and evil; taught that "the bitterest end awaits the pleasure that is contrary to right," * taught moderation, and that " a man should always keep in view the bounds and limits of things."† He declared that " Law was the ruler of gods and men." Moreover, he proclaimed that gods and men were of one family, and though the gods were far higher, yet that

---

* Isthmian, VI.　　　　　　† Pythian, II.

something divine was in all men.* And in a famous fragment (quoted by Bunsen †) he calls mankind the majestic offspring of earth; mankind, "a gentle race, beloved of heaven."

The tragic poet, Æschylus, is a figure like that of Michael Angelo in Italian art, grand, sombre, and possessed by his ideas. The one which rules him and runs darkly through all his tragedies is the supreme power of Nemesis, the terrible destiny which is behind and above gods and men. The favorite theme of Greek tragedy is the conflict of fate and freedom, of the inflexible laws of nature with the passionate longings of man, of "the emergency of the case with the despotism of the rule." This conflict appears most vividly in the story of Promêtheus, or Forethought; he, "whose godlike crime was to be kind"; he who resisted the torments and terrors of Zeus, relying on his own fierce mind.‡ In this respect, Promêtheus in his suffering is like Job in his sufferings. Each refuses to say he is wrong, merely to pacify God, when he does not see that he is wrong. As Promêtheus maintains his inflexible purpose, so Job holds fast his integrity.

Sophocles is the most devout of the Greek tragedians, and reverence for the gods is constantly enjoined in his tragedies. One striking passage is where Antigonê is asked if she had disobeyed the laws of the country, and replies, "Yes; for they were not the laws of God. They did not proceed from Justice, who dwells with the Immortals. Nor dared I, in obeying the laws of mortal man, disobey those of the undying gods. For the gods live from eternity, and their beginning no man knows. I know that I must die for this offence, and I die willingly. I must have died at some time, and a premature death I account a gain, as finishing a life filled with sorrows." § This argument reminds us of the higher-law discussions of the antislavery conflict, and the religious defiance of the fugitive slave law by all honest men.

---

* Nemean, VI.
† God in History, IV. 10.
‡ "Atrocem animam Catonis." — Horace.
§ Antigonê, 450.

Euripides represents the reaction against the religious tragedy. His is the anti-religious tragedy. It is a sneering defiance of the religious sentiment, a direct teaching of pessimism. Bunsen (" God in History ") goes at length into the proof of this statement, showing that in Euripides the theology of the poets encountered and submitted to the same sceptical reaction which followed in philosophy the divine teachings of Plato.* After this time Greek poetry ceased to be the organ of Greek religion. It is true that we have subsequent outbreaks of devout song, as in the hymn of Cleanthes, the stoic, who followed Zeno as teacher in the Porch (B. C. 260). Though this belongs rather to philosophy than to poetry, yet on account of its truly monotheistic and also devout quality, I add a translation here : † —

Greatest of the gods, God with many names, God ever-ruling and ruling
    all things !
Zeus, origin of nature, governing the universe by law,
All hail ! For it is right for mortals to address thee ;
Since we are thy offspring, and we alone of all
That live and creep on earth have the power of imitative speech.
Therefore will I praise thee, and hymn forever thy power.
Thee the wide heaven, which surrounds the earth, obeys ;
Following where thou wilt, willingly obeying thy law.
Thou holdest at thy service, in thy mighty hands,
The two-edged, flaming, immortal thunderbolt,
Before whose flash all nature trembles.
Thou rulest in the common reason, which goes through all,
And appears mingled in all things, great or small,
Which, filling all nature, is king of all existences.
Nor without thee, O Deity, does anything happen in the world,
From the divine ethereal pole to the great ocean,
Except only the evil preferred by the senseless wicked.
But thou also art able to bring to order that which is chaotic,
Giving form to what is formless, and making the discordant friendly ;
So reducing all variety to unity, and even making good out of evil.
Thus, through all nature is one great law,

* Yet, even in Euripides, we meet a strain like that (Hecuba, line 800), which we may render as follows : —
      " For, though perhaps we may be helpless slaves,
      Yet are the gods most strong, and over them
      Sits LAW supreme. The gods are under law, —
      So do we judge, — and therefore we can live
      While right and wrong stand separate forever."

† See the original in Herder's Greek text, Hellenische Blumenlese, and in Cudworth's Intellectual System.

Which only the wicked seek to disobey, —
Poor fools ! who long for happiness,
But will not see nor hear the divine commands.

But do thou, O Zeus, all-bestower, cloud-compeller !
Ruler of thunder ! guard men from sad error.
Father ! dispel the clouds of the soul, and let us follow
The laws of thy great and just reign !
That we may be honored, let us honor thee again,
Chanting thy great deeds, as is proper for mortals.
For nothing can be better for gods or men
Than to adore with perpetual hymns the law common to all.

The result of our investigation thus far is, that beside
all the polytheistic and anthropomorphic tendencies of
the old religion, there yet lingered a faith in one supreme
God, ruler of all things. This is the general opinion of
the best writers. For example, Welcker thus speaks of
the original substance of Greek religion : * —

" In the remotest period of Greek antiquity, we meet the
words θεός and δαίμων, and the names Ζεύς and Κρονίων ; anything older than which is not to be found in this religion.
Accordingly, the gods of these tribes were from the first generally, if not universally, heavenly and spiritual beings. Zeus
was the immortal king of heaven, in opposition to everything
visible and temporal. This affords us a permanent background of universal ideas, behind all special conceptions or local
appellations. We recognize as present in the beginnings of
Greek history the highest mental aspirations belonging to man.
We can thus avoid the mistaken doubts concerning this religion, which came from the influence of the subsequent manifestations, going back to the deep root from which they have
sprung. The Divine Spirit has always been manifested in the
feelings even of the most uncultivated peoples. Afterwards,
in trying to bring this feeling into distinct consciousness, the
various childish conceptions and imperfect views of religious
things arise."

§ 5. *The Gods of the Artists.*

The artists, following the poets, developed still further
the divinely human character of the gods. The architects
of the temples gave, in their pure and harmonious forms,
the conception of religious beauty and majesty. Standing

* Welcker, Griechische Götterlehre, § 25.

in some open elevated position, their snowy surface bathed in sunshine, they stood in serene strength, the types of a bright and joyful religion. A superstitious worship seeks caves and darkness; the noble majesty of the Greek temples said plainly that they belonged to a religion of light and peace.

The sculptor worked originally in company with the architect. The statues were meant to adorn the temples, the temples were made as frames and pedestals for the statues. The marble forms stood and walked on the pediments and gave life to the frieze. They animated the exterior, or sat, calm and strong, in the central shrine.

The poets, in giving a moral and human character to the gods, never quite forgot their origin as powers of nature. Jupiter Olympus is still the god of the sky, the thunderer. Neptune is the ruler of the ocean, the earth-shaker. Phœbus-Apollo is the sun-god. Artemis is the moonlight, pure, chaste, and cold. But the sculptors finally leave behind these reminiscences, and in their hands the deities become purely moral beings. On the brow of Jupiter sits a majestic calm; he is no angry wielder of the thunderbolt, but the gracious and powerful ruler of the three worlds. This conception grew up gradually, until it was fully realized by Phidias in his statues at Olympia and Elis. Tranquil power and victorious repose appear even in the standing Jupiters, in which last the god appears as more youthful and active.

The conception of Jupiter by Phidias was a great advance on that of Homer. He, to be sure, professed to take his idea from the famous passage of the Iliad where Jove shakes his ambrosial curls and bends his awful brows; and, nodding, shakes heaven and earth. That might be his text, but the sermon which he preached was far higher than it. This was the great statue of Jupiter, his masterpiece, made of ivory and gold for the temple at Olympia, where the games were celebrated by the united Hellenic race. These famous games, which occurred every fifth year, lasting five days, calling together all Greece, were to this race what the Passover was to the Jewish nation, sacred, venerable, blending divine worship and human joy. These games were a chronology, a constitution, and a church to the Pan-Hellenic race. All epochs were reckoned from them ; as events occurring in such or such an Olympiad. The first Olympiad was seven hundred and seventy-six years before Christ; and a large part of our present knowledge of ancient chronology depends on these festivals. They bound Greece together as by a constitution; no persons unless of genuine Hellenic blood being allowed to contend at them, and a truce being proclaimed for all Greece while they lasted.

Here at Olympia, while the games continued, all Greece came together ; the poets and historians declaimed their compositions to the grand audience ; opinions were interchanged, knowledge communicated, and the national life received both stimulus and unity.

And here, over all, presided the great Jupiter of Phidias, within a Doric temple, sixty-eight feet high, ninety-five wide, and two hundred and thirty long, covered with sculptures of Pentelic marble. The god was seated on his throne, made of gold, ebony, and ivory, studded with precious stones. He was so colossal that, though seated, his head nearly reached the roof, and it seemed as if he would bear it away if he rose. There sat the monarch, his head, neck, breast, and arms in massive proportions ; the lower part of the body veiled in a flowing mantle ; bearing in his right hand a statue of Victory, in his left a sceptre with his eagle on the top ; the Hours, the Seasons, and the Graces around him ; his feet on the mysterious Sphinx ; and on his face that marvellous expression of blended majesty and sweetness, which we know not only by the accounts of eyewitnesses, but by the numerous imitations and copies in marble which have come down to us. One cannot fail to see, even in these copies, a wonderful expression of power, wisdom, and goodness. The head, with leonine locks of hair and thickly rolling beard, expresses power ; the broad brow and fixed gaze of the eyes, wisdom ; while the sweet smile of the lips indicates goodness. The throne was of cedar, ornamented with gold, ivory, ebony, and precious stones. The sceptre was composed of every kind of metal. The statue was forty feet high, on a pedestal of twelve feet. To die without having seen this statue was regarded by the Greeks as almost as great a calamity as not to have been initiated into the mysteries.*

In like manner the poetic conception of Apollo was inferior to that of the sculptor. In the mind of the latter Phœbus is not merely an archer, not merely a prophet and a singer, but the entire manifestation of genius. He is inspiration; he radiates poetry, music, eloquence from his sublime figure. The Phidian Jupiter is lost to us, except in copies, but in the Belvedere Apollo we see how the sculptor could interpret the highest thought of the Hellenic mind. He who visits this statue by night in the Vatican Palace at Rome, seeing it by torchlight, has, perhaps, the most wonderful impression left on his imagination which art can give. After passing through the long galleries of the Vatican, where, as the torches advance, armies of statues emerge from the darkness before you, gaze on you with marble countenance, and sink back into the darkness behind, you reach at last the small circular hall which contains the Apollo. The effect of torchlight is to make the statue seem more alive. One limb, one feature, one expression after another, is brought out as the torches move; and the wonderful form becomes at last instinct with life. Milman has described the statue in a few glowing but unexaggerated lines: —

> " For mild he seemed, as in Elysian bowers,
> Wasting, in careless ease, the joyous hours ;
> Haughty, as bards have sung, with princely sway
> Curbing the fierce flame-breathing steeds of day ;
> Beauteous, as vision seen in dreamy sleep
> By holy maid, on Delphi's haunted steep."

> All, all divine ; no struggling muscle glows,
> Through heaving vein no mantling life-blood flows,
> But, animate with Deity alone,
> In deathless glory lives the breathing stone." †

In such a statue we see the human creative genius idealized. It is a magnificent representation of the mind

* Ottfried Müller, History of Greek Art, §§ 115, 347.
† Oxford Prize Poems, Poem for 1812.

13

of Greece, that fountain of original thought from which came the Songs of Homer and the Dialogues of Plato, that unfailing source of history, tragedy, lyric poetry, scientific investigation. In the Belvedere Apollo we see expressed at once the genius of Homer, Aristotle, Herodotus, Æschylus, Pindar, Thales, and Plato.

With Apollo is associated his sister Artemis, or Diana, another exquisite conception of Greek thought. Not the cold and cruel Diana of the poets; not she who, in her prudish anger, turned Actæon into a stag, who slew Orion, who slew the children of Niobe, and demanded the death of Iphigenia. Very different is the beautiful Diana of the sculptors, the Artemis, or untouched one, chaste as moonlight, a wild girl, pure, free, noble; the ideal of youthful womanhood, who can share with man manly exercises and open-air sports, and add to manly strength a womanly grace. So she seems in the statue; in swift motion, the air lifting her tunic from her noble limbs, while she draws a shaft from the quiver to kill a hind. No Greek could look at such a statue, and not learn to reverence the purity and nobleness of womanhood.

Pallas-Athênê was the goddess of all the liberal arts and sciences. In battle she proves too strong for Arês or Mars, as scientific war is always too strong for that wild, furious war which Mars represented. She was the civilizer of mankind. Her name Pallas means "virgin," and her name Athênê was supposed to be the same as the Egyptian Neith, reversed; though modern scholars deny this etymology.

The Parthenon, standing on the summit of Athens, built of white marble, was surrounded by columns 34 feet high. It was 230 feet long, 102 feet wide, and 68 high, and was perhaps the most perfect building ever raised by man. Every part of its exterior was adorned with Phidian sculpture; and within stood the statue of Athênê herself, in ivory and gold, by the same master hand. Another colossal statue of the great goddess stood on the summit of the Acropolis, and her polished brazen helmet and shield, flashing in the sun, could be seen far out at sea by vessels approaching Athens.

The Greek sculptors, in creating these wonderful ideals, were always feeling after God; but for God incarnate, God in man. They sought for and represented each divine element in human nature. They were prophets of the future development of humanity. They showed how man is a partaker of the divine nature. If they humanized Deity, they divinized humanity.

§ 6. *The Gods of the Philosophers.*

The problem which the Greek philosophers set themselves to solve was the origin of things. As we have found a double element of race and religion running through the history of Greece, so we find a similar dualism in its philosophy. An element of realism and another of idealism are in opposition until the time of Plato, and are first reconciled by that great master of thought. Realism appears in the Ionic nature-philosophy; idealism in Orphism, the schools of Pythagoras, and the Eleatic school of Southern Italy.

Both these classes of thinkers sought for some central unity beneath the outward phenomena. Thales the Milesian (B. C. 600) said it was water. His disciple, Anaximander, called it a chaotic matter, containing in itself a motive-power which would take the universe through successive creations and destructions. His successor, Anaximenes, concluded the infinite substance to be air. Heraclitus of Ephesus (B. C. 500) declared it to be fire; by which he meant, not physical fire, but the principle of antagonism. So, by *water*, Thales must have intended the fluid element in things. For that Thales was not a mere materialist appears from the sayings which have been reported as coming from him, such as this : " Of all things, the oldest is God; the most beautiful is the world; the swiftest is thought; the wisest is time." Or that other, that, " Death does not differ at all from life." Thales also taught that a Divine power was in all things. The successor of Heraclitus, Anaxagoras (B. C. 494), first distinguished God from the world, mind from matter, leaving to each an independent existence.

While the Greek colonies in Asia Minor developed thus the Asiatic form of philosophy, the colonies in Magna Græcia unfolded the Italian or ideal side. Of these, Pythagoras was the earliest and most conspicuous. Born at Samos (B. C. 584), he was a contemporary of Thales of Miletus. He taught that God was one; yet not outside of the world, but in it, wholly in every part, overseeing the beginnings of all things and their combinations.*

The head of the Italian school, known as Eleatics, was Xenophanes (born B. C. 600), who, says Zeller,† both a philosopher and a poet, taught first of all a perfect monotheism. He declared God to be the one and all, eternal, almighty, and perfect being, being all sight, feeling, and perception. He is both infinite and finite. If he were only finite, he could not *be ;* if he were only infinite, he could not *exist.* He lives in eternity, and exists in time.‡

Parmenides, scholar and successor of Xenophanes at Elea, taught that God, as pure thought, pervaded all nature. Empedocles (about B. C. 460) § followed Xenophanes, though introducing a certain dualism into his physics. In theology he was a pure monotheist, declaring God to be the Absolute Being, sufficient for himself, and related to the world as unity to variety, or love to discord. We can only recognize God by the divine element in ourselves. The bad is what is separate from God, and out of harmony with him.

After this came a sceptical movement, in which Gorgias, a disciple of Empedocles (B. C. 404) and Protagoras the Abderite, taught the doctrine of nescience. The latter said : " Whether there are gods or not we cannot say, and life is too short to find out."‖ Prodicus explained religion

---

* Ὁ μὲν θεὸs εἷs · κοῦτοs δὲ οὐκ, ὡs τινὲs ὑπονοῦσιν, ἐκτὸs τὰs διακοσμή-σεαs · ἀλλ' ἐν αὐτᾷ, ὅλοs ἐν ὅλῳ τῷ κύκλῳ, ἐπίσκοποs πάσαs γενέσεωs καὶ κράσεωs τῶν ὅλων. — Clem. Alex. Cohort. ad gentes.

† Monotheism among the Greeks, translated in the Contemporary Review, March, 1867. Victor Cousin, Fragments de Philosophie Ancienne.

‡ Quotations from Aristotle, in Rixner, I. § 75.

§ See Rixner, Zeller, and the poem of Empedocles on the Nature of Things (περὶ φάσεως), especially the commencement of the Third Book.

‖ His famous doctrine, that " man is the measure of all things," meant that there is nothing true but that which appears to man to be so at any moment. ' He taught, as we should now say, the subjectivity of knowledge.

as founded in utility, Critias derived it from statecraft.
They argued that if religion was founded in human nature,
all men would worship the same gods. This view became popular in Greece at the time of the Peloponnesian
War. Euripides, as we have seen, was a sceptic. Those
who denied the popular gods were persecuted by the
Athenians, but the sceptical spirit was not checked by
this course.* Anaxagoras escaped with his life only
through the powerful protection of Pericles. Protagoras
was sentenced to death, and his writings were burned.
Diogenes was denounced as an atheist, and a reward of
a talent was offered to any one who should kill him. For
an unbelieving age is apt to be a persecuting one. When
the kernel of religion is gone, more stress is laid on keeping the shell untouched.

It was in the midst of these dilapidated opinions that
Socrates came, that wonderful phenomenon in human
history. A marvellous vision, glorifying humanity ! He
may be considered as having created the science of ethics.
He first taught the doctrine of divine providence, declaring that we can only know God in his works. He placed
religion on the basis of humanity, proclaiming the well-
being of man to be the end of the universe. He preferred
the study of final causes to that of efficient causes. He
did not deny the inferior deities, but regarded them only
as we regard angels and archangels, saints and prophets ;
as finite beings, above man, but infinitely below the Supreme Being. Reverence for such beings is quite consistent with the purest monotheism.

In Plato, says Rixner,† the two polar tendencies of
Greek philosophy were harmonized, and realism and
idealism brought into accord. The school of realism
recognized time, variety, motion, multiplicity, and nature ;
but lost substance, unity, eternity, and spirit. The other,
the ideal Eleatic school, recognized unity, but lost variety,
saw eternity, but ignored time, accepted being, but omitted life and movement.

---

* Zeller, as before cited.
† Geschichte der Philosophie.

The three views may be thus compared : –

Italian Philosophy, or Eleatic.	Plato.	Ionian or Asiatic Atomic.
The One.	The One in All.	The All.
Unity.	Unity and Variety.	Variety.
Being.	Life.	Motion.
Pantheism.	Divine in Nature.	Naturalism.
Substance.	Substance and Manifestation.	Phenomena.

The philosophy of Plato was the scientific completion of that of Socrates. Socrates took his intellectual departure from man, and inferred nature and God. Plato assumed God, and inferred nature and man. He made goodness and nature godlike, by making God the substance in each. His was a divine philosophy, since he referred all facts theoretically and practically to God as the ground of their being.

The style of Plato singularly combined analysis and synthesis, exact definition with poetic life. His magnificent intellect aimed at uniting precision in details with universal comprehension.*

Plato, as regards his method of thought, was a strict and determined transcendentalist. He declared philosophy to be the science of unconditioned being, and asserted that this was known to the soul by its intuitive reason, which is the organ of all philosophic insight. The reason perceives substance, the understanding only phenomena. Being (το όν), which is the reality in all actuality, is in the ideas or thoughts of God; and nothing exists or appears outwardly, except by the force of this indwelling idea. The WORD is the true expression of the nature of every object; for each has its divine and natural name, beside its accidental human appellation. Philosophy is the recollection of what the soul has seen of things and their names.

The life and essence of all things is from God.   Plato's

---

* The sentence which Plato wrote over his door, οὐδεὶs ἀγεωμέτρητοs εἰσίτω, probably means, " Let no one enter who has not *definite* thoughts." So Goethe declared that *outline* went deepest into the mysteries of nature.

idea of God is of the purest and highest kind. God is one, he is Spirit, he is the supreme and only real being, he is the creator of all things, his providence is over all events. He avoids pantheism on one side, by making God a distinct personal intelligent will; and polytheism on the other, by making him absolute, and therefore one. Plato's theology is pure theism.*

Ackermann, in "The Christian Element in Plato," † says: The Platonic theology is strikingly near that of Christianity in regard to God's being, existence, name, and attributes. As regards the existence of God, he argues from the movements of nature for the necessity of an original principle of motion. ‡ But the real Platonic faith in God, like that of the Bible, rests on immediate knowledge. He gives no definition of the essence of God, but says,§ "To find the Maker and Father of this All is hard, and having found him it is impossible to utter him." But the idea of Goodness is the best expression, as is also that of Being, though neither is adequate. The visible Sun is the image and child of the Good Being. Just so the Scripture calls God the Father of light. Yet the idea of God was the object and aim of his whole philosophy; therefore he calls God the Beginning and the End ; ‖ and "the Measure of all things, much more than *man,* as some people have said " (referring to Protagoras, who taught that "man was the measure of all things "). So even Aristotle declared that "since God is the ground of all being, the first philosophy is theology"; and Eusebius mentions that Plato thought that no one could understand human things who did not first look at divine things; and tells a story of an Indian who met Socrates in Athens and asked him how he must begin to philosophize. He replied that he must reflect on human life ; whereupon the Indian laughed and said that as long as one did not understand divine things he could know nothing about human things.

There is no doubt that Plato was a monotheist, and

---

* For Proofs, see Ackermann, Cudworth, Tayler Lewis, and the New-Englander, October, 1869.

† Page 28, German edition. ‡ Laws, X. 893.

§ Timæus, IX. ‖ Laws, IV. 715.

believed in one God, and when he spoke of gods in the plural, was only using the common form of speech. That many educated heathen were monotheists has been sufficiently proved; and even Augustine admits that the mere use of the word "gods" proved nothing against it, since the Hebrew Bible said, "the God of gods has spoken."

Aristotle (B. C. 384), the first philologian and naturalist of antiquity, scholar of Plato, called "the Scribe of Nature," and "a reversed Plato," differing diametrically from his master in his methods, arrived at nearly the same theological result. He taught that there were first truths, known by their own evidence. He comprised all notions of existence in that of the κόσμος, in which were the two spheres of the earthly and heavenly. The earthly sphere contained the changeable in the transient; the heavenly sphere contained the changeable in the permanent. Above both spheres is God, who is unchangeable, permanent, and unalterable. Aristotle, however, omits God as Providence, and conceives him less personally than is done by Plato.

In the Stoical system, theism becomes pantheism.[*] There is one Being, who is the substance of all things, from whom the universe flows forth, and into whom it returns in regular cycles.

Zeller [†] sums up his statements on this point thus: "From all that has been said it appears that the Stoics did not think of God and the world as different beings. Their system was therefore strictly pantheistic. The sum of all real existence is originally contained in God, who is at once universal matter and the creative force which fashions matter into the particular materials of which things are made. We can, therefore, think of nothing which is not either God or a manifestation of God. In point of being, God and the world are the same, the two conceptions being declared by the Stoics to be absolutely identical."

The Stoic philosophy was materialism as regards the

* Zeller, as above. Also Zeller, "Stoics, Epicureans, and Sceptics," translated by Reichel. London : Longmans. 1870.

† Stoics, Epicureans and Sceptics, p. 140.

nature of things, and necessity as regards the nature of the human will. The Stoics denied the everlasting existence of souls as individuals, believing that at the end of a certain cycle they would be resolved into the Divine Being. Nevertheless, till that period arrives, they conceived the soul as existing in a future state higher and better than this. Seneca calls the day of death the birthday into this better world. In that world there would be a judgment on the conduct and character of each one; there friends would recognize each other, and renew their friendship and society.

While the Epicureans considered religion in all its usual forms to be a curse to mankind, while they believed it impious to accept the popular opinions concerning the gods, while they denied any Divine Providence or care for man, while they rejected prayer, prophecy, divination, and regarded fear as the foundation of religion, they yet believed, as their master Epicurus had believed, in the existence of the immortal gods. These beings he regarded as possessing all human attributes, except those of weakness and pain. They are immortal and perfectly happy; exempt from disease and change, living in celestial dwellings, clothed with bodies of a higher kind than ours, they converse together in a sweet society of peace and content.

Such were the principal theological views of the Greek philosophers. With the exception of the last, and that of the Sceptics, they were either monotheistic or consistent with monotheism. They were, on the whole, far higher than the legends of the poets or the visions of the artists. They were, as the Christian Fathers were fond of saying, a preparation for Christianity. No doubt one cause of the success of this monotheistic religion among the Greek-speaking nations was that Greek philosophy had undermined faith in Greek polytheism.

This we shall consider in another section.

§ 7. *The Worship of Greece.*

The public worship of Greece, as of other ancient nations, consisted of sacrifices, prayers, and public festivals.

13 *

The sacrifices were for victories over their enemies, for plentiful harvests, to avert the anger of some offended deity, for success in any enterprise, and those specially commanded by the oracles.

In the earliest times fruits and plants were all that were offered. Afterward the sacrifices were libations, incense, and victims. The libation consisted of a cup brimming with wine, which was emptied upon the altars. The incense, at first, was merely fragrant leaves or wood, burnt upon the altar; afterward myrrh and frankincense were used. The victims were sheep, oxen, or other animals. To Hecate they offered a dog, to Venus a dove, to Mars some wild animal, to Ceres the sow, because it rooted up the corn. But it was forbidden to sacrifice the ploughing ox. The sacrifices of men, which were common among barbarous nations, were very rare in Greece.

On great occasions large sacrifices were offered of numerous victims, — as the hecatomb, which means a hundred oxen. It is a curious fact that they had a vessel of holy water at the entrance of the temples, consecrated by putting into it a burning torch from the altar, with which or with a branch of laurel the worshippers were sprinkled on entering. The worshippers were also expected to wash their bodies, or at least their hands and feet, before going into the temple ; a custom common also among the Jews and other nations. So Ezekiel says : " I will sprinkle you with clean water and you shall be clean." And the Apostle Paul says, in allusion to this custom : " Let us draw near, having our hearts sprinkled from an evil conscience, and our bodies washed with pure water."

All these customs had a natural origin. The natural offering to the gods is that which we like best ourselves. The Greeks, eminently a social people, in the enjoyment of their feasts, wished to give a part of everything to the gods. Loving wine, perfumes, and animal food, they offered these. As it was proper to wash before feasting with each other, it seemed only proper to do the same before offering the feast to the gods.

The essential part of the sacrifice was catching and

pouring out the blood of the victim; for, in the view of the ancients, blood was the seat of life. Part of the victim was burned, and this was the portion supposed to be consumed by the god. Another part was eaten by the worshippers, who thus sat at table with the deity as his friends and companions. The joyful character of Greek worship also appeared in the use of garlands of flowers, religious dances and songs.

All the festivals of the Greeks were religious. Some were of the seasons, as one in February to Zeus, the giver of good weather; and another in November to Zeus, the god of storms. There were festivals in honor of the plough, of the threshing-floor; festivals commemorating the victories at Marathon, Salamis, etc.; of the restoration of democracy by Thrasybulus; feasts of the clothing of the images, on which occasion it was not lawful to work; feasts in commemoration of those who perished in the flood of Deucalion; feasts of nurses, feasts of youth, of women, of trades. Then there were the great national festivals, celebrated every four years at Olympia and Delphi, and every three and five years at Nemea and the isthmus of Corinth. The Panathenæic festival at Athens was held every five years in honor of Athênê, with magnificent processions, cavalcades of horsemen, gymnastic games, military dances, recitations of the Homeric poems, and competition in music. On the frieze of the Parthenon was represented by the scholars of Phidias the procession of the Peplos. This was a new dress made for the statue of Athênê by young girls of Athens, between the ages of seven and eleven years. These girls, selected at a special ceremony, lived a year on the Acropolis, engaged in their sacred work, and fed on a special diet. Captives were liberated on this occasion, that all might share in the festival.

Such festivals constituted the acme of Greek life. They were celebrated in the open air with pomp and splendor, and visitors came from far to assist on these occasions Prizes were given for foot and chariot races; for boxing, leaping, music, and even for kissing. The temples, therefore, were not intended for worship, but chiefly to contain the image of the god. The *cella*, or *adytum*, was small and often dark ; but along the magnificent portico or peristyle, which surrounded the four sides of the Doric temples, the splendid processions could circulate in full view of the multitude.* The temple was therefore essentially an out-door building, with its beauty, like that of a flower, exposed to light and air. It was covered everywhere, but not crowded, with sculpture, which was an essential part of the building. The pediments, the pedestals on the roofs, the metopes between the triglyphs, are as unmeaning without the sculpture as a picture-frame without its picture. So says Mr. Fergusson ; † and adds that, without question, color was also everywhere used as an integral part of the structure.

Priesthood was sometimes hereditary, but was not confined to a class. Kings, generals, and the heads of a family acted as priests and offered sacrifices. It was a temporary office, and Plato recommends that there should be an annual rotation, no man acting as priest for more than one year. Such a state of opinion excludes the danger of priestcraft, and is opposed to all hierarchal pretensions. The same, however, cannot be said of the diviners and soothsayers, who were so much consulted, and whose opinions determined so often the course of public affairs. They were often in the pay of ambitious men. Alcibiades had augurs and oracles devoted to his interests, who could induce the Athenians to agree to such a course as he desired. For the Greeks were extremely anxious to penetrate the future, and the power and influence of their oracles is, says Döllinger, a phenomenon unique in history.

Among these oracles, Delphi, as is well known, took the highest rank. It was considered the centre of the earth, and was revered by the Pan-Hellenic race. It was a supreme religious court, whose decisions were believed to be infallible. The despotism of the Pythian decisions was, however, tempered by their ambiguity. Their predictions,

---

* Mr. Fergusson thinks the peristyle not intended for an ambulatory, but is unable to assign any other satisfactory purpose.
† Illustrated Hand-Book of Architecture.

if they failed, seldom destroyed the faith of the believers; for always some explanation could be devised to save the credit of the oracle. Thus, the Pythian promised the Athenians that they would take all the Syracusans prisoners. They did not take them; but as a muster-roll of the Syracusan army fell into their hands, this was considered to fulfil the promise.* Aristides, the rhetorician, was told that the "white maidens" would take care of him; and receiving a letter which was of advantage, he was fully convinced that this was the "white maiden." But neither imposition nor delusion will satisfactorily explain the phenomena connected with oracles. The foundation of them seems to have been a state allied to the modern manifestations of magnetic sleep and clairvoyance.

"As the whole life of the Greeks," says Döllinger, "was penetrated by religion," they instinctively and naturally prayed on all occasions. They prayed at sunrise and sunset, at meal-times, for outward blessings of all kinds, and also for virtue and wisdom. They prayed standing, with a loud voice, and hands lifted to the heavens. They threw kisses to the gods with their hands.

So we see that the Greek worship, like their theology, was natural and human, a cheerful and hopeful worship, free from superstition. This element only arrives with the mysteries, and the worship of the Cthonic gods. To the Olympic gods supplications were addressed as to free moral agents, who might be persuaded or convinced, but could not be compelled. To the under-world deities prayer took the form of adjuration, and degenerated into magic formulas, which were supposed to force these deities to do what was asked by the worshipper.

§ 8. *The Mysteries. Orphism.*

The early gods of most nations are local and tribal. They belong only to limited regions, or to small clans, and have no supposed authority or influence beyond. This was eminently the case in Greece; and after the great Hellenic worship had arrived, the local and family gods

* Plutarch, quoted by Döllinger.

retained also their position, and continued to be reverenced. In Athens, down to the time of Alexander, each tribe in the city kept its own divinities and sacrifices. It also happened that the supreme god of one state would be adored as a subordinate power in another. Every place had its favorite protector. As different cities in Italy have their different Madonnas, whom they consider more powerful than the Madonna of their neighbors, so in Greece the same god was invoked in various localities under different surnames. The Arcadian Zeus had the surname of Lycæus, derived, probably, from Λύξ, Lux, light. The Cretan Jupiter was called Asterios. At Karia he was Stratios. Iolaus in Euripides (the Herakleidæ, 347) says: "We have gods as our allies not inferior to those of the Argives, O king; for Juno, the wife of Jove, is their champion, but Minerva ours ; and I say, to have the best gods tends to success, for Pallas will not endure to be conquered.* So, in the "Suppliants" of Æschylus, the Egyptian Herald says (838): "By no means do I dread the deities of this place ; for they have not nourished me nor preserved me to old age." †

Two modes of worship met in Greece, together with two classes of gods. The Pelasgi, as we have seen, worshipped unnamed impersonal powers of the universe, without image or temple. But to this was added a worship which probably came through Thrace, from Asia and Egypt. This element introduced religious poetry and music, the adoration of the muses, the rites and mysteries of Dêmêtêr, and the reverence for the Kabiri, or dark divinities of the lower world.

Of these, the MYSTERIES were the most significant and important. Their origin must be referred to a great antiquity, and they continued to be practised down to the times of the Roman Emperors. They seem not to belong to the genuine Greek religion, but to be an alien element introduced into it. The gods of the Mysteries are not the beings of light, but of darkness, not the gods of Olympus, but of the under-world. Everything connected with

* Buckley's translation, in Bohn's Classical Library.
† Ibid.

the Mysteries is foreign to the Hellenic mind. This worship is secret; its spirit is of awe, terror, remorse; its object is expiation of sin. Finally, it is a hieratic worship, in the hands of priests.

All this suggests Egypt as the origin of the Mysteries. The oldest were those celebrated in the island of Samothrace, near the coast of Asia Minor. Here Orpheus is reputed to have come and founded the Bacchic Mysteries; while another legend reports him to have been killed by the Bacchantes for wishing to substitute the worship of Apollo for that of Dionysos. This latter story, taken in connection with the civilizing influence ascribed to Orpheus, indicates his introducing a purer form of worship. He reformed the licentious drunken rites, and established in place of them a more serious religion. He died a martyr to this purer faith, killed by the women, who were incited to this, no doubt, by the priests of the old Bacchic worship.

The worship of Dionysos Zagreus, which was the Orphic form of Bacchism, contained the doctrines of retribution in another life, — a doctrine common to all the Greek Mysteries.

It would seem probable, from an investigation of this subject, that two elements of worship are to be found in the Greek religion, which were never quite harmonized. One is the worship of the Olympian deities, gods of light and day, gods of this world, and interested in our present human life. This worship tended to promote a free development of character; it was self-possessed, cheerful, and public; it left the worshipper unalarmed by any dread of the future, or any anxiety about his soul. For the Olympic gods cared little about the moral character of their worshippers; and the dark Fate which lay behind gods and men could not be propitiated by any rites, and must be encountered manfully, as one meets the inevitable.

The other worship, running parallel with this, was of the Cthonic gods, deities of earth and the under-world, rulers of the night-side of nature, and monarchs of the world to come. Their worship was solemn, mysterious, secret, and concerned expiation of sin, and the salvation of the soul hereafter.

Now, when we consider that the Egyptian popular worship delighted in just such mysteries as these ; that it related to the judgment of the soul hereafter ; that its solemnities were secret and wrapped in dark symbols ; and that the same awful Cthonic deities were the objects of its reverence ; — when we also remember that Herodotus and the other Greek writers state that the early religion of the Pelasgi was derived from Egypt, and that Orpheus, the Thracian, brought thence his doctrine, — there seems no good reason for denying such a source. On the other hand, nothing can be more probable than an immense influence on Pelasgic worship, derived through Thrace, from Egypt. This view is full of explanations, and makes much in the Greek mythology clear which would otherwise be obscure.

The Greek myth of Dêmêtêr and Persephonê, for example, seems to be an adaptation to the Hellenic mind and land of the Egyptian myth of Osiris and Isis. Both are symbols, first, of natural phenomena ; and, secondly, of the progress of the human soul. The sad Isis seeking Osiris, and the sad Dêmêtêr seeking Persephonê, constitute evidently the same legend ; only Osiris is the Nile, evaporated into scattered pools by the burning heat, while Persephonê is the seed, the treasure of the plant, which sinks into the earth, but is allowed to come up again as the stalk, and pass a part of its life in the upper air. But both these nature-myths were spiritualized in the Mysteries, and made to denote the wanderings of the soul in its search for truth. Similar to these legends was that of Dionysos Zagreus, belonging to Crete, according to Euripides and other writers. Zagreus was the son of the Cretan Zeus and Persephonê, and was hewn in pieces by the Titans, his heart alone being preserved by Athênê, who gave it to Zeus. Zeus killed the Titans, and enclosed the heart in a plaster image of his child. According to another form of the story, Zeus swallowed the heart, and from it reproduced another Dionysos. Apollo collected the rest of the members, and they were reunited, and restored to life.

The principal mysteries were those of Bacchus and Ceres. The Bacchic mysteries were very generally celebrated throughout Greece, and were a wild nature-worship ; partaking of that frenzy which has in all nations been considered a method of gaining a supernatural and inspired state, or else as the result of it. The Siva worship in India, the Pythoness at Delphi, the Schamaism of the North, the whirling dervishes of the Mohammedans ; and some of the scenes at the camp-meetings in the Western States, belong to the same class as the Bacchic orgies.

The Eleusinian mysteries were very different. These were in honor of Ceres ; they were imported from Egypt. The wanderings of Isis in search of Osiris were changed to those of Ceres or Dêmêtêr (the mother-earth = Isis) in search of Persephonê. Both represented in a secondary symbolism the wanderings of the soul, seeking God and truth. This was the same idea as that of Apuleius in the beautiful story of Psyche.

These mysteries were celebrated at Eleusis by the Athenians every fourth year. They were said to have been introduced B. C. 1356, and were very sacred. All persons were required to be initiated. If they refused it they were supposed to be irreligious. " Have you been initiated ? " was asked in dangerous situations. The initiated were said to be calm in view of death. It was the personal religion of the Greeks.

In the greater mysteries at Eleusis the candidates were crowned with myrtle, and admitted by night into a vast temple, where they were purified and instructed, and assisted at certain grand solemnities. The doctrines taught are unknown, but are supposed to have been the unity of God and the immortality of the soul. But this is only conjecture.

Bacchus is believed to have been originally an Indian god, naturalized in Greece, and his mysteries to be Indian in their character. The genial life of nature is the essential character of Bacchus. One of the names of the Indian Siva is Dionichi, which very nearly resembles the Greek name of Bacchus, Dionysos. He was taken from

T

the Meros, or thigh of Jupiter. Now Mount Meru, in India, is the home of the gods ; by a common etymological error the Greeks may have thought it the Greek word for *thigh*, and so translated it.

The Bacchic worship, in its Thracian form, was always distasteful to the best of the Greeks ; it was suspected and disliked by the enlightened, proscribed by kings, and rejected by communities. It was an interpolated system, foreign to the cheerful nature of Greek thought.

As to the value of the mysteries themselves, there was a great difference of opinion among the Greeks. The people, the orators, and many of the poets praised them ; but the philosophers either disapproved them openly, or passed them by in silence. Socrates says no word in their favor in all his reported conversations. Plato complains of the immoral influence derived from believing that sin could be expiated by such ceremonies.* They seem to have contained, in reality, little direct instruction, but to have taught merely by a dramatic representation and symbolic pictures.

Who Orpheus was, and when he lived, can never be known. But the probabilities are that he brought from Egypt into Greece, what Moses took from Egypt into Palestine, the Egyptian ideas of culture, law, and civilization. He reformed the Bacchic mysteries, giving them a more elevated and noble character, and for this he lost his life. No better account of his work can be given than in the words of Lord Bacon.

" The merits of learning," says he, " in repressing the inconveniences which grow from man to man, was lively set forth by the ancients in that feigned relation of Orpheus' theatre, where all beasts and birds assembled ; and, forgetting their several appetites, some of prey, some of game, some of quarrel, stood all sociably together, listening to the airs and accords of the harp ; the sound thereof no sooner ceased or was drowned by some louder noise, but every beast returned to his own nature ; wherein is aptly described the nature and condition of men, who are full of savage and unreclaimed desires of

* Republic, II. 17. See Döllinger's discussion of this subject, in " The Gentile and the Jew," English translation, Vol. I. p. 125.

profit, of lust, of revenge, which, as long as they give ear to precepts, to laws, to religion, sweetly touched by eloquence and persuasion of books, of sermons, of harangues, so long is society and peace maintained ; but if these instruments be silent, or that sedition and tumult make them not audible, all things dissolve into anarchy and confusion." *

Of the Orphic doctrines we are able to give a somewhat better account. As far back as the sixth century before Christ, there were scattered through Greece hymns, lyrical poems, and prose treatises, treating of theological questions, and called Orphic writings. These works continued to be produced through many centuries, and evidently met an appetite in the Greek mind. They were not philosophy, they were not myths nor legends, but contained a mystic and pantheistic theology.† The views of the Pythagoreans entered largely into this system. The Orphic writings develop, by degrees, a system of cosmogony, in which Time was the first principle of things, from which came chaos and ether. Then came the primitive egg, from which was born Phanes, or Manifestation. This being is the expression of intelligence, and creates the heavens and the earth. The soul is but the breath which comes from the whole universe, thus organized, and is imprisoned in the body as in a tomb, for sins committed in a former existence. Life is therefore not joy, but punishment and sorrow. At death the soul escapes from this prison, to pass through many changes, by which it will be gradually purified. All these notions are alien to the Greek mind, and are plainly a foreign importation. The true Greek was neither pantheist nor introspective. He did not torment himself about the origin of evil or the beginning of the universe, but took life as it came, cheerfully.

The pantheism of the Orphic theology is constantly apparent. Thus, in a poem preserved by Proclus and Eusebius it is said : ‡ —

---

* Advancement of Learning.
† Ottfried Müller has shown that some of these writings existed in the time of Euripides.
‡ Cudworth's Intellectual System, I. 403 (Am. ed.). Rixner, Handbuch der Geschichte der Philosophie, Anhang, Vol. I.

" Zeus, the mighty thunderer, is first, Zeus is last,
Zeus is the head, Zeus the middle of all things.
From Zeus were all things produced.   He is both man and woman ;
Zeus is the depth of the earth, and the height of the starry heavens ;
He is the breath of all things, the force of untamed fire ;
The bottom of the sea ; sun, moon, and stars ;
Origin of all ; king of all ;
One Power, one God, one great Ruler."

And another says, still more plainly : —

" There is one royal body, in which all things are enclosed,
Fire and Water, Earth, Ether, Night and Day,
And Counsel, the first producer, and delightful Love,
For all these are contained in the great body of Zeus."

§ 9. *Relation of Greek Religion to Christianity.*

One of the greatest events in the history of man, as
well as one of the most picturesque situations, was when
Paul stood on the Areopagus at Athens, carrying Christianity into Europe, offering a Semitic religion to an
Aryan race, the culmination of monotheism to one of the
most elaborate and magnificent polytheisms of the world.
A strange and marvellous scene !   From the place where
he stood he saw all the grandest works of human art, — the
Acropolis rose before him, a lofty precipitous rock, seeming like a stone pedestal erected by nature as an appropriate platform for the perfect marble temples with which
man should adorn it.   On this noble base rose the Parthenon, temple of Minerva ; and the temple of Neptune,
with its sacred fountain.   The olive-tree of Pallas-Athênê
was there, and her colossal statue.   On the plain below
were the temples of Theseus and Jupiter Olympus, and
innumerable others.   He stood where Socrates had stood
four hundred years before, defending himself against the
charge of atheism ; where Demosthenes had pleaded in
immortal strains of eloquence in behalf of Hellenic freedom ; where the most solemn and venerable court of justice known among men was wont to assemble.   There he
made the memorable discourse, a few fragments only of
which have come to us in the Book of Acts, but a sketch
significant of his argument.   He did not begin, as in
our translation, by insulting the religion of the Greeks,

and calling it a superstition; but by praising them for their reverence and piety. Paul respected all manifestations of awe and love toward those mysteries and glories of the universe, in which the invisible things of God have been clearly seen from the foundation of the world. Then he mentions his finding the altar to the unknown God, mentioned also by Pausanias and other Greek writers, one of whom, Diogenes Laertius, says that in a time of plague, not knowing to what god to appeal, they let loose a number of black and white sheep, and wherever any one laid down they erected an altar to an unknown god, and offered sacrifices thereon. Then he announced as his central and main theme the Most High God, maker of heaven and earth, spiritual, not needing to receive anything from man, but giving him all things. Next, he proclaimed the doctrine of universal human brotherhood. God had made all men of one blood; their varieties and differences, as well as their essential unity, being determined by a Divine Providence. But all were equally made to seek him, and in their various ways to find him, who is yet always near to all, since all are his children. God is immanent in all men, says Paul, as their life. Having thus stated the great unities of faith and points of agreement, he proceeds only in the next instance to the oppositions and criticisms; in which he opposes, not polytheism, but idolatry; though not blaming them severely even for that. Lastly, he speaks of Jesus, as a man ordained by God to judge the world and govern it in righteousness, and proved by his resurrection from the dead to be so chosen.

Here we observe, in this speech, monotheism came in contact with polytheism, and the two forms of human religion met, — that which makes man the child of God, and that which made the gods the children of men.

The result we know. The cry was heard on the sandy shore of Eurotas and in green Cythnus. — "Great Pan is dead." The Greek humanities, noble and beautiful as they were, faded away before the advancing steps of the Jewish peasant, who had dared to call God his Father and man his brother. The parables of the Prodigal Son and the Good Samaritan were stronger than Homer's divine song and Pindar's lofty hymns. This was the religion for man. And so it happened as Jesus had said : "My sheep hear my voice and follow me." Those who felt in their hearts that Jesus was their true leader followed him.

The gods of Greece, being purely human, were so far related to Christianity. That, too, is a human religion ; a religion which makes it its object to unfold man, and to cause all to come to the stature of perfect men. Christianity also showed them God in the form of man ; God dwelling on the earth ; God manifest in the flesh. It also taught that the world was full of God, and that all places and persons were instinct with a secret divinity. Schiller (as translated by Coleridge) declares that LOVE was the source of these Greek creations : —

> ' 'T is not merely
> The human being's pride that peoples space
> With life and mystical predominance,
> Since likewise for the stricken heart of Love
> This visible nature, and this common world
> Is all too narrow ; yea, a deeper import
> Lurks in the legend told my infant years
> That lies upon that truth, we live to learn.
> For fable is Love's world, his home, his birthplace ;
> Delightedly dwells he 'mong fays and talismans,
> And spirits, and delightedly believes
> Divinities, being himself divine.
> The intelligible forms of ancient poets,
> The fair humanities of Old Religion,
> The Power, the Beauty, and the Majesty,
> That had their haunts in dale or piny mountain,
> Or forest by slow stream, or pebbly spring,
> Or chasms or wat'ry depths ; — all these have vanished.
> They live no longer in the faith of Reason.
> But still the heart doth need a language ; still
> Doth the old instinct bring back the old names."
> *The Piccolomini,* Act II. Scene 4.

As a matter of fact we find the believers in the Greek religion more ready to receive Christianity than were the Jews. All through Asia Minor and Greece Christian churches were planted by Paul ; a fact which shows that the ground was somehow prepared for Christianity. It was ready for the monotheism which Paul substituted for their multitude of gods, and for their idolatry and image-worship. The statues had ceased to be symbols, and the minds of the Greeks rested in the image itself. This idolatrous worship Paul condemned, and the people heard him willingly, as he called them up to a more spiritual worship. We think, therefore, that the Greek religion was a real preparation for Christianity. We have seen that it was itself in constant transition; the system of the poets passing into that of the artists, and that of the artists into that of the philosophers; so that the philosophic religion, in turn, was ready to change into a Christian monotheism.

It may be said, since philosophy had undermined the old religion and substituted for it more noble ideas, why did it not take the seat of the dethroned faith, and sufficiently supply its place? If it taught a pure monotheism and profound ethics, if it threw ample and adequate light on the problem of God, duty, and immortality, what more was needed? If ideas are all that we want, nothing more. That Greek philosophy gave way before Christianity shows that it did not satisfy all the cravings of the soul; shows that man needs a religion as well as a religious philosophy, a faith as well as an intellectual system. A religion is one thing, a speculation is a very different thing. The old Greek religion, so long as it was a living faith, was enough. When men really believed in the existence of Olympian Jove, Pallas-Athênê, and Phœbus-Apollo, they had something above them to which to look up. When this faith was disintegrated, no system of opinions, however pure and profound, could replace it. Another faith was needed, but a faith not in conflict with the philosophy which had destroyed polytheism; and Christianity met the want, and therefore became the religion of the Greek-speaking world.

Religion is a life, philosophy is thought; religion looks up, philosophy looks in. We need both thought and life, and we need that the two shall be in harmony. The moment they come in conflict, both suffer. Philosophy had destroyed the ancient simple faith of the Hellenic race in their deities, and had given them instead only the abstractions of thought. Then came the Apostles of Christianity, teaching a religion in harmony with the highest thought of the age, and yet preaching it out of a living faith. Christianity did not come as a speculation about the universe, but as a testimony. Its heralds bore witness to the facts of God's presence and providence, of his fatherly love, of the brotherhood of man, of a rising to a higher life, of a universal judgment hereafter on all good and evil, and of Jesus as the inspired and ascended revealer of these truths. These facts were accepted as realities ; and once more the human mind had something above itself solid enough to support it.

Some of the early Christian Fathers called on the heathen poets and philosophers to bear witness to the truth. Clement of Alexandria,* after quoting this passage of Plato, "around the king of all are all things, and he is the cause of all good things," says that others, through God's inspiration, have declared the only true God to be God. He quotes Antisthenes to this effect: "God is not like to any; wherefore no one can know him from an image." He quotes Cleanthes the Stoic : —

> "If you ask me what is the nature of the good, listen :
> That which is regular, just, holy, pious,
> Self-governing, useful, fair, fitting,
> Grave, independent, always beneficial,
> That feels no fear or grief ; profitable, painless,
> Helpful, pleasant, safe, friendly."

"Nor," says Clement, "must we keep the Pythagoreans in the background, who say, 'God is one ; and he is not, as some suppose, outside of this frame of things, but within it ; in all the entireness of his being he pervades the whole circle of existence, surveying all nature, and blending in harmonious union the whole ; the author of his own forces and works, the giver of light in heaven, and father of all ; the mind and vital power of the whole world, the mover of all things.'"

Clement quotes Aratus the poet : —

> "That all may be secure
> Him ever they propitiate first and last.
> Hail, Father ! great marvel, great gain to man."

* Ante-Nicene Christian Library, Vol. IV. p. 71.

" Thus also," says Clement, " the Ascræan Hesiod dimly speaks of God : —

'For he is the king of all, and monarch
Of the immortals, and there is none that can vie with him in power.'

" And Sophocles, the son of Sophilus, says : —

'One, in truth, one is God,
Who made both heaven and the far-stretching earth ;
And ocean's blue wave, and the mighty winds ;
But many of us mortals, deceived in heart,
Have set up for ourselves, as a consolation in our afflictions,
Images of the gods, of stone, or wood, or brass,
Or gold, or ivory ;
And, appointing to these sacrifices and vain festivals,
Are accustomed thus to practise religion.'

" But the Thracian Orpheus, the son of Œagrus, hierophant and poet, at once, after his exposition of the orgies and his theology of idols, introduces a palinode of truth with solemnity, though tardily singing the strain : —

'I shall utter to whom it is lawful ; but let the doors be closed,
Nevertheless, against all the profane. But do thou hear,
O Musæus, for I will declare what is true.'

" He then proceeds : —

'He is one, self-proceeding; and from him alone all things proceed,
And in them he himself exerts his activity ; no mortal
Beholds him, but he beholds all.' "

Professor Cocker, in his work on " Christianity and Greek Philosophy," has devoted much thought to show that philosophy was a preparation for Christianity ; and that Greek civilization was an essential condition to the progress of the Gospel. He points out how Greek intelligence and culture, literature and art, trade and colonization, the universal spread of the Greek language, and especially the results of Greek philosophy, were " schoolmasters to bring men to Christ." He quotes a striking passage from Pressensé to this effect. Philosophy in Greece, says Pressensé, had its place in the divine plan. It dethroned the false gods. It purified the idea of divinity.

Cocker sums up this work of preparation done by Greek philosophy, as seen, —

14

"1. In the release of the popular mind from polytheistic notions, and the purifying and spiritualizing of the theistic idea.

"2. In the development of the theistic argument in a logical form.

"3. In the awakening and enthronement of conscience as a law of duty, and in the elevation and purification of the moral idea.

"4. In the fact that, by an experiment conducted on the largest scale, it demonstrated the insufficiency of reason to elaborate a perfect ideal of moral excellence, and develop the moral forces necessary to secure its realization.

"5. It awakened and deepened the consciousness of guilt and the desire for redemption." *

The large culture of Greece was evidently adapted to Christianity. The Jewish mind recognized no such need as that of universal culture, and this tendency of Christianity could only have found room and opportunity among those who had received the influence of Hellenic culture.

The points of contact between Christianity and Greek civilization are therefore these : —

1. The character of God, considered in both as an immanent, ever-working presence, and not merely as a creating and governing will outside the universe.

2. The character of man, as capable of education and development, who is not merely to obey as a servant, but to co-operate as a friend, with the divine will, and grow up in all things.

3. The idea of duty, as a reasonable service, and not a yoke.

4. God's revelations, as coming, not only in nature, but also in inspired men, and in the intuitions of the soul; a conception which resulted in the Christian doctrine of the Trinity.

The good of polytheism was that it saw something divine in nature. By dividing God into numberless deities, it was able to conceive of some divine power in

* Christianity and Greek Philosophy. By B. F. Cocker, D. D. New York : Harper and Brothers. 1870.

all earthly objects. Hence Wordsworth, complaining that
we can see little of this divinity now in nature, cries
out : —

> "Good God ! I 'd rather be
> A Pagan suckled in a creed outworn ;
> So might I, standing on this pleasant lea,
> Have glimpses that would make me less forlorn ;
> Have sight of Proteus rising from the sea,
> Or hear old Triton blow his wreathéd horn."

CHAPTER VIII.

THE RELIGION OF ROME.

§ 1. Origin and essential Character of the Religion of Rome.   § 2. The Gods of Rome.   § 3. Worship and Ritual.   § 4. The Decay of the Roman Religion.   § 5. Relation of the Roman Religion to Christianity.

§ 1. *Origin and essential Character of the Religion of Rome.*

IN the Roman state nothing grew, everything was made. The practical understanding was the despotic faculty in the genius of this people. Fancy, imagination, humor, seem to have been omitted in the character of the Latin race. The only form of wit which appeared among them was satire, that is, wit used for a serious purpose, to punish crimes not amenable to other laws, to remove abuses not to be reached by the ordinary police. The gay, light-hearted Greek must have felt in Rome very much as a Frenchman feels in England. The Romans did not know how to amuse themselves ; they pursued their recreations with ferocious earnestness, making always a labor of their pleasure. They said, indeed, that it was well *sometimes* to unbend, *Dulce est desipere in locis ;* but a Roman when unbent was like an unbent bow, almost as stiff as before.

In other words, all spontaneity was absent from the Roman mind. Everything done was done on purpose, with a deliberate intention. This also appears in their religion. Their religion was not an inspiration, but an intention. It was all regular, precise, exact. The Roman cultus, like the Roman state, was a compact mass, in which all varieties were merged into a stern unity. All forms of religion might come to Rome and take their places in its pantheon, but they must come as servants and soldiers of the state. Rome opened a hospitable asylum to them, just as Rome had established a refuge on the Capitoline Hill to which all outlaws might come and be safe, on the condition of serving the community.

As everything in Rome must serve the state, so the religion of Rome was a state institution, an established church. But as the state can only command and forbid outward actions, and has no control over the heart, so the religion of Rome was essentially external. It was a system of worship, a ritual, a ceremony. If the externals were properly attended to, it took no notice of opinions or of sentiments. Thus we find in Cicero (" De Natura Deorum ") the chief pontiff arguing against the existence of the gods and the use of divination. He claims to believe in religion as a pontifex, while he argues against it as a philosopher. The toleration of Rome consisted in this, that as long as there was outward conformity to prescribed observances, it troubled itself very little about opinions. It said to all religions what Gallio said to the Jews: " If it be a question of words and names and of your law, look ye to it; for I will be no judge of such matters." Gallio was a genuine representative of Roman sentiment. With religion, as long as it remained within the limits of opinion or feeling, the magistrate had nothing to do; only when it became an act of disobedience to the public law it was to be punished. Indeed, the very respect for national law in the Roman mind caused it to legalize in Rome the worship of national gods. They considered it the duty of the Jews, in Rome, to worship the Jewish God; of Egyptians, in Rome, to worship the gods of Egypt. " Men of a thousand nations," says Dionysius of Halicarnassus, " come to the city, and must worship the gods of their country, according to their laws at home." As long as the Christians in Rome were regarded as a Jewish sect, their faith was a *religio licita*, when it was understood to be a departure from Judaism, it was then a criminal rebellion against a national faith.*

The Roman religion has often been considered as a

* See Neander, Church History, Vol I. p. 88, American edition.

mere copy of that of Greece, and has therefore been confounded with it, as very nearly the same system.   No
doubt the Romans were imitators; they had no creative
imagination. They borrowed and begged their stories
about the gods, from Greece or elsewhere.   But Hegel
has long ago remarked that the resemblance between the
two religions is superficial. The gods of Rome, he says,
are practical gods, not theoretic ; prosaic, not poetic. The
religion of Rome is serious and earnest, while that of
Greece is gay.   Dionysius of Halicarnassus thinks the
Roman religion the better of the two, because it rejected
the blasphemous myths concerning the loves and quarrels
of the heavenly powers.   But, on the other hand, the
deities of Greece were more living and real persons, with
characters of their own.   The deities of Rome were working gods, who had each a task assigned to him.   They
all had some official duty to perform ; while the gods
of Olympus could amuse themselves as they pleased.
While the Zeus of Greece spent his time in adventures,
many of which were disreputable, the Jupiter Capitoli-
nus remained at home, attending to his sole business,
which was to make Rome the mistress of the world.   The
gods of Rome, says Hegel, are not human beings, like
those of Greece, but soulless machines, gods made by the
understanding, even when borrowed from Greek story.
They were worshipped also in the interest of the practical
understanding, as givers of earthly fortune.   The Romans
had no real reverence for their gods ; they worshipped
them in no spirit of adoring love, but always for some
useful object.   It was a utilitarian worship.   Accordingly
the practical faculties, engaged in useful arts, were deified.
There was a Jupiter Pistor, presiding over bakers.   There
was a goddess of ovens ; and a Juno Moneta, who took
care of the coin.   There was a goddess who presided
over doing nothing, Tranquillitas Vacuna ; and even
the plague had an altar erected to it.   But, after all, no
deities were so great, in the opinion of the Romans, as
Rome itself.   The chief distinction of these deities was
that they belonged to the Roman state.*

* Hegel's Philosophie in Wörtlichen Ausüzgen.   Berlin, 1843.

Cicero considers the Romans to be the most religious of all nations, because they carried their religion into all the details of life. This is true; but one might as well consider himself a devout worshipper of iron or of wood, because he is always using these materials, in doors and out, in his parlor, kitchen, and stable.

As the religion of Rome had no doctrinal system, its truths were communicated mostly by spectacles and ceremonies, which chiefly consisted in the wholesale slaughter of men and animals. There was something frightful in the extent to which this was carried; for when cruelty proceeds from a principle and purpose, it is far worse than when arising from brutal passion. An angry man may beat his wife; but the deliberate, repeated, and ingenious torments of the Inquisition, the massacre of thousands of gladiators in a Roman amphitheatre, or the torture of prisoners by the North American Indians, are all parts of a system, and reinforced by considerations of propriety, duty, and religious reverence.

Mommsen remarks,[*] that the Roman religion in all its details was a reflection of the Roman state. When the constitution and institutions of Rome changed, their religion changed with them. One illustration of this correspondence he finds in the fact that when the Romans admitted the people of a conquered state to become citizens of Rome, their gods were admitted with them; but in both cases the new citizens (*novensides*) occupied a subordinate position to the old settlers (*indigites*).[†]

That the races of Italy, among whom the Latin language originated, were of the same great Asiatic stock as the Greeks, Germans, Kelts, and Slavic tribes, is sufficiently proved by the unimpeachable evidence of language. The old Latin roots and grammatic forms all retain the analogies of the Aryan families. Their gods and their religion bear marks of the same origin, yet with a special and marked development. For the Roman nation was derived from at least three secondary sources, — the

---

[*] Römische Geschichte, von Theodor Mommsen, Kap. XII.

[†] Janus, Picus, Faunus, Romulus, were *indigites*. Funke, Real Lexicon.

Latins, Sabines, and Etruscans. To these may be added the Pelasgian settlers on the western coast (unless these are included in the Etruscan element), and the very ancient race of Siculi or Sikels, whose name suggests, by its phonetic analogy, a branch of that widely wandering race, the Kelts.* But the obscure and confused traditions of these Italian races help us very little in our present inquiry. That some of the oldest Roman deities were Latin, others Sabine, and others Etruscan, is, however, well ascertained. From the Latin towns Alba and Lavinium came the worship of Vesta, Jupiter, Juno, Saturn and Tellus, Diana and Mars. Niebuhr thinks that the Sabine ritual was adopted by the Romans, and that Varro found the real remains of Sabine chapels on the Quirinal. From Etruria came the system of divination. Some of the oldest portions of the Roman religion were derived from agriculture. The god Saturn took his name from sowing. Picus and Faunus were agricultural gods. Pales, the goddess of herbage, had offerings of milk on her festivals. The Romans, says Döllinger, had no cosmogony of their own ; a practical people, they took the world as they found it, and did not trouble themselves about its origin. Nor had they any favorite deities ; they worshipped according to what was proper, every one in turn at the right time. Though the most polytheistic of religions, there ran through their system an obscure conception of one supreme being, Jupiter Optimus-Maximus, of whom all the other deities were but qualities and attri-

---

* See Niebuhr's Lectures on the History of Rome, for facts concerning the Siculi. The sound *el* appears in Keltic, Gael, Welsch, Welsh, Belgians, Gauls, Galatians, etc. M. Grotefend (as quoted by Guigniaut, in his notes to Creuzer) accepts this Keltic origin of the Siculi, believing that they entered Italy from the northwest, and were gradually driven farther south till they reached Sicily. Those who expelled them were the Pelasgic races, who passed from Asia, south of the Caspian and Black Seas, through Asia Minor and Greece, preceding the Hellenic races. This accounts for the statement of Herodotus that the Pelasgi came from Lydia in Asia Minor, without our being obliged to assume that they came by sea, — a fact highly improbable. They were called Tyrrheanians, not from any city or king of Lydia, but, as M. Lepsius believes, from the Greek τύρρις (Latin, *turris*), a tower, because of their Cyclopean masonry. The Roman state, on this supposition, may have owed its origin to the union of the two great Aryan races, the Kelts and Pelasgi.

butes. But they carried furthest of all nations this per-
sonifying and deifying of every separate power, this
minute subdivision of the deity. Heffter * says this was
carried to an extent which was almost comic. They had
divinities who presided over talkativeness and silence, over
beginnings and endings, over the manuring of the fields,
and over all household transactions. And as the number
increased, it became always more difficult to recollect
which was the right god to appeal to under any special
circumstances. So that often they were obliged to call on
the gods in general, and, dismissing the whole polytheistic
pantheon, to invoke some unknown god, or the supreme
being. Sometimes, however, in these emergencies, new
deities were created for the occasion. Thus they came to
invoke the pestilence, defeat in battle, blight, etc., as dangerous beings whose hostility must be placated by sacrifices. A better part of their mythology was the worship
of Modesty (Pudicitia), Faith or Fidelity (Fides), Concord
(Concordia), and the gods of home. It was the business
of the pontiffs to see to the creation of new divinities.
So the Romans had a goddess Pecunia, money (from
Pecus, cattle), dating from the time when the circulating
medium consisted in cows and sheep. But when copper
money came, a god of copper was added, Æsculanus ; and
when silver money was invented, a god Argentarius arrived.

§ 2. *The Gods of Rome.*

Creuzer, in speaking of the Italian worship, says that
" one fact which emerges more prominently than any other
is the concourse of Oriental, Pelasgic, Samothracian, and
Hellenic elements in the religion of Rome." In like
manner the Roman deities bear traces of very different
sources. We have found reason to believe, in our previous chapters, that the religion of Egypt had a twofold
origin, from Asiatic and African elements, and that the
religion of Greece, in like manner, was derived from Egyptian and Pelasgic sources. So, too, we find the institutions

* Mythologie der Griechen und Romer, von Dr. M. W. Heffter. Leipzig, 1854.

14 *

and people of Rome partaking of a Keltic and Pelasgic origin. Let us now see what was the character of the Roman deities.

One of the oldest and also most original of the gods of Rome was the Sabine god JANUS. He was the deity who presided over beginnings and endings, over the act of opening and shutting. Hence the month which opened the year, January, received its name from this god, who also gave his name to Janua, a gate or door,* and probably to the hill Janiculum.†

The Romans laid great stress on all beginnings; believing that the commencement of any course of conduct determined, by a sort of magical necessity, its results. Bad success in an enterprise they attributed to a wrong beginning, and the only remedy, therefore, was to begin anew. Ovid (Fasti, I. 179) makes Janus say, "All depends on the beginning." When other gods were worshipped, Janus was invoked first of all. He was god of the year. His temple had four sides for the four seasons, and each side had three windows for the months. That his temple was open in war, but closed in peace, indicated that the character of Rome in times of war was to attack and not to defend. She then opened her gates to send her troops forth against the enemy ; while in seasons of peace she shut them in at home. This symbol accords well with the haughty courage of the Republic, which commanded victory, by not admitting the possibility of defeat. ‡

This deity is believed by Creuzer and others to have had an Indian origin, and his name to have been derived from the Sanskrit "Jan," *to be born.* He resembles no Greek god, and very probably travelled all the way from Bactria to Rome.

---

* And so our word "janitor" comes to us from this very old Italian deity.

† Ampère, L'Histoire Romaine.

‡ This seems to us more probable than Buttman's opinion, that the temple of Janus was originally by the gate of the city, which gate was open in war and closed in peace. In practice, it would probably be different.

On the Kalends of January, which was the chief feast of Janus, it was the duty of every Roman citizen to be careful that all he thought, said, or did should be pure and true, because this day determined the character of the year. All dressed themselves in holiday garb, avoided oaths, abusive words, and quarrels, gave presents, and wished each other a happy year. The presents were little coins with a Janus-head, and sweetmeats. It was customary to sacrifice to Janus at the beginning of all important business.

Janus was the great god of the Sabines, and his most ancient temple appears to have been on Mount Janiculum.* The altar of Fontus, son of Janus, and the tomb of Numa, a Sabine king, were both supposed to be there. Ovid also † makes Janus say that the Janiculum was his citadel. Ampère remarks as a curious coincidence, that this god, represented with a key in his hand, as the heavenly gate-keeper, should have his home on the hill close to the Vatican, where is the tomb of Peter, who also bears a key with the same significance. The same writer regards the Sabines as inhabiting the hills of Rome before the Pelasgi came and gave this name of Roma (meaning "strength") to their small fortress on one side of the Palatine.

In every important city of Etruria there were temples to the three gods, JUPITER, JUNO, and MINERVA. In like manner, the magnificent temple of the Capitol at Rome consisted of three parts, — a nave, sacred to Jupiter; and two wings or aisles, one dedicated to Juno and the other to Minerva. This temple was nearly square, being two hundred and fifteen feet long and two hundred feet wide; and the wealth accumulated in it was immense. The walls and roof were of marble, covered with gold and silver.

JUPITER, the chief god of Rome, according to most philologists, derives his name (like the Greek Zεὸς) from the

---

* "Quis ignorat vel dictum vel conditum a Jano Janiculum?" Solinus, II. 3, quoted by Ampère.

† "Arx mea collis erat, quem cultrix nomine nostro
Nuncupat hæc ætas, Janiculumque vocat." — Fasti, I. 245.

far-away Sanskrit word " Div " or " Diu," indicating the splendor of heaven or of day. Ju-piter is from " Djaus-Pitar," which is the Sanskrit for *Father of Heaven*, or else from " Diu-pitar," *Father of Light*. He is, at all events, the equivalent of the Olympian Zeus. He carries the lightning, and, under many appellations, is the supreme god of the skies. Many temples were erected to him in Rome, under various designations. He was called Pluvius, Fulgurator, Tonans, Fulminator, Imbricitor, Serenator, — from the substantives designating rain, lightning, thunder, and the serene sky. Anything struck with lightning became sacred, and was consecrated to Jupiter. As the supreme being he was called Optimus Maximus, also Imperator, Victor, Invictus, Stator, Prædator, Triumphator, and Urbis Custos. And temples or shrines were erected to him under all these names, as the head of the armies, and commander-in-chief of the legions ; as Conqueror, as Invincible, as the Turner of Flight, as the God of Booty, and as the Guardian of the City. There is said to have been in Rome three hundred Jupiters, which must mean that Jupiter was worshipped under three hundred different attributes. Another name of this god was Elicius, from the belief that a method existed of eliciting or drawing down the lightning ; which belief probably arose from an accidental anticipation of Dr. Franklin's famous experiment. There were no such myths told about Jupiter as concerning the Greek Zeus. The Latin deity was a much more solemn person, his whole time occupied with the care of the city and state. But traces of his origin as a ruler of the atmosphere remained rooted in language ; and the Romans, in the time of Augustus, spoke familiarly of " a cold Jupiter," for a cold sky, and of a " bad Jupiter," for stormy weather.

The Juno of the Capitol was the Queen of Heaven, and in this sense was the female Jupiter. But Juno was also the goddess of womanhood, and had the epithets of Virginensis, Matrona, and Opigena ; that is, the friend of virgins, of matrons, and the daughter of help. Her chief festival was the Matronalia, on the first of March, hence called the " Women's Kalends." On this day presents were given to women by their husbands and friends. Juno was the patroness of marriage, and her month of June was believed to be very favorable for wedlock. As Juno Lucina she presided over birth ; as Mater Matuta,* over children ; as Juno Moneta, over the mint.

The name of Minerva, the Roman Athênê, is said to be derived from an old Etruscan word signifying mental action.† In the songs of the Sabians the word " promenervet " is used for " monet." The first syllable evidently contains the root, which in all Aryan languages implies thought. The Trinity of the Capitol, therefore, united Power, Wisdom, and Affection, as Jupiter, Minerva, and Juno. The statue of Minerva was placed in schools. She had many temples and festivals, and one of the former was dedicated to her as Minerva Medica.

The Roman pantheon contained three classes of gods and goddesses. First, the old Italian divinities, Etruscan, Latin, and Sabine, naturalized and adopted by the state. Secondly, the pale abstractions of the understanding, invented by the College of Pontiffs for moral and political purposes. And thirdly, the gods of Greece, imported, with a change of name, by the literary admirers and imitators of Hellas.

The genuine deities of the Roman religion were all of the first order. Some of them, like Janus, Vertumnus, Faunus, Vesta, retained their original character ; others were deliberately confounded with some Greek deity. Thus Venus, an old Latin or Sabine goddess to whom Titus Tatius erected a temple as Venus Cloacina, and Servius Tullius another as Venus Libertina,‡ was afterward transformed into the Greek Aphroditê, goddess of love. If it be true, as is asserted by Nævius and Plautus, that she was the goddess of gardens, as Venus Hortensis and Venus

* Mater Matuta ("matutina," matinal) was a Latin goddess of the dawn, who was absorbed into Juno, as often happened to the old Italian deities. Hartung says : " There was no limit to the superficial levity with which the Romans changed their worship."
† The Etruscans worshipped a goddess named Menerfa or Menfra. — Heffter.
‡ Heffter, p. 525. *Cloaca* is derived from *cluere*, which means *to wash away*. Libertina or Libitina is the goddess of funerals.

Fruti, then she may have been originally the female Vertumnus. So Diana was originally Diva Jana, and was simply the female Janus, until she was transformed into the Greek Artemis.

The second class of Roman divinities were those manufactured by the pontiffs for utilitarian purposes, — almost the only instance in the history of religion of such a deliberate piece of god-making. The purpose of the pontiffs was excellent ; but the result, naturally, was small. The worship of such abstractions as Hope (Spes), Fear (Pallor), Concord (Concordia), Courage (Virtus), Justice (Æquitas), Clemency (Clementia), could have little influence, since it must have been apparent to the worshipper himself that these were not real beings, but only his own conceptions, thrown heavenward.

The third class of deities were those adopted from Greece. New deities, like Apollo, were imported, and the old ones Hellenized. The Romans had no statues of their gods in early times ; this custom they learned from Greece. " A full river of influence," says Cicero, " and not a little brook, has flowed into Rome out of Greece." * They sent to Delphi to inquire of the Greek oracle. In a few decades, says Hartung, the Roman religion was wholly transformed by this Greek influence ; and that happened while the senate and priests were taking the utmost care that not an iota of the old ceremonies should be altered. Meantime the object was to identify the objects of worship in other countries with those worshipped at home. This was done in an arbitrary and superficial way, and caused great confusion in the mythologies. † Accidental resemblances, slight coincidences of names, were sufficient for the identification of two gods. As long as the service of the temple was unaltered, the priests troubled themselves very little about such changes. In this way, the twelve gods of Olympus — Zeus, Poseidôn, Apollo, Arês, Hêphæstos, Hermes, Hêrê, Athênê, Artemis, Aphroditê, Hestia, and Dêmêtêr — were naturalized or identified as Jupiter, Neptune, Apollo, Mars, Vulcan, Mercury, Juno, Minerva, Diana, Venus, Vesta, and Ceres.

* Republic, II. 19. † Hartung.

Dionysos became Liber or Bacchus; Persephonê, Proserpina; and the Muses were accepted as the Greeks had imagined them.

To find the true Roman worship, therefore, we must divest their deities of these Greek habiliments, and go back to their original Etruscan or Latin characters.

Among the Etruscans we find one doctrine unknown to the Greeks and not adopted by the Romans; that, namely, of the higher " veiled deities," * superior to Jupiter. They also had a dodecad of six male and six female deities, the Consentes and Complices, making a council of gods, whom Jupiter consulted in important cases. Vertumnus was an Etruscan; so, according to Ottfried Müller, was the Genius. So are the Lares, or household protectors, and Charun, or Charon, a power of the under-world. The minute system of worship was derived by Rome from Etruria. The whole system of omens, especially by lightning, came from the same source.

After Janus, and three Capitoline gods (Jupiter, Juno, and Minerva), above mentioned, the Romans worshipped a series of deities who may be classed as follows: —

I. Gods representing the powers of nature: —

1. SOL, the Sun. A Sabine deity. In later times the poets attributed to him all the characters of Helios; but as a Roman god, he never emerged into his own daylight.

2. LUNA, the Moon. Also regarded as of Sabine origin.

3. MATER MATUTA. Mother of Day, that is, the dawn. Worshipped at the Matronalia in June, as the possessor of all motherly qualities, and especially as the protector of children from ill-treatment. As the storms were apt to go down at morning, she was appealed to to protect mariners from shipwreck. The consul Tib. Semp. Gracchus dedicated a temple to her B. C. 176.

4. TEMPESTATES, the tempests. A temple was dedicated to the storms, B. C. 259.

5. VULCANUS. This name is supposed to be from the

* "Diis quos superiores et involutos vocant." — Seneca, Quæst. Nat., II. 41.

same root as "fulgeo," *to shine.* He was an old Italian deity. His temple is mentioned as existing B. C. 491.

6. FONTUS, the god of fountains. The Romans valued water so highly, that they erected altars and temples to this divinity, and had a feast of fountains (Fontinalia) on October 13th. There were also goddesses of fountains, as Lympha Juturna, the goddess of mineral springs. Egeria is the only nymph of a fountain mentioned in Roman mythology.

7. DIVUS PATER TIBERINUS, or Father Tiber, was of course the chief river god. The augurs called him Coluber, the snake, from his meandering and bending current.

8. NEPTUNUS. The origin of this word has been a great puzzle to the learned, who, however, connect it with nebula, a cloud, as the clouds come from the sea. He had his temple and his festivals at Rome.

Other deities connected with the powers of nature were PORTUNUS, the god of harbors; SALACIA, a goddess of the salt sea; TRANQUILLITAS, the goddess of calm weather.

II. Gods of human relations: —

1. VESTA, an ancient Latin goddess, and one of the oldest and most revered. She was the queen of the hearth and of the household fire. She was also the protector of the house, associated with the Lares and Penates. Some offering was due to her at every meal. She sanctified the home.

Afterward, when all Rome became one vast family, Vesta became the goddess of this public home, and her temple was the fireside of the city, in which burned always the sacred fire, watched by the vestal virgins. In this worship, and its associations, we find the best side of Roman manners, — the love of home, the respect for family life, the hatred of impurity and immodesty. She was also called "the mother," and qualified as Mater Stata, that is, the immovable mother.

2. The PENATES and LARES. These deities were also peculiarly Roman. The Lar, or Lares, were supposed to be the souls of ancestors which resided in the home and guarded it. Their images were kept in an oratory or

domestic chapel, called a Lararium, and were crowned by the master of the house to make them propitious. The paterfamilias conducted all the domestic worship of the household, whether of prayers or sacrifices, according to the maxim of Cato, "Scito dominum pro tota familia rem divinam facere." * The Penates were beings of a higher order than the Lares, but having much the same offices. Their name was from the words denoting the interior of the mansion (Penetralia, Penitus). They took part in all the joys and sorrows of the family. To go home was "to return to one's Penates." In the same way, "Lar meus" meant "my house"; "Lar conductus," "a hired house"; "Larem mutare" meant to change one's house. Thus the Roman in his home felt himself surrounded by invisible friends and guardians. No other nation, except the Chinese, have carried this religion of home so far. This is the tender side of the stern Roman character. Very little of pathos or sentiment appears in Roman poetry, but the lines by Catullus to his home are as tender as anything in modern literature. The little peninsula of Sirmio on the Lago di Garda has been glorified by these few words.

3. The GENIUS. The worship of the genius of a person or place was also peculiarly Italian. Each man had his genius, from whom his living power and vital force came. Tertullian speaks of the genius of places. On coins are found the Genius of Rome. Almost everything had its genius, — nations, colonies, princes, the senate, sleep, the theatre. The marriage-bed is called genial, because guarded by a genius. All this reminds us of the Fravashi of the Avesta and of the Persian monuments. Yet the Genius also takes his place among the highest gods.

III. Deities of the human soul: —
1. MENS, Mind, Intellect.
2. PUDICITIA, Chastity.
3. PIETAS, Piety, Reverence for Parents.
4. FIDES, Fidelity.

* "De re rustica"; quoted by Merivale in the Preface to The Conversion of the Roman Empire.

5. CONCORDIA, Concord.
6. VIRTUS, Courage.
7. SPES, Hope.
8. PALLOR or PAVOR, Fear.
9. VOLUPTAS, Pleasure.

IV. Deities of rural and other occupations : —
1. TELLUS, the Earth.
2. SATURNUS, Saturn.   The root of this name is SAO =
SERO, *to sow.*   Saturn is the god of planting and sowing.
3. OPS, goddess of the harvest.
4. MARS.   Originally an agricultural god, dangerous to
crops ; afterwards god of war.
5. SILVANUS, the wood god.
6. FAUNUS, an old Italian deity, the patron of agriculture.
7. TERMINUS, an old Italian deity, the guardian of
limits and boundaries.
8. CERES, goddess of the cereal grasses.
9. LIBER, god of the vine, and of wine.
10. BONA DEA, the good goddess.   The worship of the
good goddess was imported from Greece in later times ;
and perhaps its basis was the worship of Dêmêtêr.   The
temple of the good goddess was on Mount Aventine.   At
her feast on the 1st of May all suggestions of the male
sex were banished from the house ; no wine must be
drunk ; the myrtle, as a symbol of love, was removed.
The idea of the feast was of a chaste marriage, as helping
to preserve the human race.
11. MAGNA MATER, or Cybele.   This was a foreign worship, but early introduced at Rome.
12. FLORA.   She was an original goddess of Italy, presiding over flowers and blossoms.   Great license was practised at her worship.
13. VERTUMNUS, the god of gardens, was an old Italian
deity, existing before the foundation of Rome.
14. POMONA, goddess of the harvest.
18. PALES.   A rural god, protecting cattle.   At his
feast men and cattle were purified.
The Romans had many other deities, whose worship

was more or less popular. But those now mentioned were the principal ones. This list shows that the powers of earth were more objects of reverence than the heavenly bodies. The sun and stars attracted this agricultural people less than the spring and summer, seedtime and harvest. Among the Italians the country was before the city, and Rome was founded by country people.

§ 3. *Worship and Ritual.*

The Roman ceremonial worship was very elaborate and minute, applying to every part of daily life. It consisted in sacrifices, prayers, festivals, and the investigation by augurs and haruspices of the will of the gods and the course of future events. The Romans accounted themselves an exceedingly religious people, because their religion was so intimately connected with the affairs of home and state.

The Romans distinguished carefully between things sacred and profane. This word " profane " comes from the root " fari," *to speak ;* because the gods were supposed to speak to men by symbolic events. A *fane* is a place thus consecrated by some divine event ; a *profane* place, one not consecrated.* But that which man dedicates to the gods (*dedicat* or *dicat*) is sacred, or consecrated.† Every place which was to be dedicated was first " liberated " by the augur from common uses ; then " consecrated " to divine uses by the pontiff. A " temple " is a place thus separated, or cut off from other places ; for the root of this word, like that of " tempus " (time) is the same as the Greek τέμνω, *to cut.*

The Roman year was full of festivals (*feriæ*) set apart for religious uses. It was declared by the pontiffs a sin to do any common work on these days, but works of necessity were allowed. These festivals were for particular gods, in honor of great events in the history of Rome, or of rural occurrences, days of purification and atonement,

---

* From the same root come our words " fate," " fanatic," etc. " Fanaticum dicitur arbor fulmine icta." — Festus, 69.

† From " sacrare " or " consecrare." Hence sacrament and sacerdotal.

family feasts, or feasts in honor of the dead. The old Roman calendar * was as carefully arranged as that of modern Rome. The day began at midnight. The following is a view of the Roman year in its relation to festivals : —

January.

1. Feast of *Janus*, the god of beginnings.
9. *Agonalia.*
11. *Carmentalia.* In honor of the nymph Carmenta, a woman's festival.
16. Dedication of the *Temple of Concord.*
31. Feast of the *Penates.*

February.

1. Feast of *Juno Sospita*, the Savior : an old goddess.
13. *Faunalia*, dedicated to Faunus and the rural gods.
15. *Lupercalia.* Feast of fruitfulness.
17. *Fornacalia.* Feast of the oven goddess Fornax.
18 to 28. The *Februatio*, or feast of purification and atonement, and the *Feralia*, or feast of the dead. Februus was an old Etrurian god of the under-world. Also, the *Charistia*, a family festival for putting an end to quarrels among relations.
23. Feast of *Terminus*, god of boundaries. Boundary-stones anointed and crowned.

March.

1. Feast of *Mars.* Also, the *Matronalia.* The Salii, priests of Mars, go their rounds, singing old hymns.
6. Feast of *Vesta.*
7. Feast of *Vejovis* or *Vedius*, i. e. the boy Jupiter.
14. *Equiria*, or horse-races in honor of Mars.
15. Feast of *Anna-Perenna*, goddess of health.
17. *Liberalia*, Feast of Bacchus. Young men invested with the Toga-Virilis on this day.
19 to 23. Feast of *Minerva*, for five days. Offerings made to her by all mechanics, artists, and scholars.

---

* The word "calendar" is itself derived from the Roman " Kalends," the first day of the month.

April.

1. Feast of *Venus*, to whom the month is sacred.
4. *Megalesia.* Feast of Cybele and Altys. It lasted six days, and was the Roman analogue of the feast of Ceres in Greece and of Isis in Egypt.
12. *Cerealia.* Feast of Ceres. Games in the circus.
15. *Fordicicia.* Feast of cows.
21. *Palililia.* Feast of Pales, and of the founding of Rome.
23. *Vinalia.* Feast of new wine.
25. *Robigalia.* Feast of the goddess of blight, Robigo.
28. *Floralia.* Feast of the goddess Flora; very licentious.

May.

1. Feast of the *Bona Dea*, the good goddess; otherwise Maia, Ops, Tellus, or the Earth. This was the feast held by women secretly in the house of the pontiff.
9. *Lemuralia.* Feast of the departed spirits or ghosts.
12. Games to *Mars.*
23. *Tubilustria*, to consecrate wind instruments.

June.

1. Feast of *Carna*, goddess of the internal organs of the body, and of *Juno Moneta.*
4. Feast of *Bellona.*
5. Feast of *Deus Fidius.*
7 to 15. Feast of *Vesta.*
19. *Matralia.* Feast of Mater Matuta.
Other lesser festivals in this month to *Summanus, Fortuna, Fortis, Jupiter Stator*, etc.

July.

1. Day devoted to changing residences, like the 1st of May in New York.
4. *Fortuna Muliebris.*
5. *Populifuga.* In memory of the people's flight, on some occasion, afterward forgotten.
7. Feast of *Juno Caprotina.*
15. Feast of *Castor and Pollux.*

Other festivals in this month were the *Lucaria, Neptu-nalia*, and *Furinalia*.

August.

1. Games to *Mars*.
17. Feast of the god *Portumnus*.
18. *Consualia*, feast of Consus. Rape of the Sabines.
23. *Vulcanalia*, to avert fires.
25. *Opeconsivia*. Feast of Ops Consiva.

September.

The chief feasts in this month were the games (*Ludi Magni* or *Romani*) in honor of Jupiter, Juno, and Minerva.

October.

13. *Fontinalia*. Feast of fountains, when the springs were strewed with flowers.
15. Sacrifice of a horse to *Mars*.

The feasts in November are unimportant.

December.

5. *Faunalia*, in honor of Faunus.
19. *Saturnalia*, sacred to Saturn. A Roman thanksgiving for the harvest. It lasted seven days, during which the slaves had their liberty, in memory of the age of Saturn, when all were equal. The rich kept open table to all comers, and themselves waited on the slaves. Presents were interchanged, schools were closed. The Senate did not sit.

Thus religion everywhere met the public life of the Roman by its festivals, and laid an equal yoke on his private life by its requisition of sacrifices, prayers, and auguries. All pursuits must be conducted according to a system, carefully laid down by the College of Pontiffs. Sacrifices and prayers of one or another kind were demanded during most of the occasions of life. Hidden in our word "inaugurate" is the record of the fact that nothing could be properly begun without the assistance of the augurs. Sacrifices of lustration and expiation were very common, not so much for moral offences as for ceremonial mistakes. The doctrine of the *opus operatum* was supreme in Roman religion. The intention was of little importance; the question was whether the ceremony had been performed exactly in accordance with rule. If not, it must be done again. Sometimes fifty or a hundred victims were killed before the priestly etiquette was contented. Sometimes magistrates must resign because the college of augurs suspected some informality in the ceremonies of their election. Laws were annulled and judicial proceedings revoked for the same reason. If the augurs declared the signs unfavorable, a public meeting must be adjourned and no business done. A single mistake in the form of a prayer would make it ineffectual. If a man went out to walk, there was a form to be recited; if he mounted his chariot, another. All these religious acts were of the nature of *charms,* which acted on the gods by an inherent power, and compelled them to be favorable, whatever their own wishes might be. The gods were, therefore, as much the slaves of external mechanical laws as the Romans themselves. In reality, the supreme god of Rome was law, in the form of rule. But these rules afterward expanded, as the Roman civilization increased, into a more generous jurisprudence. Regularity broadened into justice.* But for a long period the whole of the Roman organic law was a system of hard external method. And the rise of law as justice and reason was the decline of religion as mere prescription and rule. This one change is the key to the dissolution of the Roman system of religious practices.

The seat of Roman worship in the oldest times was the Regia in the Via Sacra, near the Forum. This was the house of the chief pontiff, and here the sacrifices were performed † by the Rex Sacrorum. Near by was the temple of Vesta. The Palatine Hill was regarded as the home of the Latin gods, while the Quirinal was that of

---

* See Merivale, The Conversion of the Roman Empire, Lect. IV. p. 74.
† Döllinger, Gentile and Jew. Funke, Real Lexicon. Festus.

the Sabine deities. But the Penates of Rome remained at Lavinium, the old metropolis of the Latin Confederation, and mother of the later city. Every one of the highest officers of Rome was obliged to go and sacrifice to the ancient gods, at this mother city of Lavinium, before entering on his office.

The old worship of Rome was free from idolatry. Jupiter, Juno, Janus, Ops, Vesta, were not represented by idols. This feature was subsequently imported by means of Hellenic influences coming through Cuma and other cities of Magna Græcia. By the same channels came the Sibylline books. There were ten Sibyls, — the Persian, Libyan, Delphian, Cumæan, Erythræan, Samian, Amalthæan, Hellespontine, Phrygian, and Tiburtine. The Sibylline books authorized or commanded the worship of various Greek gods ; they were intrusted to the Decemviri.

Roman worship was at first administered by certain patrician families, and this was continued till B. C. 300, when plebeians were allowed to enter the sacred colleges. A plebeian became Pontifex Maximus, for the first time, B. C. 253.

The pontiffs (Pontifices) derived their name (bridge-builders) from a bridge over the Tiber, which it was their duty to build and repair in order to sacrifice on either bank. They possessed the supreme authority in all matters of worship, and decided questions concerning marriage, inheritance, public games.

The Flamens were the priests of particular deities. The office was for life, and there were fifteen Flamens in all. The Flamen Dialis, or priest of Jupiter, had a life burdened with etiquette. He must not take an oath, ride, have anything tied with knots on his person, see armed men, look at a prisoner, see any one at work on a Festa, touch a goat, or dog, or raw flesh, or yeast. He must not bathe in the open air, pass a night outside the city, and he could only resign his office on the death of his wife. This office is Pelasgic, and very ancient.

The Salii were from early times priests of Mars, who danced in armor, and sang old hymns. The Luperci were another body of priests, also of very ancient origin.

Other colleges of priests were the Epulones, Curiones, Tities.

The Vestal virgins were highly honored and very sacred. Their work was to tend the fire of Vesta, and prevent the evil omen of its extinction. They were appointed by the Pontifex Maximus. They were selected when very young, and could resign their office after thirty years of service. They had a large revenue, enjoyed the highest honors, and to strike them was a capital offence. If a criminal about to be executed met them, his life was spared. Consuls and prætors must give way to them in the streets. They assisted at the theatres and at all public entertainments. They could go out to visit and to dine with their relations. Their very presence protected any one from assault, and their intercession must not be neglected. They prepared the sacred cakes, took part in many sacrifices, and had the charge of a holy serpent, keeping his table supplied with meat.

The duty of the augurs was to inquire into the divine will; and they could prevent any public business by declaring the omens unfavorable. The name is probably derived from an old Aryan word, meaning "sight" or "eye," which has come to us in the Greek αὐγή, and the German auge. Our words "auspicious" and "auspicate" are derived from the "auspices," or outlook on nature which these seers practised. For they were in truth the Roman seers. Their business was to look, at midnight, into the starry heavens; to observe thunder, lightning, meteors; the chirping or flying of birds; the habits of the sacred chickens; the appearance of quadrupeds; or casualties of various kinds, as sneezing, stumbling, spilling salt or wine. The last relics of these superstitions are to be found in the little books sold in Rome, in which the fortunate number in a lottery is indicated by such accidents and events of common life.

The Romans, when at prayer, were in the habit of covering their heads, so that no sound of evil augury might be heard. The suppliant was to kiss his right hand, and then turn round in a circle and sit down. Many formulæ of prayers were prescribed to be used on all occa-

15

sions of life. They must be repeated three times, at least, to insure success. Different animals were sacrificed to different gods, — white cattle with gilded horns to Jupiter, a bull to Apollo, a horse to Mars. Sometimes the number of victims was enormous. On Caligula's accession, one hundred and sixty thousand victims were killed in the Roman Empire.

Lustrations were great acts of atonement or purification, and are often described by ancient writers. The city was lustrated by a grand procession of the four colleges of Augurs, Pontifices, Quindecemviri, and Septemviri. Lucan, in his Pharsalia, describes such a lustration.* Tacitus gives a like description, in his History,† of the ceremonies attending the rebuilding the Capitol. On an auspicious day, beneath a serene sky, the ground chosen for the foundation was surrounded with ribbons and flowers. Soldiers, selected for their auspicious names, brought into the enclosure branches from the trees sacred to the gods. The Vestal virgins, followed by a band of children, sprinkled the place with water drawn from three fountains and three rivers. The prætor and the pontiff next sacrificed a swine, a sheep, and a bull, and besought Jupiter, Juno, and Minerva to favor the undertaking. The magistrates, priests, senators, and knights then drew the corner-stone to its place, throwing in ingots of gold and silver.

The Romans, ever anxious about the will of the gods, naturalized among themselves the Etruscan institution of the Haruspices. The prodigies observed were in the entrails of animals and the phenomena of nature. The parts of the entrails observed were the tongue, lungs, heart, liver, gall bladder, spleen, kidneys, and caul. If the head of the right lobe of the liver was absent, it was considered a very bad omen. If certain fissures existed, or were absent, it was a portent of the first importance. But the Romans were a very practical people, and not easily deterred from their purpose. So if one sacrifice failed they would try another and another, until the portents were favorable. But sceptical persons were naturally led to ask

* Book I. 592.   † IV. 593.

some puzzling questions, such as these, which Cicero puts in his work on Divination : * How can a cleft in a liver be connected, by any natural law, with my acquisition of a property ? If it is so connected, what would be the result, if some one else, who was about to *lose* his property, had examined the same victim ? If you answer that the divine energy, which extends through the universe, directs each man in the choice of a victim, then how happens it that a man having first had an unfavorable omen, by trying again should get a good one ? How happens it that a sacrifice to one deity gives a favorable sign, and that to another the opposite ? But these criticisms only arrived after the old Roman faith had begun to decline.

Funeral solemnities were held with great care and pomp, and festivals for the dead were regularly celebrated. The dead father or mother was accounted a god, and yet a certain terror of ancestral spectres was shown by a practice of driving them out of the house by lustrations. For it was uncertain whether the paternal Manes were good spirits, Lares, or evil spirits, and Lemures. Consequently in May there was the Lemuria, or feast for exorcising the evil spirits from houses and homes, conducted with great solemnity.

§ 4. *The Decay of the Roman Religion.*

"The more distinguished a Roman became," says Mommsen, "the less was he a free man. The omnipotence of law, the despotism of the rule, drove him into a narrow circle of thought and action, and his credit and influence depended on the sad austerity of his life. The whole duty of man, with the humblest and greatest of the Romans, was to keep his house in order, and be the obedient servant of the state." While each individual could be nothing more than a member of the community, a single link in the iron chain of Roman power ; he, on the other hand, shared the glory and might of all-conquering Rome. Never was such *esprit de corps* developed, never such intense patriotism, never such absolute sub-

* De Divinatione, II. 12, etc.

servience and sacrifice of the individual to the community.
But as man is manifold and cannot be forever confined to
a single form of life, a reaction against this narrow patriotism was to be expected in the interest of personal
freedom, and it came very naturally from Greek influences. The Roman could not contemplate the exuberant
development of Greek thought, art, literature, society,
without bitterly feeling how confined was his own range,
how meagre and empty his own life. Hence, very early,
Roman society began to be Hellenized, but especially
after the unification of Italy. To quote Mommsen once
more: "The Greek civilization was grandly human and
cosmopolitan; and Rome not only was stimulated by this
influence, but was penetrated by it to its very centre."
Even in politics there was a new school, whose fixed idea
was the consolidation and propagandism of republicanism;
but this Philhellenism showed itself especially in the
realm of thought and faith. As the old faith died, more
ceremonies were added; for as life goes out, forms come
in. As the winter of unbelief lowers the stream of piety,
the ice of ritualism accumulates along its banks. In
addition to the three colleges of Pontiffs, Haruspices, and
Quindecemviri, another of Epulones, whose business was
to attend to the religious feasts, was instituted in A. U.
558 (B. C. 196). Contributions and tithes of all sorts
were demanded from the people. Hercules, especially, as
is more than once intimated in the plays of Plautus,
became very rich by his tithes.* Religion became more
and more a charm, on the exact performance of which the
favor of the gods depended; so that ceremonies were
sometimes performed thirty times before the essential
accuracy was attained.

The gods were now changed, in the hands of Greek
statuaries, into ornaments for a rich man's home. Greek

* A Greek epigram, recently translated, alludes to the same fact : —

"Honey and milk are sacrifice to thee,
Kind Hermes, inexpensive deity.
But Hercules demands a lamb each day,
For keeping, so he says, the wolves away.
Imports it much, meek browsers of the sod,
Whether a wolf devour you, or a god ?"

myths were imported and connected with the story of
Roman deities, as Ennius made Saturn the son of Cœlus,
in imitation of the genealogy of Kronos. That form of
rationalism called Euhemerism, which explains every god
into a mythical king or hero, became popular. So, too,
was the doctrine of Epicharmos, who considered the
divinities as powers of nature symbolized. According to
the usual course of events, superstition and unbelief went
hand in hand. As the old faith died out, new forms of
worship, like those of Cybele and Bacchus, came in.
Stern conservatives like Cato opposed all these innova-
tions and scepticisms, but ineffectually.

Gibbon says that "the admirable work of Cicero, ' De
Naturâ Deorum,' is the best clew we have to guide us
through this dark abyss " (the moral and religious teachings of the philosophers).* After, in the first two books,
the arguments for the existence and providence of the
gods have been set forth and denied, by Velleius the
Epicurean, Cotta the academician, and Balbus the
Stoic; in the third book, Cotta, the head of the priesthood, the Pontifex Maximus, proceeds to refute the
stoical opinion that there are gods who govern the
universe and provide for the welfare of mankind. To
be sure, he says, as Pontifex, he of course believes in
the gods, but he feels free as a philosopher to deny their
existence. "I believe in the gods," says he, "on the
authority and tradition of our ancestors; but if we reason,
I shall reason against their existence." "Of course," he
says, "I believe in divination, as I have always been
taught to do. But who knows whence it comes? As to
the voice of the Fauns, I never heard it; and I do not
know what a Faun is. You say that the regular course
of nature proves the existence of some ordering power.
But what more regular than a tertian or quartan fever?
The world subsists by the power of nature." Cotta goes
on to criticise the Roman pantheon, ridiculing the idea of
such gods as "Love, Deceit, Fear, Labor, Envy, Old Age,
Death, Darkness, Misery, Lamentation, Favor, Fraud,
Obstinacy," etc. He shows that there are many gods of

* Gibbon, Decline and Fall, Chap. II.

the same name; several Jupiters, Vulcans, Apollos, and Venuses. He then denies providence, by showing that the wicked succeed and the good are unfortunate. Finally, all was left in doubt, and the dialogue ends with a tone of triumphant uncertainty. This was Cicero's contribution to theology; and Cicero was far more religious than most men of his period.

Many writers, and more recently Merivale,* have referred to the remarkable debate which took place in the Roman Senate, on the occasion of Catiline's conspiracy. Cæsar, at that time chief pontiff, the highest religious authority in the state, gave his opinion against putting the conspirators to death; for death, says he, "is the end of all suffering. After death there is neither pain nor pleasure (*ultra neque curæ, neque gaudii locum*)." Cato, the Stoic, remarked that Cæsar had spoken well concerning life and death. "I take it," says he, "that he regards as false what we are told about the sufferings of the wicked hereafter," but does not object to that statement. These speeches are reported by Sallust, and are confirmed by Cicero's fourth Catiline Oration. The remarkable fact is, not that such things were said, but that they were heard with total indifference. No one seemed to think it was of any consequence one way or the other. Suppose that when the question of the execution of Charles I. was before Parliament, it had been opposed by the Archbishop of Canterbury (had he been there) on the ground that after death all pain and pleasure ceased. The absurdity of the supposition shows the different position of the human mind at the two epochs.

In fact, an impassable gulf yawned between the old Roman religion and modern Roman thought. It was out of the question for an educated Roman, who read Plato and Zeno, who listened to Cicero and Hortensius, to believe in Janus and the Penates. "All very well for the people," said they. "The people must be kept in order by these superstitions." † 'But the secret could not be kept. Sincere men, like Lucretius, who saw all the evil

---

* Conversion of the Roman Empire, Note A.
† "Expedit civitates falli in religione," said Varro.

of these superstitions, and who had no strong religious
sense, *would* speak out, and proclaim *all* religion to be
priestcraft and an unmitigated evil.   The poem of Lucretius, " De Rerum Naturâ," declares faith in the gods to have
been the curse of the human race, and immortality to be
a silly delusion.   He denies the gods, providence, the human soul, and any moral purpose in the universe.   But
as religion is an instinct, which will break out in some
form, and when expelled from the soul returns in disguise, Lucretius, denying all the gods, pours out a lovely
hymn to Venus, goddess of beauty and love.

The last philosophic protest, in behalf of a pure and
authoritative faith, came from the Stoics.   The names of
Seneca, Epictetus, and Aurelius Antoninus gave dignity,
if they could not bring safety, to the declining religion
of Rome.

Seneca, indeed, was inferior to the other two in personal
character, and was more of a rhetorician than a philosopher.   But noble thoughts occur in his writings.   "A
sacred spirit sits in every heart," he says, "and treats us
as we treat it."   He opposed idolatry, he condemned animal sacrifices.   The moral element is very marked in his
brilliant pages.   Philosophy, he says, is an effort to be
wise and good.*   Physical studies he condemns as useless.†   Goodness is that which harmonizes with the natural movements of the soul.‡   God and matter are the two
principles of all being ; God is the active principle, matter the passive.   God is spirit, and all souls are part of
this spirit.§   Reason is the bond which unites God and
other souls, and so God dwells in all souls.‖

One of the best sayings of Epictetus is that " the wise
man does not merely know by tradition and hearsay that

---

* " Philosophia sapientiæ amor est."   " Nec philosophia sine virtute,
nec sine philosophia virtus."   Epist. XCI. 5.
† " Physica non faciunt bonos, sed doctos."   Epist. CVI. 11.
‡ " Bonum est, quod ad se impetum animi secundum naturam mo-
vet."   Epist. CXVIII. 9.
§ " Universa ex materia et Deo constant."   Epist. LXV. 24.
‖ " Socii Dei sumus et membra.   Prope a te Deus est, tecum est, in-
tus est.   Sacer intra nos Spiritus sedet, malorum bonorumque nostrorum
observator et custos.   Deus ad homines venit ; immo, in homines."
Epist. XCII. 41, 73.

Jupiter is the father of gods and men ; but is inwardly
convinced of it in his soul, and therefore cannot help acting and feeling according to this conviction." *

Epictetus declared that the philosopher could have no
will but that of the deity ; he never blames fate or fortune, for he knows that no real evil can befall the just
man. The life of Epictetus was as true as his thoughts
were noble, but he had fallen on an evil age, which needed
for its reform, not a new philosophy, but a new inspiration of divine life. This steady current downward darkened the pure soul of Marcus Aurelius Antoninus, of
whom Niebuhr says, † " If there is any sublime human
virtue, it is his." He adds : " He was certainly the
noblest character of his time ; and I know no other man
who combined such unaffected kindness, mildness, and
humility with such conscientiousness and severity towards himself." " If there is anywhere an expression of
virtue, it is in the heavenly features of M. Aurelius. His
' Meditations ' are a golden book, though there are things
in it which cannot be read without deep grief, for there
we find this purest of men without happiness." Though
absolute monarch of the Empire, and rich in the universal love of his people, he was not powerful enough to
resist the steady tendency to decay in society. Nor did
he know that the power that was to renew the life of the
world was already present in Christianity. He himself
was in soul almost a Christian, though he did not know
it, and though the Christian element of faith and hope
was wanting. But he expressed a thought worthy of the
Gospel, when he said : " The man of disciplined mind
reverently bids Nature, who bestows all things and re-
sumes them again to herself, ' Give what thou wilt, and
take what thou wilt.' " ‡

Although we have seen that Seneca speaks of a sacred
spirit which dwells in us, other passages in his works
(quoted by Zeller) show that he was, like other Stoics, a
pantheist, and meant the soul of the world. He says

* Arrian's " Discourses of Epictetus," III. 24.
† Lectures on the History of Rome, III. 247.
‡ Monolog., X. 14.

(Nat. Qu., II. 45, and Prolog. 13) : " Will you call God
the world ?   You may do so without mistake.   For he is
all that you see around you."   " What is God ?   The
mind of the universe.   What is God ?   All that you see,
and all that you do not see." *

It was not philosophy which destroyed religion in
Rome.   Philosophy, no doubt, weakened faith in the
national gods, and made the national worship seem absurd.   But it was the general tendency downward ; it was
the loss of the old Roman simplicity and purity ; it was
the curse of Cæsarism, which, destroying all other human
life, destroyed also the life of religion.   What it came to
at last, in well-endowed minds, may be seen in this extract from the elder Pliny : —

"All religion is the offspring of necessity, weakness, and
fear.   *What* God is, if in truth he be anything distinct from
the world, it is beyond the compass of man's understanding
to know.   But it is a foolish delusion, which has sprung from
human weakness and human pride, to imagine that such an
infinite spirit would concern himself with the petty affairs of
men.   It is difficult to say, whether it might not be better for
men to be wholly without religion, than to have one of this
kind, which is a reproach to its object.   The vanity of man,
and his insatiable longing after existence, have led him also
to dream of a life after death.   A being full of contradictions,
he is the most wretched of creatures ; since the other creatures
have no wants transcending the bounds of their nature.   Man
is full of desires and wants that reach to infinity, and can
never be satisfied.   His nature is a lie, uniting the greatest
poverty with the greatest pride.   Among these so great evils,
the best thing God has bestowed on man is the power to take
his own life." †

The system of the Stoics was exactly adapted to the
Roman character ; but, naturally, it exaggerated its faults
instead of correcting them.   It supplanted all other systems in the esteem of leading minds ; but the narrowness
of the Roman intellect reacted on the philosophy, and
made that much more narrow than it was in the Greek

* Zeller, Stoics Epicureans and Sceptics, p. 150.
† Quoted by Neander, Church History, I. 10 (Am. ed.).
15 *

thought. It became simple ethics, omitting both the physical and metaphysical side.

Turning to literature, we find in Horace a gay epicureanism, which always says: " Enjoy this life, for it will be soon over, and after death there is nothing left for us." Virgil tells us that those are happy who know the causes of things, and so escape the terrors of Acheron. The serious Tacitus, a man always in earnest, a penetrating mind, is by Bunsen called " the last Roman prophet, but a prophet of death and judgment. He saw that Rome hastened to ruin, and that Cæsarism was an unmixed evil, but an evil not to be remedied." * He declares that the gods had to mingle in Roman affairs as protectors ; they now appeared only for vengeance.† Tacitus in one passage speaks of human freedom as superior to fate, ‡ but in another expresses his uncertainty on the whole question.§ Equally uncertain was he concerning the future life, though inclined to believe that the soul is not extinguished with the body. ‖

But the tone of the sepulchral monuments of that period is not so hopeful. Here are some which are quoted by Döllinger,¶ from Muratori and Fabretti : " Reader, enjoy thy life ; for, after death, there is neither laughter nor play, nor any kind of enjoyment." " Friend, I advise thee to mix a goblet of wine and drink, crowning thy head with flowers. Earth and fire consume all that remains at death." " Pilgrim, stop and listen. In Hades is no boat and no Charon ; no Eacus and no Cerberus. Once dead, we are all alike." Another says : " Hold all a mockery, reader ; nothing is our own."

So ended the Roman religion ; in superstition among the ignorant, in unbelief among the wise. It was time that something should come to renew hope. This was the gift which the Gospel brought to the Romans, — hope

---

* Gott in der Geschichte, Zweiter Theil, Seite 387.
† Tacitus, History, I. 3.
‡ Ibid., Annals, IV. 20.
§ Ibid., Annals, VI. 22.
‖ Ibid., Agricola, 46.
¶ The Greek and the Jew, Vol. II. p. 147.

for time, hope beyond time.   This was the prayer for the
Romans of the Apostle Paul : " Now the God of hope
fill you with all joy and peace in believing, that ye may
abound in hope, through the power of the Holy Ghost." *
A remarkable fact, that a Jewish writer should exhort
Romans to hope and courage !

§ 5. *Relation of the Roman Religion to Christianity.*

The idea of Rome is law, that of Christianity is love.
In Roman worship law took the form of iron rules ; in
Roman theology it appeared as a stern fate ; in both as a
slavery.   Christianity came as freedom, in a worship free
from forms, in a view of God which left freedom to
man.   Christianity came to the Roman world, not as a
new theory, but as a new life.   As, during the early spring,
the power of the returning sun penetrates the soil, silently touching the springs of life ; so Christianity during
two hundred years moved silently in the heart of Roman
society, creating a new faith, hope, and love.   And as,
at last, in the spring the grass shoots, the buds open,
the leaves appear, the flowers bloom ; so, at last, Christianity, long working in silence and shadow, suddenly
became apparent, and showed that it had been transform-
ing the whole tone and temper of Roman civilization.

But wherever there is action there is also reaction,
and no power or force can wholly escape this law.   So
Roman thought, acted on by Christianity, reacted and
modified in many respects the Gospel.   Not always in a
bad way, sometimes it helped its developments.   For the
Providence which made the Gospel for the Romans made
the Romans for the Gospel.

The great legacy bequeathed to mankind by ancient
Rome was law.   Other nations, it is true, had codes
of law, like the Institutes of Manu in India, or the
jurisprudence of Solon and the enactments of Lycur-
gus.   But Roman law from the beginning was sanctified by the conviction that it was founded on justice, and
not merely on expediency or prudence.   In submitting to

* Epistle to the Romans, xv. 13.

the laws, even when they were cruel and oppressive, the Roman was obeying, not force, but conscience. The view which Plato gave as an ideal in Crito was realized in Roman society from the first. Consider the cruel enactments which made the debtors the slaves of the creditor, and the fact that when the plebeians were ground to the earth by that oppression, they did not attempt to resist the law, but in their despair fled from their homes, beyond the jurisdiction of Rome, to establish a new city where these enactments could not reach them. Only when the laws are thus enforced by the public conscience as something sacred, does society become possible; and this sense of the divinity which hedges a code of laws has been transmitted from ancient Rome into the civilization of Europe.

Cicero, in his admirable treatise on the laws, which unfortunately we have in an imperfect condition, devotes the whole of the first book to establishing eternal justice as the basis of all jurisprudence. No better text-book could have been found for the defence of what was called "the higher law," in the great American antislavery struggle, than this work of Cicero. "Let us establish," he says, "the principles of justice on that supreme law which has existed from all ages before any legislative enactments were written, or any political governments formed." "Among all questions, there is none more important to understand than this, *that man is born for justice;* and that law and equity have not been established by opinion, but by nature." "It is an absurd extravagance in some philosophers to assert that all things are necessarily just which are established by the laws and institutions of nations." "Justice does not consist in submission to written laws." "If the will of the people, the decrees of the senate, the decisions of magistrates, were sufficient to establish rights, then it might become right to rob, to commit adultery, to forge wills, if this was sanctioned by the votes or decrees of the majority." "The sum of all is, that what is right should be sought for its own sake, because it is right, and not because it is enacted."

Law appears from the very beginnings of the Roman

state. The oldest traditions make Romulus, Numa, and Servius to be legislators. From that time, after the expulsion of the Tarquins, Rome was governed by laws. Even the despotism of the Cæsars did not interfere with the general administration of the laws in civil affairs ; for the one-man power, though it may corrupt and degrade a state, does not immediately and directly affect many persons in their private lives. Law continued to rule in common affairs, and this legacy of a society organized by law was the gift of Rome to modern Europe. How great a blessing it has been may be seen by comparing the worst Christian government with the best of the despotic governments of Asia. Mohammedan society is ruled by a hierarchy of tyranny, each little tyrant being in turn the victim of the one above him.

The feudal system, introduced by the Teutonic races, attempted to organize Europe on the basis of military despotism ; but Roman law was too strong for feudal law, and happily for mankind overcame it and at last expelled it.

Christianity, in its ready hospitality for all the truth and good which it encounters, accepted Roman jurisprudence and gave to it a new lease of life.* Christian emperors and Christian lawyers codified the long line of decrees and enactments reaching back to the Twelve Tables, and established them as the laws of the Christian world. But the spirit of Roman law acted on Christianity in a more subtle manner. It reproduced the organic character of the Roman state in the Western Latin Church, and it reproduced the soul of Roman law in the Western Latin theology.

It has not always been sufficiently considered how much the Latin Church was a reproduction, on a higher

---

* " The legislation of Justinian, as far as it was original, in his Code, Pandects, and Institutes, was still almost exclusively Roman. It might seem that Christianity could hardly penetrate into the solid and well-compacted body of Roman law ; or rather the immutable principles of justice had been so clearly discerned by the inflexible rectitude of the Roman mind, and so sagaciously applied by the wisdom of her great lawyers, that Christianity was content to acquiesce in these statutes, which she might despair, except in some respects, of rendering more equitable."
— Milman, Latin Christianity, Vol. II. p. 11.

plane, of the old Roman Commonwealth. The resemblance between the Roman Catholic ceremonies and those of Pagan Rome has been often noticed. The Roman Catholic Church has borrowed from Paganism saints' days, incense, lustrations, consecrations of sacred places, votive-offerings, relics; winking, nodding, sweating, and bleeding images; holy water, vestments, etc. But the Church of Rome itself, in its central idea of authority, is a reproduction of the Roman state religion, which was a part of the Roman state. The Eastern churches were sacerdotal and religious; the Church of Rome added to these elements that of an organized political authority. It was the resurrection of Rome, — Roman ideas rising into a higher life. The Roman Catholic Church, at first an aristocratic republic, like the Roman state, afterwards became, like the Roman state, a disguised despotism. The Papal Church is therefore a legacy of ancient Rome.*

And just as the Roman state was first a help and then a hindrance to the progress of humanity, so it has been with the Roman Catholic Church. Ancient Rome gradually bound together into a vast political unity the divided tribes and states of Europe, and so infused into them the civilization which she had developed or received. And so the Papal Church united Europe again, and once more permeated it with the elements of law, of order, of Christian faith. All intelligent Protestants admit the good done in this way by the mediæval church.

For example, Milman † says, speaking of Gregory the Great and his work, that it was necessary that there should be some central power like the Papacy to resist the dissolution of society at the downfall of the Roman Empire. "The life and death of Christianity" depended, he says, "on the rise of such a power." "It is impossible to conceive what had been the confusion, the lawlessness, the chaotic state of the Middle Ages, without the mediæval Papacy."

---

* See Ranke, History of the Popes, Chap. I., where he says that the Roman Empire gave its outward form to Christianity (meaning *Latin* Christianity), and that the constitution of the hierarchy was necessarily modelled on that of the Empire.

† History of Latin Christianity, Vol. II. p. 100.

The whole history of Rome had infused into the minds of Western nations a conviction of the importance of centralization in order to union. From Rome, as a centre, had proceeded government, law, civilization. Christianity therefore seemed to need a like centre, in order to retain its unity. Hence the supremacy early yielded to the Bishop of Rome. His primacy was accepted, because it was useful. The Papal Church would never have existed, if Rome and its organizing ideas had not existed before Christianity was born.

In like manner the ideas developed in the Roman mind determined the course of Western theology, as differing from that of the East. It is well known that Eastern theological speculation was occupied with the nature of God and the person of Christ, but that Western theology discussed sin and salvation. Mr. Maine, in his work on " Ancient Law," considers this difference to have been occasioned by habits of thought produced by Roman jurisprudence. I quote his language at some length : —

" What has to be determined is whether jurisprudence has ever served as the medium through which theological principles have been viewed ; whether, by supplying a peculiar language, a peculiar mode of reasoning, and a peculiar solution of many of the problems of life, it has ever opened new channels in which theological speculation could flow out and expand itself."

" On all questions," continues Mr. Maine, quoting Dean Milman, " which concerned the person of Christ and the nature of the Trinity, the Western world accepted passively the dogmatic system of the East." " But as soon as the Latin-speaking empire began to live an intellectual life of its own, its deference to the East was at once exchanged for the agitation of a number of questions entirely foreign to Eastern speculation." " The nature of sin and its transmission by inheritance, the debt owed by man and its vicarious satisfaction, and like theological problems, relating not to the divinity but to human nature, immediately began to be agitated." " I affirm," says Mr. Maine, " without hesitation, that the difference between the two theological systems is accounted for by the fact that, in passing from the East to the West, theological speculation had passed from a climate of Greek meta-physics to a climate of Roman law. For some centuries before these controversies rose into overwhelming impor-tance, all the intellectual activity of the Western Romans had been expended on jurisprudence exclusively. They had been occupied in applying a peculiar set of principles to all combinations in which the circumstances of life are capable of being arranged. No foreign pursuit or taste called off their attention from this engrossing occupation, and for carrying it on they possessed a vocabulary as accurate as it was copious, a strict method of reasoning, a stock of general propositions on conduct more or less verified by experience, and a rigid moral philosophy. It was impossible that they should not select from the ques-tions indicated by the Christian records those which had some affinity with the order of speculations to which they were accustomed, and that their manner of deal-ing with them should not borrow something from their forensic habits. Almost every one who has knowledge enough of Roman law to appreciate the Roman penal system, the Roman theory of the obligations established by contract or delict, the Roman view of debts, etc., the Roman notion of the continuance of individual existence by universal succession, may be trusted to say whence arose the frame of mind to which the problems of West-ern theology proved so congenial, whence came the phraseology in which these problems were stated, and whence the description of reasoning employed in their solution." "As soon as they (the Western Church) ceased to sit at the feet of the Greeks and began to ponder out a theology of their own, the theology proved to be per-meated with forensic ideas and couched in a forensic phraseology. It is certain that this substratum of law in Western theology lies exceedingly deep." *

The theory of the atonement, developed by the scholas-tic writers, illustrates this view. In the East, for a thou-sand years, the atoning work of Christ had been viewed

* Maine, Ancient Law, Chap. IX.

mainly as redemption, as a ransom paid to obtain the freedom of mankind, enslaved by the Devil in consequence of their sins. It was not a legal theory, or one based on notions of jurisprudence, but it was founded on warlike notions. Men were captives taken in war, and, like all captives in those times, destined to slavery. Their captor was Satan, and the ransom must be paid to him, as he held them prisoners by the law of battle. Now as Christ had committed no sin, the Devil had no just power over him; in putting Christ to death he had lost his rights over his other captives, and Christ could justly claim their freedom as a compensation for this injury. Christ, therefore, strictly and literally, according to the ancient view, " gave his life a ransom for many."

But the mind of Anselm, educated by notions derived from Roman jurisprudence, substituted for this original theory of the atonement one based upon legal ideas. All, in this theory, turns on the law of debt and penalty. Sin he defines as " not paying to God what we owe him."* But we owe God constant and entire obedience, and every sin deserves either penalty or satisfaction. We are unable to make it good, for at every moment we owe God all that we can do. Christ, as God-man, can satisfy God for our omissions; his death, as offered freely, when he did not deserve death on account of any sin of his own, is sufficient satisfaction. It will easily be seen how entirely this argument has substituted a legal basis for the atonement in place of the old warlike foundation.

This, therefore, has been the legacy of ancient Rome to Christianity: firstly, the organization of the Latin Church; secondly, the scholastic theology, founded on notions of jurisprudence introduced into man's relations to God. In turn, Christianity has bestowed on Western Europe what the old Romans never knew, — a religion of love and inspiration. In place of the hard and cold Roman life, modern Europe has sentiment and heart united with thought and force. With Roman strength it has joined a Christian tenderness, romance, and personal

* " Non aliud peccare quam Deo non reddere debitum."

w

freedom.   Humanity now is greater than the social organization; the state, according to our view, is made for man, not man for the state.   We are outgrowing the hard and dry theology which we have inherited from Roman law through the scholastic teachers; but we shall not outgrow our inheritance from Rome of unity in the Church, definite thought in our theology, and society organized by law.

CHAPTER IX.

THE TEUTONIC AND SCANDINAVIAN RELIGION.

§ 1. The Land and the Race.   § 2. Idea of the Scandinavian Religion. § 3. The Eddas and their Contents.   § 4. The Gods of Scandinavia. § 5. Resemblance of the Scandinavian Mythology to that of Zoroaster. § 6. Scandinavian Worship.   § 7. Social Character, Maritime Discoveries, and Political Institutions of the Scandinavians.   § 8. Relation of this System to Christianity.

§ 1. The Land and the Race.

THE great Teutonic or German division of the Indo-European family entered Europe subsequently to the Keltic tribes, and before the Slavic immigration. This people overspread and occupied a large part of Northern Central Europe, from which the attempts of the Romans to dispossess them proved futile. Of their early history we know very little. Bishop Percy contrasts their love of making records, as shown by the Runic inscriptions, with the Keltic law of secrecy. The Druids forbade any communication of their mysteries by writing; but the German Scalds put all their belief into popular songs, and reverenced literature as a gift of the gods. Yet we have received very little information concerning these tribes before the days of Cæsar and Tacitus. Cæsar describes them as warlike, huge in stature; having reverence for women, who were their augurs and diviners; worshipping the Sun, the Moon, and Fire; having no regular priests, and paying little regard to sacrifices. He says that they occupied their lives in hunting and war, devoting themselves from childhood to severe labors. They reverenced chastity, and considered it as conducive to health and strength. They were rather a pastoral than agricultural people; no one owning land, but each having it assigned to him temporarily. The object of this provision was said to be to prevent accumulation of wealth and the loss of warlike habits. They fought with cavalry supported by infantry. In the time of Augustus all attempts at conquering Germany were relinquished, and war was maintained only in the hope of revenging the destruction of Varus and his three legions by the famous German chief Arminius, or Herrman.*

Tacitus freely admits that the Germans were as warlike as the Romans, and were only inferior in weapons and discipline. He pays a generous tribute to Arminius, whom he declares to have been " beyond all question the liberator of Germany," dying at thirty-seven, unconquered in war.† Tacitus quotes from some ancient German ballads or hymns (" the only historic monuments," says he, " that they possess ") the names of Tuisto, a god born from the earth, and Mannus, his son. Tacitus was much struck with the physical characteristics of the race, as being so uniform. There was a family likeness, he says, among them all, — stern blue eyes, yellow hair, large bodies. Their wealth was in their flocks and herds. " Gold and silver are kept from them by the anger, or perhaps by the favor, of Heaven." Their rulers were elective, and their power was limited. Their judges were the priests. They saw something divine in woman, and her judgments were accepted as oracles. Such women as Veleda and Aurinia were reverenced as prophets ; " but not adored or made into goddesses," says Tacitus, with a side-glance at some events at home. Their gods, Tacitus chooses to call Mercury, Hercules, and Mars ; but he distinctly says that the Germans had neither idols nor temples, but worshipped in sacred groves. ‡ He also says that the Germans divined future events by pieces of sticks, by the duel, and by the movements of sacred horses. Their leaders might decide the less important matters, but the principal questions were settled at public meetings. These assemblies were held at regular intervals, were opened by the priest, were presided over by the chief, and decided all public affairs. Tacitus remarks

---

* Cæsar, Bell. Gall., I. 36, 39, 48, 50 ; VI. 21, 22, 23.
† " Præliis ambiguus, bello non victus." — Annals, II. 88.
‡ Tacitus, Germania, §§ 2, 4, 5, 7, 8, 9.

that the spirit of liberty goes to such an extreme among the Germans as to destroy regularity and order. They will not be punctual at their meetings, lest it should seem as if they attended because commanded to come.* Marriage was sacred, and, unlike other heathen nations, they were contented with one wife. They were affectionate and constant to the marriage vow, which meant to the pure German woman one husband, one life, one body, and one soul. The ancient Germans, like their modern descendants, drank beer and Rhenish wine, and were divided into numerous tribes, who afterward reappeared for the destruction of the Roman Empire, as the Goths, Vandals, Lombards, and Franks.

The Scandinavians were a branch of the great German family. Their language, the old Norse, was distinguished from the Alemannic, or High German tongue, and from the Saxonic, or Low German tongue. From the Norse have been derived the languages of Iceland, of the Ferroe Isles, of Norway, Sweden, and Denmark. From the Germanic branch have come German, Dutch, Anglo-Saxon, Mæso-Gothic, and English. It was in Scandinavia that the Teutonic race developed its special civilization and religion. Cut off from the rest of the world by stormy seas, the people could there unfold their ideas, and become themselves. It is therefore to Scandinavia that we must go to study the German religion, and to find the influence exercised on modern civilization and the present character of Europe. This influence has been freely acknowledged by great historians.

Montesquieu says : † —

" The great prerogative of Scandinavia is, that it afforded the great resource to the liberty of Europe, that is, to almost all of liberty there is among men. The Goth Jornandes calls the North of Europe the forge of mankind. I would rather call it the forge of those instruments which broke the fetters manufactured in the South."

Geijer, in his Swedish History, tells us : —

* " Illud ex libertate vitium, quod non simul, nec ut jussi, conveniunt." — Germania, § 11.

† Esprit des Loix.

" The recollections which Scandinavia has to add to those of the Germanic race are yet the most antique in character and comparatively the most original.   They offer the completest remaining example of a social state existing previously to the reception of influences from Rome, and in duration stretching onward so as to come within the sphere of historical light."

We do not know how much of those old Northern ideas may be still mingled with our ways of thought.   The names of their gods we retain in those of our week-days, — Tuesday, Wednesday, Thursday, and Friday. Their popular assemblies, or Things, were the origin of our Parliament, our Congress, and our general assemblies. If from the South came the romantic admiration of woman, from the North came a better respect for her rights and the sense of her equality.   Our trial by jury was immediately derived from Scandinavia ; and, according to Montesquieu, as we have seen, we owe to the North, as the greatest inheritance of all, that desire for freedom which is so chief an element in Christian civilization.

Scandinavia proper consists of those regions now occupied by the kingdoms of Denmark, Sweden, and Norway. The geographical peculiarity of this country is its proximity everywhere to the sea, and the great extent of its coast line.   The great peninsula of Sweden and Norway, with the Northern Ocean on its west, the Baltic and Gulf of Bothnia on its east, penetrated everywhere by creeks, friths, and arms of the sea, surrounded with innumerable islands, studded with lakes, and cleft with rivers, is also unrivalled, except by Switzerland, in the sublime and picturesque beauty of its mountains.   The other peninsula, that of Denmark, surrounded and penetrated also everywhere by the sea, differs in being almost level ; rising nowhere, at its highest point, more than a thousand feet above the ocean.   Containing an area of only twenty-two thousand square miles, it is so penetrated with bays and creeks as to have four thousand miles of coast. Like the northern peninsula, it is also surrounded with a multitude of islands, which are so crowded together, especially on its eastern coast, as to make an archipelago.

It is impossible to look at the map of Europe, and not be struck with the resemblance in these particulars between its northern and southern geography.   The Baltic Sea is the Mediterranean of Northern Europe.   The peninsula of Denmark, with its multitudinous bays and islands, corresponds to Greece, the Morea, and its archipelago.   We have shown in our chapter on Greece that modern geography teaches that the extent of coast line, when compared with the superficial area of a country, is one of the essential conditions of civilization.   Who can fail to see the hand of Providence in the adaptation of races to the countries they are to inhabit ?   The great tide of human life, flowing westward from Central Asia, was divided into currents by the Caspian and Black Seas, and by the lofty range of mountains which, under the name of the Caucasus, Carpathian Mountains, and Alps, extends almost in an unbroken line from the western coast of the Caspian to the northern limits of Germany.   The Teutonic races, Germans, Saxons, Franks, and Northmen, were thus determined to the north, and spread themselves along the coast and peninsulas of the Northern Mediterranean.   The other branch of the great Indo-European variety was distributed through Syria, Asia Minor, Greece, Southern France, Italy, and Spain.   Each of these vast European families, stimulated to mental and moral activity by its proximity to water, developed its own peculiar forms of national character, which were afterwards united in modern European society.   The North developed individual freedom, the South social organization.   The North gave force, the South culture.   From Southern Europe came literature, philosophy, laws, arts ; from the North, that respect for individual rights, that sense of personal dignity, that energy of the single soul, which is the essential equipoise of a high social culture.   These two elements, of freedom and civilization, always antagonist, have been in most ages hostile.   The individual freedom of the North has been equivalent to barbarism, and from time to time has rolled down a destroying deluge over the South, almost sweeping away its civilization, and overwhelming in a common ruin arts, literature, and laws.   On the other hand, civilization at the South has passed into luxury, has produced effeminacy, till individual freedom has been lost under grinding despotism. But in modern civilization a third element has been added, which has brought these two powers of Northern freedom and Southern culture into equipoise and harmony. This new element is Christianity, which develops, at the same time, the sense of personal responsibility, by teaching the individual destiny and worth of every soul, and also the mutual dependence and interlacing brotherhood of all human society. This Christian element in modern civilization saves it from the double danger of a relapse into barbarism on the one hand, and a too refined luxury on the other. The nations of Europe, to-day, which are the most advanced in civilization, literature, and art, are also the most deeply pervaded with the love of freedom ; and the most civilized nations on the globe, instead of being the most effeminate, are also the most powerful.

The Scandinavian people, destined to play so important a part in the history of the world, were, as we have said, a branch of the great Indo-European variety. We have seen that modern ethnology teaches that all the races which inhabit Europe, with some trifling exceptions, belong to one family, which originated in Central Asia. This has appeared and is proved by means of glossology, or the science of language. The closest resemblance exists between the seven linguistic families of Hindostan, Persia, Greece, Rome, Germany, the Kelts, and the Slavi ; and it is a most striking fact of human history, that from the earliest period of recorded time down to the present day a powerful people, speaking a language belonging to one or other of these races, should have in a great measure swayed the destinies of the world.

Before the birth of Christ the peninsula of Denmark was called by the Romans the Cimbric Chersonesus, or Cimbric peninsula. This name came from the Cimbri, a people who, one hundred and eleven years before Christ, almost overthrew the Roman Republic, exciting more terror than any event since the days of Hannibal. More than three hundred thousand men, issuing from the pe-

ninsula of Denmark and the adjacent regions, poured like
a torrent over Gaul and Southern Germany. They met
and overthrew in succession four Roman armies; until,
finally, they were conquered by the military skill and genius of Marius. After this eruption was checked, the great
northern volcano slumbered for centuries. Other tribes
from Asia — Goths, Vandals, Huns — combined in the
overthrow of the Roman Empire. At last the inhabitants
of Scandinavia appear again under the name of Northmen,
invading and conquering England in the fifth century as
Saxons, in the ninth century as Danes, and in the eleventh as Normans again overrunning England and France.
But the peculiarity of the Scandinavian invasions was
their maritime character. Daring and skilful navigators,
they encountered the tempests of the Northern Ocean and
the heavy roll of the Atlantic in vessels so small and
slight that they floated like eggshells on the surface of
the waves, and ran up the rivers of France and England,
hundreds of miles, without check from shallows or rocks.
In these fragile barks they made also the most extraordinary maritime discoveries. The sea-kings of Norway
discovered Iceland, and settled it A. D. 860 and A. D. 874.
They discovered and settled Greenland A. D. 982 and
A. D. 986. On the western coast of Greenland they
planted colonies, where churches were built, and diocesan
bishoprics established, which lasted between four and five
hundred years. Finally, in A. D. 1000, they discovered,
by sailing from Greenland, the coast of Labrador, Nova
Scotia, and Massachusetts Bay; and, five hundred years
before the discovery of Columbus, gathered grapes and
built houses on the southern side of Cape Cod. These
facts, long considered mythical, have been established, to
the satisfaction of European scholars, by the publication
of Icelandic contemporaneous annals. This remarkable
people have furnished nearly the whole population of
England by means of the successive conquests of Saxon,
Danes, and Normans, driving the Keltic races into the
mountainous regions of Wales and North Scotland,
where their descendants still remain. Colonizing themselves also everywhere in Northern Europe, and even in

16

Italy and Greece, they have left the familiar stamp of their ideas and habits in all our modern civilization.*

§ 2. *Idea of the Scandinavian Religion.*

The central idea of the Scandinavian belief was the free struggle of soul against material obstacles, the freedom of the Divine will in its conflict with the opposing forces of nature. The gods of the Scandinavians were always at war. It was a system of dualism, in which sunshine, summer, and growth were waging perpetual battle with storm, snow, winter, ocean, and terrestrial fire. As the gods, so the people. War was their business, courage their duty, fortitude their virtue. The conflict of life with death, of freedom with fate, of choice with necessity, of good with evil, made up their history and destiny.

This conflict in the natural world was especially apparent in the struggle, annually renewed, between summer and winter. Therefore the light and heat gods were their friends, those of darkness and cold their enemies. For the same reason that the burning heat of summer, Typhon, was the Satan of Egypt; so in the North the Jotuns, ice-giants, were the Scandinavian devils.

There are some virtues which are naturally associated together, such as the love of truth, the sense of justice, courage, and personal independence. There is an opposite class of virtues in like manner naturally grouped together, — sympathy, mutual helpfulness, and a tendency to social organization. The serious antagonism in the moral world is that of truth and love. Most cases of conscience which present a real difficulty resolve them-

---

* See, for the history and religion of the Teutonic and Scandinavian race, Cæsar; Tacitus; Grimm's Deutsche Mythologie; Geschichte und System der Altdeutschen Religion, von Wilhelm Müller; Northern Mythology, by Benjamin Thorpe; The Sea-Kings of Norway, by S. Laing; Manual of Scandinavian Mythology, by G. Pigott; Literature and Romance of Northern Europe, by William and Mary Howitt; Die Edda, von Karl Simrock; Aryan Mythology, by George W. Cox; Norse Tales, by Dasent, etc. But one of the best as well as the most accessible summaries in English of this mythology is Mallet's Northern Antiquities, in Bohn's Antiquarian Library. This edition is edited by Mr. Blackwell with great judgment and learning.

selves into a conflict of truth and love.   It is hard to be
true without hurting the feelings of others ; it is hard to
sympathize with others and not yield a little of our inward truth.   The same antagonism is found in the religions of the world.   The religions in which truth, justice,
freedom, are developed tend to isolation, coldness, and
hardness.   On the other hand, the religions of brotherhood and human sympathy tend to weakness, luxury, and
slavery.

The religion of the German races, which was the natural growth of their organization and moral character,
belonged to the first class.   It was a religion in which
truth, justice, self-respect, courage, freedom, were the essential elements.   The gods were human, as in the Hellenic system, with moral attributes.   They were finite
beings and limited in their powers.   They carried on a
warfare with hostile and destructive agents, in which at
last they were to be vanquished and destroyed, though a
restoration of the world and the gods would follow that
destruction.

Such was the idea in all the faith of the Teutonic race.
The chief virtue of man was courage, his unpardonable
sin was cowardice.   " To fight a good fight," this was the
way to Valhalla.   Odin sent his Choosers to every battle-
field to select the brave dead to become his companions
in the joys of heaven.

§ 3.   *The Eddas and their Contents.*

We have observed that Iceland was settled from Norway in the ninth century.   A remarkable social life grew
up there, which preserved the ideas, manners, and religion of the Teutonic people in their purity for many hundred years, and whose Eddas and Sagas are the chief
source of our knowledge of the race.   In this ultimate
and barren region of the earth, where seas of ice make
thousands of square miles desolate and impenetrable,
where icy masses, elsewhere glaciers, are here mountains,
where volcanoes with terrible eruptions destroy whole
regions of inhabited country in a few days with lava, vol-

canic sand, and boiling water, was developed to its highest degree the purest form of Scandinavian life.

The religion of the Scandinavians is contained in the Eddas, which are two, — the poetic, or elder Edda, consisting of thirty-seven poems, first collected and published at the end of the eleventh century; and the younger, or prose Edda, ascribed to the celebrated Snorro Sturleson, born of a distinguished Icelandic family in the twelfth century, who, after leading a turbulent and ambitious life, and being twice chosen supreme magistrate, was killed A. D. 1241. The principal part of the prose Edda is a complete synopsis of Scandinavian mythology.

The elder Edda, which is the fountain of the mythology, consists of old songs and ballads, which had come down from an immemorial past in the mouths of the people, but were first collected and committed to writing by Sæmund, a Christian priest of Iceland in the eleventh century. He was a Bard, or Scald, as well as a priest, and one of his own poems, "The Sun-Song," is in his Edda. This word " Edda " means " great-grandmother," the ancient mother of Scandinavian knowledge. Or perhaps this name was given to the legends, repeated by grandmothers to their grandchildren by the vast firesides of the old farm-houses in Iceland.

This rhythmical Edda consists of thirty-seven poems.* It is in two parts, — the first containing mythical poems concerning the gods and the creation ; the second, the legends of the heroes of Scandinavian history. This latter portion of the Edda has the original and ancient fragments from which the German Nibelungen-lied was afterward derived. These songs are to the German poem what the ante-Homeric ballad literature of Greece about Troy and Ulysses was to the Iliad and Odyssey as reduced to unity by Homer.

The first poem in the first part of the poetic Edda is the Völuspa, or Wisdom of Vala. The Vala was a proph-

---

* See Die Edda, von Karl Simrock. Stuttgart, 1855. Literature and Romance of Northern Europe, by William and Mary Howitt. London, 1852. Geschichte und System der Altdeutschen Religion, von Wilhelm Müller. Gottingen, 1844. Mallet's Northern Antiquities, edited by Blackwell, in Bohn's Antiquarian Library.

etess, possessing vast supernatural knowledge. Some antiquarians consider the Vala to be the same as the Nornor, or Fates. They were dark beings, whose wisdom was fearful even to the gods, resembling in this the Greek Prometheus. The Völuspa describes the universe before the creation, in the morning of time, before the great Ymir lived, when there was neither sea nor shore nor heaven. It begins thus, Vala speaking: —

> " I command the devout attention of all noble souls,
> Of all the high and the low of the race of Heimdall ;
> I tell the doings of the All-Father,
> In the most ancient Sagas which come to my mind.

> " There was an age in which Ymir lived,
> When was no sea, nor shore, nor salt waves ;
> No earth below, nor heaven above,
> No yawning abyss and no grassy land.

> " Till the sons of Börs lifted the dome of heaven,
> And created the vast Midgard (earth) below ;
> Then the sun of the south rose above the mountains,
> And green grasses made the ground verdant.

> " The sun of the south, companion of the moon,
> Held the horses of heaven with his right hand ;
> The sun knew not what its course should be,
> The moon knew not what her power should be,
> The stars knew not where their places were.

> " Then the counsellors went into the hall of judgment,
> And the all-holy gods held a council.
> They gave names to the night and new moon ;
> They called to the morning and to midday,
> To the afternoon and evening, arranging the times."

The Völuspa goes on to describe how the gods assembled on the field of Ida, and proceeded to create metals and vegetables ; after that the race of dwarfs, who preside over the powers of nature and the mineral world. Then Vala narrates how the three gods, Odin, Hönir, and Lodur, " the mighty and mild Aser," found Ask and Embla, the Adam and Eve of the Northern legends, lying without soul, sense, motion, or color. Odin gave them their souls, Hönir their intellects, Lodur their blood and colored flesh. Then comes the description of the ash-tree Yggdrasil, of the three Norns, or sisters of destiny, who tell the Aser their doom, and the end and renewal of the world ; and how, at last, one being mightier than all shall arrive : —

> " Then comes the mighty one to the council of the gods,
> He with strength from on high who guides all things,
> He decides the strife, he puts an end to struggle,
> He ordains eternal laws."

In the same way, in the Song of Hyndla, another of the poems of this Edda, is a prediction of one who shall come, mightier than all the gods, and put an end to the strife between Aser and the giants. The song begins : —

> " Wake, maid of maidens ! Awake, my friend !
> Hyndla, sister, dwelling in the glens !
> It is night, it is cloudy ; let us ride together
> To the sacred place, to Valhalla."

Hyndla sings, after describing the heroes and princes born of the gods : —

> " One shall be born higher than all,
> Who grows strong with the strength of the earth ;
> He is famed as the greatest of rulers,
> United with all nations as brethren.

> " But one day there shall come another mightier than he ;
> But I dare not name his name.
> Few are able to see beyond
> The great battle of Odin and the Wolf."

Among the poems of the elder Edda is a Book of Proverbs, like those of Solomon in their sagacious observations on human life and manners. It is called the Havamal. At first we should hardly expect to find these maxims of worldly wisdom among a people whose chief business was war. But war develops cunning as well as courage, and battles are won by craft no less than by daring. Consequently, among a warlike people, sagacity is naturally cultivated.

The Havamal contains (in its proverbial section) one hundred and ten stanzas, mostly quatrains. The following are specimens : —

> 1. " Carefully consider the end
>   Before you go to do anything,
>   . For all is uncertain, when the enemy
>   Lies in wait in the house.

4. " The guest who enters
      Needs water, a towel, and hospitality.
      A kind reception secures a return
      In word and in deed.

7. " The wise man, on coming in,
      Is silent and observes,
      Hears with his ears, looks with his eyes,
      And carefully reflects on every event.

11. " No worse a companion can a man take on his journey
       Than drunkenness.
       Not as good as many believe
       Is beer to the sons of men.
       The more one drinks, the less he knows,
       And less power has he over himself.

26. " A foolish man, in company, had better be silent.
       Until he speaks no one observes his folly.
       But he who knows little does not know this,
       When he had better be silent.

29. " Do not mock at the stranger
       Who comes trusting in your kindness ;
       For when he has warmed himself at your fire,
       He may easily prove a wise man.

34. " It is better to depart betimes,
       And not to go too often to the same house.
       Love tires and turns to sadness
       When one sits too often at another man's table.

35. " One's own house, though small, is better,
       For there thou art the master.
       It makes a man's heart bleed to ask
       For a midday meal at the house of another.

36. " One's own house, though small, is better ;
       At home thou art the master.
       Two goats and a thatched roof
       Are better than begging.

38. " It is hard to find a man so rich
       As to refuse a gift.
       It is hard to find a man so generous
       As to be always glad to lend.

42. " Is there a man whom you distrust,
       And who yet can help you ?
       Be smooth in words and false in thought,
       And pay back his deceit with cunning.

48. " I hung my garments on two scarecrows,
       And, when dressed, they seemed

Ready for the battle.
Unclothed they were jeered at by all.

52. " Small as a grain of sand
Is the small sense of a fool ;
Very unequal is human wisdom.
The world is made of two unequal halves.

53. " It is well to be wise ; it is not well
To be too wise.
He has the happiest life
Who knows well what he knows.

54. " It is well to be wise ; not well
To be too wise.
The wise man's heart is not glad
When he knows too much.

55. " Two burning sticks placed together
Will burn entirely away.
Man grows bright by the side of man ;
Alone, he remains stupid."

Such are the proverbs of the Havamal. This sort of
proverbial wisdom may have come down from the days
when the ancestors of the Scandinavians left Central
Asia. It is like the fables and maxims of the Hitopadesá.*

Another of these poems is called Odin's Song of Runes.
Runes were the Scandinavian alphabet, used for lapidary
inscriptions, a thousand of which have been discovered in
Sweden, and three or four hundred in Denmark and Norway, mostly on tombstones. This alphabet consists of
sixteen letters, with the powers of F, U, TH, O, R, K, H,
N, I, A, S, T, B, L, M, Y. The letters R, I, T, and B very
nearly resemble the Roman letters of the same values.
A magical power was ascribed to these Runes, and they
were carved on sticks and then scraped off, and used as
charms. These rune-charms were of different kinds,
eighteen different sorts are mentioned in this song.

A song of Brynhilda speaks of different runes which
she will teach Sigurd. " *Runes of victory* must those
know, to conquer thine enemies. They must be carved
on the blade of thy sword. *Drink-Runes* must thou

---

* Hitopadesá ; or, Salutary Counsels of Vishnu Sárman. Translated
from the Sanskrit by Francis Johnson. London and Hertford, 1848.

know to make maidens love thee.   Thou must carve them
on thy drinking horn.   *Runes of freedom* must thou
know to deliver the captives.   *Storm-Runes* must thou
know, to make thy vessel go safely over the waves.
Carve them on the mast and the rudder.   *Herb-Runes*
thou must know to cure disease.   Carve them on the
bark of the tree.   *Speech-Runes* must thou know to
defeat thine enemy in council of words, in the Thing.
Mind-Runes must thou know to have good and wise
thoughts.   These are the Book-Runes, and Help-Runes,
and Drink-Runes, and Power-Runes, precious for whoever
can use them."

The second part of the poetic Edda contains the stories
of the old heroes, especially of Sigurd, the Achilles of
Northern romance.   There is also the Song of Volund,
the Northern Smith, the German Vulcan, able to make
swords of powerful temper.   These songs and ballads are
all serious and grave, and sometimes tender, having in
them something of the solemn tone of the old Greek
tragedy.

The prose Edda, as we have said, was the work of
Snorro Sturleson, born in Iceland in 1178.*   He probably transcribed most of it from the manuscripts in his
hands, or which were accessible to him, and from the oral
traditions which had been preserved in the memory of
the Skalds.   His other chief work was the Heimskrin-
gla, or collection of Saga concerning the history of the
Scandinavians.   In his preface to this last book he says he
" wrote it down from old stories told by intelligent people " ; or from " ancient family registers containing the
pedigrees of kings," or from " old songs and ballads which
our fathers had for their amusement."

The prose Edda begins with " The deluding of Gylfi,"
an ancient king of Sweden.   He was renowned for his
wisdom and love of knowledge, and determined to visit
Asgard, the home of the Æsir, to learn something of the
wisdom of the gods.   They, however, foreseeing his coming, prepared various illusions to deceive him.   Among

* See Memoir of Snorro Sturleson, in Laing's Sea-Kings of Norway.

16 *

other things, he saw three thrones raised one above another.

"He afterwards beheld three thrones raised one above another, with a man sitting on each of them. Upon his asking what the names of these lords might be, his guide answered : 'He who sits on the lowest throne is a king ; his name is Har (the High or Lofty One) ; the second is Jafnhar (i. e. equal to the High) ; but he who sitteth on the highest throne is called Thridi (the Third).' Har, perceiving the stranger, asked him what his errand was, adding that he should be welcome to eat and drink without cost, as were all those who remained in Háva Hall. Gangler said he desired first to ascertain whether there was any person present renowned for his wisdom.

"'If thou art not the most knowing,' replied Har, 'I fear thou wilt hardly return safe. But go, stand there below, and propose thy questions ; here sits one who will be able to answer them.'

"Gangler thus began his discourse : 'Who is the first, or eldest of the gods ?'

"'In our language,' replied Har, 'he is called Alfadir (All-Father, or the Father of All) ; but in the old Asgard he had twelve names.'

"'Where is this God ?' said Gangler ; 'what is his power ? and what hath he done to display his glory ?'

"'He liveth,' replied Har, 'from all ages, he governeth all realms, and swayeth all things great and small.'

"'He hath formed,' added Jafnhar, 'heaven and earth, and the air, and all things thereunto belonging.'

"'And what is more,' continued Thridi, 'he hath made man, and given him a soul which shall live and never perish, though the body shall have mouldered away, or have been burnt to ashes. And all that are righteous shall dwell with him in the place called Gimli, or Vingólf ; but the wicked shall go to Hel, and thence to Niflhel, which is below, in the ninth world.'"

Of the creation of the world the Eddas thus speak : In the day-spring of the ages there was neither seas nor shore nor refreshing breeze ; there was neither earth below nor heaven above. The whole was only one vast abyss, without herb and without seas. The sun had no palace, the stars no place, the moon no power.   After this there was a bright shining world of flame to the South, and another, a cloudy and dark one, toward the North. Torrents of venom flowed from the last into the abyss, and froze, and filled it full of ice.   But the air oozed up through it in icy vapors, which were melted into living drops by a warm breath from the South ; and from these came the giant Ymir.   From him came a race of wicked giants.   Afterward, from these same drops of fluid seeds, children of heat and cold, came the mundane cow, whose milk fed the giants.   Then arose also, in a mysterious manner, Bor, the father of three sons, Odin, Vili, and Ve, who, after several adventures, — having killed the giant Ymir, and made out of his body Heaven and Earth, — proceeded to form a man and woman named Ask and Embla.   Chaos having thus disappeared, Odin became the All-Father, creator of gods and men, with Earth for his wife, and the powerful Thor for his oldest son.   So much for the cosmogony of the Edda.

On this cosmogony, we may remark that it belongs to the class of development, or evolution, but combined with a creation.   The Hindoo, Gnostic, and Platonic theories suppose the visible world to have emanated from God, by a succession of fallings, from the most abstract spirit to the most concrete matter.   The Greeks and Romans, on the contrary, suppose all things to have come by a process of evolution, or development from an original formless and chaotic matter.   The resemblance between the Greek account of the origin of gods and men and that of the Scandinavians is striking.   Both systems begin in materialism, and are radically opposed to the spiritualism of the other theory ; and in its account of the origin of all things from nebulous vapors and heat the Edda reminds us of the modern scientific theories on the same subject.

After giving this account of the formation of the world, of the gods, and the first pair of mortals, the Edda next speaks of night and day, of the sun and moon, of the rainbow bridge from earth to heaven, and of the great Ash-tree where the gods sit in council.   Night was the

daughter of a giant, and, like all her race, of a dark complexion. She married one of the Æsir, or children of
Odin, and their son was Day, a child light and beautiful,
like its father. The Sun and Moon were two children, the
Moon being the boy, and the Sun the girl ; which peculiarity of gender still holds in the German language. The
Edda gives them chariot and horses with which to drive
daily round the heavens, and supposes their speed to be
occasioned by their fear of two gigantic wolves, from Jötunheim, or the world of darkness, which pursue them. The
rainbow is named Bifrost, woven of three hues, and by
this, as a bridge, the gods ride up every day to heaven
from the holy fountain below the earth. Near this fountain dwell three maidens, below the great Ash-tree, who
decide every man's fate. These Fates, or Norns, are
named Urd, Verdandi, and Skuld, — three words meaning
" past," " present," and " future." From Urd comes our
word " weird," and the weird sisters of Shakespeare. The
red in the rainbow is burning fire, which prevents the frost-
giants of Jötunheim from going up to heaven, which
they otherwise might do. This region of the gods is
called Asgard, and contains Valhalla, where they feast
every day, with all heroes who have died in battle ; drinking mead, but not out of their enemies' skulls, as has
been so often said. This mistake modern scholars have
attributed to a mistranslation of a word in the original,
which means " curved horns," the passage being, " Soon
shall we drink ale out of the curved branches of the
skull," that is, of an animal. Their food is the flesh of
a boar, which is renewed every day.

It is not to be supposed that Odin and the other gods
lived quietly on their Olympus without adventures.
Many entertaining ones are narrated in the Edda, had we
room to tell them. One of these describes the death of
Baldur the Good, whom all beings loved. Having been
tormented with bad dreams, indicating that his life was
in danger, he told them to the assembled gods, who made
all creatures and things, living or dead, take an oath to
do him no harm. This oath was taken by fire and water,
iron and all other metals, stones, earths, diseases, poisons,

beasts, birds, and creeping things. After this, they amused themselves at their meeting in setting Baldur up as a mark; some hurling darts or shooting arrows at him, and some cutting at him with swords and axes; and as nothing hurt him, it was accounted a great honor done to Baldur. But wicked Loki, or Loke, was envious at this; and, assuming the form of a woman, he inquired of the goddess who had administered the oath, whether all things had taken it. She said everything except one little shrub called mistletoe, which she thought too young and feeble to do any harm. Therefore Loki got the mistletoe, and, bringing it to one of the gods, persuaded him to throw it at Baldur, who, pierced to the heart, fell dead. The grief was immense. An especial messenger was despatched to Queen Hela, in Hell, to inquire if, on any terms, Baldur might be ransomed. For nine days and nights he rode through dark chasms till he crossed the river of Death, and entering the kingdom of Hela, made known his request. Hela replied that it should now be discovered whether Baldur was so universally loved as was represented; for that she would permit him to return to Asgard if all creatures and all things, without exception, would weep for him. The gods then despatched messengers through the world to beg all things to weep for Baldur, which they immediately did. Then you might have seen, not only crocodiles but the most ferocious beasts dissolved in tears. Fishes wept in the water, and birds in the air. Stones and trees were covered with pellucid dew-drops, and, for all we know, this general grief may have been the occasion of some of the deluges reported by geology. The messengers returned, thinking the work done, when they found an old hag sitting in a cavern, and begged her to weep Baldur out of Hell. But she declared that she could gain nothing by so doing, and that Baldur might stay where he was, like other people as good as he; planting herself apparently on the great but somewhat selfish principle of non-intervention. So Baldur remains in the halls of Hela. But this old woman did not go unpunished. She was shrewdly suspected to be Loki himself in disguise, and on inquiry so it turned out. Whereupon a hot pursuit of Loki took place, who, after changing himself into many forms, was caught, and chained under sharp-pointed rocks below the earth.

The adventures of Thor are very numerous. The pleasantest, perhaps, is the account of his journey to Jötunheim, to visit his enemies, the giants of Cold and Darkness. On his way, being obliged to pass the night in the forest, he came to a spacious hall, with an open door, reaching from one side to the other. In this he went to sleep, but being aroused by an awful earthquake, Thor and his companions crept into a chamber which opened out of the hall. When day came they found, sleeping near them, an enormous giant, so large, that, as it appeared, they had passed the night in the thumb of his glove. They travelled with him all day ; and the next night Thor considered himself justified in killing this giant, who was one of their enemies. Three times he launched his mallet with fearful force at the giant's head, and three times the giant awoke to inquire whether it was a leaf or an acorn which had fallen on his face. After taking leave of their enormous and invulnerable companion, they arrived at the abodes of Jötunheim, and the city of Ut-gard, and entered the city of the king, Utgard Loki. This king inquired what great feat Thor and his companions could do. One professed to be a great eater ; on which the king of giants called one of his servants named Logi, and placed between them a trough filled with meat. Thor's companion ate his share, but Logi ate meat and bone too, and the trough into the bargain, and was considered to have conquered. Thor's other companion was a great runner, and was set to run with a young man named Hugi, who so outstripped him that he reached the goal before the other had gone half-way. Then Thor was asked what he could do himself. He said he would engage in a drinking-match, and was presented with a large horn, and was requested to empty it at a single draught, which he expected easily to do, but on looking in the liquor seemed scarcely diminished. The second time he tried, and lowered it slightly. A third, and it was still only sunk half an inch. Whereupon he was laughed

at, and called for some new feat. " We have a trifling
game here," answered the king, " in which we exercise
none but children. It is merely to lift my cat from
the ground." Thor put forth his whole might, but could
only lift up one foot, and was laughed at again. Angry
at this, he called for some one to wrestle with him. " My
men," said King Utgard, " would think it beneath them to
wrestle with thee, but let some one call my old nurse Eld,
and let Thor wrestle with her." A toothless old woman
entered the hall, and after a violent struggle Thor began
to lose his footing, and went home excessively mortified.
But it turned out afterward that all this was illusion. The
three blows of the mallet, instead of striking the giant's
head, had fallen on a mountain, which he had dexterously
put between, and made three deep ravines in it, which
remain to this day. The triumphant eater was Fire itself,
disguised as a man. The successful runner was Thought.
The horn out of which Thor tried to drink was connected
with the ocean, which was lowered a few inches by his
tremendous draughts. The cat was the great Midgard
Serpent, which goes round the world, and Thor had actually pulled the earth a little way out of its place ; and the
old woman was Old Age itself.*

According to this mythology, there is coming a time in
which the world will be destroyed by fire and afterward
renewed. This will be preceded by awful disasters ; dreadful winters ; wars, and desolations on earth ; cruelty and
deceit ; the sun and moon will be devoured, the stars
hurled from the sky, and the earth violently shaken. The
Wolf (Fenrir), the awful Midgard Serpent, Loki, and Hela
come to battle with the gods. The great Ash-tree will
shake with fear. The Wolf (Fenrir) breaks loose, and
opens his enormous mouth. The lower jaw reaches to
the earth, and the upper to heaven. The Midgard Serpent, by the side of the Wolf, vomits forth floods of

* It would appear from this legend that the gods are idealizations of
human will set over against the powers of nature. The battle of the
gods and giants represents the struggles of the soul against the inexorable laws of nature, freedom against fate, the spirit with the flesh, mind
with matter, human hope with change, disappointment, loss ; "the
emergency of the case with the despotism of the rule."

poison. Heaven is rent in twain, and Surtur and the sons of Muspell ride through the breach. These are the children of Light and Fire, who dwell in the South, and who seem to belong neither to the race of gods nor to that of giants, but to a third party, who only interfere at the close of the conflict. While the battle goes on between the gods and the giants they keep their effulgent bands apart on the field of battle. Meantime Heimdall — door-keeper of the gods — sounds his mighty trumpet, which is heard through the whole universe, to summon the gods to conflict. The gods, or Æsir, and all the heroes of Val-halla, arm themselves and go to the field. Odin fights with the Wolf ; Thor with the Midgard Serpent, whom he kills, but being suffocated with the floods of venom dies himself. The Wolf swallows Odin, but at that instant Vidar sets his foot on its lower jaw, and laying hold of the upper jaw tears it apart. He accomplishes this be-cause he has on the famous shoe, the materials of which have been collecting for ages, it being made of the shreds of shoe-leather which are cut off in making shoes, and which, on this account, the religious Scandinavians were careful to throw away. Loki and Heimdall fight and kill each other. After this Surtur darts fire over the whole earth, and the whole universe is consumed. But then comes the restitution of all things. There will rise out of the sea a new heaven and a new earth. Two gods, Vidar and Vali, and two human beings, a man and woman, survive the conflagration, and with their descend-ants occupy the heavens and earth. The suns of Thor come with their father's hammer and put an end to war. Baldur, and Hodur, the blind god, come up from Hell, and the daughter of the Sun, more beautiful than its mother, occupies its place in the skies.

§ 4. *The Gods of Scandinavia.*

We can give no better account of the Norse pantheon than by extracting the passages from the prose Edda, which describe the gods. We take the translation in Mallet's Northern Antiquities : —

" OF ODIN.

" ' I must now ask thee,' said Gangler, ' who are the gods that men are bound to believe in ? '

" ' There are twelve gods,' replied Har, ' to whom divine honors ought to be rendered.'

" ' Nor are the goddesses,' added Jafnhar, ' less divine and mighty.'

" ' The first and eldest of the Æsir,' continued Thridi, ' is Odin. He governs all things, and although the other deities are powerful, they all serve and obey him as children do their father. Frigga is his wife. She foresees the destinies of men, but never reveals what is to come. For thus it is said that Odin himself told Loki, " Senseless Loki, why wilt thou pry into futurity? Frigga alone knoweth the destinies of all, though she telleth them never."

" ' Odin is named Alfadir (All-father), because he is the father of all the gods, and also Valfadir (Choosing Father), because he chooses for his sons all those who fall in combat. For their abode he has prepared Valhalla and Vingólf, where they are called Einherjar (Heroes or Champions). Odin is also called Hangagud, Haptagud, and Farmagud, and, besides these, was named in many ways when he went to King Geirraudr.' . . . .

" OF THOR.

" ' I now ask thee,' said Gangler, ' what are the names of the other gods ? What are their functions, and what have they brought to pass ? '

" ' The mightiest of them,' replied Har, ' is Thor. He is called Asa-Thor and Auku-Thor, and is the strongest of gods and men. His realm is named Thrúdváng, and his mansion Bilskirnir, in which are five hundred and forty halls. It is the largest house ever built. Thus it is called in the Grímnismál : —

> " Five hundred halls
> And forty more,
> Methinketh, hath
> Bowed Bilskirnir.
> Of houses roofed
> There 's none I know
> My son's surpassing."

" ' Thor has a car drawn by two goats called Tanngnióst and Tanngrisnir. From his driving about in this car he is called Auku-Thor (Charioteer-Thor). He likewise possesses three very precious things. The first is a mallet called Mjölnir, which both the Frost and Mountain Giants know to their cost when they see it hurled against them in the air ; and no wonder, for it has split many a skull of their fathers and kindred. The second rare thing he possesses is called the belt of strength or prowess (Megingjardir). When he girds it about him his divine might is doubly augmented ; the third, also very precious, being his iron gauntlets, which he is obliged to put on whenever he would lay hold of the handle of his mallet. There is no one so wise as to be able to relate all Thor's marvellous exploits, yet I could tell thee so many myself that hours would be whiled away ere all that I know had been recounted.'

" OF BALDUR.

" ' I would rather,' said Gangler, ' hear something about the other Æsir.'

" ' The second son of Odin,' replied Har, ' is Baldur, and it may be truly said of him that he is the best, and that all mankind are loud in his praise. So fair and dazzling is he in form and features, that rays of light seem to issue from him ; and thou mayst have some idea of the beauty of his hair when I tell thee that the whitest of all plants is called Baldur's brow. Baldur is the mildest, the wisest, and the most eloquent of all the Æsir, yet such is his nature that the judgment he has pronounced can never be altered. He dwells in the heavenly mansion called Breidablik, in which nothing unclean can enter. As it is said,—

> " 'T is Breidablik called,
> Where Baldur the Fair
> Hath built him a bower,
> In that land where I know
> The least loathliness lieth." '

" OF NJÖRD.

" ' The third god,' continued Har, ' is Njörd, who dwells in the heavenly region called Noátún. He rules over the winds, and checks the fury of the sea and of fire, and is therefore invoked by seafarers and fishermen. He is so wealthy that he can give possessions and treasures to those who call on him for them. Yet Njörd is not of the lineage of the Æsir, for he was born and bred in Vanaheim. But the Vanir gave him as hostage to the Æsir, receiving from them in his stead Hœnir. By this means was peace re-established between the Æsir and

Vanir. Njörd took to wife Skadi, the daughter of the giant Thjassi. She preferred dwelling in the abode formerly belonging to her father, which is situated among rocky mountains, in the region called Thrymheim, but Njörd loved to reside near the sea. They at last agreed that they should pass together nine nights in Thrymheim, and then three in Noátún. One day, when Njörd came back from the mountains to Noátún, he thus sang : —

> " Of mountains I 'm weary,
> Not long was I there,
> Not more than nine nights ;
> But the howl of the wolf
> Methought sounded ill
> To the song of the swan-bird."

" ' To which Skadi sang in reply : —

> " Ne'er can I sleep
> In my couch on the strand,
> For the screams of the sea-fowl.
> The mew as he comes
> Every morn from the main
> Is sure to awake me."

" ' Skadi then returned to the rocky mountains, and abode in Thrymheim. There, fastening on her snow-skates and taking her bow, she passes her time in the chase of savage beasts, and is called the Öndur goddess, or Öndurdís. . . . .'

" OF THE GOD FREY, AND THE GODDESS FREYJA.

" ' Njörd had afterwards, at his residence at Nóatún, two children, a son named Frey, and a daughter called Freyja, both of them beauteous and mighty. Frey is one of the most celebrated of the gods. He presides over rain and sunshine, and all the fruits of the earth, and should be invoked in order to obtain good harvests, and also for peace. He, moreover, dispenses wealth among men. Freyja is the most propitious of the goddesses ; her abode in heaven is called Fólkváng. To whatever field of battle she rides, she asserts her right to one half of the slain, the other half belonging to Odin. . . . .'

" OF TYR.

" ' There is Tyr, who is the most daring and intrepid of all the gods. 'T is he who dispenses valor in war, hence warriors do well to invoke him. It has become proverbial to say of a man who surpasses all others in valor that he is *Tyr-strong*, or

valiant as Tyr.   A man noted for his wisdom is also said to be
"wise as Tyr."   Let me give thee a proof of his intrepidity.
When the Æsir were trying to persuade the wolf, Fenrir, to
let himself be bound up with the chain, Gleipnir, he, fearing
that they would never afterwards unloose him, only consented
on the condition that while they were chaining him he should
keep Tyr's right hand between his jaws.   Tyr did not hesitate
to put his hand in the monster's mouth, but when Fenrir perceived that the Æsir had no intention to unchain him, he bit
the hand off at that point, which has ever since been called
the wolf's joint (úlflidr).   From that time Tyr has had but
one hand.   He is not regarded as a peacemaker among men.'

"OF THE OTHER GODS.

"'There is another god,' continued Har, 'named Bragi, who
is celebrated for his wisdom, and more especially for his eloquence and correct forms of speech.   He is not only eminently
skilled in poetry, but the art itself is called from his name
Bragr, which epithet is also applied to denote a distinguished
poet or poetess.   His wife is named Iduna.   She keeps in a
box the apples which the gods, when they feel old age approaching, have only to taste of to become young again.   It is
in this manner that they will be kept in renovated youth until
Ragnarök. . . . .

"'One of the gods is Heimdall, called also the White God.
He is the son of nine virgins, who were sisters, and is a very
sacred and powerful deity.   He also bears the appellation of
the Gold-toothed, on account of his teeth being of pure gold,
and also that of Hallinskithi.   His horse is called Gulltopp, and
he dwells in Himinbjörg at the end of Bifröst.   He is the
warder of the gods, and is therefore placed on the borders of
heaven, to prevent the giants from forcing their way over the
bridge.   He requires less sleep than a bird, and sees by night,
as well as by day, a hundred miles around him.   So acute is
his ear that no sound escapes him, for he can even hear the
grass growing on the earth, and the wool on a sheep's back.
He has a horn called the Gjallar-horn, which is heard throughout the universe. . . . .

"'Among the Æsir,' continued Har,'we also reckon Hödur,
who is blind, but extremely strong.   Both gods and men would
be very glad if they never had occasion to pronounce his name,
for they will long have cause to remember the deed perpetrated
by his hand.

" ' Another god is Vidar, surnamed the Silent, who wears very thick shoes. He is almost as strong as Thor himself, and the gods place great reliance on him in all critical conjunctures.

" ' Vali, another god, is the son of Odin and Rinda; he is bold in war, and an excellent archer.

" ' Another is called Ullur, who is the son of Sif, and stepson of Thor. He is so well skilled in the use of the bow, and can go so fast on his snow-skates, that in these arts no one can contend with him. He is also very handsome in his person, and possesses every quality of a warrior, wherefore it is befitting to invoke him in single combats.

" ' The name of another god is Forseti, who is the son of Baldur and Nanna, the daughter of Nef. He possesses the heavenly mansion called Glitnir, and all disputants at law who bring their cases before him go away perfectly reconciled. . . . .'

" OF LOKI AND HIS PROGENY.

" ' There is another deity,' continued Har, ' reckoned in the number of the Æsir, whom some call the calumniator of the gods, the contriver of all fraud and mischief, and the disgrace of gods and men. His name is Loki or Loptur. He is the son of the giant Farbauti. . . . . Loki is handsome and well made, but of a very fickle mood, and most evil disposition. He surpasses all beings in those arts called Cunning and Perfidy. Many a time has he exposed the gods to very great perils, and often extricated them again by his artifices. . . . .

" ' Loki,' continued Har, ' has likewise had three children by Angurbodi, a giantess of Jötunheim. The first is the wolf Fenrir; the second Jörmungand, the Midgard serpent; the third Hela (Death). The gods were not long ignorant that these monsters continued to be bred up in Jötunheim, and, having had recourse to divination, became aware of all the evils they would have to suffer from them ; their being sprung from such a mother was a bad presage, and from such a sire, one still worse. All-father therefore deemed it advisable to send one of the gods to bring them to him. When they came he threw the serpent into that deep ocean by which the earth is engirdled. But the monster has grown to such an enormous size that, holding his tail in his mouth, he encircles the whole earth. Hela he cast into Niflheim, and gave her power over nine worlds (regions), into which she distributes those who are sent to her, that is to say, all who die through sick-

ness or old age.   Here she possesses a habitation protected by
exceedingly high walls and strongly barred gates.   Her hall is
called Elvidnir ; Hunger is her table ; Starvation, her knife ;
Delay, her man ; Slowness, her maid ; Precipice, her thresh-
old ; Care, her bed ; and Burning Anguish forms the hang-
ings of her apartments.   The one half of her body is livid,
the other half the color of human flesh.   She may therefore
easily be recognized ; the more so, as she has a dreadfully
stern and grim countenance.

" ' The wolf Fenrir was bred up among the gods ; but Tyr
alone had the daring to go and feed him.   Nevertheless, when
the gods perceived that he every day increased prodigiously in
size, and that the oracles warned them that he would one day
become fatal to them, they determined to make a very strong
iron fetter for him, which they called Læding.   Taking this
fetter to the wolf, they bade him try his strength on it.   Fenrir, perceiving that the enterprise would not be very difficult
for him, let them do what they pleased, and then, by great
muscular exertion, burst the chain, and set himself at liberty.
The gods, having seen this, made another fetter, half as strong
again as the former, which they called Drómi, and prevailed
on the wolf to put it on, assuring him that, by breaking this,
he would give an undeniable proof of his vigor.

" ' The wolf saw well enough that it would not be so easy
to break this fetter, but finding at the same time that his
strength had increased since he broke Læding, and thinking
that he could never become famous without running some risk,
voluntarily submitted to be chained.   When the gods told him
that they had finished their task, Fenrir shook himself violently, stretched his limbs, rolled on the ground, and at last burst
his chains, which flew in pieces all around him.   He thus
freed himself from Drómi, which gave rise to the proverb "*at
leysa or læðingi eða at drepa or dróma*" (to get loose out of
Læding, or to dash out of Drómi), when anything is to be accomplished by strong efforts.

" ' After this, the gods despaired of ever being able to bind
the wolf ; wherefore All-father sent Skirnir, the messenger of
Frey, into the country of the Dark Elves (Svartálfaheim) to
engage certain dwarfs to make the fetter called Gleipnir.   It
was fashioned out of six things ; to wit, the noise made by the
footfall of a cat ; the beards of women ; the roots of stones ;
the sinews of bears ; the breath of fish ; and the spittle of
birds.   Though thou mayest not have heard of these things

before, thou mayest easily convince thyself that we have not been telling thee lies. Thou must have seen that women have no beards, that cats make no noise when they run, and that there are no roots under stones. Now I know what has been told thee to be equally true, although there may be some things thou art not able to furnish a proof of.'

" ' I believe what thou hast told me to be true,' replied Gangler, ' for what thou hast adduced in corroboration of thy statement is conceivable. But how was the fetter smithied ? '

" ' This I can tell thee,' replied Har, ' that the fetter was as smooth and soft as a silken string, and yet, as thou wilt presently hear, of very great strength. When it was brought to the gods they were profuse in their thanks to the messenger for the trouble he had given himself ; and taking the wolf with them to the island called Lyngvi, in the Lake Amsvartnir, they showed him the cord, and expressed their wish that he would try to break it, assuring him at the same time that it was somewhat stronger than its thinness would warrant a person in supposing it to be. They took it themselves, one after another, in their hands, and after attempting in vain to break it, said, " Thou alone, Fenrir, art able to accomplish such a feat."

" ' "Methinks," replied the wolf, "that I shall acquire no fame in breaking such a slender cord ; but if any artifice has been employed in making it, slender though it seems, it shall never come on my feet."

" ' The gods assured him that he would easily break a limber silken cord, since he had already burst asunder iron fetters of the most solid construction. " But if thou shouldst not succeed in breaking it," they added, " thou wilt show that thou art too weak to cause the gods any fear, and we will not hesitate to set thee at liberty without delay."

" ' " I fear me much," replied the wolf, " that if ye once bind me so fast that I shall be unable to free myself by my own efforts, ye will be in no haste to unloose me. Loath am I, therefore, to have this cord wound round me ; but in order that ye may not doubt my courage, I will consent, provided one of you put his hand into my mouth as a pledge that ye intend me no deceit."

" ' The gods wistfully looked at each other, and found that they had only the choice of two evils, until Tyr stepped forward and intrepidly put his right hand between the monster's jaws. Hereupon the gods, having tied up the wolf, he forcibly stretched himself, as he had formerly done, and used all his might to disengage himself, but the more efforts he made, the tighter became the cord, until all the gods, except Tyr, who lost his hand, burst into laughter at the sight.

" ' When the gods saw that the wolf was effectually bound, they took the chain called Gelgja, which was fixed to the fetter, and drew it through the middle of a large rock named Gjöll, which they sank very deep into the earth ; afterwards, to make it still more secure, they fastened the end of the cord to a .massive stone called Thviti, which they sank still deeper. The wolf made in vain the most violent efforts to break loose, and, opening his tremendous jaws, endeavored to bite them. The gods, seeing this, thrust a sword into his mouth, which pierced his under jaw up to the hilt, so that the point touched the palate.   He then began to howl horribly, and since that time the foam flows continually from his mouth in such abundance that it forms the river called Von.   There will he remain until Ragnarök.' "

There are also goddesses in the Valhalla, of whom the Edda mentions Frigga, Saga, and many others.

§ 5. *Resemblance of the Scandinavian Mythology to that of Zoroaster.*

These are the main points of the Scandinavian mythology, the resemblance of which to that of Zoroaster has been often remarked.   Each is a dualism, having its good and evil gods, its worlds of light and darkness, in opposition to each other.   Each has behind this dualism a dim presence, a vague monotheism, a supreme God, infinite and eternal.   In each the evil powers are for the present conquered and bound in some subterranean prisons, but are hereafter to break out, to battle with the gods and overcome them, but to be destroyed themselves at the same time.   Each system speaks of a great conflagration, in which all things will be destroyed ; to be followed by the creation of a new earth, more beautiful than the other, to be the abode of peace and joy.   The duty of man in each system is war, though this war in the Avesta is viewed rather as moral conflict, while in the Edda it is taken more grossly for physical struggle.   The tone of the theology of Zoroaster is throughout higher and more moral than that of the Scandinavians. Its doctrine of creation is not a mere development by a dark, unintelligent process, nor, on the other hand, is it a Hindoo or Gnostic system of emanation. It is neither pure materialism on the one hand nor pantheism on the other; but a true doctrine of creation, for an intelligent and moral purpose, by the conscious and free act of the Creator. But in many of the details, again, we find a singular correspondence between these two systems. Odin corresponds to Ormazd, Loki to Ahriman, the Æsir to the Amschaspands, the giants of Jötunheim to the Daêvas. So too the ox (Adudab) is the equivalent of the giant Ymir, and the creation of the man and woman, Meshia and Meshiane, is correlated to Ask and Embla. Baldur resembles the Redeemer Sosiosh. The bridge, Bifrost, which goes up to heaven, is the bridge Chinevat, which goes from the top of Albordj to heaven. The dog Sirius (Sura), the watchman who keeps guard over the abyss, seems also to correspond to Surtur, the watchman of the luminous world at the South. The earth, in the Avesta, is called Hethra, and by the ancient Germans and Scandinavians, Hertha, — the name given by Tacitus to this goddess, signifying the earth, in all the Teutonic languages. In like manner, the German name for heaven, Himmel, is derived from the Sanskrit word "Himmala," the name of the Himmalah Mountains in Central Asia, believed by the ancient inhabitants of Asia to be the residence of their gods.*

§ 6. *Scandinavian Worship.*

The religious ceremonies of the Scandinavians were simple. Their worship, like that of the followers of Zoroaster, was at first held in the open air; but in later times they erected temples, some of which were quite

---

* Physical circumstances produced alterations in the mythologies, whose origin was the same. Thus, Loki, the god of fire, belongs to the Æsir, because fire is hostile to frost, but represents the treacherous and evil subterranean fires, which in Iceland destroyed with lava, sand, and boiling water more than was injured by cold.

17

splendid. There were three great festivals in the year.
The first was at the winter solstice, and on the longest
night of the year, which was called the Mother Night,
as that which produced the rest. This great feast was
called Yul, whence comes the English Yule, the old name
for Christmas, which festival took its place when the
Scandinavians became Christians. Their festival was in
honor of the sun, and was held with sacrifices, feasting,
and great mirth. The second festival was in spring, in
honor of the earth, to supplicate fruitful crops. The
third was also in the spring, in honor of Odin. The sacrifices were of fruits, afterward animals, and occasionally,
in later times, human beings. The people believed in
divine interposition, and also in a fixed destiny, but especially in themselves, in their own force and courage.
Some of them laughed at the gods, some challenged them
to fight with them, and professed to believe in nothing
but their own might and main. One warrior calls
for Odin, as a foeman alone worthy of his steel, and it
was considered lawful to fight the gods. The quicken-
tree, or mountain-ash, was believed to possess great virtues, on account of the aid it afforded to Thor on one
occasion.

Beside the priests, the Northern nations had their
soothsayers. They also believed that by the power of
runes the dead could be made to speak. These runes
were called galder, and another kind of magic, mostly
practised by women, was called seid. It was thought
that these wise women possessed the power of raising
and allaying storms, and of hardening the body so that
the sword could not cut it. Some charms could give
preternatural strength, others the power of crossing the
sea without a ship, of creating and destroying love, of assuming different forms, of becoming invisible, of giving
the evil eye. Garments could be charmed to protect or
to destroy the wearer. A horse's head, set on a stake,
with certain imprecations, produced fearful mischief to a
foe.*

Very few remains of temples have been found in the

* Northern Mythology, by Benjamin Thorpe.

North. But (as Laing remarks in his "Sea-Kings of Norway") the most permanent remains of the religion of Odin are found in the usages and languages of the descendants of those who worshipped him. These descendants all retain, in the names of Wednesday, Thursday, and Friday, the recollections of the chief gods of this mythology. Mara (the nightmare) still torments the sleep of the English-speaking people ; and the Evil One, Nokke (so says Laing), is the ancestor of Old Nick.

Every ninth year solemn sacrifices were held in the great temple at Upsal in Sweden. The king and all citizens of importance must appear in person and bring offerings. Crowds came together on these occasions, and no one was excluded, except for some base or cowardly action. Nine human beings were sacrificed, usually captives or slaves, but in times of great calamity even a king was made a victim. Earl Hakon, of Norway, offered his son in sacrifice to obtain a victory over some pirates. The bodies were buried in groves, which thence were regarded as very sacred. One, called Odin's grove, near the temple of Upsal, was sacred in every twig and leaf.

§ 7. *Social Character, Maritime Discoveries, and Political Institutions of the Scandinavians.*

Of the manners, customs, and habits of the Scandinavians, we cannot speak at length. Society among them was divided into two classes, — the landholder or bondsmen, and the thralls or slaves. The duty of the last was to perform domestic service and till the ground, and they consisted of prisoners taken in war and their children. The business of the landholder or bondsman was war, and his chief virtue courage. His maxim was, to conquer a single opponent, to attack two, not to yield to three, and only to give way to four. To die in battle was their high ambition ; then they believed that they should pass to the halls of Odin. King Ragnar died singing the pleasure of receiving death in battle, saying, " The hours of my life have passed away ; I shall die laughing." Saxo, describing a duel, said that one of the champions fell, laughed, and died. Rather than die in their bed, some, when sick, leaped from a rock into the sea. Others, when dying, would be carried into a field of battle. Others induced their friends to kill them. The Icelandic Sagas are filled with stories of single combats, or *holm-gangs*. When not fighting they were fond of feasting; and the man who could drink the most beer was counted the best. The custom of drinking toasts came from the North. As the English give the Queen, and we the President, as the first health on public occasions, so they begin with a cup, first to Odin, and afterward to other deities, and then to the memory of the dead, in what was called grave-beer. Their institutions were patriarchal; the head of the family was the chief of the tribe and also its priest. But all the freemen in a neighborhood met in the Thing, where they decided disputes, laid down social regulations, and determined on public measures. The Thing was, therefore, legislature, court of justice, and executive council in one; and once a year, in some central place, there was held a similar meeting to settle the affairs of the whole country, called the Land-Thing or All-Thing. At this the king was chosen for the whole community, who sometimes appointed subordinate officers called Yarls, or earls, to preside over large districts. Respect for women was a marked trait among the Scandinavians, as Tacitus has noticed of their congeners, the Germans. They were admired for their modesty, sense, and force of character, rather than for the fascinations which the nations of the South prefer. When Thor described his battle with the sorceress, the answer was, "Shame, Thor! to strike a woman!" The wife was expected to be industrious and domestic. She carried the keys of the house; and the Sagas frequently mention wives who divorced their husbands for some offence, and took back their dowry. The Skalds, or Bards, had a high place and great distinction among this people. Their songs constituted the literature and history of the Scandinavians, and the people listened, not as to the inspiration of an individual mind, but to the pulsation of its own past life. Their

praises were desired, their satire feared, by the greatest
heroes and kings. Their style was figurative, sometimes
bombastic, often obscure.

Of the maritime expeditions of the Northmen we have
already spoken. For many centuries they were the terror
of Europe, North and South. The sea-kings of Norway
appeared before Constantinople in 866, and afterward a
body-guard of the emperors of the East was composed of
these pirates, who were called the Varangians. Even
before the death of Charlemagne their depredations
brought tears to his eyes; and after his death they pil-
laged and burnt the principal cities of France, and even
his own palace at Aix-la-Chapelle. They carried their
arms into Spain, Italy, and Greece. In 844 a band of
these sea-rovers sailed up the Guadalquiver and attacked
Seville, then in possession of the Moors, and took it, and
afterward fought a battle with the troops of Abderah-
man II. The followers of Mohammed and the worshippers of Odin, the turbaned Moors and the fair-haired
Norwegians, here met, each far from his original home,
each having pursued a line of conquest, which thus came
in contact at their furthest extremes.

The Northmen in Italy sold their swords to different
princes, and under Count Rainalf built the city of Aversa
in 1029.* In Sicily the Northern knights defeated the
Saracens, and enabled the Greek Emperor to reconquer the
island. Afterward they established themselves in Southern Italy, and took possession of Apulia. A league formed
against them by the Greek and German Emperors and the
Pope ended in the utter defeat of the Papal and German
army by three thousand Normans, and they afterward received and held Apulia as a Papal fief. In 1060 Robert
Guiscard became Duke of Apulia and Calabria, and at
last of the whole kingdom of Naples. Sicily was conquered by his brother, Count Roger, who, with a few
Northmen, routed vast numbers of the Saracens and completed the subjection of the island, after thirty years of
war. Meantime his brother Robert crossed the Adriatic
and besieged and took Durazzo, after a fierce battle, in

* Gibbon, Chap. LVI.

which the Scandinavian soldiers of the Greek Emperor fought with the Normans descended from the same Scandinavian ancestors.

§ 8. *Relation of this System to Christianity.*

The first German nation converted to Christianity was that of the Goths, whose teacher was Ulphilas, born 318, consecrated a bishop in 348. Having made many converts to Christianity among his people, a persecution arose against them from the pagan Goths ; and in 355, in consequence of this persecution, he sought and obtained leave to settle his converts in Mæsia. He preached with fervor, studied the Scripture in Greek and Latin, and made the first translation of the Bible into any German language. Fragments of his Gothic version are preserved at Upsal. This copy, called the " Codex Argenteus," was captured by the Swedes at Prague during the Thirty Years' War. This manuscript is of the sixth century, and, together with some palimpsests, is the only source of our knowledge of this ancient version.*

Ulphilas was an Arian, and died confessing his faith in that form of Unitarianism. Neander says it is to the credit of the orthodox historians that they do not on that account abate anything of their praise of Ulphilas for his great labors as a missionary, confessor, and doctor. His translation was, for a long time, used all over Europe by the various tribes of German descent.

Ulphilas, therefore, led the way in that work which resulted in one of the greatest events of modern history ; namely, the conversion of the German race to Christianity. It was by various families of this Teutonic stem — Goths, Vandals, Saxons, Lombards, Burgundians, Franks — that the Roman Empire was overthrown. If they had not been converted to Christianity before and during these conquests, what would have been the fate of European civilization ? The only bond uniting the modern and ancient world was the Christian faith, and this faith

---

* Smith's Dictionary of the Bible. Neander, Church History, Vol. II. Appendix.

was so adapted to the German character that it was everywhere accepted by them.* The conversion of the Anglo-Saxons by Augustin (A. D. 597), of the Germans by Boniface (A. D. 718 – 755), of the Saxons (A. D. 803), and the universal downfall of German heathenism, was a condition *sine qua non* of that union of Latin and Greek culture with the German vitality, which was at the root of modern European civilization. Previous to this the Visigoths were converted, as we have seen; then the Ostrogoths; then the Vandals and Gepidæ, — all in the fourth century. The Franks became Christians in the fifth century, the Alemanni and Lombards in the sixth. All of these tribes were converted by Arian missionaries, except the Franks. But the records of these missions have perished, for the historians were Catholics, "who," says Milman,* "perhaps destroyed, or disdained to preserve, the fame of Arian conquests to a common Christianity." "It was a surprising spectacle," says he, "to behold the Teutonic nations melting gradually into the general mass of Christian worshippers. In every other respect they were still distinct races. The conquering Ostrogoth or Visigoth, the Vandal, the Burgundian, the Frank, stood apart from the subjugated Roman population, as an armed or territorial aristocracy. They maintain, in great part at least, their laws, their language, their habits, their character; in religion alone they are blended into one society, constitute one church, worship at the same altar, and render allegiance to the same hierarchy. This is the single bond of their common humanity."

The German races also established everywhere the feudal system, that curious institution, which has been the subject of so much discussion, and has perplexed the readers of history by its incongruities. These perplexities, however, may perhaps be relieved if we see that the essential character of this institution was this, that it was an army permanently quartered on a subject people.

* See, for the conversion of the German races, Gibbon; Guizot, History of Civilization; Merivale, Conversion of the German Nations; Milman, Latin Christianity; Neander, History of the Christian Church; Hegel; Lecky, History of European Morals.
† Latin Christianity, Book III. Chap. II.

This definition contains the explanation of the whole system. The Germans had overrun and conquered the Roman Empire. They intended to possess and retain it. But being much fewer in numbers than the conquered people, how could they do this ? Suppose that when the Confederate States had been conquered by the Union Army it had been determined to hold them permanently as a conquered territory. It could be done thus. First, the original inhabitants must be disarmed and put under stringent laws, like that of the curfew, etc. Then to every private soldier in the Union Army a farm, say of fifty acres, would be assigned, on condition that whenever summoned by the captain of his company he would present himself armed to do military duty. In like manner the captain would receive, say a hundred acres, on condition of appearing with his company when summoned by his colonel. Then the colonel would receive five hundred acres, on condition of appearing with his regiment when summoned by the general. The general (*dux*, duke) must appear with his brigade when summoned by the commander-in-chief (*imperator*, emperor), and he would hold perhaps a thousand acres on this condition. All this land, thus held on condition of military service, would be held in fee, and would exemplify the actual foundation of the whole feudal system, which was simply an arrangement by which a conquering army could hold down the conquered nation.

Of course, such a system as this was one of tyranny and cruelty, and during several centuries it was tempered and softened only by the mediatorial influence of the Christian Church. This was the only power strong enough to shield the oppressed and to hold back the arm of the tyrant. Feudalism served, no doubt, some useful purposes. It was a method of riveting together, with iron nails, the conquerors and conquered, until they could come into a union of a better kind.

It was about the year 1000 that the people of the North were converted to Christianity. This process of conversion was a long time going on, and there were several relapses into paganism ; so that no precise time can be fixed for the conversion of a single nation, much less for that of the different branches of the Scandinavian stock separately situated in Sweden and Denmark, Iceland and Greenland, and colonized in England and Normandy. A mission was established in Denmark, A. D. 822, and the king was baptized; but the overthrow of this Christian king restricted the labors of the missionary. An attempt was made in Sweden in 829, and the missionary, Anschar, remained there a year and a half; but the mission there established was soon overthrown. Uniting wisdom with his ardor, Anschar established at Hamburg schools where he educated Danish and Swedish boys to preach Christianity in their own language to their countrymen. But the Normans laid waste this city, and the Christian schools and churches were destroyed. About 850 a new attempt was made in Sweden, and there the subject was laid by the king before his council or parliament, consisting of two assemblies, and they decided to allow Christianity to be preached and practised, apparently on the ground that this new god, Christ, might help them in their dangers at sea, when the other gods could not. And thus, according to the independent character of this people, Christianity was neither allowed to be imposed upon them by their king against their will, nor excluded from the use of those who chose to adopt it. It took its chance with the old systems, and many of the Danes and Normans believed in worshipping both Odin and Christ at the same time. King Harold in Denmark, during the last half of the tenth century, favored the spread of Christianity, and was himself baptized with his wife and son, believing at first that the Christian God was more powerful than the heathen gods, but finally coming to the conclusion that these last were only evil spirits. On the other hand, some of the Danes believed that Christ was a god, and to be worshipped; but that he was a less powerful god than Odin or Thor. The son of King Harold, in 990, returned to paganism and drove out the Christian priests; but his son, Canute the Great, who began to reign in 1014, was converted to Christianity in England, and became its zealous friend. But these fierce warriors

17*

made rather poor Christians. Adam of Bremen says: "They so abominate tears and lamentations, and all other signs of penitence which we think so salubrious, that they will neither weep for their own sins nor at the death of their best friends." Thus, in these Northern regions, Christianity grew through one or two centuries, not like the mustard-seed, but like the leaven, infusing itself more and more into their national life. According to the testimony of an eye-witness, Adam of Bremen, the Swedes were very susceptible to religious impressions. "They receive the preachers of the truth with great kindness," says he, "if they are modest, wise, and able; and our bishops are even allowed to preach in their great public assemblies." In Norway, Prince Hacon, in the middle of the tenth century, attempted to establish Christianity, which he had learned in England. He proposed to the great national assembly that the whole nation should renounce idolatry, worship God and Christ, keep Sundays as festivals, and Fridays as fasts. Great opposition was made, and there was danger of universal insurrection, so that the king had to yield, and even himself drink a toast to Odin and eat horse-flesh, which was a heathen practice. Subsequent kings of Norway introduced Christianity again; but the people, though willing to be baptized, frequently continued Pagans, and only by degrees renounced, with their old worship, their habits of piracy. The Icelanders embraced Christianity at their All-Thing in the year 1000, but with the condition that they might also continue their old worship, and be permitted the eating of horse-flesh and exposition of infants. When the All-Thing broke up, the assembled multitudes went to the hot-baths to be baptized, preferring for this rite hot water to cold. The Scandinavians seem at this period to have lost their faith in their old religion, and to have been in a transition state. One warrior says that he relies more on his own strength and arms than upon Thor. Another says, "I would have thee know that I believe neither in idols nor spirits, but only in my own force and courage." A warrior told King Olaff in Norway, "I am neither Christian nor Pagan. My companions and I have no other religion

than confidence in our own strength and good success."
Evidently Christianity for a long time sat very lightly on
these nations.   They were willing to be baptized and
accept some of the outward ceremonies and festivals of
the Catholic Church, which were considerately made to
resemble their old ones.

Nevertheless Christianity met many of the wants of
this noble race of men ; and, on the other hand, their instincts as a race were as well adapted to promote an equal
development of every side of Christian life.   The Southern races of Europe received Christianity as a religion of
order ; the Northern races, as a religion of freedom.   In
the South of Europe the Catholic Church, by its ingenious
organization and its complex arrangements, introduced into
life discipline and culture.   In the North of Europe Protestant Christianity, by its appeals to the individual soul,
awakens conscience and stimulates to individual and national progress.   The nations of Southern Europe accepted
Christianity mainly as a religion of sentiment and feeling ;
the nations of Northern Europe, as a religion of truth and
principle.   God adapted Christianity to the needs of these
Northern races ; but he also adapted these races, with
their original instincts and their primitive religion, to the
needs of Christianity.   Without them, we do not see how
there could be such a thing in Europe to-day as Protestantism.   It was no accident which made the founder of
the Reformation a Saxon monk, and the cradle of the Reformation Germany.   It was no accident which brought
the great Gustavus Adolphus from the northern peninsula,
at the head of his Swedish Protestants, to turn the tide
of war in favor of Protestantism and to die on the field of
Lutzen, fighting for freedom of spirit.   It is no accident
which makes the Scandinavian races to-day, in Sweden
and Norway, in Denmark and North Germany and Holland, in England and the United States, almost the only
Protestant nations of the world.   The old instincts still
run in the blood, and cause these races to ask of their
religion, not so much the luxury of emotion or the satisfaction of repose, in having all opinions settled for them
and all actions prescribed, as, much rather, light, free-

dom, and progress.   To them to-day, as to their ancestors,

> " Is life a simple art
> Of duties to be done,
> A game where each man takes his part,
> A race where all must run ;
> A battle whose great scheme and scope
> They little care to know;
> Content, as men at arms, to cope
> Each with his fronting foe."

CHAPTER X.

THE JEWISH RELIGION.

§ 1. Palestine, and the Semitic Races. § 2. Abraham ; or, Judaism as the family Worship of a Supreme Being. § 3. Moses ; or, Judaism as the national Worship of a just and holy King. § 4. David ; or, Judaism as the personal Worship of a Father and Friend. § 5. Solomon ; or, the Religious Relapse. § 6. The Prophets ; or, Judaism as the Hope of a spiritual and universal Kingdom of God. § 7. Judaism as a Preparation for Christianity.

§ 1. *Palestine, and the Semitic Races.*

PALESTINE is a word equivalent to Philistia, or the land of the Philistines. A similar name for the coast region of Syria has been found on a monument in Nineveh,* and at Karnak in Egypt.† Josephus and Philo use the term " Palestine," as applying to the Philistines ; and the accurate learning of Milton appears in his using it in the same sense. ‡ " The land of Canaan," " The land of Israel," and " Judæa " were the names afterward given to the territory of the children of Israel. It is a small country, like others as famous ; for it is only about one hundred and forty English miles in length, and forty in width. It resembles Greece and Switzerland, not only in its small dimensions, but by being composed of valleys, separated by chains of mountains and by ranges of hills. It was isolated by the great sea of sand on the east, and the Mediterranean on the west. Sharply defined on the east, west, and south, it stretches indefinitely into Syria on the north. It is a hilly, high-lying region, having all the characters of Greece except proximity to the sea, and all those of Switzerland except the height of the mountains. Its valleys were well watered and fertile. They

---

* Palaztu, on the Western Sea. Rawlinson's Herodotus, Vol. I., p. 487.
† The word has been deciphered " Pulusater." Smith's Dictionary of the Bible, Palestine.
‡ Ibid.

mostly ran north and south ; none opened a way across
Judæa to the Mediterranean. This geographical fact assisted in the isolation of the country. Two great routes
of travel passed by its borders without entering its hills.
On the west the plains of Philistia were the highway of
the Assyrian and Egyptian armies. On the north the
valley of the Orontes, separated by the chain of Lebanon
from Palestine, allowed the people of Asia a free passage to the sea. So, though surrounded by five great nations, all idolatrous, — the Babylonians, Medes, Assyrians,
Phœnicians, and Egyptians, — the people of Judæa were
enabled to develop their own character and institutions
without much interference from without. Inaccessible
from the sea, and surrounded, like the Swiss, by the
natural fortifications of their hills, like the Swiss they
were also protected by their poverty from spoilers. But
being at the point of contact of three continents, they
had (like the Mahommedans afterwards) great facilities
for communicating their religious ideas to other nations.

Palestine is so small a country that from many points
the whole of it may be overlooked.[*] Toward the east,
from all points, may be seen the high plateau of Moab
and the mountains of Gilead. Snow-capped Hermon is
always visible on the north. In the heart of the land
rises the beautiful mountain Tabor, clothed with vegetation to its summit. It is almost a perfect cone, and commands the most interesting view in all directions. From
its top, to which you ascend from Nazareth by a path
which Jesus may have trod, you see to the northeast the
lofty chain of Hermon (Jebel es Sheikh = the Captain)
rising into the blue sky to the height of ten thousand
feet, covered with eternal snow. West of this appears
the chain of Lebanon. At the foot of Tabor the plain
of Esdraelon extends northerly, dotted with hills, and
animated with the camps of the Arabs.[†] The Lake of
Galilee gleams, a silver line, on the east, with Bashan
and the mountains of Gilead in the distance, and farther

[*] Palestine, and the Sinaitic Peninsula. By Carl Ritter. Translated
by William L. Gage. New York. 1866.
[†] Ritter's Palestine, Vol. II. p. 315.

to the southeast the great plateau of Moab rises like a mountain wall beyond the Jordan. The valley of the Jordan itself, sunk far below the level of the Mediterranean, is out of sight in its deep valley ; nor is anything seen of the Dead Sea. To the northwest rises rocky Carmel, overhanging the Bay of Accha (or Acre), on the Mediterranean.

The whole country stands high. Hebron, at the south, is three thousand feet above the level of the sea ; Jerusalem is twenty-six hundred ; the Mount of Olives, twenty-seven hundred ; and Ebal and Gerizim in Samaria, the same. The valley in which Nazareth stands is eight hundred and twenty feet above the sea ; that at the foot of Tabor, four hundred and thirty-nine ; while the summit of Tabor itself is seventeen hundred and fifty. From Judæa the land plunges downward very rapidly toward the east into the valley of Jordan. The surface of Lake Galilee is already five hundred and thirty-five feet below that of the Mediterranean, and that of the Dead Sea is five hundred feet lower down.* Palestine is therefore a mountain fastness, and most of the waves of war swept by, leaving it untouched and unassailed. From Jerusalem to Jericho the distance is only thirteen miles, but the latter place is a thousand feet lower than the former, so that it was very proper to speak of a man's " going down from Jerusalem to Jericho."

The Jews belonged to what has been called the Semitic race. This family, the only historic rival of the Japhetic (or Aryan) race, is ethnologically composed of the Assyrians and Babylonians, the Phœnicians, the Hebrews and other Syrian tribes, the Arabs and the Carthaginians. It is a race which has been great on land and at sea. In the valley of the Euphrates and that of the Tigris its sons carried all the arts of social life to the highest perfection, and became mighty conquerors and warlike soldiers. On the Mediterranean their ships, containing Phœnician navigators, explored the coasts, made settlements at Carthage and Cadiz, and sailing out of the Straits

* Lynch makes it thirteen hundred feet below the surface of the Mediterranean. See Ritter.

of Gibraltar went as far north as Great Britain, and circumnavigated Africa two thousand years before Vasco da Gama. This race has given to man the alphabet, the Bible, the Koran, commerce, and in Hannibal the greatest military genius of all time.

That the different nations inhabiting the region around the Euphrates and Tigris, Syria and Arabia, belonged to one great race, is proved by the unimpeachable testimony of language. The Bible genealogies trace them to Shem, the son of Noah. Ewald,* who believes that this region was inhabited by an aboriginal people long before the days of Abraham, — a people who were driven out by the Canaanites, — nevertheless says that they no doubt were a Semitic people. The languages of all these nations is closely related, being almost dialects of a single tongue, the differences between them being hardly greater than between the subdivisions of the German group of languages.† That which has contributed to preserve the close homogeneity among these tongues is, that they have little power of growth or development. As M. Renan says, "they have less lived than lasted." ‡

The Phœnicians used a language almost identical with the Hebrew. A sarcophagus of Ezmunazar, king of Sidon, dating from the fifth century before Christ, was discovered a few years since, and is now in the Museum of the Louvre. It contains some thirty sentences of the length of an average verse in the Bible, and is in pure Hebrew. §　In a play of Plautus ¶ a Carthaginian is made to speak a long passage in his native language, the Punic tongue ; this is also very readable Hebrew. The black basalt stele, lately discovered in the land of Moab, contains an inscription of Mesha, king of Moab, addressed to his god, Chemosh, describing his victory over the Israelites. This is also in a Hebrew dialect. From

* History of Israel, translated by Russell Martineau, Vol. I. p. 231.

† New American Cyclopædia, art. Semitic Race.

‡ Quoted by Le Normant, Manual of Ancient History of the East, Vol. I. p. 71.

§ Remarks on the Phœnician Inscription of Sidon, by Professor William W. Turner, Journal of the American Oriental Society, Vol. VII. No. 1.

¶ Poenulus, Act V. Sc. 1.

such facts it appears that the Hebrews, Phœnicians, and Canaanites were all congeners with each other, and with the Babylonians and Assyrians.

But now the striking fact appears that the Hebrew *religion* differed widely from that of these other nations of the same family. The Assyrians, Babylonians, Phœnicians, and Carthaginians all possessed a nearly identical religion. They all believed in a supreme god, called by the different names of Ilu, Bel, Set, Hadad, Moloch, Chemosh, Jaoh, El, Adon, Asshur. All believed in subordinate and secondary beings, emanations from this supreme being, his manifestations to the world, rulers of the planets. Like other pantheistic religions, the custom prevailed among the Semitic nations of promoting first one and then another deity to be the supreme object of worship. Among the Assyrians, as among the Egyptians, the gods were often arranged in triads, as that of Anu, Bel, and Ao. Anu, or Oannes, wore the head of a fish ; Bel wore the horns of a bull ; Ao was represented by a serpent. These religions represented the gods as the spirit within nature, and behind natural objects and forces, — powers within the world, rather than above the world. Their worship combined cruelty and licentiousness, and was perhaps as debasing a superstition as the world has witnessed. The Greeks, who were not puritans themselves in their religion, were shocked at the impure orgies of this worship, and horrified at the sacrifice of children among the Canaanites and Carthaginians.

How then did the Hebrews, under Moses and the later prophets, originate a system so widely different? Their God was above nature, not in it. He stood alone, unaccompanied by secondary deities ; he made no part of a triad ; he was not associated with a female representative. His worship required purity, not pollution ; its aim was holiness, and its spirit humane, not cruel. Monotheistic in its spirit from the first, it became an absolute monotheism in its development. Whence this wide departure in the Hebrews from the religious tendencies and belief of the surrounding nations, who spoke the same language and belonged to the same stock ?

M. Renan considers this a question of race.* He says : " The Indo-European race, distracted by the variety of the universe, never by itself arrived at monotheism. The Semitic race, on the other hand, guided by its firm and sure sight, instantly unmasked Divinity, and without re- flection or reasoning attained the purest form of religion that humanity has known." But the Assyrians, Babylo- nians, Arabians before Mohammed, Phœnicians, and Car- thaginians, and perhaps the Egyptians, belonged to the Semitic race. Yet none of these nations attained to any monotheism purer than that of the Veda or the Avesta. The Arabs, near relations of the Hebrews, were divided between a worship like that of Babylon and Sabæism, or star-worship. No doubt in all these Semitic families the idea of one supreme god lay behind that of the secondary deities ; but this was also the case in the Aryan races. And in both this primitive monotheism receded instead of becoming more distinct, with the single exception of the Hebrews. M. Renan's view is not, therefore, sup- ported by the facts. We must look further to find the true cause, and therefore are obliged to examine somewhat in detail the main points of Hebrew history. It would be easy, but would not accord with our plan, to accept the common Christian explanation, and say, " Monotheism was a direct revelation to Moses." For we are now not able to assume such a revelation, and are obliged to con- sider the subject from the outside, from the stand-point of pure history.

§ 2. *Abraham; or, Judaism as the family Worship of a Supreme Being.*

We have been so accustomed to regard the Jewish relig- ion as a part of our own, and so to look at it from within, that it is hard to take the historic position, and to look at it from without. But to compare it with other religions, and to see what it really is and is not, this is necessary. It becomes more difficult to assume the attitude of an

* See his Essay on the People of Israel, in Studies of Religious His- tory and Criticism, translated by O. B. Frothingham.

impartial observer, because of the doctrine of verbal inspiration, so universally taught in the Protestant Church. From childhood we have looked on the Old Testament as inspired throughout, and all on the same level of absolute infallibility. There is no high, no low, no degrees of certitude or probability, where every word is assumed to be the very word of God. But those who still hold to the plenary inspiration of the Old Testament must consent, for our present purpose, to suspend their faith in this doctrine, and provisionally to look at the Old Testament with the same impartial though friendly scrutiny with which we have regarded the sacred books of other nations. Not a little will be gained for the Jewish Scriptures by this position. If they lose the authority which attaches to the Word of God, they will gain the interest which belongs to the utterance of man.

While M. Renan finds the source of Hebrew monotheism in a like tendency in the whole Semitic race, — a supposition which we have seen to be contradicted by the facts, — Max Müller regards the true origin of this tendency to be in Abraham himself, the friend of God, and Father of the Faithful. He calls attention to the fact that both Moses and Christ, and subsequently Mohammed, preached no new God, but the God of Abraham. "Thus," says he, "the faith in the one living God, which seemed to require the admission of a monotheistic instinct grafted in every member of the Semitic family, is traced back to one man." He adds his belief that this faith of Abraham in one supreme God came to him by a special revelation.

And if, by a special revelation, is meant a grand profound insight, an inspired vision of truth, so deep and so living as to make it a reality like that of the outward world, then we see no better explanation of the monotheism of the Hebrews than this conviction transmitted from Abraham through father and son, from generation to generation.

For the most curious fact about this Jewish people is, that every one of them * is a child of Abraham. All looked back with the same ancestral pride to their great progeni-

* Except the proselytes, who are adopted children.

tor, the friend of God. This has never been the case with any other nation, for the Arabs are not a nation. One can hardly imagine a greater spur to patriotism than this union of pride of descent with pride in one's nation and its institutions. The proudest and poorest Jew shared it together. There was one distinction, and that the most honorable, which belonged equally to all.

We have seen that, in all the Semitic nations, behind the numerous divine beings representing the powers of nature, there was dimly visible one Supreme Being, of whom all these were emanations. The tendency to lose sight of this First Great Cause, so common in the race, was reversed in Abraham. His soul rose to the contemplation of the Perfect Being, above all, and the source of all. With passionate love he adored this Most High God, Maker of heaven and earth. Such was his devotion to this Almighty Being, that men, wondering, said, " Abraham is the friend of the Most High God ! " He desired to find a home where he could bring up his children in this pure faith, undisturbed and unperverted by the gross and low worship around him. In some " deep dream or solemn vision " it was borne in on his mind that he must go and find such a home.

We are not to suppose, however, that the mind of Abraham rose to a clear conception of the unity of God, as excluding all other divine beings. The idea of local, tribal, family gods was too deeply rooted to be at once relinquished. Abraham, as described in Genesis, is a great Arab chief, a type of patriarchal life, in which all authority is paternal. The religion of such a period is filial, and God is viewed as the protector and friend of the family or tribe. Only the family God of Abraham was the highest of all gods, the Almighty (Gen. xvii. 1), who was also the God of Isaac (Gen. xxviii. 3) and of Jacob (Gen. xxxv. 11).

Stanley * expresses his satisfaction that the time has past in which the most fastidious believer can object to hearing Abraham called a Bedouin sheik. The type has remained unchanged through all the centuries, and the

---

* History of the Jewish Church, Lect. I.

picture in the Bible of Abraham in his tent, of his hospitality, his self-respect, his courage, and also of his less noble traits, occasional cunning and falsehood, and cruelty toward Hagar and Ishmael, — these qualities, good and bad, are still those of the desert. Only in Abraham something higher and exceptional was joined with them.

In the Book of Genesis Abraham enters quite abruptly upon the scene. His genealogy is given in Genesis (chap. xi.), he being the ninth in descent from Shem, each generation occupying a little more than thirty years. The birth of Abraham is usually placed somewhere about two thousand years before Christ. His father's name was Terah, whom the Jewish and Mohammedan traditions describe as an idolater and maker of idols. He had two brothers, Nahor and Haran ; the latter being the father of Lot, and the other, Nahor, being the grandfather of Rebecca, wife of Isaac. Abraham's father, Terah, lived in Ur of the Chaldees (called in Scripture Casdim). The Chaldees, who subsequently inhabited the region about the Persian Gulf, seemed at first to have lived among the mountains of Armenia, at the source of the Tigris ; and this was the region where Abraham was born, a region now occupied by the people called Curds, who are perhaps descendants of the old Chaldees, the inhabitants of Ur. The Curds are Mohammedans and robbers, and quite independent, never paying taxes to the Porte. The Chaldees are frequently mentioned in Scripture and in ancient writers. Xenophon speaks of the Carduchi as inhabitants of the mountains of Armenia, and as making incursions thence to plunder the country, just as the Curds do now. He says they were found there by the younger Cyrus, and by the ten thousand Greeks. The Greeks, in their retreat, were obliged to fight their way through them, and found them very skilful archers. So did the Romans under Crassus and Mark Antony. And so are they described by the Prophet Habakkuk (chap. i. 6 – 9) : —

' For lo, I raise up the Chaldeans,
   A bitter and hasty nation,

Which marches far and wide in the earth,
To possess the dwellings that are not theirs.
They are terrible and dreadful,
Their decrees and their judgments proceed only from themselves.
Swifter than leopards are their horses,
And fiercer than the evening wolves.
Their horsemen prance proudly around ;
And their horsemen shall come from afar and fly,
Like the eagle when he pounces on his prey.
They all shall come for violence,
In troops, — their glance is ever forward !
They gather captives like the sand ! "

As they were in the time of Habakkuk, so are they
to-day. Shut up on every side in the Persian Empire,
their ancestors, the Carduchi, refused obedience to the
great king and his satraps, just as the Curds refuse to
obey the grand seignior and his pashas. They can raise
a hundred and forty thousand armed men. They are
capable of any undertaking. Mohammed himself said,
" They would yet revolutionize the world."

The ancient Chaldees seem to have been fire-worshippers, like the Persians. They were renowned for the study
of the heavens and the worship of the stars, and some
remains of Persian dualism still linger among their descendants, who are accused of Devil-worship by their
neighbors.

That Abraham was a real person, and that his story
is historically reliable, can hardly be doubted by those
who have the historic sense. Such pictures, painted in
detail with a Pre-Raphaelite minuteness, are not of the
nature of legends. Stories which are discreditable to his
character, and which place him in a humiliating position
towards Pharaoh and Abimelech, would not have appeared
in a fictitious narrative. The mythical accounts of Abraham, as found among the Mohammedans and in the Talmud,* show, by their contrast, the difference between fable
and history.

The events in the life of Abraham are so well known
that it is not necessary even to allude to them. We will
only refer to one, as showing that others among the tribes
in Palestine, besides Abraham, had a faith in God similar

---

* See, for these marvellous stories, Weil, Legends of the Mussulmans.

to his. This is the account of his meeting with Melchisedek. This mysterious person has been so treated by typologists that all human meaning has gone out of him, and he has become, to most minds, a very vapory character.* But this is doing him great injustice.

One mistake often made about him is, to assume that "Melchisedek, King of Salem," gives us the name and residence of the man, whereas both are his official titles. His name we do not know; his office and title had swallowed it up. "King of Justice and King of Peace," — this is his designation. His office, as we believe, was to be umpire among the chiefs of neighboring tribes. By deciding the questions which arose among them, according to equity, he received his title of "King of Justice." By thus preventing the bloody arbitrament of war, he gained the other name, "King of Peace." All questions, therefore, as to where "Salem" was, fall to the ground. Salem means "peace"; it does not mean the place of his abode.

But in order to settle such intertribal disputes, two things were necessary : first, that the surrounding Bedouin chiefs should agree to take him as their arbiter ; and, secondly, that some sacredness should attach to his character, and give authority to his decisions. Like others in those days, he was both king and priest; but he was priest "of the Most High God," — not of the local gods of the separate tribes, but of the highest God, above all the rest. That he was the acknowledged arbiter of surrounding tribes appears from the fact that Abraham paid to him tithes out of the spoils. It is not likely that Abraham did this if there were no precedent for it; for he regarded the spoils as belonging, not to himself, but to the confederates in whose cause he fought. No doubt it was the custom, as in the case of Delphi, to pay tithes to this supreme arbiter ; and in doing so Abraham was simply following the custom. The Jewish traveller, Wolff, states that in Mesopotamia a similar custom prevails at the present time. One sheik is selected from the rest, on

---

* See my sermon on "Melchisedek and his Moral," in "The Hour that Cometh," second edition.

account of his superior probity and piety, and becomes their " King of Peace and Righteousness." A similar custom, I am told, prevails among some American tribes. Indeed, where society is organized by clans, subject to local chiefs, some such arrangement seems necessary to prevent perpetual feuds.

This " King of Justice and Peace " gave refreshments to Abraham and his followers after the battle, blessing him in the name of the Most High God. As he came from no one knows where, and has no official status or descent, the fact that Abraham recognized him as a true priest is used in the Book of Psalms and the Epistle to the Hebrews to prove there is a true priesthood beside that of the house of Levi. A priest after the order of Melchisedek is one who becomes so by having in him the true faith, though he has "no father nor mother, beginning of days nor end of life," that is, no genealogical position in an hereditary priesthood.

The God of Abraham was " The Most High." He was the family God of Abraham's tribe and of Abraham's descendants. Those who should worship other gods would be disloyal to their tribe, false to their ancestors, and must be regarded as outlaws. Thus the faith in a Supreme Being was first established in the minds of the descendants of Abraham by family pride, reverence for ancestors, and patriotic feeling. The faith of Abraham, that his God would give to his descendants the land of Palestine, and multiply them till they should be as numerous as the stars or the sand, was that which made him the Father of the Faithful.

The faith of Abraham, as we gather it from Genesis, was in God as a Supreme Being. Though almighty, God was willing to be Abraham's personal protector and friend. He talks with Abraham face to face. He comes to him, and agrees to give to him and to his posterity the land of Canaan, and in this promise Abraham has entire faith. His monotheism was indeed of an imperfect kind. It did not exclude a belief in other gods, though they were regarded as inferior to his own. His family God, though almighty, was not omnipresent. He came down to learn whether the rumors concerning the sinfulness of Sodom were correct or not. He was not quite sure of Abraham's faith, and so he tested it by commanding him to sacrifice Isaac, in whom alone the promise to Abraham's descendants could be fulfilled. But though the monotheism of Abraham was of so imperfect a kind, it had in it the root of the better kind which was to come. It was imperfect, but not false. It was entire faith in the supreme power of Jehovah to do what he would, and in his disposition to be a friend to the patriarch and his posterity. It was, therefore, trust in the divine power, wisdom, and goodness. The difference between the religion of Abraham and that of the polytheistic nations was, that while they descended from the idea of a Supreme Being into that of subordinate ones, he went back to that of the Supreme, and clung to this with his whole soul.

§ 3. *Moses ; or, Judaism as the national Worship of a just and holy King.*

In speaking of Moses and of his law, it may be thought necessary to begin by showing that such a man as Moses really existed ; for modern criticism has greatly employed itself in questioning the existence of great men. As the telescope resolves stars into double, triple, and quadruple stars, and finally into star-dust, so the critics, turning their optical tubes toward that mighty orb which men call Homer, have declared that they have resolved him into a great number of little Homers. The same process has been attempted in regard to Shakespeare. Some have tried to show that there never was any Shakespeare, but only many Shakespeare writers. In like manner, the critics have sought to dissolve Moses with their powerful analysis, and, instead of Moses, to give us a number of fragmentary writings from different times and hands, skilfully joined together ; in fact, instead of Moses, to give us a mosaic. Criticism substitutes human tendencies in the place of great men, does not love to believe in genius, and often appears to think that a num-

18

her of mediocrities added together can accomplish more
than one man of genius.

Certainly this is a mistake. The easiest and most natural solution of wonderful results is the supposition of
genius, inspiration, heroism, as their cause. Great men
explain history. Napoleon explains the history of Europe during a quarter of a century. Suppose a critic, a
thousand years hence, should resolve Napoleon into half
a dozen Napoleons ; would they explain the history of
Europe as well ? Given a man like Napoleon, and we
can understand the French campaigns in Italy and Germany, the overthrow of Austria, the annihilation of
Prussia, the splendid host of field-marshals, the Bona-
parte circle of kings, the Codex, the Simplon Road, and the
many changes of states and governments on the map of
Europe. One man of genius explains it all. But take
away the man of genius, and substitute a group of small
men in his place, and the thing is much more obscure and
unintelligible. So, given Moses, the man of genius and
inspiration, and we can understand the Exodus, understand the Jewish laws, understand the Pentateuch, and
understand the strange phenomenon of Judaism. But,
instead of Moses, given a mosaic, however skilfully put
together, and the thing is more difficult. Therefore,
Moses is to be preferred to the mosaic, as the more reasonable and probable of the two, just as Homer is prefer-
able to the Homerids, and Shakespeare to the Shakespeare Club.*

---

* Strabo, who probably wrote in the reign of Tiberius, thus describes
Moses : —

"Moses, an Egyptian priest, who possessed a considerable tract of
Lower Egypt, unable any longer to bear with what existed there, departed thence to Syria, and with him went out many who honored the
Divine Being. For Moses taught that the Egyptians were not right in
likening the nature of God to beasts and cattle, nor yet the Africans or
even the Greeks, in fashioning their gods in the form of men. He held
that this only was God, — that which encompasses all of us, earth and sea,
that which we call heaven, the order of the world, and the nature of
things. Of this, who that had any sense would venture to invent an
image like to anything which exists among ourselves ? Far better to
abandon all statuary and sculpture, all setting apart of sacred precincts
and shrines, and to pay reverence without any image whatever. The
course prescribed was that those who have the gift of divination for

We find in Moses the three elements of genius, inspiration, and knowledge. Perhaps it is not difficult to distinguish them. We see the natural genius and temperament of Moses breaking out again and again throughout his career, as the rocky strata underlying the soil crop out in the midst of gardens, orchards, and fields of corn. The basis of his nature was the hardest kind of rock, with a surging subterranean fire of passion beneath it. An awful soul, stern and terrible as Michael Angelo conceived him, the sublime genius carving the sublime lawgiver in congenial marble. The statue is as stern as law itself. It sits in one of the Roman churches, between two columns, the right hand grasping the tables of the law, the symbolic horns of power protruding from the brow, and the austere look of the judge bent upon those on the left hand. A fiery nature, an iron will, a rooted sense of justice, were strangely overflowed and softened by a tenderness toward his race, which was not so much the feeling of a brother for brethren as of a parent for children.

Educated in the house of Pharaoh, and adopted by his daughter as her child, taken by the powerful and learned priesthood of Egypt into their ranks, and sharing for many years their honors and privileges, his heart yearned toward his brethren in the land of Goshen, and he went out to see them in their sufferings and slavery. His impetuous nature broke out in sudden indignation at the sight of some act of cruelty, and he smote the overseer who was torturing the Jewish slave. That act made him an exile, and sent him to live in Arabia Petrea, as a shepherd. If he had thought only of his own prospects and position, he would not have gone near the Israelites at all, but lived quietly as an Egyptian priest in the palace of Pharaoh. But, as the writer to the Hebrews says, he " refused to be called the son of Pharaoh's daughter ; choosing rather to suffer affliction with the people of God than to enjoy the pleasures of sin for a

themselves or others should compose themselves to sleep within the Temple, and those who live temperately and justly may expect to receive some good gift from God."

season." * Another instance of his generous and tender feelings toward his nation is seen in his behavior when the people made the golden calf. First, his anger broke out against them, and all the sternness of the lawgiver appeared in his command to the people to cut down their idolatrous brethren ; then the bitter tide of anger withdrew, and that of tenderness took its place, and he returned into the mountain to the Lord and said, " O, this people have sinned a great sin, and have made them gods of gold. Yet now, if thou wilt forgive their sin — ; and if not, blot me, I pray thee, out of thy book which thou hast written." Moses did not make much account of human life. He struck dead the Egyptian who was ill-treating a Jew ; he slew the Jews who turned to idolatry ; he slew the Midianites who tempted them ; but then he was ready to give up his own life too for the sake of his people and for the sake of the cause. This spirit of Moses pervades his law, this same inconsistency went from his character into his legislation ; his relentless severity and his tender sympathy both appear in it. He knows no mercy toward the transgressor, but toward the unfortunate he is full of compassion. His law says, " Eye for eye, tooth for tooth, hand for hand, burning for burning, stripe for stripe." But it also says, " Ye shall neither vex a stranger, nor oppress him, for ye were strangers in the land of Egypt. Ye shall not afflict any widow or fatherless child." " If thou lend money to any of my people that is poor by thee, thou shalt not be to him as an usurer." " If thou at all take thy neighbor's raiment to pledge, thou shalt deliver it unto him by that the sun goeth down, for that is his covering." " If thou meet thine enemy's ox or his ass going astray, thou shalt surely bring it back to him again."

Such severities joined with such humanities we find in the character of Moses, and such we find to have passed from his character into his laws. But perhaps the deepest spring of character, and its most essential trait, was his sense of justice as embodied in law. The great idea of a just law, freely chosen, under its various aspects of Di-

---

* " Esteeming the reproach of the Christ " (that is, of the anointed, or, the anointed people) " greater riches than the treasures of Egypt."

vine command, ceremonial regulations, political order, and moral duty, distinguished his policy and legislation from that of other founders of states. His laws rested on no basis of mere temporal expediency, but on the two pivots of an absolute Divine will and a deliberate national choice. It had the double sanction of religion and justice ; it was at once a revelation and a contract. There was a third idea which it was the object of his whole system, and especially of his ceremonial system, to teach and to cultivate, — that of holiness. God is a holy God, his law is a holy law, the place of his worship is a holy place, and the Jewish nation as his worshippers are a holy people. This belief appears in the first revelation which he received at the burning bush in the land of Midian. It explains many things in the Levitical law, which without this would seem trivial and unmeaning. The ceremonial purifications, clean and unclean meats, the arrangements of the tabernacle, with its holy place, and its Holy of Holies, the Sabbath, the dresses of the priests, the ointment with which the altar was anointed, are all intended to develop in the minds of the people the idea of holiness.* And there never was a people on whose souls this notion was so fully impressed as it was upon the Jews. Examined, it means the eternal distinction between right and wrong, between good and evil, and the essential hostility which exists between them. Applied to God, it shows him to have a nature essentially moral, and a true moral character. He loves good and hates evil. He does not regard them with exactly the same feeling. He cannot treat the good man and the bad man in exactly the same way. More than monotheism, this perhaps is the characteristic of the theology of Moses.

The character of Moses had very marked deficiencies, it had its weakness as well as its strength. He was impetuous, impatient, wanting in self-possession and self-control. There is a verse in the Book of Numbers (believed by Eichhorn and Rosenmuller to be an interpolation) which calls him the meekest of men. Such a view of his

* See this well explained in The Philosophy of the Plan of Salvation, by James B. Walker.

character is not confirmed by such actions as his killing the Egyptian, his breaking the stone tables, and the like. He declares of himself that he had no power as a speaker, being deficient probably in the organ of language.   His military skill seems small, since he appointed Joshua for the military commander, when the people were attacked by the Amalekites.   Nor did he have, what seems more important in a legislator, the practical tact of organizing the administration of affairs.   His father-in-law, Jethro, showed him how to delegate the details of government to subordinates, and to reserve for himself the general superintendence.   Up to that time he had tried to do everything by himself.   That great art, in administration, of selecting proper tools to work with, Moses did not seem to have.

Having thus briefly sketched some of the qualities of his natural genius and character, let us see what were the essential elements of his legislation ; and first, of his theology, or teachings concerning God.

Monotheism, as we all know, lay at the foundation of the law of Moses.   But there are different kinds of monotheism.   In one sense we have seen almost all ancient religions to have been monotheisms.   All taught the existence of a Supreme Being.   But usually this Supreme Being was not the object of worship, but had receded into the background, while subordinate gods were those really reverenced.   Moses taught that the Supreme Being who made heaven and earth, the Most High God, was also the only object of worship.   It does not appear that Moses denied the existence of the gods who were adored by the other nations ; but he maintained that they were all inferior and subordinate, and far beneath Jehovah, and also that Jehovah alone was to be worshipped by the Jews. " Thou shalt have no other gods before me " (Exod. xx. 3 ; Deut. v. 7).   " Ye shall not go after other gods " (Deut. vi. 14). " Ye shall make no mention of the name of other gods " (Exod. xxiii. 13). " For the Lord your God is God of gods and Lord of lords " (Deut. x. 17).   The first great peculiarity of the theology of Moses was therefore this, that it taught that the Infinite and Supreme Being, who in most religions was the hidden God, was to the Jews the revealed and ever-present God, the object of worship, obedience, trust, and love. His name was Jahveh, the "I am," the Being of beings.*

In a certain sense Moses taught the strict unity of God. "Hear, O Israel ; the Lord our God is one Lord" (Deut. vi. 4), is a statement which Jesus calls the chief of the commandments (Mark xii. 29, 30). For when God is conceived of as the Supreme Being he becomes at once separated by an infinite distance from all other deities, and they cease to be gods in the sense in which he is God. Now as Moses gave to Jehovah infinite attributes, and taught that he was the maker and Lord of heaven and earth, eternal (Deut. xxxiii. 27), a living God, it followed that there was no God with him (Deut. xxxii. 39), which the prophets afterwards wrought out into a simple monotheism. "I am God, and there is no other God beside me" (Isaiah xliv. 8). Therefore, though Moses did not assert in terms a simple monotheism, he taught what contained the essential germ of that idea.

This one God, supreme and infinite, was also so spiritual that no idol, no statue, was to be made as his symbol. He was a God of truth and stern justice, visiting the sins of parents on the children to the third and fourth generation of those who hated him, but showing mercy

---

* "'Behold, when I shall come to the children of Israel, and shall say unto them, The God of your fathers hath sent me unto you, and they shall say, What is his name ? What shall I say unto them ? And God said unto Moses, I AM THE I AM. . . . . Thus shalt thou say unto the children of Israel, I AM hath sent me unto you !'

"It has been observed that the great epochs of the history of the Chosen People are marked by the several names, by which in each the Divine Nature is indicated.   In the patriarchal age we have already seen that the oldest Hebrew form by which the most general idea of Divinity is expressed is 'El-Elohim,' 'The Strong One,' 'The Strong Ones,' 'The Strong.'   "Beth-El," 'Peni-El,' remained even to the latest times memorials of this primitive mode of address and worship. But now a new name, and with it a new truth, was introduced. I am Jehovah ; I appeared unto Abraham, Isaac, and Jacob, by the name of El-Shaddai (God Almighty) ; but by my name Jehovah was I not known unto them. The only certain use of it before the time of Moses is in the name of 'Jochebed,' borne by his own mother. It was the declaration of the simplicity, the unity, the self-existence of the Divine Nature, the exact opposite to all the multiplied forms of idolatry, human, animal, and celestial, that prevailed, as far as we know, everywhere else." — Stanley's Jewish Church.

to thousands of those who loved and obeyed him.   He
was a God who was merciful, long-suffering, gracious,
repenting him of the evil, and seeking still to pardon
and to bless his people.   No doubt there is anthropomor-
phism in Moses.   But if man is made in God's image,
then God is in man's image too, and we *must*, if we think
of him as a living and real God, think of him as possessing emotions like our human emotions of love, pity, sorrow,
anger, only purified from their grossness and narrowness.

Human   actions   and   human   passions   are   no   doubt
ascribed by Moses to God.   A good deal of criticism has
been 'expended upon the Jewish Scriptures by those who
think that philosophy consists in making God as different
and distant from man as possible, and so prefer to speak
of him as Deity, Providence, and Nature.   But it is only
because man is made in the image of God that he can
revere God at all.   Jacobi says that, "God, in creating, *theo*-
morphizes man ; man, therefore, necessarily *anthropo*morphizes God."   And Swedenborg teaches that God is a
man, since man was made in the image of God.   Whenever we think of God as present and living, when we
ascribe to him pleasure and displeasure, liking and dis-
liking, thinking, feeling, and willing, we make him like a
man.   And *not* to do this may be speculative theism, but
is practical atheism.   Moses forbade the Jews to make
any image or likeness of God, yet the Pentateuch speaks
of his jealousy, wrath, repentance ; he hardens Pharaoh's heart, changes his mind about Balaam, and comes
down from heaven in order to see if the people of Sodom
were as wicked as they were represented to be.   These
views are limitations to the perfections of the Deity, and
so far the views of Moses were limited.   But this is also
the strong language of poetry, which expresses in a striking and practical way the personality, holiness, and constant providence of God.

But Moses was not merely a man of genius, he was
also a man of knowledge and learning.   During forty
years he lived in Egypt, where all the learning of the
world was collected ; and, being brought up by the daughter of Pharaoh as her son, was in the closest relations

with the priesthood. The Egyptian priests were those to whom Pythagoras, Herodotus, and Plato went for instruction. Their sacred books, as we have seen, taught the doctrine of the unity and spirituality of God, of the immortality of the soul, and its judgment in the future world, beside teaching the arts and sciences. Moses probably knew all that these books could teach, and there is no doubt that he made use of this knowledge afterward in writing his law. Like the Egyptian priests he believed in one God; but, unlike them, he taught that doctrine openly. Like them he established a priesthood, sacrifices, festivals, and a temple service; but, unlike them, he allowed no images or idols, no visible representations of the Unseen Being, and instead of mystery and a hidden deity gave them revelation and a present, open Deity. Concerning the future life, about which the Egyptians had so much to say, Moses taught nothing. His rewards and punishments were inflicted in this world. Retribution, individual and national, took place here. As this could not have been from ignorance or accident, it must have had a purpose, it must have been intentional. The silence of the Pentateuch respecting immortality is one of the most remarkable features in the Jewish religion. It has been often objected to. It has been asserted that a religion without the doctrine of immortality and future retribution is no religion. But in our time philosophy takes a different view, declaring that there is nothing necessarily religious in the belief of immortality, and that to do right from fear of future punishment or hope of future reward is selfish, and therefore irreligious and immoral. Moreover it asserts that belief in immortality is a matter of instinct, and something to be assumed, not to be proved; and that we believe in immortality just in proportion as the soul is full of life. Therefore, though Moses did not teach the doctrine of immortality, he yet made it necessary that the Jews should believe in it by the awakening influence of his law, which roused the soul into the fullest activity.

But beside genius, beside knowledge, did not Moses also possess that which he claimed, a special inspiration?

18 *   A A

And if so, what was his inspiration and what is its evidence ?   The evidence of his inspiration is in that which he said and did.   His inspiration, like that of Abraham, consisted in his inward vision of God, in his sight of the divine unity and holiness, in his feeling of the personal presence and power of the Supreme Being, in his perception of his will and of his law.   He was inwardly placed by the Divine Providence where he could see these truths, and become the medium of communicating them to a nation. His inspiration was deeper than that of the greatest of subsequent prophets.   It was perhaps not so large, nor so full, nor so high, but it was more entire ; and therefore the power that went forth from the word and life of Moses was not surpassed afterward.   " There arose not a prophet since in Israel like unto Moses, whom the Lord knew face to face."   No prophet afterward till the time of Jesus did such a work as he did.   Purity, simplicity, and strength characterized his whole conduct.   His theology, his liturgy, his moral code, and his civil code were admirable in their design and their execution.

We are, indeed, not able to say how much of the Pentateuch came from Moses.   Many parts of it were probably the work of other writers and of subsequent times. But we cannot doubt that the essential ideas of the law proceeded from him.

We have regarded Moses and his laws on the side of religion and also on that of morals ; it remains to consider them on that of politics.   What was the form of government established by Moses ?   Was it despotism or freedom ?   Was it monarchy, aristocracy, democracy, or republicanism ?   Were the Jews a free people or an enslaved people ?

Certainly the Jews were not enslaved.   They had one great protection from despotism, — a constitution.   The Mosaic law was their constitution.   It was a written constitution, and could therefore be appealed to.   It was a published constitution, and was therefore known by all the people.   It was a sacred constitution, given on the authority of God, and therefore could not be modified, except by the same authority.   This constitution therefore was a protection against despotism. A constitution like this excludes all arbitrary and despotic authority. We can therefore safely say that the law of Moses saved the nation from despotism. Thus he gave them an important element of political freedom. No matter how oppressive laws are, a government of fixed law involves in the long run much more real freedom than the government, however kind, which is arbitrary, and therefore uncertain and changeable.

But were these laws oppressive? Let us look at them in a few obvious points of view.

What did they exact in regard to taxation? We know that in Eastern governments the people have been ground to the earth by taxation, and that agriculture has been destroyed, the fruitful field become a wilderness, and populous countries depopulated, by this one form of oppression. It is because there has been no fixed rate of taxation. Each governor is allowed to take as much as he can from his subordinates, and each of the subordinates as much as he can get from his inferiors, and so on, till the people are finally reached, out of whom it must all come. But under the Mosaic constitution the taxes were fixed and certain. They consisted in a poll-tax, in the first-fruits, and the tithes. The poll-tax was a half-shekel paid every year at the Temple, by every adult Jew. The first-fruits were rather an expression of gratitude than a tax. The tithes were a tenth part of the annual produce of the soil, and went for the support of the Levites and the general expenses of the government.

Another important point relates to trials and punishments. What security has one of a fair trial, in case he is accused of crime, or what assurance of justice in a civil cause? Now we know that in Eastern countries everything depends on bribery. This Moses forbade in his law. " Thou shalt take no gift, for the gift blindeth the eyes; thou shalt not wrest the judgment of the poor, but in righteousness shalt thou judge thy neighbor."

Again, the accuser and accused were to appear together before the judge. The witnesses were sworn, and were

examined separately.   The people had cheap justice and
near at hand.   " Judges and officers shalt thou make thee
in all thy gates, throughout thy tribes; and they shall
judge the people with just judgment."

There were courts of appeal from these local judges.

There seems to have been no legislative body, since the
laws of Moses were not only a constitution but also a
code.   No doubt a common law grew up under the decisions of the local courts and courts of appeal.   But
provision was made by Moses for any necessary amendment of his laws by the reference which he made to any
prophet like himself who might afterward arise, whom the
people were to obey.*

There was no provision in the Jewish constitution for
a supreme executive.   But the law foretold that the time
would come in which they would desire a king, and it defined his authority.   He should be a constitutional king.
(Deut. xvii. 14 – 20.)

We have already said that one great object and purpose
of the ceremonial law of Moses was to develop in the minds
of the people the idea of holiness.   This is expressed
(Lev. xix. 2), " Speak unto all the congregation of the
children of Israel, and say unto them, Ye shall be holy ; for
I the Lord your God am holy."

Another object of the ceremonial law was to surround
the whole nation with an impenetrable hedge of peculiarities, and so to keep them separate from surrounding nations.   The ceremonial law was like a shell which protected the kernel within till it was ripe.   The ritual was
the thorny husk, the theology and morality were the sacred included fruit.   In this point of view the strangest
peculiarities of the ritual find an easy explanation.   The
more strange they are, the better they serve their purpose.
These peculiarities produced bitter prejudice between the
Jews and the surrounding nations.   Despised by their
neighbors, they despised them again in turn ; and this

---

* A man became a prophet only by his powers of insight and foresight ;
until that was certified to the people, he was no prophet to them.   When
it was, it was because he *convinced* them by his manifestation of the
truth ; consequently any revision of the law by a prophet was a constitutional amendment by the people themselves.

mutual contempt has produced the result desired. The Jews, in the very heart of the world, surrounded by great nations far more powerful than themselves, conquered and overrun by Assyrians, Medes, Persians, Syrians, Egyptians, Greeks, Romans, have been more entirely separated from other nations than the Chinese or the people of Japan. Dispersed as they are, they are still a distinct people, a nation within other nations. Like drops of oil floating on the water but never mingling with it, so the Jews are found everywhere, floating drops of national life in the midst of other nationalities. In Leviticus (xviii. 3) we find the command, "After the doings of the land of Egypt, wherein ye dwelt, shall ye not do; and after the doings of the land of Canaan, whither I bring you, shall ye not do; neither shall ye walk in their ordinances." They have not obeyed this command in its letter, but continue to obey its spirit in its unwritten continuation: "After the doings of the English and French and Americans shall ye not do, nor walk in their ordinances, but shall still continue a peculiar people."

§ 4. *David; or, Judaism as the personal Worship of a Father and Friend.*

Many disasters befell the Jews after their settlement in Palestine, which we should allude to were we writing the heads of their history rather than giving an account of their religion. Among these were their long conflict with the Philistines, and their subjection by that people during twenty years. The Philistines, it has been recently discovered, were not a Semitic nation, and were not in the land in the time of Moses. They are not mentioned as a powerful people in the Pentateuch or the Book of Joshua, but suddenly appear as invaders in the time of the Judges, completely defeating and subduing the Canaanites along the shore. In fact, the Philistines were probably an Indo-European or Aryan people, and their name is now believed to be the same as that of the Pelasgi. They were probably a body of Pelasgi from the island of Crete, who, by successive invasions, overran Palestine, and gave their name to it.* They were finally reduced by David; and as his reign is the culminating period of Judaism, we will devote some space to his character and influence.

The life of David makes an epoch in Jewish history and human history. Nations, like plants, have their period of flowers and of fruit. They have their spring-time, their summer, autumn, and winter. The age of David among the Jews was like the age of Pericles among the Greeks, of Augustus among the Romans, of Louis XIV. in France, of Charles V. in Spain. Such periods separate themselves from those which went before and from those which follow. The period of David seems a thousand years removed from that of the Judges, and yet it follows it almost immediately. As a few weeks in spring turn the brown earth to a glad green, load the trees with foliage, and fill the air with the perfume of blossoms and the song of birds, so a few years in the life of a nation will change barbarism into civilization, and pour the light of literature and knowledge over a sleep-ing land. Arts flourish, external enemies are conquered, inward discontents are pacified, wealth pours in, luxury increases, genius accomplishes its triumphs. Summer, with its flowers and fruits, has arrived.

When a nation is ripe for such a change, the advent of a man of genius will accomplish it. Around him the par-ticles crystallize and take form and beauty. Such a man was David, — a brave soldier, a great captain, a sagacious adventurer, an artist, musician, and poet, a man of pro-found religious experience; he was, more than all these, a statesman. By his great organizing ability he made a powerful nation out of that which, when he came to the throne, consisted of a few discordant and half-conquered tribes. In the time of Saul the Israelites were invaded by all the surrounding nations; by the Syrians on the north, the Ammonites and Moabites on the east, the

---

* Hitzig, Urgeschichte und Mythoiogie der Philister. Tacitus proba-bly referred to the Cretan origin of the Philistines, when he says that the Jews were originally natives of the island of Crete. See his account of Moses and his institutions, Historia, V. 1-6.

Amalekites and Edomites on the south, and the Philistines on the west. In the time of David all these nations were completely subdued, their cities garrisoned, and the power of the Israelites submitted to from the Euphrates to the Mediterranean.

Most great men are contented to be distinguished in one thing, and to lead a single life; but David led three lives, each distinct from the other, — the life of a soldier and statesman, the life of a poet and artist, the life of deep religious experience. We will look at his character in each of these three directions.

We have already said that David found the Israelites divided and half conquered, and left them united and conquerors. By means of his personal qualities he had made himself popular among the tribes. He was known as a brave and cautious guerilla chief. His native generosity and open-heartedness won him the love of the people. His religious tendencies gained for him the friendship of the priests, and the great influence of Samuel was always exerted in his favor. He was thus enabled to unite the people, and gain their confidence till he could make use of them in larger enterprises. The Jews were not naturally a military nation, and were never meant to be such. Yet when their strength was united they were capable, by their determination and tenacity of purpose, of extraordinary military exploits. Everything depended on their *morale*. Demoralized and weakened by doubts and scruples, or when conscious that they were disobeying the laws of Moses, they were easily defeated by any invader. The first duty of their general was to bring them back from their idolatries and backslidings to the service of God. Under Joshua it only needed two great battles to conquer the whole land of Palestine. So, reunited under David, a few campaigns made them victorious over the surrounding nations.

The early part of David's life was a perpetual discipline in prudence. He was continually beset with dangers. He had to fly from the presence and ferocious jealousy of Saul again and again, and even to take refuge with the Philistines, who had reason enough to be his

enemies. He fled from Saul to Samuel, and took shelter
under his protection. Pursued to this retreat by the
king, he had no resource but to throw himself on the
mercy of the Philistines, and he went to Gath. When
he saw himself in danger there, he pretended to be insane; insanity being throughout the East a protection
from injury. His next step was to go to the cave Adul-
lam, and to collect around him a body of partisans, with
whom to protect himself. Saul watched his opportunity,
and when David had left the fastnesses of the mountain,
and came into the city Keilah to defend it from the
Philistines, Saul went down with a detachment of troops
to besiege him, so that he had to fly again to the mountains. Betrayed by the Ziphites, as he had been before
betrayed by the men of Keilah, he went to another wilderness and escaped. The king continued to pursue him
whenever he could get any tidings of his position, and
again David was obliged to take refuge among the Philistines. But throughout this whole period he never permitted himself any hostile measures against Saul, his im-
placable enemy. In this he showed great wisdom, for the
result of such a course would have been a civil war, in
which part of the nation would have taken sides with
one and part with the other, and David never could have
ascended the throne with the consent of the whole people.
But the consequence of his forbearance was, that when
by the death of Saul the throne became vacant, David
succeeded to it with scarcely any opposition. His subsequent course showed always the same prudence. He
disarmed his enemies by kindness and clemency. He
understood the policy of making a bridge of gold for a
flying enemy. When Abner, the most influential man of
his opponents, offered to submit to him, David received
him with kindness and made him a friend. And when
Abner was treacherously killed by Joab, David publicly
mourned for him, following the bier, and weeping at the
grave. The historian says concerning this: "And all the
people took notice of it and it pleased them : as whatsoever the king did pleased all the people. For all the
people understood that day that it was not of the king to

slay Abner the son of Ner." His policy was to conciliate and unite. When Saul's son was slain by his own servants, who thought to please David by that act, he immediately put them to death. Equally cautious and judicious was his course in transferring the Ark and its worship to Jerusalem. He did this only gradually, and as he saw that the people were prepared for it.

We next will look at David in his character as man of genius, musician, artist, poet. It is not often that an eminent statesman and soldier is, at the same time, a distinguished poet and writer. Sometimes they can write history or annals, like Cæsar and Frederick the Great; but the imaginative and poetic element is rarely found connected with the determined will and practical intellect of a great commander. Alexander the Great had a taste for good poetry, for he carried Homer with him through his campaigns; but the taste of Napoleon went no higher than a liking for Ossian.

But David was a poet, in whom the tender, lyrical, personal element rose to the highest point. The daring soldier, when he took his harp, became another man. He consoled himself and sought comfort in trial, and sang his thankfulness in his hours of joy. The Book of Psalms, so far as it is the work of David, is the record of his life. As Horace says of Lucilius and his book of Odes, that the whole of the old man's life hangs suspended therein in votive pictures; and as Goethe says that his Lyrics are a book of confessions, in which joy and sorrow turn to song; so the Book of Psalms can only be understood when we consider it as David's poetical autobiography. In this he anticipates the Koran, which was the private journal of Mohammed.

" The harp of David," says Herder, " was his comforter and friend. In his youth he sang to its music while tending his flocks as a shepherd on the mountains of Judæa. By its means he had access to Saul, and could sooth with it the dark mood of the king. In his days of exile he confided to it his sorrows. When he triumphed over his enemies the harp became in his royal hands a thank-offering to the deity. Afterward he organized on

a magnificent scale music and poetry in the worship of
God. Four thousand Levites, distinguished by a peculiar
dress, were arranged in classes and choirs under master-
singers, of whom the three most distinguished, Asaph,
Heman, and Jeduthun, are known to us by specimens of
their art. In his Psalms his whole kingdom lives."

We speak of the inspiration of genius, and distinguish
it from the inspiration of the religious teacher. But in
ancient times the prophet and poet were often the same,
and one word (as, in Latin, " vates ") was used for both.
In the case of David the two inspirations were perfectly
at one. His religion was poetry, and his poetry was religion. The genius of his poetry is not grandeur, but
beauty. Sometimes it expresses a single thought or sentiment, as that (Psalm cxxxiii.) describing the beauty of
brotherly union, or as that (Psalm xxiii.) which paints
trust in God like that of a sheep in his shepherd. Of
the same sort is the fifteenth Psalm, " Lord, who shall
abide in thy tabernacle ? " the twenty-ninth, a description
of a thunderstorm ; the sixty-seventh, " O God, be merciful to us and bless us " ; the eighty-fourth, " How lovely
are thy tabernacles " ; and the last Psalm, calling on mankind to praise God in all ways.

It is a striking fact that these Hebrew lyrics, written
long before the foundation of Rome, and before the time
of Homer, should be used to-day in Christian worship and
for private devotion all over the world.

In speaking of the Vedas and the Avesta we said that
in such hymns and liturgies the truest belief of a nation
can be found. What men say to God in their prayers
may be assumed to express their practical convictions.
The Jewish religion is not to be found so surely in its
Levitical code as in these national lyrics, which were the
liturgy of the people.*

---

* " Out from the heart of nature rolled
　　The burdens of the Bible old ;
　　The litanies of nations came,
　　Like the volcano's tongue of flame,
　　Up from the burning core below, —
　　The canticles of love and woe."

EMERSON, *The Problem.*

What then do they say concerning God ? They teach his universal dominion. They declare that none in the heaven can be compared to him (Psalm lxxxix.) ; that he is to be feared above all gods (Psalm xcvi.). They teach his eternity ; declaring that he is God from everlasting to everlasting ; that a thousand years in his sight are as yesterday ; that he laid the foundations of the earth and made the heavens, and that when these perish he will endure ; that at some period they shall be changed like a garment, but that God will always be the same (Psalm xc., cii.). They teach in numerous places that God is the Creator of all things. They adore and bless his fatherly love and kindness, which heals all our diseases and redeems our life, crowning us with loving-kindness, pitying us, and forgiving our sins (Psalm ciii.). They teach that he is in all nature (Psalm civ.), that he searches and knows all our thoughts, and that we can go nowhere from his presence (Psalm cxxxix.). They declare that he protects all who trust in him (Psalm xci., cxxi.), and that he purifies the heart and life (Psalm cxix.), creating in us a clean heart, and not asking for sacrifice, but for a broken spirit (Psalm li.).

These Psalms express the highest and best moments of Jewish life, and rise in certain points to the level of Christianity. They do not contain the Christian spirit of forgiveness, nor that of love to one's enemy. They are still narrowed to the range of the Jewish land and nation, and do not embrace humanity. They are mountain summits of faith, rising into the pure air and light of day from hidden depths, and appearing as islands in the ocean. They reach, here and there, the level of the vast continent, though not broad enough themselves to become the home of all races and nations.

There is nothing in the Vedas, nothing in the Avesta, nothing in the sacred books of Egypt, or the philosophy of Greece and Rome, which so unites the grandeur of omnipotence with the tenderness of a father toward his child.

§ 5. *Solomon ; or, the Religious Relapse.*

We have seen how the religion of Abraham, as the family worship of the Supreme Being, was developed into that of Moses, as the national worship of a just and holy King. We have seen it going onward from that, ascending in the inspirations of David into trust in an infinite God as a friend, and love to him as a father. We now come to a period of relapse. Under Solomon and his successors, this religion became corrupted and degraded. Its faith was changed into doubt, its lofty courage into the fear of kings and tyrants, its worship of the Most High into adoration of the idols of its neighbors. The great increase of power and wealth in the hands of Solomon corrupted his own heart and that of his people. Luxury came in ; and, as in Rome the old puritanic virtues were dissolved by the desire for wealth and pleasure, so it happened among the Jews. Then came the retribution, in the long captivity in Babylon, and the beginning of a new and better life under this hard discipline. And then comes the age of the Prophets, who gradually became the teachers of a higher and broader faith. So, when the Jews returned to Jerusalem, they came back purified, and prepared to become once more loyal subjects of Jehovah.

The principle of hereditary succession, but not of primogeniture, had been established by an agreement between David and the people when he proposed erecting a Temple at Jerusalem. He had appointed his son Solomon as his successor before his own death. With the entrance of Solomon we have an entirely different personality from any whom we have thus far met. With him also is inaugurated a new period and a different age. The age of Moses was distinguished as that of law, — on the side of God absolute authority, commanding and forbidding; on the side of man the only question was between obedience and disobedience. Moses was the Law-giver, and his age was the age of law. In the time of the Judges the question concerned national existence and national independence. The age of the Judges was the heroic age of the Jewish nation. The Judges were men combining religious faith with patriotism ; they were religious heroes. Then came the time of David, in which the nation, having become independent, became also powerful and wealthy. After his time the religion, instead of being a law to be obeyed or an impulse to action, became ceremony and pageant. Going one step further, it passed into reflection and meditation. In the age of Solomon the inspiration of the national religion had already gone. A great intellectual development had taken the place of inspiration. So that the Jewish nation seems to have passed through a fourfold religious experience. Religion was first law, then action, next inspiration and sentiment, afterward ceremony, and lastly opinion and intellectual culture.

It is the belief of Herder and other scholars that the age of Solomon gave birth to a copious literature, born of peace, tranquillity, and prosperity, which has all passed away except a few Psalms, the Book of Proverbs, Ecclesiastes, and the Song of Solomon.

Solomon is personally a much less interesting character than David ; for policy is never so interesting as impulse, and the crimes of policy seem worse than those of passion. The first act of Solomon was of this sort. He put his brother Adonijah to death for his attempt to seize the throne. Joab, who supported Adonijah against Solomon, was also put to death, for which we do not grieve, when we remember his assassination of Abner and Amasa, shedding the blood of war in peace. But the cold, unscrupulous character of Solomon is seen in his ordering Joab to be slain in the tabernacle while holding the horns of the altar, and causing Adonijah to be taken by force from the same place of refuge. No religious consideration or superstitious fear could prevent Solomon from doing what he thought necessary for his own security. He had given Adonijah a conditional pardon, limited to good behavior on his part. But after his establishment on the throne Adonijah requested the mother of Solomon, Bathsheba, to ask her son to give him for a wife the beautiful Abishag, the last wife of David. Solomon understood this to mean, what his mother did not understand, that his brother was still intriguing to supplant him on the throne, and with cool policy he ordered him to immediate execution. Solomon could pardon a criminal, but not a dangerous rival. He deposed the high-priest for the same reason, considering him to be also dangerous. Shimei, who seems to have been wealthy and influential as well as a determined character, was ordered not to leave Jerusalem under penalty of death. He did so, and Solomon put him to death. David, before his death, had warned Solomon to keep an eye both on Joab and on Shimei, for David could forgive his own enemies, but not those of his cause ; he was not afraid on his own account, but was afraid for the safety of his son.

By the death of Joab and Shimei, Solomon's kingdom was established, and the glory and power of David was carried to a still higher point of magnificence. Supported by the prophets on the one hand and by the priests on the other, his authority was almost unlimited. We are told that " Judah and Israel were many, as the sand which is by the sea in multitude, eating and drinking and making merry. And Solomon reigned over all kingdoms from the river unto the land of the Philistines, and unto the border of Egypt ; they brought presents, and served Solomon all the days of his life. And Solomon's provision for one day was thirty measures of fine flour, and threescore measures of meal, ten fat oxen, and twenty oxen out of the pastures, and an hundred sheep, beside harts, and roebucks, and fallow deer, and fatted fowl." The wars of David were ended. Solomon's was a reign of peace. " And Judah and Israel dwelt safely, every man under his vine and under his fig-tree, from Dan even to Beersheba, all the days of Solomon. And Solomon had forty thousand stalls of horses for his chariots, and twelve thousand horsemen." " And God gave Solomon wisdom and understanding exceeding much, and largeness of heart, even as the sand that is on the sea-shore. And Solomon's wisdom excelled the wisdom of all the children of the east country, and all the wisdom of Egypt. For he was wiser than all men ; than Ethan the Ezrahite, and Heman, and Chalcol, and Darda, the sons

of Mahol ; and his fame was in all nations round about."
" And there came of all people to hear the wisdom of
Solomon, from all kings of the earth, which had heard of
his wisdom." The great power and wealth of the Jewish
court at this period are historically verified by the traditions still extant among the Arabs of Solomon's superhuman splendor.

The story (1 Kings iii. 5) of Solomon's dream, in which
he chose an understanding heart and wisdom, rather than
riches and honor, reminds us of the choice of Hercules.
It is not unlikely that he had such a dream, it is quite
probable that he always preferred wisdom to anything
else, and it is certain that his wisdom came from God.
This is the only connection we can trace between the
dream and its fulfilment.

Solomon inaugurated a new policy by entering into
alliances and making treaties with his powerful neighbors. He formed an alliance with the king of Egypt, and
married his daughter. He also made a treaty of commerce and friendship with the king of Tyre on the north,
and procured from him cedar with which to build the
Temple and his own palace. He received an embassy also
from the queen of Sheba, who resided in the south of
Arabia. By means of the Tyrian ships he traded to the
west as far as the coasts of Spain and Africa, and his own
vessels made a coasting voyage of three years' duration to
Tarshish, from which they brought ivory, gold, silver, apes,
and peacocks. This voyage seems to have been through
the Red Sea to India.* He also traded in Asia, over-
land, with caravans. And for their accommodation and
defence he built Tadmor in the desert (afterward called
Palmyra), as a great stopping-place. This city in later
days became famous as the capital of Zenobia, and the
remains of the Temple of the Sun, standing by itself in
the midst of the Great Desert, are among the most interesting ruins in the world.†

* See this point fully discussed in Ritter, Palestine (Am. ed.), Vol. I.
pp. 81 – 151.
† See Weil, Biblical Legends, for the Mohammedan traditions concerning Solomon.

The great work of Solomon was building the Temple at Jerusalem in the year B. C. 1005. This Temple was destroyed, and rebuilt by Nehemiah B. C. 445. It was rebuilt by Herod B. C. 17. Little remains from the time of Solomon, except some stones in the walls of the substructions; and the mosque of Omar now stands on the old foundation. No building of antiquity so much resembles the Temple of Solomon as the palace of Darius at Persepolis. In both buildings the porch opened into the large hall, both had small chambers on the side, square masses on both sides of the porch, and the same form of pillars. The parts of Solomon's Temple were, first, a porch thirty feet wide and fifteen feet deep ; second a large hall sixty by thirty ; and then the holy of holies, which was thirty feet cube. The whole external dimensions of the building were only sixty feet by one hundred and twenty, or less than many an ordinary parish church. The explanation is that it was copied from the Tabernacle, which was a small building, and was necessarily somewhat related to it in size. The walls were of stone, on extensive stone foundations. Inside it was lined with cedar, with floors of cypress, highly ornamented with carvings and gold. The brass work consisted of two ornamented pillars called Jachin and Boaz, a brazen tank supported by twelve brass oxen, and ten baths of brass, ornamented with figures of lions, oxen, and cherubim.

The Book of Kings says of Solomon (1 Kings iv. 32) that "he spake three thousand proverbs, and his songs were a thousand and five. And he spake of trees, from the cedar-tree that is in Lebanon even unto the hyssop that springeth out of the wall : he spake also of beasts, and of fowl and of creeping things, and of fishes." He was, according to this account, a voluminous writer on natural history, as well as an eminent poet and moralist. Of all his compositions there remains but one, the Book of Proverbs, which was probably in great part composed by him. It is true that three books in the Old Testament bear his name, — Proverbs, Ecclesiastes, and the Song of Songs. But of these Ecclesiastes was probably written afterward, and though the Song of Songs may have been written by Solomon, it was probably the work of another, living at or near his time.

But of the Book of Proverbs there cannot be much doubt. It contains some of the three thousand of which Solomon was the reputed author. It shows his style of mind very clearly, — the cool understanding, the calculating prudence, the continual reference to results, knowledge of the world as distinguished from knowledge of human nature, or of individual character. The Book of Proverbs contains little heroism or poetry, few large ideas, not much enthusiasm or sentiment. It is emphatically a book of wisdom. It has good, hard, practical sense. It is the " Poor Richard's Almanac " of Hebrew literature. We can conceive of King Solomon and Benjamin Franklin consulting together, and comparing notes of their observations on human life, with much mutual satisfaction. It is curious to meet with such a thoroughly Western intellect, a thousand years before Christ, on the throne of the heroic David.

Among these proverbs there are many of a kindly character. Some are semi-Christian in their wise benevolence. Many show great shrewdness of observation, and have an epigrammatic wit. We will give examples of each kind : —

PROVERBS HAVING A SEMI-CHRISTIAN CHARACTER.

"If thine enemy be hungry, give him bread ;
If thirsty, give him water to drink,
For thou wilt heap coals of fire on his head,
And Jehovah will reward thee."

"To deliver those that are dragged to death,
Those that totter to the slaughter,
Spare thyself not.
If thou sayest, Behold, we knew it not,
Doth not He that weighs the heart observe it ?
Yea, He that keeps thy soul knows it.
And He will render to every man according to his works.",

"Put not thyself forth in the presence of the king,
Nor station thyself in the place of great men.
Far better it is that one should say to thee,
Come up hither !
Than that he should put thee in a lower place,
In the presence of the prince."

19

"The lip of truth shall be established forever,
But the tongue of falsehood is but for a moment."

PROVERBS SHOWING SHREWDNESS OF OBSERVATION.

" As one that takes a dog by the ears,
So is he that passing by becomes enraged on account of another's quarrel."

" Where there is no wood the fire goes out;
So where there is no talebearer contention ceases."

" The rich rules over the poor,
And the borrower is servant to the lender."

" The slothful man says, There is a lion without,
I shall be slain in the streets."

" A reproof penetrates deeper into a wise man
Than a hundred stripes into a fool."

" Hope deferred makes the heart sick."

" The way of transgressors is hard."

"There is that scatters, and yet increases."

" It is naught, it is naught, saith the buyer,
But when he goeth his way then he boasteth."

PROVERBS WITTILY EXPRESSED.

" The legs of a lame man are not equal,
So is a proverb in the mouth of fools." *

" As a thorn runs into the hand of a drunkard,
So is a proverb in the mouth of a fool."†

" As clouds and wind without rain,
So is a man who boasts falsely of giving."

" A soft tongue breaks bones."

" As vinegar to the teeth, and smoke to the eyes,
So is the sluggard to him that sends him."

" The destruction of the poor is their poverty."

" A merry heart is a good medicine."

But what are human wisdom and glory? It seems that
Solomon was to illustrate its emptiness. See the king,
in his old age, sinking into idolatry and empty luxury,

---

* For he perceives the idea, but not its application to himself.
† Neither of them perceives that he is the object of the injury.

falling away from his God, and pointing the moral of his own proverbs. He himself was the drunkard, into whose hand the thorn of the proverb penetrated, without his heeding it. This prudent and wise king, who understood so well all the snares of temptation and all the arts of virtue, fell like the puppet of any Asiatic court. What a contrast between the wise and great king as described in 1 Kings iv. 20 – 34 and the same king in his degenerate old age !

It was this last period in the life of Solomon which the writer of Ecclesiastes took as the scene and subject of his story. With marvellous penetration and consummate power he penetrates the mind of Solomon and paints the blackness of desolation, the misery of satiety, the dreadful darkness of a soul which has given itself to this world as its only sphere.

Never was such a picture painted of utter scepticism, of a mind wholly darkened, and without any remaining faith in God or truth.

These three books mark the three periods of the life of Solomon.

The Song of Songs shows us his abounding youth, full of poetry, fire, and charm.

The Proverbs give his ripened manhood, wise and full of all earthly knowledge, — Aristotle, Bacon, Socrates, and Franklin, all in one.

And Ecclesiastes represents the darkened and gloomy scepticism of his old age, when he sank as low down as he had before gone up. But though so sad and dark, yet it is not without gleams of a higher and nobler joy to come. Better than anything in Proverbs are some of the noble sentiments breaking out in Ecclesiastes, especially at the end of the book.

The Book of Ecclesiastes is a wonderful description of a doubt so deep, a despair so black, that nothing in all literature can be compared to it. It describes, in the person of Solomon, utter scepticism born of unlimited worldly enjoyment, knowledge, and power.

The book begins by declaring that all is vanity, that there is nothing new under the sun, no progress in any direction, but all things revolving in an endless circle, so that there is neither meaning nor use in the world.* It declares that *work* amounts to nothing, for one cannot do any really good thing ; that knowledge is of no use, but only produces sorrow ; that pleasure satiates.† Knowledge has only this advantage over ignorance, that it enables us to see things as they are, but it does not make them better, and the end of all is despair. ‡ Sensual pleasure is the only good. § Fate and necessity rule all things. Good and evil both come at their appointed time. Men are cheated and do not see the nullity of things, because they have the world in their heart, and are absorbed in the present moment. ‖

Men are only a higher class of beasts. They die like beasts, and have no hereafter.¶

In the fourth chapter the writer goes more deeply into this pessimism. He says that to die is better than to live, and better still never to have been born. A fool is better than a wise man, because he does nothing and cares for nothing.**

Success is bad, progress is an evil ; for these take us away from others, and leave us lonely, because above them and hated by them.††

Worship is idle. Do not offer the sacrifice of fools, but stop when you are going to the Temple, and return. Do not pray. It is of no use. God does not hear you. Dreams do not come from God, but from what you were doing before you went to sleep. Eat and drink, that is the best. ‡‡ All men go as they come.

So the dreary statement proceeds. Men are born for no end, and go no one can tell where. Live a thousand years, it all comes to the same thing. Who can tell what is good for a man in this shadowy, empty life ? §§

It is better to look on death than on life, wiser to be

* Eccles. i. 2 – 11.
† Ibid. i. 12 ; ii. 11.
‡ Ibid. ii. 12 – 20.
§ Ibid. ii. 24.
‖ Ibid. iii. 1 – 11.

¶ Ibid. iii. 18 – 21.
** Ibid. iv. 1 – 3.
†† Ibid. iv. 9 – 12.
‡‡ Ibid. v. 1 – 7, 18.
§§ Ibid. vi.

sad than to be cheerful. If you say, "There *have been* good times in the past," do not be too sure of that. If you say, "We can be good, at least, if we cannot be happy," there is such a thing as being *too* good, and cheating yourself out of pleasure.*

Women are worse than men. You may find one good man among a thousand, but not one good woman.†

It is best to be on the right side of the powers that be, for they can do what they please. Speedy and certain punishment alone can keep men from doing evil. The same thing happens to the good and to the wicked. All things come alike to all. This life is, in short, an inexplicable puzzle. The perpetual refrain is, eat, drink, and be merry. ‡

It is best to do what you can, and think nothing about it. Cast your bread on the waters, very likely you will get it again. Sow your seed either in the morning or at night ; it makes no difference. §

Death is coming to all. All is vanity. I continue to preach, because I see the truth, and may as well say it, though there is no end to talking and writing. You may sum up all wisdom in six words : " Fear God and keep his commandments." ‖

The Book of Ecclesiastes teaches a great truth in an unexampled strain of pathetic eloquence. It teaches what a black scepticism descends on the wisest, most fortunate, most favored of mankind, when he looks only to this world and its joys. It could, however, only have been written by one who had gone through this dreadful experience. The intellect alone never sounded such depths as these. Moreover, it could hardly have been written unless in a time when such scepticism prevailed, nor by one who, having lived it all, had not also lived *through* it all, and found the cure for this misery in pure unselfish obedience to truth and right. It seems, therefore, like a Book of

---

* Eccles. vii. 2, 10, 15, 16.
† Ibid. vii. 26 – 28.
‡ Ibid. viii. 2, 3, 4, 11, 14 (ix. 2, 3), 15, 17.
§ Ibid. xi. 1, 2, 6.
‖ Ibid. xii. 1 – 8, 9, 12, 13.

Confessions, or the Record of an Experience, and as such well deserves its place in the Bible and Jewish literature.

The Book of Job is a still more wonderful production, but in a wholly different tone. It is full of manly faith in truth and right. It has no jot of scepticism in it. It is a noble protest against all hypocrisies and all shams. Job does not know why he is afflicted, but he will never confess that he is a sinner till he sees it. The Pharisaic friends tell him his sufferings are judgments for his sins, and advise him to admit it to be so. But Job refuses, and declares he will utter no "words of wind" to the Almighty. The grandest thought is here expressed in the noblest language which the human tongue has ever uttered.

§ 6. *The Prophets; or, Judaism as the Hope of a spiritual and universal Kingdom of God.*

Before we proceed to examine the prophetic writings of the Old Testament, it is desirable to make some remarks upon prophecy in general, and on the character of the Hebrew prophets.

Prophecy in general is a modification of inspiration. Inspiration is sight, or rather it is insight. *All* our knowledge comes to us through the intellectual power which may be called sight, which is of two kinds, — the sight of external things, or outsight; and the sight of internal things, which is insight, or intuition. The senses constitute the organization by which we see external things; consciousness is the organization by which we perceive internal things. Now the organs of sense are the same in kind, but differ in degree in all men. All human beings, as such, have the power of perceiving an external world, by means of the five senses. But though all have these five senses, all do not perceive the same external phenomena by means of them. For, in the first place, their senses differ in degrees of power. Some men's eyes are telescopic, some microscopic, and some are blind. Some men can but partially distinguish colors, others not at all. Some have acute hearing, others are deaf. And secondly, what men perceive through the senses differs according to what is about them. A man living in China cannot see Mont Blanc or the city of New York; a man on the other side of the moon can never see the earth. A man living in the year 1871 cannot see Alexander the Great or the Apostle Paul. And thirdly, two persons may be looking at the same thing, and with senses of the same degree of power, and yet one may be able to see what the other is not able to see. Three men, one a geologist, one a botanist, and one a painter, may look at the same landscape, and one will see the stratification, the second will see the flora, and the third the picturesque qualities of the scene. As regards outsight then, though men in general have the same senses to see with, what they see depends (1) on their quality of sense, (2) on their position in space and time, (3) and on their state of mental culture.

That which is true of the perception of external phenomena is also true of the perception of internal things.

Insight, or intuition, has the same limitations as outsight. These are (1) the quality of the faculty of intuition; (2) the inward circumstances or position of the soul; (3) the soul's culture or development. Those who deny the existence of an intuitive faculty, teaching that all knowledge comes from without through the senses, sometimes say that if there were such a faculty as intuition, men would all possess intuitively the same knowledge of moral and spiritual truth. They might as well say that, as all men have eyes, all must see the same external objects.

All men have more or less of the intuitive faculty, but some have much more than others. Those who have the most are called, by way of eminence, inspired men. But among these there is a difference as regards the objects which are presented by God, in the order of his providence, to their intuitive faculty. Some he places inwardly among visions of beauty, and they are inspired poets and artists. Others he places inwardly amid visions of temporal and human life, and they become inspired discoverers and inventors. And others he places amid visions of religious truth, and they are inspired prophets, lawgivers, and evangelists. But these again differ in their own spiritual culture and growth. Moses and the Apostle Paul were both inspired men, but the Apostle Paul saw truths which Moses did not see, because the Apostle Paul had reached a higher degree of spiritual culture. Christ alone possessed the fulness of spiritual inspiration, because he alone had attained the fulness of spiritual life.

Now the inspired man may look inwardly either at the past, the present, or the future. If he look at the past he is an inspired historian; if at the present, an inspired lawgiver, or religious teacher; if at the future, an inspired prophet. The inspired faculty may be the same, and the difference may be in the object inwardly present to its contemplation. The seer may look from things past to things present, from things present to things to come, and his inspiration be the same. He fixes his mind on the past, and it grows clear before him, and he sees how events were and what they mean. He looks at the present, and sees how things ought to be. He looks at the future, and sees how things shall be.

The Prophets of the Old Testament were not, as is commonly supposed, men who only uttered predictions of the future. They were men of action more than of contemplation. Strange as it may seem to us, who are accustomed to consider their office as confined to religious prediction, their chief duty was that of active politicians. They mixed religion and politics. They interfered with public measures, rebuked the despotism of the kings and the political errors of the people. Moreover, they were the constitutional lawyers and publicists of the Hebrews, inspired to look backward and explain the meaning of the Mosaic law as well as to look forward to its spiritual development in the reign of the Messiah. Prediction, therefore, of future events, was a very small part of the work of the Prophets. Their main duty was to warn, rebuke, teach, exhort, and encourage.

The Hebrew prophets were under the law. They were loyal to Moses and to his institutions. But it was to the spirit rather than to the letter, the idea rather than the form. They differed from the priests in preferring the moral part of the law to the ceremonial. They were great reformers in bringing back the people from external formalism to vital obedience. They constantly made the ceremonial part of the law subservient to the moral part of the law. Thus Samuel said to Saul: " Hath the Lord as great delight in burnt offerings and sacrifices as in obeying the voice of the Lord ? Behold, to obey is better than sacrifice, and to hearken than the fat of rams." And so afterward Isaiah declared in the name of the Lord, that the sacrifices of a wicked people were vain, and their incense an abomination.

We read of the schools of the Prophets, where they studied the law of Moses, and were taught the duties of their office. In these schools music was made use of as a medium of inspiration.

But the office of a prophet was not limited by culture, sex, age, or condition. Women, like Miriam, Deborah, Hannah, Huldah, and Noadiah ; inexperienced youths, like Jeremiah ; men of high standing in society, like Isaiah and Daniel ; humble men, like the ploughman Elisha and the herdsman Amos ; men married and unmarried, are numbered among the Prophets. Living poorly, wearing sackcloth, feeding on vegetables, imprisoned or assassinated by kings, stoned by the people, the most unpopular of men, sometimes so possessed by the spirit as to rave like madmen, obliged to denounce judgments and woes against kings and people, it is no wonder that they often shrank from their terrible office. Jonah ran to hide in a ship of Tarshish. They have called their message a burden, like Isaiah ; they have cried out like Jeremiah, " Ah, Lord God, I cannot speak, for I am a child " ; like Ezekiel, they have been obliged to make their faces harder than flints in order to deliver their message.

Dean Stanley, in speaking of the Prophets of the Old Testament, says that their theology consisted in proclaiming the unity of God against all polytheism, and the spirituality of God against all idolatry, in declaring the superiority of moral to ceremonial duties, and in announcing the supremacy of goodness above the letter, ceremony, or

19 *

dogma. This makes the contrast between the Prophets and all other sacred persons who have existed in pagan and, he adds, even in Christian times. Dean Stanley says the Prophets were religious teachers, without the usual faults of religious teachers, and he proposes them as an example to the Christian clergy. He says: " O, if the spirit of our profession, of our order, of our body, were the spirit, or anything like the spirit, of the ancient Prophets! If with us truth, charity, justice, fairness to opponents, were a passion, a doctrine, a point of honor, to be upheld with the same energy as that with which we uphold our own position and our own opinions !"

The spirit of the world asks first, Is it safe ? secondly, Is it true ? The spirit of the Prophets asks first, Is it true ? secondly, Is it safe ? The spirit of the world asks first, Is it prudent ? secondly, Is it right ? The spirit of the Prophets asks first, Is it right ? secondly, Is it prudent ? Taken as a whole, the prophetic order of the Jewish Church remains alone. It stands like one of those vast monuments of ancient days, with ramparts broken, with inscriptions defaced, but stretching from hill to hill, conveying in its long line of arches the pure rill of living water over deep valley and thirsty plain, far above all the puny modern buildings which have grown up at its feet, and into the midst of which it strides with its massive substructions, its gigantic height, its majestic proportions, unrivalled by any erection of modern time.

The predictions of the future by the Prophets of Judæa were far higher in their character than those which come occasionally to mankind through dreams and presentiments. Yet no doubt they proceeded from the same essentially human faculty. This also is asserted by the Dean of Westminster, who says that there is a power of divination granted in some inexplicable manner to ordinary men, and he refers to such instances as the prediction of the discovery of America by Seneca, that of the Reformation by Dante, and the prediction of the twelve centuries of Roman dominion by the apparition of twelve vultures to Romulus, which was so understood four hundred years before its actual accomplishment. If such presentiments are not always verified, neither were the predictions of the Prophets always fulfilled. Jonah announced, in the most distinct and absolute terms, that in forty days Nineveh should be destroyed. But the people repented, and it was *not* destroyed. Their predictions of the Messiah are remarkable, especially because in speaking of him and his time they went out of the law and the spirit of the law, and became partakers of the spirit of the Gospel. The Prophets of the Jews, whatever else we deny to their predictions, certainly foresaw Christianity. They describe the coming of a time in which the law should be written in the heart, of a king who should reign in righteousness, of a prince of peace, of one who should rule by the power of truth, not by force, whose kingdom should be universal and everlasting, and into which all nations of the earth should flow. What the Prophets foresaw was not times nor seasons, not dates nor names, not any minute particulars. But they saw a future age, they lived out of their own time in another time, which had not yet arrived. They left behind them Jewish ceremonialism, and entered into a moral and spiritual religion. They dropped Jewish narrowness and called all mankind brethren. In this they reach the highest form of foresight, which is not simply to predict a coming event, but to live in the spirit of a future time.

Thus the Prophets developed the Jewish religion to its highest point. The simple, childlike faith of Abraham became, in their higher vision, the sight of a universal Father, and of an age in which all men and nations should be united into one great moral kingdom. Further than this, it was not possible to go in vision. The difference between the Prophets and Jesus was, that he accomplished what they foresaw. His life, full of faith in God and man, became the new seed of a higher kingdom than that of David. He was the son of David, as inheriting the loving trust of David in a heavenly Father; he was also the Lord of David, by fulfilling David's love to God with his own love to man; making piety and charity one, faith and freedom one, reason and religion one, this life and the life to come one. He died to accomplish this union and to make this atoning sacrifice.

§ 7. *Judaism as a Preparation for Christianity.*

After the return from the captivity the Jewish nation remained loyal to Jehovah. The dangers of polytheism and idolatry had passed. We no more hear of either of these tendencies, but, on the contrary, a rigid and almost bigoted monotheism was firmly established. Their sufferings, the teaching of their Prophets, perhaps the influence of the Persian worship, had confirmed them in the belief that Jehovah was one and alone, and that the gods of the nations were idols. They had lost forever the sacred ark of the covenant and the mysterious ornaments of the high-priest. Their kings had disappeared, and a new form of theocracy took the place of a royal government. The high-priest, with the great council, became the supreme authority. The government was hierarchal.

Hellenic influences began to act on the Jewish mind, and a peculiar dialect of Hebrew-Greek, called the Hellenistic, was formed. The Septuagint, or Greek version of the Old Testament, was made in Alexandria about B. C. 260. In Egypt, Greek philosophy began to affect the Jewish mind, the final result of which was the system of Philo. Greek influences spread to such an extent that a great religious revolution took place in Palestine (B. C. 170), and the Temple at Jerusalem was turned into a temple of Olympic Jupiter. Many of the priests and leading citizens accepted this change, though the heart of the people rejected it with horror. Under Antiochus the Temple was profaned, the sacrifices ceased, the keeping 'of the Sabbath and use of the Scriptures were forbidden by a royal edict. Then arose the Maccabees, and after a long and bitter struggle re-established the worship of Jehovah, B. C. 141.

After this the mass of the people, in their zeal for the law and their old institutions, fell into the narrow bigotry of the Pharisees. The Sadducees were Jewish Epicureans, but though wealthy were few, and had little influence. The Essenes were Jewish monks, living in communities, and as little influential as are the Shakers in Massachusetts to-day. They were not only few, but their whole system was contrary to the tone of Jewish thought, and was probably derived from Orphic Pythagoreanism.*

The Talmud, that mighty maze of Jewish thought, commencing after the return from the captivity, contains the history of the gradual progress and development of the national mind. The study of the Talmud is necessary to the full understanding of the rise of Christianity. Many of the parables and precepts of Jesus may have had their origin in these traditions and teachings. For the Talmud contains much that is excellent, and the originality of Jesus was not in saying what never had been thought before, but in vitalizing all old truth out of a central spiritual life. His originality was not novelty, but vitality. We have room here but for a single extract.†

" ' Six hundred and thirteen injunctions,' says the Talmud, ' was Moses instructed to give to the people. David reduced them all to eleven, in the fifteenth Psalm : Lord, who shall abide in thy tabernacle who shall dwell on thy holy hill ? He that walketh uprightly,' &c.

" ' The Prophet Isaiah reduced them to six (xxxiii. 15) : He that walketh righteously,' &c.

" ' The Prophet Micah reduced them to three (vi. 8) : What doth the Lord require of thee but to do justly, and to love mercy, and to walk humbly with thy God ?

" ' Isaiah once more reduced them to two (lvi. 1) : Keep ye judgment and do justice.

" ' Amos (v. 4) reduced them all to one : Seek ye me and ye shall live.

" ' But lest it might be supposed from this that God could be found in the fulfilment of his whole law only, Habakkuk said (ii. 4) : The just shall live by his faith.' "

Thus we have seen the Jewish religion gradually developed out of the family worship of Abraham, through the national worship of the law to the personal and filial trust of David, and the spiritual monotheism of Job and the Prophets. Through all these changes there ran the one golden thread of faith in a Supreme Being who was not hidden and apart from the world, but who came to man as to his child.

* Döllinger, The Gentile and the Jew.
† See article on the Talmud, Quarterly Review, 1867.

At first this belief was narrow and like that of a child.[*]
We read that when Noah went into the ark, "the Lord
shut him in"; that when Babel was built, "the Lord
came down to see the city and the tower which the children of men had built"; that when Noah offered burnt-
sacrifices, "the Lord smelled a sweet savor"; that he told
Moses to make him a sanctuary, that he might dwell
among the Israelites.   We have seen, in our chapter on
Greece, that Homer makes Jupiter send a pernicious
dream to Agamemnon, to deceive him; in other words,
makes Jupiter tell a lie to Agamemnon.   But how is the
account in 1 Kings xxii. 20 – 23, any better?[†]

But how all this ignorance was enlightened, and this
narrowness enlarged, let the magnificent theism of the
Psalms, of Job, and of Isaiah testify.   Solomon declares
"The heaven of heavens cannot contain him, how much
less this house that I have builded."   Job and the Psalms
and Isaiah describe the omniscience, omnipresence, and
inscrutable perfections of the Deity in language to which
twenty centuries have been able to add nothing.[‡]

Thus Judaism was monotheism, first as a seed, then as
a blade, and then as the ear which the sun of Christianity was to ripen into the full corn.   The highest truth
was present, implicitly, in Judaism, and became explicit
in Christianity.   The law was the schoolmaster to bring
men to Christ.   It taught, however imperfectly, a supreme
and living God; a Providence ruling all things; a Judge
rewarding good and punishing evil; a holy Being, of
purer eyes than to behold iniquity.   It announced a moral

---

[*] An anecdote was recently related of a little girl, five years old, who
was seen walking along the road, looking up into the trees.   Being asked
what she was seeking, she replied: "Mamma told me God was everywhere, but I cannot see him in that tree."   The faith of the patriarchs
was like that of this child, — not false, but unenlightened.

[†] "And the Lord said, Who shall persuade Ahab, that he may go up
and fall at Ramoth-Gilead?   And one said on this manner, and another
said on that manner.   And there came forth a spirit, and stood before
the Lord, and said, I will persuade him.   And the Lord said unto him,
Wherewith?   And he said, I will go forth, and I will be a lying spirit in
the mouth of all his prophets.   And he said, Thou shalt persuade him,
and prevail also : go forth and do so."

[‡] See Greg, The Creed of Christendom, Chap. V.   Also, The Spirit of
the Bible, by Edward Higginson.

law to be obeyed, the substance of which was to love God with all the heart, and one's neighbor as one's self.

Wherever the Apostles of Christ went they found that Judaism had prepared the way. Usually, in every place, they first preached to the Jews, and made converts of them. For Judaism, though so narrow and so alien to the Greek and Latin thought, had nevertheless pervaded all parts of the Roman Empire. Despised and satirized by philosophers and poets, it had yet won its way by its strength of conviction. It offered to men, not a philosophy, but a religion ; not thought, but life. Too intolerant of differences to convert the world to monotheism, it yet made a preparation for its conversion. This was its power, and thus it went before the face of the Master, to prepare his way.

CHAPTER XI.

MOHAMMED AND ISLAM.

§ 1. Recent Works on the Life of Mohammed.   § 2. The Arabs and
   Arabia.   § 3. Early Life of Mohammed, to the Hegira.   § 4. Change
   in the Character of Mohammed after the Hegira.   § 5. Religious Doc-
   trines and Practices among the Mohammedans.   § 6. The Criticism of
   Mr. Palgrave on Mohammedan Theology.   § 7.   Mohammedanism a
   Relapse ; the worst Form of Monotheism, and a retarding Element in
   Civilization.   NOTE.

§ 1. *Recent Works on the Life of Mohammed.*

DR. SAMUEL JOHNSON once declared, "There are
two objects of curiosity, the Christian world and
the Mohammedan world ; all the rest may be considered
as barbarous." Since Dr. Johnson's time we have learned
to be curious about other forms of human thought, and
regard the famous line of Terence as expressing more
accurately the proper frame of mind for a Christian philosopher.   Nevertheless, Mohammedanism still claims a
special interest and excites a peculiar curiosity. It is the
only religion which has threatened Christianity with a
dangerous rivalry.   It is the only other religion whose
origin is in the broad daylight of history.   Its author is
the only one among the great men of the world who has
at the same time founded a religion, formed a people, and
established an empire.   The marvellous spread of this
religion is a mystery which never ceases to stimulate the
mind to new inquiry.   How was it that in the short
space of a century the Arab tribes, before always at war
among themselves, should have been united into an irresistible power, and have conquered Syria, Persia, the whole
of Northern Africa and Spain ?   And with this religious
outbreak, this great revival of monotheism in Asia, there
came also as remarkable a renaissance of learning, which
made the Arabs the teachers of philosophy and art to

Europe during a long period. Arab Spain was a focus of light while Christian Europe lay in mediæval darkness. And still more interesting and perplexing is the character of Mohammed himself. What was he, — an impostor or a prophet ? Did his work advance or retard human progress ? What is his position in history ? Such are some of the questions on which we shall endeavor to throw light in the present chapter.

Within a few years new materials for this study have been made accessible by the labors of Weil, Caussin de Perceval, Muir, Sprenger, Döllinger, and Arnold. Dr. Gustav Weil published his work * in 1843. It was drawn from Arabic manuscripts and the Koran. When Weil began his studies on Mohammed in 1837, he found no book except that of Gagnier, published in 1732, from which he could derive substantial aid. But Gagnier had only collected, without any attempt at criticism, the traditions and statements concerning Mohammed believed by orthodox Moslems. Satisfied that a literary want existed at this point, Dr. Weil devoted himself to such studies as should enable him to supply it ; and the result was a work concerning which Milman says that " nothing has escaped " the diligence of its author. But four years after appeared the book of M. Caussin de Perceval,† a work of which M. Saint-Hilaire says that it marks a new era in these studies, on account of the abundance and novelty of its details, and the light thrown on the period which in Arabia preceded the coming of Mohammed. Dr. A. Sprenger, an eminent German scholar, early determined to devote himself to the study of Oriental literature in the East. He spent a long time in India, and was for twelve years principal of a Mohammedan school in Delhi, where he established, in 1845, an illustrated penny magazine in the Hindoo language. After returning to Europe with a vast number of Oriental man-

* Mohammed der Prophet, sein Leben und seine Lehre. Stuttgart, 1843.
† Essai sur l'histoire des Arabes, avant l'Islamisme, pendant l'époque de Mahomet, et jusqu'à la réduction de toutes les tribus sous la loi mussulmane. Paris. 3 vols. 8vo. 1847–48.

uscripts, he composed his Life of Mohammed,[*] the result of extensive studies. Among the preparations for this work we will cite only one. Dr. Sprenger edited in Calcutta the first volume of the Içâba, which contains the names and biographies of *eight thousand* persons who were personally acquainted with Mohammed.[†] But, as if to embarrass us with riches, comes also Mr. Muir [‡] and presents us with another life of the prophet, likewise drawn from original sources, and written with learning and candor.   This work, in four volumes, goes over the whole ground of the history of Arabia before the coming of the prophet, and then, from Arabic sources, narrates the life of Mohammed himself, up to the era of the Hegira. The result of these researches is that we know accurately what Mr. Hallam in his time despaired of knowing, — all the main points of the history of Mohammed. There is no legend, no myth, to trouble us. M. Saint-Hilaire says that the French are far less acquainted with Charlemagne than the Moslems are with their prophet, who came two centuries earlier.

A Mohammedan writer, Syed Ahmed Khan Bahador, has lately published, in English, a series of Essays on the life of Mohammed, Arabia, the Arabs, Mohammedan traditions, and kindred topics, written from the stand-point of a believer in Islam. § He is dissatisfied with all the recent works on Mohammed, including those of Dr. Sprenger and Mr. Muir. He believes that the Arabic sources from which these biographies are derived are not the most authentic. The special objections, however, which this able Mohammedan urges against these European biographies by Sprenger and Muir do not affect any of the important points in the history, but only details of small moment. Notwithstanding his criticisms, therefore,

---

* Das Leben und die Lehre des Mohammed, etc. Von A. Sprenger. Berlin, 1861.

† Sprenger, Vorrede, p. xii.

‡ The Life of Mahomet and History of Islam. By William Muir, Esq. London, 1858.

§ A Series of Essays on the Life of Mohammed, and Subjects subsidiary thereto. By Syed Ahmed Khan Bahador. London : Trübner & Co. 1870.

we may safely assume that we are in a condition to understand the actual life and character of Mohammed. All that the Syed says concerning the duty of an impartial and friendly judgment of Islam and its author is, of course, true. We shall endeavor in our treatment of Mohammed to follow this exhortation.

Something, however, is always gained by hearing what the believers in a system have to say in its behalf, and these essays of the Mohammedan scholar may help us in this way. One of the most curious parts of the volume is that in which he treats of the prophecies concerning Mohammed in the Old and New Testament. Most of our readers will be surprised at learning that any such prophecies exist; and yet some of them are quite as striking as many of those commonly adduced by writers on prophecy as referring to Jesus Christ. For example (Deut. xviii. 15, 18), when Moses predicts that the Lord will raise up a prophet for the Jews, *from among their brethren;* by emphasizing this latter clause, and arguing that the Jews had no brethren except the Ishmaelites, from whom Mohammed was born, an argument is derived that the latter was referred to. This is strengthened by the declaration of Moses, that this prophet should be "*like unto me,*" since Deuteronomy xxxiv. 10 declares that "there arose no prophet *in Israel* like unto Moses."

Habakkuk iii. 3 says : "The Holy One came from Mount Paran." But Mount Paran, argues our friend, is the mountain of Mecca.

The Hebrew word translated "desire" in Haggai ii. 7, "The desire of all nations shall come," is said by Bahador to be the same word as the name Mohammed. He is therefore predicted by his name in this passage.

When Isaiah says (xxi. 7), according to the Septuagint translation, that he "saw two riders, one on an ass and one on a camel," Bahador argues that the rider on the ass is Jesus, who so entered Jerusalem, and that the rider on the camel is Mohammed.

When John the Baptist was asked if he were the Christ, or Elijah, or "that prophet," Mohammedans say that "that prophet," so anticipated, was their own.

§ 2. *The Arabs and Arabia.*

The Arabs are a Semitic people, belonging to the same great ethnologic family with the Babylonians, Assyrians, Phœnicians, Hebrews, Ethiopians, and Carthaginians.   It is a race which has given to civilized man his literature and his religion ; for the alphabet came from the Phœnicians, and the Bible from the Jews.   In Hannibal, it produced perhaps the greatest military genius the world has seen ; and the Tyrian merchants, circumnavigating Africa, discovering Great Britain, and trading with India, ten centuries before Christ, had no equals on the ocean until the time of the Portuguese discoveries, twenty-five centuries after.   The Arabs alone, of the seven Semitic families, remained undistinguished and unknown till the days of Mohammed.   Their claim of being descended from Abraham is confirmed by the unerring evidence of language.   The Arabic roots are, nine tenths of them, identical with the Hebrew ; and a similarity of grammatical forms shows a plain glossological relation.   But while the Jews have a history from the days of Abraham, the Arabs had none till Mohammed.   During twenty centuries these nomads wandered to and fro, engaged in mutual wars, verifying the prediction (Gen. xvi. 12) concerning Ishmael : " He will be a wild man ; his hand will be against every man, and every man's hand against him."   Wherever such wandering races exist, whether in Arabia, Turkistan, or Equatorial Africa, " darkness covers the earth, and gross darkness the people."   The earth has no geography, and the people no history.   During all this long period, from the time of Abraham to that of Mohammed, the Arabs were not a nation, but only a multitude of tribes, either stationary or wandering.   But of these two the nomad or Bedouin is the true type of the race as it exists in Northern Arabia.   The Arab of the South is in many respects different, — in language, in manners, and in character, — confirming the old opinion of a double origin.   But the Northern Arab in his tent has remained unchanged since the days of the Bible.   Proud of his pure blood, of his freedom, of his tribe, and of his ancient customs, he desires no change. He is, in Asia, what the North American Indian is upon the western continent. As the Indian's, his chief virtues are courage in war, cunning, wild justice, hospitality, and fortitude. He is, however, of a better race, — more reflective, more religious, and with a thirst for knowledge. The pure air and the simple food of the Arabian plains keep him in perfect health ; and the necessity of constant watchfulness against his foes, from whom he has no defence of rock, forest, or fortification, quickens his perceptive faculties. But the Arab has also a sense of spiritual things, which appears to have a root in his organization. The Arabs say : " The children of Shem are prophets, the children of Japhet are kings, and the children of Ham are slaves." Having no temples, no priesthood, no religious forms, their religion is less formal and more instinctive, like that of children. The Koran says : " Every child is born into the religion of nature ; its parents make it a Jew, a Christian, or a Magian." But when Mohammed came, the religion of the Arabs was a jumble of monotheism and polytheism, — Judaism, Christianity, idolatry, and fetichism. At one time there had been a powerful and intolerant Jewish kingdom in one region. In Yemen, at another period, the king of Abyssinia had established Christianity. But neither Judaism nor Christianity had ever been able to conquer the peninsula ; and at the end of the sixth century idolatry was the most prevailing form of worship.

At this time Mohammed appeared, and in a few years united in one faith all the warring tribes of Arabia ; consolidated them into a single nation, and then wielded their mighty and enthusiastic forces against Syria, Persia, and North Africa, triumphant wherever they moved. He, certainly, if ever man possessed it, had the rare gift of natural empire. To him, more than to any other of whom history makes mention, was given

" The monarch mind, the mystery of commanding,
  The birth-hour gift, the art Napoleon,
  Of wielding, moulding, gathering, welding, banding,
  The hearts of thousands till they moved as one."

§ 3. *Early Life of Mohammed, to the Hegira.*

But it was not as a soldier or ambitious conqueror that Mohammed began his career. The first forty years of his life were passed in the quiet pursuits of trade, or taking care of the property of Khadîjah. Serious, thoughtful, devout, he made friends of all about him. His youth was unstained by vice, and his honorable character early obtained for him the title, given him by common consent, of Al Amîn, "the faithful." At one time he tended sheep and goats on the hills near Mecca. At Medina, after he became distinguished he referred to this, saying, " Pick me the blackest of those berries ; they are such as I used to gather when I fed the flocks at Mecca. Verily, no prophet has been raised up who has not performed the work of a shepherd." When twenty-five years of age, he entered into the service of Khadîjah, a rich widow, as her agent, to take charge of her merchandise and to sell it at Damascus. When the caravan returned, and his adventure had proved successful, Khadîjah, then forty years old, became interested in the young man ; she was wise, virtuous, and attractive ; they were married, and, till her death, Mohammed was a kind and loving husband. Khadîjah sympathized with her husband in his religious tendencies, and was his first convert His habit was to retire to a cave on Mount Hira to pray and to meditate. Sadness came over him in view of the evils in the world. One of the Suras of the Koran, supposed to belong to this period, is as follows : —

Sura 103.

" By the declining day I swear !
Verily, man is in the way of ruin ;
Excepting such as possess faith,
And do the things which be right,
And stir up one another to truth and steadfastness."

About this time he began to have his visions of angels, especially of Gabriel. He saw a light, and heard a voice, and had sentences like the above put into his mind. These communications were accompanied by strong convulsions (epilepsy, says Weil), in which he would fall to the ground and foam at the mouth. Sprenger considers it to have been a form of hysteria, with a mental origin, perhaps accompanied with catalepsy. The prophet himself said : " Inspiration descends on me in two ways. Sometimes Gabriel cometh and communicateth the revelation, as one man to another. This is easy. But sometimes it is as the ringing of a bell, which rends me in pieces, and grievously afflicts me." One day, when Abu Bakr and Omar sat in the Mosque at Medina, Mohammed came suddenly upon them, lifting up his beard and looking at it ; and Abu Bakr said, " Ah thou, for whom I would sacrifice father and mother ; white hairs are hastening upon thee ! " " Yes," said the prophet, " Hûd " (Sura 11) " and its sisters have hastened my white hairs." " And who," asked Abu Bakr, " are its sisters ? " " The *Inevitable*" (Sura 56) " and the *Striking* " (Sura 101), replied Mohammed. These three are called the " terrific Suras."

But these last Suras came later than the period now referred to. At this time his visions and revelations possessed *him;* he did not possess nor control *them.* In later years the spirit of the prophet was more subject to the prophet. But the Koran is an unintelligible book unless we can connect it with the biography of its writer. All the incidents of his life took shape in some revelation. A separate revelation was given to encourage or to rebuke him ; and in his later years the too subservient inspiration came to appease the jealousy of his wives when a new one was added to their number. But, however it may have been afterward, in the beginning his visions were as much a surprise to him as to others. A careful distribution of the Suras, according to the events which befell him, would make the Koran the best biography of the prophet. As we said of David and his Psalms, so it may be said of Mohammed, that his life hangs suspended in these hymns, as in votive pictures, each the record of some grave experience.*

* " Quo fit ut omnis
Votiva pateat velut descripta tabella
Vita senis."

HORACE.

Now, it is impossible to read the detailed accounts of this part of the life of Mohammed, and have any doubt of his profound sincerity. His earliest converts were his bosom-friends and the people of his household, who were intimately acquainted with his private life. Nor does a man easily begin an ambitious course of deception at the age of forty ; having lived till that time as a quiet, peaceful, and unobtrusive citizen,* what was he to gain by this career ? Long years passed before he could make more than a handful of converts. During these weary years he was the object of contumely and hatred to the ruling tribe in Mecca. His life was hardly safe from them. Nothing could be more hopeless than his position during the first twelve years of his public preaching. Only a strong conviction of the reality of his mission could have supported him through this long period of failure, loneliness, and contempt. During all these years the wildest imagination could not have pictured the success which was to come. Here is a Sura in which he finds comfort in God and his promises . —

Sura 93.

" By the rising sunshine !
By the night when it darkeneth !
Thy Lord hath not removed from thee, neither hath he been displeased.
And verily the future shall be better than the past. . . . .
What ! did he not find thee an orphan, and give thee a home ?
And found thee astray, and directed thee ? "

In this Sura, Mohammed refers to the fact of the death of his mother, Amina, in his seventh year, his father having died a few months before. He visited her tomb many years after, and lifted up his voice and wept. In reply to the questions of his companions, he said : " This is the grave of my mother ; the Lord hath permitted me to visit it, and I asked leave to pray for her, and it was not granted. So I called my mother to remembrance, and the tender memory of her overcame me, and I wept." The child had been taken by his grandfather, Abd al Muttalib, then eighty years old, who treated him with the greatest indulgence. At his death, shortly after, Moham-

---

* The same remark will apply to Cromwell.

med was adopted by his uncle, Abu Tâlib, the chief of the tribe. Abu Tâlib brought him up like his own son, making him sleep by his bed, eat by his side, and go with him wherever he went. And when Mohammed, assuming his inspired position, declared himself a prophet, his uncle, then aged and universally respected, protected him from his enemies, though Abu himself never accepted his teaching. Mohammed therefore had good reason to bless the Providence which had provided such protectors for his orphaned infancy.

Among the earliest converts of Mohammed, after Khadîjah, were his two adopted children, Ali and Zeid. Ali was the son of his guardian, Abu Tâlib, who had become poor, and found it hard to support his family. Mohammed, " prompted by his usual kindness and consideration," says Mr. Muir, went to his rich uncle Abbas, and proposed that each of them should adopt one of Abu Tâlib's children, which was done. His other adopted son, Zeid, belonged to a Syrian tribe, and had been taken captive by marauders, sold into slavery, and given to Khadîjah, who presented him to her husband. After a while the father of Zeid heard where he was, and coming to Mecca offered a large sum as ransom for his son. Mohammed had become very fond of Zeid, but he called him, and gave him his choice to go or stay. Zeid said, " I will not leave thee ; thou art in the place to me of father and mother." Then Mohammed took him to the Kaaba, and touching the Black Stone said, " Bear witness, all here ! Zeid is my son. I shall be his heir, and he mine." So the father returned home contented, and Zeid was henceforth known as " Zeid ibn Mohammed," — Zeid, the son of Mohammed.

It is reported that when Ali was about thirteen years old Mohammed was one day praying with him in one of the retired glens near Mecca, whither they had gone to avoid the ridicule of their opponents. Abu Tâlib, passing by, said, " My nephew ! what is this new faith I see thee following ? " " O my uncle," replied Mohammed, " it is the religion of God, his angels and prophets, the religion of Abraham. The Lord hath sent me as his apostle ; and

20

thou, uncle, art most worthy to be invited to believe."
Abu Tâlib replied, " I am not able, my nephew, to separate from the customs of my forefathers, but I swear that
while I live no one shall trouble thee." Then he said to
Ali, " My son, he will not invite thee to anything which
is not good ; wherefore thou art free to cleave to him."

Another early and important convert was Abu Bakr,
father of Mohammed's favorite wife, Ayesha, and afterward the prophet's successor. Ayesha said she " could not
remember the time when both her parents were not true
believers." Of Abu Bakr, the prophet said, " I never invited any to the faith who did not show hesitation, except
Abu Bakr.· When I proposed Islam to him he at once
accepted it." He was thoughtful, calm, tender, and firm.
He is still known as " Al Sadîch," the true one. Another
of his titles is " the Second of the Two," — from having
been the only companion of Mohammed in his flight from
Mecca. Hassan, the poet of Medina, thus says of him : —

" And the second of the two in the glorious cave, while the foes were
    searching around, and they two were in the mountain, —
And the prophet of the Lord, they well knew, loved him more than all
    the world ; he held no one equal unto him." *

Abu Bakr was at this time a successful merchant, and
possessed some forty thousand dirhems. But he spent
most of it in purchasing and giving freedom to Moslem
slaves, who were persecuted by their masters for their religion. He was an influential man among the Koreish.
This powerful tribe, the rulers of Mecca, who from the first
treated Mohammed with contempt, gradually became violent persecutors of him and his followers. Their main wrath
fell on the unprotected slaves, whom they exposed to the
scorching sun, and who, in their intolerable thirst, would
sometimes recant, and acknowledge the idols. Some of
them remained firm, and afterward showed with triumph
their scars. Mohammed, Abu Bakr, Ali, and all who were
connected with powerful families, were for a long time

---

* " Mohammed once asked Hassan if he had made any poetry about
Abu Bakr, and the poet repeated these lines ; whereupon Mohammed
laughed so heartily as to show his back teeth, and said, 'Thou hast
spoken truly, O Hassan ! It is just as thou hast said.'" — Muir, Vol. II.
p. 256.

safe. For the principal protection in such a disorganized society was the principle that each tribe must defend every one of its members, at all hazards. Of course, Mohammed was very desirous to gain over members of the great families, but he felt bound to take equal pains with the poor and helpless, as appears from the following anecdote : " The prophet was engaged in deep converse with the chief Walîd, for he greatly desired his conversion. Then a blind man passed that way, and asked to hear the Koran. But Mohammed was displeased with the interruption, and turned from him roughly." * But he was afterward grieved to think he had slighted one whom God had perhaps chosen, and had paid court to a reprobate. So his remorse took the form of a divine message and embodied itself as follows : —

> " The prophet frowned and turned aside
> Because the blind man came to him.
> Who shall tell thee if he may not be purified ?
> Or whether thy admonition might not profit him ?
>   The rich man
>   Thou receivest graciously,
>   Although he be not inwardly pure.
> But him who cometh earnestly inquiring,
> And trembling with anxiety,
>   Him thou dost neglect." †

Mohammed did not encourage his followers to martyrdom. On the contrary, he allowed them to dissemble to save themselves. He found one of his disciples sobbing bitterly because he had been compelled by ill-treatment to abuse his master and worship the idols. " But how dost thou find thy heart ? " said the prophet. " Steadfast in the faith," said he. " Then," answered Mohammed, " if they repeat their cruelty, thou mayest repeat thy words." He also had himself an hour of vacillation. Tired of the severe and seemingly hopeless struggle with the Koreish, and seeing no way of overcoming their bitter hostility, he bethought himself of the method of compromise, more than seven centuries before America was discovered. He had been preaching Islam five years, and had only forty or fifty converts. Those among them who had no protectors he

---

* Muir, Vol. II. p. 128.   † Koran, Sura 80.

had advised to fly to the Christian kingdom of Abyssinia. "Yonder," said he, pointing to the west, "lies a land wherein no one is wronged. Go there and remain until the Lord shall open a way for you." Some fifteen or twenty had gone, and met with a kind reception. This was the first " Hegira," and showed the strength of faith in these exiles, who gave up their country rather than Islam. But they heard, before long, that the Koreish had been converted by Mohammed, and they returned to Mecca. The facts were these.

One day, when the chief citizens were sitting near the Kaaba, Mohammed came, and began to recite in their hearing one of the Suras of the Koran. In this Sura three of the goddesses worshipped by the Koreish were mentioned. When he came to their names he added two lines in which he conceded that their intercession might avail with God. The Koreish were so delighted at this acknowledgment of their deities, that when he added another line calling on them to worship Allah, they all prostrated themselves on the ground and adored God. Then they rose, and expressed their satisfaction, and agreed to be his followers, and receive Islam, with this slight alteration, that their goddesses and favorite idols were to be respected. Mohammed went home and began to be unhappy in his mind. The compromise, it seems, lasted long enough for the Abyssinian exiles to hear of it and to come home. But at last the prophet recovered himself, and took back his concession. The verse of the Sura was cancelled, and another inserted, declaring that these goddesses were only names, invented by the idolaters. Ever after, the intercession of idols was condemned with scorn. But Mohammed records his lapse thus in the seventeenth Sura of the Koran: —

" And truly, they were near tempting thee from what we taught thee, that thou shouldst invent a different revelation ; and then they would have inclined unto thee.
And if we had not strengthened thee, verily thou hadst inclined to them a little.
Then thou shouldst not have found against us any helper."

After this, naturally, the persecution became hotter

than ever. A second body of exiles went to Abyssinia. Had not the venerable Abu Tâlib protected Mohammed, his life might have been lost. As it was, the persecutors threatened the old man with deadly enmity unless he gave up Mohammed. But Abu Tâlib, though agreeing with them in their religion, and worshipping their gods, refused to surrender his nephew to them. Once, when Mohammed had disappeared, and his uncle suspected that the Koreish had seized him, he armed a party of Hâshimite youths with dirks, and went to the Kaaba, to the Koreish. But on the way he heard that Mohammed was found. Then, in the presence of the Koreish, he told his young men to draw their dirks, and said, " By the Lord! had ye killed him, not one of you had remained alive." This boldness cowed their violence for a time. But as the unpopularity of Mohammed increased, he and all his party were obliged to take refuge with the Hâshimites in a secluded quarter of the city belonging to Abu Tâlib. The conversion of Omar about this time only increased their rage. They formed an alliance against the Hâshimites, agreeing that they would neither buy nor sell, marry, nor have any dealings with them. This oath was committed to writing, sealed, and hung up in the Kaaba For two or three years the Hâshimites remained shut up in their fortress, and often deprived of the necessaries of life. Their friends would sometimes secretly supply them with provisions ; but the cries of the hungry children would often be heard by those outside. They were blockaded in their intrenchments. But many of the chief people in Mecca began to be moved by pity, and at last it was suggested to Abu Tâlib that the bond hung up in the Kaaba had been eaten by the ants, so as to be no longer valid. This being found to be the case, it was decided that the league was at an end, and the Hâshimites returned to their homes. But other misfortunes were in store for Mohammed. The good Abu Tâlib soon died, and, not long after, Khadîjah. His protector gone, what could Mohammed do ? He left the city, and went with only Zeid for a companion on a mission to Tâyif, sixty or seventy miles east of Mecca, in hopes of converting the in-

habitants.   Who can think of the prophet, in this lonely
journey, without sympathy ?   He was going to preach
the doctrine of One God to idolaters.   But he made no
impression on them, and, as he left the town, was followed
by a mob, hooting, and pelting him with stones.   At last
they left him, and in the shadow of some trees he betook
himself to prayer.   His words have been preserved, it is
believed by the Moslems, and are as follows : " O Lord ! I
make my complaint unto thee of the feebleness of my
strength, and the weakness of my plans.   I am insignificant in the sight of men.   O thou most merciful !
Lord of the weak !   Thou art my Lord !   Do not abandon
me.   Leave me not a prey to these strangers, nor to my
foes.   If thou art not offended, I am safe.   I seek refuge
in the light of thy countenance, by which all darkness is
dispersed, and peace comes.   There is no power, no help,
but in thee."   In that hour of prayer, the faith of Mohammed was the same as that of Luther praying for protection
against the Pope.   It was a part of the universal religion
of human nature.   Certainly this man was no impostor.
A man, going alone to summon an idolatrous city to repentance, must at least have believed in his own doctrine.

But the hour of success was at hand.   No amount of
error, no bitterness of prejudice, no vested interest in falsehood, can resist the determined conviction of a single soul.
Only believe a truth strongly enough to hold it through
good report and ill report, and at last the great world of
half-believers comes round to you.   And usually the success comes suddenly at last, after weary years of disappointment.   The great tree, which seems so solid and firm,
has been secretly decaying within, and is hollow at heart ;
at last it falls in a moment, filling the forest with the
echoes of its ruin.   The dam, which seems strong enough
to resist a torrent, has been slowly undermined by a thousand minute rills of water ; at last it is suddenly swept
away, and opens a yawning breach for the tumbling cata-
ract.   And almost as suddenly came the triumph of Mohammed.

At Medina and in its neighborhood there had long been
numerous ·and powerful tribes of Jewish proselytes.   In

their conflicts with the idolaters, they had often predicted the speedy coming of a prophet like Moses. The Jewish influence was great at Medina, and that of the idolaters was divided by bitter quarrels. Now it must be remembered that at this time Mohammed taught a kind of modified Judaism. He came to revive the religion of Abraham, Isaac, and Jacob. He continually referred to the Old Testament and the Talmud for authority. He was a prophet and inspired, but not to teach anything new. He was to restore the universal religion which God had taught to man in the beginning, — the religion of all true patriarchs and prophets. Its essential doctrine was the unity of God, and his supremacy and providence. Its one duty was Islam, or submission to the Divine will. Its worship was prayer and almsgiving. At this time he did not make belief in himself the main point ; it was to profess the unity of God, and to submit wholly to God. So that the semi-Judaized pilgrims from Medina to Mecca were quite prepared to accept his teachings. Mohammed, at the time of the pilgrimage, met with many of them, and they promised to become his disciples. The pledge they took was as follows : " We will not worship any but the one God ; we will not steal, nor commit adultery, nor kill our children (female) : we will not slander at all, nor disobey the prophet in anything that is right." This was afterward called the " Pledge of Women," because it did not require them to fight for Islam. This faith spread rapidly among the idolaters at Medina, — much more so than the Jewish system. The Jews required too much of their proselytes ; they insisted on their becoming Jews. They demanded a change of all their previous customs. But Mohammed only asked for submission

About this time Mohammed had his famous dream or vision, in which he was carried by Gabriel on a winged steed to Jerusalem, to meet all the prophets of God and be welcomed by them to their number, and then to the seventh heaven into the presence of God. It was so vivid that he deemed it a reality, and maintained that he had been to Jerusalem and to heaven. This, and the Koran itself, were the only miracles he ever claimed.

The Medina Moslems having entered into a second pledge, to receive Mohammed and his friends, and to protect them, the prophet gave orders to his followers to leave Mecca secretly in small parties, and repair to Medina. As the stout sea-captain remains the last on a sinking vessel, Mohammed stayed quietly at Mecca till all the others had gone. Only Abu Bakr's family and his own remained. The rest of the believers, to the number of about two hundred, had disappeared.

The Koreish, amazed at these events, knew not what to do. Why had the Moslems gone? and why had Mohammed remained? How dared he to stay, unprotected, in their midst? They might kill him; — but then his tribe would take a bloody vengeance on his murderers. At last they proposed to seize him, and that a number of men, one from each tribe and family, should at the same moment drive their dirks into him. Or perhaps it might be better to send an assassin to waylay him on his way to Medina. While they were discussing these alternatives, news was brought to them that Mohammed also had disappeared, and Abu Bakr with him. They immediately went to their houses. In that of Mohammed they found the young Ali, who, being asked where his father was, replied, "I do not know. I am not his keeper. Did you not order him to go from the city? I suppose he is gone." Getting no more information at the house of Abu Bakr, they sent out parties of armed men, mounted on swift horses and camels, to search the whole route to Medina, and bring the fugitives back. After a few days the pursuers returned, saying that there were no signs of any persons having gone in that direction. If they had gone that way they would certainly have overtaken them.

Meantime where were the fugitives? Instead of going north to Medina, they had hidden in a cave on a mountain, about five or six miles to the south of Mecca. Here they remained concealed three days and nights, in imminent danger from their pursuers, who once, it is said, came to the mouth of the cave, but, seeing spiders' webs spun across the opening, concluded no one could have gone in recently. There was a crevice in the roof through which

the morning light entered, and Abu Bakr said, " If one
of them were to look down, he would see us." " Think
not so, Abu Bakr," said the prophet. " We are two, but
God is in the midst, a third."

The next day, satisfied that the heat of the pursuit had
abated, they took the camels which had privately been
brought to them from the city by the son of Abu Bakr,
and set off for Medina, leaving Mecca on the right. By
the calculations of M. Caussin de Perceval, it was on the
20th of June, A. D. 622.

§ 4. *Change in the Character of Mohammed after the Hegira.*

From the Hegira the Mohammedan era begins; and
from that point of the prophet's history his fortunes rise,
but his character degenerates. He has borne adversity and
opposition with a faith and a patience almost sublime;
but prosperity he will not bear so well. Down to that
time he had been a prophet, teaching God's truth to those
who would receive it, and by the manifestation of that
truth commending himself to every man's conscience.
Now he was to become a politician, the head of a party,
contriving expedients for its success. Before, his only
weapon was truth; now, his chief means was force. Instead of convincing his opponents, he now compelled
them to submit by the terror of his power. His revelations changed their tone; they adapted themselves to his
needs, and on all occasions, even when he wanted to take
an extra wife, inspiration came to his aid.

What sadder tragedy is there than to see a great soul
thus conquered by success ? " All these things," says Satan, " I will give thee, if thou wilt fall down and worship
me." When Jesus related his temptation to his disciples
he put it in the form of a parable. How could they, how
can we, understand the temptations of a nature like that
of Christ ! Perhaps he saw that he could have a great
apparent success by the use of worldly means. He could
bring the Jew and the Gentile to acknowledge and receive
his truth. Some slight concession to worldly wisdom,

20 *						D D

some little compromise with existing errors, some hardly
perceptible variation from perfect truthfulness, and lo!
the kingdom of God would come in that very hour, instead of lingering through long centuries.   What evils
might not be spared to the race, what woes to the world,
if the divine gospel of love to God and man were inaugurated by Christ himself! This, perhaps, was one of the
temptations.   But Jesus said, "Get thee behind me,
Satan." He would use only good means for good ends.
He would take God's way to do God's work. He would
die on the cross, but not vary from the perfect truth.
The same temptation came to Mohammed, and he yielded.
Up to the Hegira, Mohammed might also have said, "My
kingdom is not of this world." But now the sword and
falsehood were to serve him, as his most faithful servants,
in building up Islam.   His *ends* were the same as before.
His object was still to establish the service of the one
living and true God.   But his *means*, henceforth, are of
the earth, earthy.

What a noble religion would Islam have been, if
Mohammed could have gone on as he began! He accepted all the essential truths of Judaism, he recognized
Moses and Christ as true teachers.   He taught that there
was one universal religion, the substance of which was
faith in one Supreme Being, submission to his will, trust
in his providence, and good-will to his creatures.   Prayer
and alms were the only worship which God required.   A
marvellous and mighty work, says Mr. Muir, had been
wrought by these few precepts.   From time beyond
memory Mecca and the whole peninsula had been steeped
in spiritual torpor.   The influences of Judaism, Christianity, and philosophy had been feeble and transient.   Dark
superstitions prevailed, the mothers of dark vices.   And
now, in thirteen years of preaching, a body of men and
women had risen, who rejected idolatry; worshipped the
one great God; lived lives of prayer; practised chastity,
benevolence, and justice; and were ready to do and to
bear everything for the truth.   All this came from the
depth of conviction in the soul of this one man.

To the great qualities which Mohammed had shown as

a prophet and religious teacher were now added those of the captain and statesman. He had at last obtained a position at Medina whence he could act on the Arabs with other forces than those of eloquence and feeling. And now the man who for forty years had been a simple citizen and led a quiet family life — who afterward, for thirteen years, had been a patient but despised teacher of the unity of God — passed the last ten years of his strange career in building up a fanatical army of warriors, destined to conquer half the civilized world. From this period the old solution of the Mohammedan miracle is in order; from this time the sword leads, and the Koran follows. To this familiar explanation of Mohammedan success, Mr. Carlyle replies with the question : " Mohammedanism triumphed with the sword ? But where did it get its sword ? " We can now answer that pithy inquiry. The simple, earnest zeal of the original believers built up a power, which then took the sword, and conquered with it. The reward of patient, long-enduring faith is influence ; with this influence ambition serves itself for its own purpose. Such is, more or less, the history of every religion, and, indeed, of every political party. Sects are founded, not by politicians, but by men of faith, by men to whom ideas are realities, by men who are willing to die for them. Such faith always triumphs at last ; it makes a multitude of converts ; it becomes a great power. The deep and strong convictions thus created are used by worldly men for their own purposes. That the Mohammedan impulse was thus taken possession of by worldly men is the judgment of M. Renan.* " From all sides," says he, " we come to this singular result : that the Mussulman movement was started almost without religious faith ; that, setting aside a small number of faithful disciples, Mahomet really wrought very little conviction in Arabia." "The party of true Mussulmans had all their strength in Omar ; but after his assassination, that is to say, twelve years after the death of the prophet, the opposite party triumphed by the election of Othman."

* Mahomet and the Origin of Islam. Studies of Religious History. Translated by O. B. Frothingham.

"The first generation of the Hegira was completely occupied in exterminating the primitive Mussulmans, the true fathers of Islamism." Perhaps it is bold to question the opinions of a Semitic scholar of the force of M. Renan, but it seems to us that he goes too far in supposing that such a movement as that of Islam could be *started* without a tremendous depth of conviction. At all events, supported by such writers as Weil, Sprenger, and Muir, we will say that it was a powerful religious movement founded on sincerest conviction, but gradually turned aside, and used for worldly purposes and temporal triumphs. And, in thus diverting it from divine objects to purely human ones, Mohammed himself led the way. He adds another, and perhaps the greatest, illustration to the long list of noble souls whose natures have become subdued to that which they worked in ; who have sought high ends by low means ; who, talking of the noblest truths, descend into the meanest prevarications, and so throw a doubt on all sincerity, faith, and honor. Such was the judgment of a great thinker — Goethe — concerning Mohammed. He believes him to have been at first profoundly sincere, but he says of him that afterward " what in his character is earthly increases and develops itself; the divine retires and is obscured : his doctrine becomes a means rather than an end. All kinds of practices are employed, nor are horrors wanting." Goethe intended to write a drama upon Mohammed, to illustrate the sad fact that every man who attempts to realize a great idea comes in contact with the lower world, must place himself on its level in order to influence it, and thus often compromises his higher aims, and at last forfeits them.* Such a man, in modern times, was Lord Bacon in the political world ; such a man, among conquerors, was Cromwell ; and among Christian sects how often do we see the young enthusiast and saint end as the ambitious self-seeker and Jesuit! Then we call him a hypocrite, because he continues to use the familiar language of the time when his heart was true and simple, though indulging himself in luxury and sin. It is curious,

* Lewes, Life of Goethe, Vol. I. p. 207.

when we are all so inconsistent, that we should find it so hard to understand inconsistency. We, all of us, often say what is right and do what is wrong; but are we deliberate hypocrites? No! we know that we are weak; we admit that we are inconsistent; we say amen to the "video meliora, proboque, — deteriora sequor," but we also know that we are not deliberate and intentional hypocrites. Let us use the same large judgment in speaking of the faults of Cromwell, Bacon, and Mohammed.

No one could have foreseen the cruelty of which Mohammed, hitherto always a kind-hearted and affectionate man, was capable toward those who resisted his purpose. This first showed itself in his treatment of the Jews. He hoped to form an alliance with them, against the idolaters. He had admitted the divine authority of their religion, and appealed to their Scriptures as evidence of the truth of his own mission. He conformed to their ritual and customs, and made Jerusalem his Kibla, toward which he turned in prayer five times a day. In return for this he expected them to receive him as a prophet; but this they refused to do. So he departed by degrees from their customs, changed his Kibla to Mecca, and at last denounced the Jews as stiff-necked unbelievers. The old quarrel between Esau and Jacob could not be appeased, nor an alliance formed between them.

M. Saint-Hilaire * does not think that the character of Mohammed changed when he became the founder of a state and head of a conquering party. He thinks " that he only yielded to the political necessities of his position." Granted; but yielding to those necessities was the cause of this gradual change in his character. The man who lies and murders from the necessity of his political position can hardly remain a saint. Plunder, cold-blooded execution of prisoners, self-indulgence, became the habit of the prophet henceforth, as we shall presently see.

The first battle against the Koreish, that of Badr, took place in January, A. D. 624. When Mohammed had

* Mahomet et le Coran, par J. Barthélemy Saint-Hilaire, Paris, 1865, p. 114.

drawn up his army, he prayed earnestly for the victory.
After a desperate struggle, the Koreish fled.   Mohammed
claimed, by a special revelation, the fifth part of the
booty.   As the bodies of his old opponents were cast into
a pit, he spoke to them bitterly.   When the prisoners
were brought before him he looked fiercely at one of
them.   " There is death in that glance," said the unhappy
man, and presently the prophet ordered him to be beheaded.   Two days after, another was ordered for execution.   " Who will take care of my little girl ? " said he.
" Hell-fire," replied Mohammed, and ordered him to be
cut down.   Shortly after the battle, a Jewess who had
written verses against Mohammed, was assassinated by
one of his followers ; and the prophet praised him for the
deed in the public mosque.   Another aged Jew, for the
same offence, was murdered by his express command.   A
quarrel between some Jews and Moslems brought on
an attack by Mohammed upon the Jewish tribe.   They
surrendered after a siege of fifteen days, and Mohammed
ordered all the prisoners to be killed ; but at last, at the
urgent request of a powerful chief in Medina, allowed
them to go into exile, cursing them and their intercessor.
Mr. Muir mentions other cases of assassination of the
Jews by the command of the prophet.   All these facts
are derived from contemporaneous Moslem historians,
who glorify their prophet for this conduct.   The worst
action perhaps of this kind was the deliberate execution
of seven or eight hundred Jewish prisoners, who had
surrendered at discretion, and the sale of their wives and
children into slavery.   Mohammed selected from among
these women one more beautiful than the rest, for his
concubine.   Whether M. Saint-Hilaire considers all this
as " yielding to the political necessities of his position,"
we do not know.   But this man, who could stand by and
see hundreds of captives slaughtered in cold blood, and
then retire to solace himself with the widow of one of
his victims, seems to us to have retained little of his
early purity of soul.

About this time Mohammed began to multiply wives,
and to receive revelations allowing him to do so beyond

the usual limit of his law. He added one after another
to his harem, until he had ten wives, besides his slaves.
His views on such subjects are illustrated by his presenting three beautiful female slaves, taken in war, one to
his father-in-law, and the others to his two sons-in-law.

So, in a series of battles, with the Jewish tribes, the
Koreish, the Syrians, passed the stormy and triumphant
years of the Pontiff King. Mecca was conquered, and
the Koreish submitted in A. D. 630. The tribes throughout Arabia acquiesced, one by one, in the prophet's
authority. All paid tribute, or accepted Islam. His
enemies were all under his feet; his doctrines accepted;
the rival prophets, Aswad and Museilama, overcome.
Then, in the sixty-third year of his age, death drew near.
On the last day of his life, he went into the mosque to
attend morning prayer, then back to the room of his
favorite wife, Ayesha, and died in her arms. Wild with
grief, Omar declared he was not dead, but in a trance.
The grave Abu Bakr composed the excited multitude, and
was chosen caliph, or successor to the prophet. Mohammed died on June 8, A. D. 632, and was buried the next
day, amid the grief of his followers. Abu Bakr and
Omar offered the prayer: "Peace be unto thee, O prophet
of God; and the mercy of the Lord, and his blessing!
We bear testimony that the prophet of God hath delivered
the message revealed to him; hath fought in the ways of
the Lord until God crowned his religion with victory;
hath fulfilled his words commanding that he alone is to
be worshipped in unity; hath drawn us to himself, and
been kind and tender-hearted to believers; hath sought
no recompense for delivering to us the faith, neither hath
sold it for a price at any time." And all the people said,
"Amen! Amen!"

Concerning the character of Mohammed, enough has
been already said. He was a great man, one of the
greatest ever sent upon earth. He was a man of the
deepest convictions, and for many years of the purest
purposes, and was only drawn down at last by using low
means for a good end. Of his visions and revelations,

the same explanation is to be given as of those received by
Joan of Arc, and other seers of that order.   How far they
had an objective basis in reality, and how far they were
the result of some abnormal activity of the imagination,
it is difficult with our present knowledge to decide.   But
that these visionaries fully believed in their own inspiration, there can be little doubt.

§ 5. *Religious Doctrines and Practices among the Moham-*
medans.

As to the religion of Mohammed, and its effects on the
world, it is easier to come to an opinion than concerning
his own character.   Its essential doctrine, as before indicated, is the absolute unity and supremacy of God, as
opposed to the old Arab Polytheism on the one hand and
the Christian Trinity on the other.   It however admits
of angels and genii.   Gabriel and Michael are the angels
of power; Azriel, angel of death; Israfeel, angel of the
resurrection.   Eblis, or Satan, plays an important part in
this mythology.   The Koran also teaches the doctrine of
Eternal Decrees, or absolute Predestination; of prophets
before Mohammed, of whom he is the successor,— as
Adam, Noah, Moses, and Jesus; of sacred books, of which
all that remain are the Pentateuch, Psalms, Gospels, and
Koran; of an intermediate state after death; of the resurrection and judgment.   All non-believers in Islam go into
eternal fire.   There are separate hells for Christians, Jews,
Sabians, Magians, idolaters, and the hypocrites of all religions.   The Moslem is judged by his actions.   A balance
is held by Gabriel, one scale hanging over heaven and
another over hell, and his good deeds are placed in one
and his bad ones in the other.   According as his scale
inclines, he goes to heaven or hell.   If he goes to heaven,
he finds there seventy-two Houris, more beautiful than
angels, awaiting him, with gardens, groves, marble palaces,
and music.   If women are true believers and righteous,
they will also go to heaven, but nothing is said about
husbands being provided for them.   Stress is laid on
prayer, ablution, fasting, almsgiving, and the pilgrimage

to Mecca. Wine and gaming are forbidden. There is no
recognition, in the Koran, of human brotherhood. It is a
prime duty to hate infidels and make war on them. Mohammed made it a duty for Moslems to betray and kill
their own brothers when they were infidels ; and he was
obeyed in more cases than one. The Moslem sects are as
numerous as those of Christians. The Dabistan mentions
seventy-three. The two main divisions are into Sunnites
and Shyites. The Persians are mostly Shyites, and refuse
to receive the Sunnite traditions. They accept Ali, and
denounce Omar. Terrible wars and cruelties have taken
place between these sects. Only a few of the Sunnite
doctors acknowledge the Shyites to be Moslems. They
have a saying, " to destroy a Shyite is more acceptable than
to kill seventy other infidels of whatever sort."

The Turks are the most zealous of the Moslems. On
Friday, which is the Sabbath of Islam, all business is suspended. Prayers are read and sermons preached in the
mosques. No one is allowed to be absent. The Ramadan
fast is universally kept. Any one who breaks it twice is
considered worthy of death. The fast lasts from sunrise
to sunset. But the rich feast in the night, and sleep during the day. The Turks have no desire to make proselytes, but have an intolerant hatred for all outside of
Islam. The Kalif is the Chief Pontiff. The Oulema, or
Parliament, is composed of the Imans, or religious teachers, the Muftis, or doctors of law, and Kadis, or ministers
of justice. The priests in Turkey are subordinate to the
civil magistrate, who is their diocesan, and can remove
them at pleasure. The priests in daily life are like the
laity, engage in the same business, and are no more austere
than they.

Mr. Forster says, in regard to their devotion : " When I
contrast the silence of a Turkish mosque, at the hour of
public prayer, with the noise and tumult so frequent in
Christian temples, I stand astonished at the strange inversion, in the two religions, of the order of things which
might naturally be expected." " I have seen," says another, " a congregation of at least two thousand souls
assembled in the mosque of St. Sophia, with silence so

profound, that until I entered the body of the building I was unaware that it contained a single worshipper."

Bishop Southgate, long a missionary bishop of the Episcopal Church of the United States, says : " I have often met with Mussulmans who seem to possess deep religious feeling, and with whom I could exercise something of a religious communion. I have sometimes had my own mind quickened and benefited by the reverence with which they spoke of the Deity, and have sometimes mingled in harmonious converse with them on holy things. I have heard them insist with much earnestness on the duty of prayer, when they appeared to have some spiritual sense of its nature and importance. I have sometimes found them entertaining elevated views of moral duty, and looking with contempt on the pleasures of this world. These are indeed rare characters, but I should do injustice to my own conviction if I did not confess that I had found them. In these instances I have been uniformly struck with a strong resemblance to patriarchal piety." He continues : " When we sat down to eat, the old Turkish Bey implored a blessing with great solemnity, and rendered his thanks when we arose. Before he left us he spread his carpet, and offered his evening devotions with apparent meekness and humility ; and I could not but feel how impressive are the Oriental forms of worship when I saw his aged head bowed to the earth in religious homage."

Bishop Southgate adds further : " I have never known a Mussulman, sincere in his faith and devout and punctilious in his religious duties, in whom moral rectitude did not seem an active quality and a living principle."

In seasons of plague " the Turks appear perfectly fearless. They do not avoid customary intercourse and contact with friends. They remain with and minister to the sick, with unshrinking assiduity. . . . . In truth, there is something imposing in the unaffected calmness of the Turks at such times. It is a spirit of resignation which becomes truly noble when exercised upon calamities which have already befallen them. The fidelity with which they remain by the bedside of a friend is at least as commendable as the almost universal readiness among the Franks to forsake it."

Five times a day the Mezzuin proclaims the hour of prayer from the minaret in these words : "There is no God but God. Mohammed is his prophet. Come to prayer." In the morning call he adds, "Prayer is better than sleep." Immediately every Mussulman leaves his occupation, and prostrates himself on the floor or ground, wherever he may be. It is very disreputable to omit this.

An interesting account is given of the domestic life of Moslem women in Syria, by Miss Rogers, in her little book called " Domestic Life in Palestine," published in 1862.

Miss Rogers travelled in Palestine with her brother, who was British consul at Damascus. The following passage illustrates the character of the women (Miss Rogers was obliged to sleep in the same room with the wives of the governor of Arrabeh, near Naplous) : —

" When I began to undress the women watched me with curiosity ; and when I put on my night-gown they were exceedingly astonished, and exclaimed, ' Where are you going ? Why is your dress white ? ' They made no change for sleeping, and there they were, in their bright-colored clothes, ready for bed in a minute. But they stood round me till I said ' Good night,' and then all kissed me, wishing me good dreams. Then I knelt down, and presently, without speaking to them again, got into bed, and turned my face to the wall, thinking over the strange day I had spent. I tried to compose myself to sleep, though I heard the women whispering together. When my head had rested about five minutes on the soft red silk pillow, I felt a hand stroking my forehead, and heard a voice saying, very gently, ' Ya Habibi,' i. e. ' O beloved.' But I would not answer directly, as I did not wish to be roused unnecessarily. I waited a little while, and my face was touched again. I felt a kiss on my fore-head, and a voice said, ' Miriam, speak to us ; speak, Miriam, darling.' I could not resist any longer ; so I turned round and saw Helweh, Saleh Bek's prettiest wife, leaning over me. I said, ' What is it, sweetness, what can I do for you ? ' She answered, ' What did you do just now, when you knelt down and covered your face with your hands?' I sat up, and said very solemnly, 'I spoke to God, Helweh.' 'What did you say to him?' said Helweh. I replied, 'I wish to sleep. God never sleeps. I have asked him to watch over me, and that I may fall asleep, remembering that he never sleeps, and wake up remembering his presence. I am very weak. God is all-powerful. I have asked him to strengthen me with his strength.' By this time all the ladies were sitting round me on the bed, and the slaves came and stood near. I told them I did not know their language well enough to explain to them all I thought and said. But as I had learned the Lord's Prayer, by heart, in Arabic, I repeated it to them, sentence by sentence, slowly. When I began, 'Our Father who art in heaven,' Helweh directly said, 'You told me your father was in London.' I replied, 'I have two fathers, Helweh; one in London, who does not know that I am here, and cannot know till I write and tell him; and a Heavenly Father, who is here now, who is with me always, and sees and hears us. He is your Father also. He teaches us to know good from evil, if we listen to him and obey him.'

"For a moment there was perfect silence. They all looked startled, and as if they felt that they were in the presence of some unseen power. Then Helweh said, 'What more did you say?' I continued the Lord's Prayer, and when I came to the words, 'Give us day by day our daily bread,' they said, 'Cannot you make bread yourself?' The passage, 'Forgive us our trespasses, as we forgive those who trespass against us,' is particularly forcible in the Arabic language; and one of the elder women, who was particularly severe and relentless-looking, said, 'Are you obliged to say that every day?' as if she thought that sometimes it would be difficult to do so. They said, 'Are you a Moslem?' I said, 'I am not called a Moslem. But I am your sister, made by the same God, who is the one only God, the God of all, my Father and your Father.' They asked me if I knew the Koran, and were surprised to hear that I had read it. They handed a rosary to me, saying, 'Do you know that?' I repeated a few of the most striking and comprehensive attributes very carefully and slowly. Then they cried out, 'Mashallah, the English girl is a true believer'; and the impressionable, sensitive-looking Abyssinian slave-girls said, with one accord, 'She is indeed an angel.'

"Moslems, men and women, have the name of Allah constantly on their lips, but it seems to have become a mere form. This may explain why they were so startled when I said, 'I was speaking to God.'" She adds that if she had only said, "I was saying my prayers," or, "I was at my devotions," it would not have impressed them."

Next morning, on awaking, Miss Rogers found the women from the neighborhood had come in "to hear the English girl speak to God," and Helweh said, "Now, Miriam, darling, will you speak to God?" At the conclusion she asked them if they could say Amen, and after a moment of hesitation they cried out, "Amên, amên!" Then one said, "Speak again, my daughter, speak about *the bread*." So she repeated the Lord's Prayer with explanations. When she left, they crowded around affectionately, saying, "Return again, O Miriam, beloved!"

After this pleasant little picture, we may hear something on the other side. Two recent travellers, Mr. Palgrave and Mr. Vambéry, have described the present state of Mohammedanism in Central Arabia and Turkistan, or Central Asia. Barth has described it as existing among the negroes in North Africa. Count Gobineau has told us of Islam as it is in Persia at the present day.* Mr. MacFarlane, in his book "Kismet, or the Doom of Turkey," has pointed out the gradual decay of that power, and the utter corruption of its administration. After reading such works as these, — and among them let us not forget Mr. Lane's "Modern Egyptians," — the conclusion we must inevitably come to is, that the worst Christian government, be it that of the Pope or the Czar, is very much better than the best Mohammedan government. Everywhere we find arbitrary will taking the place of law. In most places the people have no pro-

---

* Les Religions et les Philosophies dans L'Asie Centrale. Par M. le Comte Gobineau. Paris.

tection for life or property, and know the government only through its tax-gatherers.   And all this is necessarily and logically derived from the fundamental principle of Mohammedan theology.   God is pure will, not justice, not reason, not love.   Christianity says, " God is love "; Mohammedanism says, " God is will."   Christianity says, "Trust in God "; Mohammedanism says, " Submit to God."   Hence the hardness, coldness, and cruelty of the system ; hence its utter inability to establish any good government.   According to Mr. MacFarlane, it would be a blessing to mankind to have the Turks driven out of Europe and Asia Minor, and to have Constantinople become the capital of Russia.   The religion of Islam is an outward form, a hard shell of authority, hollow at heart.   It constantly tends to the two antagonistic but related vices of luxury and cruelty.   Under the profession of Islam, polytheism and idolatry have always prevailed in Arabia.   In Turkistan, where slavery is an extremely cruel system, they make slaves of Moslems, in defiance of the Koran.   One chief being appealed to by Vambéry (who travelled as a Dervish), replied, " We buy and sell the Koran itself, which is the holiest thing of all ; why not buy and sell Mussulmans, who are less holy ? "

§ 6. *The Criticism of Mr. Palgrave on Mohammedan Theology.*

Mr. Palgrave, who has given the latest and best account of the condition of Central and Southern Arabia,* under the great Wahhabee revival, sums up all Mohammedan theology as teaching a Divine unity of pure will.   God is the only force in the universe.   Man is wholly passive and impotent.   He calls the system, " A pantheism of force."   God has no rule but arbitrary will.   He is a tremendous unsympathizing autocrat, but is yet jealous of his creatures, lest they should attribute to themselves something which belongs to him.   He delights in making all creatures feel that they are his slaves.   This, Mr. Pal-

* A Year's Journey through Central and Eastern Arabia. By William Gifford Palgrave.   Third edition.   1866.   London.

grave asserts, is the main idea of Mohammedanism, and of the Koran, and this was what lay in the mind of Mohammed. "Of this," says he, "we have many authentic samples: the Saheeh, the Commentaries of Beydāwee, the Mishkat-el-Mesabeeh, and fifty similar works, afford ample testimony on this point. But for the benefit of my readers in general, all of whom may not have drunk equally deep at the fountain-heads of Islamitic dogma, I will subjoin a specimen, known perhaps to many Orientalists, yet too characteristic to be here omitted, a repetition of which I have endured times out of number from admiring and approving Wahhabees in Nejed.

"Accordingly, when God — so runs the tradition, — I had better said the blasphemy — resolved to create the human race, he took into his hands a mass of earth, the same whence all mankind were to be formed, and in which they after a manner pre-existed; and, having then divided the clod into two equal portions, he threw the one half into hell, saying, 'These to eternal fire, and I care not'; and projected the other half into heaven, adding, 'And these to paradise, and I care not.'

"Commentary would here be superfluous. But in this we have before us the adequate idea of predestination, or, to give it a truer name, pre-damnation, held and taught in the school of the Koran. Paradise and hell are at once totally independent of love and hatred on the part of the Deity, and of merits and demerits, of good or evil conduct, on the part of the creature; and, in the corresponding theory, rightly so, since the very actions which we call good or ill deserving, right or wrong, wicked or virtuous, are in their essence all one and of one, and accordingly merit neither praise nor blame, punishment nor recompense, except and simply after the arbitrary value which the all-regulating will of the great despot may choose to assign or impute to them. In a word, he burns one individual through all eternity, amid red-hot chains and seas of molten fire, and seats another in the plenary enjoyment of an everlasting brothel, between forty celestial concubines, just and equally for his own good pleasure, and because he wills it.

" Men are thus all on one common level, here and hereafter, in their physical, social, and moral light, — the level
of slaves to one sole master, of tools to one universal
agent. But the equalizing process does not stop here :
beasts, birds, fishes, insects, all participate of the same
honor or debasement; all are, like man, the slaves of God,
the tools and automata of his will; and hence Mahomet
is simply logical and self-consistent when in the Koran
he informs his followers that birds, beasts, and the rest
are 'nations' like themselves, nor does any intrinsic distinction exist between them and the human species, except what accidental diversity the ' King,' the ' Proud
One,' the ' Mighty,' the ' Giant,' etc., as he styles his God,
may have been pleased to make, just as he willed it, and
so long as he may will it."

" The Wahhabee reformer," continues Mr. Palgrave,
" formed the design of putting back the hour-hand of
Islam to its starting-point ; and so far he did well, for
that hand was from the first meant to be fixed.   Islam is
in its essence stationary, and was framed thus to remain.
Sterile like its God, lifeless like its First Principle and
Supreme Original, in all that constitutes true life, — for
life is love, participation, and progress, and of these the
Koranic Deity has none, — it justly repudiates all change,
all advance, all development.   To borrow the forcible
words of Lord Houghton, the ' written book' is the ' dead
man's hand,' stiff and motionless ; whatever savors of vitality is by that alone convicted of heresy and defection.

" But Christianity, with its living and loving God, be-
getter and begotten, spirit and movement ; nay more, — a
Creator made creature, the Maker and the made existing
in one ; a Divinity communicating itself by uninterrupted
gradation and degree, from the most intimate union far off
to the faintest irradiation, through all that it has made for
love and governs in love ; one who calls his creatures not
slaves, not servants, but friends, — nay sons, — nay gods :
to sum up, a religion in whose seal and secret ' God in man
is one with man in God,' must also be necessarily a religion
of vitality, of progress, of advancement.   The contrast between it and Islam is that of movement with fixedness,

of participation with sterility, of development with barrenness, of life with petrifaction. The first vital principle and the animating spirit of its birth must, indeed, abide ever the same, but the outer form must change with the changing days, and new offshoots of fresh sap and greenness be continually thrown out as witnesses to the vitality within; else were the vine withered and the branches dead. I have no intention here — it would be extremely out of place — of entering on the maze of controversy, or discussing whether any dogmatic attempt to reproduce the religious phase of a former age is likely to succeed. I only say that life supposes movement and growth, and both imply change; that to censure a living thing for growing and changing is absurd; and that to attempt to hinder it from so doing by pinning it down on a written label, or nailing it to a Procrustean framework, is tantamount to killing it altogether. Now Christianity is living, and, because living, must grow, must advance, must change, and was meant to do so: onwards and forwards is a condition of its very existence; and I cannot but think that those who do not recognize this show themselves so far ignorant of its true nature and essence. On the other hand, Islam is lifeless, and, because lifeless, cannot grow, cannot advance, cannot change, and was never intended so to do; stand-still is its motto and its most essential condition; and therefore the son of Abd-el-Wahhāb, in doing his best to bring it back to its primal simplicity, and making its goal of its starting-point, was so far in the right, and showed himself well acquainted with the nature and first principles of his religion."

§ 7. *Mohammedanism a Relapse; the worst Form of Monotheism, and a retarding Element in Civilization.*

According to this view, which is no doubt correct, the monotheism of Mohammed is that which makes of God pure will; that is, which exaggerates personality (since personality is in will), making the Divine One an Infinite Free Will, or an Infinite I. But will divorced from reason and love is wilfulness, or a purely arbitrary will.

Now the monotheism of the Jews differed from this, in that it combined with the idea of will the idea of justice. God not only does what he chooses, but he chooses to do only what is right. Righteousness is an attribute of God, with which the Jewish books are saturated.

Still, both of these systems leave God outside of the world; *above* all as its Creator and Ruler, *above* all as its Judge; but not *through* all and *in* all. The idea of an Infinite Love must be added and made supreme, in order to give us a Being who is not only above all, but also through all and in all. This is the Christian monotheism.

Mohammed teaches not only the unity but also the spirituality of God, but his idea of the divine Unity is of a numeric unity, not a moral unity; and so his idea of divine spirituality is that of an abstract spirituality, — God abstracted from matter, and so not to be represented by pictures and images; God withdrawn out of the world, and above all, — in a total separation.

Judaism also opposed idolatry and idol-worship, and taught that God was above all, and the maker of the world; but it conceived of God as *with* man, by his repeated miraculous coming down in prophets, judges, kings; also *with* his people, the Jews, mysteriously present in their tabernacle and temple. Their spirituality was not quite as abstract then as that of the Mohammedans.

But Christianity, as soon as it became the religion of a non-Semitic race, as soon as it had converted the Greeks and Romans, not only imparted to them its monotheism, but received from them their strong tendencies to pantheism. They added to the God " above all," and the God " with all," the God " in us all." True, this is also to be found in original Christianity as proceeding from the life of Jesus. The New Testament is full of this kind of pantheism, — God *in* man, as well as God *with* man. Jesus made the step forward from God with man to God in man, — " I in them, thou in me." The doctrine of the Holy Spirit is this idea, of God who is not only will and power, not only wisdom and law, but also love; of a God who desires communion and intercourse with his children, so coming and dwelling in them. Mohammed teaches a God above us; Moses teaches a God above us, and yet with us; Jesus teaches God above us, God with us, and God in us.

According to this view, Mohammedanism is a relapse. It is going back to a lower level. It is returning from the complex idea to the simple idea. But the complex is higher than the simple. The seed-germ, and the germ-cell, out of which organic life comes, is lower than the organizations which are developed out of it. The Mollusks are more complex and so are higher than the Radiata, the Vertebrata are more complex than the Mollusks. Man is the most complex of all, in soul as well as body. The complex idea of God, including will, thought, and love, in the perfect unity, is higher than the simplistic unity of will which Mohammed teaches. But the higher ought to come out of and conquer the lower. How, then, did Mohammedanism come out of Christianity and Judaism?

The explanation is to be found in the law of reaction and relapse. Reaction is going back to a lower ground, to pick up something which has been dropped, forgotten, left behind, in the progress of man. The condition of progress is that nothing shall be lost. The lower truth must be preserved in the higher truth; the lower life taken up into the higher life. Now Christianity, in going forward, had accepted from the Indo-Germanic races that sense of God in nature, as well as God above nature, which has always been native with those races. It took up natural religion into monotheism. But in taking it up, it went so far as to lose something of the true unity of God. Its doctrine of the Trinity, at least in its Oriental forms, lost the pure personal monotheism of Judaism. No doubt the doctrine of the Trinity embodies a great truth, but it has been carried too far. So Mohammedanism came, as a protest against this tendency to plurality in the godhead, as a demand for a purely personal God. It is the Unitarianism of the East. It was a new assertion of the simple unity of God, against polytheism and against idolatry.

The merits and demerits, the good and evil, of Moham medanism are to be found in this, its central idea concerning God It has taught submission, obedience, patience ; but it has fostered a wilful individualism. It has made social life lower. Its governments are not governments. Its virtues are stoical. It makes life barren and empty. It encourages a savage pride and cruelty. It makes men tyrants or slaves, women puppets, religion the submission to an infinite despotism. Time is that it came to an end. Its work is done. It is a hard, cold, cruel, empty faith, which should give way to the purer forms of a higher civilization.

No doubt, Mohammedanism was needed when it came, and has done good service in its time. But its time is almost passed. In Europe it is an anachronism and an anomaly, depending for its daily existence on the support received from Christian powers, jealous of Russian advance on Constantinople. It will be a blessing to mankind to have the capital of Russia on the Bosphorus. A recent writer on Turkey thus speaks : —

" The military strength of Mohammedanism was in its steady and remorseless bigotry. Socially, it won by the lofty ideality of its precepts, without pain or satiety. It accorded well, too, with the isolate and primitive character of the municipalities scattered over Asia. Resignation to God — a motto well according with Eastern indolence — was borne upon its banners, while in the profusion of delight hereafter was promised an element of endurance and courage. It had, too, one strikingly Arabic characteristic, — simplicity.

> " One God the Arabian prophet preached to man ;
>   One God the Orient still
> Adores, through many a realm of mighty span, —
>   A God of power and will.

> " A God that, shrouded in his lonely light,
>   Rests utterly apart
> From all the vast creations of his might,
>   From nature, man, and art.

> " A Power that at his pleasure doth create
>   To save or to destroy ;
> And to eternal pain predestinate,
>   As to eternal joy.

" It is the merit and the glory of Mohammed that, beside founding twenty spiritual empires and providing laws for the guidance through centuries of millions of men, he shook the foundations of the faith of heathendom. Mohammed was the impersonation of two principles that reign in the government of God, — destruction and salvation. He would receive nations to his favor if they accepted the faith, and utterly destroy them if they rejected it. Yet, in the end, the sapless tree must fall."

M. H. Blerzey,* in speaking of Mohammedanism in Northern Africa, says : —

" At bottom there is little difference between the human sacrifices demanded by fetichism and the contempt of life produced by the Mussulman religion. Between the social doctrines of these Mohammedan tribes and the sentiments of Christian communities there is an immense abyss."

And again : —

" The military and fanatic despotism of the Arabs has vested during many centuries in the white autochthonic races of North Africa, without any fusion taking place between the conquering element and the conquered, without destroying at all the language and manners of the subject people, and, in a word, without creating anything durable. The Arab conquest was a triumph of brute force, and nothing further."

And M. Renan, a person well qualified to judge of the character of this religion by the most extensive and impartial studies, gives this verdict : † —

" Islamism, following as it did on ground that was none of the best, has, on the whole, done as much harm as good to the human race. It has stifled everything by its dry and desolating simplicity."

Again : —

" At the present time, the essential condition of a diffused civilization is the destruction of the peculiarly Semitic element, the destruction of the theocratic power of Islamism, consequently the destruction of Islamism itself." ‡

* Article in Revue des Deux Mondes, January 15, 1868.
† Studies in Religious History and Criticism. The Future of Religion in Modern Society.
‡ Ibid., "The Part of the Semitic People in the History of Civilization."

Again : —

"Islamism is evidently the product of an inferior, and, so to speak, of a meagre combination of human elements. For this reason its conquests have all been on the average plane of human nature. The savage races have been incapable of rising to it, and, on the other hand, it has not satisfied people who carried in themselves the seed of a stronger civilization." *

NOTE TO THE CHAPTER ON MOHAMMED.

We give in this note further extracts from Mr. Palgrave's description of the doctrine of Islam.

"This keystone, this master thought, this parent idea, of which all the rest is but the necessary and inevitable deduction, is contained in the phrase far oftener repeated than understood, 'La Ilāh illa Allāh,' 'There is no God but God.' A literal translation, but much too narrow for the Arab formula, and quite inadequate to render its true force in an Arab mouth or mind.

" 'There is no God but God' are words simply tantamount in English to the negation of any deity save one alone ; and thus much they certainly mean in Arabic, but they imply much more also. Their full sense is, not only to deny absolutely and unreservedly all plurality, whether of nature or of person, in the Supreme Being, not only to establish the unity of the Unbegetting and Unbegot, in all its simple and uncommunicable Oneness, but besides this the words, in Arabic and among Arabs, imply that this one Supreme Being is also the only Agent, the only Force, the only Act existing throughout the universe, and leave to all beings else, matter or spirit, instinct or intelligence, physical or moral, nothing but pure, unconditional passiveness, alike in movement or in quiescence, in action or in capacity. The sole power, the sole motor, movement, energy, and deed is God ; the rest is downright inertia and mere instrumentality, from the highest archangel down to the simplest atom of creation. Hence, in this one sentence, 'La Ilāh illa Allāh,' is summed up a system which, for want of a better name, I may be permitted to call the Pantheism of Force, or of Act, thus exclusively assigned to God, who absorbs it all, exercises it all, and to whom alone it can be ascribed, whether for preserving or for destroying, for relative evil or for equally relative good. I say 'relative,' because it is clear that in such a theology no place is left for absolute good or evil, reason or extravagance ; all is abridged in the auto-

---

* Ibid. The Future of Religion in Modern Society, The Origins of Islamism.

cratic will of the one great Agent: 'sic volo, sic jubeo, stet pro ratione voluntas'; or, more significantly still, in Arabic, 'Kemâ yesha'o,' 'as he wills it,' to quote the constantly recurring expression of the Koran.

"Thus immeasurably and eternally exalted above, and dissimilar from, all creatures, which lie levelled before him on one common plane of instrumentality and inertness, God is one in the totality of omnipotent and omnipresent action, which acknowledges no rule, standard, or limit save his own sole and absolute will. He communicates nothing to his creatures, for their seeming power and act ever remain his alone, and in return he receives nothing from them; for whatever they may be, that they are in him, by him, and from him only. And secondly, no superiority, no distinction, no pre-eminence, can be lawfully claimed by one creature over its fellow, in the utter equalization of their unexceptional servitude and abasement; all are alike tools of the one solitary Force which employs them to crush or to benefit, to truth or to error, to honor or shame, to happiness, or misery, quite independently of their individual fitness, deserts, or advantage, and simply because he wills it, and as he wills it.

"One might at first think that this tremendous autocrat, this uncontrolled and unsympathizing power, would be far above anything like passions, desires, or inclinations. Yet such is not the case, for he has with respect to his creatures one main feeling and source of action, namely, jealousy of them lest they should perchance attribute to themselves something of what is his alone, and thus encroach on his all-engrossing kingdom. Hence he is ever more prone to punish than to reward, to inflict than to bestow pleasure, to ruin than to build. It is his singular satisfaction to let created beings continually feel that they are nothing else than his slaves, his tools, and contemptible tools also, that thus they may the better acknowledge his superiority, and know his power to be above their power, his cunning above their cunning, his will above their will, his pride above their pride; or rather, that there is no power, cunning, will, or pride save his own.

"But he himself, sterile in his inaccessible height, neither loving nor enjoying aught save his own and self-measured decree, without son, companion, or counsellor, is no less barren for himself than for his creatures, and his own barrenness and lone egoism in himself is the cause and rule of his indifferent and unregarding despotism around. The first note is the key of the whole tune, and the primal idea of God runs through and modifies the whole system and creed that centres in him.

"That the notion here given of the Deity, monstrous and blasphemous as it may appear, is exactly and literally that which the Koran conveys, or intends to convey, I at present take for granted. But that it indeed is so, no one who has attentively perused and thought over the Arabic text (for mere cursory reading, especially in a translation, will not suffice) can hesitate to allow. In fact, every phrase of the preceding sentences, every touch in this odious portrait, has been taken, to the best of my ability, word for word, or at least meaning for meaning, from the 'Book,' the truest mirror of the mind and scope of its writer.

"And that such was in reality Mahomet's mind and idea is fully confirmed by the witness-tongue of contemporary tradition."

CHAPTER XII.

THE TEN RELIGIONS AND CHRISTIANITY.

§ 1. General Results of this Survey.   § 2. Christianity a Pleroma, or Fulness of Life.   § 3. Christianity, as a Pleroma, compared with Brahmanism, Confucianism, and Buddhism.   § 4. Christianity compared with the Avesta and the Eddas. The Duad in all Religions.   § 5. Christianity and the Religions of Egypt, Greece, and Rome.   § 6. Christianity in Relation to Judaism and Mohammedanism. The Monad in all Religions.   § 7. The Fulness of Christianity is derived from the Life of Jesus.   § 8. Christianity as a Religion of Progress and of Universal Unity.

§ 1. *General Results of this Survey.*

WE have now examined, as fully as our limits would allow, ten of the chief religions which have enlisted the faith of mankind. We are prepared to ask, in conclusion, what they teach us in regard to the prospects of Christianity, and the religious future of our race.

First, this survey must have impressed on every mind the fact that man is eminently a religious being. We have found religion to be his supreme and engrossing interest on every continent, in every millennium of historic time, and in every stage of human civilization. In some periods men are found as hunters, as shepherds, as nomads, in others they are living associated in cities, but in all these conditions they have their religion. The tendency to worship some superhuman power is universal.

The opinion of the positivist school, that man passes from a theological stage to one of metaphysics, and from that to one of science, from which later and higher epoch both theology and philosophy are excluded, is not in accordance with the facts we have been observing. Science and art, in Egypt, went hand in hand with theology, during thousands of years. Science in Greece preceded the latest forms of metaphysics, and both Greek science

21 *

and Greek philosophy were the preparation for Christian faith. In India the Sánkhya philosophy was the preparation for the Buddhist religion. Theology and religion to-day, instead of disappearing in science, are as vigorous as ever. Science, philosophy, and theology are all advancing together, a noble sisterhood of thought. And, looking at facts, we may ask, In what age or time was religion more of a living force, acting on human affairs, than it is at present? To believe in things not seen, to worship a power above visible nature, to look forward to an unknown future, this is natural to man.

In the United States there is no established religion, yet in no country in the world is more interest taken in religion than with us. In the Protestant denominations it has dispensed with the gorgeous and imposing ritual, which is so attractive to the common mind, and depends mainly on the interest of the word of truth. Yet the Protestant denominations make converts, build churches, and support their clergy with an ardor seemingly undiminished by the progress of science. There are no symptoms that man is losing his interest in religion in consequence of his increasing knowledge of nature and its laws.

Secondly, we have seen that these religions vary exceedingly from each other in their substance and in their forms. They have a great deal in common, but a great deal that is different. Mr. Wentworth Higginson,* in an excellent lecture, much of which has our cordial assent, says, " Every race believes in a Creator and Governor of the world, in whom devout souls recognize a Father also." But Buddhism, the most extensive religion on the surface of the earth, explicitly denies creation, and absolutely ignores any Ruler or Governor of the world. The Buddha neither made the world nor preserves it, and the Buddha is the great object of Buddhist worship. Mr. Higginson says : " Every race believes in immortality." Though the Buddhists, as we have seen, believe in immortality, it is in so obscure a form that many of the best scholars declare

---

* The Sympathy of Religions, an Address by Thomas Wentworth Higginson. Boston, 1871.

that the highest aim and the last result of all progress in Buddhism is annihilation. He continues, "Every race recognizes in its religious precepts the brotherhood of man." The Koran teaches no such doctrine, and it is notorious that the Brahmanical system of caste, which has been despotic in India for twenty-five hundred years, excludes such brotherhood. Mr. Higginson therefore is of opinion that caste has grown up in defiance of the Vedas. The Vedas indeed are ignorant of caste, but they are also ignorant of human brotherhood. The system of caste was not a defiance of the Vedas.

Nothing is gained for humanity by such statements, which are refuted immediately by the most evident facts. The true "sympathy of religions" does not consist in their saying the same thing, any more than a true concord in music consists in many performers striking the same note. Variety is the condition of harmony. These religions may, and we believe will, be all harmonized; but thus far it is only too plain that they have been at war with each other. In order to find the resemblances we must begin by seeing the differences.

Cudworth, in his great work, speaks of "the symphony of all religions," an expression which we prefer to that of Mr. Higginson. It expresses precisely what we conceive to be the fact, that these religions are all capable of being brought into union, though so very different. They may say,

> "Are not we formed, as notes of music are,
> For one another, though dissimilar ?
> Such difference, without discord, as shall make
> The sweetest sounds."

But this harmony can only be established among the ethnic religions by means of a catholic religion which shall be able to take each of them up into itself, and so finally merge them in a higher union. The Greek, Roman, and Jewish religions could not unite with each other ; but they were united by being taken up into Christianity. Christianity has assimilated the essential ideas of the religions of Persia, Judæa, Egypt, Greece, Rome, and Scandinavia ; and each of these religions, in turn, disappeared as it was absorbed by this powerful solvent. In the case of Greece, Rome, Germany, and Judæa, this fact of their passing into solution in Christianity is a matter of history. Not all the Jews became Christians, nor has Judaism ceased to exist. This is perhaps owing to the doctrines of the Trinity and the Deity of Christ, which offend the simplistic monotheism of the Jewish mind. Yet Christianity at first grew out of Judaism, and took up into itself the best part of the Jews in and out of Palestine.

The question therefore is this, Will Christianity be able to do for the remaining religions of the world what it did for the Greeks, the Romans, and the Teutonic nations? Is it capable of becoming a universal religion?

§ 2. *Christianity a Pleroma, or Fulness of Life.*

It is evident that Christianity can become the universal human religion only by supplying the religious wants of all the races of men who dwell on all the face of the earth. If it can continue to give them all the truth their own religions contain, and add something more; if it can inspire them with all the moral life which their own religions communicate, and yet more; and, finally, if it can unite the races of men in one family, one kingdom of heaven, — then it is fitted to be and will become the universal religion. It will then not share the fate of those which have preceded it. It will not have its rise, progress, decline, and fall. It will not become, in its turn, antiquated, and be left behind by the advance of humanity. It will not be swallowed up in something deeper and broader than itself. But it will appear as the desire of all nations, and Christ will reign until he has subdued all his enemies — error, war, sin, selfishness, tyranny, cruelty — under his feet.

Now, as we have seen, Christianity differs from all other religions (on the side of truth) in this, that it is a pleroma, or fulness of knowledge. It does not differ, by teaching what has never been said or thought before. Perhaps the substance of most of the statements of Jesus may be found scattered through the ten religions of the world, some here and some there.   Jesus claims no monopoly of the truth.   He says. "My doctrine is not mine, but his who sent me."   But he *does* call himself "the Light of the World," and says that though he does not come to destroy either the law or the prophets, he comes to fulfil them in something higher.   His work is to fulfil all religions with something higher, broader, and deeper than what they have, — accepting their truth, supplying their deficiencies.

If this is a fact, then it will appear that Christianity comes, not as an exclusive, but as an inclusive system. It includes everything, it excludes nothing but limitation and deficiency.

Whether Christianity be really such a pleroma of truth or not, must be ascertained by a careful comparison of its teachings, and the ideas lying back of them, with those of all other religions.   We have attempted this, to some extent, in our Introduction, and in our discussion of each separate religion.   We have seen that Christianity, in converting the nations, always accepted something and gave something in return.   Thus it received from Egypt and Africa their powerful realism, as in the writings of Tertullian, Origen, Augustine, and gave in return a spiritual doctrine.   It received God, as seen in nature and its organizations, and returned God as above nature.   Christianity took from Greece intellectual activity, and returned moral life.   It received from Rome organization, and returned faith in a fatherly Providence.   It took law, and gave love.   From the German races it accepted the love of individual freedom, and returned union and brotherly love.   From Judaism it accepted monotheism as the worship of a Supreme Being, a Righteous Judge, a Holy King, and added to this faith in God as in all nature and all life.

But we will proceed to examine some of these points a little more minutely.

§ 3. *Christianity, as a Pleroma, compared with Brahmanism, Confucianism, and Buddhism.*

Christianity and Brahmanism. The essential value of
Brahmanism is its faith in spirit as distinct from matter,
eternity as distinct from time, the infinite as opposed to
the finite, substance as opposed to form.

The essential defect of Brahmanism is its spiritual pantheism, which denies all reality to this world, to finite
souls, to time, space, matter. In its vast unities all varieties are swallowed up, all differences come to an end.
It does not, therefore, explain the world, it denies it. It
is incapable of morality, for morality assumes the eternal
distinction between right and wrong, good and evil, and
Brahmanism knows no such difference. It is incapable
of true worship, since its real God is spirit in itself, abstracted from all attributes. Instead of immortality, it
can only teach absorption, or the disappearance of the
soul in spirit, as rain-drops disappear in the ocean.

Christianity teaches a Supreme Being who is pure
spirit, " above all, through all, and in all," " from whom,
and through whom, and to whom are all things," " in
whom we live, and move, and have our being." It is a
more spiritual religion than Brahmanism, for the latter
has passed on into polytheism and idolatry, which Christianity has always escaped. Yet while teaching faith in
a Supreme Being, the foundation and substance below
all existence, it recognizes him as A LIVING GOD. He is
not absorbed in himself, nor apart from his world, but a
perpetual Providence, a personal Friend and Father. He
dwells in eternity, but is manifested in time.

Christianity, therefore, meets the truth in Brahmanism
by its doctrine of God as Spirit, and supplies its deficiencies by its doctrine of God as a Father.

Christianity and the system of Confucius. The good
side in the teaching of Confucius is his admirable morality, his wisdom of life in its temporal limitations,
his reverence for the past, his strenuous conservatism of
all useful institutions, and the uninterrupted order of
the social system resting on these ideas.

The evil in his teaching is the absence of the supernatural element, which deprives the morality of China of
enthusiasm, its social system of vitality, its order of
any progress, and its conservatism of any improvement.
It is a system without hope, and so has remained frozen
in an icy and stiff immobility for fifteen hundred years.

But Christianity has shown itself capable of uniting
conservatism with progress, in the civilization of Christendom. It respects order, reveres the past, holds the family
sacred, and yet is able also to make continual progress in
science, in art, in literature, in the comfort of the whole
community. It therefore accepts the good and the truth
in the doctrines of Confucius, and adds to these another
element of new life.

Christianity and Buddhism. The truth in Buddhism
is in its doctrine of the relation of the soul to the laws
of nature ; its doctrine of consequences ; its assurance
of a strict retribution for every human action; its promise of an ultimate salvation in consequence of good
works ; and of a redemption from all the woes of time by
obedience to the truth.

The evil in the system is that belonging to all legal-
ism. It does not inspire faith in any living and present
God, or any definite immortality. The principle, therefore, of development is wanting, and it leaves the Mongol
races standing on a low plane of civilization, restraining
them from evil, but not inspiring them by the sight of good.

Christianity, like Buddhism, teaches that whatever a
man sows that shall he also reap ; that those who by patient continuance in well-doing seek for glory, honor, and
immortality shall receive eternal life; that the books
shall be opened in the last day, and every man be rewarded according to his works; that he whose pound
gains five pounds shall be ruler over five cities. In short,
Christianity, in its Scriptures and its practical influence,
has always taught salvation by works.

Yet, beside this, Christianity teaches justification by
faith, as the root and fountain of all real obedience. It
inspires faith in a Heavenly Father who has loved his

every child from before the foundation of the world;
who welcomes the sinner back when he repents and returns; whose forgiving love creates a new life in the
heart.   This faith evermore tends to awaken the dormant
energies in the soul of man; and so, under its influence,
one race after another has commenced a career of progress.
Christianity, therefore, can fulfil Buddhism also.

§ 4. *Christianity compared with the Avesta and the Eddas.
The Duad in all Religions.*

The essential truth in the Avesta and the Eddas is the
same.   They both recognize the evil in the world as real,
and teach the duty of fighting against it.   They avoid the
pantheistic indifference of Brahmanism, and the absence
of enthusiasm in the systems of Confucius and the
Buddha, by the doctrine of a present conflict between
the powers of good and evil, of light and of darkness.
This gives dignity and moral earnestness to both systems.
By fully admitting the freedom of man, they make the
sense of responsibility possible, and so purify and feed
morality at its roots.

The difficulty with both is, that they carry this dualistic
view of nature too far, leaving it an unreconciled dualism.
The supreme Monad is lost sight of in this ever-present
Duad.   Let us see how this view of evil, or the dual element in life, appears in other systems.

As the Monad in religion is an expression of one infinite supreme presence, pervading all nature and life, so
the Duad shows the antagonism and conflict between
truth and falsehood, right and wrong, good and evil, the
infinite perfection and the finite imperfection.   This is
a conflict actually existing in the world, and one which
religion must accept and account for.   Brahmanism does
not accept it, but ignores it.   This whole conflict is Maya,
a deception and illusion.   Yet, in this form of illusion, it
makes itself so far felt, that it must be met by sacrifices,
prayers, penances, and the law of transmigration; until
all the apparent antagonism shall be swallowed up in the
Infinite One, the only substance in the universe.

Buddhism recognizes the conflict more fully. It frankly accepts the Duad as the true explanation of the actual universe. The ideal universe as Nirvana may be one ; but of this we know nothing. The actual world is a twofold world, composed of souls and the natural laws. The battle of life is with these laws. Every soul, by learning to obey them, is able to conquer and use them, as steps in an ascent toward Nirvana.

But the belief of Zoroaster and that of Scandinavia regard the Duad as still more deeply rooted in the essence of existing things. All life is battle, — battle with moral or physical evil. Courage is therefore the chief virtue in both systems. The Devil first appears in theology in these two forms of faith. The Persian devil is Ahriman ; the Scandinavian devil is Loki. Judaism, with its absolute and supreme God, could never admit such a rival to his power as the Persian Ahriman ; yet as a being permitted, for wise purposes, to tempt and try men, he comes into their system as Satan. Satan, on his first appearance in the Book of Job, is one of the angels of God. He is the heavenly critic ; his business is to test human virtue by trial, and see how deep it goes. His object in testing Job was to find whether he loved virtue for its rewards, or for its own sake. " Does Job serve God for naught ? " According to this view, the man who is good merely for the sake of reward is not good at all.

In the Egyptian system, as in the later faith of India, the evil principle appears as a power of destruction. Siva and Typhon are the destroying agencies from whom proceed all the mischief done in the world. Nevertheless, they are gods, not devils, and have their worship and worshippers among those whose religious nature is more imbued with fear than with hope. The timid worshipped the deadly and destructive powers, and their prayers were deprecations. The bolder worshipped the good gods. Similarly, in Greece, the Chtonic deities had their shrines and worshippers, as had the powers of Blight, Famine, and Pestilence at Rome.

Yet only in the Avesta is this great principle of evil set forth in full antagonism against the powers of light

F F

and love. And probably from Persia, after the captivity, this view of Satan entered into Jewish theology. In the Old Testament, indeed, where Satan or the Devil as a proper name only occurs four times,* in all which cases he is a subordinate angel, the true Devil does not appear. In the Apocrypha he is said (Wisdom ii. 24) to have brought death into the world. The New Testament does not teach a doctrine of Satan, or the Devil, as something new and revealed then for the first time, but assumes a general though vague belief in such a being. This belief evidently existed among the Jews when Christ came. It as evidently was not taught in the Old Testament. The inevitable inference is that it grew up in the Jewish mind from its communication with the Persian dualism.

But though the doctrine of a Devil is no essential part of Christianity,† the reality and power of evil is fully recognized in the New Testament and in the teachings of the Church. Indeed, in the doctrine of everlasting punishment and of an eternal hell, it has been carried to a dangerous extreme. The Divine sovereignty is seriously infringed and invaded by such a view. If any outlying part of the universe continues in a state of permanent rebellion, God is not the absolute sovereign. But wickedness is rebellion. If any are to continue eternally in hell, it is because they continue in perpetual wickedness ; that is, the rebellion against God will never be effectually suppressed. Only when every knee bows, and every tongue confesses that Christ is Lord to the glory of God the Father ; only when truth and love have subdued all enemies by converting them into friends, is redemption complete and the universe at peace.

Now, Christianity (in spite of the illogical doctrine of everlasting punishment) has always inspired a faith in the redeeming power of love to conquer all evil. It has

---

* Job i. 6, 12 ; ii. 1 ; Zech. iii. 1 ; 1 Chron. xxi. 1.

† In the passages where Satan or the Devil is mentioned, the truth taught is the same, and the moral result the same, whether we interpret the phrase as meaning a personal being, or the principle of evil. In many of these passages a personal being cannot be meant : for example, John vi. 70 ; Matt. xvi. 23 ; Mark viii. 33 ; 1 Cor. v. 5 ; 2 Cor. xii. 7 ; 1 Thess. ii. 18 ; 1 Tim. i. 20 ; Heb. ii. 14.

taught that evil can be overcome by good. It asserts truth to be more powerful than error, right than wrong. It teaches us in our daily prayer to expect that God's kingdom shall come, and his will shall be done on earth as it is in Heaven. It therefore fulfils the truth in the great dualisms of the past by its untiring hope of a full redemption from all sin and all evil.

§ 5. *Christianity and the Religions of Egypt, Greece, and Rome.*

The Religion of Egypt. This system unfolded the truth of the Divine in this world, of the sacredness of bodily organization, and the descent of Deity into the ultimate parts of his creation. Its defect was its inability to combine with this an open spiritualism. It had not the courage of its opinions, so far as they related to the divine unity, spirituality, and eternity.

Christianity also accepts the doctrine of God, present in nature, in man, in the laws of matter, in the infinite variety of things. But it adds to this the elevated spiritualism of a monotheistic religion, and so accepts the one and the all, unity and variety, substance and form, eternity and time, spirit and body, as filled with God and manifesting him.

The Religions of Greece and Rome. The beauty of nature, the charm of art, the genius of man, were idealized and deified in the Greek pantheon. The divinity of law, organizing human society according to universal rules of justice, was the truth in the Roman religion. The defect of the Greek theology was the absence of a central unity. Its polytheism carried variety to the extreme of disorder and dissipation. The centrifugal force, not being properly balanced by any centripetal power, inevitably ends in dissolution. The defect of Roman worship was, that its oppressive rules ended in killing out life. Law, in the form of a stiff external organization, produced moral death at last in Rome, as it had produced moral death in Judæa.

Now Christianity, though a monotheism, and a monotheism which has destroyed forever both polytheism and idolatry wherever it has gone, is not that of numerical unity. The God of Christianity differs in this from the God of Judaism and Mohammedanism. He is an infinite will; but he is more. Christianity cognizes God as not only above nature and the soul, but also as in nature and in the soul. Thus nature and the soul are made divine. The Christian doctrine of the Trinity expresses this enlargement of the Jewish monotheism from a numerical to a moral unity. The God of Christ is human in this respect, that he is conceived of in the image of man. Man is essentially a unit through his will, in which lies the secret of personal identity. But besides will he has intellect, by which he comes into communion with the universe; and affection, by which he comes into communion with his race. Christianity conceives of God in the same way. He is an omnipresent will as the Father, Creator, and Ruler of all things. He is the Word, or manifested Truth in the Son, manifested through all nature, manifested through all human life. He is the Spirit, or inspiration of each individual soul. So he is Father, Son, and Spirit, above all, through all, and in us all. By this larger view of Deity Christianity was able to meet the wants of the Aryan races, in whom the polytheistic tendency is so strong. That tendency was satisfied by this view of God immanent in nature and immanent in human life.

Judaism and Mohammedanism, with their more concrete monotheism, have not been able to convert the Aryan races. Mohammedanism has never affected the mind of India, nor disturbed the ascendency of Brahmanism there. And though it nominally possesses Persia, yet it holds it as a subject, not as a convert. Persian Sufism is a proof of the utter discontent of the Aryan intellect with any monotheism of pure will. Sufism is the mystic form of Mohammedanism, recognizing communion with God, and not merely submission, as being the essence of true religion. During the long Mohammedan dominion in Turkey it has not penetrated the minds or won the love of the Greek races. It is evident that Christianity succeeded in converting the Greeks and Romans by means of its larger view of the Deity, of which the doctrine of the Trinity, as it stands in the creeds, is a crude illogical expression.

§ 6. *Christianity in Relation to Judaism and Mohammedanism. The Monad in all Religions.*

There are three religions which teach the pure unity of God, or true monotheism. These three unitarian religions are Judaism, Christianity, and Mohammedanism. They also all originated in a single race, the Semitic race, that which has occupied the central region of the world, the centre of three continents. It is the race which tends to a religious unity, as that of our Aryan ancestors tended to variety.

But what is pure monotheism? It is the worship of one alone God, separated by the vast abyss of the infinite from all finite beings. It is the worship of God, not as the Supreme Being only, not as the chief among many gods, as Jupiter was the president of the dynasty on Olympus, not merely the Most High, but as the only God. It avoids the two extremes, one of making the Supreme Being head of a council or synod of deities, and the other of making him indeed infinite, but an infinite abstraction, or abyss of darkness. These are the two impure forms of monotheism. The first prevailed in Greece, Rome, Egypt, Scandinavia. In each of these religions there was a supreme being, — Zeus, Jupiter, Ammon, Odin, — but this supreme god was only *primus inter pares*, first among equals. The other impure form of monotheism prevailed in the East, — in Brahmanism, Buddhism, and the religion of Zoroaster. In the one Parabrahm, in the other Zerana-Akerana, in the third Nirvana itself, is the Infinite Being or substance, wholly separate from all that is finite. It is so wholly separate as to cease to be an object of adoration and obedience. Not Parabrahm, but Siva, Vischnu, and Brahma; not Zerana-Akerana, but Ormazd and the Amschaspands; not the infinite world of Nirvana, nor the mighty Adi-Buddha, but the Buddhas of Confession, the finite Sakya-Muni, are the objects of worship in these systems.

Only from the Semitic race have arisen the pure monotheistic religions of Judaism, Christianity, and Mohammedanism. Each of these proclaims one only God, and each
makes this only God the object of all worship and service. Judaism says, "Hear ! O Israel, the Lord our God
is one Lord !" (Deut. vi. 4.) Originally among the Jews,
God's name as the "Plural of Majesty" indicated a unity
formed from variety ; but afterward it became in the word
Jahveh a unity of substance. "By my name Jehovah I
was not known to them" (i. e. to the Patriarchs).* That
name indicates absolute Being, "I am the I am." †

Ancient Gentile monotheism vibrated between a personal God, the object of worship, who was limited and
finite, and an infinite absolute Being who was out of sight,
"whose veil no one had lifted." The peculiarity of the
Mosaic religion was to make God truly the one alone, and
at the same time truly the object of worship.

In this respect Judaism, Christianity, and Mohammedanism agree, and in this they differ from all other religions. Individual thinkers, like Socrates, Æschylus, Cicero,
have reached the same conviction ; but these three are
the only popular religions, in which God is at once the
infinite and absolute, and the only object of worship.

Now it is a remarkable fact that these three religions,
which are the only pure monotheistic religions, are at the
same time the only religions which have any claim to
catholicity. Buddhism, though the religion of numerous
nations, seems to be the religion of only one race, namely,
the Turanic race, or Mongols. The people of India who
remain Buddhists, the Singalese, or inhabitants of Ceylon,
belong to the aboriginal Tamul, or Mongol race. With
this exception then (which is no exception, as far as we
know the ethnology of Eastern Asia), the only religions
which aim at Catholicism are these three, which are also
the only monotheistic religions. Judaism aimed at catholicity and hoped for it. It had an instinct of universality, as appeared in its numerous attempts at making
proselytes of other nations. It failed of catholicity when
it refused to accept as its Christ the man who had risen

* Exodus vi. 2.   † Exodus iii. 14.

above its national limitations, and who considered Roman tax-gatherers and Samaritans as already prepared to enter the kingdom of the Messiah.   The Jews required all their converts to become Jews, and in doing this left the catholic ground.   Christianity in the mouth of Paul, who alone fully seized the true idea of his Master, said, "Circumcision availeth nothing, nor uncircumcision, but a new creature."   In other words, he declared that it was not necessary to become a Jew in order to be a Christian.

The Jewish mind, so far forth as it was monotheistic, aimed at catholicity.   The unity of God carries with it, logically, the unity of man.   From one God as spirit we infer one human family.   So Paul taught at Athens. "God that made the world and all things therein, ... hath made of one blood all races of men to dwell on all the face of the earth."

But the Jews, though catholic as monotheists, and as worshipping a spiritual God, were limited by their ritual and their intense national bigotry.   Hereditary and ancestral pride separated them, and still separate them, from the rest of mankind.   "*We have Abraham to our Father*," is the talisman which has kept them together, but kept them from union with others.

Christianity and Mohammedanism, therefore, remain the only two really catholic religions.   Each has overpassed all the boundaries of race.   Christianity, beginning among the Jews, a Semitic people, passed into Europe, and has become the religion of Greeks, Romans, Kelts, Germans, and the Slavic races of Russia, and has not found it impossible to convert the Africans, the Mongols, and the American Indians.   So too the Mohammedan religion, also beginning among the Semitic race, has become the nominal religion of Persia, Turkey, Northern Africa, and Central Asia.   Monotheism, therefore, includes a tendency to catholicity.   But Islam has everywhere made subjects rather than converts, and so has failed of entire success.   It has not assimilated its conquests.

The monotheism of Christianity, as we have already seen, while accepting the absolute supremacy of the Infinite Being, so as to displace forever all secondary or subordinate gods, yet conceives of him as the present inspiration of all his children. It sees him coming down to bless them in the sunshine and the shower, as inspiring every good thought, as a providence guiding all human lives. And by this view it fulfils both Judaism and Mohammedanism, and takes a long step beyond them both.

§ 7. *The Fulness of Christianity is derived from the Life of Jesus.*

Christianity has thus shown itself to be a universal solvent, capable of receiving into itself the existing truths of the ethnic religions, and fulfilling them with something higher. Whenever it has come in contact with natural religion, it has assimilated it and elevated it. This is one evidence that it is intended to become the universal religion of mankind.

This pleroma, or fulness, integrity, all-sidedness, or by whatever name we call it, is something deeper than thought. A system of thought might be devised large enough to include all the truths in all the religions of the world, putting each in its own place in relation to the rest. Such a system might show how they all are related to each other, and all are in harmony. But this would be a philosophy, not a religion. No such philosophy appears in the original records of Christianity. The New Testament does not present Jesus as a philosopher, nor Paul as a metaphysician. There is no systematic teaching in the Gospels, nor in the Epistles. Yet we find there, in incidental utterances, the elements of this many-sided truth, in regard to God, man, duty, and immortality. But we find it as life, not as thought. It is a fulness of life in the soul of Jesus, passing into the souls of his disciples and apostles, and from them in a continuous stream of Christian experience, down to the present time.

The word pleroma (πλήρωμα), in the New Testament, means that which fills up; fulness, fulfilling, filling full. The verb "to fulfil" (πληρόω) carries the same significance. To "fulfil that which was spoken by the prophets," means to fill it full of meaning and truth. Jesus came, not to destroy the law, but to fulfil it; that is, to carry it out further. He fulfilled Moses and the prophets, not by doing exactly what they foretold, in their sense, but by doing it in a higher, deeper, and larger sense. He fulfilled their thought as the flower fulfils the bud, and as the fruit fulfils the flower. The sense of the fulness of life in Jesus and in the Gospel seems to have struck the minds of the early disciples, and powerfully impressed them. Hence the frequency with which they use this verb and noun, signifying fulness. Jesus fulfilled the law, the prophets, all righteousness, the Scriptures. He came in the fulness of time. His joy was fulfilled. Paul prays that the disciples may be filled full of joy, peace, and hope, with the fruits of righteousness, with all knowledge, with the spirit of God, and with all the fulness of God. He teaches that love fulfils the law, that the Church is the fulness of Christ, that Christ fills all things full of himself, and that in him dwells all the fulness of the godhead bodily.

One great distinction between Christianity and all other religions is in this pleroma, or fulness of life which it possesses, and which, to all appearance, came from the life of Jesus. Christianity is often said to be differenced from ethnic religions in other ways. They are natural religions: it is revealed. They are natural: it is supernatural. They are human: it is divine. But *all* truth is revealed truth; it all comes from God, and, therefore, so far as ethnic religions contain truth, they also are revelations. Moreover, the supernatural element is to be found in all religions; for inspiration, in some form, is universal. All great births of time are supernatural, making no part of the nexus of cause and effect. How can you explain the work of Confucius, of Zoroaster, of the Buddha, of Mohammed, out of the existing state of society, and the educational influences of their time? All such great souls are much more the makers of their age than its result; they are imponderable elements in civilization, not to be accounted for by anything outside of themselves. Nor can we urge the distinction of human and divine; for there is a divine element in all ethnic religions, and a broadly human element in Christianity.

22

Jesus is as much the representative of human nature as he is the manifestation of God. He is the Son of man, no less than the Son of God.

One great fact which makes a broad distinction between other religions and Christianity is that *they* are ethnic and *it* is catholic. They are the religions of races and nations, limited by these lines of demarcation, by the bounds which God has beforehand appointed. Christianity is a catholic religion : it is the religion of the human race. It overflows all boundaries, recognizes no limits, belongs to man as man. And this it does, because of the fulness of its life, which it derives from its head and fountain, Jesus Christ, in whom dwells the fulness both of godhead and of manhood.

It is true that the great missionary work of Christianity has long been checked. It does not now convert whole nations. Heathenism, Mohammedanism, Judaism, Brahmanism, Buddhism, stand beside it unmoved. What is the cause of this check ?

The catholicity of the Gospel was born out of its fluent and full life. It was able to convert the Greeks and Romans, and afterward Goths, Vandals, Lombards, Franks, Scandinavians, because it came to them, not as a creed, but as a life. But neither Roman Catholics nor Protestants have had these large successes since the Middle Ages. Instead of a life, Christianity became a church and a creed. When this took place, it gradually lost its grand missionary power. It no longer preached truth, but doctrine ; no longer communicated life, but organized a body of proselytes into a rigid church. Party spirit took the place of the original missionary spirit. Even the majority of the German tribes was converted by Arian missionaries, and orthodoxy has not the credit of that last grand success of Christianity. The conversion of seventy millions of Chinese in our own day to the religion of the Bible was not the work of Catholic or Protestant missionaries, but of the New Testament. The Church and the creed are probably the cause of this failure. Christianity has been partially arrested in its natural development, first by the Papal Church, and secondly by the too rigid creeds of orthodoxy.

If the swarming myriads of India and Mongolia are to be converted to Christianity, it must be done by returning to the original methods. We must begin by recognizing and accepting the truth they already possess. We must be willing to learn of them, in order to teach them. Comparative Theology will become the science of missions if it help to show to Christians the truth and good in the creeds outside of Christendom. For to the Church and to its sects, quite as much as to the world, applies the saying, "He that exalteth himself shall be abased, but he that humbleth himself shall be exalted."

§ 8. *Christianity as a Religion of Progress and of Universal Unity.*

As long as a tree or an animal lives it continues to grow. An arrest of growth is the first symptom of the decline of life. Fulness of life, therefore, as the essential character of Christianity, should produce a constant development and progress; and this we find to be the case. Other religions have their rise, progress, decline, and fall, or else are arrested and become stationary. The religions of Persia, Egypt, Greece, Rome, Scandinavia, have come to an end. As ethnic religions, they shared the fortunes of the race or nation with which they were associated. The systems of Confucius, of the Buddha, of Brahmanism, of Judæa, of Mohammed, are arrested. They remain stationary. But, thus far, Christianity and Christendom advance together. Christianity has developed, out of its primitive faith, several great theologies, the mediæval Papacy, Protestantism, and is now evidently advancing into new and larger forms of religious, moral, and social activity.

The fact of a fulness of divine and human life in Jesus took form in the doctrines of the incarnation and the Trinity. The fact of the reconciling and uniting power of this life took form in the doctrine of the atonement. Both of these doctrines are illogical and false, in their form, as church doctrines. But both of them represent most essential facts. We have seen the truths in the doctrines of incarnation and the Trinity. The truth in the atonement is, as the word itself signifies, the at-one-making power of the Gospel. The reconciliation of antagonist truths and opposing tendencies, which philosophy has always unsuccessfully endeavored to state in theory, Christianity accomplishes in practice. Christianity continually reproduces from its depths of life a practical faith in God, both as law and as love, in man, both as a free and yet as a providentially guided being. It gives us God as unity and as variety, as the substance and as the form of the world. It states the reality of evil as forcibly as any system of dualism, and yet produces a practical faith in good as being stronger than evil and sure to conquer it. In social life it reconciles the authority of human law with the freedom of individual thought and action. In the best Christian governments, we find all the order which a despotism can guarantee, with all the freedom to which a democracy can aspire. No such social organization is to be found outside of Christendom. How can this be, unless it is somehow connected with Christianity ?

The civilization of Christendom consists in a practical reconciliation of antagonist tendencies. It is a "pleroma" in social life, a fulness of concord, a harmony of many parts. The harmony is indeed by no means complete, for the millennium has not arrived. As yet the striking feature of Christendom is quantity, power, variety, fulness ; not as yet co-operation, harmony, peace, union. Powers are first developed, which are afterward to be harmonized. The sword is not yet beaten into a ploughshare, nor has universal peace arrived. Yet such is the inevitable tendency of things. As knowledge spreads, as wealth increases, as the moral force of the world is enlarged, law, more and more, takes the place of force. Men no longer wear swords by their sides to defend themselves from attack. If attacked, they call the policeman. Towns are no longer fortified with walls, nor are the residences of noblemen kept in a state of defence. They are all folded in the peaceful arms of national law. So far the atonement has prevailed. Only nations still continue to fight ; but the time is at hand when international law, the parliament of the world, the confederation of man, shall take the place of standing armies and iron-clad navies.

So, in society, internal warfare must, sooner or later, come to an end. Pauperism and crime must be treated according to Christian methods. Criminals must be reformed, and punishment must be administered in reference to that end. Co-operation in labor and trade must take the place of competition. The principles by means of which these vast results will be brought about are already known; the remaining difficulties are in their application. Since slavery fell in the United States, one great obstacle to the progress of man is removed. The next social evils in order will be next assailed, and, one by one, will be destroyed. Christianity is becoming more and more practical, and its application to life is constantly growing more vigorous and wise.

The law of human life is, that the development of differences must precede their reconciliation. Variety must precede harmony, analysis must prepare the way for synthesis, opposition must go before union. Christianity, as a powerful stimulus applied to the human mind, first develops all the tendencies of the soul; and afterward, by its atoning influence on the heart, reconciles them. Christ is the Prince of Peace. He came to make peace between man and God, between man and man, between law and love, reason and faith, freedom and order, progress and conservatism. But he first sends the sword, afterward the olive-branch. Nevertheless, universal unity is the object and end of Christianity.

INDEX

OF THE PRINCIPAL AUTHORS CONSULTED IN THE PREPARATION OF THIS WORK.

ACKERMANN (D. C.). Das Christliche im Plato. Hamburg. 1835. (Translated in Clark's Theological Library.) (Greece.)

ÆSCHYLUS, and other Greek Poets. (Greece.)

ALGER (WM. R.). A Critical History of the Doctrine of a Future Life. Philadelphia : Childs. 1864.

ALLEN (JOSEPH H.). Hebrew Men and Times. Boston. 1861. (Judæa.)

American Oriental Society, Journal of the. New Haven ; published annually. (Oriental Religions.)

AMPÈRE (J. J. A.). L'Histoire Romaine. Paris. 1864. (Rome.)

——————— La Science en Orient.

Anthropological Society of London, Memoirs of (commenced in 1863–64).

Asiatic Journal, 1816 – 1843. London.

Asiatic Researches (commenced London. 1801).

BALDWIN (JOHN D.). Pre-Historic Nations. New York. 1869.

BANHERJEA (Rev. K. M.). Dialogues on Hindoo Philosophy, comprising the Nyaya, Sánkhya, and Vyasa. London. 1861. (Brahmanism.)

BAUR (F. C.). Symbolik und Mythologie. Stuttgart. 1829.

BLEEK (ARTHUR HENRY). Avesta. The religious Books of the Parsees. Translated into English from Spiegel's German translation. Hertford. 1864. (Zoroaster.)

BÖEKH. Manetho und der Hundstern period. Berlin. 1840. (Egypt.)

BURNOUF (EUGENE). Commentaire sur le Yaçna. Paris. 1823.

——————— Introduction à l'Histoire du Buddhisme Indien. Paris. 1844.

——————— Le Bhâgavata Purana, on Histoire Poetique de Krichna. Paris. 1840.

BURNOUF (ÉMILE). Essai sur le Veda. 1863.

BRUGSCH. Histoire de l'Egypte. Leipzig. 1859.

——————— Aus dem Orient.

BUNSEN (C. C. J.). Bibelwerk. Leipzig : Brockhaus. 1858. (Judæa.)

——————— Gott in der Geschichte. Leipzig. 1857.

——————— Ægypten's Stelle in der Weltgeschichte. Hamburg. 1845 – 1867. English translation, 1868.

CHABAS (F.). Les Pasteurs en Egypt. Amsterdam. 1868.

CHASTEL (ÉTIÉNNE). Histoire de la Destruction du Paganisme dans l'Empire d'Orient. Paris. 1850.

Chinese Recorder and Missionary Journal. Foochow.

LANDSEER (JOHN). Sabæán Researches. London. 1823.
LANE (EDWARD WILLIAM). Manners and Customs of the Modern Egyptians. 2 vols. 5th edition. London. 1848.
———————— Selections from the Kuran, with an interwoven Commentary. London. 1843.
LANOYE (F. DE). Rameses the Great. New York : Scribner. 1870. (Egypt.)
LASSEN (C.). Indische Alterthumskunde. (4 Bande.) Bonn. 1847.
LATHAM (R. G.). The Natural History of the Varieties of Man. London. 1850.
———————— Descriptive Ethnology. London. 1859.
LEGGE (JAMES). The Chinese Classics, with a Translation, Critical and Exegetical Notes, Prolegomena, and copious Indexes. Hongkong. 1861–1865.
LENORMANT (FRANÇOIS). A Manual of the Ancient History of the East. London : Asher & Co. 1869. (Judæa, Egypt, Assyria, Babylon, Persia, Phœnicia, Carthage, Arabia.)
LEPSIUS (RICHARD). Letters from Egypt, Ethiopia, and the Peninsula of Sinai. London : Bohn. 1853. (Egypt.)
———————— Uber die götter der vier elemente. Berlin. 1856. (Egypt.)
———————— Das Todtenbuch der Ægypter. Leipzig. 1842.
LESLEY (J. P.). Man's Origin and Destiny. Philadelphia : Lippincott & Co. 1868. (Egypt, &c.)
LIN-LE. The History of the Ti-Ping Revolution. London. 1866. (China.)
MAINE. Ancient Law. London.
MALAN (S. C.). God in China. Shin or Shangte ? London (no date).
MACKAY (ROBERT WILLIAM). The Progress of the Intellect as exemplified in the Religious Development of the Greeks and Hebrews. 2 vols. London. 1850.
MAURY (L. J. ALFRED). Histoire des Religions de la Grèce Antique. Paris. 1857. (Greece.)
———————— Croyance et l'Antiquité. Paris. 1863.
MARIETTE (A. E.). Choix des Monuments decouverts pendant le déblayement du Sérapeum de Memphis. Paris. 1856.
———————— Mémoire sur le mère d'Apis. 1856.
MEADOWS (T. TAYLOR). The Chinese and their Rebellions. 1856. (China.)
MILMAN (HENRY HART). The History of the Jews. London. 1835. (Judæa.)
———————— The History of Latin Christianity. 4th edition. London. 1867.
Mohammedan Dynasties in Spain. Oriental Translation Fund. London. 1840. (Islam.)
MOMMSEN (THEODORE). Römische Geschichte. 3d edition. Berlin. 1861. 3 vols. 8vo. Translated into English. London. 1862. (Rome.)
MUIR (J.). Original Sanskrit Texts on the Origin and Progress of the Religion and Institutions of India. Four parts. Williams and Nordgate. 1857–1863.
MUIR (W.). Life of Mahomet and History of Islam to the Era of the Hegira. London. 1858.
MULLENS (Rev. JOSEPH). The Religious Aspects of Hindu Philosophy stated and discussed. London. 1860.

MÜLLER (C. OTTFRIED). Ancient Art and its Remains. London : Bohn. 1852. (Greece.)
———————————— Literature of Ancient Greece. London : Baldwin. 1850. (Greece.)
———————————— Die Dorier. Breslau. 1825. Translated into English by Sir G. C. Lewis. Oxford. 1830.
MÜLLER (MAX). Rig-Veda Sanhita, translated and explained. Volume I. Hymns to the Maruts, or Storm Gods. London. 1869.
———————————— History of Ancient Sanskrit Literature. 1860.
———————————— Chips from a German Workshop. 1870.
MÜLLER (WILHELM). Geschichte und System der Altdeutschen Religion. Göttingen. 1844. (Germany.)
NIEBUHR. Lectures on the History of Rome. London. 1852.
NÖLDEKE (THEODOR). Geschichte des Quorân. Göttingen. 1860.
NOTT (J. C.) and GLIDDON (GEO. R.). Types of Mankind. Philadelphia. 1854.
———————————— Indigenous Races of the Earth. Philadelphia. 1857.
OUVAROFF (M.). Essai sur les Mystères d'Eleusis. Paris. 1816.
PALGRAVE (WILLIAM GIFFORD). A Year's Journey through Central and Eastern Arabia. Third edition. 1866. London. (Islam.)
PAUTHIER (G.). Les Livres sacrés de l'Orient (containing the Chou-king, the four books of Confucius and Mencius, the Laws of Manu, and the Coran. Paris. 1843.
PERCEVAL (CAUSSIN DE). Essai sur l'Histoire des Arabs, avant Islamisme, pendant l'époque de Mahomet, et jusqu'à la réduction de toutes les tribus sous la loi Mussalmane. Paris. 3 vols. 8vo. 1847–48. (Islam.)
PICKERING (CHARLES). The Races of Men. Boston. 1846.
PICTET (A.). Les Origines Indo-Européennes, on les Aryas primitives. Paris. 1859.
PIGOTT (GRENVILLE). A Manual of Scandinavian Mythology. London : Pickering. 1839.
POOLE (MRS.). Englishwoman in Egypt. Letters from Cairo. First and Second Series. London, republished in Philadelphia. (Islam.)
PRELLER (L.). Griechische Mythologie. Leipzig. 1854.
PRIAULX (OSMOND DE B.). Quæstiones Mosaicæ. London. 1842.
PRICHARD (JAMES COWLES). The Eastern Origin of the Celtic Nations. Edited by R. G. Latham. London. 1857.
PRICHARD (J. C.) The Natural History of Man. London : Ballière. 1855. (Egypt.)
PRINSEP (JAMES). Essays on Indian Antiquities. 2 vols. London. 1858.
RAPP (ADOLPH). Die Religion und Sitte der Perser. 1865.
RAWLINSON (GEORGE). Herodotus.
———————————— Five Great Monarchies of the Ancient Eastern World. London. 1862–1868.
———————————— Manual of Ancient History. New York : Harper and Brothers. 1871. (Assyria, Egypt, Greece, Rome, &c.)
RENAN (J. E.). Articles in the Revue des Deux Mondes.
———————————— Études d'Histoire religieuse. Paris. 1857. Translated by O. B. Frothingham. New York. 1864.
———————————— Histoire générale et systèmes comparés des langues Sémitiques. Paris. 1863.

INDEX

OF SUBJECTS TREATED IN THIS WORK.

Greek worship, connected with augurs and oracles, 300.
Gylfi, deluding of, in the Edda, 369

H.

Haruspices, derived from Etruria, 338.
Havamal, or proverbs of the Scandinavians, 366.
Heathen religions must contain more truth than error, 6.
    "   " cannot have been human inventions, 6.
    "   " must contain some revelation from God, 8.
    "   " how viewed by Christ and his apostles, 9.
    "   " how treated by Paul at Athens, 10.
    "   " how regarded by the early apologists, 12.
Heimdall, warder of the gods, 380.
Herder, his description of David, 425.
Hesiod, his account of the three groups of gods, 270.
Hindoo Epics, Ramayana and Mahabharata, 128.
  " " they refer to the time succeeding the Vedic age, 128.
  " " composed before the time of Buddhism, 129.
Hindoos, antagonisms of their character, 82.
  " acute in speculations, but superstitious, 82.
  " unite luxury and asceticism, 82.
  " tend to idealism and religious spiritualism, 83.
  " their doctrine of Maya, 84.
Hindoo year, calendar of, 132.
  " " begins in April, a sacred month, 132.
Holy of Holies, in the Egyptian and Jewish temples, 252.
Homer, his description of the gods, 280.
Horace, his view of religion, 346.
Hyksôs, constitute the middle monarchy, 232.
  " expelled from Egypt after five hundred years, 233.
  " Hebrews in Egypt during their ascendency, 234, 235.
  " or Shepherd Kings in Egypt, 213.
  " a Semitic people from Asia, 232.
  " conquered Lower Egypt B. C. 2000, 233.
Hyndla, song of, extracts from, 366.

I.

Icelanders converted to Christianity, 394.
Incarnation, the fundamental doctrine of Christianity, 28.
India, always a land of mystery, 81.
  " overrun by conquerors, 81.
Infinite and finite elements in Brahmanism and Christianity, 137.

Injustice done to ethnic religions, 4.
Inspiration, its origin in the intuitive faculty, 489.
Isis and Osiris, their legend, from Plutarch, 244.
  "   "   " explanations of their myth, 246.
  "   "   " identified with the first and second order, 248.

J.

Janus, one of the oldest of Roman gods, 322.
  " presided over beginnings and endings, 322.
  " invoked before other gods, 322.
  " his temple open in war, closed in peace, 322.
  " believed by Creuzer to have an Indian origin, 322.
  " has his chief feast in January, 323.
  " a Sabine god on Mount Janiculum, 323.
Jews, a Semitic race, 399.
Job, its grandeur of thought and expression, 438.
Jones, Sir William, his life and works, 78.
  "   " progress since his time, 80.
Judaism, a preparation for Christianity, 444.
  " monotheistic after the captivity, 444.
  " influenced by Greek philosophy, 444.
  " its process of development, 445.
  " at first childlike and narrow, 446.
  " the seed of Christianity, 446.
Juno, queen of heaven, and female Jupiter, 324.
  " goddess of womanhood, 324.
  " her chief feast the Matronalia in March, 324.
  " her month of June favorable for wedlock, 325.
Jupiter, derived his name from the Sanskrit, 324.
  " had many temples in Rome, 324.
  " god of the weather, of storm, of lightning, 324.

K.

" Kings," Chinese, names and number, 47
  " teach a personal God, 57.
  " republished by Confucius, 47.

L.

Language of Ancient Egypt, 236.
Lao-tse, founder of Tao-ism, 50, 52.
  " called a dragon by Confucius, 51
  " three forms of his doctrine, 54.
Lares, gods of home, 328.

THE END.